# Contents

*Contents*

# The Paradoxes of the American Presidency

SECOND EDITION

Thomas E. Cronin
Michael A. Genovese

For conditions of borrowing, see Library Regulations

New York   Oxford
OXFORD UNIVERSITY PRESS
2004

Oxford University Press

Oxford   New York

Auckland   Bangkok   Buenos Aires   Cape Town   Chennai
Dar es Salaam   Delhi   Hong Kong   Istanbul   Karachi   Kolkata
Kuala Lumpur   Madrid   Melbourne   Mexico City   Mumbai   Nairobi
São Paulo   Shanghai   Taipei   Tokyo   Toronto

Published by Oxford University Press, Inc.
198 Madison Avenue, New York, New York, 10016
www.oup.com

Oxford is a registered trademark of Oxford University Press

**Library of Congress Cataloging-in-Publication Data**
Cronin, Thomas E.
   The paradoxes of the American presidency / Thomas E. Cronin, Michael A. Genovese.—
2nd ed.
      p. cm.
   Includes bibliographical references and index.
   ISBN 0-19-516709-0
   1. Presidents—United States. I. Genovese, Michael A. II. Title.
JK516.C73 2003
352.23′0973—dc21
                                                                                    2003049857

Printing number: 9  8  7  6  5  4  3  2  1

Printed in the United States of America
on acid-free paper

# Preface

Alexander Hamilton persuaded us an American presidency was *necessary*. Many others have demonstrated that the American presidency is *unique* and always *potentially dangerous*. Yet beyond this consensus—that the presidency is unique, necessary, and potentially dangerous—the American presidency remains a challenging institution to understand.

Much of the difficulty stems from the unusual character of the institution. The presidency is both unique and evolving. It defies simple explanations. It is dynamic, variable, and often a contradictory office. Lacking a precise constitutional delineation of powers, the American presidency is elastic and changing. Different occupants at different times may mold the institution to the nation's needs, or to suit their own needs; at other times the office and the U.S. system of separated and shared powers limit and constrain a president.

This book is an effort to understand the American presidency by viewing it through the lens of a series of paradoxes that shape and define the office. Our goal is to convey the complexity, the many-sidedness, and the contrarian aspects of the office.

A paradox is a statement that is seemingly contradictory or opposed to common sense and yet may nonetheless be true. We use the term in a general sense, that we often hold clashing or contradictory notions of what a leader should do. A more rigorous definition is as follows:

> A logical paradox consists of two contrary, or even contradictory propositions to which we are led by apparently sound arguments. The arguments are sound because when used in other contexts they do not seem to invite any difficulty. It is only in the particular combination in which the paradox occurs that the arguments lead to a troublesome conclusion. In its most extreme form a paradox consists in the apparent equivalence of two propositions, one of which is the negative of the other.
>
> John van Heijenort, "Logical Paradoxes," in Paul Edwards, ed., *The Encyclopedia of Philosophy* (New York: Macmillan Co. and Free Press, 1967), vol. 5, p. 45.

In many ways paradoxes define the presidential office, and it is the paradoxical nature of the institution that makes the search for a unified theory elusive.

This book is an interpretation and a synthesis. It is an interpretative treatment in that it offers a fresh look at this complicated institution and at the even more complicated series of leaders who have served as president.

It is also a synthesis of presidential scholarship done by able journalists, biographers, historians, and political scientists over the past fifty years. We borrow and quote liberally from the rich body of literature that has developed on the American presidency. Our bibliography acknowledges the work of those who have helped us to understand this institution.

This book is informed too by the extensive interviewing both of us have done over the past thirty years. One of us has had the opportunity to work in Congress and in the White House, and to serve on the staff at the Brookings Institution; these experiences have proved invaluable.

Finally, this book builds on and is an extension of our earlier works on the presidency, especially Cronin's *The State of the Presidency* (1980), *Rethinking the Presidency* (1982), and *The Inventing of the American Presidency* (1989); and Genovese's *The Power of the American Presidency* (2001), *The Presidential Dilemma* (1995), *The Nixon Presidency* (1990), and *The Supreme Court, the Constitution and the Presidential Power* (1980).

We thank Pauline Batrikian, Clare Clamico, Kent Jancarik, Adrianne Ralph, Ken Singer, Kelli Lee, Derek Ball, Joey Bristol, and Mahira Vallin, for thoughtful research assistance. We are grateful too for the expert secretarial assistance provided by Bernadette Bernard, JoAnn Collins, Margaret Edwards, and Donna Jones. Special thanks to Tania Cronin and Gabriela Esteva for their stalwart support and patience, our professional colleagues for their encouragement and counsel, and Whitman College and Loyola Marymount University for their institutional support. Tom Cronin also thanks the Luce Foundation and the Jerry McHugh family of Denver for their support and encouragement of his research. Karen Shapiro and Peter Labella, our editors at Oxford University Press, provided indispensable encouragement.

T.E.C. and M.G.
Autumn, 2003

# *Presidential Paradoxes*

He must have "common opinions." But it is equally
imperative that he be an "uncommon man." The public
must see themselves in him, but they must, at the same
time, be confident that he is something bigger than
themselves.

Harold J. Laski, *The American Presidency: An Interpretation*
(Harper & Brothers, 1940), p. 38

To become president, Lincoln had had to talk more rad-
ically on occasion than he actually felt; to be an effective president he was compelled to act more conserva-
tively than he wanted.

Richard Hofstadter, *The American Political Tradition*
(Vintage, 1948), p. 128

Successful leaders are able to appreciate (and live with)
the fact that their calling is replete with paradoxes. . . .
Indeed, all leadership is about resolving paradoxes and
managing a series of necessary tensions in the absence
of clear knowledge of where to draw the line.

James O'Toole, *Leadership A to Z* (Jossey-Bass, 1999), p. 201

Contradictions and paradoxes are a part of life—especially for leaders. "No
aspect of society, no habit, custom, movement, development, is without cross-
currents," writes historian Barbara Tuchman. "Starving peasants in hovels
live alongside prosperous landlords in featherbeds. Children are neglected

and children are loved."[1] In life we are confronted with paradoxes for which we seek meaning.

The same is true for the American presidency. We admire presidential power, yet fear it. We yearn for the heroic, yet are also inherently suspicious of it. We demand dynamic leadership, yet grant only limited powers to the president. We want presidents to be dispassionate analysts and listeners, yet they must also be decisive. We are impressed with presidents who have great self-confidence, yet we dislike arrogance and respect those who express reasonable self-doubt. We want leaders to be bold and innovative, yet we allow presidents to take us only where we want to go.

How are we to make sense of the presidency? This complex, multidimensional, often contradictory institution is vital to the American system of government. Political laws that seem to constrain one president, liberate another. What proves successful in one, leads to failure in another. Rather than seeking one unifying theory of presidential politics that answers all our questions, we believe the American presidency is often best understood as a series of paradoxes, clashing expectations and contradictions.

Leaders live with contradictions. Presidents learn to take advantage of contrary or divergent forces. Leadership situations commonly require successive displays of contrasting characteristics. Living with, even embracing, contradictions is a sign of political and personal maturity.

The effective leader understands the presence of opposites. The aware leader, much like a first-rate conductor, knows when to bring in various sections, knows when and how to turn the volume up and down, and learns how to balance opposing sections to achieve desired results. Effective presidents learn how to manage these contradictions and give meaning and purpose to confusing and often clashing expectations. The novelist F. Scott Fitzgerald once suggested that, "The test of a first-rate intelligence is the ability to hold two opposed ideas in the mind at the same time."[2]

The place of leadership in American democracy has always been a confused one, political scientist Erwin Hargrove reminds us, in good part because of the overriding democratic myth that the people are sovereign.[3] Alexis de Tocqueville, the discerning French aristocrat who toured the United States in the early 1830s, captured this puzzling aspect of American political life when he said the people want to be led "and they want to remain free. As they cannot destroy either of these contradictory propositions, they strive to satisfy them both at once [with democratic constitutional government]."[4]

Further, we generally have an exaggerated notion of the capacity of presidents to shape events. Historians and political scientists have learned that although a president's impact may be important, it is only occasionally decisive. In any event, presidential powers are often not as great as many people believe, and thus presidents are often unjustly condemned as ineffective. Sometimes a president will overreach or resort to unacceptable deviousness while trying to live up to popular demands.

The constitutional founders purposely left the presidency imprecisely defined. This was due in part to their fears of both the monarchy and the masses, and in part to their hopes that future presidents would create a more powerful office than the framers were able to do at the time. They knew that at times the president would have to move swiftly and effectively, yet they went to considerable lengths to avoid enumerating specific powers and duties in order to calm the then widespread fear of monarchy. After all, the nation had just fought a war against executive tyranny. Thus the paradox of the invention of the presidency: To get the presidency approved in 1787 and 1788, the framers had to leave several silences and ambiguities for fear of portraying the office as an overly centralized leadership institution. Yet when we need central leadership we turn to the president and read into Article II of the Constitution various prerogatives or inherent powers that allow the president to perform as an effective national leader.

Today the informal and symbolic powers of the presidency often account for as much as the formal, stated ones. Presidential powers expand and contract in response to varying situational and technological changes. The powers of the presidency are thus interpreted so differently that they sometimes seem to be those of different offices. In some ways the modern presidency has virtually unlimited authority for almost anything its occupant chooses to do with it. In other ways, a president seems hopelessly ensnarled in a web of checks and balances.

Presidents must constantly balance conflicting demands, cross pressures, and contradictions. Perhaps some contradictions are best left unresolved, especially as ours is an imperfect world and our political system is a complicated one. We may not be able to resolve many of these clashing expectations. At the least we should develop a better understanding of what it is we ask of our presidents, thereby increasing our sensitivity to the limits and possibilities of what a president can achieve. This might free presidents to lead and administer more effectively in those critical times when the nation has no choice but to turn to them. Whether we like it or not, the vitality of our democracy depends in large measure upon the sensitive interaction of presidential leadership with an understanding public willing to listen and willing to provide support. Carefully planned innovation is nearly impossible without the kind of leadership a competent and fairminded president can provide.

The following are some of the paradoxes of the presidency. Some are cases of confused expectations. Some are cases of wanting one kind of presidential behavior at one time, and another kind later. Some are cases where positive characteristics of presidential leadership become negative because they are excessive. Still others stem from the contradiction inherent in the concept of democratic leadership, which on the surface at least, appears to set up "democratic" and "leadership" as warring concepts. Whatever the source, each has implications for presidential performance and for how Americans judge presidential success and failure.

*Paradox #1.* Americans demand powerful, popular presidential leadership that solves the nation's problems. Yet we are inherently suspicious of strong centralized leadership and the abuse of power. Thus we place significant limits on the president's powers.

*Paradox #2.* We yearn for the democratic "common person" and simultaneously a leader who is uncommon, charismatic, heroic, and visionary.

*Paradox #3.* We want a decent, just, caring, and compassionate president, yet we also admire a cunning, guileful, and, on occasions that warrant it, even a ruthless, manipulative president.

*Paradox #4.* We admire the "above politics" nonpartisan or bipartisan approach, and yet the presidency is perhaps the most political office in the American system, which requires a creative entrepreneurial master politician.

*Paradox #5.* We want a president who can unify diverse people and interests; however, the job requires taking firm stands, making unpopular or controversial decisions that necessarily upset and divide.

*Paradox #6.* We expect our presidents to provide bold, creative, visionary, innovative, *programmatic* leadership, and at the same time to respond *pragmatically* to the will of public opinion majorities. That is to say, we expect presidents to lead and to follow, and to exercise "democratic leadership."

*Paradox #7.* Americans want powerful, self-confident presidential leadership. Yet we are inherently suspicious of leaders who view themselves as infallible and above criticism.

*Paradox #8.* What it takes to become president may not be what is needed to govern the nation.

*Paradox #9.* The presidency is sometimes too strong yet at other times too weak.

*Paradox #10.* Presidents affirm the existing order and major traditions of society, yet often must also create a new order and boldly depart from the norm.

To govern successfully, presidents must manage these paradoxes, and must balance a variety of competing demands and expectations.

*Paradox #1.* Americans demand powerful, popular presidential leadership that solves the nation's problems. Yet we are inherently suspicious of strong centralized leadership and especially the abuse of power and therefore we place significant limits on the president's powers.

We admire power but fear it. We love to unload responsibilities on our leaders, yet we intensely dislike being bossed around. We expect impressive leadership from presidents, and we simultaneously impose constitutional, cultural, and political restrictions on them. These restrictions often prevent presidents from living up to our expectations.

Our ambivalence toward executive power is hardly new. The founders knew the new republic needed more leadership, yet they feared the development of a popular leadership institution that might incite the people and yield factious or demagogic government. Indeed, if there was one thing the framers of the Constitution did not want, it was an overly powerful presidency. Thus, the early conception of the American president was of an informed, virtuous statesman whose detached judgment and competence would enable him to work well with Congress and other leaders in making and implementing national public policy. This early presidency, as envisaged by the founders, did not encourage a popularly elected leader who would seek to directly shape and respond to the public's views. On the contrary, popular leadership too grounded in the will of the people was viewed as a vice to be avoided. The founders' goal was to provide some distance between the public and national leaders, especially the president, that distance to be used to refine the popular view, to allow for leadership and statesmanship rather than to do what the people wanted done.[5] To be sure, the people should be represented through Congress, but the president was to exercise wisdom, not responsiveness; judgment, not followership.

But the presidency of 1787 is not the presidency of today. The twenty-first century presidency is a larger office, structurally similar to the original design yet politically more powerful and more closely connected to popular passions. With the evolution of the nation has come an alternative conception of the presidency—the president is, in essence, the one truly national voice and representative of the American people. New arrangements for nominating and electing presidents have reinforced this conception, as has access to the magic of television. Today's president is seen as an agent of the people who should provide popular leadership.

The demand for a responsive president often conflicts with the demand for an informed, judicious statesman. The claims of politics and popular leadership have altered and undermined the early notions of presidential behavior. And as the presidency has become the lightning rod for nearly all of society's discontents, so also have presidents sometimes sought to be all things to all people.

Still, while looking for strong, popular, presidential leadership, Americans also remain profoundly cautious about concentrating power in any one person's hands. Schooled in the tradition of negative government, Americans have historically feared the abuse of leadership power. Thus we have a constitutional system designed to thwart presidential leadership, save in times of emergencies.

Presidents are supposed to follow the laws and respect the constitutional procedures that were designed to restrict their power, yet still they must be powerful and effective when action is needed. For example, we approve of presidential military initiatives and covert operations when they work out well, yet we criticize presidents and insist they work more closely with Congress when the initiatives fail. We recognize the need for secrecy in certain government actions, yet we resent being deceived and left in the dark—again, especially when things go wrong, as in Reagan's Iranian arms sale diversions to the Contras.

Although we sometimes do not approve of the way a president acts, we often approve of the end results. Thus Lincoln was criticized for acting outside the limits of the Constitution, but at the same time he was forgiven due to the obvious necessity for him to violate certain constitutional principles in order to preserve the Union. FDR was often flagrantly deceptive and manipulative of his political opponents and sometimes as well of his staff and allies. But leadership effectiveness in the end often comes down to whether a person acts in terms of the highest interests of the nation. Most historians conclude Lincoln and Roosevelt were responsible in the use of presidential power, to preserve the Union, to fight the depression and nazism.

In short, we expect presidents, as the most visible representatives of big government and as popular leaders, to solve all kinds of problems by mustering all the powers and strengths that office now appears to confer, and then some. Yet we get upset with presidents who seem to infringe on our rights in any significant way. In a self-help, individualistic, do-it-yourself society (which we still like to think we are), we remain ambivalent about the role of centralized presidential popular leadership because, as a people, we are somewhat ambivalent about the ends of government. We need government, but we resist its powers when we can, and we dislike admitting our growing dependence on it. It is also true that while we want strong leadership, if such leadership comes in the wrong form, our enthusiasm for it diminishes. This results in a dramatic roller coaster ride of strong support for the heroic presidency model followed by equally strong condemnations of presidential power.

*Paradox #2.* We yearn for the democratic "common person" and also for the uncommon, charismatic, visionary performance.

We want our presidents to be like us, but better than us. We like to think America is the land where the common sense of the common person reigns. Nourished on a diet of director Frank Capra's "common-man-as-hero" movies, and the literary celebration of the average citizen by authors such as Emerson, Whitman, and Thoreau, we prize the common touch. The plain-speaking Harry Truman, the up-from-the-log cabin "man or woman of the people," is enticing. In practice, however, we want presidents to succeed and we yearn for brilliant, uncommon, and semiregal performances from presidents.

While we fought a revolution to depose royalty, part of us yearns for the majesty and symbolism of a royal family.

> From the beginning, American presidential style has had to lean simultaneously in two different directions; the character in the White House should behave with becoming democratic modesty. . . . But he must also express—in word, deed, bearing, personality . . . the greatness of the idea and the people he represents.[6]

We yearn for and demand both king *and* commoner. Our thirst for the heroic is so enduring that it is as if history is meaningless without heroes. At the same time, we are told the hero is the individual the democratic nation must guard itself against. "Pity the nation that needs heroes," goes a proverb. Why is this a haunting warning? Strong leaders, it is believed, can sap, diminish, and possibly even destroy the very wellsprings of self-government. Hence the notion: Strong leaders make for a weak people.

Cicero wondered whether great oratory was a national asset or a national peril. Presidents have to be persuasive, but if they are too convincing they may con us. Sometimes we are so mesmerized by the effective communicator that we fail to object, criticize, or resist: We fail to maintain the healthy skepticism so necessary in a political democracy.

An old Greek saying describes two leadership "types": hedgehogs and foxes. The hedgehog knows only one or two things but is dogged in pursuit of these goals. Foxes, on the other hand, know very many things and they go about pursuing these multiple goals. Lincoln, FDR, and Reagan are the archetype hedgehogs. They were determined to win the war or cut taxes. And they regularly simplified the goals to dramatize the need. They were wholesalers. Hoover, Ford, Carter, and George H. W. Bush were foxes who got caught up with so many muddled undertakings that they eventually became buried under the load.

Leaders must be hedgehogs *and* foxes, wholesalers *as well as* retailers. They must have macro and micro agendas. They should be willing and able to dramatize their missions, but they also must know that personal heroics need to be counterbalanced by reflective leadership.

Americans crave to be governed by a president who is greater than anyone else yet not better than themselves. We want our president to be one of the folks yet also something special. If presidents get too special, however, they get criticized and roasted. If they try to be too folksy, people get bored. We cherish the myth that nearly anyone can grow up to be president, that there are no barriers and no elite qualifications; still we don't want someone who is too ordinary.

In 1976 Governor Jimmy Carter seemed to grasp this conflict and he ran as local, down-home, farm-boy-next-door makes good. The image of the peanut farmer turned gifted governor contributed greatly to Carter's success as a national candidate and he used it with consummate skill. Early in his presidential bid, Carter enjoyed introducing himself as peanut farmer *and* nuclear physicist, once again suggesting he was down to earth but cerebral as well.

Ronald Reagan illustrated another aspect of this paradox. He was a representative all-American—small-town, midwestern, and also a rich celebrity of stage, screen, and television. He boasted of having been a Democrat, yet campaigned as a Republican. A veritable Mr. Smith goes to Washington, he also had uncommon star quality. Bill Clinton liked us to view him as both a Rhodes scholar and an ordinary saxophone-playing member of the high school band from Hope, Arkansas; as a John Kennedy and even an Elvis figure; and also as just another jogger who would stop by for a Big Mac on the way home from a run in the neighborhood. When George W. Bush was running for president, he emphasized his Texan business, baseball, and oil roots and absolutely deemphasized his elite New England prep school, Yale College, and Harvard Business School training.

A president or would-be president must be bright but not too bright, warm and accessible but not too folksy, down to earth but not pedestrian.

George W. Bush, pictured here with baseball Hall-of-Famer Nolan Ryan in 1999, played up his plain-folks, Texas baseball-owner persona throughout his 2000 presidential campaign. (*Source:* Courtesy of the National Baseball Hall of Fame Library, Cooperstown, NY.)

Democratic party presidential candidate in 1952 and 1956, Adlai Stevenson was witty and clever, talents that seldom pay in politics. Voters apparently prefer plainness and solemn platitudes, but these too can be overdone; witness Gerald Ford's talks, no matter what the occasion, that dulled our senses with the banal. People also joked that when Jimmy Carter gave a fireside chat even the fire fell asleep. The "catch 22" here is that an uncommon performance puts distance between a president and the truly common man. We persist, however, in wanting an uncommon individual as president.

We are often torn between demanding dynamic, charismatic leadership from our presidents and wanting presidents to heed our views. The preeminently successful presidents radiated courage and hope and stirred the hearts and minds of Americans with an almost demagogic ability to simplify and convince. "We need leaders of inspired idealism," said Theodore Roosevelt, "leaders to whom are granted great visions, who dream greatly and strive to make their dreams come true, who can kindle the people with the fire from their own burning souls."[7]

Do we pay a price when we get, permit, or encourage heroic popular leadership in the White House? Does it diminish the vitality of nongovernmental America? Does it possibly dissipate citizen and civic participation and responsibility? We haven't studied these effects carefully enough to know. We do know, however, that those heroic, larger-than-life presidents sometimes have inadvertently weakened the office for their successors. The impressive and often bold performances of Jefferson, Jackson, Lincoln, Wilson, and FDR may well have made it difficult for their successors to lead. The stretching of the powers and the strenuous performance often invited backlash. It was as if the presidency had roamed too far from the normal and acceptable. Invariably, a leveling of their successors seemed to take place.

There is another related problem with the notion of heroic presidential leadership. Most of the time those who wait around for heroic leaders in the White House are disappointed. This is because most of the time presidents do not provide galvanizing, brilliant policy leadership. In practice, the people make policy more often than presidents do; solutions percolate up rather than being imposed from the top down. Indeed, on many of the more important issues the people generally have to wait for presidents to catch up. In the over-all scheme of the untidy policy making process the public often is out in front, as they were in the move to get out of Vietnam, as they were in civil rights and in demanding better and more sustained arms control negotiations. Thus the old question of who leads whom gets raised. Presidents, much of the time, are shrewd followers; it is only in national emergencies that they sometimes can become heroic, pace-setting, or in-advance-of-their-times leaders.

*Paradox #3.* We want a decent, just, caring, and compassionate president, yet we admire a cunning, guileful, and, on occasions that warrant it, even a ruthless, manipulative president.

There is always a fine line between boldness and recklessness, between strong self-confidence and what the Greeks called "hubris," between dogged determination and pigheaded stubbornness. Opinion polls indicate people want a just, decent, and intellectually honest individual as our chief executive. Almost as strongly, however, the public also demands the quality of toughness.

We may admire modesty, humility, and a sense of proportion, but most of our great leaders have been vain and crafty. After all, you don't get to the White House by being a wallflower. Most have aggressively sought power and were rarely preoccupied with metaphysical inquiry or ethical considerations.

Franklin Roosevelt's biographers, while emphasizing his compassion for the average American, also agree he was vain, devious, and had a passion for secrecy. These, they note, are often the standard weaknesses of great leaders. Significant social and political advances are made by those with drive, ambition, and a certain amount of brash, irrational self-confidence.

One psychologist believes Americans insist that our country's leaders display moral judgment, "but nothing dismays them as much as an office-holder who appears publicly anguished or in conflict over the ambiguities of an issue."[8]

George McGovern and Gerald Ford were criticized for being "too nice," "too decent." Being a "nice guy" is sometimes equated with being soft and afraid of power. The public dislikes the idea that a chief executive might be spineless or sentimental. Gerald Ford, Jimmy Carter, and Bill Clinton were all criticized by their own staffs for failing to "crack the whip" and discipline their advisers.

Would-be presidents simultaneously have to win our trust by displays of integrity while possessing the calculation, single-mindedness, and pragmatism of a jungle fighter.

Ronald Reagan seemed to understand these conflicting signals. He talked often of his concern for the truly needy and he portrayed himself as a devout believer in traditional values. This was manifest in his unusually strong pro-school prayer, pro-life/anti-abortion, and pro-family values positions. At the same time, his family relationships were hardly ideal.

Perhaps Dwight Eisenhower reconciled these clashing expectations better than recent presidents. Blessed with a wonderfully seductive, benign smile and a reserved, calming disposition, he was also the disciplined, strong, no-nonsense five-star general with all the medals and victories to go along with it. His ultimate resource as president was this reconciliation of decency and proven toughness, likability alongside demonstrated valor. Some of his biographers suggest his success was at least partly due to his uncanny ability to appear guileless to the public yet act with ample cunning in private.

While Americans want a president who is somewhat religious, they are wary of one who is too much so. Presidents often go out of their way to be photographed going to church or in the presence of noted religious leaders. Nixon and Reagan, who were not religious in the usual sense, held highly publicized Sunday services in the White House and spoke at fundamentalist religious gatherings.

One of the ironies of the American presidency is that those characteristics we condemn in one president, we look for in another. Thus a supporter of Jimmy Carter's once suggested that Sunday school teacher Carter wasn't "rotten enough," "a wheeler-dealer," "an s.o.b."—precisely the virtues (if they can be called that) that Lyndon Johnson was most criticized for a decade earlier. President Clinton was viewed as both a gifted Southern Baptist–style preacher by some admirers and at the same time character challenged by his critics.

We seem to demand a double-faced personality. We demand the sinister as well as the sincere, the cunning as well as the compassionate, President Mean and President Nice, the president as Clint Eastwood and the president as Mr. "Won't You Be My Neighbor" Rogers—tough and hard enough to stand up to Khrushchev and North Korea, to Saddam Hussein and Osama bin Laden, or to press the nuclear button, yet compassionate enough to care for the ill fed, ill clad and ill housed. In this case, the public seems to want a kindhearted s.o.b. or a clean wheeler-dealer, hard roles to cast and an even harder role to perform over eight years.

Former President Nixon, in writing about leaders he worked with, said a modern-day leader has to employ a variety of unattractive qualities on occasion in order to be effective, or at least to appear effective. Nixon may have carried these practices too far when he was in office, but his retirement writings are instructive nonetheless:

> In evaluating a leader, the key question about his behavioral traits is not whether they are attractive or unattractive, but whether they are useful. Guile, vanity, dissembling—in other circumstances these might be unattractive habits, but to the leader they can be essential. He needs guile in order to hold together the shifting coalitions of often bitterly opposed inter-

est groups that governing requires. He needs a certain measure of vanity in order to create the right kind of public impression. He sometimes has to dissemble in order to prevail on crucial issues.[9]

Nixon should know. Despite his notable failings, Nixon was sometimes an effective foreign affairs president.

We want decency and compassion at home, but demand toughness and guile when presidents have to deal with our adversaries. We want presidents to be fierce or compassionate, nice or mean, sensitive or ruthless depending on what we want done, on the situation, and, to some extent, on the role models of the recent past. But woe to a president who is too much or too little possessed of these characteristics!

Leaders need to balance their competing impulses. Because leadership is wholly contextual, what works in one setting may fail in another. Thus, to be effective across issues and time, leaders must be flexible in matching style to circumstance.

In other words, leaders have to be uncommonly active, attentive listeners. They must squint with their ears. Along with listening we expect leaders to decide, and make judgments. Leaders such as Hamlet wait too long. Others, like King Lear or Sophocles' King Creon of Thebes, listen little and act in haste.

Ambition is essential if a leader is to make a major difference. And, to gain power and retain it, one must have a love of power, and this love is often incompatible with moral goodness. In fact, it is often more linked to qualities of pride, duplicity, and cruelty. It raises all the worst fears associated with some of Machiavelli's slash-and-burn tactics.

Too, the intentional use of coercion, force, and even killing may, under certain circumstances, be morally and legally justifiable. The moral dilemma often becomes a choice between two competing evils. The key, usually, is whether the leader is seeking only self-aggrandizement. Leadership divorced from worthy purposes is merely manipulation or deception and, in the extreme, repressive tyranny. We insist that leaders, whatever their style, act with integrity and remain committed to larger purposes and commonly held goals.

Still, a paradox remains. "Power, or organized energy, may be a man-killing explosive or a life-saving drug," wrote Saul Alinsky. "The power of a gun may be used to enforce slavery, or to achieve freedom."[10] And so it is with leadership. Good leaders respect the preciousness of human life. Elements of calculation, abrasiveness, manipulation, and egoism are endemic in leadership. But a president must also be able to consider people in all of their relationships, in the wholeness of their lives, and not just as a means for enhancing profit or productivity.

A person who permits a cynical shell to harden around the heart will not long be able to exercise creative leadership. "The exercise of the heart is that of experiencing, thinking critically, willing, and acting, so as to overcome egocentrism and to share passion with other people . . . and to respond to their needs with the help one can give," writes Michael Maccoby.[11] Presidents who are hell bent on success rarely ponder whether the ends justify their means. Yet we ask that they raise questions of integrity and motivation with themselves.

It was said of the nineteenth-century statesman Henry Clay that he was so brilliant and capable and yet also so corrupt that "like a rotten mackerel in the moonlight, he both shines and stinks." This phrase lives on because it is clever and also because it speaks to a moral ambiguity most Americans find hard to comprehend. "We look for heroes to represent us, although we rarely find them," writes prize-winning journalist Alan Ehrenholt. "We take a certain perverse pleasure in unmasking hypocrites and dispatching blow-hards who fail to deliver on their promises. The leaders we have trouble dealing with are those of obvious talent and genuine achievement who turn out to have displayed appalling ethical insensitivity—or worse."[12] Nixon and Clinton are only the beginning of the list of such leaders.

Abraham Lincoln reminded us that few things are wholly good or wholly evil. Most public policies or ideological choices are an indivisible compound of the two. Thus, our best judgment of the balance between them is continually demanded. The best of presidents are balanced individuals; they are sure of themselves, yet not dogmatic; they are self-confident, yet hopefully willing to learn from their mistakes. They somehow also combine effectiveness and integrity.

*Paradox #4.* We admire the "above politics" nonpartisan or bipartisan approach, yet the presidency is perhaps the most political office in the American system, a system in which we need a creative entrepreneurial master politician.

The public yearns for a statesman in the White House, for a George Washington or a second "era of good feelings"—anything that might prevent partisanship or politics as usual in the White House. Former French President Charles de Gaulle once said, "I'm neither of the left nor of the right nor of the center, but above." In fact, however, the job of president demands that the officeholder be a gifted political broker, ever attentive to changing political moods and coalitions.

Many of our early presidents unambiguously condemned parties while blatantly reaching out for party support when they needed to get their programs through Congress. "It is one of the paradoxes of the office," wrote historian Robert J. Morgan, "that a President must seek to balance his position as chief of his party with an equal need for support of his policies from all quarters of the nation regardless of partisan lines. He owes his office to the efforts of the party which put him there and, yet, once in power, his success as a leader rests in no little measure upon his securing a broad base of popular approval."[13]

Franklin Roosevelt illustrates this well. Appearing so remarkably non-partisan while addressing the nation, he was in practice one of the craftiest manipulators and political-coalition builders to occupy the White House.[14] He could punish friends and reward enemies when needed, or vice versa. He did not always succeed—for example when he tried to "pack the Court" in 1937 and to purge some Democratic members of Congress in 1938.

Presidents are often expected to be above politics in some respects while being highly political in others. Presidents are never supposed to act with their eyes on the next election, yet their power position demands they must. They are neither supposed to favor any particular group or party nor wheel and deal and twist too many arms. Instead, a president is supposed to be "president of all the people," above politics: "a unifier not a divider," as George W. Bush said he would be when he ran for the White House in 2000.

A president is also asked to lead a party, to help fellow party members get elected or reelected, to deal firmly with party barons, interest group chieftains, and congressional political brokers. His ability to gain legislative victories depends on his skills at party leadership and on the size of his party's congressional membership. Jimmy Carter once lamented that "It's very difficult for someone to serve in this office and meet the difficult issues in a proper and courageous way and still maintain a combination of interest-group approval that will provide a clear majority at election time."[15]

To take the president out of politics is to assume, incorrectly, that a president will be generally right and the public generally wrong, that a president must be protected from the push and shove of political pressures. But what president has always been right? Over the years, public opinion has usually been as sober a guide as anything else on the political waterfront. And, lest we forget, having a president constrained and informed by public opinion is the defining characteristic of a democracy.

The fallacy of antipolitics presidencies is that only one view of the national interest is tenable, and a president may pursue that view only by ignoring political conflict and pressure. Politics, properly conceived, is the art of accommodating the diversity and variety of public opinion to meet public goals. Politics is the task of building durable coalitions and majorities. It isn't always pretty. "The process isn't immaculate and cannot always be kid-gloved. A president and his men must reward loyalty and punish opposition; it is the only way."[16]

> A president has to be far more than a party leader; but if he is not at least that he usually will fail—fail to accomplish his goals, however worthy, and fail to perpetuate the influence of the forces and considerations that elected him. Governing takes politics; it also takes persistence.[17]

Factions and partisan coalitions are a reality in American politics—even if many of our founders tried to wish them away. Paradoxically, men like Alexander Hamilton, John Adams, and Thomas Jefferson, all of whom had condemned political parties in the 1780s, vigorously reached out for party support only a few years later. Jefferson, the man who unambiguously proclaimed that if he "could go to heaven but with a party, I would not go there at all," became one of the most astute party leaders in American presidential history.

No president can escape politics. Presidents must first be elected by their party. And presidents who are effective must rely on party leaders in Congress and the states.

In their attempts to be unifying leaders, presidents often avoid polarizing conflicts. One of the lessons of history, however, is that early confrontation of controversial and divisive issues may avoid later violence. Further, sharpening conflict is often an important leadership responsibility. After he had left the White House, Harry Truman said a president "who is any damn good at all makes enemies. I even made a few myself when I was in the White House, and I wouldn't have been without them." The desire for a nonpolitical presidency sometimes is a staunchly status quo desire to curb presidents, like Harry Truman and Franklin Roosevelt, from becoming advocates and coalition builders for humanitarian progress through political reform.

If past is prologue, presidents will go to considerable lengths to portray themselves as unconcerned with their own political future. They will do so in large part because the public applauds a divorce between the presidency and politics. People naively think that we can somehow turn the job of president into that of a managerial or strictly executive post.

Yet the presidency is a highly political office, and it cannot be otherwise. Moreover, its political character is for the most part desirable. A president separated from, or somehow above, politics might easily become a president who doesn't listen to the people, doesn't respond to majority sentiment or pay attention to views that may be diverse, intense, and at odds with his own. Presidents may not always wish to obey the will of the majority—in fact, leadership sometimes requires them to publicly argue against majority sentiment—but they cannot be unmindful of the will of the people. A president indifferent to or somehow "above" politics would be a president who would become too easily isolated from the processes of government and from the thoughts and aspirations of the people.

This clashing expectation will endure. A standard diagnosis of what's gone wrong in an administration will be that the presidency has become too politicized. Yet it is futile to try to take the president out of politics. A more useful approach is to realize that certain presidents try too hard to hold themselves above politics, or at least to give that appearance, rather than engage in it deeply, openly, and creatively. A democratic president has to act politically regarding controversial issues if any semblance of government by consent is to be achieved.

In sum, political skills are a necessity, not a liability, for those presidents who want to be effective. High-minded declarations that "I'm above politics" may be appealing, yet just as an intelligent home owner would seldom think of hiring someone who boasted of being without plumbing skills to solve a plumbing problem, a prudent voter should remain skeptical of candidates who boast they are not political and have disdain for politics.

*Paradox #5.* We want a president who can unify us, yet the job requires taking firm stands, making unpopular or controversial decisions that necessarily upset and divide us.

A president should be a national unifier and a *harmonizer* while at the same time the job requires priority setting and *advocacy* leadership. Such tasks are near opposites.

Presidents, it is expected, must pull us together. Presidents must build coalitions and seek consensus. Presidents must not be too far ahead of their times if they are to be successful.

> He must see what he sees with the eyes of the multitude upon whose shoulders he stands. To get anywhere he must win understanding; to win it, the policy he pursues must never be so remote from the view about him that he cannot get that understanding. At bottom, his real power is in the popular support he can rally. . . . [18]

The United States is one of the few in the world that calls on its chief executive to serve as its symbolic, ceremonial head of state *and* as its political head of government. Elsewhere, these tasks are spread around. In some nations there is a monarch and a prime minister; in others there are three visible national leaders—a head of state, a premier, and a powerful party chief.

In the absence of an alternative office or institution, we ask our president to act as a unifying force in our lives. Perhaps it all began with George Washington, who so artfully performed this function. At least for a while he truly was a unique symbol of our new nation. He was a healer and an extraordinary man for several seasons. Today we ask no less of our presidents than that they should do as Washington did.

We have designed a presidential job description, however, that often forces our contemporary presidents to act as national dividers. Presidents must necessarily divide when they act as the leaders of their political parties, when they set priorities to the advantage of certain goals and groups at the expense of others, when they forge and lead political coalitions, when they move out ahead of public opinion and assume the role of national educators, when they choose one set of advisers over another, when they decide we should enter into a military campaign. A president, as a creative executive leader, cannot help but offend certain interests.

The opposite is, of course, also true. Presidents obsessed with striving to protect their power and popularity by choosing to act can run into difficulties as well. Presidents may avoid divisive conflict in favor of short-run, low-risk policymaking. Such a president may seem effective but may in reality undermine the confidence of the American people and the credibility of the presidency in the long run.

The nation is torn between the view that a president should primarily preside over the nation and merely serve as a referee among the various powerful interests that actually control who gets what, when, and how and a second position, which holds that a president should gain control of government processes and powers so as to use them for the purpose of furthering public, as opposed to private, interests.

The president is sometimes seen as the great defender of the people, the ombudsman or advocate general of "public interests." But this should be viewed as merely a claim, for many presidents have acted otherwise, even antagonistically, to mass or popular preferences.

Hence, we alternately want our presidents to stir things up or calm things down, to enlarge conflict or to lessen conflict. Much depends, too, on how you define leadership. And only the narrowest conception of leadership would call solely for the avoidance of conflict.

The public demands results, yet often judges presidents on the basis of means. Whereas the public will usually approve of the ends of certain policies, they may disapprove of the means. Means often require sacrifice, and this can turn the public against a president.

Leaders are forever having to decide how much harmony or stirring up is needed to achieve objectives. All organizations need action and decisiveness, yet they also need shared values, community, and integration. The truly effective president understands how to use selective conflict for revitalization.

*Paradox #6.* We expect our presidents to provide bold creative, visionary, innovative, *programmatic* leadership and at the same time to *pragmatically* respond to the will of public opinion majorities; that is to say, we expect presidents to lead and to follow, to exercise "democratic leadership."

We want both pragmatic and programmatic leadership. We want principled leadership and flexible, adaptable leaders. *Lead us,* but also *listen to us.* We want presidents with creative plans who will also respond to facts and be able to improvise according to varying contexts.

Most people can be led only where they want to go. "Authentic leadership," wrote James MacGregor Burns, "is a collective process." It emerges from a sensitivity or appreciation of the motives and goals of both followers and leaders. The test of leadership, according to Burns, "is the realization of intended, real change that meets people's enduring needs." Thus a key function of leadership is "to engage followers, not merely to activate them, to commingle needs and aspirations and goals in a common enterprise, and in the process to make better citizens of both leaders and followers."[19]

Leadership at its best unlocks the talent and energy of the nation. Strong presidential leadership can provide a vision that empowers all of us to rise above the routine and make real contributions to our common purpose. Yet Americans rebel against too much of this hierarchical leadership, and we emphatically resist being led too far in any one direction.

We expect vigorous, innovative leadership when crises occur. Once a crisis is past, however, we neither need nor want them around. We do expect presidents to provide us with bold, creative, and forceful initiatives "to move us ahead," but we resist radical new ideas and changes and usually embrace "new" initiatives only after they have achieved some consensus.

Most of our presidents have been conservatives or "pragmatic liberals." They seldom ventured much beyond the crowd. They followed public opinion rather than shaped it. John F. Kennedy, the author of the much-acclaimed *Profiles in Courage,* was often criticized for presenting more profile than courage. Kennedy responded to his critics by pointing out that he had barely won election in 1960 and that great innovations should not be forced on the public by a leader with such a slender mandate. He also said that caution is needed, that the important issues are complicated, technical, and best left to the administrative and political experts. Seldom did Kennedy attempt to change the political context in which he operated. Instead he resisted, "the new form of politics emerging with the civil rights movement: mass action, argument on social fundamentals, appeals to considerations of justice and morality. Moving the American political system in such a direction would necessarily have been long range, requiring arduous educational work and promising substantial political risk."[20]

Leadership requires radiating hope, grounded in reality. Be dedicated to "visions" and be passionately committed to carrying them out. Be flexible enough to change direction quickly. The art of the possible is wanted, the challenges of bringing about the doable and the desirable, yet creative dreaming also is required. A constant balance, reconciling dreams and reality, intuition and logic, is needed.

We occasionally look to idealists and prophets because we know that major breakthroughs and reforms often come only from the principled few, not the conventional political or organizational leaders. This is true, in part, because majority opinion often stifles new approaches. As most politicians know: if you oppose your constituents too directly on an issue too close to their hearts, you are not going to get elected, or re-elected.

Presidents can get caught coming and going. The public wants them to be both leaders of the country and representatives of the people. We want them to be decisive and exercise their own judgment; we want them to be responsive to public opinion, especially to the "common sense" of *our* opinions. It was perhaps with this in mind that many have defined the ideal democratic leader as an "uncommon man of common opinions."

Americans may admire consistency in the abstract, but in politics consistency has its costs. Everett Dirksen, a popular Republican U.S. senator from Illinois, used to say, "I'm a man of fixed and unbending principle—but my first fixed and unbending principle is to be flexible at all times."

Franklin D. Roosevelt proclaimed that the presidency is preeminently a place for moral leadership. But he was also an opportunist and pragmatist just as Lincoln and Theodore Roosevelt were before and as Kennedy, Reagan, and Clinton would be after him. Former California governor and erstwhile presidential candidate Jerry Brown once told an interviewer that "a little vagueness goes a long way in this business."

Those men knew that political leadership responsibilities in America meant sometimes being detached, vague, and uncommitted, while at other times taking a stand and being passionately committed. Timing often determined their success or failure. But perhaps more important, the lesson for those who want political power in America is that they must narrow their range of ideas and ideals to conform to the prevailing political and economic climate of opinion.

Our paradoxical desire for programmatic yet pragmatic leadership is compounded by the reality that what we find desirable in one president we condemn in another. This factor often renders the lessons of history immaterial, and makes such a thing as standard pragmatic or programmatic leadership difficult, if not impossible.

A president who becomes too committed risks being called rigid; a president who becomes too pragmatic risks being called wishy-washy. However, the more a president tries to please everyone and respond only to immediate pressures, the more that president is likely to be drawn away from the more significant remote problems of the day. The more pragmatic presidents become, the more they are shaped by events rather than being shapers of them.

Most candidates view a campaign as a fight to win office, not an occasion for adult education. Barry Goldwater in 1964 ran with the slogan "We offer a choice not an echo," referring to his unusually thematic strategy, but Republican party regulars who yearned to win the election preferred "a chance, not a choice." Once in office, presidents often operate the same way—the electoral connection looms large as an issue-avoiding, controversy-ducking political incentive. Most presidents strive to maximize their options, and hence leave matters up in the air or delay choices.

We want idealism *and* realism, optimism *and* levelheadedness. Be inspirational, we tell the president, but also be realistic—don't promise more than you can deliver. We ask our presidents to stir our blood, and rekindle a sense of glory about our nation, but also to appeal to our reason. Too much inspiration will invariably lead to dashed hopes, disillusionment, and cynicism. The best leaders often suffer from one of their chief virtues—an instinctive tendency to raise aspirations, to summon us to transcend personal interests and subordinate ourselves to dreaming dreams of a bolder, more majestic national community.

Most Americans want to be inspired. We savor the upbeat rhetoric and promises of a brighter tomorrow. We genuinely want to hear about New Nationalism, New Deals, New Frontiers, Great Societies, New American Revolutions, and New Covenants; we want our fears to be assuaged during a "fireside chat" or a "conversation with the President"; we want to be told "the torch has been passed to a new generation of Americans . . . and the glow from that fire can truly light the world." We want something to believe. We want fearless leaders to tell us that the "only fear we have to fear is fear itself," that "we are Number One," that a recession has "bottomed out," or that "America is back standing tall again." To understate the state of the nation is to seem unpresidential.

Presidents who do not raise hopes are criticized for letting events shape their presidency rather than making things happen. A president who eschewed inspiration of any kind would be rejected as un-American. For people everywhere America has been the land of promise, of possibilities, of dreams. No president can stand in the way of this truth, regardless of the current dissatisfaction about the size of big government in Washington and its incapacity to deliver the services it promises.

Do presidents overpromise because presidential aspirants are congenital optimists, or because they are pushed by the demanding public? Or are competing candidates engaged in an escalating spiral of promise heaped upon promise as they try to outbid each other for votes? Surely the public demands it, but only self-confident optimists need apply in the first place. Whatever the source, few presidents have been able to keep all their major promises and fulfill their intentions. Poverty was not ended; a Great Society was not realized. Vietnam dragged on and on. Watergate outraged a public that had been promised an open presidency. Energy independence, balanced budgets, and an end to terrorism remain an illusion.

Charlie Brown of Peanuts cartoon fame once said, "I have very strong opinions, but they don't last long." So also American public opinion shifts—sometimes quickly, sometimes slowly. There are times when we want presidents to be engaged actively as innovators, and on other occasions we would like to see them sit back and let things run their course.

Historically, conservatives have been more opposed to a strong presidency than liberals. This changes, especially when conservatives occupy the White House. Conservatives may fear a powerful planning presidency at home, but they want an assertive presidency, such as that of Reagan or George W. Bush, for national security leadership. Liberals, of course, have generally applauded a strong presidency when it has been in the hands of an FDR or Clinton. Overall, in the debate over the proper range of presidential power our attitudes are shaped considerably by the party and by the kind of leader in the White House at the time.

American historian Arthur M. Schlesinger, Sr., when writing about public mood shifts in America, once claimed that "a period of concern for the rights of the few has been followed by one of concern for the wrongs of the many. . . . An era of quietude has been succeeded by one of rapid movement."[21] A period of affirmative government is followed by backlash and a period of lull.

This examination of shifting public mood is of interest because a president is constrained by the dominant national mood or climate of expectations. Sometimes the coming of a new president can help to recast or shift the national mood. More often, however, the national mood responds to major events, or challenges.

*Paradox #7.* Americans want powerful, self-confident presidential leadership. Yet we are inherently suspicious of leaders who are arrogant, and above criticism.

We cherish our three branches of government with their checks and balances and theories of dispersed and separated powers. We want our presidents to be successful and to share their power with their cabinets, Congress, and other "responsible" national leaders. In theory, we oppose the concentration of power, we dislike secrecy, and we resent depending on any one person to provide all of our leadership.

But Americans, at least on occasion, also yearn for dynamic, aggressive presidents—even if they do cut some corners. We celebrate gutsy presidents who made a practice of manipulating and pushing Congress. We perceive the great presidents to be those who stretched their legal authority and dominated the other branches of government. It is still Jefferson, Jackson, Lincoln, and the Roosevelts who get top billing. Whatever may have been the framers' intentions for the three branches, most experts believe that most of the time, especially in crises, our system works best when the presidency is strong and when we have a self-confident, assertive president.

There is, of course, a fine line between confidence and arrogance, firmness and inflexibility. We want presidents who are not afraid to exert their will, but at what point does this become antidemocratic, even authoritarian?

We want presidents to consult widely and use the advice of cabinet members and other top advisers. We like the idea of collegial leadership and shared responsibility. But do we want presidents to sacrifice their own ideas and priorities to those of their cabinet officers? No. We elect the president, not the advisers. While we want presidents to be open minded, we also admire the occasional "profile in courage" type of decision. One of the most fondly remembered Lincoln stories underscores this point. President Lincoln supposedly took a vote at a cabinet meeting and it went entirely against him. He announced it this way: "Seven nays and one aye, the ayes have it." But most of the time, Abraham Lincoln followed the leadership of Congress, his advisers, and the general public.[22]

> A president who is believed not to make up his own mind rapidly loses the power to maintain the hold. The need to dramatize his position by insistence upon his undoubted supremacy is inherent in the office as history has shaped it. A masterful man in the White House will, under all circumstances, be more to the liking of the multitude than one who is thought to be swayed by his colleagues.[23]

We want simultaneously a secular leader and a civil religious mentor; we praise our three-branched system, but we place capacious hopes upon and thus elevate the presidential branch. Many people believe only the president can give us sustained leadership, can dramatize and symbolize our highest expectations of ourselves as an almost "chosen" people with a unique mission.

Although a president is expected to exude hope, reassurance, and an "I'm OK we're OK" sense of confidence, the public nevertheless likes to see presidents visibly wrestling with crises. We admire the solitary executive embattled in conflict sitting alone, making the tough decision, exerting will. Presidents learn that more political support is available when the United States is at odds with an enemy. It is almost easier to go to the brink of war than to defend advances in detente or new arms agreements. President Kennedy found "the politics of confrontation" with Cuba as well as with Khrushchev politically helpful. President Reagan benefited from a military mission with Grenada, and both Presidents G. H. W. Bush and George W. Bush won praise and popular support for "winning" the Gulf War and the war in Afghanistan.[24]

Presidents are simultaneously asked to build a lasting peace and to maintain United States superiority as the superpower. Promote peace, yes. But don't yield anything to the enemy. Moreover, presidents who wish to appear presidential must accentuate the nation's sense of being in a severe predicament. They perceive that a sense of heightened crisis must be created. FDR did it, as did Kennedy, especially in the summer of 1961 when he launched his "everybody build a fallout shelter" program. Ronald Reagan's claims of a "window of vulnerability" and the "evil empire" of the Soviet Union may have been partly the product of a desire to alarm the public into action.

The danger of falling under the "leadership" of one who lacks will or confidence to lead persists. Humility is admirable, while excessive humility paralyzes. Significant advances in the world have often been made by confident innovators.

Leaders must face all the complexities of the situation but they must also act. Leaders are conscious of the flaws in their own organization, yet minimize the risks. They know their followers often want and need relentless optimism about impending battles. Shakespeare's *Henry V* provided this almost irrational, gamble-all, whatever-the-odds call to arms. Winston Churchill in the midst of World War II also personified this dimension.

"Any self-doubts the leader may have, especially in the battlefield, must be concealed at all costs," wrote military historian John Keegan. "The leader of men in warfare can show himself to his followers only through a mask, . . . made in such form as will mark him to men of his time and place as the leader they want and need."[25]

Rare is the great commander, the truly successful executive, or the politician who is not self-centered and conceited. Similarly, the politician who does not exude the desire for leadership is not likely to be effective or remembered. A leader must be self-confident enough to believe he or she is indispensable.

Untempered confidence, however, is dangerous. Hitler oozed it. So did Melville's mad Captain Ahab. Both had vision, purpose, and enormous drive.

The question is whether these large egos are subject to reasonable self-control. Self-discipline is key. An unrestrained ego that constantly needs to be fed and isn't placed in disciplined service to worthy ends is an ego that invariably corrupts.

Leaders, of course, must believe in themselves, but they cannot afford to discredit the ideas, plans, counsel, or criticism of others. Leaders who encourage thoughtful dissent in their organizations are, according to several studies, likely to produce better organizational decision-making. Effective presidents encourage and reward criticism without retaliating against the critics. Hitler eliminated his critics. Ahab ignored his. In *Antigone,* Sophocles' King Creon listened almost entirely to himself, which proved fatal. His son, Haemon, chided him in vain, saying, "Let not your first thought be your only thought. Think if there cannot be some other way. Surely, to think you own the only wisdom and yours the only word, the only will, betrays a shallow spirit, an empty heart."

But Creon dismisses his son's advice, saying, "Indeed, am I to take lessons at my time of life from a fellow of his age?" He ignores everyone else as well until it is too late.

Presidents are a little like Creon. A fine line separates self-confidence from conceit, boldness from recklessness, mindless adherence to the course from reevaluation and redirection. The challenge is how to blend the competing impulses and combine them effectively in particular situations.

*Paradox #8.* What it takes to become president may not be what is needed to govern the nation.

To win a presidential election takes ambition, money, years of hard work, masterful public relations strategies, as well as some luck. It requires the formation of an electoral coalition. To govern a democracy requires much more. It requires the formation of a *governing* coalition, and the ability to compromise and bargain.

"People who win primaries may become good presidents—but 'it ain't necessarily so'" wrote columnist David Broder. "Organizing well is important in governing just as it is in winning primaries. But the Nixon years should teach us that good advance men do not necessarily make trustworthy White House aides. Establishing a government is a little more complicated than having the motorcade run on time."[26]

Ambition and determination are essential for a presidential candidate, yet too much of either can be dangerous. A candidate must be bold and energetic, but in excess these characteristics can produce a cold, frenetic candidate. To win the presidency obviously requires a laser-like single-mindedness, yet our presidents must also have a sense of proportion, be well rounded, have a sense of humor, be able to take a joke, and have hobbies and interests outside the realm of politics.

To win the presidency many of our candidates (Lincoln, Kennedy, and Clinton to cite a few) had to pose as being more progressive or even populist than they actually were, to be effective in the job they are compelled to appear more cautious and conservative than they often want to be. One of Carter's political strategists said, "Jimmy campaigned liberal, but governed conservative." Bill Clinton pointed out toward the end of his first year in office, "We've all become Eisenhower Republicans."[27]

Another aspect of campaigning for the White House is the ambiguous position candidates take on issues in order to increase their appeal to the large bulk of centrist and independent voters. The following is a typical view replete with paradox: "I want my presidential candidate to have clear-cut policies, to be as clear and precise as possible on his positions, not hazy and ambiguous—to run a campaign that educates people and persuades them to adopt the candidate's positions. But I also want my candidate to win—I realize they have to be ambiguous to build the winning coalitions."[28]

Policy positions are seldom comprehensively outlined; bumper-sticker slogans and entertaining TV ads are designed to please most people and offend few. Such presidential pledges as LBJ's "We will not send American boys to fight the war that Asian boys should be fighting," Richard Nixon's "open presidency" (1968) and "peace is at hand" (1972), Carter *and* Reagan's "I will balance the budget," and as noted previously, George W. Bush's "I'm a uniter, not a divider" are illustrative.

One of the most difficult aspects of campaigning is to win without proving you are unworthy of the job you are seeking. Thus it is a common temptation for all candidates, including some incumbents, to run a "bureaucrats-are-bums," anti-Washington outsider, kind of campaign. There is something more than a little deceitful, and certainly a lot that is ironic, in a presidential candidate who is trying to get to Washington by saying that he is running "against Washington," and one hoping to be elected to the most powerful office in the world by proclaiming that he is against big government. An irony of the 1980s is that Reagan campaigned against big government yet left bloated deficits, a proliferation of defense programs, and a bigger government than anyone ever would have imagined in 1980.

We expect a president to be able to work closely and effectively with Congress and civil servants. Candidates who bad-mouth Washington officials will breed resentment; if they get to the White House, they will have a difficult time winning sustained cooperation from these same officials. Candidates who get too pious about how ethical standards have to be raised in Washington will be called hypocrites if their own top aides are caught in compromised conflict-of-interest positions.

We often also want both a "fresh face," an outsider, as a presidential candidate *and* a seasoned, mature, experienced veteran who knows the corridors of power and the back alleyways of Washington. That is one of the reasons Colin Powell fascinated so many people. Frustration with past presidential performances leads us to turn to a "fresh new face" uncorrupted by Washington's politics and its "buddy system." But inexperience, especially in foreign affairs, has sometimes led to blunders by the outsiders.

New nominating rules combine with the requirements of the media and this "high tech" campaign age to sharpen the clash between what is required of a successful candidate and the successful president.

To be a winning candidate, the would-be president must put together an electoral coalition involving a majority of voters advantageously distributed across the country. The candidate must thus appeal to all regions and interest groups and cultivate the appearance of honesty, sincerity, and experience. Note that this is not all bad. It's good to travel around the country, meeting people, learning about their problems and testing ideas on diverse audiences. As Jimmy Carter put it, "I was a hell of a better American because I had to go around the country and learn about the different regions and people. . . . You have to be able to stand up under pressure and have the physical endurance and ability to express yourself . . . and let the public learn about you as you learn about them."[29]

Once elected, however, the electoral coalition has served much of its purpose and a governing coalition is the order of the day.

Candidates depend on television to transform candidacy into incumbency. Studies find that candidates spend well over half their funds on radio and television broadcasting. Moreover, this is how most people "learn" about the candidates. At least two-thirds of the American public report television is the way they follow candidates, and about half of the public acknowledges that their best understanding of the candidates and issues is derived from television coverage. This may change in the twenty-first century as the Internet becomes omnipresent and as more political watchdog groups report on candidates via this medium.

While important, television has mixed and confusing effects for the presidency. Faults are exaggerated and "looking good" often becomes as important as doing well.

Thus, what it takes to become president may differ from what it takes to *be* president. To become president takes a determined, and even a driven, person, a master fund-raiser, a person who is glib, dynamic, charming on television, and hazy on the issues. But once president, the person must be well rounded, careful in reasoning, clear and specific in communications, and not excessively ambitious.

*Paradox #9.* The presidency is sometimes too strong, yet other times too weak.

Presidents are granted wide latitude in dealing with events abroad. At times, presidents can act unilaterally, without the express consent of Congress. While the constitutional grounds for such action may be dubious, the climate of expectations allows presidents to act decisively abroad. This being the case, the public comes to think the president can do the same at home. But this is usually not the case. A clashing expectation is built into the presidency when strength in some areas is matched with weakness in other areas.

It often seems that our presidency is *always too strong* and *always too weak:* Always too powerful given our worst fears of tyranny and our ideals of a "government by the people"; always too strong, as well, because it now possesses the capacity to wage nuclear war (a capacity that doesn't permit much in the way of checks and balances and deliberative, participatory government); yet always too weak when we remember nuclear proliferation, the rising national debt, the budget deficit, lingering discrimination, poverty, and the clutch of other fundamental problems yet to be solved.

The presidency is always too strong when we dislike the incumbent. Its limitations are bemoaned, however, when we believe the incumbent is striving valiantly to serve the public interest as we define it. The Lyndon Johnson presidency vividly captured this paradox: many who believed he was too strong in Vietnam also believed he was too weak to wage his War on Poverty. Others believed the opposite.

Since President Washington took office we have multiplied the requirements for presidential leadership and made them increasingly difficult to fulfill. Students of the presidency usually conclude that more power, not less, will be needed if presidents are to get the job done.

But if the presidency is to be given more power, should it not also be subject to more controls? Perhaps so. But what controls will curb the power of a president who abuses the public trust and at the same time not undermine the capacity of a fair-minded president to serve the public interest? The riddle here arises because we sometimes disagree over which days are good and which are bad. Thus Ford's extensive use of the veto power was applauded by some and condemned by others, as was his pardon of Nixon. Likewise, Clinton's efforts to end the ban on gays in the military was seen by some as a strengthening of human rights and equality, by others as condoning or encouraging what they saw as immoral behavior.

*Paradox #10.* Presidents are order *affirming* and order *creating.* Presidents celebrate traditional American values and the American way of doing things yet an effective president often has to help us create bold new traditions and a new order where, as Lincoln once reminded us, the dogmas of the past become irrelevant to new challenges.

Presidents serve as the primary agents of modernization in the United States. No nation can stagnate and long endure. But political change is resisted. Since we fear change, and a variety of political roadblocks stand in the way, how are needed reforms enacted?

In order to promote change, presidents must simultaneously affirm and create order. They begin by affirming the past, and use that past to undo the present and recreate it on the basis of past values.[30]

Abraham Lincoln understood this better than most. In his Gettysburg Address and Second Inaugural Address, Lincoln affirmed the nation's commitment to past values, but reinvented the future by reinterpreting those values to reflect modern necessity. He paid tribute to the framers of the Constitution while elevating the principles of the Declaration of Independence above the Constitution. In effect he promoted a conservative revolution: conservative in that it grounded itself in the security of known values from the past, but revolutionary in that it reordered those values to place political democracy and equality above all else. Lincoln affirmed the reordered traditional values of the collective past as a way to affirm a new vision for the future.[31]

In a way, all presidents are compelled to couch reform and modernization in the comforting, familiar clothing of past values. To be forward-looking we must affirm the past. Change, to be acceptable, must be grounded in deeply rooted American values.

## CONCLUSION

*Leadership* means many things to many people. For some it has a rich, positive meaning. For others it connotes manipulation, deception, or even oppression.

Neither presidents nor the general public should be relieved of their respective responsibilities for trying to fashion a more effective and fair-minded leadership system simply because the presidency is an office full of clashing expectations. We cannot throw up our hands and say, "Well, no one makes a person run for that crazy job in the first place."

All leaders face countervailing pressures that pull them in different directions. Sisyphus of Greek mythology was a man condemned forever to roll a rock up a hill only to have it roll down before reaching the top. "I have discovered the secret that after climbing a great hill," Nelson Mandela said, "one only finds that there are many more hills to climb."[32]

We have to select presidents who understand these dilemmas and have a gift for the improvisation necessitated by their contrary demands. Too often we have selected persons who have simply learned to manipulate these contending expectations for short-term electoral purposes.

We need to probe the origins and to assess the consequences of the clashing expectations and to learn how presidents and we as the public can better coexist with them. It is apparent that they often serve to confuse us in our evaluation of presidents, and they create tremendous ambiguity for presidents.

When Americans realize that the presidency is incapable of dealing with everything well and that democratic politics, in general, is not suited to provide quick answers to every social and economic malaise, then we will be more responsible in the way we judge presidents.

# Electing Presidents

He shall hold his Office during the Term of four Years. . . . No person except a natural born Citizen, or a Citizen of the United States at the time of the Adoption of this Constitution, shall be eligible to the Office of President; neither shall any person be eligible to that Office who shall not have attained to the Age of thirty-five years, and been fourteen Years a Resident within the United States.

U.S. Constitution, Article II

If Jefferson is elected, the Bible will be burned, the French "Marseillaise" will be sung in Christian churches, and we may see our wives and daughters the victims of legal prostitution; soberly dishonored; speciously polluted.

Reverend Timothy Dwight, President, Yale University, quoted<br>in D.C. Coyle, Order of the Presidency (1960), p. 43

The [2000] presidential election leaves us all baffled, bothered and bewildered. It should be some consolation, though, that this is not the first time the republic has endured tight elections and confusing results. Nor is it the first time the winner of the popular vote has been denied the presidency. Nor is it the first time the Electoral College has been a source of trouble.

Arthur Schlesinger, Jr., "It's a Mess, But We've Been Through<br>It Before," Time, November 20, 2000, p. 64.

The presidential election of 2000 was full of paradoxes and surprising twists and turns. It was a cynic's paradise and a democrat's nightmare. It took weeks after the election before the U.S. Supreme Court essentially settled the election by approving a process whereby the candidate who had won the popular vote by more than a half-million votes was declared the loser.

The candidate with more training for the job and more experience lost his bid for the White House. Indeed, for the fourth time in a generation, the election, as validated by the electoral college, went to a non-Washingtonian, an outsider governor. This happened despite the fact that Al Gore, as vice president, had been a key partner in an administration that could claim to have helped influence, if not to have guided, an enormously robust period of peace and prosperity—usually thought to be the two key advantages of incumbents seeking to win reelection.

Moreover, "elaborate academic models and sophisticated polling" predicted the loser would be the winner, and ultimately the outcome of the November 7, 2000, election "depended on bungling, dedicated, and even random acts by obscure election officials" in Florida more than it did on the American voters.[1] Further, it was an embarrassment for the role of the United States as a "leading" democracy. After decades of U.S. "mentoring" of elections in other nations, presumably to ensure that democratic participation and voters really mattered, the United States found itself trying to explain to others why we couldn't get a vote count right and that many voters had been misled by flawed ballot designs. There exists, too, the possibility that the loser won the election, in both the popular and electoral counts. After 105 million voters voted, it was ultimately a handful of Supreme Court justices who forcibly "selected" a president by a narrow 5–4 vote, coincidentally split largely along partisan and ideological lines.[2]

Americans love their country, celebrate democratic ideals, and generally prize the American presidency, yet we are far less bullish and reverential about the way we elect presidents. Quite a few Americans were bewildered by the presidential election of 2000, are baffled by the electoral college, and are embarrassed by the always huge role money plays in presidential elections. Then, too, people see the selection process as an often self-defeating system that is more like a demolition derby, a process of eliminating good people rather than encouraging good candidates to run for the White House. Many worry as well at the paradox noted in Chapter 1, that the qualities needed to govern are not necessarily the same as those needed to win the White House.

This chapter explores and explains how we elect our presidents. The following questions are discussed: Who becomes president? What do we look for in prospective presidents? What must a person do to be taken seriously as a presidential candidate? How important are the primaries? Are national conventions still needed? What about the so-called advantages of incumbency? What has been the effect of the Twenty-second Amendment? Why do people vote or not vote for a president? What about the controversial electoral college and its role in presidential elections? And finally, does the selection process do what we need in democratic and quality-of-outcome terms? After all, a presidential election is about more than merely determining who will assume office. It is also, or should be, the great conversation a democracy has concerning its future.

## WHO BECOMES PRESIDENT?

Our presidents are usually middle-aged white male Protestant lawyers of European lineage from the larger states. Thirty-seven of our forty-three presidents trace ancestry to the British Isles, three were Dutch, and two were German. All but one, John Kennedy, were Protestants. About half have been lawyers and served in Congress. Most others have held state or community elective office. A handful were military heroes.

Gone are the days when party leaders could select a presidential candidate. Today, with the proliferation of primary elections, candidates who are well financed and can devote themselves to full-time campaigning often have an advantage over public figures who occupy office. Candidates such as Jimmy Carter and Ronald Reagan had the advantage over most of their rivals. Wealthy individuals such as H. Ross Perot and Steve Forbes can "buy" their way into a race.

In one sense, there is an "on-deck" circle of at most thirty to forty individuals in any given presidential election year: governors, prominent U.S. senators, a few members of the House of Representatives, and a handful of recent governors or vice presidents who have successfully kept themselves in the news media. These men, and an occasional woman, form the core of electables whom "The Great Mentioner," that mythic conglomeration of prominent media figures, is willing to anoint as serious candidates.

No doubt there are talented business entrepreneurs, educators, or other outstanding individuals who might make as capable a president as any of the activist politicians who inevitably become the serious candidates. Seldom, however, are these nonprofessional politicians willing to enter the political thicket at age 56 or 61. Billionaire H. Ross Perot, who won 19 percent of the popular vote in 1992 and 8 percent in 1996, is an exception to the rule. Even he could barely stomach the process.

Some, perhaps many, do not want to spend two or three years on the campaign trail or raise the thirty to forty million dollars needed to run. Others may be reluctant to disclose their finances and subject their families and themselves to the brutal public scrutiny involved in a presidential race. General Colin Powell readily acknowledged in 1996 that his wife's objection to his running for president was a major factor in his decision not to seek the presidency. He also stated, vaguely, that he hadn't quite felt the call to political service. The demanding presidential campaign, especially with its more than thirty primary elections, is unappealing even to seasoned politicians.

The general public harbors a disdain for politicians. When asked about their career aspirations for their children, parents rate "politician" or even "president" low on their list. In 1955, only three out of ten thought politics was a good profession for their sons. A similar finding occurred in 1965. In 1991 Gallup questions included aspirations for daughters, and the results were the same as for sons. A recent Gallup poll found that only 8 percent of teenagers said public office was an attractive career goal.

A 1996 Princeton Survey Research Associates poll found that 63 percent said they would not want a child to seek the presidency. And a 1996 *Time*/CNN poll found 61 percent saying they did not want their child to run for president. A 1992 survey asked, "Which one of these would you most like to see one of your children grow up to be?": 38 percent said university president; 28 percent chose head of a large corporation; 11 percent said a sports star; only 7 percent said president of the United States.[3] Americans grew more patriotic after the September 11, 2001 terrorist attack and trust in government rose slightly, at least for a while. Yet the overall pattern persists: Americans are suspicious and often skeptical of politicians.

As noted, our candidates are drawn from a narrow range of backgrounds. Eight of the nineteen presidents since 1900 were attorneys, eight were members of Congress, nine served as governors, and seven had been vice president. Only George H.W. Bush was elected president while running as an incumbent vice president; the other six became president on the death or resignation of the incumbent president, or were elected after leaving the vice presidency.

By about January of each presidential election year one or two frontrunners have emerged from the pack to go on to the semifinal—the nominating convention. Both parties and the public are usually presented with a virtual *fait accompli*. In practice, name familiarity, access to large financial resources, and the substantial spare time necessary to prepare for the primaries give certain candidates advantages over others.

A presidential candidate must be at least 35 years old, must have lived within the United States for fourteen years, and must be a natural born citizen. Whether a person born abroad of American parents is qualified to serve as president has never been decided. Scholars believe, however, that such a person would be considered "natural born" even if not native born.

Yet in addition to the constitutional requirements, American voters have a tough, unwritten set of demands for anyone presumptuous and driven enough to want to become president. We are often disappointed in the quality of our candidates because we invariably measure them against an idealized composite of what our greatest presidents and world leaders did, rather than against what our past presidents looked like prior to their becoming presidents. We remember past presidents primarily for their victories and on their best days.

Of course we should ask a lot of our presidential candidates. We rightly ask not only who should serve in the White House, but what kind of leadership we want from our government, what kind of leadership role our country should play in the world, and how much all of us should accept our civic responsibilities.

Most of us yearn for so many talents and qualities in our presidents that it comes close to wanting "God—on a good day." We want vision, character, organizational competence, intelligence, stamina, inspiration, judgment, wisdom, emotional stability, and strength, and we want someone who shares our political beliefs.

When looking for a new president, we also want a leader who can bring us together and bring out the best in us. But this is a tough assignment in a nation shaped by stalwart individualism and irreverence for government and centralized leadership institutions.

We justifiably look at candidates with an unforgiving eye, but perhaps we are unfair with pop quizzes, trick questions, and denunciation of candidates for doing things we ourselves might have done. We simultaneously want a candidate to be like us and better than us.

Our ideal candidate, in addition to sharing our dreams and policy values, would have the following attributes:

**Courage.** The willingness to take risks and try to serve all the people and not just those who bankrolled his or her candidacy. The intellectual courage to do what is right even when it is not popular or easy. And the guts not to give up after legislative or political defeats.

**Experience** and competence in bringing people together in teams to solve major policy problems; great skills as a negotiator and builder of policy agreements.

**Political savvy.** An understanding of the necessity of politics and the ability to be an effective politician, one who works regularly with people of all political views and who recognizes that coalition building is a central as well as constant part of the job.

An **understanding** of history and constitutionalism. A solid grasp of how governments and markets work and how trade and diplomacy operate, and a respect for the U.S. Constitution and the constraints it puts on leadership and government. Helpful, too, would be a sophisticated understanding and respect for the diverse political culture in the United States.

The **ability** and judgment to recruit wise advisors and effective administrators, and the wisdom to delegate to teams of colleagues. This requires, too, an understanding of the strategic tools for governing and an ability to empower public servants and volunteers at all levels of government.

**Listening,** learning, and teaching skills. A leader has to both listen to us and lead us. We want leaders who give us a sense not only of who they are, but more importantly, of who we are, and what we as a nation might become.

**Programmatic** ideas and wisdom, and the ability to define plans, clarify options, and help set the nation's policy agenda. A president has to be preoccupied with the large, compelling issues of our day (economic opportunities for everyone, freedom, trade, nuclear proliferation, racism, equality, etc.)—a forest person, not overwhelmed by the trees or leaves.

**Communication** and motivational skills. Ideas and wisdom are of little use if a president cannot rally the public and empower teams and constituencies to enact new plans. Having speaking and media conference skills and the ability to inspire and build new political coalitions is crucial.

**Tenacity** and discipline balanced with emotional strength and humility. Self-confidence and self-esteem are also essential. A thick skin helps in this generally thankless job, as do the ability to laugh at oneself and to admit flaws and mistakes. Not wanted are persons who are defensive, rigid, torn by self-doubt or self-pity, or who blame their problems on "enemies."

**Intellectual honesty.** We want presidents we can trust, who have a basic respect for others and a commitment to serve the public interest. A sense of decency, integrity, and fair play.

**Morale-building** and community-building skills. The presidency is far more that just a political or constitutional job; it is also an institution and office that has to help us through crises and transitions, and help unify us when we experience national setbacks and tragedy. Presidents at their best help remind us of our mutual obligations, shared beliefs, and the trust and caring that can hold us together in traditions and duty.

Do we ask too much of our presidential candidates? Sure we do. History conditions different cultures to expect different things of their leaders. In the United States we exaggerate the capacity of what even heroic presidents can do to change the course of events.

But we aren't likely to lower our expectations.

The overriding factors that influence how people vote in presidential elections are their *party orientation,* their *public policy preferences,* the way they perceive the *integrity, character, and judgment* of the candidates, and *retrospective judgments* on the performance of the incumbent or their political party.

Parties may be decaying as organized, vital institutions in America, but they are still important factors when votes are counted. Americans are not as partisan as they were in the early twentieth century; they now are better educated, have multiple sources of political information, and are no longer dependent on party leaders for welfare, patronage, or certain other intermediary services. Still, roughly two-thirds of Americans identify themselves as Democrats or Republicans. Most of the time, Republicans vote Republican, Democrats vote Democrat. Republicans, however, are a more cohesive party in the general election. Thus 92 percent of Republicans voted for Reagan in 1984 and 91 percent voted for G.H.W. Bush in 1992 and, likewise, 91 percent voted for his son in 2000.

Democrats, for most of the post–World War II era, are more numerous, less unified, and less predictable than Republicans. Democrats gave Walter Mondale only 73 percent of their vote in 1984, Dukakis 82 percent in 1988, Clinton only 77 percent in 1992, and Gore received just 86 percent of the "Democratic" vote in 2000.

The core of party loyalists upon whom candidates have traditionally relied has shrunk. The public is less attached to parties and more dependent on television for voting cues, which forces presidents to "go public" in an effort to woo the independent-minded voters. Thus, candidates often feel the need to reinvent themselves at each campaign to better conform to what they perceive voters' preferences to be, and to tailor their message to the current fashion. While it is important for leaders to be flexible, they must also have character. There is a difference between a candidate willing to bend, and one who will break.

Issues or public policy preferences play an even more complicated role in how people cast their presidential vote. In certain years, like 1800, 1860, 1896, 1936, 1964, and 1992, issues played a larger, more clear-cut role. In other years, 1956, 1960, 1984, and 2000, issues weren't as important. Sometimes both major candidates take the same position on a major issue, as in 1968 when both Nixon and Hubert Humphrey said they favored ending the war, honorably, in Vietnam.

Issues seem to be less important in many elections because of the tendency for both parties to offer candidates who take moderate policy stands to appease widespread public opinion. Thus, both candidates often echo the public mood rather closely. Moreover, candidates' policy preferences are often deliberately highly ambiguous. Clear-cut policy stands are infrequent and inconspicuous as candidates devote much more attention to their concerns about general goals, problems, and past performance.

While candidates often try to avoid specific controversial issues, such issues do serve a broader and in many ways more important function: They allow candidates to simplify complexity for voters. Effective candidates provide meaning, purpose, and hope in a confusing world. They help make sense of the times. A candidate, or president, who can give comfort, assurance, and hope amid confusion can generate loyal and wide support.

Honesty and integrity top the list of desired characteristics. We are keenly aware, more so because of Watergate, the Iran-Contra scandal, and Clinton's various failings, of the need for a president to set a tone, and to serve as an example, of credibility. Dishonesty and duplicity are qualities we dislike. Indeed, one of the reasons Al Gore lost in 2000 is that he was viewed as somewhat less honest than his rival, George W. Bush. Two-thirds of the American people in 2000 thought the word "dishonest" aptly described Bill Clinton, with whom, of course, Al Gore had been associated for the previous eight years.[4]

Moreover, George W. Bush was viewed more positively than Al Gore on the qualities "honesty" and "strength of leadership." Bush was viewed as less likely to traffic in unfair political attacks on his opponent and as less likely to say *anything* to get elected. These differences in perceptions of character may have played a decisive role in the outcome of the election in 2000.

Most voters look for a moderate candidate. They generally vote against extremists of any kind and for the middle-of-the-road, don't-rock-the-boat candidates. This has led to an aphorism that "the only extreme in American politics that wins is the extreme middle." Ronald Reagan is somewhat of an exception to this rule, yet the public seldom saw Reagan as an extremist; his rhetoric was often comforting and nurturing to the point that he appeared to be mainstream.

In the post–Cold War era, questions of nuclear arms and foreign policy have been less meaningful to voters. In 1992, Americans elected a president who had no foreign policy experience and had avoided the draft during the Vietnam War, and in 2000 another candidate with no foreign policy experience was elected president. In recent years, the terms of debate have changed as voters turned inward, and the ideological cleavages have been less over foreign affairs than over domestic issues such as the economy, crime, education, the environment. The irony here is that regardless of the lack of electoral importance for presidential campaigning, foreign affairs often come to dominate a president's agenda, as happened with G. W. Bush.

Personality and character also count. In local elections people often just rely on party labels. But with governors, U.S. senators, and especially presidents, and with the availability of extensive television coverage, people plainly intrude their own personal judgment about who is most fit to serve in office.

Some people deplore the fact that a candidate's personality and style are evaluated as equal to or more important than issues and substance. But a candidate's personality and emotional strengths are perfectly legitimate and, indeed, proper subjects for voters to weigh. There is little doubt that a candidate's sense of self-confidence and personal style of conduct can and usually do affect how he or she would behave in office. "Presidents do far more than respond to the issue preferences of the voters. They have enormous discretionary power, and their personalities can importantly affect the way they handle issues and decide public policy."[5]

The basic insecurities of certain presidents have also led to failure in the White House. We have reason to be alert to whether a candidate can accept criticism and whether he demands absolute loyalty from subordinates. "The great danger is that a President who feels threatened by events or harassed by 'enemies' will precipitate a crisis in order to shore up his own inner doubts and confound his opposition."[6]

Elections are also judgments about the past and hopes for the future. We base our vote in part on a retrospective assessment of how well or poorly we think the incumbent president or their party did in governing the nation. We base our vote in part on how confident we are in where the country is going. If we feel good about the state of the economy and the direction we think the country is headed, we are more likely to reward the incumbent party.

What then do we look for in our presidents? We want persons who are self-confident and self-aware, persons who are not defensive and compulsive.

Political scientist James David Barber, a pioneer in studying presidential personality, urged voters to look first at a candidate's character. The issues of an election year will change, but the character of the president will last. Politics, he said, is politicians. There is no way to understand the former without understanding the latter. We need to look closely at the rhetoric, skill, and world view of presidential candidates. Barber said Wilson, Hoover, Johnson, and Nixon displayed tendencies toward compulsiveness and rigidity and were not as desirable as FDR, Truman, and JFK. These latter candidates combined a high volume and fast tempo of activity with marked enjoyment of politics and people. These "activist-positives," as Barber called them, manifested strong self-esteem and distinct success in relating to their environment.[7]

Barber's analysis, while helpful, has notable limitations. It would not have encouraged us to consider favorably Abraham Lincoln. Political scientist Jeffrey Tulis suggests Lincoln's effective presidential performance was more due to his political philosophy and skill than his "active-negative" character. And Barber's theory is less than helpful when applied to Gerald Ford, Jimmy Carter, and George H.W. Bush, all of whom Barber initially viewed as healthy active-positive types, yet all of whom proved to be merely average, at best, in presidential effectiveness. In short, psychological style and personality do not necessarily predict a president's performance and effectiveness. Barber raised important questions, yet his provocative writings raised almost as many questions as they answer.[8]

Still, questions of character often loom large in presidential politics. During the 1988 primaries, Democratic candidate Gary Hart was forced to withdraw from the race when he was discovered on a pleasure yacht, the "Monkey Business," with a woman other than his wife. During the 1992 primaries, candidate Bill Clinton had to defend himself against charges by a woman that she had had a long-term affair with the then governor. As president, Clinton had to fend off legal charges of improper behavior allegedly committed during his presidency and while he was governor of Arkansas. Polls regularly found that voters thought Clinton did a good job as president, and many people liked him, yet even his supporters found his character lacking.

In 1996, Americans reelected a president about whom they had serious character-related reservations. Voters did not ignore or dismiss the character question when they voted. But since all elections are judgments about past performance, an incumbent president is judged in good part on the quality of the job done. Character matters, yet performance generally matters more.

To what extent are questions of private moral character relevant to presidential politics? While the president is, in many ways, a moral or symbolic spokesperson for the nation, must the person who fills the office be personally "pure" to be a good president? It doesn't seem so. The public may want its presidents to be of the highest character, but a look at the private lives of our great presidents reveals an array of personal foibles.

The only modern president who might have passed today's "character test" is Richard Nixon. In his private life Nixon was seemingly upright. In his public life, however, Nixon left much to be desired. In a test of character "which Nixon passes and FDR fails, something is evidently amiss with our current prejudices about the kind of character we desire in political leaders."[9]

Precisely what do we mean by character? Some people with roguish private lives exhibit great public integrity. Others of spotless private life exhibit public qualities of duplicity. Today, journalists and rival candidates search the backgrounds of candidates, looking for any indiscretion. If found, that candidate is savaged and often drummed out of the race. Is it fair to base our judgments of character on isolated events that may have occurred years ago, and from which the candidate may have drawn useful lessons?

Questions about presidential character are as old as the office itself. In 1800, ministers denounced Thomas Jefferson from their pulpits as "godless," and Andrew Jackson was pilloried as a barbarian and adulterer.

The election of 1884 provides a fascinating case study of character in politics. In that election, Democratic candidate Grover Cleveland was charged with fathering a child out of wedlock. Cleveland took responsibility, and agreed to pay for the child's upbringing. This became a prime issue for his opponent James G. Blaine. The dilemma was that while Cleveland had character questions about his private life, his public or political reputation was spotless. Blaine, on the other hand, had a fine private life, but was generally thought of as a public crook. Voters selected Cleveland.

Today we see a person's private life as a barometer that reveals the truth about the person's public life. But a review of history suggests that this is not

The 1884 election put the character issue firmly in the forefront. Grover Cleveland was elected despite being pilloried in the press for allegedly fathering a child out of wedlock. (*Source:* Originally published in *Puck Magazine*, circa 1884.)

so. Presidents, like the rest of us, are human, they make mistakes. Some learn from their mistakes, others don't. The perfect person does not exist. Our presidents come with a wide array of strengths and weaknesses. To disqualify candidates because it is revealed they made mistakes years ago seems shortsighted. Does Bill Clinton's early experimentation with pot disqualify him for the presidency? Should George W. Bush's youthful drinking and D.U.I.s have prevented him from running for president, twenty or twenty-five years later? Plainly, Bush had learned from his mistakes and reformed.

We must also remember that, on occasion, we punish presidents for doing what they believe is right. Few presidents exhibit a "profiles in courage" type of leadership because it is electorally dangerous. President Ford's principled stand on the Nixon pardon, and Carter's insistence that we do the honorable thing about the Panama Canal, serve as examples of how politically hazardous speaking truth to power can be.

Can a president be too nice, too honorable? Both Ford and Carter were decent people. Would they have been more effective if they had been more Machiavellian?

Judging character is especially difficult given the varied motives of those who pursue political careers. Some enter politics for the wrong reasons—to fill a void or need that arises from low self-esteem. Others go into politics for more noble reasons—to accomplish good things for the nation. It is often difficult to tell.

One clue into character may be how a person deals with adversity or defeat. FDR's polio would have overwhelmed most people, but Roosevelt overcame adversity, and in doing so, was even more convincing when he told us we had nothing to fear but fear itself. In Roosevelt's case, adversity made him stronger. His character was forged in the fire of personal crisis.

Yes, presidents lie. But is there a difference between the behavior of FDR prior to U.S. entry into World War II and Nixon's lies about Watergate? The essential difference is that FDR misled with the public good in mind, and Nixon misled to save himself. In the long run, historians judge FDR's methods as questionable but his goals and outcome as honorable. Historians see Nixon's actions as self-serving and dishonorable.

While no single definition of character adequately covers all our needs, the following qualities are certainly admirable in the person who becomes president:

- Courage of conviction
- Internal moral compass
- Respect for others
- Commitment to the public good
- Respect for democratic standards
- Trustworthiness
- Generosity of spirit

- Compassion and empathy
- Optimism, hope, and emotional strength
- Sense of decency and fair play
- Inner strength and self-confidence

Is there a useful model for judging character in presidents? The following three tests may serve as a beginning: (1) Does the behavior exceed the boundaries of what most reasonable people would think of as normal? (2) Is there a clear pattern of this behavior, and not an isolated act or event? (3) Does it affect the job performance?

In the end, questions of presidential character serve as yet another example of the paradoxical nature of presidential politics. What we applaud in one president we condemn in another. In the end, the real test of presidential character may well be, "Did this president bring the best out in all of us?"

However much we seek the well-rounded leader, we usually get ambitious, vain, and calculating candidates who do not know what is to be done (though they are willing to try). The people who run and win view presidential campaigns less as dialogues or programs for adult education than as a fight to win office, a fight to get there. Once they get there, they will experiment and see what works. The voters may like a person who knows all the answers—but few candidates make commitments that are not reversible once in office. One of the first laws of presidential politics seems to be to promise a fresh approach yet avoid specificity, to give the appearance of executive ability yet not spell out what one intends to execute—at least not in any risky detail.[10]

## THE INVISIBLE PRIMARY

Not too many years ago political analysts held that nothing that happened before the New Hampshire presidential primary (held in February of presidential election years) had much meaning. In times past, it was a confession of weakness for a presidential candidate to get too organized before the New Hampshire primary. Now, however, candidates work for three and even four years before that primary to prepare for their race. Thus Jimmy Carter announced his candidacy for the White House on December 12, 1974, almost two full years before the 1976 election, and he admits he made his decision in 1972, four years before the election. And Senator Bob Dole (R-Kan.) began his bid for the 1996 presidential nomination almost immediately after the 1992 race was over. Many of the Democrats running for their party's 2004 nomination got started in 2001. Hence, "the invisible primary"—the determining events of an election that actually occur a year or more before the New Hampshire primary.[11] Since 1936 active candidates who ranked as most popular within their party in the Gallup poll taken one month before New Hampshire's primary have won their party's nomination almost every time. Pre-primary activity is significant. A candidate needs to be convincing on at least several "tracks" before he or she gets contender status. All of the following are needed:

- To become as well known as possible
- To raise substantial sums of money
- To attract and organize a staff
- To pay numerous visits to key caucus and primary states, especially Iowa and New Hampshire
- To identify core issues and build a supportive constituency
- To become identified as a spokesperson for a few key issues
- To devise a "winning" strategy
- To speak at scores of party functions (the rubber-chicken circuit)
- To devise an effective relationship with the media
- To develop a psychological preparedness and a self-confidence that radiates hope and likability

These do not necessarily occur in this order, and this short list does not exhaust the self and organizational testing of this period. However, without these a candidate has little chance of being taken seriously.

The first need of a would-be president is to become known. No other effort commands as much time as the battle to gain name recognition. Candidates like Roosevelt, Eisenhower, Kennedy, Reagan, Al Gore, and George W. Bush had a leg up on most others because they had become celebrities or had inherited a well-known name even before they ran for the presidency. Candidates like Carter, Dukakis, Clinton, and Howard Dean, on the other hand, had to go out and become known the hard way—by crisscrossing the nation, visiting city after city, and giving unremitting, bone-numbing speeches and interviews.

The second major need for a presidential candidate is money. Large sums are needed to pay for staff, for travel, and later in the campaign for crucial television and radio advertising. In the 2000 Republican primary race, George W. Bush raised more money than had ever been raised to run for president. He was thus able to outspend challenger John McCain dramatically to win his party's nomination. Money is convertible into many other resources. It is exceedingly difficult to raise money for a presidential race unless you look like a "winner" or unless you take especially strong positions on controversial issues. A conservative such as Barry Goldwater, George Wallace, Ronald Reagan, or Phil Gramm can more easily raise early money than a moderate such as Howard Baker, Bruce Babbitt, Paul Tsongas, or Richard Lugar. Making matters worse, the national media generally follow the "star system" of giving primary coverage to those who are already well known or to the controversial candidates who command intense followings.

The process of raising money in large sums is compromising and often corrupting.[12] The burden of having to raise millions for a presidential race is at the heart of why many able persons do not consider running for the office.

It is also at the heart of why some people are turned off by our political process. Two Republican presidential hopefuls in 1996, former Defense Secretary Dick Cheney and former HUD Secretary Jack Kemp, decided not to seek the office, citing among their chief reasons the distastefulness of raising large sums of money. As Kemp noted, "There are a lot of grotesqueries in politics, not the least of which is the fund-raising side."[13] Several top prospects dropped out of the race or failed to enter because of the difficulty of raising money, while the candidates of considerable wealth such as H. Ross Perot and Steve Forbes could enter almost at will. This raises serious questions about the selection process. When does a political contribution become a bribe? When does systematic campaign soliciting become equivalent to a conspiracy to extort funds? The late Hubert Humphrey, who twice ran for president, put it bluntly:

> Campaign financing is a curse. It's the most disgusting, demeaning, disenchanting, debilitating experience of a politician's life. It's stinky. It's lousy. I just can't tell you how much I hate it. I've had to break off in the middle of trying to make a decent, honorable campaign and go up to somebody's parlor or to a room and say, "Gentlemen, and ladies, I'm desperate. You've got to help me . . ."
>      . . . And you see people—a lot of them you don't want to see. And they look at you, and you sit there and you talk to them and tell them what you're for and you need help and, out of the twenty-five who have gathered, four will contribute. And most likely one of them is in trouble and is somebody you shouldn't have had a contribution from.[14]

Reliance on big money has made the presidential selection process vulnerable to charges of corruption. In the aftermath of the Watergate scandal, the Congress passed legislation for public financing of presidential elections. Enacted in 1974, the campaign finance reform called for public disclosure of all contributions exceeding one hundred dollars, established ceilings on contributions, created a system of federal subsidies, and established spending limits. This law was challenged in court, and in *Buckley v. Valeo* (424 U.S. 1, 1976) the Supreme Court viewed money as speech, and not as property, and determined that while the Congress could regulate contributions and expenditures of campaign organizations, it could not prevent or limit independent individuals or groups from exercising free speech (and spending) rights.

The Congress then passed the Federal Election Campaign Act (FECA), to revise existing laws to keep them in line with constitutional standards. These new guidelines have been in effect since the 1976 presidential election. Since that election, campaign organizations have discovered various loopholes in the law that allow campaigns to get around the law.[15]

First the "independent" money exemption allows individuals and organizations to spend money for or against candidates as long as the effort is not conducted with the advice or assistance of a candidate's campaign organization. This has opened the door for independent spending on behalf of a candidate, or, as is more likely, negative campaign ads against a candidate. Second, the spending of what is called "soft money" allowed party organizations to raise and spend money for a variety of purposes in support of the campaign.

To run a winning primary campaign in 2000, George W. Bush had to spend over $50 million. Enormous time was spent on fund raising. When asked why he robbed banks, Willie Sutton said, "Because that's where the money is." Where do would-be presidents go for their money? Wealthy individuals, corporate elites, and to California for Hollywood money (known as "the Beverly Hills Primary"). Lamar Alexander attended nearly three hundred fund-raising events in 1995, prompting him to comment, "I feel like a trained dog." Another 1996 Republican aspirant, U.S. Senator Arlen Specter, spent four hours on the phone every morning soliciting contributions.[16]

While it would be unfair to say that money literally buys elections, it is nonetheless clear that money plays a significant role in determining who the eventual winner will be. Almost always, the primary candidate who spends the most money wins.

Campaign contributions are often given to reward and influence candidate positions. Steel magnate Henry C. Frick complained of Teddy Roosevelt, "We bought the son of a bitch and then he did not stay bought."[17] Most campaign contributions are seen as investments in the future, and contributors do expect, and often get, a return on their investments.

Incumbent presidents have always used the lure and trappings of the office to elicit campaign contributions, but no president in the past twenty years elevated it to the art form practiced by the Clinton White House. In an elaborately orchestrated series of "coffees" and "sleep-overs" (in the Lincoln bedroom), the president invited big donors to the White House in hopes that they would contribute to the Clinton reelection effort. The campaign of 1996 was costly, with each nominee receiving $61.8 million from the government, and the party national committees raising over $80 million in "soft money." President Clinton's fund-raising efforts were unusual *only* for the brazen manner in which the White House was used to raise money.[18]

Campaign spending in 2000 dwarfed all previous campaigns, with Bush and Gore spending about $163 million, plus the parties spending over $80 million in "soft money." In 1996, Clinton and challenger Bob Dole spent about $116 million.[19] In the Republican primaries, George W. Bush spent more money than any candidate in history, and these resources helped him defeat challenger John McCain.

More recently, the Congress has approved new "reforms" aimed at disallowing "soft money" contributions in presidential campaigns, yet whether these reforms will work remains to be seen.

Attracting loyal staff, identifying key issues, becoming identified with vital issues, and devising a sensible strategy are all vital to the successful launching of a candidacy. Often underestimated is the capacity to establish a good working relationship with reporters and television interviewers. In an age of candidate-centered campaigns, where political parties are of decreasing importance, the electoral role of the media has greatly increased. Some candidates, great speakers who are superb at raising funds, perform poorly when interviewed by the press. Sometimes, too, the great stump speaker looks foolish and too "hot" on television. Friends of former Vice President Hubert Humphrey said Humphrey and television were not made for each other. He was an outstanding orator at political rallies, yet he talked too fast and too much for the television viewer. Ronald Reagan was masterful at giving a prepared speech yet when interviewed one-on-one made errors, and his handlers were forced to restrict press access to their candidate.

What might be called the psychological test—how a candidate reacts to the strain, the temptations, and the intense public scrutiny of the campaign—is one of the most important measures of a candidate. Arthur Hadley asked, "How much does the candidate want the presidency? How much of his private self and belief will be compromised to the public man? To what extent will he abandon family, friends and other normal joys of life, and how does he handle this isolation?"[20]

Some candidates develop self-doubts. Some develop a tendency to tell audiences what they want to hear, and over the course of a few weeks they become inconsistent and look ridiculous. Others, such as Edmund Muskie, become plagued by a need for more sleep. Muskie also found his presidential bid in 1972 exacerbated by his inability to control his temper. In 1988, Gary Hart seemed to challenge reporters to catch him in an act of indiscretion, and they did. Both Bill Clinton in 1992 and George W. Bush in 2000 gained energy and voice during their campaigns, similar to the way that John F. Kennedy grew and honed his political and campaigning skills in 1960. The exacting invisible primary period is always an exhausting ordeal and a formidable test, as well, of whether an individual can hold up physically and can control himself emotionally.

## PRESIDENTIAL PRIMARIES

Presidential primaries began as an outgrowth of the Progressive movement's efforts in the early twentieth century to eliminate "boss rule" and encourage popular participation in government. Presidential primaries began to take shape after 1905 when the La Follette Republicans in Wisconsin provided a system for the direct election of members of the state's delegation to the national nominating convention. Now most of the big, electoral-rich states are using some type of presidential primary.

The concept of popular participation in the nomination of the presidential party nominees evolved slowly. First we relied on the congressional caucus system, which did not allow for direct popular participation at all. Until 1828 members of Congress from each party met and selected the person they wanted as their nominee. With the growth of democratic sentiment and the coming of the Age of Jackson, the national nominating convention system began to emerge as the replacement. In 1828 state legislatures and state party conventions were relied on to nominate party nominees. After that, national conventions took hold, although it was not until 1840 that national party conventions were accorded full recognition.

Not until 1912 did primaries begin to be used regularly (about twelve states used them that year) in enough places to begin to have a serious impact on the presidential nominations. Many party leaders, however, have never been enthusiastic about primaries, in large part because they believe they undermine the two-party structure by strengthening the hand of candidate loyalists and issue-oriented zealots at the expense of the party regulars. Primaries allow people to vote who may have little or no loyalty to the party and no interest in the party's future. In fact, those voting in party primary races generally hold more extremist views than party regulars. Thus primaries favor more ideological candidates (to the left in the Democratic party, to the right in the Republican party). These candidates may do well among committed activists within one wing of the party, yet can spell disaster in the general election where the electorate is more moderate. The Republicans in 1964 with Barry Goldwater, and the Democrats in 1972 with George McGovern, are examples of what can happen when crusading issue activists capture the nomination only to be trounced in the general election.

The importance of primaries has waxed and waned during the past century, but they have become increasingly important. Candidates now view the primaries as essential in winning the nomination. Most delegates are won in these primary contests.

The rules for primaries vary from state to state and from party to party. Usually, however, voters elect delegates directly or by showing a preference for a presidential candidate. Some of the early primaries, such as those in New Hampshire and Wisconsin, or "Super Tuesday" in the South, can be important in giving a psychological lift to a front-runner or a new challenger. Later primaries can be important in giving the final edge to one candidate over others as the front-runner heads into the national convention. Rarely, however, do the later primaries have an impact, since the front-runner usually has a sufficient number of committed delegates before the California primary. This has led California and a number of other states to "front-load" their primaries, moving them earlier in the calendar year. This gives a great advantage to those who are well known, well funded, and well organized early in the process, and inhibits a lesser-known candidate from building momentum over time. This has created a rush to the starting line, as only those candidates who do well early have a chance of winning. It has also scared away capable but lesser-known candidates who might otherwise have run.

In recent years the system of presidential primaries has become one of the most passionately debated aspects of the presidential selection process. Critics say it is a case of "democracy gone mad," and a "very questionable method of selecting presidential candidates." It is especially good at eliminating candidates.

Nearly always, the criticism of the primaries ends up focusing on these alleged flaws: the system takes too long, costs too much, highlights entrepreneurial personalities at the expense of issues, makes pseudoenemies out of true political allies, invites factionalism, undermines parties, often favors colorful ideological candidates over moderates, and frequently does not even affect the outcome of the nomination process. Critics point to the Goldwater and McGovern nominations as prime examples of flaws in the primary system.

Primary voters are older, have higher incomes, are more educated, and are more ideological and politically active than are primary nonvoters. Turnout is relatively low. This leads some analysts to conclude that as a democratic institution designed to stimulate popular participation, the presidential primary has limited effectiveness, and has turned off rather than turned on potential voters.

The frequent and sustained criticism of primaries leads some observers to suggest that we should abolish or at least reform them. Many people support a national primary, a one-shot winner-take-all event in August or September of election year. Others favor regional (multistate) primaries or a return to state conventions as a better means by which to select competent presidential nominees.

The primary system has its blemishes, but it has also served us reasonably well. Although "the people" do not fully control the nominating process, primaries have increased the public's potential to influence who will be convention delegates and has opened the process to some candidates and ideas that might otherwise have been excluded.

Primaries have decreased the party leaders' control over the nomination process. Students of our party system worry about this. They would prefer a system that sends responsible party regulars of the state and local parties to the national convention, not bound by rigid instructions from a primary verdict but as representatives, free to seek out the national interest according to their best judgment. They believe these party regulars would be delegates concerned with the majority of the party's rank and file and also with the acceptability and electability of a candidate as well as that candidate's ability to serve effectively as president. This view celebrates party regulars as those who are most informed and best qualified to select the nominee.

Another criticism of the primary system stems from the undue weight placed on the first primary in New Hampshire. Does this small state reflect the nation or does the very conservative nature of the state give undue advantage to more conservative candidates? In an effort to offset the power of the New Hampshire primary, many states have "front-loaded" their primaries, that is, moved them up in the calendar so as to have a greater impact. But the probable impact of front-loading has been to give New Hampshire even greater influence, as winning that primary is seen as essential if a candidate is to be regarded as credible in those primaries that follow shortly thereafter.

It is true that primaries do allow, on occasion, for a Goldwater or a McGovern to be nominated. But primaries also allow for fresh faces, and young new blood to emerge, as happened in 1960, 1976, 1992, and 2000. The 1976 and 1992 campaigns showed that the Democrats, for example, could emerge from the primaries as a fairly unified party. By giving candidates several opportunities to present themselves to the public, our present procedures make it possible for a candidate to win substantial support during a relatively short time period. Abolishing this aspect of the presidential selection process could limit the infusion of new blood into the presidential race. Further, to return to the choosing of the nominee by a small establishment group is unacceptable to most Americans today who see politics as unsavory. People are demanding more involvement, not less. That Americans fail to utilize the very thing they demand to have only reinforces the paradoxical nature of presidential politics.

Modest participation in the primaries prompts reform suggestions. Universal voter registration or the motor-voter bill (allowing people to register to vote at the time they register for a driving license) slightly increases participation. Newspapers and television could do a better job of getting to the heart of candidates' views, exploring inconsistencies, and piecing together the candidates' positions on various policies.

One of the virtues of the primary system is that candidates are required to present themselves to the people. Candidates have to organize their thoughts, to clarify and define key issues. They are required to communicate with all kinds of people and to react under pressure. Most of the time it is an excellent learning experience for both candidates and the public. It also allows room for the people to sharpen and alter their initial views of candidates.

The chances of destroying or eliminating an outstanding front-runner in the primaries are slim.

Primaries were designed to give the people the right to be involved in the choice of their party's nominee and should not be abandoned because qualified persons choose not to run. While more must be done to encourage the best people to seek the office, we need not sacrifice the democratic integrity of the process to attain our goals. The national party convention can still draft a "dark horse" if there is no popular favorite. Primaries may be imperfect, but so are democratic societies. They are an inexact, expensive, and overlong way of coming up with nominees, but the system is not as flawed as critics contend.[21] And many of these flaws can be modified (not necessarily fixed) to make the process more congenial to the integrity of the process.[22]

Return to state conventions or the ancient congressional caucus procedure would serve only to increase the influence of political bosses and special interests, who find it easier to bring pressure to bear on a few individuals in those old "smoke-filled rooms" than on entire electorates. Moving to a national or even a regional primary would lessen contact between candidate and voter, virtually prevent the less well-known candidate from running, and increase reliance on television advertising.

## NATIONAL CONVENTIONS

National conventions have performed (or tried to perform) several functions. They have nominated presidential candidates acceptable to most factions within the party. By winning plurality victories in the primaries a candidate can secure the nomination without being acceptable to virtually all elements within a party. It is only the acquiescence of these other interests at the convention that signals to the party's rank and file that the nominee is the legitimate party standard-bearer. Carter and Ford won that legitimization at the 1976 conventions; Al Gore and George W. Bush did so in 2000. Goldwater and McGovern failed at their conventions in 1964 and 1972, respectively.

It has always been the purpose of a convention to select or ratify nominees who possess a strong likelihood of winning voter support in November. The goal is to produce a winning ticket. Thus a second function of the convention is to shape the vice presidential choice in such a way as to both strengthen the ticket and reconcile factional cleavages within the party.

A more general function of conventions is trying to unify a party that is not inherently unified. This is a time not to examine differences but to seek unity in the face of disagreements and diversity. It is naturally in the party's interest to build enthusiasm and rally the party faithful to work for the national ticket.

Conventions also hammer out party platforms. Platforms are generally less meaningful than the campaign statements of the presidential candidates, but they are a useful guide to the major concerns of a party. They are often inclusive "something-for-everyone" reports. A platform is invariably a compromise of sectional views, diverse caucuses (women, blacks, etc.), and the policy preferences of dominant party elites. The winning candidate is often willing to concede a plank in the platform to the wishes of one of the runner-ups in the primaries. This can be a quid pro quo offer to a faction or a candidate-based organization within the convention that must be won over to unite the party.

If the party has an incumbent president, the platform is often drafted in the White House or approved by the president and his top policy advisers. Seldom does the party adopt a platform critical of its incumbent president.

Criticism of the national party nominating conventions has been loud and frequent. President Eisenhower called them a national disgrace, and social critic H. L. Mencken once wrote that "There is something about a national convention that makes it as fascinating as a revival or a hanging." Critics contend conventions are too big, noisy, unwieldy, unrepresentative, irresponsible, and a waste of time. Others say they function with too much concern for selecting a winner rather than the best qualified person. Similarly, critics say vice presidential choices are often made too hastily, with much regard for balancing the ticket and little regard for selecting a person who may eventually become president. They give as examples the selections of Agnew (1968), Eagleton (1972), and Quayle (1988).

Television and the proliferation of presidential primaries have altered the role of modern conventions. Today, conventions are less about selecting candidates and more about political theater and marketing; less about where the party wishes to lead the nation and more about entertainment. Bill Greener, who managed TV coverage at the 1996 Republican convention, said:

> We don't make the rules to the game. We are dealing with the rules. And the rules are: You get an hour and don't forget in that hour we have got our commercials to air and our station breaks, and don't forget that we need time to showcase our talent, and don't forget that even before we think about going to the podium we have got to establish the presence of our anchor and our four floor correspondents, and don't forget that after that we are going to take a commercial break, and then we are going to go back to the anchor, and then we *might* take what you've got going at the podium. And that's just the way it is.[23]

Yet another complaint about national conventions has came about in the wake of the Democratic party's reforms of the early 1970s. A commission was established to try to improve the delegate selection processes and to "open up" the Democratic party. The basic goal of these reforms was to end the traditional dominance of regular party leaders and to make the Democratic convention more representative of the party rank and file.

A key criticism, however, is that according to the new rules many, perhaps even a majority, of the delegates to the Democratic convention, are not acting as responsible members of a party, with all the memories, past participation in, and commitment to its future. Instead, they are acting as members of a candidate-centered organization whose loyalties are almost exclusively to specific candidates and their issues. This may lead, critics charge, to allowing the "zealots" to rule.

This is a serious charge, but it does not stand up to critical analysis. "Greater participation . . . does not mean that party leaders must automatically lose. All it means is that party leaders must compete with nonleaders for influence."[24] Nor are issue activists inclined to be party wreckers. "The groups advantaged by the [new participatory] process are not homogeneous, they are not necessarily more or less representative than the party organization people they have replaced . . . and their participation does not necessarily guarantee continued internal divisions in the Democratic party."[25]

While it is true that party activists and convention delegates are more ideological (in the sense of being more left or right) than the general public, it is not true that this leads them to nominate extremists for the presidency. Of the ten individuals nominated over the last six election cycles, only Ronald Reagan leaned to the political extreme, and he rarely seemed extreme to the voters who elected him twice.

One wag commented that "Democrats have to control their left-wing nuts and Republicans have to worry about their right-wing nuts." And we should not be surprised when committed true believers get active in politics in pursuit of their cherished agenda items. At the 1996 Republican convention, 21 percent of the delegates identified themselves as members of the religious right. Only 15 percent of the public has such an affiliation. Seventy percent of the delegates said they were conservative. Only 34 percent of the public so identifies itself. Did these "zealots" nominate a right-wing radical? No. They chose Bob Dole (or, more accurately, the primary voters did). On the Democratic side, 43 percent of the delegates said they were liberal, yet only 16 percent of the voters and 21 percent of Democrats so identify themselves. Did they nominate a leftist? No. "New Democrat" Bill Clinton was their nominee.

On balance, the national conventions have served us rather well, if imperfectly. New rule changes, the far greater role of television, and the reality that nominees are more and more "selected" and "nominated" in the state primaries require us to reexamine the traditional functions of the convention. Although substantial change has taken place, the conventions still serve many intended goals. Despite their deficiencies, they have nominated some capable leaders, Lincoln, the Roosevelts, Wilson, FDR, Eisenhower, and JFK among them. Conventions have had many triumphs and only a few outright failures.

Conventions remain a uniquely American pageant. Where most Western democracies select their leader (prime minister) from a closed party caucus, away from the hustle and bustle of mass politics, in the United States selecting a president is the people's job, as messy and chaotic as this process may be.

Many of the criticisms of the convention process are really criticisms of elections in general. Elections may not be our finest hour, they may not always address our better selves, they may not be the ideal way to select leaders, but they remain the most reliable of the known available devices.


## INCUMBENCY: ADVANTAGE OR DISADVANTAGE?

The advantages of incumbency for a president seeking reelection are traditionally revered as a political article of faith. For a sitting president, the benefits of incumbency are easily distinguishable: instant recognition; full access to government research resources; ability to dominate events and make news and to attract constant media exposure; party organizational structure at one's disposal; ability to dispense government contracts; and some ability to manipulate the economy.

Regardless of a president's record of accomplishment, an incumbent president is supposed to benefit from a public relations machine that shows the president as a person of action, a commander in chief, a traveling statesman, and a strategic crisis manager. Not the least of a president's assets is a loyal White House staff that, in the unavoidable blurring of presidential and political functions, performs a myriad of services. A president and the national party can also raise money far more easily than the opposition, and the resources of the office provide millions of dollars' worth of publicity.

A rival for the presidency is generally a political candidate and little more. He or she is a seeker whose motives are unclear, a pursuer with a feverish gleam in his or her eye. Such candidates covet what their rival already possesses. The most they can give are promises.

Perhaps the most important asset for the incumbent is the selective or manipulative use of government contracts, patronage, and other political controls over the economy. President Nixon's manipulation of milk prices is alleged to have aided his campaign treasury in the 1972 election. In what was called "the incumbency-responsiveness program," Nixon aides sought to maximize their control over the federal government's enormous resources to their best advantage. Federal grants were evaluated according to political benefits. Political appointments and ambassadorships were sometimes promised in exchange for large campaign contributions. And corporations were "encouraged" to contribute to the upcoming Nixon campaign in a near-extortionist manner.

But is incumbency really that much of an advantage? Political scientist Edward Tufte, who studied the relationship of the economy's performance and election outcomes, concluded that short-run economic performance has a good deal to do with ensuring an incumbent's reelection. Tufte found positive support going back to 1918 for the not surprising hypothesis "that an incumbent administration, while operating within political and economic constraints and limited by the usual uncertainties in successfully implementing economic policy, may manipulate the short-run course of the national economy in order to improve its party's standing in upcoming elections and to repay past political debts."[26] Today, however, presidents have less opportunity to manipulate the economy in this manner. With an enormous national debt and budget challenges, presidents have less discretionary money and fewer resources to throw at the voters in the months before an election. Incumbents can and often have lost. Indeed, incumbency is sometimes as much a burden as a benefit. Since the Jacksonian era, which inspired the rise of mass political parties and the party convention system, five presidents have been denied party renomination: Tyler, Fillmore, Pierce, Andrew Johnson, and Arthur. Another nine, John Adams, Van Buren, Cleveland, Benjamin Harrison, Taft, Hoover, Ford, Carter, and George H. W. Bush, were defeated for a second term after winning their party's nomination. Against these fourteen failures, incumbent presidents have been successful in winning both the nomination and the election only sixteen times, including three reelection triumphs by Franklin Roosevelt.

One of the paradoxes of recent years can be seen in the incumbency advantage being transformed into the incumbency disadvantage. In 1968, incumbent Lyndon Johnson was compelled not to seek renomination when faced with mass protests over his Vietnam policy. His successor, Richard Nixon, was forced to resign from office one step ahead of impeachment. Nixon's successor, Gerald Ford, nearly lost his nomination bid and ended up losing the election in 1976, and the man who defeated him, Jimmy Carter, also faced a serious nomination challenge and lost in his 1980 bid for reelection. Reagan's successor George H.W. Bush lost in his 1992 reelection bid to Bill Clinton. Plainly, being the incumbent can sometimes be dangerous to the president's political health.

On paper, Democratic presidential candidate Al Gore should have been able to benefit from the optimism associated with economic prosperity. The public believed that the economy was doing well and that the country was on the right track in 2000. Yet Gore received little advantage from this asset.

Political scientist Gerald Pomper speculates that this may have been the case because the economic good times of the 1980s and 1990s had gone on so long that voters might have come to see the condition as almost natural. Yet a more compelling explanation holds that "Gore did not properly exploit the advantages offered by his administration's economic record . . . Gore would briefly mention the record of prosperity but then emphasize his plans for the future."[27] Gore preached an anticorporate populism, perhaps in hopes of fending off Ralph Nader's challenge on his left, yet in doing so failed to reap the benefits of the Clinton-Gore economic record.

Incumbency, then, is a double-edged sword. It can help a president who presides over a period of prosperity and peace and projects an image of being in charge of events. But it can just as readily act against a president associated with troubled, perplexing times, who does not seem to be in full possession of his office. If prosperity favors the incumbents, depression favors the challengers. Distrust of politicians and low morale in the nation favor the challengers; strong confidence in the national government favors the incumbent.

An incumbent is necessarily on the defensive: His record is under detailed scrutiny, his administration's every flaw and unfulfilled promise is exposed to microscopic examination. The American people can conveniently, if often unfairly, blame a whole range of problems on the president, whereas the astute challenger presents a smaller target. The challenger can talk about secret plans and make a rash of promises without being specific about what they would cost and who would wind up paying for them. A challenger is also in a far better position to present illusory problems as real ones and to play upon public fear about such things as missile gaps, inflation, immigrants, and crime in the streets in ways that may distort reality while conveniently winning headlines. The challenger can take the offensive and try to convince the voters that a new president would do better.

The incumbent is often judged against the idealized model of the perfect president, and not unnaturally, is found wanting. Paradoxically, the incumbent may at times be the symbol of the nation's pride, but just as readily may be the nation's most convenient scapegoat.

In the past generation the presidency has gradually acquired more responsibility for peace, prosperity, and improvement in the quality of life than it has the authority to implement. It is a case of demanding more of the presidency, even when the capacity to act is often limited. The "what have you done for us lately" refrain is even more recurrent in an age of heightened single-issue, narrow special-interest-group politics.

## THE GENERAL ELECTION: WHAT MATTERS?

In 2000, while 105 million voters (or 51.2 percent) turned out to vote, at least another 100 million who were eligible to participate in the selection of the president did not vote. As is well known, people with higher family incomes are more likely to vote than those with lower incomes. Older people, with the exception of the infirm, vote more often than younger people. Women vote in higher percentages than men. White turnout nowadays is only slightly higher than African-American turnout, but Hispanic voting is decidedly lower. The more formal education one has, the more likely one is to vote.

Why do so many people not vote in presidential elections? The easiest explanation is that people are lazy and apathetic about national issues. Paradoxically, however, American citizens are more aware of and interested in political issues than are citizens in most other democracies, yet American participation in elections is far lower.

There are a variety of reasons for not voting. Most states require advance voter registration. As can be seen in Table 2.1, some people say they are too busy, too ill, or don't feel the outcome of the election will make that much difference.

One analysis of lower voter turnout in recent years suggests it is also partly due to the fact that political parties have declined in importance, that the media dwells so much on the negative aspects of candidates and campaigning, and that presidential campaigns go on for so long that elections become a mind-numbing experience. One remedy might be to shorten the nominating process, writes political scientist Thomas E. Patterson.[28]

In general, voters who vote participate out of a sense of duty, believing that it is a part of their civic responsibility. Most also believe that their vote matters, that their political and economic interests are at stake. They want their party nominee to win because they either strongly or mildly adhere to the policies championed by their party. (See Figure 2.1 for information on voter turnout patterns over the past two hundred years.)

So *political parties* do matter. In addition, *candidate appeal* and *special issues* being debated in a particular election can matter a lot. But for issues to really matter requires that the issues in question matter to a large number of voters and that the main candidates take clearly opposing stances on the issues. But rarely do candidates focus on only one issue and candidates often blur their issue positions in order to broaden their appeal.

During the election of 2000, issues, even important ones, did not seem to influence the outcome as much as party identification and candidate and character appeal. While Gore was viewed as more "competent," George W. Bush was seen as more "likable" and honest.

Candidates such as Dwight Eisenhower in 1952, John F. Kennedy in 1960, and Ronald Reagan all benefited from the candidate appeal factor.

Presidential candidates are not free agents who can choose among strategies at will. Strategy is seldom based on mere choice, it is usually forced by circumstance. For example, about every eight or twelve years

**TABLE 2.1**
**Why People Don't Vote**

| | |
|---|---|
| Too busy, conflicting schedule | 20.9% |
| Illness or disability (own or family's) | 14.8 |
| Not interested, felt vote would not make a difference | 12.2 |
| Out of town or away from home | 10.2 |
| Other reason, not specified | 10.2 |
| Did not like candidates or campaign issues | 7.7 |
| Refused or don't know | 7.5 |
| Registration problems | 6.9 |
| Forgot to vote (or send in absentee ballot) | 4.0 |
| Inconvenient polling place or hours or lines too long | 2.6 |
| Transportation problems | 2.4 |
| Bad weather conditions | 0.6 |

*Source:* U.S. Bureau of the Census, "Reasons for Not Voting, by Sex, Age, Race and Hispanic Origin, November 2000," at www.census.gov.

there is a strong underlying desire to throw out the party in office. (In 1920, 1932, 1952, 1960, 1968, 1980, and 1992 voters seemed in part to be punishing those in office who were unable to improve things.) Slogans such as "It's time for a change" or "Throw the rascals out" are a familiar refrain as voters turn incumbents out of office with an almost predictable alternation.

Between 65 and 75 percent of the voters usually have made up their minds as to how they will vote by the end of the national conventions (late August of election year, a good eight or ten weeks before election day). The basic organizational effort of a candidate must be aimed at stirring up the support of voters at the grass roots. The strategy that makes the most sense is to get out all possible supporters and potential supporters and independents and to target only secondary resources at converting the opposition. Supporters need general reassurance on both substantive and stylistic matters, but opponents want to know specific policy plans and program ideas.

A lot depends on how candidates conduct themselves. Our election process usually, although not always, excludes broad policy questions. Of necessity, then, in addition to observing the candidates' party, the people assess the contenders not so much on what they believe but on how good a job they might do. This is why we carefully watch how they answer tricky questions and whether they keep their cool with hecklers as well as in heated presidential debates. Looking "presidential" is an important part of the voter's equation when deciding on a preferred candidate.

More than anything else, presidential electoral politics is coalitional politics. Interest groups help to get others involved in a campaign. They help mobilize voters on election day. Groups are seldom neutral. They lean to one party or one kind of candidate over others. Groups want access to the political system and they want someone favorable to their interests in the White House.

Candidates find the general election fraught with dynamic tensions. Issue-oriented enthusiasts urge them to "speak out on the vital issues." Party

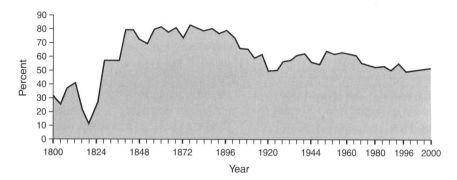

**Figure 2.1** Voter Turnout in Presidential Elections, 1800–2000 (*Source:* Howard W. Stanley and Richard G. Niemi, *Vital Statistics on American Politics, 1999–2000* [CQ Press, 2000]. See also "National Voter Turnout in Federal Elections," 1996–2000, at www.infoplease.com/ipa/A0781453.html.)

regulars urge them to work closely with the party bosses. Television consultants urge them to devote most of their time to brief television spots and talk-show appearances. Public relations aides urge them to invoke patriotic symbols and quote from prestigious heroic sources. Campaign managers generally argue that debating all the issues and trying to educate the public is the worst possible way to run a campaign. Issues that attract some groups repulse others.

Do elections matter? They do, although elections seldom give a president or country a specific mandate. The 1996 elections are a good example. Clinton won because of a strong economy and because Dole was a weak candidate who ran a weak campaign. But the voters did not give Clinton a policy mandate. A national election in the United States is not a plebiscite or referendum on a number of specific issues. Because of candidates' policy ambiguity, we often vote without a clear idea of what the candidates will do if elected.

Candidates who win by a large margin usually claim they have won a mandate from the people. Such a claim is often unjustified, however, especially in elections such as those of 1964, 1972, and 1984 where the "landslide" was more a factor of the personal popularity of a president or of the negative perceptions about the defeated than positive perceptions about the victor.

Presidents invariably claim some sort of mandate, believing that if the public and Congress believe the claim they will have an easier time governing. A mandate is based on three features: the *size* of a president's electoral victory; the *type* of election (issue oriented or personal); and the *number* of candidates from the president's party elected to Congress (the president's coattails and the aggregate numbers).

An election can produce various types of mandates. A *positive mandate* (e.g., Reagan in 1980) comes as the result of a significant margin of victory in a race in which a significant number of candidates from the president's party were elected to Congress, major issues were contested, and one side won a clear victory. Positive mandates usually mean that the president can accomplish significant elements of his campaign platform. A *negative mandate* (e.g., Nixon in 1968 and Clinton in 1992) is a repudiation of the incumbent president or party and normally does not serve as much of a guide to future action, nor does it grant the victor significant power. A *marginal mandate* (e.g., Reagan in 1984 and Clinton in 1996) normally results from a relatively issueless campaign and confers no measurable margin of power. Or, as was the case in 2000, an election can confer *no mandate* at all.

The debate over whom to vote for usually centers around which candidate is best equipped to handle the job and the problems at hand rather than around the detailed specifics of how to solve the big issues of the day. Thus, our elections represent mandates to get the job done, but we leave the means up to the judgment of the president. Elections sometimes set limits on what can be done, but they usually only moderately determine the precise future course of public policies.[29]

Unlike their parliamentary counterparts, elections in the United States do not confer *power.* They merely grant office, which grants the opportunity to seize power. Presidents must work at translating an electoral victory into political power.

Presidential elections are important in terms of who is to handle the issues and with what broad leeway. But elections seldom are direct policy-making events. The general mood in the nation on issues and the partisan and ideological balance in the recently elected Congress are probably as important, if not much more so, in shaping how a president will act. Note the qualities that appeared to matter most to voters in 2000. (See Figure 2.2.)

## THE ELECTORAL COLLEGE DEBATE

The election of 2000 was puzzling. Some of our worst fears about the anachronistic electoral college came true. Popular vote winner Al Gore lost to electoral winner George W. Bush. Bush carried 30 states and won 271 electoral votes. Gore won 20 states and the District of Columbia and won 267 electoral votes.

The Florida vote ended up in nearly a statistical tie, yet all 25 electoral votes went to Bush, rather than a proportional allocation of 12.5 electoral votes to each of the leading contenders.

There were at least two puzzling aspects of the election in 2000. Bush and Gore all but ignored California, New York, and Texas, the three largest states in terms of population and electoral votes. These states were conceded well in advance—California and New York to Gore and Texas to Bush.

Both before and after the 2000 election, the American public favored abolishing the electoral college and moving to the more simple and presumably much more democratic "one-person–one-vote" direct election procedure for selecting a president. Between 60 and 70 percent of Americans reg-

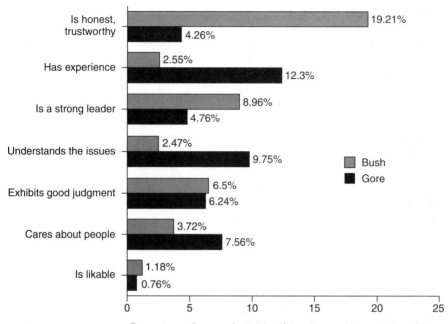

**Figure 2.2** Qualities that Mattered Most in the 2000 Presidential Election (*Source:* www.cnn.com/ELECTION/2000/results/index.epolls.html.)

ularly support this system in various surveys. Yet weeks after the Bush-Gore election was settled, there was little public clamor and even less political maneuvering for amending the U.S. Constitution to effect this change.

As we were reminded in 2000, presidents are elected by the electoral college and not directly by the voters. Many people and many political observers grumble about the electoral college system, but nothing seems to get done about it. Even people like Nobel Prize winning former president Jimmy Carter think it is a waste of time to talk about changing it. "I would predict," said Carter, "that 200 years from now, we will still have the Electoral College."[30]

The electoral college system was adopted for a variety of complicated reasons at the Constitutional Convention of 1787 and ever since it has been one of the most regularly debated provisions in the Constitution.[31]

## HOW THE ELECTORAL COLLEGE WORKS TODAY

In making their presidential choice every four years, voters technically do not vote for a candidate but rather choose between slates of "presidential electors" selected by state political parties. In almost all of the states, the slate that wins a plurality of popular votes in the state casts all the electoral votes for that state. In Maine and Nebraska, the plurality of the votes in congressional districts determines two and three of their four and five electoral votes respectively. This is called the district plan.

Candidates cannot afford to lose the popular vote in many of the most populous states. The electoral college system plainly gives a disproportionate power to the largest states.

Each state has one electoral vote for each senator and each representative. The District of Columbia has three votes, which were granted by the Twenty-third Amendment to the U.S. Constitution. There are 538 votes in today's electoral college and one must earn 270 or more to win. George W. Bush's much debated 271-vote electoral victory was plainly a close call.

A president is not officially elected on election day. Victorious slates of electors travel to their respective state capitols on the first Monday after the second Wednesday in December—no wonder most people don't remember how this system works!—where they cast ballots for their party's presidential ticket. Ballots are then sent from each state capitol to Congress, where early in January they are formally counted by House and Senate leaders and the next president is finally announced.

There is yet another unusual and rather undemocratic aspect to the electoral college. In the event that no candidate secures a majority of electoral votes, the decision then goes to the House of Representatives. This has happened twice, once in 1800 and again in 1824. It was a possibility in 1968, 1992, and again in 2000. In the House, the delegation from each state casts a single vote. If a delegation is evenly divided, this state forfeits its vote. Thus the influence of a third-party "spoiler" candidate can on occasion pose a significant threat to the two main parties, because the House of Representatives chooses a president from among the top three candidates. Consecutive ballots are taken until a candidate wins a majority (26) of the state delegations.


## THE CASE FOR RETAINING THE ELECTORAL COLLEGE

Defenders of the electoral college contend we should not lightly dismiss a system that has served us reasonably well for so long. Not surprisingly, neither George W. Bush nor leading Republicans find fault with a system that served them well in 2000.

Defenders are fond of the old saying that "the evil best known is the most tolerable" and "when it is not necessary to change, it is necessary not to change." They also cite John F. Kennedy, who once defended the electoral college by arguing that the question does not merely involve certain technical details of the election process, but a whole solar system of subtle, interrelated institutions, principles, and customs.

Defenders emphasize that ours is a federal system, not a unified, centralized, hierarchical, or nationalized system. They remind us that our nation was founded as a republic with a number of checks and balances, and that the electoral college is one of those balancing checks.

Supporters of the electoral college process claim eliminating this system might:

- weaken the existing two-party system and encourage splinter parties, possibly triggering numerous contingency elections
- weaken the federal character of America's constitutional system
- encourage presidential candidates to pay less attention to smaller states as they concentrate on major metropolitan areas
- encourage even more simplistic media-oriented campaigns

Perhaps the greatest fear of moving from the electoral college system to a direct vote system is that relatively small third parties or single-cause candidates might be able to magnify their strength. "In direct elections," writes historian Arthur Schlesinger, Jr., "they could drain enough votes, cumulative from state to state, to prevent the formation of a national majority—and to give themselves strong bargaining positions in a case of a run off."[32]

Defenders of the electoral college argue, often passionately, that the current system is an essential part of the subtle structure of federalism. This, they contend, has helped thwart factionalism and helped encourage liberty. The electoral college also imposes a state-oriented strategy upon presidential candidates. Each candidate must forge a coalition of supporters within each state, especially the big states.

## THE CASE FOR THE DIRECT ELECTION OF PRESIDENTS

The direct election method means that the person who gets the most votes wins. There is no electoral college. Advocates of the direct popular system contend everyone's vote should count equally, people should vote directly for the candidate, and the candidate who gets the majority of votes should be elected.

With the electoral college method, a president can be elected who has fewer popular votes than his opponent, as was the case in 1824 when John Quincy Adams, with 30.92 percent of the vote, defeated Andrew Jackson, with 41.34 percent of the vote. This happened again in 1876 when Rutherford B. Hayes, with 47.95 percent of the popular vote, won over Samuel J. Tilden, with 50.97 percent of the vote; and in 1888, when Benjamin Harrison, with 47.82 percent, won over Grover Cleveland, with 48.62 percent. And, of course, it happened most recently in 2000 when George W. Bush won 47.9 percent of the popular vote while Al Gore won 48.4 percent. This can happen because all of a state's electoral votes are awarded to the winner of the state's popular vote regardless of whether the winning candidate's margin is one vote or three million votes.

Ironically, the major "defect" here, the unit-rule provision, is not part of the Constitution. This winner-take-all formula (unit rule) is merely a state practice, first adopted in the early nineteenth century for partisan purposes and gradually accepted by the rest of the states to ensure maximum electoral weight for their state in the national election.

But because the rest of the states use the winner-take-all rule, the electoral college benefits large "swing" states at the expense of the middle-sized states. The unit-rule arrangement magnifies the relative power of residents in large states. As political scientist Larry Longley suggests, each of the voters in the ten largest states might, by their vote, "decide not just one popular vote, but how a bloc of 33 to 54 votes are cast—if electors are faithful." Hence, the electoral college has a major impact on candidate strategy.

As the presidential election of 2000 reminded us, the logic of the electoral college forces the serious candidates to concentrate only on the competitive "saving" or "battleground" states. In fall 2000, only about 15 states were still "in play," effectively eliminating the vast majority of the states, including as we've noted California, New York, and Texas, from the election process.

The smaller states are advantaged by the "constant two" electoral votes. Thus, Alaska may get one electoral vote for every 40,000 popular votes, whereas Minnesota may get one for every 200,000 popular votes. In the 1990s, "the seven states with 3 electoral votes each had a ratio of 268,000 or fewer citizens per electoral vote, while every state with 13 or more electoral votes had a ratio of 475,000 or more citizens per electoral vote."[33]

In contrast to the complexities and dangers of the electoral college system, the direct-vote method is appealing in its simplicity. Since it is based on a one-person–one-vote principle, it more clearly makes a president the agent of the people and not of the states. Governors and senators are elected by statewide direct popular voting, and they are supposed to be agents of the state. The president, however, should be president of the people, not president of the states—or at least this is what reformers say.

Most of those who favor a direct popular election of the president base their views on the undemocratic character of the electoral college. They say it doesn't treat voters equally, it discourages turnout, and it discriminates against third parties and independent presidential candidates. They point out that those living in large states and small states get more influence. They point out that Democrats in Kansas or Idaho and Republicans in the District of Columbia can be discouraged from even turning out to vote since votes are cast in bloc and the chances of their party winning are small.

Thus there are major questions of fairness and democracy that constantly get raised in the debate over the electoral college and its alternatives. A direct popular vote would eliminate undesirable and undemocratic biases. Stephen J. Wayne wrote "It would better equalize voting power both among and within states. . . . The large, competitive states would lose some of their electoral clout by the elimination of winner-take-all voting. Party competition within the states and perhaps nationwide would be increased. Candidates would be forced to wage campaigns in all fifty states. No longer could an area of the country be taken for granted. Every vote would count in a direct election."[34]

Critics of the electoral college system invariably also attack the contingency election procedure and would change the contingency procedure to a popular runoff. The current system provides that if no presidential candidate wins an absolute majority of the electoral votes (270 under present arrangements), the members of the House of Representatives choose a president from the top three vote getters. The members vote as a part of their state delegation with each state having just one vote. Thus, Alaska and California, Delaware and New York, Wyoming and Texas get one vote.

If this contingency procedure had to be used in future elections, it would obviously be a big boon for small states. But more important, critics lament, it would be an incredibly undemocratic way to select a president. Further, the intrigues in the House might prove unseemly, especially in a three-person, three-party race.

Thus, proponents of the direct vote say it is the most forthright alternative and far preferable to the present system. They contend that voters, when they are choosing a president, think of themselves as national citizens, not as residents of a particular state. According to the American Bar Association, the present system is "archaic, undemocratic, complex, ambiguous, indirect and dangerous."[35] The direct popular vote system, proponents claim, is simple, democratic, and clear-cut.

Although we may not especially like or even understand fully the electoral college system, we are likely to be stuck with it, for better or worse, for at least the coming generation. Still, plenty of reform suggestions will continue to be debated, and deserve to be debated. They are summarized as follows:

1. The direct vote system just discussed.[36]
2. The district system, as used in Maine and Nebraska.
3. A proportional allocation of the vote within the states, similar to that used in many European countries. Thus, in Florida in 2000 Gore and Bush would have received 12.5 state electoral votes each, rather than all 25 going to Bush.[37]
4. A national bonus plan, which would award 102 bonus electoral votes to the winner of the popular vote—a system that strives to preserve the best aspects of the electoral college yet virtually guarantees that the popular vote winner wins.[38]

In the aftermath of the confusing 2000 presidential election, a wide array of ideas surfaced, many dusted off from earlier efforts at reform. Most efforts were, as noted, some type of direct vote or proportional allocation. One intriguing, if unlikely, proposal called for a new format for voting that asks voters to choose not only their first choice, but also their second and third choices. If no candidate receives 50 percent, the candidate with the fewest votes among the top three would be eliminated. Those who voted for the eliminated candidate would then have their second choice receive their vote. This is repeated with lesser candidates until only two candidates remain and there is a clear winner. It is, in essence, a built-in "instant runoff" procedure, a runoff without having to hold a new election.[39] While this and similar ideas attracted interest, it was instructive how quickly demands for reform faded and the United States went on as usual, as if the bizarre events of the presidential election of 2000 had never happened.

## CONCLUSION

Our presidential selection process is neither tidy nor easy to understand. It is and will continue to be under criticism because of its expense and length, because of the biases of the electoral college, and because many people believe it tests candidates more for their fund-raising and media skills than for the ability to govern and make tough economic and foreign policy choices.

The election process has evolved in varying and often unpredictable ways since the framers met in Philadelphia. It seeks to achieve a variety of often contending and conflicting purposes. Yet it is one of the grand compromises so often found in the structure of the American political system that seek to paper over regional, political, and even ideological differences. Old tensions of how strong a central government we really want and of how strong and powerful a central leader we are willing to tolerate are never far behind the scenes. Questions of just how much democracy we really want and how much we actually trust the judgment of the average citizen are also often involved in our attitudes about the presidential election system. The whole selection process is part of the continuing American quest to preserve a politics of compromise, coalitions, moderation, and pragmatism. The politics produced by such a quest is not always pretty, is not always democratic, and, as we have tried to suggest, has its share of paradoxes.

# Rating and Understanding Presidents

Lincoln never ceased to be a common man: that was his source of strength. But he was a common man with genius, a genius for things American, for insight into the common thought, for mastery of the fundamental things of politics . . . for judging men and assessing arguments.

Woodrow Wilson, *Mere Literature and Other Essays* (1896)

Great presidents possess, or are possessed by, a vision of an ideal America. Their passion is to make sure the ship of state sails on the right course. If that course is indeed right, it is because they have an instinct for the dynamics of history. . . . Great presidents [also] have a deep connection with the needs, anxieties, dreams of the people.

Arthur M. Schlesinger, Jr., "The Ultimate Approval Rating,"
*The New York Times Magazine,* December 15, 1996

The great presidents were great because they not only brought about change but also left a legacy—principles, institutional arrangements, and policies that defined an era . . . When decisive action was required, they took it. Even when such efforts are necessary, however, they risk weakening the capacity of citizens to fend for themselves. Indeed, . . . the presidency is a nondemocratic office . . . the need to execute requires presidents to flout the popular will.

Mark Landy and Sidney M. Milks, *Presidential Greatness*
(Lawrence: University Press of Kansas, 2000), p. 3.

The Triumvirate: the presidents most often portrayed as the three greatest in U.S. History—(from right to left) Abraham Lincoln, George Washington, and Franklin Delano Roosevelt. (*Source:* All three images reproduced from the collections of the Library of Congress.)

George W. Bush's approval rating soared from 51 percent in the Gallup poll before September 11, 2001, to 90 percent a few weeks later—the single highest jump in the more than sixty-year history of the Gallup poll. Later millions of people in the United States and elsewhere around the world marched in protest against Bush's unilateralism and preemptive war against Iraq. Still later some Americans worried whether Bush had misled them about the reasons for going to war. Most presidents lose public approval the longer they serve in the White House. In contrast, Bill Clinton was more popular toward the end of his presidency, after he was impeached, than in his first year when he was trying to reform an unfair health care system, advance gay rights, and so on. Harry Truman is more popular now than he was when he was in office. Indeed, his many critics back then used to say "to err is Truman." What explains the way in which presidents get approved and criticized, remembered and forgotten?

A nation reveals a lot about itself by the leaders it remembers and honors, by those it rates as great and by those it forgets. American historians and biographers agree that Lincoln, Washington, and Franklin D. Roosevelt were our great presidents, followed by Jefferson, Wilson, Jackson, and possibly Theodore Roosevelt. Presidents Polk and Truman also win favorable approval.[1]

The average American is ahistorical. Americans like presidents whom they know or at least about whom they have first-hand stories. Thus recent Gallup poll popular favorites are John F. Kennedy, Ronald Reagan, Harry Truman, FDR, and to a lesser extent Dwight Eisenhower.[2]

Experts and citizens alike forget Buchanan, Pierce, Harding, Fillmore, Hoover, and Andrew Johnson, among others.

Americans were tough on King George III, and we continue to be rough in how we treat our own governing elites. We love our country but we have never loved our government. Presidents, as symbols of government, are regularly scrutinized and blamed for the ills of government. They have to prove themselves or pay an exacting penalty.

The most glaring paradox in how we evaluate presidents is the confused standards by which we judge leaders. While we are "results oriented" we are also deeply concerned about means. We demand that presidents succeed, and criticize them if they do not. But they must not demand too much of us, push the system too far, call for too many sacrifices, or trample on our rights and liberties.[3] Like people everywhere, we want heroic leadership *and* a government by the people. We want presidents to lead yet also to be responsive to us.

We say we want leadership, yet we are reluctant followers.

What follows is a discussion of how what we want from presidents has changed over time. Moreover, as discussed in Chapter 1, we not only hold contradictory expectations about our presidents, we have also redefined their job in such a way that being an effective president is an incredible challenge.

Here are a few factors that affect how we evaluate and understand presidents and public opinion:

- The American public has always rewarded those presidents who provided, or at least presided over, periods of peace and prosperity and who displayed integrity and courage.

- A president can be popular and a splendid communicator yet also ineffective. What the public thinks about presidents is not always what historians and political biographers will conclude. Thus JFK, Reagan, and Clinton were often popular with the public yet are viewed as merely average and indeed as "overrated" presidents by informed students of the presidency.

- Presidents go to great lengths to win public support for themselves and their initiatives for the simple reason that public support is viewed as a strategic resource in winning support in Congress, in the bureaucracy, in diplomatic endeavors, as well as, occasionally, in the courts.

- Public approval of presidents is less shaped by charisma or election results than by the times, the economy, the context of the challenges presidents have to face, and their success in dealing with such challenges.

- Finally, presidential leadership involves more than becoming popular; Americans expect presidents on occasion to rise above doing what might be conventionally popular in favor of doing the courageously right thing—that is, to lead us, to educate us, and to bring out our better, more idealistic selves. We don't want presidents to pander only to our selfish, short-term interests.

Figure 3.1 displays how statistical samples of Americans have rated their presidents when asked, "Do you approve or disapprove of how [President X] is handling his job as president?" Notice the gyrations and the gravity-like

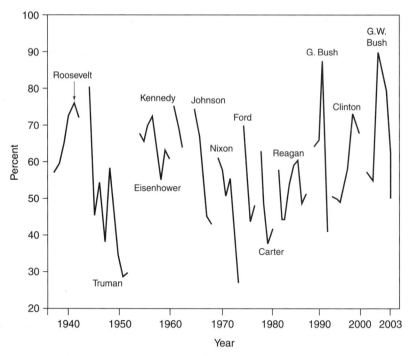

**Figure 3.1** Presidential Approval Ratings, Gallup Poll, 1938–2003    (*Sources:* Calculated by the editors; 1938–1980: *The Gallup Opinion Index,* October– November 1980, 13–38; 1981–2001: *The Gallup Report,* July 1988, 19–20; The Gallup Poll, "Reagan Regaining Public Confidence," press release, October 9, 1988; The Gallup Organization [www.gallup.com], unpublished data from the Gallup Poll.)

pull of diminished approval that presidents usually face over the course of their terms.

## WHAT DO WE EXPECT OF OUR PRESIDENTS?

Alexander Hamilton wrote in 1788 that the office of president would never fall to the lot of anyone not in an eminent degree endowed with the requisite qualifications. Indeed he predicted the office would be regularly filled by individuals noted for ability and virtue. This was too optimistic a prediction; our presidents have varied dramatically in skill and character. Moreover, what we expect of a president has varied over the course of our history. The framers of the Constitution were not of one mind, and the final constitutional provisions were compromises, sometimes even guesses. They left much to be worked out.

One expectation, however, has remained constant. We want prudent and intellectually honest leaders who exercise their powers to the fullest when emergencies arise or when the country or the Constitution is threatened. We want presidents who will place the country and the Constitution ahead of their own personal or partisan interests. At the same time, the framers and citizens worried that a president capable of exercising robust executive power in a crisis situation could also become a demagogue and the worst kind of tyrant. The tension between robust executive power and popular rule is an enduring one. Hence, checks, both formal and informal, would always be needed to safeguard liberty. An appreciation of this paradox has given rise to an ambivalence toward presidents and presidential power.

As America expanded presidential powers and responsibilities, and as we moved away from Whig notions of limited presidential leadership, this ambivalence only grew more intense. We yearn for effective leaders to become president yet only sometimes do we want them to have the powers and resources necessary to do the job. Events throughout the past few generations again and again raised concern about the abuse of power and the possible irresponsible actions of an even moderately empowered president. We have come to understand that presidential power can be used to achieve both noble and ignoble ends. "What seems like a paradox at first now acquires logic."[4] Limited tenure, as now required by the Twenty-second Amendment, and additional statutory checks and accountability procedures such as inspectors general and ethics codes are some of the devices we now use to try to keep strong power from becoming irresponsible power.

The growth of presidential power came in fits and starts over our first 140 years. But since Franklin D. Roosevelt, the office and its power have steadily grown. It did not grow because of presidential fiat or reckless abandonment of earlier constitutional principles. It occurred because times changed, popular expectations changed, and Congress passed laws and delegated increased responsibilities to presidents, especially during crisis periods. As the United States emerged as a preeminent world economic and military power, presidential power grew.

## WHAT DID THE FRAMERS EXPECT OF PRESIDENTS?

The framers of the Constitution were torn between their fears of executive tyranny and the need for executive power. They feared the possibility of an arbitrary and ruthless leader. However, even the most vigorous champions of a strong executive insisted that the president would not become a monarch. Alexander Hamilton, in *Federalist* 69, compared the powers of a president with those of a king, and argued persuasively that presidents would possess far less power than the English monarch.

The framers were deliberately vague about the precise character of presidential powers, yet they provided the office with a potential for growth. Over the short run, they wished a president to be no more than an equal partner in a triumvirate, to be restrained by the judicial and especially by the legislative branch. They took care, in drafting the Constitution, to construct a governmental system that did not depend on a strong, popular leader. Even to admit the need for strong leadership was to leave open the possibility for the exercise of discretion and thus power. Unchecked power was thought dangerous. According to many historians, the framers, in a burst of intellectual cleverness, devised a constitutional system that made great political and presidential leadership all but impossible, except in times of crisis. Yet, Alexander Hamilton believed prosperity would be realized not from the absence of power, but from the presence of decisive executive power and leadership.

The framers obviously hoped for wise and virtuous statesmen to be presidents, individuals who would work closely with Congress and respond to the "sense of the community." Implicit, if not explicit, in their early expectations was the notion that each president, as well as members of Congress, would be preoccupied with what ought to be done rather than with what shortsighted temporary majorities might desire. They thus sought to insulate the president from the pressures of popular whim, and likewise to protect the other branches from the dangers inherent in a president armed with the support of the masses.

The reason for providing distance between the people and the presidency is clear. It was to allow ample scope for leadership and statesmanship. In a representative democracy, or republic, public opinion would not always be identical with the public interest. There is more than a hint in Hamilton's conception of national leadership that sometimes a president would have to have the power "to do what the laws would do if the laws could foresee what should be done, as well as the power to make exceptions in the execution of the laws, exceptions governed by a judgment as to whether it would be good to apply them or not."[5]

Hamilton's prediction came true more quickly than he had imagined. President George Washington set a few precedents for unilateral executive action not exactly envisioned by the framers. He saw to it that he alone would lead the executive branch of government. He issued the Neutrality Proclamation of 1793 without the consent of Congress. He withheld information from Congress he thought should not be disclosed for reasons of national security. Washington seldom assumed these leadership responsibilities over the objection of the other two branches of government or the people. Congress willingly conceded to Washington most of the executive powers he exercised, especially those in foreign policy matters. By making the president commander-in-chief and allowing him to appoint ambassadors and to negotiate treaties, the framers provided important foreign policy and symbolic roles for the newly invented presidency.

Once Washington established these early practices, however, executive assertiveness was somewhat limited. Monarchial fears of the anti-federalist opponents of the Constitution were not realized. With only a few exceptions, Adams, Jefferson, Madison, and Monroe regularly deferred to Congress. In essence these early presidents did so because they believed the voice of the people and their duly elected representatives in Congress must be heeded.

The framers, and the American voters of the day, did not expect regular and extensive domestic and economic policymaking leadership as much as administrative efficiency. Washington, in taking executive action yet always acknowledging the power and importance of Congress, set the prudent example.

What was expected of our early presidents was an executive role with neither tyrannical nor hereditary powers, restrained by representatives of the people yet able to protect the people, at least on occasion, from their own representatives. Under George Washington, Americans in the 1790s got what they wanted and more.

## WHAT WAS EXPECTED IN THE NINETEENTH CENTURY?

Early presidents did not have to conduct presidential campaigns as we know them today. Due to the natural restrictions of travel and the absence of modern media tools, they remained distant from the average citizen. To be sure, presidents traveled about the country for occasional ceremonial visits. The early presidents also held weekly social gatherings and were accessible even to casual visitors in the nation's capitol. Many presidents deemed it a requirement of the job to take an occasional "bath in public opinion," to paraphrase Lincoln.

Still, presidents in this period were not expected to provide popular leadership. Elected representatives, it was believed, would be better able to make important decisions than the average citizen. Being physically removed from the workings of government, the general public had fewer expectations of their representative, and of the president. Moreover, the impact of the national government on the average citizen was decidedly less than it is today. Not until much later in the nineteenth century did the notion take hold of a president as a direct representative of the American people.

The typical nineteenth-century president was expected to be a "constitutional executive," a dignified presider over the administrative branch who would not tread on the responsibilities of the other branches. Although the nineteenth century eventually witnessed remarkable industrial growth based on individual initiative, most of that growth operated independently from any governmental restrictions. Freedom *from* government seemed to permeate all aspects of economic and social life.

The doctrine of laissez faire was widely accepted. Government might help, yet only in a limited way. Public expectations of the president were not geared toward greatness, but toward efficiency in those limited responsibilities assigned to the presidency.

Other factors also made the public expect less of presidents in the nineteenth century than today. Presidents before McKinley (1897–1901) were not expected to make the United States a world power. Thus, when we look back and judge presidents, we rate them largely according to domestic affairs, often forgetting they had fewer responsibilities than today.

To say that nineteenth-century presidents had less to do does not mean crises and emergencies did not arise. The Civil War was the greatest crisis the nation and our constitutional system ever faced. Rather it means the public seldom viewed presidents the way we do today.

With the exception of Lincoln's crisis leadership, the presidency was rarely a dominant and often not even a particularly visible leadership institution in America. For much of the first half of the century, government was dominated by congressional leaders such as Daniel Webster, Henry Clay, and John Calhoun. Andrew Jackson, forceful executive that he was, did not approve of a forceful national government prior to taking office. Abraham Lincoln, before he was elected president, counseled against a strong presidency. And save in matters of war or security, President Lincoln regularly deferred to Congress and his cabinet.[6]

Not until Theodore Roosevelt did the general public consciously expect a president to provide sustained assertive leadership.[7] Populist manifestoes of the late nineteenth century began to change attitudes, as people turned to popular movements, popular political figures, and the central government as possible remedies for their economic problems. The crusade to elect William Jennings Bryan was illustrative of this new development. Attitudes toward presidents and presidential leadership began to change.

Teddy Roosevelt used the "bully pulpit" of the presidency to set the nation's programmatic agenda. And in doing so over time he also expanded expectations for the office. Woodrow Wilson echoed and extended Roosevelt's conception. Wilson wrote that the presidency should respond to and help enact the progressive sentiments of the people. Since the country had expanded in so many ways, now the presidency must expand. The people, Wilson suggested, should look to their presidents to promote the conscience of the nation.[8]

Were Roosevelt and Wilson responsible for changing the expectations of the presidency, or were they merely in office when the public began to expect and demand more? Probably more the latter than the former, but doubtless both factors were at work.

## PUBLIC ATTITUDES TOWARD PRESIDENTS IN RECENT TIMES

Public attitudes toward the presidency are subject to certain cycles. After strong presidents, who are often crisis or war presidents, the public yearns for a lessened presidential role, a return to normalcy. After a weak leader, and especially after a series of weak leaders, we yearn for strength. Presidents live in the shadows of their immediate predecessors, and presidents often pay for the sins of a predecessor. After the presidencies of Theodore Roosevelt and Woodrow Wilson, the Harding-Coolidge-Hoover administrations assumed a more passive posture.

Coolidge once said nine out of ten problems brought to his office could be safely ignored and did not require his leadership attention. After Franklin

Roosevelt served there was a backlash; the public supported the Twenty-second Amendment in an apparent effort to punish the institution (as well as reaffirm the two-term tradition). After the Kennedy-Johnson-Nixon administrations there was another backlash to presidential power, as Ford and Carter provided a return to normalcy and rectitude in the White House. However, Ford and Carter paid for the political excesses of Nixon by being severely constrained by a more energized Congress.

Yet seldom does a president actually relinquish any powers associated with the office. The more passive ones may not use the powers in a vigorous way, yet even the three Republican presidents of the 1920s (Harding, Coolidge, Hoover) attempted to protect the powers of the office they inherited by "consciously trying to steer a middle course between the extreme activism of Wilson and the passivity that had destroyed Taft."[9]

President Franklin D. Roosevelt set a precedent for executive leadership that remained popular as the national government became more and more involved in everyday life. Roosevelt established a pattern that most chief executives would inevitably follow: proposing legislation, lobbying to get proposals enacted, rallying public opinion in support of his measures, creatively using the newly invented electronic media, and inserting himself into ongoing international diplomatic negotiations.

In the beginning of the Republic there was at best grudging acceptance that a president would intervene in the affairs of Congress. Now it is taken for granted that presidents regularly initiate and seek to win support for their measures. The FDR performance irretrievably altered people's views of presidents and the presidency. General Dwight Eisenhower added the reputation of a national hero to the luster of the office. Then, partly due to the youthful enthusiasm and glamor of the Kennedy administration, people and scholars were captivated by the magic of the office. The mystique of the "textbook presidency" prevailed. After Lyndon Johnson won a landslide reelection and enjoyed a sustained honeymoon with Congress, he was able to pass vital civil rights legislation and he got the Great Society programs off to a rousing start. The power of the modern presidency appeared virtually unlimited. Public and scholarly celebration of the presidency reached a peak.

Then came Vietnam, increased secrecy and deception, Watergate scandals, obstruction of justice, and an increasingly frustrated American public. For a period, this dissatisfaction was reflected by a profound anti-Washington sentiment. Public approval of presidents declined and expectations of presidents were briefly lowered.

Presidents Johnson, Nixon, Ford, and Carter were criticized and found wanting. Yet after a brief infatuation with the idea of turning to Congress for national leadership (notably in the 1973–80 period), Americans revived their demand for decisive and assertive presidential leadership. Ronald Reagan won election in part because he played upon this yearning. "Reagan's apparent self-assurance, good humour, decisiveness and faith in the eternal verities seemingly struck a responsive chord among a demoralized public," according to two public opinion specialists. "His presentation of self, whether natural or stage-managed, communicated a sense of pride in the nation and its past."[10] Reagan's likability, his talent for speaking plainly, his ability to convey his love of the country, and his ability to give the people he was talking to, whether an individual or the public at large, the impression of liking them made him a rare political phenomenon. Reagan called for and promised a more powerful presidential performance. He charmed and often entertained the nation.

Several political scientists in recent years have suggested it is important to evaluate presidents in the context of the nation's political cycles. Some presidents come to power as the result of the rise of new political coalitions. These new coalitions may have developed in response to major problems that governments are asked to solve. But once in power for a presidential term or two, the dominant coalition often faces divisions and degenerates in ways that make it difficult to lead.

Thus Andrew Johnson and FDR came to power as a result of new coalitions and new challenges for government, whereas Franklin Pierce and Jimmy Carter "both came to power at a time when the dominant coalition had degenerated into myopic sects that appeared impervious to the most basic problems facing the nation."[11]

These cycle or "political times" theories can be complicated to explain, yet they are helpful in warning that it is extremely difficult to compare and contrast presidents as if they all faced similar circumstances and enjoyed similar political environments and resources.

## THE PARADOXES OF BILL CLINTON

The Clinton presidency proved to be one of the most fascinating roller coaster rides in U.S. history. Bill Clinton was a masterful politician: smart, resourceful, creative, energetic, with a deft touch and a rhetorical flair. He was also a man with some notable character flaws. His affairs and his dishonesty about them led to distrust and to the most extensive investigations ever conducted into the behavior and "sins" of a president.

Bill Clinton was a president of contradictions, possibly the most paradoxical president since Richard Nixon. Like Nixon, Clinton was a man of extremes: flawed character, yet remarkable political skill; a man who made huge blunders, but also political successes; a man whom the people did not trust, but to whom they gave high job approval ratings. Like Nixon's Watergate, Clinton's conduct is perplexing: How could such a smart and politically astute president do such dumb things? Clinton's irresponsible behavior jeopardized his entire presidency and diminished the presidency itself.

Bill Clinton's accomplishments were many, especially given the nature and behavior of his political opponents who attacked him and his wife, Hillary Clinton. Reacting to the Reagan years, in which the nation shifted from a center-left to a center-right political orientation, Clinton moved the

Even in the throes of his impeachment, Bill Clinton's approval ratings remained reasonably high—perhaps due to the robust economy over which he presided. (*Source:* Copyright © Peter Turnley/CORBIS.)

Democratic party toward the political center. His "Third Way" (between the liberal left of the Democratic party and the hard right of the Republicans) allowed him to offer a moderate alternative to political extremes.

More than anything else, however, Clinton was saved by a robust economy—low inflation, high employment, and balanced budgets—that coincided with his second term in office. Whether Clinton or the economic cycles that occur in this country deserve the credit is difficult to assess, but good economic times lift public approval ratings. Clinton also enjoyed some successes in domestic politics: during his administration the Family Leave Act was passed, environmental protection was extended (against stiff Republican opposition), and gun control was extended through the Brady Bill.

Ironically, Clinton's highest public approval came when the scandals involving Monica Lewinsky, the White House intern with whom Clinton had sexual encounters, were constantly in the news—and when he was being impeached by the House of Representatives. At the very same time Americans disapproved of Clinton's personal conduct, they approved, at one point even at the 81 percent level, of Clinton's "handling of the economy." One scholar says the Lewinsky scandal prevented Clinton's approval from being even higher than it was.[12]

Clinton's legacy will always be dogged by the character issue. He was a man of large appetites and inadequate personal discipline. He pressed his legal claims in the Lewinsky case to their limits and thereby left the presidency weaker and more defenseless: presidential immunity, privilege, and privacy have all been eroded due to Clinton's actions.

Like most presidents, Bill Clinton's record is mixed: some successes, some failures. If Clinton's successes seem bigger than most, his failures, too, seem larger than life. In the long run, historians will probably put Clinton in the middle of the pack of presidents: not great, not a failure.[13]

## QUALITIES AMERICANS LOOK FOR IN THEIR PRESIDENTS

We appear to have a tough, unwritten code of conduct for our nation's chief executive. We demand much. Part of this comes from our inflated image of what "the great" presidents did. Our selective memories about the past glories and victories under our favorite presidents result in our holding incumbents to unusually high standards. A president is expected to be an agenda setter—"greater than anyone else, but no better than anyone else," wrote John Steinbeck. "We are related to the President in a close and almost familial sense; we inspect his every move and mood with suspicion. . . . We subject him and his family to close and constant scrutiny and denounce them for things that we ourselves do everyday."[14]

According to polls, how we evaluate presidents varies with the times and depends partially on who has recently been president and on who is now in office. Polls in the late 1950s and early 1960s showed the general public wanted strong presidential leadership. They also wanted checks on presidents. People recognized presidents had to play an increasingly central role as a foreign policy leader. People had considerable faith in the dedication of presidents to the public interest.[15] In the mid-1970s, that faith in the notion that "the president knows best" sharply diminished, only to increase again in the mid-1980s.

Experts usually rate experience, vision, and intellectual capacity over honesty. But this is not the case with the average person. *Honesty* and *credibility* are top qualities the public wants in a president. The average voters say they want a leader whose words they can both understand and believe and whose intentions are trusted. When George H.W. Bush enjoined the public to "Read my lips, no new taxes," and later was compelled to break that vow, the public was unforgiving. Likewise, when candidate Clinton promised a middle-class tax cut but broke that vow, he lost political capital as well as credibility.

Surveys show the public rates honesty as a top quality a president should have, as well as compassion, intelligence, toughness/decisiveness, and decision-making ability. Experience and knowledge of economic issues are also cited frequently (see Table 3.1 and Figure 3.2).

## HOW AMERICANS EVALUATE INCUMBENT PRESIDENTS

Do presidents shape public opinion or do they merely follow public opinion? This debate is as old as it is unanswerable. Long before the advent of polls, President Lincoln said public sentiment is everything. With public support, nothing can fail; without it, nothing can succeed. Lincoln, who was fortunate

**TABLE 3.1**
**Assessing Candidates: Standards and Qualities**

| | |
|---|---|
| Q. What is the single most important standard by which you judge a presidential candidate? | |
| Honesty | 41% |
| Political beliefs same as own | 37 |
| Moral character | 15 |
| Party affiliation | 2 |
| Personal appearance and presence | 1 |
| Don't know/No answer | 3 |
| Q. What is the single most important skill you look for in evaluating a candidate's credentials for the presidency? | |
| Experience in national-level politics | 32% |
| Knowledge of economic issues | 30 |
| Experience in foreign affairs | 20 |
| Experience in business or other nonpolitical fields | 10 |
| Other | 2 |
| Don't know/No answer | 5 |

*N* = 1001.

*Source:* "The American Public's Experience with Recent Presidential Elections," a national survey of public awareness and personal opinion (New York: The Hearst Corporation, 1988). Interviews were done in late October 1987. Also see *Times Mirror Center for the People & the Press,* "Voter Anxiety," *Los Angeles Times,* November 14, 1995, p. 22; and *The Roper Center,* "Americans Rate Their Society and Chart Its Values," *The Public Perspective* 8(2) (February/March 1997).

to live through the most trying of times without Gallup and Harris polls reporting his considerable public disfavor, would warn us today that in evaluating presidents we should take care not to take polls too seriously, for the sources of positive or negative evaluations are often superficial. He would doubtless also say the influence between a people and their president is reciprocal: presidents must be both leaders and followers of public opinion.

With the coming of professional polling organizations in the 1930s, we began to accumulate extensive data about what people thought of presidents. The Gallup Organization surveyed the general public on this question occasionally in the late 1930s and regularly under Harry Truman. Several patterns are evident as one examines the ups and downs of presidential approval over a fifty-year period.

- Presidents tend to be more popular in their first year than they are later. (Clinton was an exception.)

- Presidential approval ratings often rise during the "honeymoon" early months in office.

- Over time, however, approval ratings usually drop, with a number of zigs and zags caused by specific events, conditions, or crises.

- Presidents typically lose popularity during midterm elections when the "guns" of the opposition party are aimed directly at the White House. (2002 was an exception.)

- Domestic crises typically cause approval evaluations to drop.

- International or terrorist crises, regardless of what a president does, typically cause us to rally around our president in the short run.
- Republican presidents are typically less approved at the beginning of their presidencies than Democrats who served just before them. (Eisenhower, Nixon, Reagan, G.W. Bush)
- Americans give an initial high approval evaluation to vice presidents who are thrust suddenly into the presidential job at a time of death or emergency. (Truman, LBJ, Ford)
- Presidents often enjoy a rebound late in the first term—especially when they begin to be evaluated in comparison with likely opponents.
- If a president is reelected, the pattern often repeats itself, although approval ratings drop more quickly and tend to be lower than during the first term.

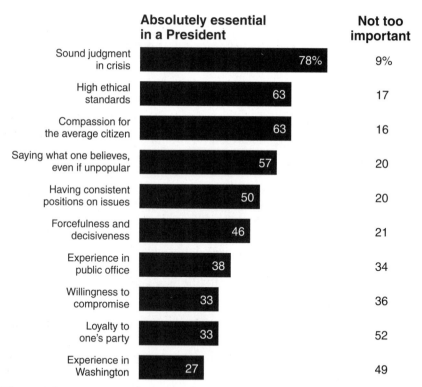

| | Absolutely essential in a President | Not too important |
|---|---|---|
| Sound judgment in crisis | 78% | 9% |
| High ethical standards | 63 | 17 |
| Compassion for the average citizen | 63 | 16 |
| Saying what one believes, even if unpopular | 57 | 20 |
| Having consistent positions on issues | 50 | 20 |
| Forcefulness and decisiveness | 46 | 21 |
| Experience in public office | 38 | 34 |
| Willingness to compromise | 33 | 36 |
| Loyalty to one's party | 33 | 52 |
| Experience in Washington | 27 | 49 |

**Figure 3.2** Essential Qualities Americans Want in a President. (A surveyor asked the following: "First I'm going to read you a list of personal characteristics or qualities. If '5' represents an absolutely essential quality in a President, and '1' a quality that is not too important, where on this scale . . . ?") (*Source:* Survey by Princeton Research Associates for the Pew Research Center, July–September 1999.)

While these patterns are persistent, they are not inevitable. It is premature to be definitive when we are examining just ten or twelve presidencies.

One of the more confusing aspects of presidential accountability is the way the American people find it convenient to blame presidents for a whole range of problems, regardless of whether the problems have been subject to presidential influence and solution. Presidents are the focus of attention and receive blame, and sometimes praise, for events over which they have little or no control.

The majority of the public is politically inattentive and will notice only mistakes, while failing to appreciate successes. Decline in approval of the president is partly a function of the inability and unlikelihood of a president to live up to the buildup he receives during the presidential honeymoon (or perhaps the hopes and promises he raised during his campaign). Heightened expectations are invariably followed by disappointment. Sometimes the disappointment warrants despair and retribution; often unfairly people turn on a president almost as if he were the sole cause of everything that is wrong in their lives.

One of the most difficult paradoxes for a president to deal with stems from the public's desire to have contradictory things of government. The public demands budget cuts yet not service cuts (for them at least); we want tax cuts yet also demand that entitlements be fully funded. In one USA Today/CNN/Gallup poll, 82 percent of the sample reported that it was a "major concern" that the Republican majority in Congress "reduce the budget." At the same time, 69 percent responded that it was a "major concern" that the Republicans provide a "tax cut for most Americans."[16]

Most presidents concede that those who use presidential power must understand that by using it they may dissipate it. No president has had as much power in his last year in office as he had in his first. Several presidential resources wane as the years roll by. The presidential honeymoon comes to an end. Prominent politicians who are rivals for the office begin, after a short grace period, to attack a president's positions, partisan followings crystallize, and the ranks of those who disapprove of the president begin to swell. Presidential promises, at least some of them, go unachieved. Presidential achievements often fail to get acknowledged, or at least remembered. Factions in the president's own party inevitably develop. Press criticism increases. And persons whose pressing claims go unheeded become disaffected.

A vicious cycle can develop. As popularity wanes a president loses valuable public support, and he may eventually find himself in an ever-deepening hole of credibility. Unpopular chief executives are far less able to influence public opinion. Such a president may often avoid divisive issues in favor of "not making waves." And the more presidents strive to achieve favorable evaluations and thus protect their public support, the more they engage in short-term transitory policies—policies that may not be good for the country in the long run. We also "have the paradox that governments following public opinion polls," writes Samuel Kernell, "begin to look more and more incompetent. As they look incompetent, confidence in government begins to disintegrate."[17]

The frequency and duration of these dynamic ebbs and flows of approval between the president and the public are not well understood. Most presidents lose popularity during congressional elections when the opposition party takes the offensive against the incumbent administration, and most presidents' popularity declines considerably in the public-opinion polls over time (Table 3.2). Eisenhower, however, was generally immune to this cyclic factor, perhaps due to his "don't rock the boat" demeanor in office. Legislative activists like Truman and Johnson suffered most in the polls, whereas Eisenhower and Nixon, until Watergate, enjoyed more stable support. Is more expected of Democrats? Johnson enjoyed a comfortable margin of American trust for at least two years, then suddenly it was gone.

Legislative activists suffered declines in public approval, in part because they were outspoken on domestic issues. (Reagan was often outspoken as well, yet he portrayed himself effectively as reasonable and willing to compromise.) Perhaps the expectations generated by these administrations were more difficult to fulfill, and the greater heterogeneity of the Democratic party made opposition to any presidential action more likely. Each time presidents are forced to act on such controversial domestic issues as racial integration, health care reforms, or the separation of church and state they risk losing the support of intense minorities. How does a president please both conservative southerners and blacks, Baptists and Catholics, farmers and consumers? The temptation to become the people's source of inspiration

TABLE 3.2
Average Yearly Presidential Approval Rating, 1953–2003

| Year | Approval | Year | Approval | Year | Approval | Year | Approval |
|------|----------|------|----------|------|----------|------|----------|
| 1953 | 69% | 1966 | 54% | 1979 | 37% | 1992 | 41% |
| 1954 | 65 | 1967 | 44 | 1980 | 38 | 1993 | 49 |
| 1955 | 72 | 1968 | 42 | 1981 | 57 | 1994 | 46 |
| 1956 | 72 | 1969 | 61 | 1982 | 43 | 1995 | 47 |
| 1957 | 63 | 1970 | 56 | 1983 | 45 | 1996 | 56 |
| 1958 | 54 | 1971 | 50 | 1984 | 56 | 1997 | 58 |
| 1959 | 64 | 1972 | 56 | 1985 | 60 | 1998 | 64 |
| 1960 | 61 | 1973 | 41 | 1986 | 60 | 1999 | 61 |
| 1961 | 76 | 1974 | 26 | 1987 | 48 | 2000 | 60 |
| 1962 | 72 | 1975 | 47 | 1988 | 53 | 2001 | 67 |
| 1963 | 62 | 1976 | 46 | 1989 | 66 | 2002 | 78 |
| 1964 | 70 | 1977 | 62 | 1990 | 67 | | |
| 1965 | 67 | 1978 | 45 | 1991 | 70 | | |

*Source:* The Gallup Organization, Princeton, New Jersey.

for every worthy policy can overcommit the political resources, as well as the institutional prestige, of the presidency. Presidents learn, sometimes after the fact, that they must follow public opinion as well as lead it.

The public's rhythmic "issue-attention cycle" tends to restrict the president's leeway in seeking solutions to the nation's domestic problems. Economist Anthony Downs persuasively argued that "American public attention rarely remains sharply focused upon any domestic issue for very long, even if it involves a continuing problem of crucial importance to society. . . . Each of these problems suddenly leaps into prominence, remains there for a short time and then, though still largely unresolved, gradually fades from the center of public attention."[18]

Another problem occurs when a president is forced to act on a controversial issue; he is likely to create intense and often unforgiving opponents among his former supporters.

Even without taking action, a president can come under attack from those who voted for him but find themselves neglected in the distribution of federal patronage or contracts or otherwise disappointed by their inability to influence future presidential policies. Because modern press and television coverage gives so much emphasis to the presidency, it serves to quicken and intensify these reactions. Precisely because a president can gain immediate publicity, he is expected to communicate his views and solve problems without delay. Precisely because he is supposed to be a shaper of public opinion, he is expected to inspire the country to great causes.

Leading the public is believed to be one of the key sources of power for a president. But the ability to move the nation and generate public support takes time and effort; it is not automatically conferred upon assuming office, nor is it always translated into political clout. Presidents spend considerable time and effort trying to build popular support for both themselves and their programs. Their efforts often fail.[19]

A president with popular support (and other skills to complement popularity) can exert pressure on Congress and is somewhat more likely to get his program passed.[20] As a result, presidents are keenly aware of fluctuations in popularity, and routinely engage in efforts aimed at dramatizing themselves in the hope of increasing their popularity.

Is popularity a source of power? Many scholars believe popularity is indeed a convertible source of political power; that presidents can convert popularity into congressional votes, better treatment by the media, and less criticism by political opponents. While hard evidence to support these claims is scarce, one must remember that in politics, *perception* often counts as much as and sometimes more than *reality*. If a president can convince Congress that he is popular and that to defy him is politically dangerous, the battle is half won. In his first two years in office this is precisely what Ronald Reagan was able to do. Democrats in Congress were afraid Reagan's popularity might really have been as wide and as deep as Reagan claimed, and thus many in Congress were more inclined to vote for his legislative proposals. This perception of power strengthened Reagan's bargaining position.

In the aftermath of the 9-11 terrorist attack, President George W. Bush's popularity soared to 90 percent. This led Democrats to be cautious in their criticism of the president, and softened their opposition to many of his policies. It also helped Republicans reclaim control of the U.S. Senate and wider margins in the U.S. House of Representatives in the November 2002 midterm elections.

Yet we must not make too much of Reagan's or any other president's ability to move public opinion. After all, on one of the issues nearest and dearest to Reagan's heart, aid for the rebels in Nicaragua (the Contras), Reagan failed, despite Herculean efforts, to sway the public or Congress to support his goals. In the end, Reagan was forced to act unilaterally, but he was never able, in spite of his much deserved sobriquet "the great communicator," to convince the public they should accept his proposals.

Can presidents convert popularity into power? Political scientist George Edwards is skeptical. After a thoughtful study of the relationship between the two, Edwards concluded that while popularity may help, there is no certainty that popular presidents will get their legislative programs through Congress.[21]

Public support may empower presidents but it is not an easy thing to attain. And that is the challenge for presidents, to gain public support *and* convert it into political power.

But how can presidents *lead* public opinion? Franklin Roosevelt said "All our great Presidents were *leaders* of thought at times when certain historic ideas in the life of the nation had to be clarified." His cousin Theodore Roosevelt observed, "People used to say of me that I . . . divined what the people were going to think. I did not 'divine' . . . I simply made up my mind what they ought to think, and then did my best to get them to think it."[22]

Great presidents take risks. Those who merely want to be loved sometimes sacrifice conviction for wanting to be loved. Harding was popular yet also a failure. JFK was popular yet often cautious. FDR once said, "Judge me by the enemies I've made." Historian Arthur M. Schlesinger, Jr., suggests that effective presidential leadership is provided by those who follow their convictions and, at least on important issues, ignore middle-of-the-road pragmatism:

> We hear much these days about the virtues of the middle of the road. But none of the top nine (highly rated presidents) can be described as a middle-roader. Middle-roading may be fine for campaigning, but it is a sure road to mediocrity in governing. The middle of the road is not the vital center: it is the dead center. . . . The Greats and Near Greats all took risks in pursuit of their ideals. They all provoked intense controversy. They all, except Washington, divided the nation before reuniting it on a new level of national understanding.[23]

Polls and popularity ratings force a president to dance to a different and much faster tune. With one eye always focused on popularity, presidents may be less likely to make the tough choices, the hard decisions. Flattering the public has a greater short-term benefit than speaking a harsh truth.

The relationship between presidents and the public they serve and lead is a complex one. To govern, a president must have a fairly high level of popular support. But the avenues open to a president for attaining that support are limited. Public demands and expectations are high and often contradictory. The public wants presidents to deliver good news, not hard reality.

Political scientist Jeffrey Cohen suggests that presidents try to resolve this challenge by being symbolically responsive when they believe they need to be, yet they try to retain substantive control over public policy. Thus, although presidents know they have to respond to the public's policy preferences they are wary of doing so if the policy outcomes will not be positive and if the policy really is not what the president wants. Cohen writes, "if presidents try to curry public favor by implementing policies that follow public wishes, and if these policies fail, it will be the president, not the public, that bears the brunt of the blame."[24]

Presidents, Cohen concludes, are intuitively protective of their reputation as well as their programmatic agenda, so they will not blindly follow or pander to the public when it is not in their interest to do so. There is a growing body of research aimed at trying to understand this complicated paradox of when to lead, when to follow, where to respond substantively, and when to hold back or merely respond symbolically.[25]

## WHY DOES POPULARITY DECLINE?

As suggested, presidents who have served during the past two generations have generally lost popularity the longer they remained in office. Eisenhower and Clinton are exceptions. Different administrations have encountered different problems, advocated different programs, and presented different images to the public. Presidents during these years have employed a number of distinctive leadership styles. Inevitably the public becomes disenchanted and their earlier more optimistic expectations diminish.

Today, when only about 50 percent of eligible citizens vote, a president can and often is elected by only slightly more than a quarter of the adult population. Moreover, many of these people frequently, and rationally, vote retrospectively rather than prospectively. That is, many people vote against an incumbent because of the incumbent's record and failings rather than for the prospective and only dimly understood programs of the challenger. This was clearly the case in 1976, 1980, and again in 1992. The new president "won" because we were voting out the incumbent president. This, in part, was also Gore's problem in 2000.

Presidents have usually had the support of a majority of Americans just after their inauguration. A rallying around the newly elected president customarily takes place. Most people, including many who did not vote or who did not vote for the victor, give new presidents the benefit of the doubt. Most Americans want to have positive feelings about the presidency, and the inauguration is a great American political and ceremonial event. In the election campaign leading up to the inauguration, voters are told to expect more from the president than they are currently receiving. Promises are made: "I'll get the nation moving again"; "I will never lie to you"; "I'll balance the budget"; "No new taxes"; "I'm a unifier not a divider." In many cases expectations become unrealistic.

The heroic view of what might be accomplished is promoted by journalists who write or talk about the possibilities of the first one hundred days and in doing so sometimes attribute to the president the entire responsibility for the nation's economy. The problem is compounded by Americans who want to believe their presidents can make a major difference. Polls regularly provide persuasive evidence that people do believe a president can make a difference, that Franklin Roosevelt did make things happen, that America would have been much different if John F. Kennedy had not been assassinated, that presidents can reduce unemployment or inflation, increase governmental efficiency, pursue an effective foreign policy, and strengthen the national defense and homeland security.

To win the presidency, presidents have to make promises. Once in office, they find themselves battling with the Congress and colliding with the Supreme Court on occasion, unable to exert as much influence over the federal bureaucracy as they had presumed and constrained by public opinion, the press, interest groups, and other forces. A president's power today to make and implement policies is limited by the decentralized character of politics and government in America, which often results in gridlock.[26] America's growing interdependence with the rest of the world and the economies of other nations, as well as the rise of worldwide terrorism, also serves to limit the flexibility of the office.

Thoughtful people realize presidents are indeed constrained and should be constrained. But no matter, they still hold presidents responsible. Presidents are a convenient, highly visible scapegoat for the nation's problems. We oversimplify issues, we personalize them, and television is constantly featuring the president on the evening news. When things go wrong, people notice. Yet when things go right, people are usually complacent. Reality may be far more complex, yet it is easier for busy people to ascribe blame to a specific person.

In recent years scholars have tried to determine why presidential popularity declines. While findings from this research are inconclusive, the more compelling suggestions for why presidents lose public approval are the following:

- Expectations are too high at the outset.
- There are negative perceptions of the economic direction of the nation.
- Major negative or divisive events, such as Vietnam, Watergate, the Iranian hostage episode, or Whitewater, occur and drag on as an unresolved condition.

- The president's economic policy performance is viewed as weak, indecisive, or unwise.
- There are continuous bad news and negative media coverage associated with the government's performance in economic and foreign policy matters.

The American people evaluate presidents on the basis of the quality of social, economic, and international policy outcomes. Yet the public's perceptions of presidential performance are usually inexact or hazy. One scholar concludes, "the public evaluates the president more on the basis of how it thinks the government is performing on economic policy than how it thinks the economy is performing."[27] Solving economic problems ranks high on the American public's roster of priorities, and the relative weight individual citizens give to economic progress affects their evaluations of a modern president. Their evaluation may not be based on their own situation as much as on their general judgment of how the nation is doing. "When the economy falters, support for the president erodes not so much because citizens blame the president for their private hardships, however vivid, immediate, and otherwise important they might be—but because citizens hold the president accountable for the deterioration of national economic conditions. In evaluating the president, citizens seem to pay more attention to the nation's economic predicament," [than to their own].[28]

One study of the fluctuations of presidential popularity acknowledges some support for a cycle theory in which a brief honeymoon period is followed by a decline over the next three years followed by an upswing of approval in the fourth year. This fourth-year upswing occurs because the public is comparing the incumbent with an all-too-human alternative (i.e., the other party's presidential candidate) or because of a reluctance to make a break from the familiar to the unknown. Yet the economy's impact on presidential popularity is an additional key variable explaining public approval and disapproval of presidents. Unemployment, especially among white-collar workers and married men, is the single most important factor in an incumbent's approval rating. A cycle phenomenon and a citizen's rational response to economic developments are both at work.[29]

While nearly all scholars agree economic realities such as inflation and disposable income usually do have an effect on how people judge presidential performance, the overall picture of economic variables shaping presidential popularity remains muddled.[30] Other kinds of domestic, international, or political events have a way of arising to override people's normal concern with economic issues. "It may well be true that in the absence of foreign or domestic crises for extended periods of time, people evaluate presidential performance largely on the basis of economic conditions. But "normal times," it appears, "are not the norm." Certainly, some people hold presidents responsible for the economy. "Perhaps everybody does at one time or another. But in general it appears that current events—both international and domestic—and the day-to-day policy decisions that the president must make take precedence in people's minds."[31] Thus sometimes the economy takes a back seat.

This verdict is persuasive for many if not all cases. Lyndon Johnson lost public approval more because of civil rights disturbances and the divisiveness of his Vietnam policies than because of economic developments; the economy was actually quite good at the time of his major popularity losses. Nixon lost his popularity and his claim to office not because of economic factors, but because of all the things associated with Watergate. Ford experienced one of the biggest single Gallup poll declines in polling history, more than twenty points, because of his pardon of former President Nixon. And Reagan's public approval took a twenty-point nose dive after the Iran-Contra affair disclosures. On the other hand, Carter, Reagan, G.H.W. Bush, and Clinton usually seemed to be judged according to the general public's perceptions of inflation and the so-called "misery index" of leading economic indicators.

The Clinton presidential years coincided with a robust economy, even an economic boom in his second term. Unemployment and inflation were at thirty-year lows and even the nation's budget was balanced for a short while. Clinton had difficulty averaging a 50 percent approval rating in his first term, yet economic prosperity helps explain favorable public opinion in his final years. Clinton was also aided by the Republican party takeover in the House of Representatives and the way Speaker Newt Gingrich overplayed his so-called mandate to redirect the nation from Capitol Hill. Clinton used the takeover to recenter his administration and used Gingrich as a foil for his leadership strategies. All this happened while Clinton was being investigated, lambasted, and impeached for improper personal behavior.[32]

George W. Bush received higher than expected public approval ratings in the 2001–2003 period despite recessions, doubtless because of the rally of support for his efforts to combat terrorism.

Another reason presidents lose popularity is because we have faulty memories. We forget past presidents also had difficulty controlling events and solving problems quickly. We also forget that all leaders, even our heroes, made mistakes. We often judge our presidents according to a model of the perfect, ideal, heroic president. Interestingly, in their fourth years many presidents gain back some of their public support. Truman, Eisenhower, Nixon, Reagan, and Clinton are illustrative. This is partly so, as suggested earlier, because in their fourth year presidents get compared with a real-life alternative—to Dewey, Stevenson, McGovern, Mondale, and Dole, respectively, not to the model of the perfect presidency.

When asked, people often acknowledge they hold unfair or unrealistic expectations about what presidents can accomplish. Thus when people are asked, "Why do you think presidents almost always lose popularity the longer they stay in office?," they suggest blame is cast for these reasons:

- Presidents can't please everybody.
- People only see their good points at first.

- Presidents are scapegoats for our problems.
- The job is too much for one individual.
- They make too many promises they can't keep.
- They're only human—they make mistakes too.
- Some presidents can't cope with new problems.
- Familiarity and overexposure breeds either contempt or boredom—and sometimes both.
- Presidents often have to make unpopular decisions.
- Presidents are not as powerful as people often think.
- People don't always look at the overall record of a president.
- People are fickle.

In sum, people do hold presidents accountable and responsible. They do judge them on their record, on whether they follow through on their pledges, and on their overall job performance. Our support for presidents is influenced by how long they have been in office, but for the most part questions of peace, prosperity, and integrity are more important. The public is relatively quick to reward but quicker to punish, depending on a president's performance and actions in office. Hence, although presidents have limited opportunities to shape or lead public opinion, they are forced by upcoming elections, by ongoing polls, and by their desire to be responsive to act on the desires of the American public.

## HOW AMERICANS EVALUATE AND RANK PRESIDENTS

The unwritten presidential job description, the one we carry around in our heads, calls for a president to be a visionary problem solver, a unifying force for the nation, a healer and sage. Thus, every four years we search anew for a fresh superstar who is blessed with the judgment of Washington, the brilliance of Jefferson, the genius of Lincoln, the political savvy of FDR, and the youthful grace of JFK. Expectations always rise. Yet an exaggerated sense of the possibilities of the perfect, or what can be called our notion of "the textbook president," inevitably blind us to the limits of what a president can accomplish.

It is instructive, both for future presidents and for our understanding of the presidency, to know more about what the people judge to be effective presidential leadership.

One difference in the evaluation between the public and experts is the perspective of time. The public is plainly influenced by what historians have termed *presentism*. The people are more likely to remember presidents who were good ones in their own lifetimes, rather than past presidents who were perhaps great in the judgment of history. People who remember the youth and excitement of John Kennedy or the charm and patriotism of Ronald Rea-

**TABLE 3.3**
**Ranking of Presidents in the Gallup Polls, 1975, 1985, 1991, and 2003**

| | Year | | | |
|---|---|---|---|---|
| President | 1975 | 1985 | 1991 | 2003 |
| John F. Kennedy | 52% | 56% | 48% | 13% |
| Abraham Lincoln | 49 | 48 | 42 | 15 |
| Franklin D. Roosevelt | 45 | 41 | 28 | 9 |
| Bill Clinton | | | | 11 |
| George W. Bush | | | | 11 |
| Harry S. Truman | 37 | 26 | 18 | 4 |
| George Washington | 25 | 25 | 24 | 7 |
| Ronald Reagan | | 21 | 22 | 10 |
| George H. W. Bush | | | 27 | 2 |
| Dwight D. Eisenhower | 24 | 16 | 12 | 1 |
| Richard M. Nixon | 5 | 11 | 7 | 1 |
| Jimmy Carter | | 9 | 9 | 3 |
| Thomas Jefferson | 8 | 7 | 5 | 2 |
| Theodore Roosevelt | 9 | 7 | 10 | 2 |
| Lyndon B. Johnson | 9 | 5 | 3 | 0 |
| Woodrow Wilson | 5 | 1 | 2 | 0 |

*Source:* Compiled by the authors from Gallup poll data.

gan, especially in comparison to their successors who seem ineffective or dishonest, rank Kennedy and Reagan as greater than Thomas Jefferson. (See Tables 3.3 and 3.4.)

Popularity while in office is not a useful gauge for judging reputation. After all, Harry Truman received some of the lowest popularity ratings in history, yet his reputation today is very high. As political scientist James Ceaser reminds us,

> It is worth emphasizing how little approval ratings have to do with any last-ing judgment of presidential performance. A President's legacy derives from his accomplishments or failures, and no President will be long remem-bered for having an average approval rating of more than 60 percent, nor quickly forgotten for having an average lower than 45 percent. As an instru-ment of presidential power, a high approval rating has some value as a reminder to others of the potential "cost" they might have to pay in oppos-ing a popular President. Yet it is important to remember that an approval rating is a lag, rather than a lead, indicator. What determines the score will be the public's assessment of conditions, performance, and persona. An astute President should accordingly be prepared in most cases to sacrifice his standing today, if by doing so he can affect positively the future assess-ment of these factors.[33]

All rankings of presidents, whether by the public or by experts, rein-force our inclination to attribute more power to presidents than they really had. When great deeds get done, we invariably attribute more of the cause to presidents than is reasonable; the same is true of great failures.

**TABLE 3.4**
**Presidential Favorites**

*Question:* "Looking back on the past American Presidents, living or dead, which ONE of them would you want to have running this country today?" (July 1996)

| | |
|---|---|
| John F. Kennedy | 28% |
| Ronald Reagan | 13 |
| Franklin D. Roosevelt | 8 |
| Abraham Lincoln | 8 |
| Harry S. Truman | 8 |
| George Bush | 5 |
| Dwight D. Eisenhower | 4 |

*N* = 979.

*Source:* From *The New York Times*/CBS News Poll, July 11–13, 1996, Copyright © 1996 by the New York Times Co. Reprinted by permission.

Still, with this important reservation, we can look at the Gallup poll surveys asking the public to choose past presidents and what they remembered about them. Again the top choice was Kennedy, because he was "a strong leader," "concerned for the people," and "had the confidence of the people." Number two, Franklin Roosevelt, provides an exception to the rule. He was chosen for what were viewed as good policies and programs, his ability to handle economic problems, and his image as an effective leader. The public remembered Truman for his forcefulness, his forthrightness and outspokenness, and his leadership. The public admired Eisenhower because he had the confidence of the people, he was a leader, and he seemed forceful. "Greatness," in the public eye, is based upon certain intangible qualities, those chiefly being leadership and the way the president made the people feel. Enthusiasm gives the nation a lift. Inspiration or bold and contagious self-confidence can cover up a lot of ineffective or inadequate policy. In choosing their most admired or least admired president, what criteria are used by the general public?

What Americans expect of a president depends on varying factors. Not least of these is who is president, who was recently in office, and what the times demand. If recent presidents appear to have been weak, the public will likely call for more decisiveness. If the recent presidents or president seem to have been too dominant in relation to Congress, the public demands honesty or a cooperative president.

In short, the public likes assertive, activist, and honest presidents. We set high personal standards for our presidents, and most of us, in addition, demand them to solve major problems. The public does not always base its evaluation of presidents on policies, issues, or achievements. The public remembers presidents who seemed to be great leaders, and just as important, ones who made them proud of their country. They then use these historic examples as paragons to judge candidates and incumbents. Our evaluations of presidents are based partly on the times they served. In this sense the public is sometimes guilty of a lack of perspective. Experts, on the other hand, are more often concerned with how a president handled the cultural and economic demands of the day, the content of a president's program, and the president's success in carrying it out.

Both expert and average citizens alike are influenced by the cycles of American politics. People cannot emancipate themselves from their own age and country. To be sure, historians and biographers are expected to transcend the present, yet they, too, seldom entirely succeed.

## HOW EXPERTS EVALUATE PRESIDENTS

There is no commonly accepted standard on what constitutes presidential greatness. In general experts judge presidents on the basis of four factors: the scope of the problems they faced; their efforts (actions) and intentions (vision) in dealing with these problems; what they were able to accomplish; and the long-term results. Experts are critical in judging presidents who were corrupt, whose administrations were rife with corruption, or who were lacking in character.

This last point raises an interesting dilemma. While we are clear that public corruption, that is, abuse of public trust, criminality, improper use of government for personal gain, leads to negative ratings, what of private corruption? Does a president's (or candidate's) private behavior, his personal character, give clues to performance in the White House? How important is what we call character?

The word *character* comes from the Greek *charakter,* meaning the mark of a coin or seal. Euripides defined character as "a stamp of good repute on a person." Some of our highly regarded presidents were men of dubious personal character in their private relations. Recently press attention has focused on extramarital relations presidents and candidates may have had, the implication being that such affairs should disqualify a candidate from the presidency. Yet if that is our standard of judgment, several of our most popular presidents—Jefferson, FDR, Eisenhower, Kennedy, Clinton, and others—would be disqualified from office.

While the president represents the nation and serves as a symbol of who we are, and while logic tells us that character is important, in terms of presidential performance there is little correlation between "high" personal moral character and performance in office. Some of our presidents with checkered backgrounds performed well, and others who were considered to be of the highest private character were political failures.[34]

The process of rating presidents is fraught with potential biases. The actions of presidents look different from different historical vantage points. There are dangers in trying to assess the effectiveness and achievements of a presidency too early, say within twenty-five years. Sometimes a spate of new biographies about a former president will cast a favorable light upon a presidency, or conversely, may condemn a previously respected administration.

The charge is made, too, that most of the experts polled in these surveys are university professors or writers who tend to be more liberal, progressive, or Democratic in their political orientation. While this is true, one study found the ranking by conservatives and liberals "remarkably similar." Serious disagreement in the ranks of the top ten most favored presidents apparently involved only the relative placement of Franklin Roosevelt.[35] Still the charge cannot be entirely ignored. Experts on the presidency are generally biased in favor of activist Democratic presidents and those who succeeded as wartime presidents.

A survey conducted in 2000 by the conservative Federalist Society and cosponsored by *The Wall Street Journal,* deliberately included both law school professors and more scholars of a Republican persuasion. The detailed survey of over seventy experts again found Washington, Lincoln, and FDR as the great presidents, with Jefferson, Theodore Roosevelt, and Jackson as leading near-great presidents. But Republicans Ronald Reagan and Dwight Eisenhower rose in these rankings at the same time that Democrats Woodrow Wilson and JFK won less respect than in many earlier surveys. Overall, however, the Federalist Society's rankings were similar to those in the Arthur Schlesinger, Jr., study of historians[36] (see the results in Table 3.5).

Presidents who served during times of crisis are often ranked higher. Crisis, of course, does not ensure greatness. Madison, Pierce, Buchanan, Andrew Johnson, and Hoover all faced crises yet their responses seemed ineffective. On the other hand, Lincoln, Wilson, FDR, and Truman all rank as great or above average because they responded to crises effectively. Although severe crises do not necessarily bring forth great leadership, the so-called "greats" served in periods of military, social, and economic upheaval, and to the extent the tests were met justifiably enhanced their reputations. The old question of whether great times make for great leadership or great leaders make great times is never satisfactorily settled.

Activist, assertive presidents who contested rivals and rival institutions and expanded the normal responsibilities of the presidency and left the office larger than they found it are invariably rated as great or near-great presidents. Could it be that historians and political scientists, especially those who get polled in these presidency evaluations, are biased in favor of a vigorous, vital presidency? Presidents like John Quincy Adams, Taft, and Coolidge suffer in this context because they are often compared, and unfavorably so, with their contemporaries such as Jackson, Theodore Roosevelt, Wilson, and FDR, all of whom infused enormous personal energy into the presidency. Experts, along with the general public, seem to have a bias in favor of presidents with energy and presidents who, because they are unsatisfied with the status quo, enlarge the presidential role.

Another bias that renders rankings problematic is the difficulty in judging some presidents solely on their performance in office. Their achievements over a lifetime are often a complicating factor. Thus Washington, Jefferson, Madison, and Eisenhower were distinguished Americans quite apart from their presidencies. Grant was a great general yet a weak president. Madison was a superb constitutional architect, yet at best an average president. Hoover had been an outstanding success in business and a splendid war relief administrator and cabinet member, but was far less successful as a president. Jimmy Carter won great praise and a Nobel Prize for his humanitarian efforts, but received lower marks for his presidential leadership. It is difficult to separate the presidential years from the overall career.

Whether a president dies in office from natural causes or is assassinated may also affect later rankings. While Harding and McKinley provide less evidence for this supposition, the public surely views Lincoln, FDR, and Kennedy differently, and one suspects more favorably, because of their deaths in office.

An additional problem arises. Can we objectively compare presidents from different eras? Just as presidents cannot be experts on all areas of policy, historians cannot be experts on all presidents. And, as noted earlier, biographers and historians have to be mindful of the varying cultural and political climates in which presidents served.[37] Yet, isn't this what is necessary to make fair, objective judgments? Seldom are presidents faced with the same situation. Thus, we honor Jefferson and Polk for adding vast areas to the territory of the United States, yet recent presidents cannot duplicate that feat. Sometimes it is not possible to distinguish vision and foresight until years later, as with Andrew Johnson's purchase of Alaska in 1867.

## WHAT IS PRESIDENTIAL GREATNESS?

Any attempt to define "presidential greatness" is necessarily subjective. We all have biases. We all live in a fixed historical era. We almost always approach the task with an eye on contemporary problems and with a partisan bias of some kind. Still, it is worthwhile to attempt such a definition.

Experts judge presidents as effective or outstanding when they acted greatly in challenging times. Did the president have the courage to fight for what was right? Did they bring out the best in the American people? Did they display common sense, decisiveness, and good judgment in picking priorities, associates, and fights? The lesser presidents often shy away from rather than join a conflict. They fear that decisiveness or polarization will lead to blood in the streets, even though history often teaches that courageous and early confrontation of divisive issues often avoids even worse violence later.

Also, moral courage stands out. Were they willing and able to stand up and be counted, as Lincoln and FDR were, when the nation and the nation's allies were challenged by the forces of hate and oppression? The great presidents were persons of principle and commitment, prepared to sacrifice popularity to what they knew was right.

An almost universally accepted aspect of great leadership is the willingness and ability to take risks, to act boldly when situations necessitate vision. Presidents are asked to educate and shape public opinion—even as they consult it. The question, to be sure, is more difficult than it first seemed, because determinations of what is popular and what is right are hard to make. Still, we can look back and find examples of presidential courage, of bucking the popular trends, and conclude satisfactorily that these actions were correct.

Thus George Washington faced intense hostility over the Jay Treaty, yet saw it through. Adams was prepared to break up his party to avoid war with France, and did both. Lincoln defied public opinion by removing General McClellan of the Army of the Potomac, and Truman displayed similar courage nearly a century later in removing General Douglas MacArthur. Though these actions were unpopular at the time, history vindicated them.

Experts look for accomplishments and whether the president provided leadership for the common cause. Historian Henry Steele Commager in 1977 formulated this list of five common denominators for those he considered great presidents.

- All believed the president should be both a symbol and leader, all identified themselves with the whole people, all had programs they wished to see adopted, and all worked actively to get them through Congress.
- All ranged themselves on the side of the people, of an enlarged scope for government, and of progress and reform.
- Few were good administrators, nor was the art of the politician a contribution to greatness.
- All possessed wisdom, sagacity, and intelligence.
- All were men of principle, prepared to sacrifice popularity for what they thought was right.[38]

Political scientist Clinton Rossiter once suggested that presidents who wanted to be judged as "truly eminent" by historians must stretch the Constitution. Other students of the presidency have observed that, much as they may admire the checks and balances, presidents must do what needs to be done. Sometimes this is called the doctrine of necessity. Thus it is said of Lincoln that he exercised both constitutional and extra constitutional powers yet saved the union, and in doing so, he saw to it that the Constitution endured. So also in various ways Jefferson, FDR, and others either stretched or ignored their explicit oaths to follow the Constitution to pursue what they thought was right.

Those presidents generally considered "great" were also often the ones who regularly challenged Congress. They exercised many of the powers that were thought to be solely congressional. Some of them even seemed to enjoy "kicking Congress" (and sometimes the Supreme Court) around.

While these vigorous presidents may win praise from both the expert and public, they may also make life difficult for those who come after them. Thus, Lincoln "made the office so strong that, like Jefferson and Jackson, he weakened it for his successors in the inevitable morning after."[39] Richard Nixon and some of Reagan's National Security Council aides tried to ignore

Congress and, on occasions, the Constitution as well. But they were condemned and punished rather than praised. Just how far can the Constitution be stretched?

What did the great presidents do? George Washington, more than any other individual, converted the paper Constitution into an enduring document. With commanding prestige and character he set the precedents that balanced self-government and leadership, constitutionalism and statesmanship. Washington's success made possible the success of the Republic. That Washington owned at least two to three hundred slaves and became wealthy as a result of their labor is hard for many modern Americans to accept. He held contradictory and varied ideas about the institution of slavery and only at the end of his life did he begin to set his slaves free.[40]

Jefferson, a genius in his generation, was a skilled organizer and a resourceful chief executive and party leader. He made his share of mistakes yet he adapted the office to countless new realities. His expansion of territory with the Louisiana Purchase, an achievement breathtaking in its consequences, assures him special status. Lincoln saved the union and will be remembered as the foremost symbol of democracy, union, and tenacious leadership in our hour of ultimate crisis. FDR saw the nation through its worst economic crisis and rallied the nation and the world to defeat nazism and Hitler. In a time of dictatorships he managed a democratic response to the depression.

These accomplishments are admirable. Still, in this line of reasoning, they raise as many questions as are answered. If presidents alone were responsible for all those notable and enduring accomplishments, it is little wonder that our expectations are so high. Plainly, a variety of people and institutions contributed to the achievements.

History seldom adequately honors the economic and movement leaders and reform activists who often provide as much or more of an era's leadership than does the president of the time.[41] Rarely do we take opportunity levels, resources, situation, or context into account when we judge presidents. Yet the best of the good ones will surround themselves with talented independent-minded aides, advisers, and administrators. Rarely do we judge presidents—on their own terms—on how successful they were in achieving their goals. Great leadership depends on its surroundings, on teams of leaders, and on people who demand leadership. Doubtless luck—sometimes "dumb luck"—also plays a part in greatness. Timing and being at the right place at the right time also help. Many of "the great" presidents also made great mistakes. The great presidents typically look better in death than they did while they were among the living.

We learn perhaps as much by those we judge as failures. Harding is ranked near or at the bottom by the experts because his administration was so corrupt. Loyalty to his friends was fatal. Others rank near the bottom because they lacked integrity, a program, or political skill. While Nixon had notable achievements, particularly his China policy, he is viewed as one of the worst because he lied to the American public, plotted a cover-up of ille-

**TABLE 3.5**
**New York Times Magazine Ratings of Presidential Performance—1996**

| | |
|---|---|
| *Great:* | Lincoln, FDR, Washington |
| *Near Great:* | Jefferson, Jackson, Wilson, Theodore Roosevelt, Truman, Polk |
| *Average (High)* | John Adams, Eisenhower, Cleveland, McKinley, Kennedy, LBJ, Monroe |
| *Average (Low)* | Madison, J. Q. Adams, Van Buren, Hayes, Arthur, Harrison, Taft, Ford, Carter, Reagan, Bush |
| *Below Average* | Tyler, Taylor, Fillmore, Coolidge |
| *Failure* | Pierce, Buchanan, A. Johnson, Grant, Harding, Hoover, Nixon |

*Source:* Arthur M. Schlesinger, Jr., "The Ultimate Approval Rating," *The New York Times Magazine,* December 15, 1996, pp. 48–49. Copyright © 1996 by the New York Times Co. Reprinted by permission.

gal and unconstitutional activities, resigned in disgrace, and, in the eyes of many, thoroughly disgraced the integrity and dignity of the presidency. Some at the bottom of the lists were good and decent individuals but were mediocre leaders, overshadowed by other people, overtaken by events, for example, Buchanan, Pierce, Grant, Fillmore, Andrew Johnson, Tyler, and Taylor.

Surveys typically ask scholars to pay special attention to presidential performance in ranking presidents. Thus the 1996 *New York Times Magazine* poll asked historians to judge performance in office. "The standard was not lifetime achievement but performance in the White House. The scholars were to decide for themselves how presidential performance was to be judged." Historian Arthur M. Schlesinger, Jr., added, "It was supposed that historians would know greatness—or failure—when they saw it. . . ."[42] And so they ranked presidents as great, near great, average, below average, and failure. (See Table 3.5.)

A *Chicago Tribune* survey specifically suggested leadership categories and asked scholars and biographers to award points on the basis of these qualities, skills, and achievements. Presidents in that survey were compared on the basis of leadership qualities, accomplishments and crisis management, political skills, appointments, character, and integrity. These are sensible if still general categories. (See Tables 3.6 and 3.7.) Future surveys should use these and similar probing categories. Nonetheless, its findings were generally the same as more informal surveys.[43]

Evaluating and understanding the Reagan presidency raises additional problems. Reagan enjoyed high personal popularity at the end of his first term and in the early part of his second term. His landslide reelection had a lot to do with his popularity, as did his uncanny ability to portray himself as a self-confident, strong, and "effective" president. His early success in winning many of his important measures in Congress added to this aura of competence. Yet, with adversity and scandal, Reagan experienced somewhat greater disapproval.

Contrary to conventional wisdom, Reagan's first-term public approval ratings were not consistently high. People approved of *him* more than they approved of his initiatives or his performance. Reagan's policies were more

**TABLE 3.6**
**President Ranking by "Experts" (Murray/Blessing Poll)**

| Great | Near Great | Above Average |
|---|---|---|
| Abraham Lincoln | Theodore Roosevelt | John Adams |
| Franklin D. Roosevelt | Woodrow Wilson | Lyndon B. Johnson |
| George Washington | Andrew Jackson | Dwight D. Eisenhower |
| Thomas Jefferson | Harry S. Truman | James K. Polk |
| | | John F. Kennedy |
| | | James Madison |
| | | James Monroe |
| | | John Quincy Adams |
| | | Grover Cleveland |

| Average | Below Average | Failure |
|---|---|---|
| William McKinley | Zachary Taylor | Andrew Johnson |
| William Taft | Ronald Reagan | James Buchanan |
| Martin Van Buren | John Tyler | Richard Nixon |
| Herbert Hoover | Millard Fillmore | Ulysses S. Grant |
| Rutherford B. Hayes | Calvin Coolidge | Warren G. Harding |
| Chester A. Arthur | Franklin Pierce | |
| Gerald Ford | | |
| Jimmy Carter | | |
| Benjamin Harrison | | |

*Source:* Robert K. Murray and Tim Blessing, *Greatness of the White House* (University Park: The Pennsylvania State University Press, 1994), p. 16. Copyright 1994 by the Pennsylvania State University. Reproduced by permission of the Publisher.

controversial than Reagan himself. While he proved adept at deflecting personal criticism, communicating with the public, and maintaining reasonably congenial relations with Congress, his policies sometimes divided the country. His tax cuts, for example, produced the largest deficits in the nation's history. His aid to the Contra rebels and his Iran-Contra scandal disappointed many people.

Political scientists and historians rate Reagan less highly than the average citizen does. Whereas the public judges him largely on his rhetoric and means, at least in the short run, the experts pay more attention to policy outcomes and results.

Our fascination with presidential effectiveness and failure reveals much about ourselves, about qualities we admire and those we dislike. It tells us, too, about our dreams and national character. We yearn for heroism and courage in literature, film, sports, and our own lives. And so too we look for certain heroic qualities, Mount Rushmore qualities, in our presidents. We delight in presidents who have triumphed when they faced ultimate tests. We are diminished by those who reveal the darker side of human nature and public life.

Leadership at the presidential level is full of risks. Sometimes risk-taking does not pay off, as with Johnson's Vietnam policies. FDR risked his political life and reputation by arranging secret naval deals with the British, and his

**TABLE 3.7**
**The Best and the Worst Presidents, According to the Experts**
**(58 Presidential Historians and Political Scientists)**

| The Ten Best | The Ten Worst |
| --- | --- |
| 1. Abraham Lincoln (best) | 1. Warren Harding (worst) |
| 2. George Washington | 2. James Buchanan |
| 3. Franklin D. Roosevelt | 3. Franklin Pierce |
| 4. Thomas Jefferson | 4. Ulysses Grant |
| 5. Theodore Roosevelt | 5. Andrew Johnson |
| 6. Woodrow Wilson | 6. Millard Fillmore |
| 7. Harry S. Truman | 7. Richard Nixon |
| 8. Andrew Jackson | 8. John Tyler |
| 9. Dwight Eisenhower | 9. Calvin Coolidge |
| 10. James Polk | 10. Herbert Hoover |

*Source:* Steve Neal, "Putting Presidents in Their Places," *Chicago Sun-Times,*
November 19, 1995, pp. 30–31.

policies were handsomely rewarded. Nothing may be more dangerous than to be constantly guided by instant and temperamental national poll results. For while the public often affords a president popularity on the basis of means, it is ends that ultimately determine the common good. The means may require sacrifice and alienation.

The presidency is not and should not be a place for pandering to the polls. In one sense,

> Dr. Gallup renders us a disservice by his repeated polls on popular standings. Excessive acclaim, while personally gratifying, may be a bad sign as far as eminence is concerned. . . . Presidents who achieved reform, like Wilson and Franklin Roosevelt, were bound to make foes among the dislodged. President Eisenhower was so popular as to raise the suspicion that he had not disturbed enough the entrenched interests.[44]

One instance of a president appearing to pander to the polls and public sentiment came from President Ford. At a press conference he was asked whether he favored a stiff tax on a gallon of gasoline as a form of price rationing to dampen demand. Columnist George Will recalls his answer and condemns Ford's reasoning: "No, today I saw a poll that showed that 81% of the American people do not want to pay more for a gallon of gasoline. . . . "Therefore," said Ford, "I am on solid ground in opposing it." The problem is that all ground seems solid when your ear is to it, and as Churchill said, "It is hard to look up to someone in that position."[45]

A democratic republic puts its faith in the people, faith that they will not merely elect presidents who will be responsive to their desires, but also do what is right. Americans want to be heard, yet they also want leaders who will independently exercise their own judgment. We honor leaders who refuse to be intimidated by contrary public opinion data. Although presidents, to be sure, must take care not to be so self-assured they become insen-

Ronald Reagan is a prime example of a president whose popularity with the American public exceeded his rating by political scientists and historians. (*Source:* Reproduced from the collections of the Library of Congress.)

sitive to criticism and counsel, they also need a certain inner sense of what has to be done. In the end, the best of presidents are likely to be those who can accurately interpret or anticipate the sentiments of the nation and rally the people and other political leaders to do what must be done, and what the public will later learn to respect. These presidents will commonly be strong political leaders with a vision, if not a detailed program, of where they think the nation should go. We will ask of them: Did they preserve, protect, and enrich the liberty, the rights, and the economic opportunities of all the people? Did they so engage with the public to educate and build support for what was right and to encourage the many alternative sources of leadership in a nation with such ample talent? (See Table 3.8.)

## THE POPULARITY DILEMMA

Presidents serve a variety of functions for the American public. Political scientist Fred Greenstein summarizes the psychological connection between president and people noting that the president serves as a symbol of national unity, stability, and the American way of life; an outlet for effect, for feeling good about America; a cognitive aid, simplifying complexity into a single symbol; and a means of vicarious participation in the political world.[46]

**TABLE 3.8**
**The Best and the Worst U.S. Presidents, ranked by 73 scholars**
**in History, Politics, and Law (October, 2000 survey)**

| The Eleven Best | The Ten Worst |
| --- | --- |
| 1. George Washington (best) | 1. James Buchanan (worst) |
| 2. Abraham Lincoln | 2. Franklin Pierce |
| 3. Franklin Roosevelt | 3. Warren Harding |
| 4. Thomas Jefferson | 4. Andrew Johnson |
| 5. Theodore Roosevelt | 5. Millard Fillmore |
| 6. Andrew Jackson | 6. John Tyler |
| 7. Harry Truman | 7. Richard Nixon |
| 8. Ronald Reagan | 8. U.S. Grant |
| 9. Dwight Eisenhower | 9. Zachary Taylor |
| 10. James Polk | 10. Jimmy Carter |
| 11. Woodrow Wilson | |

*Source:* James Lindgren, "Rating the Presidents of the United States, 1789–2000:
A Survey of Scholars in History, Political Science, and Law," sponsored by the
Federalist Society and *The Wall Street Journal* (Washington, D.C.: Fall 2000), a
report. See also James Lindgren and Steven Calabresi, "Ranking the Presidents,"
*The Wall Street Journal,* November 16, 2000, p. A26.

Because the president serves as both head of government (the nation's chief politician) and head of state (the symbolic representation of the nation), the president is simultaneously the chief divider of the nation and its chief unifier. Ronald Reagan was a masterful head of state. In the aftermath of the Challenger disaster Reagan took on the role of high priest and national healer for a nation devastated by tragedy. This role allowed Reagan, the nation's top politician, to rise above politics and become a symbol for the nation.

Invested in the office of the presidency is high respect, but also high expectations (added to by presidential campaign promises). Yet the president's powers are not always commensurate with the responsibilities or the public's expectations. Often this leads to frustration, and also to a decline in popularity. Likewise, if the public continues to demand that the government deliver on contradictory expectations (e.g., lower taxes *and* more government services), presidents are put in no-win situations. Given this paradox, what's a president to do?

Political scientist Theodore Lowi claimed that presidents resolve this dilemma by resorting to rule by political manipulation. Impression management replaces policy achievement. Appearances are everything.[47] Political scientists Paul Brace and Barbara Hinckley maintained that excessive reliance on appearances has led to the development of a "public-relations presidency . . . concerned primarily with maintaining and increasing public support."[48]

What then is the proper function of a leader in a democratic system? Should the leader follow the public's wishes? Or attempt to educate the public? Should presidents attempt to *act,* to move the government in the direction they believe is best? Should a president find out what the people want and merely attempt to give it to them? Or should presidents speak truth, however unpleasant, to power?

Leading in a democratic society unveils a web of paradoxes and contradictions that can never be wholly resolved. And while the founders feared a president who might fan the embers of popular passions, it is clear that in our time the president has become the embodiment of the nation's government and is looked to as symbol-in-chief.

During his presidency, Jimmy Carter often tried to educate the people on the limits of America's power, thereby treating the public with the respect due an educated citizenry in a democracy. But Carter was unable to convince people that they had to settle for less and accept limits. This failure opened the door for Ronald Reagan who, in 1980, scoffed at limits. He flattered the public and told them to buy and spend. They did. Carter spoke of a tough reality, Reagan offered an easier path with less sacrifice. Carter lost, Reagan won.

## THE DOUBLE-EDGED SWORD OF THE MEDIA

The lens through which we observe the presidency is the media. Some argue that television has created an "electronic throne" from which the president gains access to the people. Others contend the media are a constant thorn in the side of presidents, always tearing them down. Do the media serve as lapdog or watchdog? The paradox here is that to a degree, both views are correct.

Television has both *enlarged* and *shrunk* the presidency. It has enlarged the presidency by focusing a disproportionately large amount of attention on the presidency at the expense of Congress (if there is a balance of power, it rarely shows on television). It has shrunk the presidency by an overexposure that has led to the trivialization and/or intrusion of the press into the most personal and private of presidential activities. Before the 1992 election, Bill and Hillary Clinton were asked by Mike Wallace of "60 Minutes," "Are you prepared to say you never had extramarital affairs?" And after the election a young woman, with TV cameras running, asked Clinton, "Mr. President, the world's dying to know, is it boxers or briefs?"

The media are a two-edged sword that cuts both ways. Some presidents effectively use the media. Others are used by it. Kennedy and Reagan, handsome, poised, witty, self-assured, were able to use the media to their advantage. Nixon, Ford, Carter, and George H.W. Bush, stiff, nervous, awkward, fared less well. Clinton often, but not always, has been able to win good media coverage, largely due to his superior interpersonal skills.

Generally, presidents get somewhat favorable press coverage.[49] But in the aftermath of Vietnam, Watergate, and Clinton's scandals, reportage has become much more critical. In an age of cynicism, the media have seen their role as more adversarial and, along with the proliferation of cable television, more personal and intrusive.[50]

As political scientist Larry Sabato noted:

> It has become a spectacle without equal in modern American politics: the news media, print and broadcast, go after a wounded politician like sharks in a feeding frenzy. The wound may have been self-inflicted, and the politician may richly deserve his or her fate, but the journalists now take center stage in the process, creating the news as much as reporting it, changing both the shape of election-year politics and the contours of government.[51]

Even the more responsible media outlets have been affected. Both print and electronic journalists have had to respond to market demands, with print imitating the *USA Today* "light news" format, and television adopting the fast cut, short, quick shots of MTV. Style wins out over substance. The average "sound bite," the time devoted to candidate statements, has shrunk from forty-two seconds in 1968 to seven seconds in recent years.

Few presidents were criticized as much as Bill Clinton. After the Clinton years, accusations that the media were biased in favor of liberals rang hollow. Still, as one of Clinton's perceptive biographers notes, while Clinton had impressive leadership skills he compromised himself by an almost obsessive desire to be liked by the public. "Clinton may have lost a great deal of his moral authority well before Lewinsky by snuggling too close to us—by polling every last whim, by trying too hard to please. It is entirely possible that the Clinton era will be remembered by historians primarily as the moment when the distance between the president and the public evaporated forever."[52]

Recent presidents and their White House public relations teams devote a lot of energy to managing the news and increasing a president's public support. They do so because higher presidential public approval ratings make it easier for a president to persuade Congress and other constituencies to support his or her strategic priorities.

Politically, the president is the nation's center of attention. But rarely can a president reach out and touch "real people." The media serve as the president's conduit for reaching the public. Through the media, especially television, the public sees presidents, hears about their ideas, gets interpretations of how well or poorly they are doing their job. In this way, the media are a prime intermediary between a president and the public. Presidents cannot succeed without the media, yet the media often are a president's toughest critics.

In the 1960s, television changed politics and the presidency. Television gave the president instant access to our homes, and made the president an intimate member of our extended family. Today, there are even more outlets through which presidents can communicate. Web sites, town hall meetings, and satellite and cable television have all given presidents choices in how to connect with the public. These new outlets are replacing older methods such as press conferences as preferred means of communication. (See Table 3.9)[53]

The media's fascination with presidents, their families, even their pets, has led to increased attention lavished on the president who serves as the

TABLE 3.9
**Presidential News Conferences with White House Press**

| President | Average per Month | Total Number |
|---|---|---|
| Herbert Hoover (1929–33) | 5.6 | 268 |
| Franklin D. Roosevelt (1933–45) | 6.9 | 998 |
| Harry Truman (1945–53) | 3.4 | 334 |
| Dwight Eisenhower (1953–61) | 2.0 | 193 |
| John Kennedy (1961–63) | 1.9 | 64 |
| Lyndon Johnson (1963–69) | 2.2 | 135 |
| Richard Nixon (1969–74) | 0.5 | 37 |
| Gerald Ford (1974–77) | 1.3 | 39 |
| Jimmy Carter (1977–81) | 0.8 | 59 |
| Ronald Reagan (1981–89) | 0.5 | 44 |
| George Bush (1989–93) | 3.0 | 142 |
| Bill Clinton (1993–99) | 2.0 | 192 |

*Source: Weekly Compilation of Presidential Documents,* vol. 31, *Annual Index* (p. C12); Interview, White House Press Office, December 27, 2000.

nation's "Celebrity-in-Chief." The gravitational pull of the presidency gives the president a readymade bully pulpit, yet it also has a down side. In an era of "in your face" investigative reporting, everything and anything a president does is fodder for tabloid journalists. The president has become a pop cultural icon. The micro coverage of the president sometimes trivializes the office, the person, and politics itself.

Since the media serve as the president's conduit to the public, and because so much is riding on good press coverage, no president can afford to ignore, or even leave to chance, relations with the media. Presidents must devise and implement strategies for attaining good press, and efforts at media manipulations are quite common.

Because presidents are limited in what they can accomplish, and given that the public expects presidents to deliver the goods, sometimes, when faced with an inability to achieve policy results, presidents will resort to political grandstanding to give the impression that they are doing something. Few White House operators used image management better than the Reagan team.[54]

The strategy of presidential power in the media age is called "going public." Samuel Kernell saw an unending political campaign where presidents go public in an effort to increase political clout within the Washington community.[55]

In this, the United States has come a long way from what the creators of the presidency envisioned. The inventors of the presidency feared a president who was too closely linked to the public because this might undermine deliberation and reason, subverting the routines of representative government. Over time, such concerns gave way to the unstoppable logic of the electronic media and the need to use whatever levers a president could find to increase power.

Upon entering office, presidents feel compelled to announce their intention of having an "open presidency." Such efforts are always short-lived. Presidents soon become concerned with the release of bad news, or leaked information, and begin to engage in news (or information) management and "spin control."

Presidents can wield a carrot or a stick in dealing with the press. Some presidents revert to a "blame the messenger" strategy and attack the media. While press harassment can have an effect, most presidents mix strategic approaches ranging from co-optation to condemnation.

It is important to link the media strategy to the president's political agenda. In this, presidents are advised to follow the Haldeman strategy. Richard Nixon's chief-of-staff, Bob Haldeman insisted that before something went on the president's agenda or schedule, the staff member who proposed it had to tell (1) what the expected headline would be; (2) what the photo accompanying the headline would be; and (3) how the first paragraph of the story would read. The Reagan administration followed a variant of this model. Key aides met early each morning to decide what the story of the day would be. They also developed long-term strategies for shaping the agenda. George W. Bush's White House staff has both learned from these models and refined them.

By thinking strategically with a media focus presidents can command media attention and shape coverage of the president's agenda. Presidents often choreograph every step, "wallpaper" stories with attractive visuals, and when things sour, send the spin doctors out to do damage control.

There are times when the media are the lapdogs for the president,[56] and at other times, the media check presidential power. If a president does not actively use the media, he may become its victim.

Are the media biased? If so, are they biased in favor of the left or right of the political spectrum? During the twelve years of Republican presidents from 1980 to 1992, conservatives insisted the press was hostile first to Ronald Reagan and then to George H.W. Bush. But was this accurate? The media do a strange mating dance where presidents are concerned, and one may be inclined to level the charge of bias when your preferred president is being criticized in the press. Indeed, Bush did get rough treatment from the media in 1992. If that is the point at which one measures bias, it might appear that indeed the press was out to get Bush. But if you choose a different point of time to measure bias, say, the first year or second term of the Clinton presidency, a different picture emerges. Clinton was pummeled in the media during his eight years in office.[57]

Rather than look on the media as primarily leftish, it may be more helpful to see the media as following rather than leading public opinion. When a president is up, they tend to be somewhat gentle (George H.W. Bush in 1991, Reagan in 1984, Nixon in 1972); when a president is faltering, they become more critical (Nixon in 1974, George H.W. Bush in 1992, Clinton in general).

Presidents dislike the press because it catches their inconsistencies, mistakes, and failure to deliver on promises. But, to govern, presidents must work with and through the media, and presidents must think and act strategically where the media are concerned. Good press makes governing a bit easier; bad press makes governing difficult. Of course, the best way to get a good press is to do a good job.

## CONCLUSION

The presidency was designed more to be an administrative than a political or leadership position. All this has changed and public views of what presidents should do are significantly different than in the 1790s or even a few generations ago.

We expect a lot from our contemporary presidents. We know they cannot all be "Mt. Rushmore presidents," but still we want the best for our nation's sake and our own.

Presidents go to considerable length to win public support for themselves and their policies because they believe it is the most important way they can win the cooperation of Congress to enact their programs. But, as this chapter describes, some presidents can become popular yet not necessarily effective. Also, the public does not evaluate presidents in the same way that expert historians, biographers, and political scientists do. Today's media are critical of incumbent presidents as they strive to be watchdogs and avoid the inevitable spin every White House dishes out.

Public support for presidents follows certain patterns, yet these patterns are not exact and the exceptions are sometimes as interesting as the patterns themselves.

Scholars note that when ranking presidents we often learn more about the raters than the rated. Even the most serious efforts at evaluating presidencies invariably involve some subjective or partisan biases.

Still even those who are skeptical about presidential rankings suggest general variables for evaluating presidencies. Thus Arthur M. Schlesinger, Jr., writes, "To succeed, presidents must have a port to seek and must convince Congress and the electorate of the rightness of their course. Politics in a democracy is ultimately an educational process, an adventure in vision and consent."[58] Presidential historian James MacGregor Burns says these qualities are necessary for presidential greatness: "They are character, competence, courage, conviction and commitment."[59]

Political scientist Richard M. Pious offers still another set of evaluation guidelines. His top presidents would have had a successful response to a great challenge facing the nation and the successful use of presidential powers. Second, the president would have helped create a new political regime and offered "transformative leadership involving fundamental values." Further, his top president would have converted uncertainty into risk and provided successful risk management, all of which strengthened the moral and intellectual authority and legitimacy of both the government and the presidency.[60]

The United States has had several excellent presidents yet Americans have reserved the label "great" president to just one a century, Washington in the eighteenth century, Lincoln in the nineteenth century, and FDR in the twentieth century. Along the way we have liked Teddy Roosevelt, JFK, and Ronald Reagan, yet affection toward these presidents is a different matter than their place in history. In the end, we know a lot more about presidents than we know about what will make a president great. Still, the enduring challenge or paradox for current and future presidents remains: summon us to live up to our highest shared ideals of a generous, benevolent country that is a shining beacon for liberty and freedom, yet pay close attention to our immediate needs such as jobs, security, lower taxes, cheap oil, and prosperity.

# Presidential Power and Leadership

Taken by and large, the history of the presidency is a history of aggrandizement, but the story is a highly discontinuous one. Of the . . . individuals who have filled the office not more than one in three has contributed to the development of its powers; under other incumbents things have either stood still or gone backward. That is to say, what the presidency is at any particular moment depends in important measure on who is President. . . .

Edward S. Corwin, *The President: Office and Powers* (New York University Press, 1957), pp. 29–30

Though the powers of the office have sometimes been grossly abused, though the presidency has become almost impossible to manage, and though the caliber of the people who have served as chief executive has declined erratically but persistently from the day George Washington left office, the presidency has been responsible for less harm and more good, in the nation and in the world, than perhaps any other secular institution in history.

Forrest McDonald, *The American Presidency: An Intellectual History* (University Press of Kansas, 1994), p. 481

Anyone can lead where people already want to go; true leaders take them where only their better selves are willing to tread. That's where the leader's own values come in. They must want to do something with their power, not just for the powerful.

Jonathan Alter, *Newsweek*, December 3, 1990

"Power" is an often used yet little understood concept. The problem is particularly vexing when we wrestle with the concept of presidential power. What do we mean by power? How much power does a president have? How much power should the president wield in a constitutional democracy? What are the appropriate limits to be placed on presidents?

The very term *democratic leadership* is paradoxical. How can a democracy—government of, by, and for the people—countenance one person, or even a small team of people, leading? It sounds so antidemocratic.[1] The words *leader* and *leadership* imply that someone provides command or direction. The word *democracy* implies widespread participation and rule by the people. The two seem irreconcilable.

While there is certainly a tension between democracy and leadership, it can be a creative tension that enhances and supports both democracy and leadership. Yet, all too often this potentially creative tension degenerates into forms of behavior that can undermine both democracy and leadership.

Before we can examine what democratic leadership might look like, we will discuss presidential power and leadership. For while democratic leadership may be our goal, the road to achieving it can be difficult.

## THE PRESIDENT AND THE SYSTEM

The presidency is part of a system. This system consists of a constellation of political participants: Congress, courts, public, media, interest groups, and bureaucrats—all of whom share a claim to power. The president is a part of this system, often a vital part, yet a president is not in control of the system.[2]

Ours is a constitutional system of shared, separated, overlapping, dispersed and fragmented powers. No one influential figure controls the levers of power; they are spread out across the system. This lessens the likelihood of tyranny. But it also makes it difficult to achieve necessary change. The system is slow and cumbersome, designed to make leadership deliberate and usually difficult as well.

Leadership is difficult precisely because the framers of our Constitution wanted it, except in emergencies, to be so. The men who invented the presidency did not wish to create a *ruler;* their experience with kings of England soured them to this prospect. Instead, they hoped to create the conditions where *leadership* might from time to time flourish. A ruler commands; a leader influences; a ruler wields power; a leader persuades. Presidents have *limited and shared powers.* The paradox here is that our expectations are high, we demand much of our presidents, yet the resources at the disposal of the president are limited and the system in which a president operates can easily frustrate efforts at presidential leadership. We have created a "leadership aversion system"[3] and demanded that presidents take control and lead. Is it any wonder that we are often disappointed in presidents? In effect, we set them up to fail and then turn on them when they do.

## AMERICA'S ANTILEADERSHIP CULTURE

Several hurdles stand in the way of strong presidential leadership. A system organized around a separation of powers as opposed to a fusion of power (Great Britain fuses legislative and executive power, for example) structurally inhibits strong leadership. America's *political culture* also undermines strong leadership.

Ours is in many ways an antiauthority and therefore an antileadership culture. Political scientist Samuel Huntington refers to "the American Creed," which consists of a commitment to individualism, egalitarianism, democracy, and freedom.[4] Admirable goals all, yet not especially supportive of strong leadership or strong deferential followership. Political scientist Clinton Rossiter captured this paradox when he wrote, "We have always been a nation obsessed with liberty. Liberty over authority, freedom over responsibility, rights over duties—these are our historic preferences. . . . Not the good man, but the free man has been the measure of all things in this "sweet land of liberty"; not national glory, but individual liberty has been the object of political authority and the test of its worth."[5]

How does this American creed affect our attitudes toward leadership? While it creates a fundamentally antileadership disposition, the American propensity for individualism does generate a type of hero worship that feeds into the heroic model of the presidency. Thus we honor Washington the patriot, Jefferson and Jackson the great democrats, Lincoln and FDR the saviors. But such hero worship masks, in some ways, our stronger stance of antileadership and antiauthority.

In general, the antiauthority strain of the American creed has personified our culture. Max Lerner has written that "American thinkers have been at their best in their anti-authoritarianism."[6] From Jefferson and Madison to Calhoun and Thoreau, some of America's most profound and influential thinkers reflected deep strains of individualism and antiauthoritarianism. The implications of this for leadership were not lost on that thoughtful French observer of the American scene, Alexis de Tocqueville, who wrote,

> When it comes to the influence of one man's mind over another's, that is necessarily very restricted in a country where the citizens have all become more or less similar . . . and since they do not recognize any signs of incontestable greatness or superiority in any of their fellows, are continually brought back to their own judgment as the most apparent and accessible test of truth. So it is not only confidence in any particular man which is destroyed. There is a general distaste for accepting any man's word as proof of anything.[7]

It is difficult, except in a crisis, for presidents to ask the people to make major sacrifices for the common good, to move beyond self interest. When Jimmy Carter asked citizens to turn their thermostats down to 68 degrees Fahrenheit in an oil crisis, he was rebuked. When President Clinton called on the American people to provide military peace forces in Somalia, Haiti, and Bosnia, Americans were hesitant if not hostile to such urgings. George W. Bush learned about this hesitancy as the "post-victory" struggles continued on and on in Afghanistan and Iraq.

The United States lacks a defined "public philosophy" of the role and purpose of government in a post–Cold War era. The lack of a public philosophy often reflects a lack of consensus as to what we as a people should do, where we as a nation need to move. In the absence of a national consensus, presidents have a difficult time moving our separated system.

Our sense of a shared community, or of a social contract, has generally remained murky. We are not "one nation indivisible" as much as a collection of individuals. We rarely pull together for the common good. In part, we are a "nation," a loose-knit collection of individuals, and in part we are a confederation of tribes.[8]

Yet effective leadership requires a supporting consensus behind governmental authority and presidential initiatives. Disharmony and conflict have often characterized the American political system. A divided nation, a polarized nation, cannot be a well-governed nation. "Where did we go wrong?," leadership expert Warren Bennis asked, "America has always been at war with itself. We have always dreamt of community and democracy but always practiced individualism and capitalism. We have celebrated innocence but sought power. We are the world's leading sentimentalists, and it's a very short step from sentimentality to cynicism."[9]

While Americans occasionally demonstrate patriotic fervor, they seldom demonstrate a deep sense of community. From a strong commitment to community, one can elicit a consensus upon which to build leadership. When the public lacks a strong sense of community, leaders have a difficult time pulling the nation together (except in a crisis) to respond collectively, politically, as one nation.

## THE MOODS AND CYCLES OF AMERICAN POLITICS

Leadership does not occur in a vacuum. There are different "seasons" of leadership, times when presidents are afforded more or less room to exercise power.[10]

These cycles take many forms: the business cycle of economic growth followed by recession; the political pendulum of liberalism followed by a conservative period; strong presidents followed by weak ones; the mood swing of public confidence in government followed by a retreat into private interests and cynicism; the foreign policy shifts from isolationism to international involvement. These cycles are, for the most part, beyond the control of presidents, but they do have an impact on presidential power.[11]

There are times when, and conditions under which, presidents are afforded considerable leverage and power. There are also times when presidents are kept on a short leash.

Thus, in the aftermath of the war in Vietnam and of Watergate, the public turned against the government and presidential power and the United States entered a period when we questioned everything a president did. Thus Presidents Ford and Carter were restricted in their opportunities to exercise power. The public was more cynical and suspicious, the press was more skeptical, the Congress was willing to reassert its authority, and if that weren't enough, the economy was sluggish. Even if Ford and Carter had been highly skilled, gifted politicians, their level of political opportunity was so low there was little way they could have been successful.

FDR, by contrast, a highly skilled politician, also benefited from a level of opportunity that was unusually high. He came to office at a time when the public demanded strong leadership, when the Congress was willing to accede power to the president. Thus the mixture of high skill and high opportunity allowed FDR to pursue both power and success.

Political time is also important.[12] During periods of change and social disruption, certain types of leadership will be more necessary, while during periods of normalcy, a different type of leadership may be required. Likewise, a different sort of leadership is required during periods of crisis. Clearly there is not one leadership style for all seasons. Effective leaders are able to adjust to these different seasons.

Several cycles are especially relevant to presidential leadership. One is the *succession cycle.* Political scientist Valerie Bunce noted that major policy shifts are most likely when new leaders come to power.[13] Thus, leadership change is connected to policy change. Another cycle is the *cycle of decreasing popularity.* Over time, presidents tend to lose popular support (as stated in the last chapter), which makes it more difficult for them to put together political coalitions as time progresses. Another presidential cycle is the *cycle of growing effectiveness.*[14] The president's learning curve is at its lowest at the beginning of a term and rises as time goes by. Yet the president's power is usually at its zenith early in the terms, when knowledge is lowest.

The cycle that seems most relevant to presidential leadership deals with the long-term ebb and flow of American politics. Historians Arthur M. Schlesinger and Arthur M. Schlesinger, Jr., suggest that this cycle is like a pendulum swinging back and forth. The United States alternates between periods of "conservatism versus innovation" (Emerson), "diffusion versus centralization" (Henry Adams). Arthur M. Schlesinger, Jr., describes these mood swings as "a continuing shift in national involvement, between *public purpose* and *private interest.*"[15]

The roots of this repeating cycle doubtless lie deep in human nature and the U.S. structure of government, and the pattern follows roughly a thirty-year alternation between the pursuit of public purpose and of private interest. In the twentieth century there were a few periods of high governmental activism in support of public purpose: Theodore Roosevelt and Woodrow Wilson from 1901–9 and 1913–17, Franklin D. Roosevelt from 1933–35, and John F. Kennedy and Lyndon Johnson from 1963–66. There have also been "high tides of conservative restoration—the 1920s, the 1950s, the 1980s."[16]

We must view political change as a connection between leader (office holder) and follower (citizen) at different points in time. This allows us to broaden our horizons to the complex and interconnected nature of political change in a democracy. Leaders do not always lead; followers do not always follow. Different political climates require different types of political leadership and a different set of political skills.

So much of a president's power is contextual, that is, different contexts or situations present presidents with different power opportunities. Some presidents have a high level of political opportunity; others a low level.

One's level of political opportunity is based upon factors such as crisis versus normal conditions (as the post 9-11 political environment demonstrated, a crisis president has expanded powers), the results of the previous election (landslide versus a close election), the number of a president's political party in Congress (a large majority versus divided government), issue ripeness, and public demand for action. *Opportunity,* combined with *resources,* and *skill,* determine how much power a president is likely to have.[17]

## THE VAGARIES OF PRESIDENTIAL POWER

All presidents on assuming office receive similar formal constitutional powers. The founding fathers arranged for an office broadly defined as well as vaguely outlined. Power granted, they believed, should be a wide discretionary residual power available when other governmental branches failed to meet their responsibilities or failed to respond to the urgencies of the day. Power was available, but it would be subject to various checks and balances. The president is open to challenges and vetoes from a number of other political institutions.[18]

As Edward S. Corwin and others have pointed out, there is a plasticity in our fundamental conception of the presidency and its powers.[19] The exact dimensions of executive power at any given moment are largely the consequence of the incumbent's character and energy combined with the overarching needs of the day, the challenges to system survival and regeneration. Some presidents have been power maximizers. Jackson, Lincoln, and the Roosevelts are illustrative. Certain of them became shrewd party leaders. Some saw themselves as direct agents of the American people, as the people's choice with mandates to carry out in exchange for the grant of powers. Still others employed the "take care that the laws be faithfully executed" clause of the Constitution to broaden the notion of executive power well beyond the boundaries envisioned by most of the framers of the Constitution. Plainly, an office underdefined on paper has become enlarged with the accumulation of traditions and with the cumulative legacy of some often brilliant achievements.

Tocqueville rightly observed that if executive power was weaker in the United States than in European countries (in the early 1800s), the reason was more in circumstances than in laws. He added that "it is generally in its relations with foreign powers that the executive power of a nation has the chance to display skill and strength."[20] If the United States had remained a small nation, isolated and removed from the other nations of the world, the role of the executive would doubtless have remained weak, certainly much weaker than the presidency we have come to know today. Had the presidential office been incapable of expanding, the nation may well not have survived. Presidential powers and presidential leadership have been essential for both progress and stability.

One of the more persisting of presidential paradoxes from the standpoint of presidents is the realization that the office carries much less power, however power is defined, than the candidates had thought when they ran for the office. Lyndon Johnson did his best to pyramid available power resources to the office soon after he found himself there. But he never stopped complaining that his responsibilities always exceeded his powers. Thus it is not surprising that although LBJ did not have much advice for his successor, he did have these words of caution:

> Before you get to the presidency you think you can do anything. You think you're the most powerful leader since God. But when you get in that tall chair, as you're gonna find out, Mr. President, you can't count on people. You'll find your hands tied and people cussin' you. The office is kinda like the little country boy found the hoochie-koochie show at the carnival, once he'd paid his dime and got inside the tent: "It ain't exactly as it was advertised."[21]

Political scientist Richard Neustadt's celebrated *Presidential Power,*[22] first published in 1960, studied this same problem. His work is a veritable manual of personal power: how to get it, how to keep it, and how to use it. Presidents Kennedy and Johnson were influenced by Neustadt's thinking, as were other presidents. Kennedy studied it and employed Neustadt as a consultant on staffing and varied policy questions. Johnson almost naturally seemed to conduct himself according to the Neustadt power principles.

*Presidential Power* was a call for presidents to exercise their power wisely and fully. How do his views hold up in the twenty-first century? After Vietnam, Watergate, Iran-Contra, the Clinton impeachment and a new foreign policy of "preemptive war," does Neustadt's position still inform? Have the intervening decades validated his basic premises?

## CONCEPTIONS OF PRESIDENTIAL POWER

*Presidential Power* was rightfully hailed as a pioneering contribution to our understanding of the operational realities of presidential leadership. It was widely read in the 1960s and it remains a classic.

Neustadt's *Presidential Power* broke away from the traditional emphasis on leadership traits, the compartmentalized listings of functional tasks, and the then-dominant tendency to study the presidency in legal or constitutional terms. Instead, Neustadt used organizational and administrative behavior as frames of reference for the study of what presidents must do if they want to influence events and why and how presidents often lose the ability to influence. His stress was on the *shared* powers of the office rather than the separation of powers. He emphasized the reciprocal character of influence, the constant personal calculations and trade-offs that motivate people to cooperate or not to cooperate with presidential initiatives.

His message was that the presidency is neither as powerful as many people think nor should its strengthening be feared as many others believe. Neustadt called on future presidents to acquire as much power as they could, for he noted that the formal institutional powers were fragile, even puny, compared with the responsibilities.

Neustadt said presidential power is the power to *persuade,* and the power to persuade comes through *bargaining.* Bargaining, in turn, comes primarily through getting others to feel it is in their own self-interest to cooperate. Presidents are depicted as being constantly challenged by threats to their power and constantly needing to enhance their reputation as a shrewd bargainer. Tenacity and proper timing are also essential.

Neustadt viewed Franklin D. Roosevelt as a many-splendored prototype. Roosevelt had that rare combination of self-confidence, ambition, political experience, sense of purpose, and Neustadt's elusive term *sensitivity to power,* that was necessary to harness formal authority with effective personal performance and thus make the presidency work. "Roosevelt had a love affair with power in that place. It was an early romance and it lasted all his life."[23] "[He] saw the job of being President as being FDR."[24] "Roosevelt always knew what power was and always wanted it."[25] In short, Roosevelt had the will to power, the driving ambition, and the uncommon sense of knowing how to deal with people; these combined almost always to leave him in the driver's seat.

Neustadt was impressed with the way Roosevelt juggled assignments, kept people guessing, put men of clashing temperaments, outlooks, and ideas in charge of his major projects. FDR loved dividing authority and keeping his organizations temporary and overlapping. To some people this might have been the art of manipulation, but to Neustadt it was the essence of leadership. Roosevelt remained the Neustadt model, particularly his robust, playful temperament: "Roosevelt's sense of fun combined with Roosevelt's sort of confidence remain for me what they were . . . a target at which to aim."[26]

Neustadt's analytical treatment of presidential power was a description of how to strengthen the hand of a president one liked. Neustadt's propositions, slightly rephrased, are as follows:

1. To be a leader, a president must have a will for power. If he lacks a consuming hunger for power and a penchant for shrewdly handling people, then he is not suited for the office.
2. The skill of a president at winning others over to his support is the necessary energizing factor to get the institutions of the national government into action. He and only he supplies the agenda for action for the Washington political community.

3. A president cannot be an introvert, or above the battle, or above politics, or simply work from within the confines of his own ideas; a sensitivity to the thoughts and feelings of others and an ability to create solutions that compromise contesting points of view are what distinguishes effective leadership from nonleadership.

4. The members of Congress act the way they think they have to in order to get reelected and to "look good." A president's job is to get members of Congress and other influential members of the government community to think his requests are in their own best interests.

5. A president has to ride events and crises to gain attention. Most Americans grow attentive only as they grow directly concerned with what may happen in their lives.

6. A president should never rely on others to determine his power stakes. He should be his own intelligence officer, his own expert on crucial power relationships. Moreover, he should be concerned with details, gossip, and the intricacies of human sensitivities. A president who delegates the job of being chief politician to others is a president who will not exercise much influence.

7. The lesson from cases is that when it comes to power, nobody is expert but a president, and if he too acts as a layman, it will be fatal.

8. Popularity and public prestige produce favorable credit for a president among the professional Washington community. But public disapproval heightens and encourages resistance from the Washington community (defined as members of Congress, bureaucrats, the press, governors, diplomats, etc.).

9. Presidential power is not easy to come by and even the most skillful of presidents will have to be flexible, always sensitive to the need for multiple channels of information, always frugal in using power resources to get their way, and always employing the art of persuasion in a bargaining situation, thereby avoiding at almost all costs the direct issuing of a confrontational command.

Thus, *Presidential Power* held out hope that a shrewd and artfully manipulative leader could and would be a powerful Hamiltonian engine of change. An aggressive, ambitious politician, determined to get his way and ever distrustful of the motives of others, seemed to be the remedy for the post-Eisenhower years. Neustadt concluded that a key problem of the presidency at the time was how the presidency could regain control over the drifting Washington policy apparatus. Forceful leadership was needed, and only the president could fill the leadership vacuum.

Neustadt's greatest contribution to the understanding of the presidency is his notion that the power of a president rests ultimately on his ability to persuade others. Because a president shares authority with other institutions, he cannot merely command. Rather he must constantly bargain and trade in an effort to achieve results.

## UNRESOLVED QUESTIONS

What of the problems and concerns raised by *Presidential Power?* How help-ful is it as a guide to understanding presidential leadership?

Perhaps the most frequent criticism of this analysis is that it seemed too preoccupied with the will to power, the acquisition of power, and stockpiling the power, divorced from any discussion of the purposes to which power should be put. Such an emphasis on means without any clear discussion of ends left the impression that the art of leadership is tantamount to the art of manipulation. Neustadt was faulted too for his failure to emphasize the role that a "sense of direction" plays in presidential leadership, and how a presi-dent would call on or consider ideological values in his power exchanges.

One critic went so far as to suggest that Neustadt "baptizes" political ambition just as Dale Carnegie and self-help manuals baptize greed. Many readers would have liked a more thoughtful discussion of the ends of presi-dential power, of the ethical boundaries. What are the higher claims on a president and how does the creative president join together the ethic of responsibility and the ethic of ultimate ends?

Put another way, Neustadt's methodology "does not allow political sci-ence to distinguish between the use and the abuse of presidential power."[27] Neustadt made little claim beyond this, although he did suggest that a pres-ident's sensitivity to the means of power has a good deal to do with "viable" public policy. To some people, this seems as if in Neustadt's terms, public purpose *is* linked directly to presidential purpose.

In any event, Neustadt did not apologize for his focus on the means of leadership. Although certain critics did, and with some reason continue to contend that the analysis and discussion of power devoid of content is a shal-low, even an empty, exercise. In Neustadt's defense it can be said that the ends were, and perhaps still remain, implicitly embedded in the liberal vision of the 1960s.

A second criticism of Neustadt's book was that it is too approving of the personalization of presidential power. It seems to say: Find the right presi-dent and teach him or her what power is all about and progress will be real-ized. It portrays presidents as potential saviors. If only we had the Second Coming of Franklin Roosevelt, all would be well. It comes close to suggest-ing we need a charismatic larger-than-life figure on whom to lean to make the system work. Further, the book speaks almost exclusively about the Washington political community and makes little or no reference to the peo-ple's role or to social movements.

Two problems arise from this emphasis on FDR and on presidents as the answer to our needs. First, Neustadt failed to take into account the degree to which presidents are almost invariably stabilizers or protectors of the status quo rather than agents of redistribution or progressive change. Neustadt gave little attention to the way the prevailing American elite values, and market capitalism,[28] often limit a president's freedom. Bruce Miroff wrestles with some alternative interpretations in his *Pragmatic Illusions: The Presidential Politics of John F. Kennedy.*[29] One gets the impression from reading Neustadt that he thought a president can roam at will, providing he is shrewd enough to be able to persuade others that their interests are the same as his. In fact, however, all of our presidents have had to prove their political orthodoxy and their acceptability to a wide array of established powers, especially corporate leaders, entrenched interest-group leaders, and so on. Thus, Neustadt raised hopes that the presidency will be an instrument for the progressive transformation of American politics.[30]

Just how much and how often can we turn to the White House and hope that a benevolent and bright president will provide truly inspired leadership? Sometimes we must turn there, yet a reading of history suggests that breakthroughs and leadership often come from the bottom (or at least the middle) up. Civil rights workers, consumer organizers, women's rights activists, environmental protectionists, tax-revolt champions, and antiwar protestors are illustrative of the catalysts that more often than not bring about policy change in the United States. John W. Gardner, himself a citizen-activist, cautions that "crusading citizens' groups may not always be wise, witness the Prohibitionists. Or they may be wise but unsuccessful in persuading their fellow citizens. For every citizens' group that changes the course of history, there are thousands . . . that never create a ripple."[31]

In Neustadt's defense it can be said that although his treatise reads like a hymn of praise for FDR, the author really did not go so far as to say: Defer completely to your president and trust him. He appears instead, at least most of the time, to say that without a good engineer the train just won't go.

There is also an elitist cast to Neustadt's formulation. There is an implicit, if not explicit, fear of the masses juxtaposed with a robust faith in the great leader. This was, of course, a prevailing view among most academics at the time. Roosevelt may have been a grand manipulator and sometimes deceptive as well, but wasn't this increasingly necessary? Leaders need a free hand. It was as if Roosevelt on occasion deceived people, including the American people, much as the physician who lies to the patient "for the patient's own good." Walter Lippmann, George Kennan, Hans Morganthau, and others had previously and often eloquently argued a similar case. What was needed was an activist helmsman to define the national interest, to subdue or avoid the passions of the electorate and the parochialisms of the special-interest groups and Congress. Look to your presidents for leadership, for in Lippmann's oft-quoted words, "The unhappy truth is that the prevailing public opinion has been destructively wrong at the critical junctures."

Did Neustadt's call for strong presidential leadership betray a liberal bias? For most of the post–World War II era, the heroic/strong presidency that Neustadt promoted was considered the model for political progressives of his day. Neustadt and others advocated a powerful activist presidency in pursuit of more government intervention in problem solving. From the 1950s through the 1970s, conservatives advocated more limited government, less presidential power, and a smaller role for the federal government.

But as testimony to the seductive lure of the heroic presidency model, by the 1980s even conservatives had been converted to presidential power.

The heroic presidency could, conservatives found, be used to pursue the conservative agenda. Emboldened by Ronald Reagan's rhetorical skills and the promise of a "Reagan Revolution," conservatives saw the presidency as a vehicle for political power. Conservative centralizers sprang up all over. Neustadt's strong presidency view became a philosophy for multiple political leanings.[32]

## POWER-MAXIMIZING STRATEGIES

Any essay dealing with presidential power must deal with presidential weakness as well as strength. The founders left the president vulnerable to several potential veto points, most notably the Congress. The framers did not want executive impotence—had that been their goal they could have stuck with the Articles of Confederation. But neither did they want executive dominance—had that been their goal they could have adopted the British parliamentary model with a fusion of executive and legislative power. They chose instead an executive office of limited powers that operated in a separation-of-powers model which fragmented power. Of course, such a system had consequences for the president's ability to lead.

Left to its own devices, the presidency has limited powers and is vulnerable to the will or whim of Congress and others. Neustadt rightly focuses our attention on the need for presidents to be conscious of their power positions.

As students of the presidency know, rarely can a president act alone. A president is usually dependent on the compliance or cooperation of others to achieve his or her goals. The presidency gives the occupant of the White House little more than the opportunity to govern.

In this Neustadt points us in the right direction. Presidents cannot merely command, they must persuade. But they must do much more. For presidents to be effective, and govern within the bounds of democratic leadership, they must also develop a sophisticated "strategic sense." They must know what to accomplish and how to accomplish it. And, their means and goals must aim to further the will of the people, empower citizens, and strengthen democratic accountability. Success is not measured merely by getting one's way but also by the ends to which policies are directed.

By strategic sense, we mean the ability to devise an overall plan that is designed to integrate means and ends, that shows what to do and how to do it, that links smaller tactical steps to a broad guiding vision.

Few presidents take the time to think strategically. They tend to think short term, in an "I'll cross that bridge when I come to it," manner. They are more reactive than proactive. The world has a way of forcing presidents to respond rather than create. Someone once said that presidents cannot see beyond the next election. Today the time frame of presidential activity has shortened. Due to the proliferation of opinion polls, instant television analysis, and talk radio punditry, presidents feel compelled to worry how something will look on CNN in the next hour or two. This is unfortunate.

To overcome the roadblocks built into the system a president must develop a strategic sense of governing. Some elements of presidential leadership remain fairly constant over time—the Constitution, the separation of powers. Others are variable—the skill level of a president, the context or situation at hand, the nature of a president's mandate, the president's party strength in Congress. The president must develop a strategy designed to maximize political capital.[33]

Presidential leadership refers to more than mere officeholding. Leadership is a complex phenomenon involving *influence*—the ability to move others in desired directions. Successful leaders are those who can take full advantage of their opportunities, resources, and skills. Institutional structures, the immediate situation, the season of power, the political culture, the regime type, and the dynamics of followership define the opportunities for the exercise of leadership. The resources at a leader's disposal include constitutional and statutory powers, intermediaries, media, level of popularity, nature of the congressional majority, and policy arena. We often mistake resources for power. A successful leader converts resources to power. This does not happen automatically. To convert resources to power requires skill.

The leader's style, political acumen, experience, political strategy, management skills, vision, ability to mobilize political support, character traits, and personal attributes provide a behavioral repertoire, a set of skills. Opportunities, resources, and skills interact to determine the potential for success or failure in attempts to lead and influence.

Presidents who can play to the optimum their cards of opportunity, resources, and skill have a chance of succeeding.

But few presidents are FDR, and few face the opportunities for leadership that FDR enjoyed. Power is dispersed, it "exists only as a potential. Leadership is the means by which the president can exploit that potential. This is no easy task."[34]

A president has vast responsibilities, with high public expectations and limited power resources. But as an institution, the presidency has proven to be elastic; it stretches to accommodate skilled leaders in situations of high opportunity, but contracts to hem in less skilled leaders. Noting the variable nature of the power potential in the presidency, Robert Dahl has written, "The presidency is like a family dwelling that each new generation alters and enlarges. Confronted by some new need, a president adds on a new room, a new wing; what began as a modest dwelling has become a mansion; every president may not use every room, but the rooms are available in case of need."[35]

The variable nature of presidential power has left presidency scholars a bit schizophrenic regarding the proper scope and limits of presidential power. When presidents performed credibly (1930s to early 1960s), they called for an enlarged institution. As presidents faltered (1960s to 1980s), they called for restrictions on presidential power, and when the United States faced terrorist attacks in 2001, demands were heard for an enlarged presidency. This variability is reactive, it is based on the subjective judgments derived from the short-term political performance of presidents. Such evaluations miss the key point: the *normal* state of the presidency is one of constrained power. To be successful, a president must overcome nature, or at least the nature of power built into the system. Thus, it is better to look at the requirements for leadership generically, at the preconditions necessary for the exercise of political leadership, than merely to react to the current temporary occupant of the Oval Office. In doing this we can see which threads run through the *presidency* as well as see how well a *president* performed.

The founders wanted a government of energy, yet a specific type of energy, energy that resulted from consensus, cooperation, and collaboration. What model or type of leadership is required to move such a system? A model based on consensus, not fait accompli; influence, not command; agreement, not independence; cooperation, not unilateralism. Such a model of power requires presidents to think strategically.[36]

## PRESIDENTIAL LEADERSHIP

The words *leadership* and *power* are often used interchangeably. This is misguided. Leadership suggests influence; power is command. Leaders inspire and persuade; power wielders order compliance. Leaders induce followership; power holders force compliance. Officeholders have some power by virtue of occupying an office. Leaders, on the other hand, must earn followership. The officeholder uses the powers granted by virtue of position. The leader tries to reshape the political environment, "he seeks to change the constellation of political forces about him in a direction closer to his own conception of the political good."[37]

Occasionally, a president can act on his own authority, "independent" of others. President George H. W. Bush's 1989 decision to overthrow the government of Manuel Noriega in Panama is an example of this form of claimed power. But such unilateral acts are the exception, not the rule. In most cases, presidents share power. Therefore, the informal "powers" usefully discussed by Neustadt become important to presidents who wish to promote political change.

All presidents have some power, some ability to command. Yet such power is short term and limited. It ceases to exist the moment the president leaves office. Its effects can often be undone by a new president.

A president's formal power, for so long the focal point of presidential studies,[38] includes constitutional authority, statutes, delegated powers, and those areas where others follow a president's command. But with the publication of Neustadt's *Presidential Power,* the ability to persuade took center stage in presidential studies. Rather than take an "either/or" approach to the debate over formal versus informal powers, one should see these two potential sources of strength as complementary, as presidential options in the pursuit of their goals. While presidents derive some of their power from constitutional sources, they derive other parts from political and personal sources.

Effective presidents use *all* the resources available to them. They assess the situation and determine where their best chance for success rests, and are flexible enough to make the adjustments necessary to optimize their power. True leadership occurs when presidents are able to exploit the multifaceted nature of opportunities to both command and influence.

For better or worse, only presidential leadership can regularly overcome the natural lethargy built into the American system and give focus and direction to government. Congress can, on occasion, take the lead on select policy, as was the case when the Congress overcame presidential opposition from Ronald Reagan and imposed economic sanctions on the white minority government of South Africa. The Gingrich-led Congress in 1995 provides a few examples. But such cases are infrequent. Congress simply is not institutionally well designed to provide consistent national leadership over extended periods of time. In the late twentieth and early twenty-first centuries, the citizens have most often looked to the White House for leadership and direction. If the president does not lead, gridlock usually results. In this sense, John F. Kennedy's view that "The presidential office is the vortex into which all the elements of national decision are irresistibly drawn,"[39] is persuasive. Presidential leadership usually remains the key for moving the machinery of government.

## THE BUILDING BLOCKS OF PRESIDENTIAL LEADERSHIP

### Vision

The most important "power" a president can have is to present to the public a clear and compelling *vision*. An attractive, meaningful, positive vision that is rooted in building blocs of the past, addresses needs and hopes of the present, and portrays an image of a possible future opens more doors to presidential leadership than all the skills and resources combined. A powerful vision can transform a political system, recreate the regime of power, and chart a course for change. Vision energizes and empowers, inspires and moves people and organizations. A president with a compelling vision can be a powerful president.

Few presidents use to the fullest what Theodore Roosevelt referred to as "the bully pulpit" to develop a public philosophy for governing. Rather than attempting to educate and lead the public, most presidents serve as managers or clerks of public business. But if presidents wish to craft significant change, and not merely preside, they must use the bully pulpit to promote a moral and political vision in support of change.

Visions are empowering. They are derived from the core values of a community, flow from the past, are about the future. Visions inspire, give meaning and direction to a community, are roadmaps. Visions are about achieving excellence. A visionary leader gives direction to an organization and gives purpose to action. Visionary leadership charts a course for action.

"Leaders," wrote Warren Bennis and Burt Nanus,

> define what has previously remained implicit or unsaid; then they invent images, metaphors, and models that provide a focus for new attention. By so doing they consolidate or challenge prevailing wisdom. In short, an essential factor in leadership is the capacity to influence and organize meaning for members of the organization. . . . Communication creates meaning for people. Or should. It's the only way any group, small or large, can become aligned behind the overarching goals of an organization.[40]

Visionary leaders are remembered and have an impact after they have left office. Thus, long after FDR, John Kennedy, Martin Luther King, Jr., and Ronald Reagan were gone from public life, the power of their ideas and the impact of their words remain symbolic and emotional forces in the political arena.

Ronald Reagan was able to inspire followers because he was skilled at presenting his vision. In contrast, the Bushs often had trouble with providing a compelling vision that rallied the nation.

No other politician in America is better positioned to present a vision to the public than a president. Already the focus of much media and public attention, presidents can become "highlighters" of important issues to be addressed as a part of the president's agenda.

Teddy Roosevelt employed what he referred to as a "bully pulpit," actively shaping and educating the public about key issues on his agenda. (*Source:* Reproduced from the collections of the Library of Congress.)

## Skill

For successful political leadership, skill is important, but skill is never enough. Even the most skilled of individuals face formidable roadblocks. Skill helps determine the extent to which a president takes advantage of or is buried by circumstances, but circumstances or the political environment set the parameters of what is possible regarding leadership. President Reagan referred to the "window of opportunity," his way of talking about how open or closed circumstances were for exercising presidential leadership. Skilled presidents facing a closed window (e.g., the opposition party controlling Congress during a period of economic troubles where the president's popularity is low) will be limited in what they can accomplish. Presidents of limited skill, when the window of opportunity is open, will have much greater political leverage, even though their skill base is smaller. It is thus entirely possible for a president with limited skill to be more successful than a president with great skill. If one is dealt a weak hand, there is only so much skill can do. But if one is dealt four aces, what Machiavelli called "fortuna" (fortune), not skill, determines outcome.

This is not to say that skill is unimportant. But in the constellation of factors that contribute to success or failure, skill is but one, and probably not the most important element.

Before an election one often hears political cynics whine, "It doesn't matter who gets elected, they all end up doing the same thing anyway." Social science lends some support to this cynical view. After all, social scientists widely believe the institution, role, expectations, time, and other factors play a significant role in determining behavior. While the cynic has a point, it should not be taken too far. Individuals *are* constrained, but individuals do matter.[41]

One way of looking at the skill/opportunity dilemma is to focus on what is referred to as a president's "political capital." Is a president's political capital like a bank account where a one-time deposit is made at the beginning of his term and he invests carefully and draws on that account prudently, lest he run out of resources? Or can a president add to his bank account from time to time, renewing his resources?

President George H. W. Bush seemed to think that his capital was a fixed sum, and in spending it, he dissipated it. Bill Clinton, on the other hand, did not view his political capital as a fixed asset. He regularly spent, then tried to replenish his assets as best he could. As President Clinton noted,

> . . . even a President without a majority mandate coming in, if the President has a disciplined, aggressive agenda that is clearly in the interest of the majority of the American people—I think you can create new political capital all the time, because you have access to the people through the communications network. If you have energy and sort of an inner determination that keeps you at the task, I think you can re-create political capital continuously throughout the Presidency. I have always believed that.[42]

Do leaders make a difference? Yes, sometimes. As political scientist Erwin C. Hargrove writes, "Surely the issue is not, Do individuals make a difference? but under what conditions do they make a difference? The relative importance of leaders varies across institutions and across time and place. . . . The task of scholarship is to integrate the study of individuals with the social and institutional forces that move them and that they, in turn, may influence."[43]

At what point do individuals matter? When is skill an important variable in presidential success? While it may sound obvious, it is nonetheless important to note that "effectiveness in achieving goals was enhanced if skill and task were congruent."[44] To that we would add a third element: opportunity level. Skill, matched to task when the window of political opportunity is open, usually leads to goal attainment. Plainly the effectiveness of a leader is greater or lesser depending on the historical situation and the opportunities available to them.

The impact of individual presidents who made a difference in specific policy areas is unmistakable: Lyndon Johnson and civil rights and the war on poverty, Richard Nixon and China, Jimmy Carter and human rights, Ronald Reagan and tax cuts, George H.W. Bush and the Gulf War, Bill Clinton and the Brady bill and NAFTA (North American Free Trade Agreement), George W. Bush and the war on terrorism. These presidents made choices, moved in new directions, made a difference. Yes they were limited, yet they were able to overcome the natural lethargy of the system and succeed in selected policy arenas. That in most areas and on most issues presidential behavior appears more similar than dissimilar should not obscure the fact that on some issues at some times, some presidents can make a difference.

The problem is that determining what role skill played in these events is a slippery task. Could another president have opened doors to China? Perhaps, yet maybe not. Could any president emphasize human rights in his foreign policy? Probably. So where are we left? When does skill matter? How can we recognize or measure political skill? Regrettably, it is probably too elusive a concept to measure precisely. Suffice it to say that high levels of skill, task congruence, and high opportunity usually lead to presidential success, and low levels of these often lead to failure.[45]

To beg the question: If skill is of some importance, it is useful to ask, what skills are most useful to a president? Political experience is often cited as a requirement for effective leadership, and while this sounds like common sense, the correlation between experience and achievement is not strong. After all, some of our most experienced national leaders were, in many respects, failures (Hoover, LBJ, Nixon, and George H.W. Bush come to mind). But overall, more experience is better than less experience, although by no means a guarantee of successful performance. This suggests that other factors determine to a great degree the success or failure of a president.

Ronald Reagan and Bill Clinton serve as excellent examples of amateurs, in Washington, D.C., terms, who sometimes behaved amateurishly in the White House. Reagan in Beirut, and Clinton in Somalia, placed American military personnel in harm's way without sufficient support or protection and against the recommendations of more experienced advisers. In both cases, Americans were attacked and some killed (over 220 marines in Beirut and a dozen in Somalia) before changes in policy led to increased safety precautions. In both cases, leaders with little or no foreign policy experience made blunders that probably could have been avoided. More experienced hands might have known better.

Political skills are always in short supply, and a president with a high level of political acumen can sometimes gain the upper hand. By political skill we mean a good sense of timing (knowing when an issue is "ripe," when to move, when to hold back), task competence, a power sense, situational skills (crisis versus routine decision skills), policy skills (to develop sound workable programs), and political savvy (you need to love playing politics, as FDR did, not hate politics, as Nixon did). Of FDR's love of and for politics, James MacGregor Burns has written, "If other leaders bent under the burdens of power, Roosevelt shouldered his with zest and gaiety. He loved being President; he almost always gave the impression of being on top of his job. Cheerfully, exuberantly, he swung through the varied presidential tasks. . . . The variegated facets of the presidential job called for a multitude of different roles, and Roosevelt moved from part to part with ease and confidence."[46]

Presidents also need people skills. They must know how to persuade, bargain, cajole, and co-opt. They must be masters of self-presentation. They must be able to motivate and inspire, to gain trust and influence. Charisma helps. In short, occupants of the White House must master the art of "presidential schmoozing." Presidents must simultaneously appeal to Main Street (the average citizen), Wall Street (the business community), and Easy Street (the wealthy). It is a difficult juggling act even for the most accomplished of leaders.

Personality skills are also a significant part of the arsenal of presidential requirements.[47] All presidents have a strong drive for power. Some hold it within healthy bounds; others, like Nixon, destroy themselves. To be effective, presidents should be self-confident, secure, flexible, and open. Presidents who are consumed by self-doubt, insecurity, and rigidity (Barber's "negative" characters) are often dangerous and more apt to abuse power.

Presidents also need self-knowledge. We all have our weaknesses, but we do not all let our weaknesses consume us. Good presidents recognize their strengths *and* weaknesses, and attempt to deal constructively with weakness. Thus, presidents who are inexperienced in foreign policy may need to compensate by surrounding themselves with very experienced foreign policy insiders.

Managerial skills are also important if a president is to succeed.[48] Upon taking office presidents tend to see only the personal as important; the historical and institutional are often downplayed.

And a president must have personal skills. By this we mean they must be disciplined, intelligent, have stamina, show sound judgment, and act with maturity. Good presidents are creative, empathetic, and expressive. They should be relentlessly optimistic. They must also have a sense of humor, and learn to control their temper. President Reagan's self-effacing sense of humor served him well; it disarmed opponents and won over much of the public.

## Political Timing

The "when" of politics also matters greatly: when major legislation is introduced, when the public is ready to accept change, when Congress can be pressured to act, when to lead and when to follow, when to push and when to pause. A sense of political timing, part of the overall "power sense" all great leaders have, helps a president know when to move, when to retreat, when to push, and when to compromise. The transition and the honeymoon are especially important periods.

Getting a good start ("hitting the ground running") is a key element of political success, and during the transition, the eleven-week period between the November election and the January inauguration, some of the most important work of an administration is done. Here the groundwork is laid for much that will follow and a tone is set that shapes the way others see the new administration. During the transition, the president makes key decisions on who the top advisers will be, who will fill important cabinet positions, how the staff will be structured, what decision style will be employed, whether to pursue a partisan strategy or try to woo the opposition, how to mobilize the public, and what issues the administration will push during the first year. These "who, what, where, why, and when" of politics set the stage for not only how the administration will operate but how the public, Congress, and media will view and respond to the new administration.

"Power is not automatically transferred, but must be seized. Only the *authority* of the presidency is transferred on January 20; the *power* of the presidency—in terms of effective control of the policy agenda—must be consciously developed."[49] To seize power, presidents must adopt a strategic approach to the transition, one that leaves little to chance and that deals self-consciously with the use of power.

Presidential scholars agree that a president's first one hundred days and first six to ten months are crucial periods for setting the agenda. It is important to win at least a few key legislative victories as soon as possible.

Strong presidents such as Woodrow Wilson, Franklin Roosevelt, Lyndon Johnson, and Ronald Reagan began with clear goals and pushed Congress to approve bold new programs. Indeed, each new president is in effect invited in the first year to share a vision and a national agenda with attentive Washington, national, and international audiences.

When Reagan took office, for example, his administration self-consciously chose to focus on a select few big-ticket items: tax cuts and increased defense spending. Nearly all else, including important foreign policy matters, were put on the back burner. This allowed the Reagan administration to concentrate its energies and also conveyed an image that this president could succeed. He appeared to be, and for a time was, influential.

Scholars often point to the Reagan honeymoon as an example of how to get the most out of early opportunities. Reagan had an attractive personality, a compelling television presence, a vision that he ably shared, and a clear focus on only a few key ideas. During his transition, his key advisers put together, with little involvement from the president-elect, a narrow, focused agenda and initiated a public relations and legislative blitzkrieg that ended in the president gaining much of his early legislative agenda. This in turn added to the aura of power surrounding Reagan, and made it easier for him to win subsequent contests because the Congress "feared" him.

In contrast, George H. W. Bush virtually relinquished the advantages offered by the honeymoon period. He got off to a slow start and appeared more concerned with managing a response to events as they happened than with shaping events by his actions. His early weeks were marked by caution.

Bush signaled early on that there was not going to be a Bush Revolution, a New Deal, or a Great Society. Pundits searching for a label suggested it might be the "Beige" or "Bland Deal." Conservative columnist George Will noted the absence of any large purpose or specificity and labeled Bush the "pastel president." A *Wall Street Journal* evaluation of George H. W. Bush's first one hundred days found him blending into the landscape, reacting to events, and allowing Congress or others to set the national agenda. Bush rarely gave the American people a sense of where he wanted to lead.[50]

George W. Bush had a different problem. He assumed office in a disputed election, only after a razor-thin Supreme Court majority interceded and selected him president. Bush had to establish his legitimacy and viability to a skeptical nation. To his credit, Bush did assert his authority and was able to head off challenges to his legitimacy. Yet he was regularly challenged with recessions, terrorism, and enormously complicated foreign policy events in Afghanistan, Iraq, and North Korea.

A president's strategic sense must also take into account other key elements of presidential power maximization: popularity and public opinion, relations with and the number of the president's party members in Congress, media relations, management skills, control of the agenda, and coalition and consensus building.

## MORE POWER TO THE PRESIDENCY: AN ENDURING THEME

Americans may have lost confidence in many of their leaders, yet they have not lost hope in the efficacy of strong purposive leadership. Back in the 1970s, all the revelations about the crimes of Watergate and the dramatic resignation of a president lulled people into believing perhaps that "the system worked," that checks checked and balances balanced. Perhaps the very cataloging of the misuses of presidential powers solved, or seemed to solve, the problem. By 1980 people were asking, "Whatever happened to the imperial presidency?" Since the end of the Watergate era, the public has been more comfortable with efforts at strong presidential leadership. They welcomed Ronald Reagan's efforts at moving the system, and have generally been more responsive to calls for presidential power. In the wake of the terrorist attack against the United States in late 2001, the public seemed somewhat comfortable with an assertion of presidential power that was expansive.

In the aftermath of the wounded or imperiled presidency of the Watergate era, could Congress furnish the leadership necessary to govern the country? Most scholars and writers said no. Even in the wake of the Gingrich-led Republican House of the mid-1990s, most commentators questioned the ability of Congress to present coherent national policies. The conventional answer was that "we will need a presidency of substantial power" if we are to get on top of our domestic problems and maintain our leadership position in foreign affairs.

Americans still yearn, at least on occasion, for dynamic, reassuring, and strong leadership. Watergate, Iran-Contra, and Bill Clinton's scandals notwithstanding, we still celebrate the gutsy, aggressive presidents—even if many of them did violate the legal and constitutional niceties of our separation-of-powers ideal. We remember Kennedy's command of press conferences, Lyndon Johnson's mastery of Congress, Reagan's humor, and Bill Clinton's speaking ability. The era of the strong president is here to stay. People want it that way.

The central challenge is not to reduce the president's power to lead, to govern, and to persuade, but to ensure that the president is held accountable for the means he or she uses to lead, to govern, and to persuade.[1]

How you stand on the question of how strong the presidency should be depends usually on what policies you favor and how these policies are advanced or hampered by the president or by Congress. It matters too, of course, whether you like the person who is in the White House. If you approve of a president and most of that president's policies, the tendency is to believe that the president should be, to paraphrase Woodrow Wilson, free to be as big a leader as he or she can be.

## CONCLUSION

Bold, effective, sustained presidential leadership is uncommon. In those rare periods of leadership, presidents are able to animate citizens and mobilize government, develop a vision and establish an agenda, move Congress and lead the bureaucracy. Such presidents recast the arena of the politically possible. It has not happened often. The forces arrayed against a president usually have the upper hand. The power of lethargy is considerable.

The preconditions for effective presidential leadership are rarely in syncopation: skill, the right timing, a consensus, a governing coalition, popularity, vision, and a mandate. Presidents, to be effective leaders in a democratic system, must bring Hamiltonian energy to a Madisonian system for Jeffersonian ends. Few presidents can achieve this.

To succeed, presidents must be masters of the light (education, vision, mobilization) and the heat (power, bargaining). Given the incredible array of skills and circumstances necessary for presidents to succeed, no wonder many of them fail to live up to our expectations.

Some of the difficulty rests with individual presidents who lack valid programmatic ideas as well as sufficient political skill. Part of the challenge rests with the structural design of the American constitutional system, which separates and fragments power.

A tension will always exist between the need for leadership and the demands of democracy. The English historian James Bryce reminded us that "Perhaps no form of government needs great leaders so much as democracy."[52] But what kind of leadership? The strong, powerful direction of a heroic leader, or the gentle guiding hand of a teacher? We fear, as noted, that "strong leaders make a weak people," but can the people come together and accomplish their goals with weak leadership?[53] Proponents of robust democracy realize that leadership has rarely fit comfortably with democracy in America. "The claim of leaders to political precedence violates the equality of democratic citizens," writes Bruce Miroff. "The most committed democrats have been suspicious of the very idea of leadership. When Thomas Paine railed against the 'slavish custom of following leaders,' he expressed a democrat's deepest anxiety."[54]

This tension has not prevented Americans from looking to strong leaders to guide the republic, especially during an emergency. As historian Arthur M. Schlesinger, Jr., noted,

> The American democracy has readily resorted in practice to the very leadership it had disclaimed in theory. An adequate democratic theory must recognize that democracy is not self-executing: that leadership is not the enemy of self-government but the means of making it work; that followers have their own stern obligation, which is to keep leaders within rigorous constitutional bounds; and that Caesarism is more often produced by the failure of feeble governments than by the success of energetic ones.[55]

There are ways to bring leadership and democracy together in a creative tension that calls for a role for the leader while also promoting participation and practices among the citizenry. Just as Abraham Lincoln gave us a succinct definition of democracy as "government of the people, by the people, and for the people," so too did one of America's other Mt. Rushmore leaders give us an appropriate definition of democratic leadership. Thomas Jefferson believed that the primary duties of a leader in a democracy were "to inform the minds of the people, and to follow their will."[56]

Informing the minds of the people speaks to the role of leader as educator. In a democracy, the leader has a responsibility to educate, enlighten, and inform the people. He or she must identify the problems and mobilize the people to act. By informing or educating the citizenry, the leader also engages in a dialogue, the ultimate goal of which is to involve leader and citizen in the process of developing a vision, grounded in the values of the nation, that will animate future action.

The leader's task in a democracy is to look ahead, foresee problems, focus the public's attention on the work that must be done, provide alternative courses of action, chart a path for the future, and move the nation in support of ideas. Former President Jimmy Carter nicely adds that "a government's ultimate goals are to preserve security and to insure justice: to treat people fairly, to guarantee their rights, to alleviate suffering and to try to resolve disputes peacefully."[57] No small order.

# Presidents in a Separated System

And people talk about the powers of a President, all the powers that a Chief Executive has, and what he can do. Let me tell you something. . . . The President may have a great many powers given to him in the Constitution and may have certain powers under certain laws which are given to him by the Congress of the United States; but the principal power that the President has is to bring people in and try to persuade them to do what they ought to do without persuasion. That's what the powers of the President amount to.

Harry S. Truman, *Public Papers of the Presidents of the United States* (U.S. Government Printing Office, 1949), p. 247

I find that when things go badly, it becomes our business. When the stock market goes down, letters are addressed to the White House. When it goes up, we get comparatively few letters of appreciation. But when you have high unemployment, it is because the President hasn't gotten the country moving again.

John F. Kennedy, quoted in H. W. Chase and A. H. Lerman, eds., *Kennedy and the Press* (Crowell, 1965), pp. 426–27

You have heard about the man tarred and feathered and ridden out of town on a rail? A man in the crowd asked him how he liked it, and his reply was that if it wasn't for the honor of the thing, he would much rather walk.

Abraham Lincoln, reply to a friend who asked how it felt to be president, c. 1862

Anyone searching for the paradoxes of the American presidency need look no further than the president's informal as well as formal job description: high expectations yet limited power; many demands, few resources. We expect presidents to accomplish great things, yet tie their hands. Of course, the job of the president has changed and enlarged dramatically since 1789. While the constitutional provisions relating to presidential power remain virtually unchanged, the responsibilities and expectations placed on the office have increased significantly.

Historians still debate the motives of the framers of the U.S. Constitution. Were they great democrats or protectors of the propertied interests? Did they attempt to empower or enfeeble government? Did they retreat from full democracy because they feared the people or because they were responsible leaders who saw a representative government as most likely to protect liberty and achieve stability?[1]

Whether great advocates of or traitors to robust democracy, it is clear the framers harbored concerns about both mass-based democracy and executive tyranny. These concerns are evident when one examines the inventing of the American presidency.

To understand what is expected of presidents today, we need to examine the invention of the presidency as well as its evolution over time. Only then can we fully appreciate the many roles and demands placed on the presidency.

### THE PRESIDENCY AS DEFINED AND DEBATED IN 1787

The presidential job description as outlined in the Constitution was a series of compromises. The framers wanted a presidency strong enough to do what was asked of it and yet not one that would use governmental authority for selfish ends or contrary to the general welfare. In almost every instance presidential powers were shared powers. Perhaps only the pardon power was a truly imperial grant of power.

Despite the administrative, diplomatic, commander-in-chief, and veto powers granted to them, presidents found they had to act within a set of strong constitutional, political, and social restraints. They had to be sensitive to the dominant elites, the cultural "rules of the game," and, of course, the threat of being impeached or turned out of office at the next election.

The writers of the U.S. Constitution created, by design, what some call an "antileadership" system of government. Their goal was less to provide for an efficient system of government than one that would not jeopardize liberty. Freedom was their goal; governmental power their concern. The constitutional framers who toiled through that hot summer of 1787 in Philadelphia thus created an executive institution, a presidency, that had limited powers.

The framers primarily wanted to counteract two fears: the fear of the mob (democracy, or mobocracy), and the fear of monarchy (centralized, tyrannical executive power). The menacing image of England's King George III, against whom the colonists rebelled and whom Thomas Paine called "the Royal Brute of Britain," served as a powerful reminder of the dangers of a strong executive. To contain power they set up an executive office that was constitutionally rather weak (Congress had, on paper at least, most of the power), based on the rule of law, with a separation of powers, ensuring a system of checks and balances.

To James Madison, the chief architect of the Constitution, a government with too much power was a dangerous government. A student of history, he believed human nature drove people to pursue self-interest, and therefore a system of government designed to have "ambition checked by ambition" set within rather strict limits was the only hope to establish a stable government that did not endanger liberty. Realizing that "enlightened statesmen" would not always guide the nation, Madison embraced a checks and balance system of separate but overlapping and shared powers. Madison's concern for a government that controlled and limited powers is seen throughout his writings, yet nowhere is it more vivid than when he wrote in *Federalist Papers No. 51,* "You must first enable the government to control the governed; and in the next place, oblige it to control itself."[2]

Yes, government was to have enough power to govern, but no, it could not have enough power to overwhelm freedom. If one branch were empowered to check another, tyranny might be thwarted. There is scant concern in Madison's writings for the needs of a strong government. Thus, the Constitution was both an enabling and a constraining document.

Alexander Hamilton emerged as the chief defender of a powerful executive. An advocate of strong central government, Hamilton promoted, especially in the *Federalist Papers,* a version of executive power different from Madison's dispersed and separate powers. Where Madison wanted to check authority, Hamilton wished to enhance authority; where Madison believed the new government's powers should be "few and defined," Hamilton wanted to infuse the executive with "energy": A feeble executive implies a feeble execution of the government. A feeble execution is but another phrase for a bad execution; and a government ill executed, whatever it may be in theory, must be, in practice, a bad government.[3]

Hamilton wanted a strong president within a more centralized government. Yet such a system would undermine Madison's determination to check government power—the presidency, a unitary office headed by one person, would have no internal check. Thus Madison insisted on the need for strong external checks, that is, a strong Congress. While Madison may have won the day at the Convention, creating a presidency with fairly limited powers, history has generally been on Hamilton's side.

Looming in the background was the influential presence of Thomas Jefferson. Friendly toward small government and democracy, Jefferson was suspicious of power. But Jefferson's vision of a decentralized government, an agrarian economy, and a robust democracy was given little attention at the convention.

The Madisonian model calls for both protections against mass democracy and limits on governmental power. This is not to say the founders wanted a weak and ineffective government—had that been their goal they could have kept the Articles of Confederation. But they did want a government that could not act too easily. The theory of government the Madisonian design necessitates is one of consensus, coalition, and cooperation on the one hand and checks, vetoes, and balances on the other.

The result is, as stated, a rather weak presidency with few independent powers. The paradox thus created, especially in the modern period, is, again, how can a president bring Hamiltonian energy to this Madisonian system for Jeffersonian ends? The framers did not make it easy for the government to act or for presidents to lead. That was decidedly not their intent. And they left the powers and contours of the office somewhat vague—expecting Washington to fill in the gaps. This created, in Edward S. Corwin's words, "an invitation to struggle" for control of government.[4] A modern efficiency expert, looking at the framers' design for government, would likely conclude that the system could not work well: too many limits, too many checks, not enough power, not enough leadership. But this is the way the framers wanted it.

The Constitution does not clearly spell out the power of the presidency. Article I is devoted to the Congress, the first and constitutionally the most powerful branch of government. Article II, the executive article, deals with the presidency. The president's power cupboard is, compared with that of the Congress, nearly bare or at least vague. Section 1 gives the "executive power" to the president, but does not reveal whether this is a grant of tangible power or merely a title. Section 2 makes the president commander-in-chief, but reserves the power to declare war for the Congress. Section 2 also gives the president power to grant reprieves and pardons, power to make treaties (with the advice and consent of the Senate), and power to nominate ambassadors, judges, and other public ministers (with the advice and consent of the Senate). Section 3 calls for the president to inform the Congress on the state of the union and to recommend measures to Congress; grants the power to receive ambassadors; and imposes on the president the duty to see that the laws are faithfully executed. These powers are significant, yet in and of themselves do not suggest a strong or independent leadership institution.

Thus, the president has two types of power: *formal,* the ability to command; and *informal,* the ability to persuade. The president's formal powers are limited and (often) shared. The president's informal powers are a function of skill, situation, and political time. While the formal powers of the president remain fairly constant over time, the informal powers are variable, dependent on the skill of the individual president. This is not to say a president's formal powers are static—over time presidential power has increased significantly—but the pace of change has been such that it was over one hundred years before the presidency assumed primacy in the U.S. political system.

The structure of government dispersed or fragmented power; there is no recognized, authoritative vital center; power is fluid and floating; no one branch could easily or freely act without the consent of another branch; power was designed to counteract power; ambition to check ambition. It was a structure designed to force a consensus before the government could act. The structure of government created by the framers did not create *a* leadership institution, but three separate semiautonomous institutions that shared power. One scholar concluded, "the framers designed a system of shared powers within a system that is purposefully biased against change."[5]

## THE PRESIDENCY AS REDEFINED BY WASHINGTON AND HIS SUCCESSORS

As noted, the Constitution was the result of bargains and compromises. One area of dispute was the power the new president would be granted. Unable to come to terms with this question, the framers were forced to leave the powers of the president somewhat ambiguous. This was not especially troublesome because they knew who the first president would be: George Washington. The framers held Washington in such high regard that they were confident he would set the proper tone for the office.

George Washington loomed large in the early republic. Washington sailed in uncharted waters and is credited with establishing generally sound precedents.[6] He lent dignity to this newly invented presidency, developed a version of consensus leadership where possible and executive independence where necessary, was guided by the rule of law and recognized the limits of his power, and generally remained true to the requirements of constitutional government. Above all, he established the legitimacy of the office of president.[7]

Keenly aware that as the first occupant of the presidential office his every act of commission and omission would be noticed, scrutinized, and perhaps established as precedent, Washington was careful to establish the independence of the office yet still respect the integrity of the Congress. Shortly after his inauguration he commented that "many things which appear of little importance in themselves . . . may have great and durable consequences from their having been established at the commencement of a new general government."[8] Washington also imposed his regal persona and his republican sentiments on the new office, and in effect, brought to life what the framers had merely invented.

Following Washington, the power of the presidency rose and fell depending on circumstances, the will of the president, and the demands of the time.[9] Thomas Jefferson (1801–9) stretched the powers of the presidency, using the nascent political party to aid in achieving his goals.[10] Andrew Jackson (1829–37) asserted the independence of the presidency and linked his power to the people. Jacksonian democracy represented a broadening of democracy and a connection between the president and the people about which the framers were suspicious. Jackson portrayed himself as the "tribune of the people" and asserted a brand of leadership linked to popularity.[11]

Abraham Lincoln (1861–65) demonstrated that during a crisis, the powers of the presidency could be expanded. Using a combination of claimed emergency and war powers, Lincoln took bold action during the Civil War, blockading Southern ports, calling up the militia, arresting persons suspected of disloyalty, suspending the writ of habeas corpus, all without congressional authorization. Lincoln knew he had intruded into areas of congressional authority, yet claimed the doctrine of necessity as his justification.[12]

During the presidency of Theodore Roosevelt (1901–9) the United States emerged as a world power, intent on making its mark on the international stage. TR aggressively asserted presidential power both at home and abroad, and reestablished presidential primacy. Roosevelt used the presidency as a "bully pulpit" and contributed to the rise of what is called the "rhetorical presidency,"[13] seeing the president as the "steward of the people." Viewing power expansively, TR asserted that "it was not only his right but his duty to do anything that the needs of the nation demanded unless such action was forbidden by the Constitution or by the laws. . . . Under this interpretation of executive power I did and caused to be done many things not previously done by the president and the heads of the departments. I did not usurp power, but I did greatly broaden the use of executive power."[14]

The presidency of Woodrow Wilson (1913–21) further established the United States as a world power and the presidency as a pivotal center or lever of American government. Wilson used powerful rhetorical skills in conjunction with a reliance on party and programmatic leadership to establish the presidency as the guiding force for the nation. Combined with his leadership during World War I, Wilson elevated the office of presidency to one of national and international leadership.[15]

Mixed in between the Jeffersons, the Lincolns, and the TRs were a series of lesser or even lackluster presidents who often diminished the office. For every Jackson, there was a Tyler; for every Lincoln, a Grant; for every Wilson, a Harding. Yet if there were presidential underachievers along with those who stretched the boundaries of presidential power, clearly the institutional trend was in the direction of growing influence.

## THE PRESIDENCY AS REDEFINED BY FDR AND THE MODERN PRESIDENTS

The institution of the presidency as we know it today was born in the 1930s. The stepchild of depression and war, it was during the Franklin D. Roosevelt era (1933–45) that the presidency became a truly modern institution.

The economic depression of 1929 and the world war a decade later contributed to the presidency-centered nature of our national government, and the leadership style and skill of FDR confirmed the United States (for better or worse) as a presidential nation.

FDR, considered by presidential scholars to be one of the nation's greatest presidents, was a powerful and effective chief executive. Under his leadership the presidency became the prime mover of the American system, and people began to look to the federal government and to the presidency as the nation's problem solver. The federal government had grown, and with it presidential responsibilities, ending the era in which presidents such as Calvin Coolidge could claim that his greatest accomplishment was "minding my own business."

Roosevelt's success transformed both the presidency and public attitudes about it. He created expectations of presidential power and leadership that would be imposed on his successors. The "heroic" model of the presidency was established as a result of FDR's leadership, and for the next forty years, presidential scholars would often promote the model as good and necessary. FDR's successors would labor in his dominant shadow.[16]

If Roosevelt was an important president, the myth of FDR took on even greater stature. An inflated view of Roosevelt passed for fact in popular and scholarly mythology of the presidency. He was, of course, not as powerful as many remembered him.

Truman assumed the presidency in the final days of World War II. In an effort to hasten an end to the war, Truman ordered atomic bombs to be dropped on Japan. After the war, it was Truman and his advisers who implemented the "containment" policy toward the Soviet Union, a policy each succeeding president would, more or less, follow until the end of the Cold War. Truman presided over the Marshall Plan for European recovery, helped establish the North Atlantic Treaty Organization (NATO), and led the United States back to a postwar domestic economic revival. It was also under Truman that the Korean War began.

To the surprise of most of his contemporaries, Truman became an effective president, though his popularity could never match that of FDR, and it would be only much later that his contribution was fully appreciated. This created a sense in which people said, "Surely if *he* can do the job, there must be something inherent in the office which brings out greatness in even the most common of men." Thus was born the "FDR halo," which could be passed down from president to president, a kind of magic that seemed to confer special powers on the occupant of the White House.

When Dwight D. Eisenhower became president in 1953, the Republican lent a bipartisan air to the majesty of the office. While not an activist president, Ike did manage to exert a hidden-hand type of leadership in an era where the public seemed anxious to take a break from the hurly-burly world of politics.[17] After all, the United States had been through a depression in the '30s, a world war in the '40s, and a nascent cold war in the late '40s and early '50s, and by the Eisenhower era the American people welcomed a low-profile leader. Ike, with a low-key, almost apolitical style, gave them what they wanted. He was popular, especially for a president who seemed to do little, and his popularity extended across the entire eight years of his tenure.

If the FDR halo seemed to be in limbo during the Eisenhower years, Ike's successor was determined to revive it. John Kennedy proposed an activist administration. Yet try as he might, President Kennedy's legislative proposals often fell prey to unresponsive leaders in Congress. Stymied by an intransigent Congress that took the system of checks and balances quite seriously, the Kennedy legislative record was at best mixed. The first Roman Catholic ever to be elected president, Kennedy barely won the presidency in 1960. Kennedy was responsible for the Bay of Pigs fiasco in Cuba, placed thousands of military advisers in Vietnam, and successfully led the nation through the Cuban missile crisis. His few progressive domestic initiatives, however, were blocked by a Congress controlled by conservatives in his own party. Kennedy did achieve tax cuts that stimulated economic growth, started the Peace Corps, and outlined the need for civil rights reform.

Scholars were as captivated as anyone at the prospect of a strong president leading the fragmented system to new heights, overcoming the chains of the checks and balances, and achieving mighty and good ends. A sampling of quotes from the classic *The American Presidency* by Clinton Rossiter, first published in 1956, gives an indication of the status and esteem in which even the conservative Rossiter held the presidency.

- Few nations have solved so simply and yet grandly the problem of finding and maintaining an office or state that embodies their majesty and reflects their character . . .

- There is virtually no limit to what the President can do if he does it for democratic ends and by democratic means . . .

- He reigns, but he also rules; he symbolizes the people, but he also runs their government . . .

- The President is not a Gulliver immobilized by ten thousand tiny cords, nor even a Prometheus chained to a rock of frustration. He is, rather, a kind of magnificent lion who can roam widely and do great deeds so long as he does not try to break loose from his broad reservation.[18]

Rossiter wrote that the American presidency was "one of the few truly successful institutions created by men in their endless quest for the blessings of free government." He concluded:

> It is, finally, an office of freedom. The Presidency is a standing reproach to those petty doctrinaires who insist that executive power is inherently undemocratic; for, to the exact contrary, it has been more responsive to the needs and dreams of giant democracy than any other office or institution in the whole mosaic of American life. . . . The vast power of this office has not been "poison," as Henry Adams wrote in scorn; rather, it has elevated often and corrupted never, chiefly because those who held it recognized the true source of the power and were ennobled by the knowledge.[19]

Rossiter was not alone in his celebration of the presidency and presidential power. Plenty of other scholars joined in the chorus, viewing the president as the indispensible agent of reform. We can thus see the intellec-

John F. Kennedy's inclination to be an activist president was often stymied by a recalcitrant Congress. (*Source:* Reproduced from the collections of the Library of Congress.)

tual origins of what is called the "textbook presidency," a charismatic leader who was good, powerful, and essential.

A presidency-centered model that came to dominate thinking was more than an operating style of government, it was also a philosophy of governing. It was an operating style in that it promoted a system of government in which the president was to direct or lead the people and the other branches of government from a perch of great power. It was a philosophy of government in that it legitimized a strong central government, which took power away from the other branches and, perhaps more important, took power from the people, and vested responsibility in the hands of government (the president) to solve problems. This diminished democratic responsibility in the people (a Jeffersonian goal), and promoted responsibility and power in the leadership class (a Hamiltonian goal). It also failed to recognize the potential danger of the heroic leadership model.

Lyndon Johnson's notable legislative achievements in the wake of the tragic assassination of John Kennedy confirmed for many the wisdom of the strong presidency model. The FDR halo was revived. Lyndon Johnson temporarily brought the strong presidency model back to life.

If the public suspended its skepticism about a strong presidency and placed its faith in the heroic model, why did scholars go along? There were voices in the wilderness, warning of the dangers of unchecked presidential power,[20] but in general scholars, like the public, were intrigued by or perhaps seduced by the strong presidency.

Just when the public was lulled into a false sense of complacency and security concerning the benevolence of presidential power, however, the war in Vietnam and the reaction against it caused everyone to rethink our assumptions.

U.S. involvement in Vietnam began quietly, escalated incrementally, and eventually led to tragedy. By 1968, the United States was engaged in a war it could not win and from which it could not (honorably) withdraw. It was a "presidential war," and it brought the Johnson administration to its knees.

As U.S. involvement escalated, and as victory seemed further and further away, blame was placed squarely on the shoulders of President Johnson. While the Constitution gives the power to declare war to the Congress, since the Truman administration, presidents had generally acted unilaterally in Vietnam. By the time Johnson came to office, presidents had been setting policy in Vietnam for twenty years, virtually unencumbered by the Congress. The tragedy of Lyndon Johnson is that after a positive start, after important legislative successes, the problem of Vietnam would overwhelm him and the nation. The nation was torn apart. The strong presidency, so long seen as critically important for the American system, now seemed too powerful, too unchecked, in short, a threat. After years of hearing calls for "more power to the president," by the late 1960s the plea was to rein in the overly powerful White House.

It was a rude awakening. All the hopes, all the trust, all the expectations that had been entrusted to the presidency had been jolted.

If Vietnam led to questions about the power of the presidency, Johnson's successor Richard Nixon would raise new concerns about that power. With the constitutional crisis known as Watergate, Richard Nixon, named an "unindicted co-conspirator" by a grand jury, became the nation's first president to resign from office.

As a reaction against the perceived abuses of power by Johnson and Nixon, Congress attempted to reassert its power. The Ford and Carter presidencies, rather than being imperial, seemed imperiled. It was a time of presidents being constrained.

In the 1980s, Ronald Reagan began to resurrect presidential power. Yet his several successes were matched, if not overshadowed, by enormous budget deficits and the Iran-Contra scandal.

Americans yearned for a strong leader, one who could solve problems, one who would flex America's muscles. Enter Ronald Reagan, a presidential knight in shining armor. Reagan seemed to be everything Ford and Carter weren't: strong and self-assured. He made promises, spoke about grand visions, built expectations. He attempted to return to an era of American grandeur.

Claiming a bold mandate and focusing on several key economic items, Reagan managed to get much of his agenda enacted. But after an impressive start, Reagan faltered. Initial success in dealing with Congress gave way to frustration and defeat. The president could not overcome the system's road-blocks, and, unwilling to accept the limits placed upon the office, he and members of his administration went beyond the law and abused power.

Reagan's engaging personality and ready wit helped make him popular, and while his borrow-borrow, spend-spend approach to policy may have added to America's military might, it also left the nation on the brink of economic insolvency. The United States went from being the world's largest creditor/lender nation in 1980 to becoming the world's largest debtor/borrower nation in the late 1980s.

The presidency under George H. W. Bush was in a state of suspended animation. A man of grayness or beige, Bush seemed to many people a manager at a time when the nation needed a leader. The end of the Cold War opened a window of opportunity to exert creative leadership. But Bush was shackled by a vastly depleted resource base (the legacy of Reagan's economic miscalculations) and an intellectual cupboard that was bare (little vision for a post–Cold War future). Bush often seemed a passive observer in a dramatically changing world.

Bush was at his best when he had a clear goal to achieve (e.g., the Gulf War), a goal imposed upon him by events. But when it came time for him to choose, to set priorities, to decide upon direction, he floundered. As columnist George Will commented, "When the weight of the [presidency] is put upon a figure as flimsy as George Bush, the presidency buckles. . . ."[21]

The Clinton presidency proved to be one of the most paradoxical and fascinating roller-coaster rides in history. Bill Clinton was a brilliant rogue. He was a masterful politician. He was also a man severely character challenged. His serial affairs and dishonesty about them resulted in the most extensive investigations ever launched into the conduct of a president.

He was a gifted empathizer yet also a national seducer. He brought out the worst in his adversaries as he tried to bring out the best in the American people. In the end, he was saved by the enemies who so hated him that they overplayed their hand and ended up turning the public against the accusers. In 1995, after the Republican electoral landslide, Clinton looked like a lame if not a dead duck. But Newt Gingrich, in all his self-indulgence, led by a slash-and-burn style of politics, stepped in to help orchestrate a governmental shutdown that made Clinton look good, and probably granted him victory in the 1996 presidential contest. And during the dark days of impeachment, when Clinton's adversaries had in their hands a credible case for impeachment, his enemies again stepped in and saved him. Independent Counsel Kenneth Starr and the House Republicans offered an alternative that forced the public into the president's corner, again saving him from himself.

Clinton's "Third Way" (between the liberal left of the Democratic party and the hard right of the Republicans) often allowed him to "triangulate" himself between two political extremes, and offer voters a moderate alternative to the old style left-right models.

History will probably place Clinton somewhere in the middle of the pack of presidents. Not great, not a failure. His many political successes will salvage something, yet his personal faults will haunt him. He is indeed a complex, contradictory man, and his presidency reflected his talents as well as his complexity.

After a hotly disputed election, George W. Bush, son of George H. W. Bush, assumed the presidency. Bush initially promoted tax cuts and education reform. But his presidency changed dramatically after the terrorist attack against the United States on September 11, 2001.

The attack changed the political circumstances under which Bush governed, and created a "crisis presidency." Power shifted to the White House, as the public, Congress, and much of the world community rallied behind the president.

The 9-11 attack gave the administration, at least for a while, a focus. It also removed many of the normal restraints that impeded presidential authority prior to the attack. The public rallied behind the president. Congress supported Bush. The Democratic opposition gave Bush nearly a free hand to act. Other nations, again, at least for a while, gave support.

How would Bush use this power? The president already had in place an experienced foreign and defense policy team. They were given a clear goal: stop terrorism. And the usually complex world was reduced to a simple equation: terrorists were the enemy, they had to be defeated! It was a single-minded goal and it gave drive and focus to the administration.

Initially, the president's goal was clear: go after the Al Qaeda terror network and overthrow the Taliban government in Afghanistan. An international coalition helped weaken the Al Qaeda network, and a short, successful war in which the Taliban were overthrown gave the president key early victories in the war against terrorism.

But when the president turned his attention to Iraq and Saddam Hussein, a long time thorn in the side of the United States, things got more complicated and more messy. The administration was determined to overthrow Hussein, and when initial efforts to take the case for war to the United Nations failed to generate support for a war in Iraq, the administration cobbled together what it called the "coalition of the willing" (essentially the U.S. and Great Britain) and launched a war against Iraq.

The war generated vigorous opposition from nations across the globe, including, France, Germany, Russia and other allies. World opinion, which was strongly supportive of the United States in the year after the 9-11 terrorist attack, turned against the United States.

A Gallup Poll taken in January of 2003 asked if respondents had a positive or negative attitude towards U.S. foreign policy. The results were disturbing. In Spain, negative reactions outstripped the positive 57 percent to 9 percent, in Russia 55 percent to 11 percent, in Argentina 58 percent to 13 percent and in Pakistan 46 percent to 8 percent. Results such as these led British historian Sir Michael Howard to note "a year after September 11, the United

States finds itself more unpopular than perhaps it has ever been in its history."[22]

Amid this wave of opposition to U.S. policy, the administration has promoted the use of a "first strike" policy. Stressing preemption over deterrence, military superiority over all possible rivals and a willingness to use force as a tool of policy, it was a policy that according to a *New York Times* editorial, "bristles with bold assertions of American power."[23]

The president also faced criticism for undermining certain constitutional rights and liberties of U.S. citizens. His attorney general, John Ashcroft, used the USA Patriot Act and also claimed inherent rights in wartime to imprison citizens without charge, deny them the right to see an attorney, prevent them from being brought to court for hearings, and even imprison children in detention camps in Cuba without access to an attorney. While the courts gave the president considerable leeway in these areas, critics argued that the president was unnecessarily violating the Constitution and denying Americans their constitutional rights.

In the aftermath of the war against Iraq, the president was forced to defend himself against claims that he had misled the public, Congress, and the international community in the run up to war. George W. Bush made the case for war on the basis of claims that Iraq had weapons of mass destruction, and was thereby a direct and imminent threat to the United States and our allies. But after the war it seemed the administration had oversold the case and in some instances, knowingly fudged the data.[24]

## THE JOB OF THE MODERN PRESIDENT

Nowadays a president is asked to do countless things that are not spelled out with any clarity in the Constitution. We want the president to be a national cheerleader as well as an international peacemaker, a moral leader as well as the nation's chief economic manager, a politician-in-chief, and a unifying representative of all the people. We want every new president to be everything, at least of virtue, that all our great presidents have been. No matter that the great presidents were not as great as we think they were. Rightly or wrongly, we believe our greatest presidents were individuals of talent, tenacity, and optimism, leaders who could clarify the vital issues of the day and mobilize the nation for action. Our great presidents were transforming leaders who could not only move the enterprise forward but could summon the highest kinds of moral commitment from the American people.

Yet rarely is a president a free agent. They nearly always mirror the fundamental forces of society: the values, the myths, the quest for order and stability, and the vast, inert, and usually conservative forces that maintain the existing balance of interests. Ours is a system decidedly weighted against radical leadership, a system that encourages most presidents, most of the time, to respond to the powerful, organized, and already represented interests at the expense of the unrepresented. Moreover, a president today must preside over a highly specialized and sprawling bureaucracy as well.

Reality, as well as expectations, expanded and recast the presidency, and has organized it around three major interrelated policy areas that we may call subpresidencies: (1) foreign affairs and national security, (2) aggregate economics, and (3) domestic policy, or "quality of life," issues. A president's time is absorbed by one or another of these competing policy spheres, and the staff and cabinet have come to be organized around these three substantive areas.

## The Foreign Affairs Presidency

Modern presidents concentrate on foreign and national security policy, often at the expense of the other policy areas. This is understandable. Since World War II, the United States has been the hegemonic, or dominant, power of the Western alliance. Since the break up of the Soviet Empire in 1989, the United States has been recognized as the major superpower in the world. Yet today, with the war against terrorism, matters of foreign policy continue to loom large. U.S. world leadership for the past sixty years has been linked to presidential power: a strong America necessitated, so many believed, a strong presidency. Thus, presidents focused increased attention on foreign affairs.

To be sure, an exclusively foreign, economic, or domestic problem is a rarity, and many issues intersect all three areas. Critical problems such as trade, inflation, energy development, drug abuse, or environmental problems, not to mention war, require planning and policy leadership that cut across the three presidencies. Still, a close examination of how presidents have spent their time in recent decades suggests that foreign policy matters (often crises) have driven out domestic policy matters. Economic matters usually come in second.

The founding politicians never intended a president to be the dominant agent in national policymaking, yet they did anticipate the president to be the major influence in foreign affairs. In the eighteenth century, foreign affairs were generally thought to be an executive matter. The first task for a national leader is the nation's survival and national defense. Today, especially in the nuclear age, foreign policy responsibilities cannot be delegated: they are executive in character and presidential by constitutional tradition or interpretation. After the Bay of Pigs tragedy, President Kennedy vividly emphasized the central importance of foreign policy: "It really is true," he told a visiting Richard Nixon, "that foreign affairs is the only important issue for a President to handle. . . . I mean, who gives a s . . . if the minimum wage is $1.15 or $1.25, in comparison to something like this [the Bay of Pigs]?"[25]

Kennedy frequently said the difference between domestic and foreign policy was the difference between a bill being defeated and the country being wiped out. Both Kennedy and Nixon were personally more fascinated with foreign policy than with domestic or economic policy. Both wanted history to record that they had laid the foundation for peace not only in their own time but also for generations to come. President Carter spent more time on the Middle East issue than on any other matter during his first three years in office. Panama Canal politics and relations with the Soviet Union and China were preoccupations as well. He confessed he liked dealing with foreign policy because his capacity to act unilaterally seemed much greater in the foreign than in the domestic realm. President Reagan, after an initial flirtation with economic policy, spent most of his last six years concentrating on foreign affairs. George H. W. Bush had almost exclusively a foreign policy focus.[26] Bill Clinton, who had an ambitious domestic and economic policy agenda, found himself spending more and more time on foreign affairs as problems such as Haiti, Bosnia, Russia, the Middle East, and North Korea forced their way onto his agenda. And George W. Bush was forced to devote most attention to the war against terrorism and his efforts in Iraq.

White House advisers from all the recent administrations agree presidents spend at least half of their time on foreign policy or national security deliberations. In some instances, this emphasis on foreign policy and national security has occurred by choice, most notably for President Nixon, who said, "I've always thought this country could run itself domestically—without a President; all you need is a competent Cabinet to run the country at home. You need a President for foreign policy; no Secretary of State is really important; the President makes foreign policy."[27] President G. H. W. Bush also had a much greater personal interest in foreign affairs as opposed to domestic policy. President Johnson, on the other hand, was strongly disposed by experience toward domestic programs, but was unable to prevent his presidency from being consumed by military affairs.

In addition, presidents naturally work hardest where they see both hope of success and leeway for significant personal impact. Former Nixon counsel Leonard Garment pointed to yet another reason when he explained Nixon's preference for foreign policy in this way to Theodore White: "In foreign policy, you get drama, triumph, resolution—crisis and resolution so that in foreign policy Nixon can give the sense of leadership. But in domestic policy, there you have to deal with the whole jungle of human problems."[28]

But presidents cannot focus on foreign affairs to the exclusion of the nation's domestic needs. George H. W. Bush is a case in point. After successfully winning the Persian Gulf War, Bush's popularity rose to historically unprecedented levels. Yet between January of 1991 and November of 1992, a slow economy and domestic drift led to electoral defeat.

Most scholars believe there are significant differences in the institutional balance of power when one compares the realms of domestic policy with foreign policy. Presidents, it is believed, have greater power in the foreign policy arena than they do in domestic and economic policy.

In the 1960s political scientist Aaron Wildavsky argued that since the end of the Second World War, presidents have been more successful at attaining their policy goals from Congress in foreign policy than in the domestic arena. Thus, Wildavsky concluded, a president is usually more effective in international affairs and foreign policy-making. Commenting on the power of the presidency in the international arena Wildavsky asserted, "there has not been a single major issue on which Presidents, when they were serious and determined, have failed."[29]

While Wildavsky's "two presidencies" notion may be oversimplified, it does highlight certain patterns. In foreign affairs, presidents can assert their will by being proactive, and force the Congress to be reactive. By setting policy, the president sets in motion events of his choosing. If Congress wishes to intercede, it does so in response to acts already taken. The initiative usually belongs to the president.

Constitutionally, the president may be on shaky ground, but in practical terms, it is difficult to stop a strong, assertive president in foreign affairs. Clinton's NATO intervention into Bosnia and George W. Bush's unilateral actions in response to the war against terrorism are cases in point. While all presidents claim their use of foreign policy power is grounded in the Constitution, such claims of independent authority are generally flimsy. It is the Congress, even in foreign affairs, that has the broadest and clearest constitutional mandate, but its power has atrophied due to lack of use.[30] Even the power to declare war, which is expressly granted to the Congress, has often slipped through the hands of the legislature. The *War Powers Act* and the Constitution notwithstanding, it is the president who, by acting, exercises primacy in war and foreign affairs.[31]

Much of foreign policy involves diplomatic activities that are generally under the purview of the executive, and in most areas, presidents simply presume authority to act. Likewise, much activity in foreign affairs does not require legislation,[32] and, to make matters worse (or better if you are a president), during a crisis presidents proceed with considerable authority and few checks.

Perhaps the chief power presidents have is the presumption that they speak for the nation to the world. This allows a president the opportunity to act, to make decisions, to announce policies, thereby preemptively eliminating most potential challengers. By preemptive initiatives, the president may tie the hands of potential rivals on the congressional side. To defy the president on a matter of national security often risks appearing unpatriotic, especially in moments of international crisis. Thus, presidents can sometime both muffle potential critics and force the Congress to submit to their will. Examples of Teddy Roosevelt sending the fleet halfway around the world in defiance of congressional budget restrictions, then saying, "I sent the fleet . . . will they leave them there?"; George H.W. Bush sending U.S. troops to the Middle East following the 1991 Iraqi invasion of Kuwait, preparing for war, building public support, *then* challenging Congress to issue a vote of support, or Clinton sending U.S. troops to Haiti in 1994, are examples of how presidents, by acting and forcing the hand of Congress, can get their way.[33]

Over the course of a term, presidents spend more and more time dealing with foreign affairs perhaps in part because they so often get frustrated being rebuffed in domestic and economic policy. They also, in recent years, became preoccupied with foreign and defense policy because the United States has troops in and is highly involved in military activities in South Korea, Bosnia, Afghanistan, the Phillipines, the Republic of Georgia, Kuwait, Iraq, and elsewhere.[34] Since presidents need to be seen as accomplishing things in order to maintain their reputation as "the leader," they almost naturally gravitate to the area in which their power in greatest. The irony, of course, is that the president has the greatest power in the area where he or she is probably most (potentially) dangerous and in need of controls and checks and balances, and is most controlled in the least dangerous area and the area most in need of leadership.

## The Economic Presidency

The second largest portion of presidential policy time is spent on macroeconomic policy; issues of monetary and fiscal policy such as trade and tariff policy, inflation, unemployment, the stability of the dollar, and the health of the stock market.

In the early days of the Republic, presidents had less involvement in the development of economic policies. The nation was young, not yet a world power, and Congress was in primary control of determining the budget and setting economic policy. Presidents began to get more involved in setting economic policy with passage of the Budget and Accounting Act of 1921. This law directed the president to formulate a national budget and created a Bureau of the Budget. The Pandora's box was opened. Beginning with Franklin D. Roosevelt, presidents began to expand their control over economic and budgetary matters.

During the 1930s, with the depression, the Supreme Court began to give judicial sanction to governmental and presidential intervention in the economy. The Constitution thus shifted from a limiting to an empowering document in presidential economic management. Since then, we have witnessed the development of a more "controlled" economy and the growth of presidential power in the economic sphere. In the post–World War II period, the passage of the Employment Act of 1946 further focused economic policy-making in the executive branch.

While the expectations of presidential responsibility and control of the economy have grown enormously over the past sixty-five years, the powers given to the president to manage the economy have not risen accordingly, creating yet another presidential paradox. We expect presidents to bring about economic breakthroughs, but rarely give them the power necessary to work miracles.

In recent years, presidential involvement in economic policy has grown to the point where primary responsibility for economic management largely rests in the White House. Historical circumstance, presidential desire, legislative acquiescence, and public expectation have all contributed to the emergence of a powerful, but limited, presidency in economic affairs. While congressional efforts to recapture their constitutional duty over the "power of the purse" are evident (e.g., the Congressional Budget and Impoundment Control Act of 1974), the president remains the central, yet not controlling, figure in setting economic policy for the nation.

A president can scarcely hide from the hard, visible quantitative economic indicators: unemployment rates, consumer price and inflation rates, the gross domestic product, interest and mortgage rates, commodity prices, oil import price levels, and stock-market and bond-market averages. In the era of instant cable and Internet news, these figures are available to everyone, at any time, and the American people increasingly judge and measure their presidents on whether they can cope aggressively with recession and inflation, can offer effective economic game plans (preferably without tax increases), and can use the nation's budget as an instrument for ensuring a healthy and growing economy. The complex issues of tax reform and income redistribution are always on the agenda of national politics.

But a president's statutory responsibilities for maintaining full employment and pursuing stabilization policies are not matched by political resources or available expertise. In most areas of our economy the public is relatively weak or unorganized, but an uneven performance by the economy will call down on a president immediate pressure from wealthy businesspeople, unions, and farmers and from their friends in Congress.

A further paradox of the president's role as economist-in-chief of the nation relates to the contradictory demands we place on the government. We want to cut spending, cut taxes, and cut the deficit, but we do not want any of "our" favorite programs cut (and every line in the budget is somebody's favorite). Most people want the government to do more but spend less. In a robust economy, the hard choices become easier, but in a staggering economy or one burdened with debt, all choices become painful—as George W. Bush found out in recent years.

## The Domestic Presidency

Presidents concentrate on those areas in which they believe they can make the greatest impact, in which the approval of interest groups and the public can be most easily rallied. Yet, involvement in domestic policy is costly both financially and politically. Moreover, newly elected presidents find that budgets are virtually fixed for the next year and a half if not longer, and that in domestic matters they are dependent on Congress, specialized bureaucracies, professions, and state and local officialdom. Is it surprising, then, that the implementation of domestic policy can become the orphan of presidential attention? Is it possible presidents rationalize that they must concern themselves with foreign and macroeconomic policy as they lose heart with the complicated, hard-to-affect, divisive domestic problems?

From Roosevelt through George W. Bush, presidents have complained that progress on the domestic front was more difficult than they had imagined. Presidents also regularly complain there are greater limits on their ability to bring about favorable results in the domestic sphere than they had imagined. Clinton's efforts to restructure national health care programs and policy is a notable example. George W. Bush's efforts to "reform" the tax system is another.

Jimmy Carter learned early and often about the limits of his domestic leadership powers. One hilarious example of this lesson concerned a mouse that had climbed inside a wall of the Oval Office and died. The odor became offensive one day just as Carter was about to greet a visiting diplomat. An emergency call went out to the General Service Administration (the agency that maintains and oversees federal property), but GSA refused to respond, insisting that it had already exterminated all the mice in the White House. The dead mouse, the GSA officials reasoned, had obviously come in from outside of the building and was therefore the responsibility of the Department of the Interior. However, Interior officials objected; they contended that the mouse was not their concern because it was now inside the White House. An exasperated Carter finally ordered officials from both agencies to his office where he angrily told them, "I can't even get a damn mouse out of my office. . . ." A special task force representing the two agencies was established and they proceeded to get rid of the mouse!

## THE MULTIDIMENSIONAL PRESIDENCY

Within each of these presidencies or policy subpresidencies, a president is asked to provide functional leadership in seven activity areas: crisis management, symbolic leadership, priority setting and program design, recruitment of advisers and administrators, legislative and political coalition building, program implementation and evaluation, and oversight of government routines and early warning of problem areas. These are not compartmentalized, unrelated functions but rather a dynamic, seamless assortment of tasks and responsibilities. This job description does not exhaust all presidential activity; rather, the examples in Table 5.1 attempt to classify the major functional as well as substantive responsibilities of the office. Of course, political activity solely for personal enhancement (such as reelection) should be acknowledged as a presidential preoccupation just as staying elected is a prime objective for most legislators.

In practice, no president can divide the job into tidy compartments. Instead, a president must see to it that questions are not ignored simply

**TABLE 5.1**
**The Presidential Job Description**

| Types of Activity | The Three "Subpresidencies" | | |
| --- | --- | --- | --- |
| | Foreign policy and national security | Macroeconomics | Domestic policy and programs |
| Crisis management: | Wartime leadership; missile crisis, 1962; Gulf War, 1991; war against terrorism, 2001; Iraq War, 2003 | Coping with recessions, 1982, 1992, 2002–3 | Confronting coal strikes of 1978; LA riots, 1992; LA earthquake, 1992 |
| Symbolic and morale-building leadership: | Presidential state visit to Middle East or to China | Boosting confidence in the dollar | Visiting disaster victims and morale building among government workers |
| Priority setting and program design: | Balancing pro-Israel policies with need for Arab oil | Choosing means of dealing with inflation, unemployment | Designing a new welfare program, health insurance, education reform |
| Recruitment leadership (advisers, administrators, judges, ambassadors, etc.): | Selection of secretary of defense, U.N. ambassador | Selection of secretary of treasury, Federal Reserve Board governors | Nomination of federal judges |
| Legislative and political coalition building: | Selling Panama or SALT treaties to Senate for approval, Homeland security coordination | Lobbying for energy-legislation package | Winning public support for transportation deregulation, tax cuts |
| Program implementation and evaluation: | Encouraging negotiations between Israel and Egypt | Implementing tax cuts or fuel rationing | Improving quality health care, welfare retraining programs, education |
| Oversight of government routines and establishment of an early-warning system for future problem areas: | Overseeing U.S. bases abroad; ensuring that foreign-aid programs work effectively | Overseeing the IRS or the Small Business Administration | Overseeing National Science Foundation or Environmental Protection Agency |

because they fall between or cut across jurisdictional lines. Presidents must act alternately, and often simultaneously, as crisis managers and as symbolic, priority-setting, coalition-building, and managerial leaders. Ultimately, all these responsibilities mix with one another. Being president is a little like being a juggler who is already juggling too many balls and is forever having more balls tossed into the game.

## Crisis Management

A crisis is a situation that occurs suddenly, heightens tensions, carries a high level of threat to a vital interest, provides only limited time for making decisions, and possesses an atmosphere of uncertainty. Crisis management involves both precrisis planning and the handling of the situation during a crisis.

When crises and national emergencies occur, we instinctively turn to the president. Presidents are asked during a time of crisis to provide not only political and executive leadership but also the appearance of confidence, responsible control, the show of a steady hand at the helm. Popular demand and public necessity force presidents nowadays to do what Lincoln and Franklin Roosevelt once did during the national emergencies of their day, namely, whatever is required to protect the union, to safeguard the nation, and to preserve vital American interests.

In normal times, the checks and balances of the U.S. political system can be formidable, severely limiting presidential initiatives. But in a political crisis, most of these checks evaporate, and the president is given wide discretionary leeway in the exercise of executive prerogative or emergency powers. While the Constitution contains no explicit provisions for government during a crisis, in an emergency a president can invoke emergency statutes or merely assume power and become the nation's crisis manager-in-chief (as did Lincoln in the Civil War, Franklin Roosevelt during the Great Depression, and Kennedy during the Cuban missile crisis).[35]

The most significant factor in the swelling of the presidential establishment in the post-1939 era has been the accretion of new presidential roles during national emergencies, when Congress and the public have looked to the president for decisive responses. The Constitution neither authorized presidents to meet emergencies nor forbid them to do so. All strong presidents have taken advantage of this omission. The Great Depression and World War II in particular caused sizable increases in presidential staffs. After the Russians orbited Sputnik in 1957, President Eisenhower added science advisers; after the Bay of Pigs in 1961, President Kennedy enlarged his national security staff. The Cold War commitments as President Kennedy enumerated them in his Inaugural Address, to "pay any price, bear any burden, meet any hardship, support any friend, oppose any foe," and the presence of nuclear weapons fostered the argument that only presidents could move with sufficient quickness and intelligence in national security matters. When major crises occur, Congress traditionally holds debates but just as predictably delegates authority to the president, charging him to take whatever actions are necessary to restore order or regain control over the situation.

Primary factors underlying the transformation of the presidency of the Constitution to the modern crisis-management presidency are the invention of nuclear weapons, the emergence of the Cold War, the permanence of large standing armies, and the interdependent role of the United States in the world economy, and the international war against terrorism. Constant crises in national security have dominated American thinking throughout the twentieth century. Such crises include the Japanese bombing of Pearl Harbor in 1941, the North Korean invasion of South Korea in 1950, the Russian launching of Sputnik in 1957, the offensive missiles placed in Cuba by the Russians in 1962, the Viet Cong offensives in South Vietnam in the mid and late 1960s, and the various Middle East wars and incidents of the 1960s through the 1990s.

Nowhere was the crisis presidency more visible than in the aftermath of the 9-11 terrorist attack. The George W. Bush presidency began with Bush facing formidable odds. The table was set for deadlock. But on September 11, 2001, everything changed. A terrorist attack destroyed the World Trade Center in New York City and shook the nation's sense of self and security. President Bush responded, trying to reassure the nation. He declared war on the terrorists and those nations who had assisted them. The nation faced a crisis and, in this threat, the public rallied behind the president.

On September 10, Bush faced a vast array of checks and balances; after 9-11 he was handed enhanced extraconstitutional power. George W. Bush did not become a political genius overnight. The context of his leadership did, however, change dramatically, adding to his power. What he does with that power will determine his place in history. Crises take the measure of a leader. A crisis gives the leader a freehand to act. Time will tell the wisdom of Bush's actions.

## Symbolic, Morale-building, and Shamanistic Leadership

The American presidency is more than a political or constitutional institution. It is a focus for intense emotions. The presidency serves our basic need for a visible and representative national symbol to which we can turn with our hopes and aspirations. The president has become an icon who embodies the nation's self-understanding and self-image. Thus, we place the president on a high pedestal, yet we demand democratic responsiveness. The president is at once our national hero and national scapegoat.

Presidents are the nation's number-one celebrity; most everything they do is news. Merely by going to a sports event, or a funeral, by celebrating a national holiday, or visiting a particular nation, presidents not only command attention, they convey meaning. By their actions presidents can arouse a sense of hope or despair, honor or dishonor.

Although Americans like to view themselves as hardheaded pragmatists, they, like humans everywhere, cannot stand too much reality. People do not live by reason alone. Myths and dreams are an age-old form of escape. People will continue to believe what they want to believe. And people turn to national leaders just as indigenous people turn to shamans—yearning for meaning, healing, empowerment, legitimacy, assurance, and a sense of purpose.[36]

Americans expect many things from their presidents—honesty, credibility, crisis leadership, agenda-setting and administrative abilities, and also certain of the tribal leader or priestly functions we associate with primitive or religious communities. In a way, the president serves as high priest, national leader, and hand-holder-in-chief. A president's personal conduct affects how millions of Americans view their political loyalties and civic responsibilities. Of course, the symbolic influence of presidents is not always evoked in favor of worthy causes, and sometimes presidents do not live up to our expectations of moral leadership. Still, a great many people find comfort in an oversimplified image of presidents as *warrior-captains* firmly at the helm of the ship of state, as *emancipators or liberators* in the Exodus tradition, as *priests and prophets* of our civil religion, and as *defenders of the democratic faith* and *evocative spokesmen* of the American Dream.

United in this one institution are multiple roles that are on the surface confusing and conflicting. A president's unifying role as a head-of-state and symbol-in-chief, especially in times of crisis, often clashes with his advocacy of program initiatives and partisan responsibilities. Further, presidents invariably take advantage and borrow from their legitimacy as representative and symbolic head-of-state to expand their political and partisan influence.

The framers of the U.S. Constitution did not fully anticipate the symbolic and morale-building functions a president would have to perform. Certain magisterial functions such as receiving ambassadors and the granting of pardons were conferred. Yet the job of the presidency demanded symbolic leadership from the very beginning. Washington and his advisers would readily recognize that in leadership at its finest, the leader symbolizes the best in the community, the best in its traditions, values, and purposes. Effective leadership infuses vision and a sense of significant meaning into the enterprise of a nation.

George Washington was one of the few continental figures of his day. He was already a warrior-hero. He had commanded with distinction the revolutionary patriots for over eight years. In victory he became a prime symbol of that crusade. His integrity and judgment, his lengthy service both in and out of uniform to his country, and his devotion to his troops and his countrymen, set him apart from his fellow founders.

Washington wasn't a great philosopher, orator, lawyer, or even organizer. Even his military abilities have been questioned. He was not especially imaginative and, although his mind was keen, it was slow in operation.

But the new nation needed a hero. America had no heritage of celebrated public servants other than those in England, and hence it was essential for national pride to endow our first hero with lavish praise. His countrymen did precisely this. And Washington understood their need and not only accepted it graciously, he used it as a means of legitimizing both his new office and the new national government he had labored so long to bring into being.[37]

No matter how ably others had explained the Constitution, and especially the provisions for presidential leadership, it was now up to President Washington to carry out the promise of the office and establish the precedents to be followed as long as the country survived. Washington was fully aware that the process of making the Constitution work had only just begun. He knew that written documents do not implement themselves. He appreciated that a living, real constitution includes customs, traditions, practices, interpretations, and precedent setting to fill out the vagueness of the written provisions.

In some ways Washington became the nation's first secular priest or societal shaman. In helping his countrymen to transcend their ordinary definitions of reality he helped instill a new nationalism and a new sense of purpose. His combination of *warrior* and *priest, liberator* and *definer* of a national vision presaged additional extraconstitutional responsibilities for future American presidents.[38]

**The warrior-symbol**   In deciding to make the executive office also the place for commander-in-chief responsibilities, the framers fused together the roles of executive leadership and military or security leadership. This unification, which had been absent under the Articles of Confederation and especially during the American Revolution, guaranteed that Americans would expect presidents to know about war, be capable of wartime leadership, and, if possible, have military experience. Not surprisingly, then, we have elected several military heroes. Presidents Washington, Jackson, Grant, Teddy Roosevelt to a lesser extent, and Eisenhower all benefited from their military achievements, which enhanced their legitimacy as presidential candidates. And the presidency itself, because of these warrior-presidents, took on additional meaning. Each brought to the office some of the aura of legend and the charisma of reputation and authority earned in defense of the nation-state. While this never guaranteed effectiveness in presidential performance, particularly in the case of Grant, it expanded the public's acceptance of presidential authority—and in four of their cases it helped achieve for them rather high evaluations for their presidencies. By contrast, President Clinton had difficulties establishing his legitimacy in part due to his lack of military experience.

Military heroes rise to leadership roles in every society and ours is no exception. On balance, the military veterans who have become president have generally bent over backward to not unnecessarily militarize the presidency. Yet the emergence of the nation as the leading military power in the world necessarily blurs the distinction between the job of the president as political and as national security leader. Whereas national security was once merely one of the jobs of the president and only occasionally demanding, it now compels the modern president to spend at least half of his time planning strategy and presiding over a sprawling military complex, often with as many as 500,000 troops in uniform stationed in all reaches of the world.

**The emancipator-liberator symbol**   The Exodus or emancipator "paradigm" or theory of emergency leadership is one that is deeply embedded in the cultural consciousness of the West. One writer describes the Exodus as an account of deliverance not only in religious terms, but also in a secular, this-worldly account. The Exodus paradigm is one of liberation, of a march to freedom. Americans, like the Israelites, in their own way have had to march, and have had to have leaders and discipline, to free themselves from oppression and depression.

The American Revolution, although in many ways a conservative revolution, was a war of liberation and a determined, disciplined, focused striving to bring about a deliverance. If an aspiration, hope, and promise motivated that rebellion, forceful and committed leadership was needed to help realize the triumph. And the story and legend of George Washington are inextricably linked to this, our own story of liberation.

Yet perhaps it is the story of Abraham Lincoln that epitomizes the emancipator-liberator role of the American political leader. Political scientist Clinton Rossiter once wrote of Lincoln as the supreme American myth, the richest symbol in the American cultural experience. "He is," wrote Rossiter, "the martyred Christ of democracy's passion play. And who, then, can measure the strength that is given to the President because he holds Lincoln's office, lives in Lincoln's house, and walks in Lincoln's way?" Rossiter goes so far as to say the final greatness of the presidency lies in the truth that it is not just an office of incredible power, but a breeding ground of indestructible myth.[39]

Lincoln's special role in American civic and cultural life comes not from his revelation of God's will, but because he revealed and unlocked the higher aspirations and promise of America. In his ability to be a common man with uncommon instincts he preserved the nation, presided over our worst ordeal, and encouraged the rebirth and liberation the nation so urgently needed.[40]

Lincoln, caught up in the turbulent social forces of his time, helped point the way to a resolution of the nation's most perplexing moral problem. The Lincoln myth is not that he was a political saint, but rather that he acted so as to encourage the country toward self-improvement and the liberation of the nation's more generous impulses toward one another.

In his actions, and even more in the legends that developed around him after his death, the Lincoln story is rich in meaning and symbol. Lincoln helped his nation renew human hopefulness, he appealed to our better angels. Lincoln also added considerably to the legitimacy of the presidency and expanded the public's expectations of the possibilities of presidential moral leadership.[41]

Eighty years later, Franklin Roosevelt's determined personal leadership designed to cope with the devastation of the Great Depression also fit the emancipator-liberator symbolic role. Again the legend and myths that developed are often enlarged out of proportion. Yet in politics, the perception of the image is usually as important and more lasting than the reality. Today Roosevelt is remembered for his willingness to risk his political career to stake out bold new measures needed to rescue the nation from its worst economic disaster.

Similarly, his risking all to come to the aid of the Allies in defeating fascism is also interpreted as leadership of liberation. Somehow, whether during the aftershocks of Pearl Harbor, the invasion of Normandy, or Roosevelt's personal diplomacy and personal visits to the troops in North Africa, the president seemed to be engaged in bringing new meaning to the mission of America. While a wide variety of meanings were doubtless conveyed, the emancipator-liberator, the leader in defense of freedom, always loomed large and forms the FDR legend today—"a Soldier of Freedom" as one of his biographers puts it, and, we might add, the foremost architect as well of the modern American presidency.

**Presidents as defenders of the faith**   Every four years Americans elect a politician to serve as president. Yet we also yearn for a high priest of sorts, because despite our separation of church and state, we need performed for us some of the same functions that shamans, medicine men, and other practitioners of ritualistic arts perform in other societies. Having no national religion, we look nonetheless for spiritual meaning. And we often look to our presidents as high priests.

In our time, Ronald Reagan had an uncanny understanding of the symbolic roles a capable president must perform. He had a conscious appreciation of the need for the president to reaffirm our basic goals, to celebrate liberty and freedom, and to participate fully in the rituals that both give meaning to American life and help people understand the larger events of which they are a minor part. Few presidents have been better than Reagan at helping the nation observe its ritual occasions such as Memorial Day, July Fourth, Thanksgiving, and Veteran's Day or participate in the Olympics, summit diplomacy, and similar ceremonies. No one was better at performing national chaplain services—as Reagan did in comforting Americans after the Challenger disaster or as he grieved with and gave meaning to those who mourned the deaths of U.S. Marines in Lebanon. Reagan understood that Americans have a civil religion and semisacred symbols and that these reflect our human need to make sense of eclectic experiences and give meaning, form, order, and assurance.

Much of this commingling of the political and the culturally symbolic in presidential performance is an altogether understandable human response to societal yearnings. Leaders sometimes have no choice but to fulfill tribal roles, no matter how pragmatic, educated, sophisticated, or secular the society. Rituals are ceaselessly reinvented by the human heart.

There is nothing wrong with the symbolic powers that come with the job. They can become a problem, however, when they lead the public to believe symbolism equals accomplishment, or when ceremonial and symbolic requirements keep presidents from performing their other demanding duties. This was one of the criticisms of the Reagan presidency.

Sometimes a president invokes the warrior, priest, defender-of-the-faith images that come with the job and help legitimize presidential authority to give credibility to decisions or actions that are not deserving of our approval. Perhaps Richard Nixon's enemies list, his deceptiveness in obstructing the judicial investigation of the Watergate break-in, and his extensive invocation of executive privilege best illustrate abuse of the office. Nixon portrayed himself as a leader, like Lincoln, embattled in crisis and needing more deference, loyalty, secrecy, and imperial authority.

The amplification of the symbolic roles of the American president may do a disservice in diminishing competing forms of democratic leadership. Our system was not designed to achieve the acquiescence of the many in the rule of the favored few. It is sometimes said that people are ruled by their imaginations; yet it is perhaps more valid to suggest they are governed by the weaknesses of their imaginations.

No one, certainly not the founding politicians, ever intended that presidents would be the sole interpreter of the meaning of America. Most assuredly we want a nation that is capable of rich dialogue about our purposes, vision, and future aspirations. We also want a nation of leaders, not a nation dependent on a single leader and a single, centralized leadership institution. Our strength has always come from our diversity, our willingness and eagerness to debate, listen to alternative viewpoints, and nurture dissent. A top-heavy leadership structure with undue reverence and deference to the presidency would undermine much that is precious to the American experiment.

If the profound symbolism of the presidency has costly implications for the quality of the relationship between citizens and the presidency, it affects fully as much the ways in which presidents and their associates conceive of themselves and their jobs. The reverence and loyalty rendered a new president are a rich resource, yet an overindulgent citizenry can distort the president's psychological perspective and sense of right and wrong.

On balance, we turn to presidents for more symbolic meaning and ritual leadership than was ever intended—and more than is probably desirable. Such dependence has consequences.

### Vision, Priority Setting, and Program Design

Presidents, by custom, have become responsible for proposing new initiatives in the areas of foreign policy, economic growth and stability, and the quality of life in America. This was not always the case. But beginning with Woodrow Wilson and particularly since the New Deal, a president is expected to promote peace, prevent depressions, and formulate domestic programs to resolve countless social problems.

Reagan presents an interesting case of a president who shaped the national policy agenda, because he was a more ideologically committed president than most of his predecessors. Reagan's conservatism helped him develop a vision, a policy agenda, and a program of action. There is a good and a bad side to being an ideologue. It can be good in that a committed ideology can simplify complex problems; on the bad side, many problems do not lend themselves to simple solutions. On the good side, ideology can help get an administration marching in the same direction; on the bad side, people may march like lemmings, over a cliff. On the good side, ideology highlights certain variables in problem solving; on the bad side, it hides or obscures other equally important variables. On the good side, ideology gives passion to purpose; on the bad side it can also degenerate into crusading extremism.

George W. Bush campaigned as a moderate, stressing education and softening some of the hard right stances that alienated centerist voters from the Republican Party. He spoke of "compassionate conservatism" and convincingly presented himself as a nonideological pragmatist. But in the aftermath of the 9-11 tragedy, and emboldened by popular support and success in the 2002 mid-term elections, Bush moved further to the political right, and on issues such as the environment, faith-based programs, taxes, civil liberties, and certain foreign policy issues, Bush emerged more as a conservative than his pragmatic father.

Because power in the American system is not clearly given to any one branch, a policy entrepreneur can, on certain issues, capture control of the policy agenda. If this can be done, a president may be able to force an otherwise reluctant Congress to at least meet part of his policy goals. And no one is better positioned to attract attention than the president. If presidents are to lead and not merely preside, they must shape and try to influence the agenda.

Presidents are often criticized for not being programmatic enough, for not being more passionately committed. The fact is, presidents, by force of habit, almost always want to extend their personal influence, not their ideology, over people and programs. They are generally suspicious of long-range planning. Politicians inherently fear being in advance of their time. They enjoy flexible processes and eschew explicit platforms forever visited on them by well-meaning expert advisers. Presidents are constantly being asked to plan, to forecast, to prevent us from going down the path to policy disasters, yet their instinct is "to leave their options open."

The essence of the modern presidency lies in its potential capability to resolve societal problems.

An effective president will attempt to clarify many of the major issues of the day, define what is possible, and harness the governmental structure so that new initiatives are possible. A president, with the cooperation of Congress, can set national goals and propose legislation.

## Recruitment Leadership

A president's most strategic formal resource is the ability to recruit able people who share the president's convictions to fill high-level positions in both the executive and judicial branches. According to what might be called the "good-person theory," a presidency is only as good as its staffs, cabinet, and counselors. Quality and loyalty are what is wanted. In practice, the view that a president dominates the recruitment and appointment process is misleading.

After running for the presidency for several years, the successful candidate often finds that the people courted during the campaign—delegates, press, financial contributors, machine leaders, advance aides, or political strategists—do not have the skills or experience needed to manage the executive branch. Kennedy repeatedly complained, "People, people, people! I don't know any people [for the cabinet and other top posts]. I only know voters! How am I going to fill these 1,200 jobs?"[42] Almost half of Kennedy's eventual cabinet appointees were unknown to him. Carter supposedly had almost 3,000 posts to fill, but in an effort to restore dignity to his cabinet officers he permitted them to allocate a large portion of the vacancies.

In the postelection rush many appointments are made on the basis of subjective judgments or ethnic or geographical representation and from too limited a field of candidates. Ironically, at the time when presidents have the largest number of jobs to fill and enjoy their greatest drawing power, they have less time and information available to take advantage of this major prerogative than at any other point. Later in their term, presidents have fewer vacancies and usually less prestige; candidates from outside the government are wary about being saddled with troubled programs and recognize that little can be accomplished in an administration's last year or two.

A president sometimes errs in recruiting only like-minded appointees; this can lead to an amiability and conformity in thinking. Social psychologist Irving Janis pointed out that this leads to a dangerous inclination to seek concurrence and groupthink at the expense of critical judgment.[43] The cult of loyalty to President Nixon doubtless encouraged the suspension of critical and objective thinking on the part of many of the people involved in the Watergate affair.

Some potential appointees do not want to live or even be near Washington, D.C. Others balk at the idea of having to disclose their financial background and income. Others do not care to live in the glare of an intrusive media, or have every detail of their past in print on the front page of the newspapers. Involvement with past administrators or too close an association with past scandals or major industries connected with a new assignment may be enough to occasion congressional hostility to a presidential nomination. Congress is more sensitive these days to any kind of potential conflict of interest, especially when there is divided government. Both George H. W. Bush and Clinton were forced to withdraw nominees when relatively minor past blemishes were brought to light by the opposition. In 1997, Clinton was forced to withdraw both CIA nominee Tony Lake and William Weld, his nominee for U.S. Ambassador to Mexico. Likewise, George W. Bush had to pull nominee Linda Chavez as labor secretary nominee after it was revealed that she knowingly employed an illegal immigrant. Dozens of presidential nominees have had their chances ended when a key senator or senators refused to hold confirmation hearings.

Effective presidents shrewdly use their recruitment resource not only as a means of rewarding campaign supporters and enhancing their ties to Congress but also as a vital form of communicating the priorities and policy directions of their administrations. One student of the appointment process described the importance of this function:

A President's nominees are the primary link between him and the millions of men and women in the federal bureaucracy. Most of these men and women are located in the executive branch of the government and technically they work for the President. But he has little power to hire and fire them, he cannot control their political loyalties, and he lacks the time and resources to supervise their activities. His executive appointees must act as his surrogates in dealing with the federal bureaucracy. The quality and the character of the people he chooses to serve in executive positions will have a major impact on the ability of his transient administration to control the permanent government.[44]

Even when presidents have recruited able and loyal persons to their administration they run the risk of high turnover. The average cabinet member has stayed in the post for only about two and a half years, although President Clinton's cabinet averaged a bit longer.

## Legislative and Political Coalition Building

To govern in the United States is to build coalitions, to form alliances and power networks. In relatively few areas can a president act unilaterally and not face challengers to his authority. Custom and the design of the U.S. system necessitate coalition building by political leaders.

The centrifugal force of American politics pulls the system apart and encourages independent entrepreneurship. Power is not fused as in parliamentary democracies, presidents and members of Congress are elected relatively independent of one another, parties do not develop a great deal of cohesion among the branches. Political scientists Benjamin Ginsberg and Martin Shefter agree that since elections fail to provide clear governing coalitions, the president and Congress end up resorting to "politics by other means" in order to influence policy.[45]

This dilemma highlights the essential difference in what it takes to get elected and what it takes to govern. Getting elected requires the development of an "electoral coalition." Governing requires the development of a "governing coalition." These may be different, even contradictory things.

To get elected, Bill Clinton made appeals to a wide variety of traditionally Democratic interest groups, hoping to pull a sufficient number of these groups together to ensure his election. It was a successful electoral strategy. But was it good for governing? As soon as the election was over, all these groups approached Clinton demanding he keep his promises and deliver the goods. Clinton tried to deliver on his promises. Thus, he broadened federal support for abortion rights (which garnered some backlash) and attempted to allow openly gay persons to serve in the military. This generated an incredible backlash—opposition from the military and fundamentalist religious groups all but paralyzed the new administration in the honeymoon period and did significant political damage to the new president precisely at the time he should have been at his power peak. In effect, Clinton's honeymoon was in part sacrificed at the altar of his electoral coalition.

One of the misleading indications of presidential power or success is the so-called presidential box score used by the *Congressional Quarterly* to indicate successes and failures in legislative programs. If Congress has approved a majority of a president's legislative program, the *Congressional Quarterly* may headline its story, "Congress Acts Favorably on President X's Requests." The impression often given is that a president is not only devoted to high principle but has also given independent, creative, galvanizing impetus to legislative progress. It is as if the president is the chief legislator; the Congress is mainly passive and has yielded its legislative authority.

However, box scores must be used with caution. First, they are often deceptive because legislative measures are by no means equal in importance. Moreover, scores fail to distinguish between measures that were central and those peripheral to presidential priorities. Further, they are skewed by the high percentage of presidential requests in the areas of defense and foreign policy, which Congress approves somewhat more readily than other matters. They show nothing of those programs a president wanted but, recognizing the overwhelming likelihood of defeat, never requested at all. Much of what a president does not achieve consists of what is never requested, rather than of what is proposed but does not get passed. Finally, sometimes a president merely anticipates what is going to pass Congress and adds an endorsement at a late stage in its legislative development.

Another area in which Congress influences presidential initiatives is in the shaping of legislation. Many scholars conclude nowadays that Congress merely delays and amends and is basically incapable of creating legislation or formulating policy. In fact, however, Congress sometimes plays the dominant role in initiating legislation; the formulation as well as the enactment of virtually all major legislation relating to domestic and economic policy is the result of extensive conversations between the presidency and Congress and between both of these institutions and pivotal interest groups.[46]

Much of the policy presidents supposedly formulate and propose as their own is derived directly from traditional party priorities, from previous presidents, or from Congress. Just as the celebrated New Deal legislation had a fairly well-defined prenatal history extending back several years before its espousal by FDR, so also recent investigations into the origins and enactment of most of the New Frontier and Great Society legislative programs, for example, broader medical-care programs, federal aid to education, and the more activist stance on civil rights, indicate they too were the fruition of past recommendations by the Democratic party.

Presidents have major resources with which they can enhance their political coalition and legislative lobbying roles. First, they can achieve a closer contact with the American public than any other politician in the country. The president can and often does appeal directly to the people for their support. This does not always work, yet when a president can define an issue and rally the public's concern, Congress and other power centers usually will take careful note.

A second resource is the use of patronage. Patronage today refers not only to jobs and favors rendered but also to campaign trips into districts and states, invitations to the White House, and countless considerations that a president can exchange in an effort to win friends and influence votes. The president's congressional liaison office, with a staff of sometimes up to twenty in recent years, works full time trying to employ these possibilities for maximum advantage.

The third resource is a president's role as a political party leader. Although a president has no formal position in the party structure, a president's influence over national policies and appointments and celebrity status command respect from party leaders. Presidents need the party's support to enact their program. Presidents find they must bargain and negotiate with party leaders just as they do with other independent power brokers.

### Policy Implementation and Evaluation

Implementation, the carrying out and realization of presidential goals, is a crucial, if underappreciated, part of a president's job. The provisions made within the executive office to ensure presidential control over implementation simply do not guarantee this happens. Repeatedly, federal programs fail to accomplish desired goals. When such failures occur, it is relatively easy to blame the original legislation rather than examine what happened after a bill became a law. Of course, poorly written legislation can yield poor results. But students of national policymaking now realize even the best legislation can fail owing to problems encountered during implementation. Sometimes these problems can lead to the outright failure of a program; more often, however, they mean excessive delay, underachievements of desired goals, or costs far above those originally expected.

Implementation is a process involving a long chain of decision points, all of which need to be cleared before a program can be successfully carried out. At each decision point is a public official or community leader who holds power to advance—or delay—the program. The more decision points a program needs to clear, the greater the chance of failure or delay. Special problems result if the successful implementation of a national program depends on the cooperation of state and local officials. The state or locality may be eager to help; another might be opposed to a program and try to stop it. The advent of new federalism and the vast growth in the number and scope of federal grant-in-aid programs have added to the problem of implementation.[47]

If anything has been learned by students of the presidency, it is that policymaking does not end once a law is passed (or when a court decision or presidential executive order is handed down). The implementation of such laws, especially the development of specific guidelines and regulations, can have just as great an impact on public policy as the law itself. The ultimate responsibility for the implementation of the nation's governmental decisions rests with the president.

Presidential decisions transmitted to the bureaucracy often have a way of getting watered down or ignored. The routines of governmental bureaucracies are geared to maintaining the status quo. That's fine if a president merely wants to maintain the status quo. But most presidents want to change at least some policies. Yet policies persist from one administration to the next remarkably unchanged. Resistance to change is reinforced by several factors, chief of which are (1) inadequate communication and determination by a president, (2) the alliances between bureaucrats and the appropriate special interests and congresspersons, and (3) inadequate information and evaluation processes.

Another major factor minimizing presidential influence in the implementation stage is the fact executive branch departments are more the creation of Congress than the White House. Special-interest groups often effectively capture administrative as well as legislative officials and succeed in fragmenting the organization to their own ends.

Congress, even when it is dominated by the president's party, often does not want to increase presidential discretion within executive agencies. The congressional committee structure in large measure parallels executive-branch organization, and what often appear to be structural absurdities in the executive branch may persist because of long-standing jurisdictional disputes within the Congress. Citing their responsibility of administrative review, these committees jealously protect what they consider to be their prerogative to determine how the departments and agencies they oversee are to be restructured. In addition, members of Congress guard those areas in which they have developed expertise and the close relations with government officials and extragovernmental clientele. A committee reorganization could diminish a member's sources of campaign finance or even jeopardize his or her chances for reelection.

Some observers suggest presidents have ignored the managerial side of their responsibilities because of a lack of incentives or rewards in this area. In the words of one public administration expert, "No President has been able to identify any significant political capital that might be made out of efforts to improve management except for the conservative purpose of economizing or reducing costs."[48] Others feel that the way in which our civil-service system is organized encourages bureaucratic reluctance or resistance.[49] Still others remind us that the president frequently lacks authority to issue directions to operating departments.

In sum, the array of formal powers and accumulated "chief executive" prerogatives that we commonly associate with the modern presidency do not, in fact, guarantee the achievement of very much.

## Oversight and Early-Warning System

Still another part of the job of the modern president is the design of oversight and early-warning systems and putting these to effective use. Often, little presidential time or stamina remains for inquiring into those routine activities that make up the great bulk of federal governmental work. Unfortunately, routine activities that are neglected or improperly monitored and evaluated can escalate to crisis proportion. But, for the most part, presidents must delegate large amounts of discretion to political subordinates and career professionals, and their influence over routine activities is felt only indirectly: through appointees, budgetary examinations, or legislative clearance. Presidents may view these activities as self-executing, or may even attempt to dissociate themselves from them, but much of the administrative and executive burden of the presidency consists of imaginative supervision of program implementation. The functional task of a president in the leadership of federal implementation activities is much more than merely issuing directives to the cabinet. It entails compromise, coalition building, education, and political leadership just as much as does the winning of congressional or public support. The quality of bread-and-butter service and assistance programs is important to the average American; a president, like it or not, is held responsible for the general quality of governmental performance.

Only through the skillful monitoring of routine governmental activities can a president know whether citizens are getting a fair return on their taxes. Only by a more imaginative use of presidential resources in overseeing these activities can the activities be prevented from becoming sources of crises themselves. To be sure, supervision and reform must come not only from presidents but also from other quarters as well. But how effective a president is in fashioning an executive oversight and review system is crucial. On the one hand, presidents must be able to delegate vast responsibilities to talented managers; on the other hand, they must have an early-warning system that alerts them through, among other means, their managers about inadequate government performance, about experimentation that yields negative results, and about progress in research and development that could provide corrective feedback.

In short, an effective organization is a learning organization—a system that ensures governmental activities concerned with implementation and routine would be brought to a president's attention when necessary and as they affected priority-setting and political-leadership tasks instead of only when they become matters of crisis management. Interior and transportation officials, for example, should detect evidence of impending fuel shortages sufficiently in advance to permit a president to commission studies and devise remedial strategies before the crisis occurs. Homeland security officials should be alert to pending terrorist threats.

If one of the purposes of presidential power is to execute federal laws faithfully and to help avert costly crises, the presidency must be organized systematically as a learning agency, capable of anticipating and preventing system overload, communications failures, and corruption or ineptness in the operations of the executive branch.

## CONCLUSION

Several underlying incentives help shape the performance of the presidential job. As they have operated in the recent past, these incentives ensure that certain responsibilities get special attention, whereas others become neglected. Preoccupation with problems of national security and macroeconomics leaves little time for leadership in the area of domestic policy. Crisis management, symbolic leadership, and priority setting also crowd out the tasks of lobbying and program implementation and supervision. Creative follow-through is seldom adequate; the routines of government often go neglected. Program evaluation and the imaginative recruitment of program managers for appropriate tasks never receive the sustained attention they merit. On balance, White House officials often do what is easy to do or what they perceive as urgent, sometimes to the neglect of doing what is important.

Presidents tend to concentrate on selected areas of the presidential job. In part this may be because we have created a nearly impossible presidential job description—we give our presidents too much to do and too little time in which to do it. In part, however, recent presidents have also been, or so it would appear, lulled into responding to those parts of their job that are more glamorous, more prominent. Presidential activity in symbolic, priority-setting, and crisis contexts conveys an image of strength, vigor, and rigor.

The true measure of presidents' effectiveness is their capacity to integrate multiple responsibilities in order to avoid having initiatives in one area compound problems in another or having problems go unattended merely because they defy the usual organizational boundaries. Another challenge of presidential leadership is the intricate balancing of each aspect of the presidential job with the others. A close examination of presidential performance in recent years relative to the whole matrix of the job suggests that presidents are strong in some areas and weak in others, and that the overarching job of synthesis and integration is seldom performed adequately.

Those who devise structural solutions to what are essentially political questions are likely to be disappointed. In the twenty-first century we shall get improved presidential performances only when we have a clearer idea of what we want to do as a nation and when we understand better the mix of incentives that now shape the way presidents respond to their political and executive duties, and to the times.

CHAPTER 6

# *Presidents and Congress*

All the public business in Congress now connects itself
with intrigues, and there is great danger that the whole
government will degenerate into a struggle of cabals.

John Quincy Adams, *Diary,* January 1819

(Congress is) functioning the way the Founding Fathers
intended—not very well. They understood that if you
move too quickly, our democracy will be less responsible to the majority. . . . Exhaustion and exasperation are
frequently the handmaidens of legislative decision. . . .
I don't think it's the function of Congress to function
well. It should drag its heels on the way to decision.

Congressman Barber B. Conable, Jr., *Time,* October 22, 1984

Our republic, we know, was designed to be slow-
moving and deliberative. Our founding fathers were
convinced that power had to be entrusted to someone,
but that no-one could be entirely trusted with power.
They devised a brilliant system of checks and balances
to prevent the tyranny of the many by the few. They
constructed a perfect triangle of allocated and checked
power. . . . There could be no rash action, no rush to
judgment, no legislative mob rule, no unrestrained
chief executive.

The difficulty with this diffusion of power in today's
cyberspace age is that everyone is in check, but no-one
is in charge.

Sen. William S. Cohen, (R-Maine) (later secretary of defense),
*Washington Post National Weekly Edition,* January 28–
February 4, 1996, p. 29

Major Pierre L'Enfant, the principal designer of the nation's capital, had more than design in mind when he located the president and Congress at opposite ends of an avenue. Congress, he decided, would be housed atop Jenkins Hill, giving it the high ground. The president would be housed about one mile away, at the end of a long street that would serve as a threadlike link connecting these two institutions. Not only did the Constitution separate the executive and legislative branches, but geography would as well.[1]

Yet for the U.S. system to work, both branches must frequently find ways to bridge the gap, and join what is separated. The framers saw the separation of powers not as a weakness but as a source of strength, as a way to ensure deliberation and as a way to prevent tyranny. Cooperation between president and Congress was what the framers required if energetic government was to be achieved. But how was a president to develop the collaboration of the branches necessary to make the system of separate institutions sharing power work?

The relationship between president and Congress is the most important one in the American system of government, and while presidents spend considerable energy courting the media and appealing to the public, they do so primarily to gain leverage with the Congress. For, in the long run, presidents must get Congress to accept their proposals. Only Congress can allocate resources, and presidents who consistently attempt to go around the Congress cannot long succeed. A president may not like it, but sustained cooperation with Congress is a necessity.[2] Presidents may act semiautonomously of the Congress in a few areas, but most of the president's goals require a partnership with Congress.

This is no easy matter. As one long-time presidential adviser noted, "I suspect that there may be nothing about the White House less generally understood than the ease with which a Congress can drive a president quite out of his mind and up the wall."[3]

## THE PRESIDENT'S CONSTITUTIONAL PLACE

In matters requiring legislative authorization Congress ultimately has the upper hand. While a president may be seen as leader of the nation, agenda setter, vision builder, and legislator-in-chief, it is often Congress that has the final say. And since there are multiple veto points in Congress, any of which may block a president's proposal, the forces wishing to prevent change almost always have the upper hand. The American system has many roadblocks, yet few avenues for positive change.

Many people expect presidents to lead the Congress. But public expectations notwithstanding, a president's legislative powers are constitutionally (Article II, Section 3) thin. The Constitution grants Congress "all legislative power" but establishes a relationship of mutual dependence and power sharing. The more ambitious a president's agenda, the more dependent that president is on congressional cooperation. Presidents have the veto power. They report on the state of the union, and extraconstitutionally they may suggest legislation, lobby Congress, set the agenda, and build coalitions. Still, overall presidential powers over Congress are limited.[4]

The peculiar paradox is that in a real sense, as many have noted, no one is in charge. Responsibility and power are fragmented. This often creates a fascinating blame game, with presidents blaming the Congress for the ills of the nation and the Congress blaming the president. This was illustrated during the Reagan presidency when Reagan, who never once in eight years submitted a balanced budget to the Congress, railed against the big-spending Democrats in Congress, and Democrats countered, attacking the president as a budget buster. Who was right? Both were. Because we separate power, both could lay blame yet neither had to accept responsibility. Accountability in such a system is difficult to maintain.

In this the U.S. system stands in contrast to parliamentary systems such as that of Great Britain. Rather than having a separation of powers, parliamentary systems have a *fusion* of power. The prime minister is elected from and by the majority party in the Parliament. Prime ministers are responsible to, yet also have power over, the majority party, and are thereby granted more legislative power than a U.S. president possesses. Fusing the executive and legislative powers together creates more power and greater accountability. If things go well or ill, the voters know who is responsible.

## HISTORICAL EVOLUTION

Congress was established as the dominant branch of government, and the first few presidents were minimally involved in the legislative process. But the founders' vision soon gave way to political reality, and slowly presidents began to pull power into the White House. Congress was often a willing participant in giving additional power to the presidency. The rise of the legislative presidency did not follow a clear unobstructed path. Some of the more ambitious chief executives such as Jefferson used the newly forming political parties to exert influence in Congress. Others such as Jackson exploited popular opinion to gain influence. Still others such as Lincoln and FDR gained additional powers during crisis.

Sprinkled between these power-aggrandizing presidents were less assertive or weaker chief executives. Thus, an institutional ebb and flow characterizes power relations between president and Congress. Over time, however, this tug of war has moved toward a stronger president in the legislative arena. Today, "What was designed as a congressionally centered system has evolved into a presidentially centered . . . system."[5] Still, Congress has a way of frustrating even the most skilled of presidents, especially when there is divided government, with the control of the presidency and Congress in the hands of vying political parties.[6]

While the popular expectation is that the president is the "chief legislator" who "guides Congress in much of its lawmaking activity,"[7] reality is often different. The decentralized nature of power in Congress, the multiple access and veto points within the congressional process, the loosely organized party system, the independent/entrepreneurial mode of the legislators, the weakness of the legislative leadership, all conspire against presidential direction and leadership.[8] This means that presidents often impact Congress only "at the margins," and are more "facilitators" than leaders.[9]

The theory on which the U.S. government is based hinges on a reasonable amount of cooperation between the two branches. As Justice Robert Jackson wrote in 1952, "while the constitution diffuses power the better to secure liberty, it also contemplates that practice will integrate the dispersed powers into a workable government."[10]

## WORKING WITH CONGRESS

Immediately on a new president's taking office, members of Congress take the measure of the person. Will the president stand firm? Will the president bend? Will the new president work with us or act independent of Congress? Will the president be highly partisan or bipartisan? Will the president be able to intimidate us, or can we lead the White House? Who will set the tone?

From early August of 1990 through much of January 1991 President George H. W. Bush deftly maneuvered the United States in the direction of what became known as Operation Desert Storm to liberate Kuwait. Bush said initially his decision to send troops to Saudi Arabia was a "wholly defensive" mission. Yet he increasingly enlarged our military presence, and he rallied both the United States and a twenty-eight-nation coalition to prepare for war against Iraq's Saddam Hussein. In December of 1990 Bush signaled cabinet officials that he wanted to go to war to liberate Kuwait. He is reported also to have told foreign leaders in the coalition that if he decided to go to war, he would do so whether Congress agreed or not.[11]

Congress eventually, after heated arguments, passed resolutions supporting the use of military force to liberate Kuwait. There was, however, no formal declaration of war. Critics assert that American presidents now have more personal power to make war than do the leaders of any other major democracy. And they lament that this is precisely what the framers of the Constitution set out to prevent.[12]

The tumultuous Senate confirmation hearings of Clarence Thomas are yet another example of the politics of shared powers. Presidents nominate individuals to fill vacancies on the Supreme Court, but the Senate has the power to confirm or deny such nominations. The Clarence Thomas hearings raised issues of sexual harassment and integrity as well as debates about liberal and conservative court policy. Thomas eventually won confirmation in a 52–48 roll-call vote—the closest for a confirmed Supreme Court nominee in more than one hundred years.[13] Judge Thomas termed the last segment of his hearings "a high-tech lynching" and said, near the end of the proceeding, that he was no longer interested in whether he got the job; he just wanted to clear his name. The hearings angered a lot of people, and "senators in both parties admitted to a common embarrassment at the institution's failure to deal better with the divisive issues before them."[14]

Sparring between President Clinton and House speaker Newt Gingrich in 1995 over who would control the nation's public policy agenda may have seemed unusual, but in historical terms it merely reflects the ongoing struggle between the president and Congress.

After the 9-11 terrorist attack against the United States, President George W. Bush proposed the creation of a Homeland Security Agency. But Bush and the Democrats clashed over several issues, most importantly over Bush's attempt to exempt employees in the proposed agency from labor regulations. In the end it was only after the 2002 mid-term election, where the Republicans recaptured control of the Senate, that the Democrats relented and ceded to Bush much of what he wanted.

These are examples of skirmishes between the president and Congress as they try to adapt the Constitution of 1787 to today's realities. In this chapter we begin by looking at our system of separate branches and the conflict between the branches. We then treat two interpretations of the relationships between the presidency and Congress. In the second half of the chapter, we examine some of the measures Congress has taken in recent decades to try to reassert its authority in its continuing struggle with the White House.

## THE POLITICS OF SHARED POWER

The framers anticipated presidents and Congress would often disagree over policy, for they gave the president veto power over legislation but gave the Congress the power to override that veto. They gave the power to nominate top personnel to the president but gave the Senate power to confirm top personnel. They authorized presidents to negotiate treaties but required the Senate's approval by a two-thirds vote before the president could ratify a treaty and make it part of the law of the land. The framers also knew from their study of history that heads of government were more prone to going to war than were the people's representatives, so they vested the final authority for war in the legislature.

Constitutional democracy in the United States was designed to be one of both shared powers and division. The framers wanted disagreement as well as cooperation because they assumed that the checks and balances within the government would prevent a president and Congress from "ganging up" against the people's liberties. The framers actually made such disagreements inevitable by providing a president, Senate, and House of Representatives elected by different constituencies and for different lengths of service.

The United States is notable among major world powers because it is neither a parliamentary democracy nor a wholly executive-dominated government. Our Constitution invites both Congress and president to set policy and govern the nation. Leadership and policy change are encouraged only when two, and sometimes all three, branches of government concur on the desirability of new directions. At one time Congress was the dominant partner, but recently, as we have noted earlier, presidents seem to hold the upper hand, despite constitutionally specified restraints.

The politics of shared power has often been stormy, as the Persian Gulf War, Iran-Contra affair, Clarence Thomas confirmation hearings, the Clinton health care proposal, and George W. Bush's proposed tax cuts in 2003 illustrate. The politics of shared powers is characterized by changing patterns of cooperation and conflict depending on the partisan and ideological makeup of Congress, the popularity and skills of the president, the strength of the political parties, and various events that shape the politics of the times. As we discuss later, the politics of shared powers in an era of divided government can aptly be described as the politics of Congress's varying success at asserting itself in relation to the initiatives and leadership provided by presidents.

Divided government has become the norm rather than the exception. Since 1952 there has been a split in partisan control of the presidency and Congress for about two-thirds of the time. Only Presidents John Kennedy, Lyndon Johnson, Jimmy Carter, and for a brief time Bill Clinton, enjoyed majority control by their own party in Congress, and even they had considerable trouble getting support for many of their legislative programs. President George H. W. Bush, with control of both Houses of Congress as a result of the 2002 mid-term elections, should have somewhat smoother legislative sailing.[15]

The opposition party in Congress regularly mounts its own programs. It will, when possible, defeat a president's policy initiative and substitute its own. This effort becomes all the more troublesome, of course, when Congress is controlled by the opposition party. Certainly Presidents Bush, Reagan, and Clinton had their troubles with a House of Representatives controlled by the opposition.

The politics of shared power necessitates the development of agreement between a president and Congress. The model, or theory of government, on which the American system was founded is based on consensus and coalition building. Consensus means agreement about *ends;* coalitions are the *means* by which the ends are achieved. Since power is fragmented and dispersed, something (crisis) or someone (usually, a president) has to pull the disparate parts of the system together.

Power can only be legitimately exercised when the different parts of the system act together. Power, which in many ways floats in the American system, has to be harnessed and channeled. For this to happen, a working consensus on what to do has to be developed, and a coalition of forces has to be formed.[16]

A consensus can be formed if the president has a clear, focused agenda; if the president can forcefully and compellingly communicate a vision; and if the public is ready to embrace that vision. If a president can develop a consensus he can then muster the power to form the coalitions necessary to bring the vision to fruition.

Simply placing a legislative package at the doorstep of Congress is not enough. Presidents must work to build support within and outside Congress. They must build coalitions. The office does not guarantee political leadership; it merely offers incumbents an invitation to lead politically. It is in this sense that those best suited to the job are those who can creatively shape their political environment and savor the rough-and-tumble give-and-take of political life.

Of course, building coalitions is easier said than done. Institutional combat, not power sharing, characterizes this relationship, as both branches attempt to usurp power and govern autonomously.

## THE PRESIDENT IN THE LEGISLATIVE ARENA

Although separation of powers and divided government are obstacles, they are not insurmountable barriers to good public policymaking. Presidents and Congress can legislate when the leaders of both institutions bargain and compromise in ways that overcome the roots of division. In fact, while the Constitution disperses power and invites a continuous struggle between these two branches, it also requires the two branches to collaborate. And usually they do. Even when the relationship is regarded as hostile, "bills get passed and signed into law. Presidential appointments are approved by the Senate. Budgets are eventually enacted and the government is kept afloat. This necessary cooperation goes on even when the White House and the Capitol are divided between the two major parties."[17]

Under what conditions are presidents likely to establish their agenda and get congressional support? Put another way, when is the Congress most likely to follow a president's lead? And when is it likely that a president will follow the lead of Congress?

Several factors lend themselves to presidential success in dealing with Congress. First, in a crisis, the president is accorded additional deference, and the Congress usually supports the president. Second, when a president has a clear electoral mandate (when the campaign was issue oriented, the president won by a wide margin, and the president's party has a sizable majority in Congress), the Congress sometimes will follow. Third, a president can exert pressure on members of Congress when he won the election by a landslide and ran ahead of the member in his or her own district (usually referred to as "presidential coattails"). Part of President Clinton's problems with Congress can be traced to the fact he ran behind most members in their districts, did not face an emergency, and did not win a clear electoral mandate in 1992 or 1996.

Fourth, presidential popularity is often said to be a source of power over Congress. But how easily can a president translate popularity into power? Many social scientists are dubious, believing that popularity has only a marginal impact on presidential success within Congress.[18] Others argue that popularity does translate into power.[19]

Fifth, skill does make a difference, but how much of a difference? As is the case with popularity, scholars disagree, some arguing that skill is of little importance,[20] others that it is important.[21] One scholar warns that

> it is important to depersonalize somewhat the study of presidential leadership and examine it from a broader perspective. In this way there are fewer risks of attributing to various aspects of presidential leadership consequences of factors largely beyond the president's control. Similarly, one is less likely to attribute incorrectly the failure of a president to achieve his goals to his failure to lead properly. Things are rarely so simple.[22]

High skill levels may give a president greater leverage to win in the congressional process. Skills such as knowledge of the congressional process and needs, good timing, bargaining, deal-making, persuasion, and coalition-building skill; moving the public; setting the agenda; self-dramatization; arm twisting; trading; consultation and co-optation, and even threats can all be used to advance the president's goals.

Lyndon Johnson, one of the more skilled of the modern presidents vis-à-vis Congress, emphasized that a White House had to work continuously to build bridges with Congress. He urged his aides and cabinet members to get to know the members of Congress as well as they knew their family.

President Johnson perfected what some called "the Johnson treatment." Journalists Rowland Evans and Bob Novak described it as follows:

> Its tone could be supplication, accusation, cajolery, exuberance, scorn, tears, complaint, the hint of threat. It was all of these together. It ran the gamut of human emotions. Its velocity was breathtaking, and it was all in one direction. Interjections from the target were rare. Johnson anticipated them before they could be spoken. He moved in close, his face a scant millimeter from his target, his eyes widening and narrowing, his eyebrows rising and falling. From his pockets poured slips, memos, statistics. Mimicry, humor, and the genius of analogy made The Treatment an almost hypnotic experience and rendered the target stunned and helpless.[23]

Lyndon Johnson could be relentless, but he was afforded that luxury only partly due to personal skills. He had other significant advantages that made his power more robust and his threats more credible than many of his successors. One of the most important of these power resources is party support.

Partisan support in Congress is the sixth major factor shaping presidential success with Congress. Parties can serve as a bridge linking the institutional divide between the president and Congress. Lyndon Johnson had such a large majority of party members in Congress that even if several dozen Democrats abandoned the president, he could still get his majority in Congress. George H. W. Bush on the other hand faced a Congress in control of the opposition, and was thus stymied.

Linked to this is the seventh factor: the nature of the opposition in Congress. How many votes do they have? How ideologically driven are they? How cohesive are they? How willing are they to work with the president? In

1981, President Reagan faced a Senate controlled by his own party but a House controlled by the Democrats. Reagan was able, via skill, luck, and circumstance, to win over enough Democrats (referred to as the "Boll Weevils") to win several significant legislative battles. By contrast, while President Clinton had majorities in both houses during his first two years in office, the Republican opposition was so unified against the president (on Clinton's 1993 economic package, not one Republican senator supported the President) that Clinton had a difficult time with Congress.[24] Yet, in spite of these difficulties, Clinton achieved a lofty 86.4 percent bill passage rate in his first two years in office. In 1995, the year after the Republican takeover of Congress, Clinton's success rate plummeted to 36.2 percent, the lowest score of any president in modern times. Clinton began to move more to the center and averaged close to 50 percent in his next five years (see Table 6.1).

Due to the nature of partisan politics, the eighth factor that shapes presidential success or failure in Congress is the nature of consultation between the two branches. One of the lessons President Clinton learned is that a president must consult, not only with the president's own partisans but with the opposition as well. Attempting to gain cooperation and agreement must be the first step. A president also needs to set up an effective legislative liaison office that listens and works closely with the leadership on the Hill. Then

**TABLE 6.1**
**Success Rate History of Modern Presidents with Congress**

| Eisenhower | | Nixon | | Reagan | | Clinton | |
|---|---|---|---|---|---|---|---|
| 1953 | 89.0% | 1969 | 74.0% | 1981 | 82.4% | 1993 | 86.4% |
| 1954 | 82.8 | 1970 | 77.0 | 1982 | 72.4 | 1994 | 86.4 |
| 1955 | 75.0 | 1971 | 75.0 | 1983 | 67.1 | 1995 | 36.2 |
| 1956 | 70.0 | 1972 | 66.0 | 1984 | 65.8 | 1996 | 55.1 |
| 1957 | 68.0 | 1973 | 50.6 | 1985 | 59.9 | 1997 | 56.62 |
| 1958 | 76.0 | 1974 | 59.6 | 1986 | 56.1 | 1998 | 51 |
| 1959 | 52.0 | | | 1987 | 43.5 | 1999 | 37.8 |
| 1960 | 65.0 | **Ford** | | 1988 | 47.4 | 2000 | 55 |
| | | 1974 | 58.2% | | | | |
| **Kennedy** | | 1975 | 61.0 | **G.H.W. Bush** | | **G.W. Bush** | |
| 1961 | 81.0% | 1976 | 53.8 | 1989 | 62.6% | 2001 | 87% |
| 1962 | 85.4 | | | 1990 | 46.8 | 2002 | 88 |
| 1963 | 87.1 | **Carter** | | 1991 | 54.2 | | |
| | | 1977 | 75.4% | 1992 | 43.0 | | |
| **Johnson** | | 1978 | 78.3 | | | | |
| 1964 | 88.0% | 1979 | 76.8 | | | | |
| 1965 | 93.0 | 1980 | 75.0 | | | | |
| 1966 | 79.0 | | | | | | |
| 1967 | 79.0 | | | | | | |
| 1968 | 75.0 | | | | | | |

*Source:* Updated from *Congressional Quarterly Reports.*

Lyndon Johnson's long career as "Master of the Senate" prior to his becoming President—as well as, ironically, his association with the martyred JFK—helped him carve out one of the highest success rates in getting legislation through Congress. (*Source:* Copyright © Bettmann/CORBIS.)

too, a president needs to appreciate the policy values and political needs of the national legislators. Presidents sometimes need to follow as well as lead, especially when there are better ideas to be found in Congress.

Finally, the type of agenda a president pursues has a significant impact. George H.W. Bush had a thin legislative agenda, and he pursued it only half-heartedly. Bill Clinton had an ambitious agenda, making it more difficult to get the Congress to go along. Given the antipolitics mood of the times, it is surprising Clinton did as well as he did in his first term. An ambitious agenda is difficult to pass in good times, but in tough times, the tough choices appear to be impossible choices.

In recent decades the inside bargaining skills necessary to cut deals have been replaced by or supported by major marketing or self-promotion efforts. In the loose bargaining regime of the Congress, presidents think their time is better spent appealing directly to the public for support, which may translate into clout in Congress. But ultimately presidents must cut deals in Congress.[25]

Congress can, of course, play a major role in setting and sometimes shaping the national public policy agenda. It may be difficult for a plural institution to lead, yet Congress sometimes acts as a leadership and law-making as well as representative institution. When is this the case? This happens when a party enjoys strong majorities in both chambers, when a president is vulnerable, such as at the end of a term, or is politically wounded (as Nixon was in 1973 and 1974), and when Congress has strong leaders, as when Sam Rayburn and Lyndon Johnson exercised impressive leadership toward the end of the Eisenhower presidency.

But the central question under consideration here is: Can a president lead Congress? The answer remains: Yes, yet not often, and not usually for long. A mix of skill, circumstances, luck, popularity, party support, timing, and resources need to converge if effective collaboration of these two highly political branches is to occur.

What follows is a consideration of some of the resources and realities that can affect presidential-congressional leadership.

## THE PRESIDENTIAL VETO

A president can veto a bill by returning it, together with specific objections, to the house in which it originated. Congress, by a two-thirds vote in each chamber, may override the president's veto (see Table 6.2). Another variation of the veto is known as the pocket veto. In the ordinary course of events, if the president does not sign or veto a bill within ten weekdays after receiving it, it becomes law without the chief executive's signature. But if Congress adjourns within the ten days, the president, by taking no action, can kill the bill.

The veto's strength lies in the usual failure of Congress to get a two-thirds majority of both houses. Historically Congress has overridden less than 7 percent of presidents' general vetoes. Yet a Congress that could repeatedly mobilize a two-thirds majority against a president can almost take command of the government. This is a rare situation, but such was the fate of Andrew Johnson in the 1860s.[26]

Presidents can also use the veto power in a positive way. They can announce that bills under consideration by Congress will be turned back unless certain changes are made. They can use the threat of the veto against some bills Congress wants badly in exchange for other bills that the president may want. A presidential veto can also protect a national minority from hasty, unfair legislation passed in the heat of the moment. But the veto is essentially a negative weapon of limited use to a president who is pressing for action.

The presidential veto power has stirred little controversy. Carter vetoed only thirty-one bills, Nixon vetoed forty-three, Ford sixty-six, and Reagan seventy-eight. George H. W. Bush vetoed forty-six bills, and Clinton vetoed thirty-seven bills.

In short, there is little Congress can do when confronted with a veto. It must either get enough votes to override the veto or modify the legislation and try again. Presidents are able to make the vast majority of their regular vetoes stick.

**TABLE 6.2**
**Presidential Vetoes, 1789–2002**

|  | Regular vetoes | Pocket vetoes | Total vetoes | Vetoes overriden |
|---|---|---|---|---|
| Washington | 2 | — | 2 | — |
| Madison | 5 | 2 | 7 | — |
| Monroe | 1 | — | 1 | — |
| Jackson | 5 | 7 | 12 | — |
| Tyler | 6 | 3 | 9 | 1 |
| Polk | 2 | 1 | 3 | — |
| Pierce | 9 | — | 9 | 5 |
| Buchanan | 4 | 3 | 7 | — |
| Lincoln | 2 | 4 | 6 | — |
| A. Johnson | 21 | 8 | 29 | 15 |
| Grant | 45 | 49 | 94 | 4 |
| Hayes | 12 | 1 | 13 | 1 |
| Arthur | 4 | 8 | 12 | 1 |
| Cleveland | 304 | 109 | 413 | 2 |
| Harrison | 19 | 25 | 44 | 1 |
| Cleveland | 43 | 127 | 170 | 5 |
| McKinley | 6 | 36 | 42 | — |
| T. Roosevelt | 42 | 40 | 82 | 1 |
| Taft | 30 | 9 | 39 | 1 |
| Wilson | 33 | 11 | 44 | 6 |
| Harding | 5 | 1 | 6 | — |
| Coolidge | 20 | 30 | 50 | 4 |
| Hoover | 21 | 16 | 37 | 3 |
| F. Roosevelt | 372 | 263 | 635 | 9 |
| Truman | 180 | 70 | 250 | 12 |
| Eisenhower | 73 | 108 | 181 | 2 |
| Kennedy | 12 | 9 | 21 | — |
| L. Johnson | 16 | 14 | 30 | — |
| Nixon | 26 | 17 | 43 | 7 |
| Ford | 48 | 18 | 66 | 12 |
| Carter | 13 | 18 | 31 | 2 |
| Reagan | 39 | 39 | 78 | 9 |
| Bush, G.H.W. | 29 | 17 | 46 | 1 |
| Clinton | 37 | 1 | 37 | 2 |
| **TOTALS:** | 1,486 | 1,064 | 2,549 | 106 |

*Source:* U.S. Senate Historical Office, Senate Library.

## THE LEGISLATIVE VETO

Since the 1930s and most especially since the 1970s, Congress has exercised what came to be known as the legislative veto. Using this device, Congress would draft a law broadly but incorporate a provision allowing Congress to review and veto the executive branch's implementation of the law. The legislative veto could be put into effect by a majority vote of one house, both houses, or sometimes even by a single congressional committee, depending on how the law was written.

Whatever the form, the legislative veto allowed Congress to delegate general power to the executive branch and then take it away without having to secure presidential approval. In effect, it permitted Congress to legislate without exposing its handiwork to a presidential veto, as the framers intended. The Constitution stipulates that every bill, resolution, or vote for which the agreement of the Senate and the House of Representatives may be necessary, shall be presented to the president for approval or veto. Joint resolutions were regularly submitted to the president, but concurrent resolutions were not. In the past this made little difference, because concurrent or simple one-house resolutions were mainly used to express congressional opinion and had no force of law.

But the legislative veto was also used to keep presidents in check. Arms sales had to be submitted to Congress for its scrutiny. Presidential use of military troops abroad had to be reported to Congress and was subject to recall by unilateral congressional action. In short, angered by presidents who had either lied to or ignored Congress, assertive legislators tried to use the legislative veto to recapture congressional power.

The legislative veto originated in 1932 when Congress passed a resolution allowing President Herbert Hoover limited authority to reorganize the executive branch agencies. The resolution stipulated that the president's proposals would not be put into effect for ninety days, during which time either house of Congress, by a simple resolution, could veto the proposal. For the next fifty-one years, the legislative veto became a standard practice.[27]

Between 1932 and mid-1983 more than two hundred pieces of legislation included some provision for a legislative veto. The device was used to ensure that bureaucratic regulations conformed to congressional intentions. This was important in the 1970s because of the rapid increase in the number of such regulations, which often have the same or nearly the same force as laws. In any given year in the late 1970s or early 1980s, Congress might have passed a few hundred public laws; but the administrators in about 708 executive branch agencies were responsible for twenty times as many regulations.

Then, in 1983, Chief Justice Warren Burger, speaking for a Supreme Court majority in a 7–2 decision (*INS v. Chadha*), said that to maintain the separation of powers, the carefully defined limits on the power of each branch must not be eroded. The legislative veto was found unconstitutional. Said Burger: "With all the obvious flaws . . . we have not yet found a better way to preserve freedom than by making the exercise of power subject to the carefully crafted restraints spelled out in the Constitution." In effect, the Court told Congress that to obtain more influence over an agency or the presidency, Congress should pass a law that accomplished this explicitly. In the words of dissenting Justice Byron White, the Court's decision "strikes down in one fell swoop provisions in more laws enacted by Congress than the Court has cumulatively invalidated in its history."[28]

In this historic decision, the Court tried to curb a weapon Congress had sometimes used effectively to intimidate executive branch officials. Clearly, the existence of the legislative veto stimulated compromise and understandings between executive and legislative officials. Some observers viewed the decision as just one in a long series of Supreme Court rulings that generally approve and encourage an assertive and increasingly powerful presidency.

Because of this decision, Congress has been a little more explicit about the policy directions it sets. It is also exercising some options that make it clear to executive departments that if congressional committees are displeased by the actions of the departmental officials, congressional retribution in the form of reduced appropriations is likely. Congress has found ways to exercise the functional equivalent of a legislative veto.[29] Dozens of such quasi-legislative vetoes have been signed into law in the past decade. Further, there have been scores of informal agreements between the branches.

These quasi-legislative vetoes and similar agreements survive, despite the Court's ruling, because they serve a purpose. They give the executive branch the flexibility it desires and that Congress might otherwise not provide, while allowing the Congress to retain a certain amount of ongoing control. "The legislative veto procedure represented a classic quid pro quo," says Louis Fisher. "It attempted to reconcile the interests of both branches: the desire of (executive) agencies for greater discretionary authority and the need of Congress to maintain control short of passing another public law."[30] Hence legislative vetoes or agreements similar to them are likely to be with us for the near future.

## PRESIDENTS AND CONGRESS IN FOREIGN AFFAIRS

Although the framers of the U.S. Constitution may not have anticipated the degree to which presidents would become so centrally involved in the making of domestic public policy, scholars have justified the need for strong dynamic presidents who would help overcome the fragmentation of power in the country and in Congress. The creaky machinery of our government, they contend, can be made to work only if we give a president the proper amount of help and authority.

If the constitutional framers expected presidents to play a relatively minor role with respect to domestic policy, they had different expectations with respect to foreign and national security matters. That is why they made the president the agent in making and ratifying treaties, with senatorial consent, and also gave the president control over the military forces.

Although foreign affairs in the eighteenth century were generally thought to be an executive matter, the framers did not want the president to be the only or even the dominant agent. Various powers vested in Congress by the Constitution were explicitly designed to bring the national legislature into the making of foreign and military policy. Indeed, a good part of the Constitution was written to deprive the executive of control over foreign policy and foreign relations, which under the English system were so dramatically vested in the king. Thus the framers gave Congress as a whole the sole power to declare war, and they plainly intended the Senate to serve as a partner in the shaping and making of foreign policy. Constitutional scholar

Leonard W. Levy goes even further: "The framers meant, at the most, that the president should be a joint participant in the field of foreign affairs, but not an equal one."[31]

But as the world leadership role of the United States has increased, so also has the foreign policy role and the power of the president. From 1940 onward, "the Oval Office is where foreign policy for better or worse has been made."[32] Policies that have succeeded in recent decades—the Marshall Plan, the Truman Doctrine, the Panama Canal Treaty, the Camp David Accords, and the North American Free Trade Agreement—have been those in which presidents encouraged careful collaboration and debate in Congress. When presidents have involved Congress and the people in the shaping of new foreign policies, those policies have generally won legitimacy and worked. "The policies that have failed have tended to be those adopted by presidents without meaningful debate—Roosevelt's Yalta policy toward Poland, Kennedy's intervention in the Bay of Pigs . . . Reagan's Iran-contra policy, among others."[33]

## THE "IMPERIAL PRESIDENCY" ARGUMENT

No matter what the circumstances, though, most people expect Congress to exercise fully the system of constitutional checks to rein in the president, and vice versa. Late in the 1960s and in the early 1970s, a number of events made many fear that Congress had become too passive and the presidency too powerful.

In the early 1970s, the Vietnam War was finally winding down, but not without leaving the nation reeling from the protests, civil unrest, and loss of lives associated with that unpopular and largely unsuccessful war. The nation's grief and outrage were fueled, too, by revelations that both Johnson and Nixon had misled Congress and acted in some instances without congressional approval in making and conducting the war. These disconcerting events were compounded by the Watergate scandals and the growing realization that a president of the United States had acted to obstruct justice. These developments led Arthur M. Schlesinger, Jr., a historian and former adviser to John F. Kennedy, to write *The Imperial Presidency,* charging that presidential powers were so abused and expanded by 1972 that they threatened our constitutional democracy.[34]

Schlesinger and other proponents of the "imperial presidency" view contended the problem stemmed in part from ambiguity concerning the president's power as commander-in-chief; it is a vaguely defined office, not a series of specific functions. Schlesinger and others acknowledged that Johnson and Nixon did not create the imperial presidency; they merely built on some of the more questionable practices of their predecessors. But some observers insisted there is a distinction between the abuse and the usurpation of power. Abraham Lincoln, Franklin Roosevelt, and Harry Truman temporarily usurped power in wartime. Johnson and Nixon abused power, deceiving Congress, misusing the Central Intelligence Agency, and manipulating public opinion and the electoral process.

Secrecy has often been used to protect and preserve a president's national security power. Nixon, it is said, pushed the doctrine beyond acceptable limits. Before Eisenhower, Congress expected to get the information it sought from the executive branch, and instances of secrecy and executive privilege were the rare exceptions. By the early 1970s, however, these practices had become the rule. And a Congress that knows only what the president wants it to know is not an independent body.

After the 9-11 attack against the United States, President George W. Bush assumed expanded powers and circumvented the Congress in a variety of ways, including issuing executive orders as a way of establishing policies without the consent of Congress, claiming powers to intern U.S. citizens without a charge or trial and without access to an attorney, and expanding the use of secrecy in the executive branch. This led to charges of the imposition of a new imperial presidency, yet initially, the public was unmoved by such criticisms.[35]

Schlesinger's views are a useful point of departure for discussing the alleged too-powerful presidency. The chief complaints involve such presidential activities as war making, emergency powers, diplomacy by executive agreement, and government by veto.

## PRESIDENTIAL WAR-MAKING POWERS BEFORE 1974

The Constitution delegates to Congress the authority to declare the legal state of war (with the consent of the president), but in practice the commander-in-chief often starts the fighting or initiates actions that lead to war. This power has been used by the chief executive time and time again. In 1846, President James K. Polk ordered American forces to advance into disputed territory. When Mexico resisted, Polk informed Congress that war existed by act of Mexico, and a formal declaration of war was soon forthcoming. William McKinley's dispatch of a battleship to Havana harbor, where it blew up, helped precipitate war with Spain in 1898. The United States was not formally at war with Germany until late 1941, but prior to the Japanese attack on Pearl Harbor, Franklin Roosevelt ordered the navy to guard convoys to Great Britain and to open fire on submarines threatening the convoys. Since World War II presidents have sent forces without specific congressional authorization to Korea, Berlin, Vietnam, Lebanon, Grenada, Cuba, Libya, Panama, Kuwait, and Haiti—in short, around the world.

From George Washington's time until today, a president, by ordering troops into battle, has often decided when Americans will fight and when they will not. When the cause has had political support, the president's use of this authority has been approved. Abraham Lincoln called up troops, spent money, set up a blockage, and fought the first few months of the Civil War without even calling Congress into session.

It became obvious that presidents needed the power to respond to sudden attacks and to protect the rights and property of American citizens. One State Department official once described this enlarged mandate as follows:

> In the twentieth century the world has grown much smaller. An attack on a country far from its shores can impinge directly on the nation's security. . . . The Constitution leaves to the President the judgment to determine whether the circumstances of a particular armed attack are so urgent and the potential consequences so threatening to the security of the U.S. that he should act without formally consulting the Congress.[36]

Congress was angered when it learned (several years after the fact) that in 1964 President Johnson won approval of his Vietnam initiatives on the basis of misleading information. Under Nixon in 1969 and 1970 a secret air war was waged in Cambodia with no formal congressional knowledge or authorization. The military also operated in Laos under Nixon without formally notifying Congress. It was to prevent just such acts as these that the framers of the Constitution had given Congress the power to declare war; many members of Congress believed that what happened in Indochina in the 1960s and 1970s was the result of the White House's bypassing the constitutional requirements. They also agree, however, that presidential excesses came about because Congress either agreed too readily with presidents or did little to stop them.

During hostilities, especially if the military action is not an all-out war with the nation's vital interests clearly at stake, such as World War II, the country and Congress typically rally behind a president. As casualties mount and fighting continues, support usually falls off. In both Korea and Vietnam, presidential failure to end the use of American ground forces led to increased political trouble. Eisenhower swept into power in 1952 saying, "I shall go to Korea," thus arousing hope among voters that he would end the Korean conflict. Nixon won in 1968 when Johnson was forced out over Vietnam. But even though Congress may have been misled during the Vietnam War, it enthusiastically supported the president and went along with his actions. Not until the war turned sour did senators and representatives begin to charge misrepresentation. Why, then, were they so easily talked into approving funds for the war? (They continued to pass appropriations for it right up to April 1975.) The general lesson appears to be that the country, Congress, and the courts tend to go along with a president's judgments about military actions overseas. It is also true that presidents who involve the nation in a limited war for limited stakes do so at great political peril; unless they get the war over quickly and with few casualties, they face the prospect of defeat in the next election.

There are additional reasons why no formal congressional declaration of war has been issued since 1941. During a state of war the president assumes certain legal prerogatives that Congress might not always be willing to grant. There are also international legal consequences of a formal declaration of war regarding foreign assets, the rights of neutrals, and so on, which

our allies would not always be willing to recognize and which would be difficult to insist upon. Moreover, there is the psychological consequence of
declaring war, compounded by the fact that, according to Article II, Section
2, of the United Nations Charter, war is illegal except in self-defense.

The end of the war in Vietnam, the 1974 impeachment hearings, and the
resignation of President Nixon gave Congress new life.[37] It set about to
recover its lost authority and discover new ways to participate more fully in
making national policy. We now examine Congress's more notable efforts to
reassert itself.

## THE CONTINUING DEBATE OVER WAR POWERS

The dispute over war powers arises because of some seemingly contradictory passages in the Constitution, which state that Congress has the power
to declare war, that the executive power shall be vested in the president, and
that the president shall be the commander-in-chief of the army and navy.

In 1973 Congress overrode Richard Nixon's presidential veto and
enacted the War Powers Resolution, which declared that henceforth the
president can commit the armed forces of the United States only: (1) after a
declaration of war by Congress; (2) by specific statutory authorization; or (3)
in a national emergency created by an attack on the United States or its
armed forces. After committing the armed forces under the third circumstance, the president is required to report to Congress within forty-eight
hours. Unless Congress had declared war, the troop commitment must be
ended within sixty days. The president is allowed another thirty days if the
chief executive claims the safety of U.S. forces requires their continued use.
A president is also obligated by this resolution to consult Congress "in every
possible instance" before committing troops to battle. Moreover, at any time,
by concurrent resolution not subject to presidential veto, Congress may
direct the president to disengage such troops. A concurrent resolution is
passed when both chambers of Congress wish to express the "sense" of their
body on some question. Both houses must pass it in the same form. These
resolutions are not sent to the president and do not have the force of law.
Because of a 1983 court ruling, the question of whether Congress can
remove the troops by concurrent resolution or legislative veto is now in
doubt.

Not everyone was pleased by the passage of the War Powers Resolution
of 1973.[38] Nixon vetoed it because he said it encroached on presidential powers. Purists in Congress and elsewhere said it was clearly unconstitutional,
yet cited reasons different from Nixon's. They said it gives away a constitutional power plainly belonging to Congress, namely, the war-making or war-
declaring power, for up to ninety days.

Still other observers, however much they may have thought this resolution was defective, believed nonetheless that war powers legislation was of
symbolic and institutional significance because it reflected a new determi-

nation in Congress at the time. Presidents had been put on notice that the commitment of American troops is subject to congressional approval. According to the resolution, presidents have to persuade Congress and the nation that their actions are justified by the gravest of national emergencies.

Even so, all recent presidents have opposed the War Powers Resolution as unwise and overly restrictive. They claim it gives Congress the right to force them to do what the Constitution says they do not have to do, withdraw American forces at some arbitrary moment. The War Powers Resolution has not really been tested in the courts because it raises political questions judges generally seek to avoid.

In 1982 President Reagan reported to Congress, along the lines suggested in the War Powers Resolution, after he sent troops into Lebanon. Congress arranged a compromise favorable to the White House and sent it to Reagan for his signature. He made clear in a written statement that his compliance did not "cede any of the authority vested in me under the Constitution as president and as commander in chief. . . . Nor should my signing be viewed as any acknowledgement that the president's constitutional authority can be impermissibly infringed by statute."[39]

At other times, as in Grenada and Libya, when Reagan used the military in overseas operations the president did not invoke the War Powers Resolution. He generally acted as though he did not need any authorization. How did Congress react? Members grumbled but took no action.

President George H. W. Bush insisted, like Reagan before him, that he had an obligation to conduct national security and military affairs as he saw fit—unrestricted by the War Powers Resolution. Bush pointed out that presidents throughout history have had to order military actions without congressional authorization. His sending of troops to Panama in 1989 was in this tradition.

Bush maintained he sent troops to Saudi Arabia in 1990 in response to a request from the Saudis. But when it became clear that Iraq's Saddam Hussein would not pull out of Kuwait, Bush marshaled the support of the United Nations and then sought the support of Congress for offensive military action in the Persian Gulf. "The current situation in the Persian Gulf, brought about by Iraq's unprovoked invasion and subsequent brutal occupation of Kuwait, threatens vital U.S. interests," wrote Bush to Congress. He requested both chambers to adopt a resolution stating that Congress supports the "use of all necessary means to implement U.N. Security Council Resolution 678."[40]

Bush's letter to Congress was the first time since 1964 that a president had asked Congress for a show of support for military engagement. After a soul-searching debate, the House approved the requested resolution 250–183; the Senate by a more narrow 52–47. A majority of the Congress, controlled by Democrats, acted to support a Republican president. It is not clear what Bush would have done if Congress had not given him his support. He is reported to have told journalists that he had the authority to act without such a vote, but plainly he wanted to have their political support.

Bill Clinton sent U.S. troops to Somalia, Haiti, and, under NATO auspices, Bosnia. In all cases, American soldiers were placed in danger of attack by adversaries. But President Clinton acted on his own, without direct congressional authorization, although Congress rather grudgingly did pass both supportive and restricting resolutions with respect to Clinton's sending troops on a Bosnian peacekeeping mission.

In the early months of the war against terrorism, in 2001 and 2002, President George W. Bush acted unilaterally in a number of areas, including the arrest, without recourse to legal counsel, of U.S. citizens. The congressional response to such usurpations of power was meek. Further, Bush was able to prosecute the war in Afghanistan with little congressional oversight, and was able to initiate a United Nations resolution against Iraq with little congressional involvement. He claimed to have unilateral authority to invade Iraq, if events warranted it. Such claims, rather than reviving accusations of an imperial presidency, were mostly ignored in Congress.

What are the lessons of the War Powers Resolution of 1973? On the one hand, Congress tried to reassert itself, and tried to get tough about unilateral presidential war making. On the other hand, presidents have mostly ignored the resolution and viewed it as a nuisance. In the 1990s many members of Congress recognized that the 1973 approach was not effective and perhaps not wise. Those who want to strengthen the resolution and force presidents to comply with it to the letter do not have the votes to get their colleagues to confront the White House. Many Republicans would prefer to scrap the resolution altogether, saying it has not worked and it is not proper for Congress to undermine a president who has to act fast in today's military emergencies, never mind what the Constitution may imply on the matter.[41]

Another group in Congress would like at some point to modify the War Powers Resolution to make it workable. They would have Congress establish a special consultative group of some eighteen congressional leaders who would meet with the president before decisions are made committing American troops to situations where hostilities are probable.

Constitutional and political questions will continue to surround the war-making powers as long as our constitutional democracy survives. The constitutional debate over the precise character of this power continues even as practical accommodations in our constitutional system evolve.

## CONGRESS AND THE INTELLIGENCE AGENCIES

Presidents have also been charged with abusing the intelligence and spying agencies. The Central Intelligence Agency (CIA) was established in 1947, when the threat of "world communism" led to a vast number of national security efforts. At that time, Congress recognized the dangers to a free society inherent in such a secret organization. Hence it was stipulated that the CIA was not to engage in any police work or to perform operations within the United States.

From 1947 to the mid-1980s, no area of national policymaking was more removed from Congress than CIA operations. In many instances Congress acted as if it really did not want to know what was going on. Said one senator: "It is not a question of reluctance on the part of CIA officials to speak to us. Instead it is a question of our reluctance, if you will, to seek information and knowledge on subjects which I personally, as a Member of Congress and as a citizen, would rather not have."[42] There is much evidence that both Congress and the White House were lax in supervising intelligence activities. By 1973, the CIA was accused of plotting assassinations, experimenting with mind-altering drugs, carrying out extensive foreign paramilitary operations, and perhaps most important, spying on American citizens during the Watergate era.

Congress has tried to reassert control over the CIA. It now requires the agency to report to two committees, the House and the Senate oversight committees, any plans for clandestine operations. In 1976, in an unprecedented exercise of power, Congress amended the Defense Appropriations Bill to terminate American covert intervention in Angola.

Presidents have criticized Congress for weakening the CIA, for going too far in making covert operations too difficult. President Carter especially pressed this case during the Iranian and Afghanistan crises of 1980. President Reagan gave the CIA a new era of prominence and enhanced powers; its role in coordinating American assistance to the Nicaraguan Contras is perhaps the most striking example. President Bush, a former CIA director himself, generally continued to be highly supportive of the CIA, yet the end of the Cold War and the dissolution of the Soviet Union understandably caused the CIA budget to be reduced in the 1990s.

Former CIA Director Stansfield Turner says congressional oversight of the CIA is useful. It forces intelligence officers to exercise greater judiciousness, he contends, and to maintain a healthy sense of the national temper. He also believes congressional oversight strengthens the hand of the CIA director in controlling what has always been a notoriously independent agency.[43]

After the Reagan administration's covert selling of arms to Iran was revealed, Congress considered a variety of proposals to place additional curbs on the CIA. None became law. President George H.W. Bush, for his part, worked with congressional leaders to keep them informed about CIA covert activities, as he was required to do under existing law. President Clinton's CIA directors James Woolsey, John Deutch, and George Tenet had to report to Congress on a more regular basis.

Still, for all the talk of greater congressional control, the CIA and recent presidents have not been much hampered in carrying out the operations they have deemed necessary.[44] This is not to say Clinton or Congress has been especially pleased by the CIA in recent years. The CIA has plainly not had an easy transition from the Cold War to the post–Cold War era.

In an age of anti-terrorism, the role of the CIA is being expanded and some of the safeguards initiated in the 1970s are being weakened. President

George W. Bush increased the scope and authority of the CIA to combat terrorism, and lifted some of the restrictions on domestic activity by the CIA. Concerns for stopping terror at home have trumped the fears generated by the excesses of previous years, and the CIA has an increased role in shaping policy, operations at home and abroad, and in advising the president.

## THE 1974 CONGRESSIONAL BUDGET AND IMPOUNDMENT CONTROL ACT

During the Nixon administration, some members of Congress used to joke that ours was a system of checks and balances all right. Congress wrote the checks, and the White House kept the balance. They were referring to President Nixon's frequent use of the power to impound funds appropriated by Congress.

By impounding funds a president forbids an executive branch agency to spend money even though the money has been appropriated by Congress. Impoundment may be necessary to accommodate a change in events (if a war ends, for example) or to alter a managerial approach (to carry out a project more efficiently). Before Nixon, impoundments were infrequent and usually temporary; they generally involved small amounts of money. Nixon stretched the use of impoundments to new lengths. He claimed that the Democratic Congress was spending too much and causing huge deficits. Congress responded that Nixon was using impoundment to set policy and that he was violating the Constitution, which states: "No Money shall be drawn from the Treasury, but in Consequence of Appropriations made by Law." Congress took this to mean it had the final say in fiscal policymaking. But Congress not only complained, it acted as well by passing the 1974 Congressional Budget and Impoundment Control Act.

This Act repealed the 1921 language used by Nixon to justify his impoundments. It also stipulated two new procedures, rescissions and deferrals, by which a president, at least temporarily, can override appropriations decisions or delay spending. A president may propose to cancel, or rescind, enacted appropriations or subsections of a larger appropriations bill, but unless Congress agrees (with a majority vote in both houses) to the rescission within forty-five days, the money must be spent by the executive branch. The new item veto certainly is a strengthened variation of this same authority.

Recent presidents have used this provision, which has cut billions from the budget, and Congress has mostly gone along with presidential suggestions for rescission. Some have complained, however, that this provision creates too much paperwork. Reports need to be sent to Congress even when a few thousand dollars are not spent for simple managerial and efficiency purposes. Others complain about the vagueness of the law. Still, this involvement by Congress and the need for presidents to win congressional approval for impoundment have reclaimed some of the diminished power of the purse for Congress.

The second provision, permitting the deferral of spending by the executive, has caused considerable confusion. According to the law, a president may propose to defer spending funds already appropriated for up to a year. The law requires only that the executive notify Congress of these deferrals and that new notification be filed with Congress to continue a deferral into a second year. The law permits either the Senate or the House to overturn a deferral. But in 1983 the Supreme Court invalidated legislative vetoes and in effect said that the only way to counter a president's deferral of funds was to pass a law doing so.

The Congressional Budget and Impoundment Control Act of 1974 also responded to the fact that since the days of President Roosevelt congressional influence over federal spending had diminished, while that of the Office of Management and Budget in the executive office of the president had increased. With no budget system of its own, only many separate actions and decisions, Congress had become dependent on the president's budget proposals. Members of Congress grew to appreciate the old saying, "The one who controls the purse has the power."

The 1974 act created a permanent budget committee for each chamber of Congress and a Congressional Budget Office (CBO). This office provides budgetary and fiscal experts and computer services to give Congress technical assistance in dealing with the president's proposals. Some members of Congress hoped the CBO would provide hard, practical data to guide the drafting of spending legislation. Others saw it as a potential "think tank" that might propose standards for spending and national priorities. Optimists hoped this budget reform act would help Congress react more effectively and in a timely fashion to the president's budget proposals. They hoped, too, it would tie separate spending decisions to fiscal policy objectives.

In fact, the CBO is most frequently used to provide routine cost estimates of spending and tax bills and to keep track of the overall budget level. Its budgetary timetable gives Congress three additional months to consider the president's recommendations. By May 15 of each year, Congress adopts a tentative budget that sets target totals for spending and taxes. These targets serve as guides for the committees considering detailed appropriations measures. By September 15 Congress is supposed to adopt a second resolution that either affirms or revises the earlier targets. If necessary to meet the final budget totals, this resolution must also dictate any changes in expenditures and revenues.

How has the "reformed" budget process worked in recent years? The quality of information produced by the CBO has improved congressional deliberation on the budget; the new budget committees in each house have worked reasonably well; and the budget resolutions have provided a vehicle for certain helpful debates on key economic issues. But overall the new budgetary process has not diminished the budgetary powers of the president. Nor has it reversed the spiraling national debt. Confusion still surrounds the budgetary process. The whole point of this new budget process was to force Congress to make choices, to put together in one place the spending claims and the revenues, and to decide what it wants. Yet Congress only reluctantly applies cuts to the "sacred cows" of Medicare, defense, agricultural subsidies, and senior citizen entitlement programs.

Many people believe the problem is structural and not the result of personal faults of members of Congress. Congress reflects many competing local pressures, while presidents reflect national pressures. Congress may well have to restructure itself to strengthen places where overall consensus can be built. But this would mean weakening subcommittees and curbing the recent tendencies to disperse power—something Congress is unlikely to do. Yet if it cannot do this, Congress will very likely have to respond to the choices and priorities set by presidents.

## BUDGET REFORM REVISITED: GRAMM-RUDMAN-HOLLINGS

After several years in which virtually no one believed the budget process had worked well, Congress, with White House support, voted to approve the Balanced Budget and Emergency Deficit Reduction Act of 1985 (popularly known by the names of its sponsors in the U.S. Senate, Phil Gramm, Warren Rudman, and Ernest "Fritz" Hollings). After years of being unable to cure the problem of deficit spending, Congress opted for more surgery. This legislation set maximum allowable deficit levels on a declining basis from 1986 to 1991, when the deficit was supposed to be at zero; Congress later set 1993 as the date to be at zero. In 1996, they set a seven-year target. The reduction of deficits was intended to be achieved through across-the-board spending cuts. Initially Gramm-Rudman (as it is usually called) had given the comptroller general of the General Accounting Office the final word in ordering the president to trim spending and reduce deficits. But a 1986 Supreme Court ruling (*Bowsher v. Synar,* 478 U.S. 714) said that giving this authority to the comptroller general would violate the separation of powers doctrine because the comptroller general is an officer of Congress. Congress reverted to a fallback position that requires both houses to pass a resolution making the spending cuts. Then Congress sends this resolution to the president to order the cuts. Certain programs, such as for Social Security or interest on the national debt, are exempt from this process, but almost all domestic and military spending is subject to these cuts.

Even some of the sponsors of this budget-balancing measure called it a "bad idea whose time had come." They insisted it was needed to bring a dose of reality that would force hard choices about domestic spending, military spending, and taxes. It is far preferable, proponents argued, than the processes of the previous decade, during which no choices were made and annual deficits soared.

Critics of Gramm-Rudman called it the worst form of congressional posturing and fear it will bring about an unprecedented shift of power from the legislative to the executive branch. "With this additional power," said Senator Bill Bradley (D-N.J.), a president, "if he plays hard ball, could dismantle the nondefense portion of the budget and wreak havoc with America's poor."[45]

Some critics have noted other aspects of this measure that transfer power to the executive. Thus, Gramm-Rudman legislation requires the president to bring future federal budgets into line with the deficit-reduction schedule by reducing, or even eliminating, cost-of-living allowances and similar automatic spending increases previously enacted in entitlement programs.

After a few years during the Clinton presidency when we had budget surpluses, we once again have an enormous deficit and debt. Congress and the president found countless ways to evade the Gramm-Rudman deficit targets. The savings and loan bailout, for example, was handled outside these targets. Too often Congress simply voted to exclude spending outlays from Gramm-Rudman calculations.

A major goal of all recent budget reforms was to force policy and priority consensus where none had existed. "Budgeting rules, however, have not changed the desire of presidents and members of Congress to represent and to be reelected," writes James Thurber. "It is clear that the executive-legislative divisions over budget policy remain as entrenched as ever. Increased budgetary discipline by Congress and the President is not a simple matter of legislation."[46]

## CONFIRMATION POLITICS

The framers regarded the confirmation process and its advice and consent by the Senate as an important check on executive power. Alexander Hamilton viewed it as a way for Congress to prevent the appointment of "unfit characters."

Presidents have never enjoyed exclusive control over hiring and firing in the executive branch. The Constitution leaves the question somewhat ambiguous: "The President . . . shall nominate, and by and with the Advice and Consent of the Senate, shall appoint Ambassadors, other public Ministers and Consuls, Judges of the Supreme Court, all other officers of the United States." The Senate jealously guards this right to confirm or reject major appointments. During the period of congressional government after the Civil War, presidents had to struggle to keep their power to appoint and dismiss. Presidents in the twentieth century gained a reasonable amount of control over top appointments. Presidents won more influence, in part, because public administration experts warned that chief executives without compatible cabinet level appointees of their choice cannot otherwise be held accountable.

Today the U.S. Senate and the president often struggle over control of top personnel in the executive and judicial branches. The Senate has taken a somewhat tougher stand. Time spent evaluating and screening presidential nominations has increased. "Our tolerance for mediocrity and lack of independence from economic interests is rapidly coming to an end," said one senator. Another summed it up this way: "Surely, we have learned that one item our government is short on is credibility." Senators are especially concerned about potential conflicts of interest and about related character and integrity concerns.

The Senate rejected several nominations of Presidents George H.W. Bush, Reagan, and Clinton including turning down Bush's choice for secretary of defense, John Tower. Tower, a prominent former senator, was accused of having a drinking problem and perhaps a too-cozy tie to several defense contractors. Tower denied the charges, promised not to drink liquor if he was confirmed, yet still failed to win confirmation. He was the first cabinet nominee to be rejected since 1959, when a rejection came late in Eisenhower's second term, not during the "honeymoon" first year as was the case with Bush's defeat with Tower.

President Clinton often watched in frustration after several of his nominees for attorney general, CIA director (Tony Lake in 1997), surgeon general, and judges and ambassadors withdrew after their nominations raised stiff opposition in the Senate.

The Senate's role in the confirmation process was never intended to eliminate politics but rather to use politics as a safeguard. Some conservatives in recent years object that the Senate has rejected occasional nominees because of their political beliefs and thus has interfered with the executive power of presidents. In such instances, so this complaint goes, the Senate's decision is not a reflection of the fitness of a nominee but rather of the political strength of the president.

The Senate's participation in recent years has become more thorough and more independent. "Unfortunately, the process has also become more tedious, time-consuming, and intrusive for the nominees," according to one study. "For some, this price is too high, particularly in conjunction with the requirements of the Ethics in Government Act of 1978. For others, the process is annoying and distasteful but not enough of a roadblock to prevent them (nominees) from going forward."[47]

Because of the tradition called "senatorial courtesy," a president is not likely to secure Senate approval for appointments against the objection of the senators from the state where the appointee is to work, especially if these senators are members of the president's party, even if his party does not control the Senate. Thus, for nearly all district court judgeships and a variety of other positions, senators can exercise what is in fact a veto. This veto can be overridden only with great difficulty. Further, it is usually exercised in secret and is subject to little accountability. But this form of patronage is sufficiently important to senators that senatorial courtesy is likely to continue.

There is a difference between judicial appointments, especially those to the Supreme Court, and administration appointments. The Senate plays a greater role in judicial appointments because of both the life terms judges and justices serve and the fact that they constitute an independent and, as we discuss in Chapter 8, vital branch of the government.[48] There is, as noted, an argument that when it comes to cabinet-level positions in the executive branch, a president ought to be able to choose those who share the president's views and will carry out the general views of the White House. In contrast, a president is not expected to have or to enjoy partisan loyalty from those nominated to the bench. Thus Presidents George H. W. Bush and Reagan had more difficulty in winning confirmation for their nominations to the Supreme Court than they had with their cabinet nominations. Court nominees regularly endure aggressive political and policy scrutiny.

The confirmation provisions in the Constitution have fulfilled most of the intentions of the framers. The Senate has been able to use its power to reject unqualified nominees. It has sometimes also been able to prevent those with conflicts of interest from taking office. In addition, senators have been able to use the confirmation process to make their views known to prospective executive officials. Indeed, the very existence of the confirmation process generally deters presidents from appointing weak, questionable, or "unfit characters." Yet, by and large, presidents have still been able to appoint the people they want to important positions.[49]

## FUSING WHAT THE FRAMERS SEPARATED

A few reformers believe relations between the president and Congress are so bad that what we have is a "constitutional disorder"[50] and only major reforms can right the wrong the framers inflicted upon us. The "wrong" in this case is said to be the separation of powers that fragments and shares political power between the different branches. These commentators see the separation as a weakness that often leads to divided government, which brings about divisive politics, which ends up in deadlock.

This separation is a structural problem, and the proposed cure is the *fusion* of executive and legislative power. The model is British parliamentary democracy.[51] In *Constitutional Reform and Effective Government,* James L. Sundquist offers a parliamentary critique of American government.

Failed government is the problem for which Sundquist suggests the U.S. system has no real cure. What happens "when a president fails as a leader?" Stalemate. But would a system organized along more parliamentary lines solve this problem? Sundquist believes there is much we can learn from the Canadian and British parliamentary systems, yet warns against wholesale grafting of the parliamentary model onto the U.S. system. He writes that "for most constitutional reformers the parliamentary system represents only a source of ideas for incremental steps that might bring more unity to the American government, each step to be considered on its own merits in terms of its adaptability to American tradition and institutions. Parliamentary democracy is not a model to be adopted in its entirety, supplementing the entire U.S. constitutional structure with something new and alien."[52]

Throughout this work, Sundquist is sensitive to how proposed parliamentary reforms might fit into the American system. He focuses his concern on five areas: divided government, length of terms of office, reconstructing failed governments, fostering interbranch collaboration, and altering the checks and balances.

In recent years, divided government has been the norm, leading to a higher probability of deadlock. The solution? Sundquist examines four proposals: (1) a presidential-congressional team ticket, (2) changing the ballot format to make ticket splitting more difficult, (3) separating the presidential and congressional elections by a short time period, and (4) arbitrarily assigning the president's party enough seats in the Senate and House to gain a majority (a bonus seat plan).

Sundquist also looks at plans to lengthen or adjust the terms of office for the president and Congress, examining the four-eight-four plan, the eight-year Senate term, the six-six-three plan, repeal of the Twenty-second Amendment, and eliminating the mid-term elections. The goal in all of these plans is to link the electoral fate of the legislature more closely with that of the president, thereby promoting opportunities for true mandates and presidential coattails.

How to reconstruct a failed government? All too often in recent years, the United States has faced, for various reasons, failed governments. In a presidential system there is little short of impeachment that can be done to remedy this situation. Says Sundquist:

> All governments descend into periods of ineffectiveness, when for any of a wide range of causes leadership fails, public confidence is lost, and conflicts within the government deepen and remain unresolved. When this occurs, parliamentary systems possess a safeguard; their governments can be dissolved at any time and new elections can then install new leaders with a fresh mandate from the people. Or weak leaders can be replaced with stronger ones even in the absence of new elections, without provoking a constitutional crisis . . . the United States, in contrast, is in bondage to the calendar. The nation's leader is elected for four years, and no matter what his failures the office is his as a kind of property right until his term's scheduled expiration—with two exceptions. He may be removed under the impeachment clause of the Constitution if he is convicted of "treason, bribery, or other high crimes and misdemeanors." He may also be relieved of his duties under the Twenty-fifth Amendment, adopted in 1967, if the vice president and a majority of the cabinet declare him to be unable to perform the functions of his office and, in the event the president disputes that finding, two-thirds of both houses of Congress confirm his incapacity.[53]

To overcome this problem, Sundquist looks at several reforms: special elections, no confidence votes, and other "safety valves."

In an effort to promote greater collaboration between the branches, Sundquist offers several proposals, all designed to modify the separation of powers. Among these are such ideas as allowing members of Congress to serve in the president's cabinet, giving cabinet officers a place in the Congress, and, most important of all, strengthening political parties. He notes: "Whatever can be done to strengthen political party organizations will serve to improve cohesion between the executive branch and the President's party in the Congress. The party is still the web that infuses the organs of government with a sense of common purpose."[54]

But in the long run, Sundquist laments, "proposals for formal institutional linkages between the branches . . . hold little promise."[55]

Still, Sundquist offers more than an exercise in intellectual calisthenics. After examining a multitude of reform proposals, he gives, in order of importance, his own formula for constitutional reform: (1) a team ticket; (2) four-year House terms, eight-year Senate terms; (3) a method of special elections to reconstitute a failed government; (4) removal of the prohibition against dual officeholding (to permit members of Congress to serve in the executive branch); (5) a limited item veto; (6) restoration of the legislative veto; (7) a new war powers amendment; (8) approval of treaties by a majority of both houses; and (9) a national referendum to break deadlocks.

While these are not a panacea to break us out of the deadlock of stalemated government, and while Sundquist is not optimistic about the chances for implementation, he does offer an integrated package of reform proposals designed to marry some aspects of the parliamentary model to the idiosyncrasies of America's traditions and institutions.

James MacGregor Burns, in his *The Power to Lead,* takes a similar reformist approach, examining the symptom of failed government and prescribing the cure of a parliamentary alternative. Burns, like Sundquist, sees antileadership tendencies intentionally built into the Constitution, and this leads to either deadlock or the overpersonalization of politics.[56]

Mainstream political scientists disagree with the prescriptions put forward by Sundquist and Burns. They say a president who enjoys both a working majority in Congress and a strong party might be too free to impose his or her own program on the nation. And if the Twenty-second Amendment were voided, this vigorous president might, over time, be able to dominate the judicial branch as well. Critics also say these schemes are designed almost entirely to strengthen the White House and weaken Congress.

Defenders of our presidential system say it generally serves us well. It is a system, they say, that reflects the cautious temperament of the American people. The vitality of the system depends on new ideas and new people, not on importing parliamentary features. In parliamentary systems the parties are so tightly organized that they often become rigid. The American system was intended to have tension in it. It sometimes swings a bit too far in one or another direction, yet it generally works. It is, moreover, especially well designed to protect the liberties of individuals and minorities and it has succeeded in preventing authoritarianism.

Finally, opponents of the Sundquist-Burns proposals say the principle of separation of power is no less valid today than it was in 1787. The national legislature was designed to prevent tyranny of any one leader and tyranny of the majority. Yes, the system is often slow and cautious and hostile to bold leadership initiatives. Yet isn't this appropriate to its responsibilities and primary function? Most Americans want a certain amount of deadlock and delay on policy initiatives that emerge out of presidential or party brainstorming. The genius of the American Congress, then and now, is its capacity for deliberation, debate, and prudent reflection.[57]

## THE CONTINUING STRUGGLE

Most observers now believe Congress has not won back many of its allegedly lost powers, and they are skeptical of Congress's ability to match the president's advantages in setting the nation's long-term policy direction over the long run. Ronald Reagan demonstrated that a popular president who knew what he wanted could not only influence the national policy agenda but also win considerable cooperation from the Congress. George W. Bush and his father demonstrated that a president could win considerable public and congressional support for his foreign policy and military initiatives, even with Congress controlled by the opposition party.

The American public may be skeptical and critical about its political leaders, yet it has not really lost a belief in the efficacy of strong, purposeful leadership. Whether or not people believed in Ronald Reagan's policy priorities, many supported his view that the country needed a strong president who would strengthen the presidency and make the office a more vital center of national policy than it had been in the years immediately following the Watergate scandals. Whether people were critical of Clinton's character or not, Americans generally recognized his leadership efforts to encourage trade, promote new jobs, and advance the cause of civil rights and environmental protection.

A central question during the 1970s was whether, in the wake of a somewhat diminished presidency, Congress could furnish the necessary leadership to govern the country. Most people, including many members of Congress, did not think Congress could play that role. The routine answer now in the twenty-first century is that the United States needs a presidency of substantial power if we are to solve the terrorism, trade, deficit, productivity, and other economic and national security problems we currently face. We live in a continuous state of emergency. Terrorism or nuclear warfare could destroy our country. Global competition of almost every sort highlights the need for swift leadership and a certain amount of efficiency in government. Many people realize, too, that weakening the presidency may, as often as not, strengthen the vast federal bureaucracy and its influence over how programs are implemented more than it would strengthen Congress.

Congress simply is not structured for sustained leadership and direction. Power in Congress is too fragmented and dispersed. Congress can, on occasion, provide leadership on various issues, yet it is far less able to adapt to changing demands and national or international crises that arise than is the presidency. The presidency is a more fluid institution and thereby can usually more quickly adjust and adapt.

Congress's efforts to reassert itself were more a groping and often unsystematic, if well-intentioned, attempt to be taken seriously than a concerted effort to weaken the presidency. It did not take long for observers to appreciate that when a president is unable to exercise authority and leadership, no one else can usually supply comparable initiative. Not only did we reaffirm the pre-Watergate view that the presidency is usually an effective instrument for innovation, experimentation, and progress, but a majority of Americans concurred that to the extent the country is governable on a national basis, it must be governed from the White House by a president and top advisers who can figure out a way to gain the cooperation of various coalitions.

# CHAPTER 7

## *Presidents and Political Parties*

No free country has ever been without parties, which are a natural offspring of Freedom.

James Madison, from a speech at the Constitutional Convention 1787

The spirit of party serves always to distract the public councils, and enfeeble the public administration. It agitates the community with ill-founded jealousies and false alarms; kindles the animosity of one part against another; foments occasional riot and insurrection.

George Washington, Farewell Address to the People of the United States, September 19, 1796

[The president] is the party nominee and the only party nominee for whom the whole nation votes. . . . He can dominate his party by being spokesman for the real sentiment and purpose of the country, by giving direction to opinion, by giving the country at once the information and the statements of policy which will enable it to form its judgments alike of parties and of men. . . . He may be both the leader of his party and the leader of the nation, or he may be one or the other. If he can lead the nation, his party can hardly resist him.

Woodrow Wilson, *Constitutional Government in the United States* (Columbia University Press, 1908), pp. 67–69

The Constitution deliberately created a separate legislative branch and a separate executive. Yet making our Madisonian system of separate powers work effectively requires some help to encourage meaningful cooperation. One of the devices that has often served this intermediary function is the American political party.

A political party at its best brings like-minded people together, that is, people who share similar policy perspectives. Thus members of Congress and a president who are members of a common party not only can talk more easily across the branches, but can devise collaborative mechanisms to produce agreed on legislation, treaties, budgets, and similar political decisions. One of the great paradoxes of the president-party relationship is that while the party can be one of the useful tools of presidential leadership, it is less developed and less appreciated than should be the case.

It is often said that presidents are leaders of their political parties. In fact, however, a president has no formal position in the party structure. In theory, the supreme authority in our parties is the national presidential convention. More directly in charge of the national party, at least on paper, is the national committee (and each national committee has a national chairperson).

In practice, successful presidents usually control their national committees and, often, their national conventions as well. Although the national committee picks the national party chair, a president almost always lets the committee know whom he wants. Modern presidents hire and fire national party staff almost at will. Several of our recent presidents have ignored their national party committees.

Political parties once were a prime source of influence for a president. It used to be said, for example, that our most effective presidents were effective in large part because they had made use of party support and took seriously their party leadership responsibilities. But as our parties have declined in organizational importance, there has been more of an incentive for presidents to "rise above" party or "go public."

Today, the presidential-party relationship is strained. National party chairpersons come and go. Few party chairpersons of the president's party have enjoyed much influence. And many were regarded at the White House as little more than clerks. Clinton's Democratic National Committee's fundraising operation, especially some of its Asian contributions, proved especially embarrassing in 1996.

The central concern in this chapter is the awkward alliance between presidents and their parties. Both president and party need each other. Yet each sometimes becomes frustrated and even annoyed with the other. What has been the role of the president as party leader? What of presidents' use of party as an appeal to Congress for support of their programs? Why the apparent growing divorce between presidents and their parties? What are the limits on presidents as party leaders and the limits of the party as a check on presidents? Could something be done to encourage more cohesion between presidents and parties?

## PRESIDENT AS PARTY LEADER?

Our earliest presidents vigorously opposed the development of political parties. They viewed them as factions and divisive—something to be dreaded as the greatest political evil. The Constitution makes no mention of political parties. In his Farewell Address of 1796, George Washington warned against the "spirit of party generally," and said the nascent parties were "the curse of the country." But if the inventors of the presidency bemoaned the emergence of parties, they soon came to accept them as inevitable, and many even attempted to use parties to their advantage.

The president's role as party leader developed over time; it was a role grafted onto the presidency. The president serves as the party's "most eminent member," titular leader of the national committee, and most visible spokesperson for the party, and he initiates the party's program.

But the president is also, in many ways, independent from the party. Today, the party does not control the nomination; it is comparatively weak and relatively undisciplined; there are separate national, state, and local organizations; presidential involvement can be sporadic; and ordinarily, presidents need support from the opposition to pass their proposals and have them accepted as legitimate.

However, the president needs the party. The grids usually lock if the president, with help from the party, cannot grease the machinery of government: "To be successful, to be powerful the president needs the lubricating of party. Since Washington, all the presidents considered great or near great were active and powerful party leaders. And failures neglected or failed to adequately use party."[1]

One of the chief reasons presidents seek ways other than legislation to make policy is that they are so often unable to get Congress to pass their proposals. This sometimes leads to use of administrative tactics, or engaging in *fait accompli* acts, going public, or moving beyond the law. But if the president has a strong party on which to rely (as long as this party has a majority in Congress), the temptation to achieve results by other means is not as great. Parties can help presidents govern while helping maintain democratic accountability.

By 1800, the contest for the presidency had become a battle between political parties. The Jefferson-led Republicans took on and defeated the John Adams-led Federalists. But even Jefferson, sometimes called the founder of what later became the Democratic party, had doubts about party contests for the presidency. He disliked the Federalist party and its narrow, elitist constituency. He hoped the Federalist party would shrivel and collapse, thus allowing the more representative Republicans to remain in permanent control. Jefferson's party was in fact dominant for two generations.

Parties just naturally arose. They represented fundamental ideological and cultural divisions in American society. Out-of-power interests coalesced to put their own candidates in contention for the presidency. Party clashes became routine. The evolution of political parties had much to do with the

Presidents are often, though not always, seen as the leader of their party. John Adams (left), leader of the Federalist Party, was defeated in the election of 1800 by Thomas Jefferson (right), standard-bearer of the Democratic-Republican Party. *(Source:* Both images reproduced from the collections of the Library of Congress.)

successful functioning of both presidency and Constitution. They solved in part the problem of presidential recruitment. They served also as a means of checking presidents, of keeping them responsive to concerned grass-roots citizens, for to remain in office a president would have to win renomination from his political party.

As they evolved, parties helped narrow down the number of candidates, prepared platforms, and creatively mediated among the diverse interests that were pressing claims and pushing ideological views on future office-holders. Parties usually were able to find the common middle ground among more or less hostile groups so that agreement could be reached on general principles.

Moreover, the parties enabled officeholders to overcome some of the limitations of our formal constitutional arrangements. Political parties facilitated coordination among the branches. President Jackson especially used his resources to promote partisan control of government. Jackson's achievements as party leader transformed the office, so much so that he is sometimes called the "first modern president."

> The President became both the head of the executive branch and leader of the party. The first six Presidents usually acted in a manner that accorded Congress an equality of power. However, starting with Andrew Jackson the President began more and more to assert his role not simply as head of the executive branch but as leader of the government. By the skillful use of his position as head of the party he persuaded Congress to follow his lead, thereby allowing him to assume greater control of the government and to direct and dominate public affairs.[2]

Many historians and political scientists believe the effective presidents have been those who, like Jackson, strengthened their position by becoming strong party leaders. Cooperation and achievement could be achieved through party alliances. "Since the office did not come equipped with the necessary powers under the Constitution, they had to be added through a historical process by the forceful action of vigorous Presidents whose position was strengthened by the rise and development of political parties."[3]

Few presidents have been able to duplicate Jackson's success. Most have found it exceedingly difficult to serve as an activist party builder and party leader while trying to serve also as chief of state and national unifier. President William Taft lamented that the longer he was president, "the less of a party man I seem to become."[4] President William McKinley said he could no longer be president of a party for "I am now President of the whole people."[5] Others complain they cannot simultaneously be faithful party leaders and serve the nation impartially.

What, at least in theory, are the obligations of a president as a party leader? These vary, of course, depending on one's conception of the presidency and the party system. The textbook model has generally held that the president should promote party platforms, reward party loyalists, punish party mavericks, run proudly with the party ticket, and heed the interests and advice of party leaders. The president should be a party builder and strengthen the party ranks by communicating the party's purpose and positions. Presidents, it is believed, should be as much the product of their parties as they are the leader. It should be a two-way street, with parties serving to check ambition and to ensure accountable leadership. A president is expected to consult regularly with local, state, and national party committee officials.

Presidential practice is different. Few of our recent presidents have spent much time working with party officials save as it was necessary for their renomination. Most presidents of late have mistreated their national party committees.

The Nixon presidency in many ways was the ultimate in presidential hostility toward its own party. Nixon dumped Republican Party Chairman Ray Bliss, who was acknowledged as a brilliant party builder. Nixon time and again sought to divorce himself from the Republican label and from supporting Republican candidates. Nixon regularly ignored Republican Party officials and set a similar tone for his White House staff. Once, when National Chairman Robert Dole had been trying for some time to see the president, a White House aide is alleged to have said to Dole: "If you still want to see the president, turn on your television set tonight at 7:00. The president will be on then." Nixon yearned to be above partisan responsibilities. He wanted to be a bipartisan foreign policy leader. Accordingly, Nixon's definition of presidential leadership was that a president is there to make global decisions that no one else can make. He also thought party officials do not know enough to clarify foreign policy issues, not to mention to make foreign policy decisions. Thus Nixon would be the peace-maker, the statesman, the globe-trotting diplomat.

But when a president strives to be above party, critics say, he and his aides may grow dependent on secretive and covert political operations. The campaign abuses of 1972 are one result. A president who divorces himself from his party is potentially an arbitrary president, one who may be too much in the business of self-promotion at the expense of party and public interests. A president out of touch with party politics usually feels little accountability to the people who are close to the grass-roots realities of political life.

The record of recent presidents as party builders is mixed. Ronald Reagan benefited from the efforts of Bill Brock who served as Republican party chair from 1977 to 1981. In the aftermath of the Watergate crisis, Brock rebuilt the party. Under his leadership Republicans gained seats in Congress, raised large sums of money, and aided in the campaigns of Republicans. His efforts helped recapture the Senate in 1980, and paved the way for Ronald Reagan.

As president, Reagan was sensitive to party needs. Since Reagan was not actively involved in the day-to-day workings of his presidency he had time to cultivate party members and satisfy the partisan needs of members of Congress. He was especially willing to have photo sessions with Republican members of Congress, big donors, and the party faithful. This, along with Bill Brock's efforts, greatly enhanced the Republican party, and helped Reagan govern. But in his 1984 reelection bid, Reagan eschewed party and ran a more personalized campaign. He won in a landslide but failed to help his party, and thus had rough going in his relations with Congress during his second term.

George H. W. Bush ran a slashingly partisan campaign in 1988, but tried to govern in a less partisan manner, calling for a "kinder, gentler" America. This may reflect the split personality of George Bush, who tended to see politics as a dirty business, but government as an honorable enterprise.[6] It also reflected Bush's weak political position as he faced a Congress controlled by the opposition. Bush's position was further complicated by the fact that he was not trusted by the far right wing of his party, and even faced a nomination challenge from the right by Pat Buchanan in 1992.

Bill Cinton came to office with something unusual: his party in control of both houses of Congress. But the Democrats were divided and undisciplined. Clinton, who had been governor of a one-party state, initially tried to govern in a "Democrats only" manner. This proved unsuccessful as the Democrats soon came to realize they could pressure the president to give them special favors in exchange for votes and the Republicans, using the filibuster to an unprecedented degree, stalled and delayed the president's program. In effect, Clinton was held hostage by both parties.

The mid-term elections of 1994 as well as the 1996 election changed the political climate. For the first time in forty years, the Republicans gained control of both the House and the Senate. Ironically, President Clinton benefitted by this, as he defined himself in contrast to Newt Gingrich and converted politics into a more personal, Clinton vs. Gingrich battle.

Bucking the conventional wisdom, presidential advisor Karl Rove pushed George W. Bush to actively recruit, fund, and promote Republican candidates in preparation for the 2002 mid-term election. Such party-building by presidents has a limited history of success and often backfires. But in the heat of the war against terrorism, Rove believed the president could rally the public behind the Republican efforts to combat terror and pick up seats in Congress. Bush campaigned aggressively and tirelessly, and in the end, the strategy paid dividends when the Republicans picked up seats in the House and recaptured a majority in the Senate.[7]

## LIMITS ON PRESIDENTIAL PARTY LEADERSHIP

Once in office, presidents often bend over backward in an attempt to minimize the partisan appearance of their actions. This is so in part because the public yearns for a "statesman" in the White House, for a president who is above politics. Presidents are not supposed to act with their eyes on the next election; they are not supposed to favor any particular group or party.

Herein lies another of the paradoxes of the presidency. On the one hand, presidents are expected to be pure and neutral public servants, avoiding political and party considerations. On the other hand, they are supposed to lead their party, help cooperative members of Congress get reelected, and work closely with party leaders. Also, they must build political coalitions and drum up support, including party support, for what they believe needs to be done.

To take the president out of partisan politics, however, is to assume incorrectly that the president will be so generally right and the leaders and rank and file of their party so generally wrong that the president must be protected from the push and shove of political pressures. But what president has always been right? Having a president constrained and informed by party platforms and party leaders is what was intended when our party system developed. How often this was actually done is difficult to estimate.

Another profound limitation on the modern presidents as party leader is the requirement that they must now communicate to citizens by television. Television is the main source of information for the citizen. Television is also a major weapon in the arsenal of presidential leadership. But it also apparently forces the president to bypass party structures—the nonpartisan direct television appeal has replaced the party rally. As a result, the party has lost one of its main functions, namely, being a source of information and communication between citizens and their government.

Presidents know that appeals to party during television addresses are not politically wise. Presidents are instructed by their pollsters and marketing managers to rely on popular appeals and encourage popular leadership rather than party leadership. Party organization thereby becomes subordinate. Time and again, a personalized entrepreneurial politics emphasizing the president triumphs over a politics emphasizing party purposes and party issues.

Television has also provided a means for third-party and extraparty interests to communicate their views to the public and bypass traditional party structures. Ross Perot and George Wallace were beneficiaries of the availability of television time. Television shows and news coverage of people like Pat Robertson, Rush Limbaugh, and Ralph Nader have helped to promote yet other alternatives to the regular two-party process. Little known "partyless" candidates who are wealthy, such as Steve Forbes, can spend millions of dollars in primaries, bypassing the party by going directly to voters, and become serious candidates without the party.

Another related but more subtle factor in lessening the role presidents play in party activities is the fact that for at least a generation now, ours has been a candidate-financed election system, not a party-financed system. A few states, such as Wisconsin, are an exception to this pattern. Most candidates now raise their own funds and organize their own staffs and campaign committees. Generally speaking, the ablest organizers, campaigners, and media consultants have worked for candidates—candidates for the presidency and candidates for Congress. As the parties have grown weaker and as candidate-based organizations have become the routine, people who have remained as workers with party organizations are often less talented, or so at least is the perception of many people now involved in elective politics. The most talented campaign people now are usually in the White House or in Congress, either in office or in staff positions. So much is this the case that elected officeholders and their staffs often do not take "the party people" seriously.

Not surprisingly, these candidate-oriented professionals look down on party officials, and especially party staffers. What have they ever won? This may not be as it should be, but it is the way attitudes get formed in the world of the practitioners.

Ironically, just as the American voter has become less partisan, the American legislator has become more partisan. Voters, several generations removed from a realigning election (the last genuine realignment took place in the 1932–34 period; in recent years there has been de-alignment), are less committed to any one particular party, more inclined to ticket-split, more likely to vote for the person over party, and less dependent on party as a cue in voting. But in Congress, partisanship (and party voting) has increased in the past two decades. This paradox speaks volumes to the nature of partisan bickering and ideological savagery that has taken place in the past decade in American politics.[8]

Every recent White House has had an aide, usually a senior aide, assigned the function of liaison with the national committee staff of the president's party. Such persons (Kenneth O'Donnell for Kennedy, Marvin Watson for Johnson, Tim Kraft for Carter, Ed Meese and others for Reagan, Harold Ickes in Clinton's first term, and Karl Rove for George W. Bush) meet with the chairperson of the national committee, arrange for an occasional presidential visit to state and national party fund-raising functions, and host visits from visiting party delegations. Sometimes, for example, a state party chairperson or even a state party committee will be invited to the White House for staff briefings and perhaps even a lunch with the president. The liaison aide also oversees sensitive party patronage decisions and handles suggestions and complaints coming from national committee members and state chairpersons.

But the work of this White House aide has been overshadowed by the gradual development in the contemporary White House of an office of interest-group liaison. With a notable institutionalization in the Nixon White House, this staff (sometimes numbering as high as twenty-nine or more staffers) has sought an outreach to ethnic, professional, labor, business, religious, and every conceivable citizen-interest organization. Aides such as William Baroody, Jr. (Nixon and Ford), Midge Costanza and Anne Wexler (Carter), Elizabeth Dole (Reagan), and Rahm Emmanuel (Clinton) have pioneered this effort of working directly with groups that once enjoyed their access to politics primarily through the political parties. These aides bring delegations of interest-group leaders to the White House for briefings. They provide an opportunity for the groups to bring their views and grievances directly to top White House aides. In addition, these White House aides try to provide information and inside know-how to group leaders, with the hope they will back the president's programs in Congress and try to get their organization to support the president.

In sum, these are several, but by no means all, of the limits that make it difficult for a president to serve aggressively as a party leader. We have not bothered to elaborate on the well-worn observation that our parties become truly national only for the purposes of electing a president and organizing the national legislature. Although national committees now enjoy greater influence in the conduct of presidential nominations, they still have little influence over our decentralized party structure between elections. Hence, a president's practical influence over the party is sharply limited. A president's power as party leader comes to an end when the president needs it most. The president is virtually unable to recruit party candidates for Congress or other offices and has little or no influence in the selection of state and local party officials. A president's once vast influence over patronage appointments is now considerably circumscribed. Presidents and cabinet members must weigh patronage claims of the party against their own need for expertise and talented assistance. Patronage has its limits. President after president is amazed at the ingratitude of those who have been on the receiving end (and, of course, for every one person who wins a position, a lucrative contract, or some other presidential favor, there are several more who felt they should have won it instead).

## THE "NO-PARTY" PRESIDENCY

Are we moving to a no-party presidency?[9] Parliamentary regimes such as Great Britain have strong disciplined parties, and the prime minister can rely on the party in the Parliament to gain passage of his or her proposals. But in the United States, with weak, undisciplined parties, presidential power is more personalized. While parties matter in the United States, they do not matter as much as in Britain or other European democracies.

These factors undermine party in this country:

- An antiparty bias exists in the political culture.
- Our history is generally one of weak parties.
- The nomination process is not in the control of party regulars.
- The party does not run campaigns.
- Office seekers are entrepreneurs first, partisans second.
- Parties are not the prime fund raisers, individual office seekers are.
- Presidents have short coattails.
- Presidents do not often rely on party, choosing other governing strategies such as
  - direct appeals to the public
  - bipartisanship
  - administrative or managerial strategies
  - taking action on their own
- Patronage has shifted from partisan to personal systems as presidents seek ideological and personal loyalty over party loyalty.

Presidents encounter a number of disincentives when determining what approach to take toward party leadership. In the nominating and governing processes, it is often more useful to eschew party than embrace party. As Robert Harmel writes,

> the context of presidential politics provides few incentives for presidents to lead their party organizations, and most recent presidents have acted accordingly. While none has totally abandoned his party, it can be said without exaggeration that the record has been one of neglect more than active party leadership.[10]

Given the difficulties presidents have in exerting effective party leadership, it may seem surprising that presidents *do* spend some of their precious resources on party. But as difficult as party leadership may be, the alternative, to allow the parties to deteriorate, is far worse. The demise of party has a number of adverse consequences. If party is of little and only sporadic use to presidents, it is at least of some use. In a process where the president's resource cupboard often seems relatively bare, party *may* serve as an aid in moving the machinery of government. It may not be much, but at least it is something.

## PRESIDENTS AND USE OF PARTY APPEAL IN CONGRESS

Presidential control of party supporters in Congress has seldom been great. "Party discipline," wrote Arthur Schlesinger, Jr., "far from being a novelty of our fallen times, is one of the conditions that American democracy has endured from the start."[11] Of course, the situation varies from time to time. If Ronald Reagan enjoyed surprising party unity for his 1981 economic package, he enjoyed it less on social issues and defense spending matters. President Carter experienced a lack of party discipline among the Democrats in Congress. He found members of his own party were strong-minded and independent. Appeals to party were of marginal benefit; Carter found he needed Republican votes as well to secure most of his victories.

George H. W. Bush, facing Democratic control of both houses of Congress, presented an unambitious legislative package to the Congress and failed to push his proposals through. Bill Clinton, after early success in Congress, faced a legislature controlled by the Republicans in 1995 and was forced to alter both his agenda and his operating style. His attempt to pressure an unfaithful Democrat, Senator Richard Shelby of Alabama, led the senator to switch parties after the 1994 mid-term elections.

This led to government shutdowns, negative politics, impeachment, and partisan squabbling. After the 2000 election, President George W. Bush had a razor-thin majority in the House and a 50–50 split in the Senate. But after some self-inflicted wounds, Bush lost control of the Senate when Vermont Senator Jim Jeffords bolted the Republican Party over being slighted by the White House on both policy concerns (education funding) and personal matters (not being invited to the White House to celebrate the "Teacher of the Year" honor which was awarded to a Vermont teacher). Jeffords became an Independent, and voted with the Democrats, ceding control of the Senate to the Democrats.

The mid-term election of 2002 provided President Bush with additional Republican seats in the House, and a majority in the Senate (51–48). Bush's successful showing in mid-term elections that normally go against a president's party were the result of the continued importance of 9–11 and the ongoing war against terrorism, plus an effective barnstorming campaign in which President Bush aggressively campaigned for Republicans across the country. In picking up seats in the House and Senate, Bush boosted his numbers in Congress and increased the chances he might use party as a vehicle for governing.[12]

Presidential attempts to unseat or purge disloyal members of Congress in the president's party have not worked. Roosevelt's celebrated "purge" of nonsupportive Democrats in the congressional elections of 1938 was mainly in vain. Anti–New Deal Democrats won reelection or election for the first time in most of the places where he tried to wield his influence.[13]

Presidential coattails, once thought to be a significant factor in helping to elect members of a president's party to Congress, have had little effect in recent years (see Table 7.1). Members usually get reelected because of the quality of their constituency services and the fact they can take advantage of incumbency, not on whether they have worked cooperatively with the White House. Congressional races are not notably affected by national issues or national trends (1994 and 2002 were exceptions). Time and again, presidents

**TABLE 7.1**
**Presidential Coattails, 1932–2000**

| Year | President | Party | Gains or losses of president's party | |
|------|-----------|-------|-------|--------|
| | | | House | Senate |
| 1932 | Roosevelt | Democrat | +90 | +9 |
| 1936 | Roosevelt | Democrat | +12 | +7 |
| 1940 | Roosevelt | Democrat | +7 | −3 |
| 1944 | Roosevelt | Democrat | +24 | −2 |
| 1948 | Truman | Democrat | +75 | +9 |
| 1952 | Eisenhower | Republican | +22 | +1 |
| 1956 | Eisenhower | Republican | −3 | −1 |
| 1960 | Kennedy | Democrat | −20 | +1 |
| 1964 | Johnson | Democrat | +37 | +1 |
| 1968 | Nixon | Republican | +5 | +7 |
| 1972 | Nixon | Republican | +21 | −2 |
| 1976 | Carter | Democrat | +1 | +1 |
| 1980 | Reagan | Republican | +33 | +12 |
| 1984 | Reagan | Republican | +14 | −2 |
| 1988 | Bush | Republican | −3 | −1 |
| 1992 | Clinton | Democrat | −10 | 0 |
| 1996 | Clinton | Democrat | — | −2 |
| 2000 | Bush | Republican | −3 | −4 |

*Source:* Adapted and updated from Harold W. Stanley and Richard G. Niemi, *Vital Statistics on American Politics,* (Washington, D.C.: Congressional Quarterly Press, 1992), pp. 124–25.

have found in mid-term congressional elections that they can do little to help members of their own party who are in trouble. Ford campaigned vigorously in 1974 for dozens of members of Congress only to see most of them defeated. Carter experienced similar disappointments in 1978, especially in Senate races. In the 1994 mid-term elections President Clinton's party lost fifty-two seats in the House and eight in the Senate.

Presidents today have little retaliatory leverage to apply against uncooperative legislators. Members of Congress, as a result of various congressional reforms, have more and more resources (trips home, large staffs, more research facilities, more home offices and office staffs in their districts, and so forth) to help themselves win reelection. With the dramatic growth of government programs and governmental regulation, members of Congress are in a good position to make themselves nearly indispensable to local officials and local business people, who need to have a Washington "friend" to cut through the red tape and expedite government contracts or short-circuit some federal regulation. These kinds of developments have enhanced reelection chances for most members while at the same time making them less dependent on the White House and less fearful of any penalty for ignoring presidential party appeals.

From the president's vantage point, it is seldom helpful to punish party mavericks. In this reformed Congress, with power more dispersed and decentralized and where nearly everyone has a piece of the action, there is just too much risk for a president to single out a few party "disloyalists" for retribution. White House congressional relations aides know all too well that it is best to abide by the motto of "no permanent allies, no permanent enemies." You may lose someone on a vote today, but his or her vote may be crucial on some other measure next week. Then, too, a president has fewer patronage plums or perquisites these days with which to persuade a wavering member of Congress. More and more patronage jobs of the past are now civil service positions or are selected on the basis of merit. More and more governmental contracts or so-called "pork-barrel" expenditures come under close congressional or press scrutiny or are subject to some funding formula.

In short, a president's appeal to his fellow party members in Congress is effective only some of the time. It sometimes will help, but this kind of appeal is more unpredictable today than in the past. Party caucuses may be a bit stronger in Congress, but legislators know that neither the White House nor fellow members in Congress will penalize them if they can claim that "district necessities" forced them to differ with the party on a certain vote—even a key vote. Presidents doubtless will contrive to encourage party cohesion, but just as clearly, party support will vary on the kinds of measures the president is asking them to support and on whether or not parties continue to lose importance in national political life.

## PROPOSALS TO INCREASE COHESION BETWEEN PRESIDENT AND PARTY

In spite of the revival of the Republican Party in the past decade, experts still see the party system as weak and offer proposals that might revitalize the parties and help them recapture some of their historic mediating and moderating influence in U.S. political life.

Of course, most Americans couldn't care less, and are indifferent to the purposes of our parties. Moreover, even some informed observers say they do not know whether there is much realism in trying to resuscitate the parties. Critics of party renewal efforts sometimes contend there is too much nostalgia for a romanticized two-party system that seldom or never really existed.

Still, rethinking public policy toward the parties is much needed. In the campaign to revive and protect them, the following are the measures, at least bearing on the presidency, one hears most often. We will examine some of their merits and defects.

The most ambitious proposal seeks to replace the Madisonian system of separated powers with a parliamentary system of fused executive and legislative powers similar to that of Great Britain. Observers note that parliamentary systems are more efficient than presidential types of democracies. Parliamentary governments tend to have strong, programmatic, disciplined parties.

A bipartisan committee of scholars and practitioners calling itself the Committee on the Constitutional System, founded in 1981, calls the weak party structure in the United States the chief flaw of the American system. The committee promotes parliamentary reforms so as to bridge the wide gap between the president and Congress, and party plays a prominent role in strengthening that bond. Among the proposals of the committee relating directly to party are:

1. Grant all party nominees for the House and Senate seats as uncommitted voting delegates at the national convention.
2. Make it easier to vote straight-line party tickets by having one line or lever for a party vote.
3. Create a Congressional Broadcast Fund to be used by the party to air TV spots.
4. Have strong party discipline in Congress.

Political scientist James MacGregor Burns, a proponent of these reforms, offers a slightly different list of party reforms.[14] Parties have changed a lot since the 1960s, Burns says, mostly for the worse. To strengthen coherent, unified national parties, controlled from the grass roots, Burns would make major changes in the presidential selection process: participation in primaries would be based on active party membership and statewide primaries would be discouraged; instead delegates would be selected in local caucuses. State party committees could select at-large delegates to reward party officers and party loyalty, and Burns would make certain elements of the party platform mandatory for the party nominees to uphold.

Some proponents of party renewal say federal funding of presidential elections should be abolished or at least significant portions of this public financing should be channeled through the parties and not go directly to the candidates. They say federal funding bypasses parties too much and encourages autonomous, entrepreneurial political adventurers who are unaccountable to anyone. Campaign funds, these purists argue, should go to the party organization. Party regulars or party establishments would then have some control and, thereby, more of a function. Candidates would have to demonstrate their loyalty and their willingness to run with the ticket and on the platform as a quid pro quo of getting adequate financial help. This would presumably tie a candidate, and perhaps later the officeholder, to a closer relationship to the national committee. Moreover, it is pointed out by veteran observers that the two national committees already have experienced accounting offices and these staffs could help reduce the staff work, start-up costs, and probable errors of a newly formed candidate organization. Campaign financing legislation encourages separate candidate committees to be set up to receive and account for public funds, at least in primary elections. If candidates trusted their national committees and national committee staffs, the funds could, at least in theory, come through these party officers to the candidates (this could be done at both the primary and general election stage).

However, the abuses of the pre-1974 system of private financing to candidates had to be remedied. It was predominantly a private candidate-financed system in which candidates and their campaign teams raised enormous sums of money from wealthy donors. If the party got involved, it was to serve the needs of the candidate and not to call the shots itself. The party fundraising apparatus had been reduced to financial middle-man (if it was used at all) for the candidate. In the 1972 Nixon campaign, things got so out of hand that Congress was forced to confront the abuses of this system.

In response to these kinds of situations and the Watergate revelations, Congress passed the Campaign Reform Act of 1974, which substituted a publicly financed candidate system for a privately financed candidate system. National party committees receive some public funds for running the quadrennial national conventions. But as with many reform efforts, the unintended consequences of these reforms closed some loopholes yet opened others. One of the more controversial "new" funding mechanisms is the use of "soft" money by political parties. Money can be donated to the party itself for party-building efforts and that is perfectly legal, as long as there is no direct connection between party and the candidate. Of course, this is a distinction without much difference. In the past several presidential election cycles, soft money donations have been a key element in the efforts of both parties to skirt campaign financing limitations and pour special interest money into presidential campaigns.[15]

Why did this campaign finance reform bypass the parties? Most members of Congress just didn't want to strengthen party committees; members of Congress have little interest in giving party officials more power over who gets money in national elections. Congress obviously was thinking of itself as well. If public financing is extended to congressional campaigns, the last thing a member wants is to have to submit to local and state party officials for campaign funds. As things stand now, the candidate raises his or her own funds. It is a highly individualistic arrangement, and few members of Congress will entrust so important a career lifeblood factor to party bosses. Especially is this the case with officeholders who had to buck the party to get elected merely a few years ago. Further, in its weakened state, party machinery sometimes gets taken over by extremist factions.

If public funds are made available to the national committees, it will probably be done through indirect side payments of some kind or another. Thus, Congress in 1979 approved a lower postal rate for parties to use in fund-raising efforts. Another subsidy, which would make sense, is the provision of free television time to national party committees to present their views and purposes to the American people. Modest assistance of this kind may help to prop up the major parties. Too much funding of the parties, however, might cement into permanence the present parties at the expense of some future party that would be deserving of a chance to catch on.

## PROSPECTS

One of the many reasons politicians rely on the media and go public rather than use the party organization is that the media route is easier. Keeping a party organization intact or rebuilding a political party in a community is an exacting undertaking. It is no accident that more and more groups in America are single-issue organizations. It is difficult to hold a multiissue group together for long, and that is what a party is. We need to have a better understanding of why this is and why there appear to be patterns of party organization and practices of local parties that apparently ensure decay. Could it be otherwise? Might different practices or different incentives help overcome the ruts and the rot?

There have been some healthy signs in the past years. The party caucuses and party conferences in Congress have shown signs of life. Indeed, the Democratic Party caucus in the House of Representatives in the mid-1970s was instrumental in revitalizing that institution. The House Republicans Conference was instrumental in fashioning strategies that led to the Republican takeover of Congress in the mid-1990s. Party caucuses were used to help modernize and democratize the House of Representatives. The party caucus is also a place to discuss party commitments and adapt old commitments to new policy problems. Reagan benefited from notable party caucus loyalty from Republicans in the early 1980s.

Parties need to be preserved: they need to be made constructive and a vital part of the political process. Those who are aware of the chaos and paralysis produced by thousands of new interest groups, each having an impact directly on the government in narrow public policy areas, long for almost any instrument that might prevent direct parochial impact and encourage intermediary processes of trade-off, mediation, and so forth. Stronger parties would obviously help here.

Parties help to give the electorate reasonable choices at the election booth. They can provide a forum for candidates of somewhat common perspectives to agree on broad purposes. They certainly will continue to be important in organizing the legislative branch. Perhaps, too, they sometimes will formulate strategies that can help us overcome some of our toughest economic policy questions.

Perhaps most important to the preservation of parties is a commitment to avoid further weakening of them. To move to the direct election plan might encourage splinter and single-issue parties and further weaken our major parties. Similarly, a national primary might be a severe blow to our party system. Political scientist Austin Ranney views the national primary proposal with alarm, saying it not only would greatly weaken state parties but would mean "a virtual end to the national parties as anything more than passive arenas for contests between entrepreneurial candidate organizations."[16]

Can parties as institutions be made to serve as a more effective check on presidents? This might be desirable, but again, the weakened condition of the parties and the history of party fragmentation and lack of discipline suggests that the prospects are not inviting.[17] One should not overlook, however, the role party officials and party stalwarts have played in checking and balancing presidents of their party. Johnson was forced to quit his 1968 bid less by Eugene McCarthy's insurgency than by Robert Kennedy and party regulars in Wisconsin and elsewhere making it clear he was unacceptable to broad segments within the Democratic Party. So also, Nixon was forced to resign when it was clear that stalwarts in his own party—people like Senators Barry Goldwater, Hugh Scott, and others—could no longer support him.

Parties need to be protected and preserved even if they are not likely to be much strengthened. Presidents in the future, as in the past, will find party leadership a necessary yet exacting task. The incentive is to ignore the party. The four-year term with the necessity of renomination at least ensures that most presidents in the first term will recognize the importance of the party to their political survival. A political party should retain the threat of dumping a president who has turned his back on his party's pledges or has ignored the party platform. We shall have some presidents in the tradition of the Jacksons, Wilsons, and Roosevelts who will serve as party leaders, but just as likely, we will have presidents in the Eisenhower mold, who eschew party responsibilities.

We have not had a president in recent decades who has gone the extra mile and tried to be a vigorous party leader. And while George W. Bush did make an effort in this direction in 2002, the incentive system may be stacked against it. Parties will endure, but in the future as in the past, they will serve us in direct proportion to our taking them seriously and our willingness to make them work.

We need to remember political scientist Clinton Rossiter's warning that there can be "No America without democracy, no democracy without politics, no politics without parties."[18] Likewise we will rarely have effective presidencies without healthy political parties that have integrity.

# Presidents and the Court

[The Supreme Court] has been in angry collision with the most dynamic and popular Presidents in our history. Jefferson retaliated with impeachment. Jackson denied its authority; Lincoln disobeyed a writ of the Chief Justice; Theodore Roosevelt, after his Presidency, proposed a recall of Judicial decisions; Wilson tried to liberalize its membership; and Franklin D. Roosevelt proposed to "reorganize" it.

Robert H. Jackson, *The Struggle: Judicial Supremacy* (New York: Vintage Books, 1941), p. x

For most practical purposes the President may act as if the Supreme Court did not exist. . . . The fact is that the Court has done more over the years to expand than contract the authority of the Presidency. . . . In the nature of things judicial and political, the Court can be expected to go on rationalizing most pretensions of most Presidents. It is clearly one of the least reliable restraints on presidential activity.

Clinton Rossiter, *The American Presidency* (New York: Harcourt, Brace and World, 1960), pp. 56, 58–59

We rely on the courts to enforce what the Constitution promises us.

But in one area the courts have disappointed us. In time of war, actual or threatened, they have repeatedly abdicated their function, bowing to claims of national security.

Anthony Lewis, "Marbury v. Madison v. Ashcroft," *The New York Times,* February 24, 2003, p. A21

The history of presidential–Supreme Court relations is generally one of the nation's highest court encouraging an expansive view of presidential power. Although the Supreme Court has occasionally halted presidential action or declared a presidential act unconstitutional, the Court has more frequently labored to approve or legitimize the growth of presidential power.

The framers of the Constitution intended the Court to serve, along with the presidency, as a check on the anticipated or at least potential excesses of the national legislature. The Court, they hoped, would comprise wise, virtuous, and well-educated statesmen who would interpret and preserve the Constitution, especially from legislative encroachment. Most of the framers believed the Court would work hand in hand with the executive. Some even viewed it as part of the executive department or at least engaged in the same functions, namely executing, interpreting, and applying the laws.

Both president and Court have a national constituency. But where the president serves many masters, the Court serves only one: the Constitution. Both are expected to restrain Congress when needed.

Presidents and the Court have had their share of clashes. This is to be expected. The Constitution stands as the supreme law of the land in a nation governed by laws, not individuals. The rule of law has a key limiting and empowering function for our government. Yet the Constitution is sometimes ambiguous, sometimes silent on matters of grave concern; the law is flexible and changing, open to interpretation. Differences of opinion, interest, and interpretation are inevitable. In most yet by no means all encounters between presidents and courts, presidents emerge victorious. The exceptions are notable. Jefferson was told by the Marshall Court that he had acted wrongly. Lincoln, after his death, was rebuffed for using military courts in areas where they were not justified. FDR saw several New Deal initiatives struck down by the Court as unconstitutional. Truman was ordered by the Court to release steel mills from federal control. Richard Nixon's policy and political intentions were overturned by the federal courts on at least seventy-five occasions, most notably in the summer of 1974 when the Supreme Court directed him to release White House tapes for use in criminal investigations. And Bill Clinton in areas such as executive privilege and executive immunity often found himself rebuked by the courts.[1]

Here are some basic characteristics of two hundred and fifteen years of presidential–Supreme Court relations.

• There is no getting politics out of a nomination to the Supreme Court. Picking justices is a political act. Presidents usually want to "pack" or at least shape the Court, but they possess no special legal or constitutional right to impose their views on a whole branch for a generation. The Constitution entitles a president only to try, not necessarily to succeed.

• Presidents nominate Supreme Court justices and their nominees are usually confirmed by the U.S. Senate. Most justices conform to the general intentions of the presidents appointing them. However, about 25 percent of the justices deviate and become "wayward justices." That is, they vote and write decisions contrary to the views and values of those who appointed them. Several factors encourage justices, once on the bench for awhile, to grow independent from the presidents who nominated them.

• The Supreme Court is generally a friend of the presidency and supports the use of presidential power, especially in wartime or in the conduct of foreign affairs. Indeed the judiciary has played a significant role in the trend toward executive primacy in foreign policymaking.

• The justices can thwart presidential initiatives and are most likely to do so if evidence exists that Congress would agree with the Court, and if there is clear absence of any authority for the presidential action either in the Constitution or in congressional statutes. They are also likely to weigh in against a president when a president's public approval is reasonably low, at the end of a term or after the president has left office or died.

• Presidents take an oath of office, typically administered by the Chief Justice, pledging to uphold the Constitution and not necessarily what the Supreme Court says about the Constitution. Presidents reserve the right to interpret the Constitution for themselves. They may, as they usually do, defer to the judgment of the Court, yet they do not have to accept or agree with the judicial reasoning.

This chapter explores these realities and seeks to understand the following questions and paradoxes. How do presidents select people for the Supreme Court? Why do some nominees get rejected? Why do some justices grow noticeably independent once on the Court? What were the Lincoln and FDR experiences with the court and why did Roosevelt try to "pack the Court"? When, and in what circumstances, has the Court acted to expand the prerogatives of the chief executive? When and in what instances has the Court restrained the presidency? Can we expect the judiciary to constrain a powerful and popular president bent on exercising his or her will? Finally, do national security considerations justify virtually any means, constitutional or otherwise, a president wishes to adopt to ensure U.S. sovereignty and survival?

## PRESIDENTIAL NOMINATIONS TO THE COURT

At the federal convention of 1787 in Philadelphia many delegates believed the national legislature should appoint the justices. The important Virginia plan had suggested this method. But it was opposed as impractical. It had not worked well in the states. The legislature would be too large to make such personnel decisions. And there were other objections. Yet strong opposition to legislative appointment was met with equally strong opposition to appointment by the chief executive.

Alexander Hamilton, in an effort to break the deadlock, proposed that all major officials be nominated by the president with the Senate having the right to approve or reject them. Although Hamilton's proposal was an ingenious compromise, delegates rejected the concept of two-branch participation in the appointment process twice before approving it only in the last month of their deliberations.

In modern times, presidents have to look at the judicial selection process as a partnership venture between the White House and the Senate. A judicial nominee must win a majority confirmation in the Senate. Presidents usually get their way with cabinet and top executive department nominations. The widely accepted view is that presidents are entitled to the assistance in the executive branch of people they respect and trust and whose views are compatible with their own. The Supreme Court, however, is different. It's a separate branch and most members of the Senate nowadays think they have a co-equal responsibility for who should sit on the nation's highest court.[2]

The U.S. Constitution is silent as to the criteria that should guide a president in selecting a Supreme Court nominee. As Terry Eastland, a former Reagan and Bush administration aide, writes: "This is a matter clearly within the president's discretion." However, "the considerations that have decisively influenced presidents in judicial selection have included political patronage, geographical balance, judicial philosophy, and—especially in recent years—race and gender."[3] Judicial values and judicial philosophy are plainly now the dominant criteria.

Most presidents understandably seek to nominate to the bench persons who share their policy preferences. In effect, presidents make predictions about the likely future performance and policy opinions of their potential nominees. If a president can nominate two or three members to the Court, that president's political philosophy can extend beyond his term in office. Thus presidents pay a great deal of attention to whom they shall nominate. In many instances this has led to nomination of close friends, advisers, and loyal partisans. Yet party label alone is not enough or even, in some instances, a key factor. President Theodore Roosevelt wrote to his friend Henry Cabot Lodge and outlined some of his views about what was important as he considered Massachusetts Chief Justice Oliver Wendell Holmes, Jr., as a Supreme Court nominee. To Lodge he wrote, "I should like to know that Judge Holmes was in entire sympathy with our views, that is, with your views and mine . . . , before I would feel justified in appointing him . . ."[4]

In recent decades, presidents have been slightly more partisan in judicial selection. Jimmy Carter did not get the opportunity to appoint any justices to the Supreme Court, but Ronald Reagan was able to appoint three: Sandra Day O'Connor, Antonin Scalia, and Anthony Kennedy. Reagan also elevated William Rehnquist to chief justice in 1986. George H. W. Bush appointed David Souter and Clarence Thomas. Bill Clinton appointed two justices to the Court. Ruth Bader Ginsburg and Stephen G. Breyer. All these justices came from the appointing president's party. (See Table 8.1.)

The appointment of federal judges also reflects the partisan interests of the president and his party (See Table 8.2). Only 13 of 108 members of the Supreme Court came from a party other than the president's. And, as

**TABLE 8.1**
**Supreme Court Appointments, 1972–2003**

| Name | Year of appointment | Law school | Appointing president | Prior judicial experience | Prior government experience |
|---|---|---|---|---|---|
| William H. Rehnquist | 1972 | Stanford | Nixon | — | Assistant U.S. Attorney General |
| John Paul Stevens | 1975 | Chicago | Ford | U.S. Court of Appeals | — |
| Sandra Day O'Connor | 1981 | Stanford | Reagan | Arizona Court of Appeals | State Legislator |
| Antonin Scalia | 1986 | Harvard | Reagan | U.S. Court of Appeals | — |
| Anthony M. Kennedy | 1988 | Harvard | Reagan | U.S. Court of Appeals | — |
| David H. Souter | 1990 | Harvard | Bush | U.S. Court of Appeals | New Hampshire Attorney General |
| Clarence Thomas | 1991 | Yale | Bush | U.S. Court of Appeals | Chair, Equal Employment Opportunity Commission |
| Ruth Bader Ginsburg | 1994 | Columbia | Clinton | U.S. Court of Appeals | — |
| Stephen G. Breyer | 1995 | Harvard | Clinton | U.S. Court of Appeals | U.S. Senate Aide |

Table 8.3 reveals, Republican presidents tend to appoint more white men to the bench than do Democrats, who appoint a higher percentage of women and minorities to federal judgeships.

Presidents have been influenced by a variety of factors when searching for potential Supreme Court nominees. First, as noted earlier, is finding someone who shares their ideological and philosophical views. Second, presidents are politicians and they naturally want praise and political credit for their appointments. Reagan's first nominee, Sandra Day O'Connor, conveniently satisfied both these standards. She was a strong Reagan supporter and her appointment won considerable praise for the president, especially from women's groups.

Still other factors are at work. Nominees have to be confirmed by a majority of the U.S. Senate. Presidents and their aides consult leading senators, especially those from a prospective nominee's home state. They also often consult with members of the Senate Judiciary Committee, the committee responsible for confirmation hearings and initial screening. Presidents also generally take into account the wishes of public and private sector leaders and interest groups who have a known interest in the nomination.

Who gets nominated and confirmed? They have all been lawyers, and in recent years most have been graduates of distinguished law schools such as

**TABLE 8.2**
**Party Affiliation of District Judges and Court of Appeals Judges Appointed by Presidents**

| President | Party | Appointees from same party |
|-----------|-------|----------------------------|
| Roosevelt | Democrat | 97% |
| Truman | Democrat | 92 |
| Eisenhower | Republican | 95 |
| Kennedy | Democrat | 92 |
| Johnson | Democrat | 96 |
| Nixon | Republican | 93 |
| Ford | Republican | 81 |
| Carter | Democrat | 90 |
| Reagan | Republican | 94 |
| Bush | Republican | 89 |
| Clinton | Democrat | 88 |

*Sources:* Sheldon Goldman, "Judicial Selection Under Clinton: A Midterm Examination," *Judicature* (May/June 1995), p. 280; Sheldon Goldman and Elliot Slotnick, "Clinton's Second: Term Judiciary Selection Under Fire." *Judicature* (May/June 1999).

Harvard, Yale, Stanford, Chicago, and Northwestern. Almost all have been active in politics in some way or another. Some have served in local or state elective office. Some have been party leaders. Some were actively involved in presidential campaigns. A few even ran for the presidency themselves (Taft, Hughes, and Earl Warren). Approximately 30 percent served as executive branch officials in the national government before their appointment to the Court. Nine were attorneys general, four were solicitors general, at least eighteen held cabinet-level posts, and over a dozen held various other Department of Justice positions.

Perhaps the most common background in the recent past has been some experience serving as a state or federal judge. Dwight Eisenhower, Richard Nixon, Ronald Reagan, and Bill Clinton all wanted candidates who had judicial experience. Why? In part because they believed this was ideal training for service on the nation's highest court. They also recognized it was easier to discern the predictable future responses of a potential Court member if that person's decisions could be studied.

The Constitution nowhere stipulates, however, that Court members be lawyers. Nor is there any congressional statute insisting on judicial experience. Yet no one today disputes the need for *legal* experience. The desirability of *judicial* experience, however, is less clear. Several distinguished justices did not have prior judicial experience, including John Marshall, Earl Warren, Louis Brandeis, Robert Jackson, and Lewis F. Powell. Intelligence and temperament, as well as being well read, would seem to be just as important as lower court experience. However, most future court nominees are likely to come from the lower federal courts.

**TABLE 8.3**
**A Profile of Presidential Appointees to the Lower Federal Courts**

| | Number of appointees | | | | | | | |
|---|---|---|---|---|---|---|---|---|
| | Johnson | Nixon | Ford | Carter | Reagan | Bush | Clinton | G. W. Bush (01–02) |
| *Gender* | | | | | | | | |
| Male | 159 | 226 | 63 | 217 | 340 | 149 | 266 | 82 |
| Female | 3 | 1 | 1 | 41 | 28 | 36 | 110 | 18 |
| *Ethnicity or race* | | | | | | | | |
| White | 152 | 218 | 58 | 202 | 344 | 165 | 285 | 84 |
| Black | 7 | 6 | 3 | 37 | 7 | 12 | 62 | 9 |
| Hispanic | 3 | 2 | 1 | 16 | 15 | 8 | 24 | 6 |
| Asian | | 1 | 2 | 2 | 2 | | 5 | 6 |
| Native American | | | | 1 | | | 1 | 0 |
| Arab American | | | | | | | 1 | 1 |
| *ABA ratings* | | | | | | | | |
| Exceptionally/well qualified | 89 | 117 | 31 | 145 | 203 | 109 | | |
| Qualified | 68 | 110 | 32 | 110 | 165 | 76 | | |
| Not qualified | 4 | | 1 | 3 | | | | |
| *Total number of appointees* | 162 | 227 | 64 | 258 | 368 | 185 | 376 | 100 |

Note: One Johnson appointee did not receive an ABA rating. George W. Bush did not use ABA ratings. Clinton ABA ratings not available.

Sources: Updated and adapted from Sheldon Goldman, "Bush's Judicial Legacy: The Final Imprint." *Judicature* 282 (1993); *Alliance for Justice*, Judicial Selection Project Annual Report, 1993; and Alliance for Justice Judicial Selection Project Annual Report, 1995 (Washington, D.C.: Alliance for Justice, January 1996). Reprinted by permission of Alliance for Justice.

Future presidents will probably consider these political factors:

(1) whether his choice will render him more popular among influential interest groups; (2) whether the nominee has been a loyal member of the President's party; (3) whether the nominee favors presidential programs and policies; (4) whether the nominee is acceptable (or at least not "personally obnoxious") to the home-state Senators; (5) whether the nominee's judicial record, if any, meets the Presidential criteria of constitutional construction; (6) whether the President is indebted to the nominee for past political services; and (7) whether he feels "good" or "comfortable" about his choice.[5]

Issues of race and gender will also doubtless play a role in presidential Court nomination decisions.

## CONFIRMATION BATTLES

As noted, our Constitution does not vest the process of Supreme Court appointments solely in the president. Article II, Section 2, provides that a president shall have power, "by and with the advice and consent of the Senate," to appoint Supreme Court justices. If a president decides simply to assert his power to pack the court with good friends or unqualified or extremist persons, senators from the opposition party, or even from the president's own party, often try to use their constitutional power to defeat him. Over the history of the Republic the senate has rejected twenty-six presidential nominees to the Court (see Table 8.4). This amounts to about 15 percent of those nominated. This rejection rate increases about 25 percent for presidents in their last year in office and when the Senate is controlled by the opposition party. More important, this check on presidential power has forced presidents to not appoint persons who would fail to win Senate approval. In yet other instances some potential nominees may have taken themselves out of consideration precisely because they feared grueling confirmation hearings.[6]

Why are some nominees rejected? Sometimes it is because a president is highly unpopular in the country and in the Senate. President Andrew Johnson's stock in the Senate was so low he probably could not have had any nominee of his confirmed; his one nominee fell victim to Senate rejection.

On occasion a practice known as "senatorial courtesy" contributes to the rejection of a nominee. This occurs when one or both senators from a nominee's home state indicate to the White House that they strongly oppose the proposed Court appointment. This practice is more common in cases of federal district judge appointments, yet it has in times past under-cut a presidential Supreme Court appointment.

The political and philosophical views of a nominee can sometimes stir up the opposition of major interest groups and the opposition party, as was the case in Reagan's 1987 nomination of Robert Bork. This can especially harm

TABLE 8.4

## Supreme Court Nominations Rejected, Postponed, or Withdrawn Due to Senate Opposition

| Nominee | Year nominated | Nominated by | Actions |
|---|---|---|---|
| William Paterson[a] | 1773 | Washington | Withdrawn |
| John Rutledge[b] | 1795 | Washington | Rejected |
| Alexander Wolcott | 1811 | Madison | Rejected |
| John J. Crittenden | 1828 | J. Q. Adams | Postponed |
| Roger B. Taney[c] | 1835 | Jackson | Postponed |
| John C. Spencer | 1844 | Tyler | Rejected |
| Reuben H. Walworth | 1844 | Tyler | Withdrawn |
| Edward King | 1844 | Tyler | Postponed |
| Edward King[d] | 1844 | Tyler | Withdrawn |
| John M. Read | 1845 | Tyler | No action |
| George W. Woodward | 1845 | Polk | Rejected |
| Edward A. Bradford | 1852 | Fillmore | No action |
| George E. Badger | 1853 | Fillmore | Postponed |
| William C. Micou | 1853 | Fillmore | No action |
| Jeremiah S. Black | 1861 | Buchanan | Rejected |
| Henry Stanbery | 1866 | Johnson | No action |
| Ebenezer R. Hoar | 1869 | Grant | Rejected |
| George H. Williams[b] | 1873 | Grant | Withdrawn |
| Caleb Cushing[b] | 1874 | Grant | Withdrawn |
| Stanley Matthews[a] | 1881 | Hayes | No action |
| William B. Hornblower | 1893 | Cleveland | Rejected |
| Wheeler H. Beckham | 1894 | Cleveland | Rejected |
| John J. Parker | 1930 | Hoover | Rejected |
| Abe Fortas[e] | 1968 | Johnson | Withdrawn |
| Homer Thornberry | 1968 | Johnson | No action |
| Clement F. Haynsworth, Jr. | 1969 | Nixon | Rejected |
| G. Harrold Carswell | 1970 | Nixon | Rejected |
| Robert H. Bork | 1987 | Reagan | Rejected |
| Douglas H. Ginsburg | 1987 | Reagan | Withdrawn |

a = Reappointed and confirmed.

b = Nominated for chief justice.

c = Taney was reappointed and confirmed as chief justice.

d = Second appointment.

e = Associate justice nominated for chief justice.

*Source:* Adapted from *Storm Center: The Supreme Court in American Politics,* 3rd ed., by David M. O'Brien. Copyright © 1993, 1990, 1986 by David M. O'Brien. Reprinted by permission of Addison-Wesley Educational Publishers, Inc.

a candidacy when the opposition party controls the U.S. Senate, as it did when Nixon, for example, tried to appoint Clement Haynsworth in 1969. Many senators, especially Democrats, viewed Haynsworth as too conservative. The senate rejected another of Nixon's nominees, Florida Judge G. Harrold Carswell, mainly on the basis of inadequate professional competence. Opposition to Carswell came fast and strong. One respected law school dean suggested this nominee presented more slender credentials than any other nominee for the Supreme Court put forth that century, and after the confirmation hearings were completed, most senators agreed with this verdict.

Sometimes the Senate rejects a nominee to signal its opposition to the policy or recent record of the incumbent Supreme Court. Sometimes senators are unsure of the political reliability of a nominee. And sometimes the Senate merely makes a mistake, as some observers believe it did when it rejected President Herbert Hoover's 1930 nomination of Judge John J. Parker of North Carolina.

The Senate usually takes its constitutional responsibility seriously. Senators view an appointee to the Court as more consequential than most members of a president's cabinet. Court nominees are seen as more important because of their longer tenure, their independence from the White House, and their impact over a whole range of important public policy issues. Usually the Senate Judiciary Committee and then the Senate itself scrutinize these nominees closely. Poor selections such as Madison's choice of Alexander Wolcott, Grant's choice of George Williams, and Nixon's choice of Harrold Carswell have been rejected often enough to set reasonable standards. Although the Senate rejected only four nominees in the twentieth century, presidents and White House advisers with any sense of history are aware that the Senate jealously prizes this shared power of appointment.

In late 1987, Reagan's nomination of Robert H. Bork incited sharp differences of opinion about how much the Senate should take into account the philosophical views of a nominee. Some Democrats in the Senate proclaimed that the framers had intended the broadest role for the Senate in choosing members of the Court and hence they had wide authority in checking into a nominee's constitutional views and values. At least one Republican senator disagreed, saying that for the Senate to require that judicial candidates pledge allegiance to the political and ideological views of particular senators or interest groups could lead to paralyzing the Senate in a gridlock of competing interest groups, each hawking its own agenda. However, a New York Times/CBS News public opinion survey at the time found that Americans believed senators should attach importance to nominee's positions on constitutional issues when judging the nominee's fitness in the confirmation process. (See Table 8.5 for the poll data.)

The Clarence Thomas, Bush nomination fight in 1991 was one of the most divisive in U.S. history. Thomas barely won confirmation by a 52 to 48 vote, but both his nomination and especially his confirmation battle triggered a major political backlash for George H. W. Bush and to some extent for the U.S. Congress.[7]

During the Clinton years, confirmation politics often were deeply partisan events. While partisanship has always played a part in the process, an intense partisanship affected confirmation politics in the 1990s. "The Republicans rewrote the rules when Clinton was in office," said judicial scholar Sheldon Goldman. The process has broken down, he added, "The partisanship has gotten out of hand. The 'advise and consent' process has turned into 'obstruct and delay.'"[8]

**TABLE 8.5**
**Judging Supreme Court Nominees: Should Their Views and Values Be Considered by the Senate?**

Q. "When senators decided how to vote on confirming a president's nominee for the Supreme Court, after satisfying themselves about the nominee's legal experience and background, how much importance should a senator attach to the nominee's positions on major constitutional issues?"

| | |
|---|---|
| A lot | 62% |
| A little | 25 |
| None | 6 |
| No answer | 7 |

*Source:* Based on a New York Times/CBS News poll of 745 people interviewed by telephone, July 21–22, 1987, reported in *The New York Times,* July 24, 1987, p. 10. Copyright © 1987 by the New York Times Co. Reprinted by permission.

Republicans blocked many Clinton nominees, delaying the holding of hearings on others, and refused to even deal with still others. It was a strategy designed to prevent the president from filling seats on the bench. And when George W. Bush became president in 2001, and the Democrats controlled the Senate, they did much the same.

This led a frustrated Bush to propose process changes in the confirmation system, setting specific deadlines for the president and Senate to act on judicial nominations.[9] But such efforts went to the back-burner when Republicans regained control of the Senate in 2003, and Bush's judicial nominees fared somewhat better with their partisans in control of the process.

## WAYWARD JUSTICES

Once confirmed, new members of the Court are in no way obliged to the president who appointed them. There is always an element of unpredictability in how justices will vote in future years. Loyalty to the president who appointed them is not considered a proper reason for judgment on the Court. Even justices who have "pleased" their sponsoring president acknowledge that they think and act differently once they join the Court.

Justice William H. Rehnquist said that any president who attempts to leave a lasting ideological stamp in the Court will typically fail. Unexpected legal developments, the Court's time-honored tradition of independence, the role of precedent, the influence of eight colleagues already there, and other factors undermine a president's efforts to leave a mark on the Court.

Dwight Eisenhower regretted his appointments of Chief Justice Earl Warren and Justice William Brennan. Both provided indispensable judicial leadership in civil rights, reapportionment, and criminal procedure issues. Cordial relations between Warren and Eisenhower diminished perceptively soon after the landmark *Brown v. Board of Education* (1954)[10] decision.

Years later, Ike told friends "the appointment of that dumb son of a bitch Earl Warren" was his biggest mistake as president.[11]

How often do presidents fail to get what they want in the people they appoint to the Supreme Court? One student of the judiciary concludes about 25 percent of the justices have "deviated" from the expectations presidents held for them. In some instances, such as the Earl Warren case, we can relate judicial performance to presidential expectations with considerable precision. More often assumptions have to be made based on the general political views of the presidents and on the situations in which they operated. In still other cases of short tenure, it is near impossible to discern the "loyalty" or "deviation" of a justice. Political scientist Robert Scigliano examined the fit or lack of fit between justices and presidents and concluded:

> ... that about three-fourths of those justices for whom an evaluation could be made conformed to the expectations of the Presidents who appointed them to the Supreme Court . . .
>
> Our conclusion is an important one in that it indicates limitations upon the ability of Presidents to influence the policies of the court through appointments and assures us, retrospectively at least, of a certain, but crucial, measure of judicial independence from Presidential attempts to bring the Court closely into line with the executive branch of government.[12]

Why have so many justices disappointed the presidents who appointed them? Sometimes it is because the presidents and their advisers failed to examine closely the already known views of the prospective nominee. Woodrow Wilson apparently overlooked some of the doctrinal conservatism of McReynolds. Eisenhower apparently engaged in some wishful thinking in his selection of Earl Warren. Ike was also in debt to Warren politically for his help in the late stages of the 1952 presidential nomination battle. Warren had not done a lot, but what he did do, Eisenhower greatly appreciated.

The constitutional obligations of the court are different from those of being a friend or adviser to a president. The Court is not supposed to be a rubber stamp for anyone, and most of the justices come to view themselves as virtually sovereign in their own right. The Court, moreover, decides when violations of the law, including violations by the executive branch, occur. The Court further is charged with keeping the president and others in the executive branch in their constitutional place. The *Marbury v. Madison* (1803), *Ex parte Milligan* (1866), *Youngstown Sheet and Tube Co. v. Sawyer* (1952), and *U.S. v. Nixon* (1974) tradition is important to the Court and its new justices become defenders of this tradition.[13]

Justices are clearly affected as well by the Court's long-standing inclination to honor precedent except in unusual situations. The philosophy, interest, and training of the vast majority in the legal profession tend toward conservatism. Concern with precedent and respect for the past and for authorities, existing customs, vested rights and usages, and established relations characterizes the method of thinking in the legal profession. "No lawyer sufficiently devoted to the law to know our existing rules, the history of them, and the justification for them, will depart from them lightly," wrote Robert H. Jackson, shortly before FDR appointed him to the Court. "The contribution of legal philosophy to the balance of social forces will always be on the conservative side."[14] The job of the justices, most would agree, is not to promote the president's powers or policy initiatives, but rather to ensure that the political trends of the day don't overwhelm our enduring values of due process, liberty, and equality.

Life tenure adds an incentive to think, act, and decide independently. The framers knew that what Alexander Hamilton called "the least dangerous branch" would need to be at least somewhat free from the influences of ambition and interest if they were to perform their responsibility. Life tenure gives justices "high honor, high responsibility, and guaranteed tenure and salary, so that they need neither seek higher office nor worry about retaining the one they have. These conditions, at once emancipating and greatly demanding, result in judicial behavior which may not conform either to presidential expectations or to the views that the justices expressed before joining the Court."[15]

Once a justice is on the Court, a president cannot effectively threaten, intimidate, or retaliate against a wayward or hostile justice. There may be times and circumstances when presidential "jawboning" would sway a decision but, as the following examples suggest, they would be the exception to the rule. Jefferson tried in vain to have a justice impeached. FDR tried to reorganize or pack the Court. Nixon, in a crucial case involving him, hinted he might not comply with the Court's decision. None of these presidential intrigues worked.

Thus, there is, as there should be, a certain amount of unpredictability in the judicial appointment process. Presidents can never be certain their nominees will be approved by the Senate. Nor can a president ever be sure a justice will not change when he or she dons the judicial robes. A Yale law professor put it well: "You shoot an arrow into a far distant future when you appoint a Justice and not the man himself can tell you what he will think about some of the problems that he will face."[16]

## PRESIDENT LINCOLN AND THE COURT

Lincoln did not believe in a dominant role for the American presidency, at least not in normal times. As a Whig Party member in earlier years, he believed Congress should make the law, and he believed in a strong cabinet. He also thought presidents should rarely use the veto power.

Lincoln, however, came to office in extraordinary times. In one sense, he owed his election in 1860 to Chief Justice Roger B. Taney. For the Taney Court's controversial 1857 *Dred Scott* decision split the Democratic Party into northern and southern wings over the issue of slavery. Lincoln rose to prominence because he opposed the Taney Court decision, and he won election because of the Democratic schism.[17]

Lincoln's expansion of presidential powers came because of the wartime emergencies he faced soon after he came to office. He would defer to Congress and his cabinet on domestic matters but would use his powers as commander-in-chief to the fullest. Indeed, he would push them beyond the boundaries the country had hitherto known.

Fellow members of Lincoln's Republican party were determined to reform the Supreme Court as Lincoln came to office. Some wanted to call a national convention to modify the power of the Court through a constitutional amendment. Others pushed a "court-packing" scheme that would have enlarged the Court to thirteen members. Still others proposed even more radical remedies.

Lincoln chose a more elusive and generally a politically successful approach. He would do what he deemed necessary to fight and win the Civil War and he would, whenever possible, try to prevent the Court's interference by denying it an opportunity to become involved in controversial cases. Lincoln exercised broad constitutional power, and in nearly every case he sought congressional approval only after he acted unilaterally. With Congress and public opinion on his side, Lincoln was usually not challenged by the Court.

Yet Lincoln clashed with the Court on some occasions, and the federal judiciary ruled against him in several cases (though many of these came after his assassination). His wartime leadership expanded the scope of executive power and tested the Court's ability to restrain a president in times of war or crisis.

Faced with the secession crisis in 1861, Lincoln, with Congress out of session, proclaimed a blockade of southern ports and ordered the navy to enforce the blockade. The blockade-running shipowners whose ships were seized went to court and challenged the legality of Lincoln's blockade. The owners claimed that under international law a blockade was legal only in a declared state of war. Yet no such declaration existed. Hence, they claimed, Lincoln's blockade was illegal and unconstitutional until July 1861, when Congress sanctioned the war.

Crucial constitutional questions were raised or raised anew as this case came before the Court. Was the blockade valid without a congressional declaration of war? Can a president commit the nation to military action without congressional approval? Are undeclared wars sanctioned by the U.S. Constitution?

The Court ruled (5–4) that a state of war had existed at the time of the blockade and its institution, thus justifying a resort to these means of subduing a "hostile force." Lincoln "won," yet only by a narrow margin. Still, the case established significant constitutional precedent. A president may determine the existence of an emergency and he can take whatever measures are necessary to meet it. A president cannot declare war, yet as commander-in-chief he may commit the nation to military action, especially in an ongoing domestic crisis. The president, at least in certain cases, can wage a "defensive war."

Had this case been brought up soon after the event itself, Lincoln might not have won. The Court delayed hearing the blockade cases for a year. By the time of the decision Lincoln had made three appointments to the Court; they constituted three of the five pro-Lincoln or pro-presidential power votes. Chief Justice Taney voted against Lincoln's position. Lincoln's initial war-making acts were thus held valid, the blockade was legitimated, the condemnation of the seized ships was sustained, and a convenient dual theory of the Civil War was outlined: it was both an insurrection, a hostility within a nation, and a hostility between independent nations.

During this time Lincoln created a national army out of state militias, calling up 75,000 volunteers for three months of military service, which the law authorized him to do. But he went beyond the law a short time later when he called up 42,000 volunteers to serve for three years in the army, thereby doubling the army's size and necessitating major spending for unauthorized projects. Congress later gave him retroactive approval, yet he was exercising his powers to their fullest. He also suspended the right of habeas corpus (a court order stipulated in the Constitution directing an official having a person in custody to produce the person in court and explain to the judge why he or she is being held).

The central issue in another clash that Lincoln had with Chief Justice Taney rested on whether the Constitution expanded in wartime to provide enlarged presidential discretion and authority. Lincoln insisted necessity forced him to take whatever measures were needed to subdue the enemy. On this and similar occasions, Lincoln believed measures otherwise unconstitutional might become lawful by being indispensable for the preservation of the Constitution through the preservation of the nation. Usually, however, Lincoln insisted the Constitution did provide the necessary authority for him to act as he had acted.

The Constitution, Lincoln believed, was nothing without the nation. National survival was his prime duty. Preserving all the rights and liberties provided for in the Constitution was a secondary duty, at least for the time being.

Chief Justice Taney disagreed. He wrote the president saying he had no constitutional power to suspend the writ of habeas corpus. A president certainly "does not faithfully execute the laws if he takes upon himself legislative power, by suspending the writ of habeas corpus, and the judicial power also by arresting and imprisoning a person (Merryman) without due process of law."[18] Taney lectured Lincoln that Merryman should be set free and that the President should reconsider his misuse of powers belonging to Congress.

Lincoln ignored Taney's judgment, although later in a special message to Congress Lincoln asked: "Are all the laws but one to go unexecuted and the government itself go to pieces lest that one be violated?"—which is a classic validation of executive power beyond the law for the alleged needs of national security. Taney's verdict wasn't a Supreme Court decision, it came in a directive from Taney acting as a circuit court judge and thus had less binding force than had it come as a Court decision. More important, in this case Lincoln enjoyed public opinion support and popular acquiescence for his extension of executive power. Even Taney conceded he could not match the president's power.

Lincoln, through his secretary of state, instituted censorship and military arrest and trials, and continued to ignore or even suspend habeas corpus requirements in cases of persons accused of aiding the Confederacy. Throughout this period Lincoln resisted the federal courts, and Taney in particular, on the ground a president's duty to obey judicial rulings may be suspended, in special circumstances, by the higher responsibility to "preserve, protect, and defend the Constitution." One part of the Constitution may be disregarded temporarily, he implied, in order to save the government as a whole.

What is the lesson to be drawn from this clash between Taney and Lincoln? At first glance it was simply a question of Taney as Supreme Court justice striving to preserve respect for the law. Lincoln as president was determined to preserve the Union. Constitutional historians draw additional verdicts. Clinton Rossiter comes close to saying that if a president has public support, he can virtually disregard both the Constitution and federal courts.

> The one great precedent [here] is what Lincoln did, not what Taney said. Future Presidents will know where to look for historical support. So long as public opinion sustains the President, as a sufficient amount of it sustained Lincoln in his shadowy tilt with Taney and throughout the rest of the war, he has nothing to fear from the displeasure of the courts. . . . [19]

Others concluded that Lincoln's sweeping assertions of authority revealed an inability of Congress and the Court to curb a dynamic president determined to act decisively in times of emergency. His leadership stunned even some of those who sympathized with the northern cause. Thus, the abolitionist Wendell Phillips called Lincoln an "unlimited despot." Lincoln may have lacked mass backing for certain of his war policies and civil liberties violations, yet he could count on the popular acquiescence that proved to sustain his leadership.

Taney died in October of 1864, just before Lincoln won reelection to the White House. Two years later, Taney, who while in office could never curb Lincoln's sweeping definition of emergency powers, won at least a symbolic victory in the Supreme Court in the case of *Ex-parte Milligan* (1866). It vindicated the Taney judgment in *Ex-parte Merryman* (1861). The Court, with Lincoln dead and at least a couple of Lincoln appointees now voting with the majority, ruled Lincoln's use of military courts outside the war zone unconstitutional.

As long as civil courts are open and operating, the Court said, an accused is entitled to a civil trial by jury. Congress had not clearly authorized the imposition of martial law. Thus Lincoln and the executive branch had acted unconstitutionally.

Note, however, that this after the fact "slap-on-the-wrist" decision came a full year or so after the Civil War was over. It had not restrained or affected Lincoln or his presidential performance. Many analysts point to this decision as typical of the timidity of the Court or its inability to act as a reliable check on a president during wartime. If the Court was unable or unwilling to restrain a prudent leader like Lincoln, will it be able to restrain a determined, guileful, and ambitious future president? Will future presidents learn from the Lincoln lesson that emergency actions in the gray area of the Constitution are unlikely to be met with Court resistance, at least not during the emergency or during their lifetime?

Lincoln scholar Richard N. Current disputes the suggestion that Lincoln was a despot or an American Cromwell. Lincoln, he writes, continued to be sensitive to the constitutional limits on executive action. Not only did he retain his Whiggish habits of deferring rather than dictating to Congress, he almost never used the veto and he continued to consult widely. Lincoln would sometimes even acknowledge he had little legal basis for what he had done, and he'd ask Congress for appropriate authority.

> Never did Lincoln show any hankering for the perquisites or trappings of exalted power. If absolute power corrupts absolutely, he was absolutely safe from corruption. As a young man, he warned against future politicians of a dictatorial bent. . . .
>
> Such, in actual life, were the concerns of the Lincoln whose image, more or less distorted, later presidents were to exploit. When, regardless of their party, they represented themselves as true followers, they were indeed doing as he had done, for he had said again and again that he was the true follower of the honored dead of both parties of the past. But when his successors asserted the broadest presidential power and took him as their prototype, they were making a very dubious use of history and biography. . . . Neither by word nor by deed did he give any real justification for the idea of "executive privilege" or of an "imperial president."[20]

## FRANKLIN D. ROOSEVELT AND THE COURT

Like most strong presidents, Franklin D. Roosevelt had a series of clashes with the Court. Like Lincoln, FDR came to office during an emergency, and the times demanded extraordinary leadership. Roosevelt was more than happy to provide it. The Supreme Court, on the other hand, would not always approve his interpretation of what needed to be done.

Roosevelt's New Deal emergency relief and recovery programs had their presumed constitutional basis in emergency executive powers or in the power of Congress to provide for the general welfare and to regulate interstate commerce. The combined efforts of FDR and a generally cooperative Congress became the most far-reaching assertion to date of national emergency leadership.

The Supreme Court of the early Roosevelt years was hardly a body receptive to FDR's spacious uses of executive and federal power. Most of its members were appointees from the Harding, Coolidge, and Hoover years.

Roosevelt's first two years passed without notable clashes with the Court. This changed in 1935. Between early 1935 and mid-1936 the Court ruled against the New Deal in several decisions. Among other actions, it held unconstitutional important parts of the National Industrial Recovery Act, the Railroad Retirement Act, a federal farm mortgage relief act, the Agricultural Adjustment Act, and the Bituminous Coal Conservation Act. The Court also told Roosevelt he was without inherent power, which FDR had claimed, to remove a Federal Trade commissioner.

The Supreme Court was not the only part of the federal judiciary hostile to Roosevelt. Hundreds of injunctions restraining officers of the federal government from carrying out various congressional acts were granted by federal district judges.

To Roosevelt and his advisers the Court's actions amounted to a reckless, partisan, and irresponsible claim of judicial supremacy. The Court had virtually nullified vital, core chunks of the New Deal recovery effort. Robert H. Jackson, a top FDR Justice Department official, who would later become a Supreme Court member, describes the Court's attack on the New Deal:

> In striking at New Deal laws, the Court allowed its language to run riot. It attempted to engraft its own nineteenth century laissez faire philosophy upon a Constitution intended by its founders to endure for ages. . . . The Court not merely challenged the policies of the New Deal but erected judicial barriers to the reasonable exercise of legislative powers, both state and national, to meet the urgent needs of a twentieth-century community.[21]

Then came 1936. Roosevelt won by a landslide. It was a defeat for the Court almost as much as it was a Roosevelt victory. Tensions were high. Senator Burton K. Wheeler proposed a constitutional amendment that would allow Congress to overrule a Supreme Court decision merely by reenacting it by a two-thirds vote in both houses. Neither FDR nor his advisers wanted to go that far, yet they warned that some means had to be found to adapt the legal system and judicial interpretation to contemporary national needs.

On February 5, 1937, a frustrated Roosevelt, emboldened no doubt by his impressive reelection victory, introduced his famous reorganization or "court-packing" plan to Congress. Jefferson, Jackson, and Theodore Roosevelt all altered or threatened to alter the size of the Court, thus Roosevelt's actions were not entirely unprecedented. Yet the scope of his proposal (from nine to fifteen) was an almost revolutionary court-packing effort.

FDR's plan recommended that if a federal judge (Supreme Court or lower courts) who had served at least ten years waited more than six months after his seventieth birthday to resign or retire, a president could add a new judge to the bench. A president, in fact, could appoint as many as six new justices to the Supreme Court and forty-four new judges to the lower federal courts.

Roosevelt's objective was obvious. Although claiming he sought efficiency and elimination of crowded backlogs facing the courts, everyone realized he was seeking to gain quick control of the Supreme Court. He told friends that what the Court needed were some Roosevelt appointments. "Then we might get some good decisions out of them." He had had no opportunity to appoint a justice in his first term. He believed he had no choice but to act now, and to act boldly.

The plan stirred angry protests. Even Roosevelt Democrats worried it might destroy the independence of the judiciary. Several Roosevelt confidants such as James Farley, Harry Hopkins, and Rexford Tugwell disagreed with FDR's strategy. The less than candid reasons he gave for the plan damaged his credibility. Chief Justice Charles Evans Hughes blasted the Roosevelt scheme, saying that adding members to the Court would actually hinder rather than promote efficiency in Supreme Court operations. Most all of the members of the then sitting Court resented FDR's attempt to make the Court more submissive to his political will. Justice Louis Brandeis, the Court's eldest member, was irked by the arbitrary and indiscriminate attack on age. Still the plan was given reasonably serious consideration in Congress—a Congress controlled by Democrats—until the Senate Judiciary Committee wrote a scathing report on the measure, which helped defeat it.[22]

Other reasons for the plan's defeat came as a result of changes by and on the Court itself. The Court began upholding as constitutional key New Deal measures that came before it. Two of the justices (Hughes and Roberts) shifted sides. Then in May of 1937 one of the conservatives announced his retirement. These developments gave FDR pretty much what he wanted, a likely 6–3 working majority. Other developments in Congress, also were at work, but the end result was a defeat for FDR's devious plan.

Scholars often say Roosevelt lost the battle yet won the war. Plainly his 1936 election victory combined with his subsequent campaign to alter the Court's size had an impact on the Court. "A switch in time," it was said "saved nine." The presidential power of appointment combined with congressional authority to determine the Court's size proved to be useful guns behind the door. Still this was one of the worst political defeats of the Roosevelt presidency.

In the end, however, FDR got what he wanted and won significant changes.

As with Lincoln, Franklin Roosevelt's most important ally in his conflicts with the Court was public opinion. Ultimately, the Court came to legitimize Roosevelt's more sweeping use of national power because he enjoyed the support of the public. Whether public opinion should sway the judgments of the judiciary is of course another matter, and one of the most profoundly debated aspects of the role of the Court and constitutional review in our democratic republic.

Roosevelt enjoyed even stronger public support for the foreign policy and wartime measures he initiated. Conservative Republican George Sutherland, a Harding appointee, shared Roosevelt's view of a strong president for foreign policy. Justice Sutherland said in the *U.S. v. Curtiss-Wright Export Corporation* case in 1936 that in foreign policy, "with its important, complicated, delicate and manifold problems, the president alone has the power to speak or listen as a representative of the nation." Congress had delegated broad powers in foreign affairs to the president and even extended the normal pattern. Sutherland called the president the sole organ of the nation, and came close to calling the president "the sovereign." It appeared from this that virtually any delegation of foreign policy power to a president would be upheld.

Political scientist David Gray Adler summarizes its impact:

> There can be little doubt that the opinion in *United States v. Curtiss-Wright Export Corp.* in 1936 has been the Court's principal contribution to the growth of executive power over foreign affairs. Its declaration that the president is the "sole organ of foreign affairs" is a powerful, albeit unfortunate, legacy of the case. Even when the sole-organ doctrine has not been invoked by name, its spirit, indeed its talismanic aura, has provided a common thread in a pattern of cases that has exalted presidential power above constitutional norms.[23]

Once again in 1942, in *Ex-parte Quirin,* the Supreme Court expanded presidential power in a period of wartime. The case involved the manner in which eight German saboteurs who had landed on American shores with explosives should be tried. Franklin Roosevelt ordered a secret military trial and closed the civil courts to them. Judicial scholar David J. Danelski explains this complex, fascinating, and tortured case well, but his conclusion is of primary concern here:

> For the executive branch, the Saboteurs' Case was a constitutional and propaganda victory; it expanded Executive power, and it allayed public fears of subversion. For the Supreme Court, it was an institutional defeat. If there is any lesson to be learned from the case, it is that the Court should be wary of departing from its established rules and practices, even in times of national crisis, for at such times the Court is especially susceptible to co-optation by the executive.[24]

In 1944, another significant delegation of power was added to the list of precedents for presidential emergency leadership. The Court, in the *Korematsu v. U.S.* case (in which the Court approved the actions of the executive branch when in the early 1940s it forced West Coast Japanese-Americans to relocate to the Rocky Mountain region) gave the president foreign policy or national security powers even when these powers extended into the domestic arena.[25] A president's war powers were found to take precedence even over the constitutional rights of U.S. citizens on American soil. The Court based, as it did in the *Curtiss-Wright* decision, much of its decision on the reality of congressional approval of the president's action. Also, Roosevelt still had public opinion on his side. When a president has both Congress and the public supporting an initiative or a policy, nine out of ten times the Court is likely to legitimize it as constitutional.

Two later Presidents, Truman and Nixon, sometimes found themselves in the situation where neither Congress nor the public stood by them. The Court is more tempted to strike presidential actions down when a president stands alone. Such was Truman's fate in the 1952 *Youngstown Sheet and Tube Co. v. Sawyer* case.[26] Nixon suffered a series of defeats before the Court, including his impoundment policy, wiretapping, and the famous tapes case, *U.S. v. Nixon* (1974).

On balance, the Court will limit presidents mainly when presidents ignore congressional mandates, attempt to alter the structure of government, or seriously tread on individual liberties. (Even then the Court may find rationales for supporting extension of presidential power.) The Court becomes more bold than it otherwise might be when presidents lose the backing of the American public. Still, the judicial history of noninterference with the growth of presidential power contains just enough exceptions to make it unpredictable.

## MOVING BEYOND THE LAW

Given the many roadblocks and agents that have a veto that clutter a president's path, it is not surprising that the more ambitious and goal-oriented presidents get frustrated as other actors block their way. Well-organized opposition in Congress, demanding special interests, an uncooperative business community, an adversarial press, and others can at times seem to gang up on the White House.

When faced with these multiple opposing forces, most presidents feel trapped. The choice may appear to be either to accept defeat or take bold action on behalf of what presidents claim is the national interest. Making the complex separation of powers work is difficult under the best of circumstances, in normal times it may seem impossible to get the system moving. Thus, rather than accept defeat some presidents are tempted to cut corners, move beyond the law, stretch the constitutional limits a bit.[27]

When all else fails, and it so often does, some presidents, knowing their future political success, not to mention their historical reputation, is at stake, simply cannot resist going beyond the law. If the choice is deadlock or illegality, some presidents will choose the latter. After all, presidents are convinced that what they want is for the best interests of the nation, so why let a corrupt Congress, an uninformed public, or a hostile press stand in the way of progress (self-defined by the president)?

Presidents not well grounded in the virtues of the American system may see the system itself as the enemy and thus feel justified in going beyond the law. Richard Nixon with Watergate[28] and Ronald Reagan with the Iran-Contra scandal are two pronounced examples.[29] Clinton and George W. Bush in some of their antiterrorism initiatives also illustrate this.

Some presidents get away with it (e.g., Reagan, Clinton); some do not (Nixon). But when the choice seems to be to stay within the law and fail

(Ford, Carter) or go beyond the law and maybe you will succeed and maybe you won't get caught, the temptation is too great for some leaders to resist.

An attitude of arrogance may overtake the president and top staff. "We know best" and "they are blocking progress" lead to the belief that the "slight" abuse of power is being done for the greater good. But such an attitude leads to the imperial presidency, and to further abuses of power.[30]

President Reagan was convinced that communism was an evil that had to be fought at all costs, that the Marxist government in Nicaragua was a serious and direct threat to the United States, that the Congress was soft on communism, and that public opinion, which opposed U.S. intervention, was uninformed in spite of herculean efforts by the administration. Therefore, Reagan was faced with the difficult choice of either accepting the will of Congress, the voice of the people, and the law or acting on what he believed to be in the national interest. He acted.

Putting aside for a moment the question of whether Reagan was correct about the threat Nicaragua posed, one thing is clear: the Reagan administration decided that the law was wrong and that they would not be bound by law. This was one of the chief reasons the framers insisted on checks and balances: to control abuses of power.[31]


## THE PRESIDENT'S EMERGENCY POWER

Is a president ever justified in stretching the Constitution? While the word *emergency* does not appear in the Constitution, the founders may have envisioned the possibility of a president exercising "supraconstitutional powers" in time of national emergencies.[32]

During a crisis, a president often assumes extraconstitutional powers. The branches that, under normal circumstances, are designed to check and balance a president will usually defer to the president in times of national emergency. A president's institutional position offers a vantage point from which he can more easily exert crisis leadership, and the Congress, Court, and public usually accept the president's judgments.

The idea that there is a different set of legal and constitutional standards for normal conditions than for emergency conditions raises some unsettling questions regarding democratic governments and constitutional systems. Can democratic regimes function in any but prosperous, peaceful circumstances? Or must the United States constantly rely on the strength of a despot or "constitutional dictatorship" to save it from disaster? Are constitutional governments incapable of meeting the demands of crisis?

In most instances, democratic political theorists have seen a need to accept a certain amount of authoritarian leadership in times of crisis. Locke called this executive "prerogative," Rossiter referred to a "constitutional dictatorship." To Rousseau it was an application of the "general will." In cases of emergency, many theorists suggest that democratic systems, to save themselves from destruction, must defer to the ways of totalitarian regimes. In other words, to preserve democracy one must abandon democracy.

For British theorist John Locke, in emergency situations the Crown retains the prerogative "power to act according to discretion for the public good, without the prescription of the law and sometimes even against it."[33] While this prerogative could properly be exercised only for the "public good," one cannot escape the conclusion that this is shaky ground on which democratic governments and democratic theory must stand. And what if an executive acts wrongly? Here Locke was forced to abandon secular concerns: " . . . the people have no other remedy in this, as in all other cases where they have to judge on earth, but to appeal to Heaven."[34]

Rousseau, writing in the *Social Contract,* noted:

> The inflexibility of the laws, which prevents them from adapting themselves to circumstances, may, in certain cases, render them disastrous, and make them bring about a time of crisis, the ruin of the State.
> . . . If . . . the peril is of such a kind that the paraphernalia of the laws are an obstacle to their preservation, the method is to nominate a supreme ruler, who shall silence all the laws and suspend for a moment the sovereign authority. In such a case, there is no doubt about the general will, and it is clear that the people's first intention is that the State shall not perish.[35]

The chief difference between Locke and Rousseau on this matter rests in Rousseau's refusal to rely on an "appeal to heaven" in cases of possible abuse of the power of the "supreme magistracy." Rousseau said this power must have strictly enforced time limitations as a protection against a complete takeover of the system. Yet once extraordinary power is assumed by an individual ruler, who can be sure that such time limits can and will be adhered to?

Political scientists J. Malcolm Smith and Cornelius P. Cotter summed up this problem in the writings of democratic theorists when they noted that ". . . democratic political theorists tacitly admit the existence of a fatal defect in any system of constitutional democracy: Its processes are inadequate to confront and overcome emergency."[36]

Political historian Clinton Rossiter's *Constitutional Dictatorship* is a discussion of the same problem.[37] The "constitutional dictatorship" is an admission of the weakness of democratic theory, or of its failure to cover the full range of governing requirements. To save democracy, we escape from it. To protect democracy, we reject it. Democratic theory, then, according to the democratic theorists, is incomplete; in cases of emergency, one is called on to reject democracy for the more expedient ways of the dictator. In this manner, democratic theory may open the door to a strong, power-aggrandizing executive.

Nowhere in the Constitution is it specified that a president will have additional powers in times of crisis or emergency. History, however, has shown us that in times of national emergency the powers of a president have greatly expanded, and while former Justice Abe Fortas writes that, "Under the Constitution, the president has no implied powers which enable him to make or disregard laws,"[38] under the microscope of political reality we can see that this is precisely what American presidents have done.

The consequence of this view of an enlarged reservoir of presidential power in emergencies was characterized by constitutional scholar Edward S. Corwin as "constitutional relativity."[39] By this Corwin envisioned a constitution broad and flexible enough to meet the needs of an emergency situation as defined and measured by the Constitution. The Constitution can be adapted, in short, to meet the needs of the times. If the times call for quasi-dictatorial action by the executive, the Court could find this acceptable.

The dilemma of emergency situations in democratic systems is not easily answered. If the potential power of the state is used too little or too late, the democratic state faces the possibility of destruction. If used arbitrarily and capriciously, the system could accept a form of permanent dictatorship. In a modern sense, the constant reliance on the executive to solve the many "emergencies" (self-defined by the executive) facing America could very well lead to the acceptance of the overly powerful executive and make the meaning of the term *emergency* shallow and susceptible to executive manipulation.

With each new "emergency" in American history, the public and our political institutions seem to have become more accustomed to accepting an enlarged definition of presidential power to meet it. In the twenty-first century, it seems hardly a debatable point to say that a president is expected to assume responsibility and added powers to meet both domestic and foreign crises.

The Court under Rossiter's constitutional dictatorship will generally recognize the need for the president to have inflated powers with which to deal with the impending crisis, and will allow for a "flexible" interpretation of the powers of the president. For as Rossiter noted, "In the last resort, it is always the executive branch in the government which possesses and wields the extraordinary powers of self-preservation of any democratic, constitutional state."[40]

Under Rossiter's theory, the Court recognizes the emergency and allows the president to assume additional powers. But the constitutional dictator must recognize the limits of his responsibilities. Franklin D. Roosevelt, after claiming/requesting of Congress a grant of an unusually large amount of power in 1942, assured the legislature that: "When the war is won, the powers under which I act automatically revert to the people—to whom they belong."[41] The executive, in short, is to return the extraordinary powers he was granted during the crisis to their rightful place. But serious questions remain as to (1) whether presidents have in fact returned this power, and (2) whether, even if the president desired to do so, a complete or even reasonable return to normalcy is possible after the dictatorial or quasi-dictatorial power is placed in the hands of one person. In sum, can a democracy survive without a strong executive, and conversely, can a democracy exist with one?

## PRESIDENTIAL ACTION IN TIMES OF EMERGENCY

In practice a president's emergency power has indeed been great in comparison to powers under normal circumstances. When faced with a crisis situation, presidents have made exaggerated claims of power, have acted on these claims, and generally have gotten away with these excessive, and often extralegal, uses of power. History provides us with clear examples of the enormous power of a president in an emergency situation.[42]

Presidents on occasion act with little regard for the wishes and dictates of the other branches. The necessity for quick, decisive, often extraconstitutional actions, which the crisis may demand, places a heavy burden on the president, or so at least president think. Being the only leader able to move quickly, the president must shoulder the burden of meeting the crisis. According to Richard Longaker, "In time of crisis constitutional limitations bend to other needs."[43]

For the crisis presidency to be seen as legitimate, (1) a president must face a genuine and a widely recognized emergency; (2) Congress and the public must, more or less, accept that the president should exercise supraconstitutional powers; (3) Congress may, if it chooses, override presidential acts; (4) the president's acts must be public so as to allow Congress and the public to judge them; (5) there must be no suspension of the next election; and (6) the president should consult with Congress where possible. Lincoln and Roosevelt met (more or less) these requirements, Nixon and Reagan often did not. Clinton's was a mixed case indeed.[44]

Even when the above requirements are met, however, one should not be sanguine about presidential usurpations of power. As the Supreme Court reminded us in *Ex-parte Milligan* (1866): "wicked men, ambitious of power, with a hatred of liberty and contempt of law, may fill the place once occupied by Washington and Lincoln."

After the terrorism of 9-11 the public rallied behind George W. Bush in support of his efforts to battle the terrorist network responsible for the attack on the United States. While generally the president pursued his goals with reason and proportionality, some of the administration's actions proved controversial. The attorney general questioned the patriotism of anyone who objected to administration actions, and ordered the detention, without being charged with a crime, without access to an attorney, and without recourse to judicial appeal, of American citizens and non-nationals.[45]

Bush was further able to get the Congress to quickly pass the U.S. Patriot Act into law, and later establish a new cabinet post, the Office of Homeland Security. He orchestrated a successful war against Afghanistan, whose Taliban government had been harboring the terrorists of Al Qaeda. All of this was done either with the near rubber stamp approval of Congress or on the president's own claimed authority, independent of congressional authorization.

But Bush's actions raised concern when in late 2002, the administration announced a major shift in U.S. strategic policy when they released "The

National Security Strategy of the United States of America." This report announced the replacement of deterrence with a new policy of preemption. This announcement was made on the authority of the president alone, without congressional involvement or authorization. It was a major transformation of U.S. strategic policy, was solely a presidential policy, and paved the way for a preemptive strike on Iraq.

## COURT DECISIONS AND PRESIDENTIAL POWER

Five types of Supreme Court decisions are possible when presidential powers come into question (Table 8.6). Most of the time, as noted earlier, the Court approves or *expands* presidential authority. It often also *legitimizes* presidential power. The Court can also *avoid* or duck the question on the grounds it is a political matter to be settled by Congress and the president. On rare occasions a *two-sided decision* is possible, when the Court may restrict an individual president but add to the power of the office. The Nixon tapes decision in 1974 is illustrative of a two-sided ruling. The Court ordered Nixon to yield his tapes. The Court also, and for the first time, recognized executive privilege as having constitutional standing. Sometimes, of course, in a clash of views the Supreme Court *restricts* or curbs a president and presidential powers.

How often do we see the Supreme Court handing down these kinds of decisions? The two-sided rulings are rare. The Court, over its history, has often avoided questions affecting presidential power. Justices, for example, rarely want to deal with questions about the legality of a war such as in Vietnam.

When sensitive issues of national security arise the Court often invokes what is commonly called the doctrine of "political questions" to avoid head-on collisions with the president. The doctrine rests on the separation of powers theory, which holds that the Supreme Court exercises judicial power and leaves policy or political questions to the president and Congress. Chief Justice John Marshall invented the "political question" doctrine as early as 1803 when he said that matters in their nature political are not for this Court to delve into. He affirmed this later, as in 1829 when he refused to rule on a boundary dispute between the United States and Spain. The judiciary shall not, said Marshall, decide foreign policy. Questions such as foreign boundaries, he added, are more political than legal.

Expanding and legitimizing decisions are common. They are several times more likely than restricting decisions. Nearly every analyst of Court-presidency relations emphasizes the Court's role in the expansion of presidential powers. Most of the time the Supreme Court has supported the vigorous actions of our strong presidents. One scholar concluded that "in every major constitutional crisis between the executive and the judiciary, the president has emerged the victor." He also said the judiciary can neither force the president to do anything, "nor prevent him from doing anything he may

**TABLE 8.6**
**Types of Court Decisions Regarding Presidential Power**

| Type of decision | Definition | Example |
| --- | --- | --- |
| *Expanding:* | Decision adding power to presidency | *U.S. v. Curtiss-Wright Export Corp.* (1936). Recognizes it is necessary for presidents to have more power in foreign than in domestic affairs. |
| *Legitimizing:* | Decision giving Court approval for presidential activities that were questioned | *Korematsu v. U.S.* (1944). Approved FDR and executive powers to intern Japanese-American citizens in World War II. |
| *Avoiding:* | Decisions the Court decided "not to decide"; avoids getting involved | *Massachusetts v. Laird* (1970). Denied to hear a case that questioned the president's broad power in the Vietnam War, thus avoiding a decision on the war. |
| *Two-Sided:* | Decisions going against a president yet adding power to institution of the presidency | *U.S. v. Nixon* (1974). Nixon told to yield tapes, yet court recognizes "executive privilege" as valid in serious national security situations. |
| *Restricting:* | Decisions curbing or even diminishing presidential power | *Youngstown Sheet and Tube Co. v. Sawyer* (1952). Truman and his Secretary of Commerce told they had exceeded their power in seizing the nation's steel mills to prevent a strike. Truman based his action on general powers of his office. Court held he could take no such action without express authorization from Congress. |

decide to do."[46] Although his sweeping verdict exaggerated the case, many students of presidential-judicial relations modify this judgment only slightly today.[47]

The Supreme Court has been and will very likely continue to be a supportive ally in most potential showdowns, especially in the case of emergency or national security contexts.

## PRO-PRESIDENCY COURT RULINGS: EXPANDING OR LEGITIMIZING PRESIDENTIAL POWER

Many of the cases cited here are cases in which the highest court in our nation essentially gave or approved of power that had been previously undefined or undetermined. The issue at stake is whether presidents are able to cite a law or precise wording in the Constitution, or whether their broad and vague "executive power" allow them to conduct certain activities.

*The Prize Cases* (1863) were not the first dealing with presidential power to come before the Court, yet they are the first dealing with extraordinary, independent actions taken during a crisis. The Supreme Court ruled five to four that Lincoln could wage war with the South, under his authority as commander-in-chief, without congressional declaration. Presidential discretion was deemed sufficient for exercising this power. Indeed it was deemed to be within the broad grant of executive power found in Article II of the Constitution. The maxim that "There are two Constitutions, one for peace, the other for war" has its roots in these Civil War decisions.[48]

Before 1863, under international law ships could be legally taken as prizes only when a conflict had been recognized as a war between two belligerent powers. Thus, if the Supreme Court said the South did not have belligerent status, it appeared the justices would have had to rule the blockade as illegal. They decided instead to give primacy to executive discretion.

Another pro-presidency landmark case, *In re Neagle* (1890),[49] dealt not with foreign affairs but rather with the domestic task of effectively carrying out the functions of government. David Neagle, deputy U.S. marshal in the San Francisco region, was assigned to travel with Supreme Court Justice Stephen J. Field. Field's life had been threatened by a Californian, whom Field had sentenced to prison. The U.S. attorney general assigned Neagle to help protect Field. In implementing his assignment Neagle had to shoot, fatally it turned out, the man who in fact did try to attack Field.

The central question involved in this case was whether a president has either the constitutional or the prerogative sources of power to execute orders of the kind that assigned Neagle to his duties. Is a president limited to enforcing only acts of Congress?

Here again the Supreme Court ruled the president had been granted broad executive powers that he must be able to use at his discretion to administer properly the laws of the land. The Court openly acknowledged it was interpreting the word *law* in a liberal manner, the only conceivable manner that would serve the interests of justice in this instance. The president's executive order was clearly constitutional under the "faithfully execute" clause of the Constitution. The president's duty to fulfill this clause is consequently not limited to the enforcement of acts of Congress, according to their express terms, "but includes also the rights, duties and obligations growing out of the Constitution itself, our international relations, and all the protection implied by the nature of the government under the Constitution."

This decision strengthened and expanded the powers of the presidency. This broad interpretation was underlined a few years later in a subsequent Court case that legitimized President Grover Cleveland's sending troops into the Chicago area to deal with a railroad strike. Workers at the Pullman railroad company in 1894 had gone out on strike over certain wage reductions. The American Railway Union carried out a secondary boycott against the Pullman company, a boycott that eventually threatened violence. A federal court issued an order seeking to halt the boycott on the grounds the strike crippled interstate commerce. Union President Eugene V. Debs and his aides ignored the court order, were arrested, and were convicted of contempt and sentenced to prison. President Grover Cleveland had dispatched federal troops to Chicago and ordered the U.S. attorney in Chicago to halt the strike. Debs not only ignored these federal initiatives but petitioned the

Supreme Court for a writ of habeas corpus, challenging his detention as illegal. Writing for the Court in this famous *in re Debs* (1895) case, Justice David J. Brewer affirmed sweeping executive emergency powers. His pro-presidency opinion:

> While it is not the province of the government to interfere in any matter of private controversy between individuals, or to use its great powers to enforce the rights of one against another, yet, whenever the wrongs complained of are such as affect the public at large, and are in respect of matters which by the Constitution are entrusted to the care of the nation, and concerning which the nation owes the duty to all the citizens of securing to them their common rights, then the mere fact that the government has no pecuniary interest in the controversy is not sufficient to exclude it from the courts, or prevent it from taking measures therein to fully discharge those constitutional duties.[50]

In a 1926 landmark decision, *Myers v. United States,* the Court in a 6–3 decision granted a president, and presumably the presidency, with further administrative power, authorizing presidents to remove governmental officials without obtaining the consent of Congress. Frank Myers, postmaster for Portland, Oregon, was removed by President Woodrow Wilson without Wilson's securing Senate consent. Myers brought suit for salary for the remainder of his term. Back in 1876 Congress had passed a law providing for Senate participation in the removal of postmasters. Thus the question now, in the 1920s, was: May Congress limit a president's removal power?

Here is a rare instance in which the Supreme Court went against the wishes of Congress, at least as represented by the old statute under which Myers claimed to have his job protected. As we have seen, the Court usually defers to congressional judgment when Congress has specifically addressed the issue at hand, yet in this case the Court did not. The majority in this case believed a strict separation of powers is necessary if the executive is to function effectively. The 1876 law was simply overturned as unconstitutional, for as Chief Justice Taft put it in his majority opinion, it was found to violate Article II of the Constitution. Taft said a president's power of removal of executive officers appointed by the executive with the advice and consent of the Senate is full and complete without Senate consent. Taft went on to say the sole power of removal is essential to the president if he is to faithfully execute the laws.

Justices Louis Brandeis and Oliver Wendell Holmes, Jr., in dissent, made the same arguments the majority would make in a case nine years later that would greatly narrow the *Myers* decision. Brandeis said Congress was given the power to establish offices and tenure; it was not specifically denied the right to participate in removals, so it should be able to do so. Removal, to Brandeis, was a condition or qualification of tenure. He added an observation widely cited today: "The separation of the powers of government did not make each branch completely autonomous. It left each, in some measure, dependent upon the others, as it left to each power to exercise, in some respects, functions in their nature executive, legislative and judicial. . . . The doctrine of separation of powers was adopted by the Convention of 1787, not to promote efficiency but to preclude the exercise of arbitrary power. The purpose was not to avoid friction, but, by means of the inevitable friction incident to the distribution of the government powers among three departments, to save the people from autocracy. . . ."[51]

Perhaps the next major expansion of presidential power came in a case previously discussed in the section on Franklin Roosevelt. In the *United States v. Curtiss-Wright Export Corporation* (1936), the Court in a 7–1 decision chose to affirm and expound at length on the broad foreign powers held by the president. The executive, the Court said, was the sole spokesman of the nation, not of the Constitution, of the national government, or of Congress. To many observers this expansive decision came close to saying the president was "the sovereign." Congress could delegate, or so it seemed, virtually any foreign policy authority to the White House.[52]

A year later, in *United States v. Belmont* (1937), a near unanimous Court ruled the national executive has the sole right to enter into executive agreements with other nations. State laws or policies do not supersede presidentially arranged international agreements even if they are not precisely in treaty form requiring Senate approval. Implicitly, if not explicitly, the Court ruled executive agreements had the binding force of treaties. Although an international compact is not always a treaty, the federal government has sole claim to "external affairs" and the external powers of the United States are to be exercised without regard to state policies or laws.[53]

In 1944, an even more decisive delegation of authority was added to the long list of pro-presidency precedents. The Court, in the already noted *Korematsu* and related cases, gave the president national security powers even when those powers extended primarily to domestic public policy considerations. On February 19, 1942, President Roosevelt issued an executive order empowering the secretary of war to clear the three West Coast states and parts of Arizona of all persons of Japanese descent, 70,000 of whom were American citizens, and place them in detention centers.

Fred T. Korematsu, an American-born citizen of Japanese descent, violated the civilian exclusion order, a part of the implementation of FDR's general order, and was given a suspended sentence of five years of probation by the federal court. He appealed his case and the Court began to consider his and similar cases in May 1943.

Lawyers for Mr. Korematsu in 1943 (and in later years when his conviction was overturned) said Roosevelt in effect was using his commander-in-chief authority to condemn a race to imprisonment. No charge had been issued; no trial conducted. With his action, FDR called into question several constitutional rights for all American citizens: personal security, the right to move about freely, and the right to not be deprived of those rights except on an individual basis after trial by jury. The force of the Fifth Amendment that guaranteed equal treatment under the law and due process was weakened. The character of U.S. citizenship and the wartime powers of the military over citizenry were also called into question.

On December 18, 1944, the U.S. Supreme Court ruled against Korematsu, effectively legitimizing FDR's actions as constitutional. During the trial, no claim was made that Korematsu was a disloyal citizen. His "crime" consisted solely of refusing to leave the restricted West Coast region, in the state where he was a citizen near the house where he was born.

Justice Hugo Black, writing for the majority, said Korematsu was not excluded from the West Coast because of hostility to him or his race. He was excluded because we were at war with the Japanese Empire, and because the properly constituted military authorities feared an invasion of our West Coast and therefore felt constrained to take appropriate security measures. The presence of an "unascertained number of disloyal members" of the Japanese group deemed, he said, the exclusion necessary. Black noted that he and his colleagues were aware of the hardships imposed by these presidential orders, "But hardships are part of war, and war is an aggregation of hardships. Compulsory exclusion of large groups of citizens from their homes, except under circumstances of direct emergency and peril, is inconsistent with our basic governmental institutions. But when under conditions of modern warfare our shores are threatened by hostile forces, the power to protect must be commensurate with the threatened danger. . . ."[54]

Justices Frank Murphy, Robert Jackson, and Owen J. Roberts dissented. Justice Roberts said the indisputable facts in the case exhibited a clear violation of constitutional rights. Justice Murphy believed the decision placed the Court in "the ugly abyss of racism." Justice Jackson said the armed services must protect a society, not merely its Constitution. His dissent was particularly disturbing; in effect, he said the army actions were unconstitutional, yet he also appeared to acknowledge that the Court could not be expected to do much, if anything, about such actions in wartime.

*Korematsu* is an example of the Supreme Court's reluctance to question and its readiness to affirm a president's determination of necessity under the conditions of wartime. In dissent, Justice Murphy said the judicial test of whether the executive, on a plea of military necessity, can validly deprive an individual of his rights must be reasonably related to a public danger that is so immediate as not to admit of delay and not to permit the intervention of ordinary constitutional processes to alleviate the danger. He obviously thought the situation did not warrant the conviction.

Scholars now regard the *Korematsu* decision as one of the Court's dismal blunders. Racism, hysteria, and misleading military judgments all were at work. One legal scholar concludes:

> Given the tensions of the period after Pearl Harbor, one might charitably advance the excuse of wartime hysteria for the harried members of Congress and the executive branch who made the initial decisions. No such excuse can be entertained for the justices of the Supreme Court who abandoned their most sacred principles at the first whiff of grapeshot.[55]

One of the ironic expansions came about as a result of the *U.S. v. Nixon* case in 1974. The case involved an appeal made by the Nixon administration to vacate an order by federal district court Judge John Sirica requiring Nixon to release tapes and transcripts of sixty-four White House conversations that had been subpoenaed by Watergate Special Prosecutor Leon Jaworski. The executive branch claimed the president had the right under the doctrine or custom of "executive privilege" to withhold the tapes. It was essential, it claimed, for presidents to be able to speak freely with their advisers without fear that such conversations would be available for public consumption.

Although the Court, speaking through Chief Justice Warren Burger, held Nixon's claims erroneous, it also believed it was its duty to define executive privilege. The Court seemed to say national security considerations would weigh heavily in balancing executive privilege against a competing constitutional claim. In the case at hand, in the summer of 1974, national security was not being threatened, this was a criminal case, and hence Nixon had to yield the tapes. To be sure, then, the Court limited President Nixon's claims of executive privilege, yet only after acknowledging for the first time the constitutionality of executive privilege.

In *Goldwater v. Carter 444 U.S. 996* (1979), the Supreme Court in effect approved President Jimmy Carter's termination of the 1954 Mutual Defense Treaty with Taiwan. U.S. Senator Barry Goldwater and certain others in Congress had challenged the president's authority to end such pacts, yet they never brought it to a vote. Most members of the Court considered this a matter that should be settled between the legislative and executive branches and that it thus was "not ripe for judicial review." In effect the Court said if Congress refrains from confronting the president on a matter such as this, it is not our task to do so. Only when there is an irreconcilable conflict between the two branches would the Court enter this kind of treaty dispute. The Supreme Court's order to a lower court to dismiss the challenge to Carter's actions was hailed by the Justice Department and presidentialists as a victory for the president's prerogatives in the foreign affairs field.

Doubtless Carter's action made sense in improving the evolving relations between the United States and the People's Republic of China. Indeed, the termination of the 1954 treaty was one of the conditions for the normalization of relations between the two nations. Yet the Rehnquist decision in this case is viewed by some analysts as another case of judicial obeisance to presidential dominance in foreign policymaking. Criticizing this Court decision as an act of timidity and a mistake, David G. Adler wrote:

> When a court invokes the political question principle in the face of very dubious presidential action, it causes tremors among those who favor government of limited powers. It is understandable that the Court, when it is confronted with important questions involving the separation of powers doctrine, will proceed cautiously, so as not to encroach upon the powers of one or the other departments. It is one thing for [the] Court to exercise judicious interpretation; it is quite another to shy behind the smokescreen of the political question doctrine when it prefers to evade a difficult problem.[56]

The Court deferred to the presidency again in mid-1981 when it upheld the executive agreements by Carter and Reagan that helped end the Iranian hostage crisis. Carter and later Reagan agreed to transfer large sums of Iranian funds and security out of the country in 1981 in exchange for release of the hostages. Yet an estimated 450 lawsuits were filed in U.S. courts by American companies laying claim to these assets as partial compensation for broken contracts and seized property. Justice William H. Rehnquist, speaking for a unanimous Court, emphasized the Court was making no sweeping decision in favor of the presidency in all such instances, only in the narrow set of circumstances involved in this case. "But where, as here, the settlement of claims has been determined to be a necessary incident to the resolution of a major foreign policy dispute between our country and another, and where, as here, we can conclude that Congress acquiesced with the President's action," Rehnquist wrote, "we are not prepared to say that the President lacks the power to settle such claims."[57]

A divided Supreme Court in June of 1982 ruled 5–4 that a president enjoys absolute immunity from civil damage suits for official actions exercised while on duty in the White House. Toward the end of 1995 President Clinton, however, found himself facing charges of sexual harassment. Paula Corbin Jones accused the president of improperly approaching her while Clinton was governor of Arkansas. She was a state employee at the time. In 1997, the Supreme Court ruled unanimously that a sitting president is not immune from civil suits of this type, and the Paula Jones case was allowed to proceed. Eventually, a settlement was reached between the parties.

Several post–9-11 actions by President George W. Bush and Attorney General John Ashcroft headed for the courts. The actions taken by this administration in response to the terrorist attack against the United States have some precedent in history, as do court decisions challenging the constitutionality of such acts. The courts are asked to adjudicate on a vexing set of concerns: does the *rule of law* apply in a crisis? What are the proper limits on a president acting without the consent of the Congress during a crisis? Must the United States, in order to defend itself, undermine the Constitution?[58]

Although FDR suffered some initial setbacks, he eventually got most of what he wanted from the Court and indeed shaped, with his nine appointments, a decidedly pro-national government and pro-presidency Court. Nixon also suffered several setbacks. He lost a number of cases both in the Supreme Court and in lower federal courts. And during the Clinton years, the courts decided several cases against the president. The next section reviews some notable Court decisions constraining presidential power.

## PRESIDENTIAL LOSSES BEFORE THE SUPREME COURT

On this side of the ledger, the cases are less numerous. The Court has taken decisive stands against presidents only after the Civil War, during the first New Deal, briefly near the end of the Korean War, during the Watergate affair, and recently in the second Clinton term (the Paula Jones case and

Whitewater executive privilege issues). Moreover, these anti-presidency stands were often tempered by the fact that they generally were not direct, independent, or confrontational challenges to a president. Thus the Court stood up to Lincoln only after his assassination. The Court backed off after its brief though significant foray against the early New Deal legislation, and reacted to Watergate only after the press, the public, and Congress were already "up in arms."[59] The Court, then, has not been a very secure protector of rights and freedoms during times of crisis.

Still, when a president went directly against provisions of the Constitution or an explicit congressional directive, or both, the Court was inclined to stop him from treading further. And the Court, understandably enough, is usually a bit bolder in these assertions when the president has suffered a notable decline in public approval.

Because we have treated some of these cases earlier, especially in the discussions of Lincoln and FDR, and because the major pattern in the Court-presidency relationship has been in expanding presidential power, we shall discuss these restraining decisions in briefer detail. Note, however, that these counterpoint decisions are no less important; they are merely the exceptions to the pattern.

The first significant case arose in Jefferson's term when Chief Justice John Marshall, Jefferson's antagonist, explicated the doctrine of judicial review. The *Marbury v. Madison* (1803)[60] decision, while cleverly avoiding a direct confrontation with the president, gave the Court the means for serving as the primary interpreter of what laws or executive action conform to the U.S. Constitution. In the process of handing down this decision John Marshall also said President Jefferson and his Secretary of State James Madison acted improperly. More important, however, was the establishment of the Court and its authority to serve as a vital branch if not exactly a coequal branch with the other two branches of government.

A year later, the Court in a unanimous decision instructed executive branch officials to pay for damages in the seizure of a Danish vessel, a seizure the Court said took place because of improper or invalid presidential instructions. The *Little v. Bareme* case involved the following question: Whether a naval captain could be found civilly liable for following what the Court found to be an executive order that went beyond what Congress had authorized.[61]

Chief Justice John Marshall confessed that initially he believed that although President John Adams' instructions of 1799 could not give a right for the seizure, they might yet excuse the navy captain, Captain Little, from paying damages. He added, however, "I was mistaken." The instructions were invalid and therefore furnished no protection for the navy captain, who obeyed his president at his peril, because the congressional legislation in question authorized only the seizure of vessels proceeding to French ports. Executive instructions cannot, the Court ruled, ever change the nature of an administrative transaction or legalize an act that would have been a plain trespass. If the Congress had been silent on the matter, the president's general authority as commander-in-chief would probably have been sufficient, but once Congress had prescribed the manner in which the law was to be carried out the president and all other executive officials were obliged to respect the limitations imposed by congressional statute.

Another major case arose during a military emergency (just as nearly all limiting or presidency-constraining decisions arose during unusual circumstances), the Civil War, during which Lincoln had suspended the writ of habeas corpus. Chief Justice Taney, acting in his additional role as a circuit court judge, ruled Lincoln had no constitutional power to suspend the writ. Lincoln never complied with this order, and a major lesson was learned. Rarely again would the Court attempt to stop a presidential action while it was taking place. Presidents can seldom if ever be enjoined from taking an action, only reprimanded once they have taken it. Still, *Ex-parte Merryman* (1861) was important in that a Supreme Court justice recognized limits to presidential power, even in wartime.

In *Ex-parte Milligan* (1866), the Court did place clear limitations on the emergency powers of the president, limiting his military authority. Of course this happened after the fact, after the war was over and after Lincoln had died. And in the *Korematsu* case of 1944, when the danger to the Union was almost nonexistent, a different Court ignored this *Milligan* Civil War precedent and granted to the chief executive all the powers Lincoln had assumed and more. Thus, in many respects these two Civil War limitations can be said to be insignificant in the overall definition of presidential power, even as they are important because they were among the first weak attempts by the Supreme Court to recognize that individual rights deserve to be considered as important as a strong national executive.

Other clashes between the Court and the presidency arose again in emergency circumstances, during the height of the Depression. Once more, the Court believed the president lacked the constitutional authority to act alone in "saving the Union." Roosevelt's multiple plans to shore up the economy or regulate economic behavior met with Court disfavor. The Court's several rulings about the unconstitutionality of the early New Deal measures have already been discussed. Congress, in one sense, had erred by giving Roosevelt too general a mandate. Had FDR been carrying out specific congressional plans, he would have probably won the Court's approval in most instances (although it is doubtful Congress could have agreed on specific plans for him to administer). These anti–New Deal Court rulings represented a distinction the Supreme Court has always made between foreign and domestic affairs. In foreign affairs, a president hardly needs even a general mandate from Congress. But domestic and economic affairs have usually required more detailed statutes from Congress.

This maxim was proved true once again in the 1935 case of *Humphrey's Executor v. United States.*[62] In this case, a congressional prescription for removing a Federal Trade Commission commissioner was violated by Franklin Roosevelt. And the Court responded by narrowing and in some ways overturning the *Myers* decision it had made just nine years earlier. In this 1935 ruling, the Court acknowledged that Congress, in creating agencies to carry out judicial and legislative duties, could restrict a president's removal power in specified cases, and thus it overruled FDR. *Humphrey* became one of only a handful or so of the actual major precedents serving to limit presidential powers.[63]

Another case in which a president was limited came during what most people might consider less than a national crisis, although President Truman apparently thought otherwise. This was the *Youngstown Sheet and Tube Co. v. Sawyer* (1952) case. Sawyer was Truman's secretary of commerce who was instructed by Truman to seize and operate certain steel mills that otherwise would have been shut down by union strikes (or, depending on your outlook, by the failure of the steel mill companies to improve pay and benefits).

The Korean War was dragging on and on. The pending shutdown of the steel mills so concerned Truman that he appealed to both sides but to no avail. Steel supplies were low already and some Pentagon officials believed a major Chinese offensive was in the making. The United States Steel Corporation was willing to meet the United Steel Workers terms, but only if it could get some relief from the wartime price controls the Truman administration was exercising over the steel industry. Truman refused this. He also refused to invoke provisions of the Taft-Hartley Act, recently passed by Congress over his veto, that might have permitted yet another way out of the impasse.

With deadlock and a prolonged strike likely to occur, Truman faced a dilemma: shutdown of the mills for even a short time could seriously impair, he believed, the Korean supply effort and jeopardize the lives of American soldiers. On the other hand, this executive action was a bold initiative sure to arouse critics and possibly legal and constitutional objections.

Truman, however, was privately advised by his close friend and the man he had nominated as chief justice, Fred Vinson, to go ahead with the steel seizure. Vinson based his recommendations on legal grounds. Moreover, Truman placed considerable faith on a memorandum that Associate Justice Tom Clark, another of his appointees to the Court, had prepared for him while Clark was earlier serving as Truman's attorney general. Clark had informed the president he could use various inherent powers of the presidency to settle labor disputes of this type.

Truman had appointed four of the then sitting members of the Court. The rest were FDR appointments. Hence, Truman thought his steel seizure plan would win approval in the Court if it did come to a test.

In any event, Truman seized, through his secretary of commerce, all the steel mills affected by the strike. This accounted for eighty-six companies, over two hundred steel mills, 600,000 workers, and 95 percent of the nation's steel production.

The seizure was implemented without much administrative trouble. Executive order number 10340 was issued and all employees of these mills now worked for the U.S. government and did so at the same wages as before. Every company was ordered to fly the American flag above its mills. Everyone complied. Yet the steel companies didn't like it and they soon filed suit in federal district court. The district court agreed with the steel mills and issued a preliminary injunction against the seizure. Hours later, the court of appeals issued a stay of the preliminary injunction and the seizure was allowed to continue until the Supreme Court could be brought into the matter.

Meanwhile Truman, his popularity already low, was attacked for being a bully, a usurper, a lawbreaker, and an architect of a labor dictatorship. "Newspapers, magazines, steel executives, business organizations, and Republicans [exceeded] their own performances of the Roosevelt years. They attacked Truman as a Caesar, an American Hitler or Mussolini, an author of evil. . . ."[64] Within a few days the Court responded and heard the case. The steel companies hammered away at the unconstitutionality of Truman's actions. He had, they said, acted without congressional approval and without constitutional justification.

Truman's Justice Department countered with every plausible precedent, especially from the Lincoln and FDR eras. It didn't work. Justice Hugo Black, speaking for a 6–3 majority, agreed with the steel companies. No clause in the Constitution justified Truman's action, nor had it been authorized by Congress. Although Black commanded the majority in this ruling, every single justice, on both sides of the issue, wrote his own opinion. This resulted in an overall set of opinions consuming nearly 130 pages. More questions were probably raised than settled in this case, and even as Truman's initiative was being denied, several members of the Court implied he could probably have seized the mills if he had relied on emergency powers granted his office under several congressional acts rather than on the inherent powers of the office he claimed he possessed. Still, the reality was that Truman had to get the government out of the steel mills and thus suffered one of the worst setbacks of his presidency.

The Court in effect ruled that the Korean crisis was not a full-scale emergency justifying the full invocation and exercise of presidential war powers. This case obviously had serious political ramifications. Truman long remained furious about this decision and bitter toward his appointee and former Attorney General Tom Clark, who voted against him.

> That damn fool from Texas that I first made Attorney General and then put on the Supreme Court! I don't know what got into me. He was no damn good as Attorney General, and on the Supreme Court, it doesn't seem possible but he's been even worse. He hasn't made one right decision that I can think of. And so when you ask me what my biggest mistake was, that's it. Putting Tom Clark on the Supreme Court of the United States.[65]

Other notable cases limiting executive power involve Nixon. Richard Nixon several times tested the limits of the office, sometimes succeeding in gaining power for the office and sometimes having his authority curbed. In the celebrated Pentagon Papers case, or *New York Times Co. v. United States* (1971),[66] the Supreme Court acted for the first time under wartime conditions since it had done so belatedly during and after the Civil War to protect

Richard Nixon tested the limits of executive power throughout his Presidency. The Supreme Court's unanimous vote in *U.S. v Nixon* (1974) sealed the fate of his administration—Nixon resigned shortly thereafter. (*Source:* Copyright © CORBIS.)

institutional liberties against inroads from the executive branch. Vietnam was, however, an undeclared war, being waged at that time without much public or congressional support and by a somewhat unpopular president.

The Nixon administration attempted to halt publication in *The New York Times* and the *Washington Post* of a collection of classified but leaked essays and documents entitled "History of U.S. Decision-Making Process on Vietnam Policy." The real question, the only question on which, ultimately, this decision is based, is whether publication of these articles and documents would have yielded "direct, immediate, and irreparable damage to our nation and its people."

Nixon and the Justice Department said the publication of the so-called "Pentagon Papers" assaulted the principle of government control over classified documents. There are other parts of the Constitution that grant power and responsibilities to the president, they claimed, and the First Amendment was never intended to make it impossible for the president to function or to protect the security of the nation.

The Court was not persuaded. They ruled six to three in favor of *The New York Times* and permitted publication. The reasoning of the justices, however, is not simple to explain. There were six separate opinions for the majority and one for the three dissenters. The common bond linking the six majority judges was that the executive branch had simply failed to prove that the publication of these documents posed a major threat: "Any system of prior restraint of expression comes to this Court bearing a heavy presumption against its constitutional validity," the Court said. "The Government thus carries a heavy burden of showing justification for the enforcement of such a restraint."[67]

While the Supreme Court in this important case did not allow the Nixon administration to run roughshod over the First Amendment, it left the door open for executive discretion. Several justices acknowledged that had the publication of the Pentagon Papers truly threatened national security, they might have allowed for prior restraint. The Court still would not put an absolute limit on executive authority.

Justices Black and Douglas saw no need for this flagrant, indefensible suppression of information. A few others said it was the function of Congress, not the executive, to decide when an emergency might be great enough to justify this sweeping type of restraint.

A second decision that somewhat limited presidential power was a unanimous one in *United States v. U.S. District Court* in 1972.[68] Here the Supreme Court ruled that domestic surveillances required a warrant from the courts. And in fact, a lower court extended this decision to foreign wiretaps (made for national security purposes), and the Carter administration later pledged to do no wiretapping without prior judicial approval.

In this case the Court insisted there was a difference between domestic security and national security, and ruled that warrants would be required for domestic surveillance. The Court did recognize, it is important to note, that wiretaps for national security might sometimes be upheld, although they did not necessarily address that question in this case.

Critics of Nixon's and of the growing expansion of presidential power especially welcomed this decision. Clear limits, they believed, were placed on the executive through this opinion. Consequently the FBI had to disconnect several wiretaps.

There are indications, however, that the executive branch's compliance with this Court ruling has subverted its spirit. In practice, the executive branch pretty much wins regular approval through convenient procedures the judiciary and the Justice Department subsequently established.

Several questions remain unsettled in this area. Our political system still has a way to go to work out acceptable methods whereby both the rights of individual citizens to their privacy, and the responsibilities of the chief executive to ensure that national security interests, are reconciled in domestic wiretapping cases. Still, while some abuses may continue, the Supreme Court was effective in raising crucial issues and in halting a few of the obnoxious abuses of the Fourth Amendment that occurred in the Nixon years.

During the Clinton years, the courts were especially active in confronting and narrowing the scope of presidential power. This increased activity reflects the confluence of four factors. First, Clinton kept pressing the limits of his power and prerogatives, sometimes in service to the needs of the office, sometimes in service to his own self-interest. Second, the Republicans who controlled Congress demonstrated an especially hostile attitude toward

Clinton, and often refused to bargain and compromise on key issues, thus guaranteeing a series of legal showdowns. Third, an independent counsel, Kenneth Starr, went after the president with a zeal that called into question his judgment and his motives. And finally, a politicized Supreme Court was intent on keeping President Clinton on a short leash. This combination almost guaranteed that clashes between the president and Congress would turn into multiple court battles.[69]

The legal controversies that enveloped Clinton, from questions of executive privilege to immunity, from presidential warmaking to the pardon power, from secrecy to lawyer-client privilege, erupted into a series of court cases, many of which went against the president. In an atmosphere of partisanship and personal rancor, policy differences were elevated into personal battles that made compromise hard to achieve.

The possibility of accommodation between the executive and the legislature became more remote with the aggressive investigatory pursuit of the president by Kenneth Starr. The flames of personal acrimony between the president and prosecutor, fanned by presidential arrogance and prosecutorial zeal, placed the two on a collision course that led to the impeachment of the president.

All three branches were ensnared and forced to confront issues and resolve disputes that, in more temperate times, likely would have been resolved by more informal means. But requests from both Congress and the independent counsel for information—for notes, memos, diaries, e-mail communications, and files—were met with executive refusal. Resistance replaced accommodation, acrimony trumped goodwill, and entrenchment dictated the use of subpoenas, grand juries, and courtroom trials. Thus it was that law and politics, public opinion and political wrangling, and personal posturing and constitutional maneuvering propelled the three branches into a dispute over presidential power and independence.

In the end, the courts shrank the powers of the presidency in some key areas. In the Paula Jones lawsuit, the president's lawyers sought immunity from the suit while the president was in office, asking that the case be postponed until after Clinton left office. The Supreme Court eventually decided that the president enjoys no immunity, even temporary, from civil suits for unofficial acts.[70] This makes future presidents more open to court challenges and gives presidents less protection from lawsuits, frivolous and otherwise.

Ironically, it was the Clinton deposition in the Jones case (aired in excruciating detail on the evening news) that led to perjury charges by Kenneth Starr against the president. In that deposition, Clinton was asked a series of leading questions about his relationship with Monica Lewinsky, a former White House intern. Clinton's answers were untruthful. This opened a door for the independent counsel to recommend the president be impeached. To add insult to injury, Clinton eventually settled the Jones case out of court. Had he done so earlier, he might have avoided impeachment altogether.

Clashes between the president and Congress often involved Clinton's claims of executive privilege. In a variety of areas—investigations of Agriculture Secretary Mike Espy, the administration's anti-drug policy, U.S.–Haiti policy, the Lewinsky scandal, even investigations of the First Lady—Clinton refused to give Congress information and materials it requested.

Presidents have long claimed that discussions with aides were privileged and could be kept from Congress. In past conflicts over such information, presidents usually struck a compromise with Congress. But during the Clinton years, all sides took an all-or-nothing approach. Thus, the courts were called to intervene. And in the end, the Court sided with Congress, leaving Clinton and future presidents more vulnerable and less protected. On the other hand, when the same courts were asked, in the early days of the presidency of George W. Bush, to force Vice President Dick Cheney to reveal with whom he had discussed a controversial energy policy, the courts sided with Cheney and against the Government Accounting Office, the investigatory arm of Congress.

## CONCLUSION

Supreme Court justices tend to share with presidents a similar national perspective and a common outlook about the national interest. However, they have different obligations and operate in a different political forum with different responsibilities. More often than not, the Supreme Court and the lower federal courts have aided presidents, as new demands and emergencies encouraged presidents to stretch the formal powers of the office. This trend or pattern is now well established and is rooted in Sutherland's famed 1936 *Curtiss-Wright* decision. This judicial deference exists especially in wartime and when presidents enjoy high popularity.

The Court is well aware that only a president is elected by the nation. Still it is a paramount function of the Court to insist that presidents do not go beyond what is necessary or to try to singularly embody the nation's sovereignty. No president should be allowed to make the law or disregard for long the general commands of the U.S. Constitution.

Strong presidents invariably look for ways to expand their prerogatives and authority. Often, of course, this may be due to the emergencies confronting the nation. Their popularity or prestige does have an important bearing on whether they can win victories in their clashes with the Court.[71] Strong presidents try to nominate new justices who will advance their policies and values. For several generations now it has become common practice for presidents to appoint justices with a clear reference to their policy leanings, and this is likely to continue.

One of the strengths of the Supreme Court is its ability to function as an independent and at least a somewhat unpredictable institution. No president can shape it for long. As noted, members of the Court develop their own independent constitutional philosophies, the more so the longer they remain on the Court.

We cannot expect the Supreme Court to be the sole or even main accountability check on presidents, yet we must encourage a vitality and independence and a climate of expectations in the country that will maintain a Supreme Court that is not intimidated by the other two branches. Our system functions best when Congress, the president, and the Court each energetically promote its own independent vision of good government. Preferring a strong presidency should not lead one to want a corresponding weakness in the other two branches, but rather a corresponding strength and assertiveness.

# Presidents as Chief Executives

A good cabinet ought to be a place where the large outlines of policy can be hammered out in common, where the essential strategy is decided upon, where the president knows that he will hear, both in affirmation and in doubt, even in negation, most of what can be said about the direction he proposes to follow.

Harold J. Laski, *The American Presidency: An Interpretation* (Harper & Brothers, 1940), pp. 257–58

Cabinet meetings in the Bush White House were stilted, boring affairs. Instead of creative ferment and the clash of ideas, there were droning reports. . . . The truth is, Cabinet meetings are an anachronism.

Dan Quayle, *Standing Firm* (Harper Paperback, 1995), p. 109

Many of the embarrassing blunders that have done the most damage to recent presidencies were not the result of external "enemies" sabotaging the president but resulted from the actions of loyal subordinates in the White House . . . [Presidents] should be aware of the major elements of administration proposals, they should make major staff decisions, and they should be aware of what their immediate staff aides are doing in their names.

James P. Pfiffner, ed., *The Managerial Presidency,* 2d edition (College Station: Texas A&M University Press, 1999), p. 7

A president may be but one person, yet the presidency is an institution—a collection of people and departments organized to, at least in theory, assist a president in making wise decisions and effectively implementing the laws of the land. But, "The plain fact is," writes Peri E. Arnold, "that no modern president has fully managed the executive branch."[1] We recruit politicians, not managerial leaders, to the White House, yet we evaluate them every day on how well they are running the government, managing the bureaucracy, and leading their cabinet departments.

Most presidents are indifferent managers. They lack the time to manage effectively. Their success has come from campaigning and appealing for public support and they generally have little experience managing large, complex bureaucracies like the executive branch of the U.S. government. Moreover, presidents are reluctant to expend too much of their personal political capital on administrative matters.

Sometimes presidents lack the skill to manage effectively. Yet inattention to matters of personnel and implementation can cause considerable problems. Indeed, many of the mistakes and even blunders of recent presidential administrations can be traced to lack of attention to the managerial and administrative responsibilities that are an important part of being president.[2]

## PRESIDENTS AND THE CABINET

The presidential cabinet in America is a misunderstood political institution. This is in part because the cabinet in some parliamentary systems has substantial influence as a policymaking group. This is not the case in the United States. Paradoxically, however, enormous media coverage is paid to a president's cabinet appointments and much fanfare is given to a new president's first cabinet meetings.

The American cabinet is too big and too divisive a group to function effectively in policymaking. Many cabinet members are appointed as much for their representativeness as for their policy or managerial expertise. Then, too, there is usually a lot of turnover in the cabinet, so much so that cabinet secretaries are unlikely to form a cohesive policymaking team.[3] They serve mainly as presidential emissaries to a department and as policy advisers to the president singly or occasionally as part of a selective team, for example as a member of the national security or economic policy team.

President Jimmy Carter, an engineer and more of a manager than most presidents, talked of his growing frustrations in trying to make the cabinet into a policymaking group. He acknowledged that he used his cabinet less and less as his four years wore on. "After a few months, the cabinet meetings became less necessary," Carter wrote. "As a result, in the first year we had thirty-six sessions with the full cabinet, then, during the three succeeding years, twenty-three, nine and six such meetings respectively."[4]

President Bill Clinton enjoyed more stability or continuity in his cabinet than most presidents. Still, he rarely felt the need to hold cabinet meetings.

In his first two and one-half years in office, Clinton did hold twelve full cabinet meetings, but the longer he stayed in office, the fewer cabinet meetings he held.

The way the cabinet is used and the value of the cabinet to a president obviously fluctuates according to the personality and the needs of the president and changing national conditions. It also changes over the course of an administration. After reviewing the origins of the cabinet and how cabinet members are selected, this chapter will assess how presidents, their top advisers, and cabinet members have interacted and managed, or mismanaged, the executive branch of government.

The framers discussed at length the possibility of creating some form of executive council that would comprise the president, heads of the departments, and the chief justice of the Supreme Court, yet they decided to leave things flexible. The Constitution makes no provision for a cabinet. It merely implies there are to be principal offices of the executive departments. The first Congress passed statutes that provided for the creation of three departments, State, War, and Treasury. An attorney general was also authorized, yet this would be a part-time adviser, not the head of a department.

From the outset President George Washington regarded his officers as assistants and advisers. "He began the practice of assembling his principal officers in council. And this practice became in the course of time a settled custom. The simple truth is that the cabinet is a customary, not a statutory body."[5] The term *cabinet* was probably first used in 1793, but mention of it in statutory language did not occur until 1907. Presidents over the course of our history have used the cabinet in greatly differing ways.

Thus President Andrew Jackson did not even convene his cabinet as a group during his first two years in office, whereas President James Polk held at least 350 cabinet sessions during his four years. Lyndon Johnson told his cabinet secretary that the thing that bothered him most about cabinet meetings was they were so dull; he said, "I just don't want them falling asleep at the damned [cabinet] table."[6] Reports had it that President Reagan did indeed doze off on a few occasions, prompting one wag to quip that the "cabinet room seats 12 and sleeps one."

As a general rule, recent presidents have often met with their full cabinet in formal cabinet meetings their first year or two in office and then, like Carter and Clinton, worked out other arrangements to get together with them singly or in small groups. A president who wants to dispense with cabinet meetings simply does so. Still, presidents and their staffs have to work out processes for regular communication with cabinet heads.

## SELECTING CABINET ADVISERS

Few acts of presidential leadership are as important as the appointment of a president's cabinet members and senior advisers. Presidents are thought to have a free hand in choosing their cabinet members, yet this is not exactly the way it works. In addition to administrative competence and experience, loyalty and congeniality are basic considerations in selections. Other factors are at work as well. Party rivals often have to be disarmed and placated either with an appointment to the cabinet or selection as the vice presidential running mate. Reagan's selection of George H. W. Bush as vice president and Alexander Haig as his first secretary of state are examples. Regional, ethnic, gender, and geographical considerations are almost always important. Nowadays, for example, it is a custom to have at least one African American, one Hispanic, one westerner, and one southerner in the cabinet, and several women.[7] After capturing the presidency, a president usually goes about selecting the cabinet in such a way as to try to win the confidence of major sections and sectors of the nation. "I knew," wrote Richard Nixon, "that some of my choices for Cabinet posts would have to serve, even if only symbolically, to unite the country and 'bring us together.'"[8]

President Carter and his top campaign aides said he was going to appoint a crop of fresh faces from a new generation, not from the generation that had already served in high posts for previous administrations. Carter's attitude on this matter ran counter to the usual theory that to be effective in Washington you should have had extensive earlier experience learning the ropes there.

In theory a president can nominate anyone for a cabinet post. In practice the constraints are many.[9] First, each cabinet member has to be confirmed by a majority of the members in the U.S. Senate. Nowadays, nominees are being examined more carefully at both ends of Pennsylvania Avenue and by interest groups and the media. This automatically precludes those who will not submit to this process. Others are unwilling to give up their much higher salaries and fringe benefits. Some are unwilling to join the cabinet because it would mean having to give up a seat in the Senate or would hinder their chances of running for a national leadership position. Still others sometimes pose conditions under which they would accept nomination and the conditions are not acceptable to the president. Others are put off by the conflict-of-interest regulations and the Ethics in Government Act that recent presidents have imposed on all top appointees.[10]

It has also become harder to attract many talented individuals to cabinet-level positions due to the media culture of "gotcha" politics in Washington, D.C. Both recent and past mistakes get spotlight attention and top administrative appointees are attractive targets. Their public and private lives become an open book for the press and for opposition critics. The assault can be painful. Also, the power and influence of at least some cabinet positions has declined relative to that of key White House operatives such as Henry Kissinger in the Nixon-Ford era or Karl Rove in the George W. Bush White House.

A president has to select certain cabinet officers because of the needed expertise they will bring to the administration and the policy needs of certain departments. Typically, for example, the secretary of defense is someone who has worked closely with that department in some previous capacity. The labor secretary will often be someone who has had extensive nego-tiating background and, if a Democrat, some advisory ties to the AFL-CIO leadership. A treasury secretary is traditionally viewed as the financial com-munity's representative in the cabinet. In selecting a treasury secretary a president-elect usually wants someone who can simultaneously serve as a "spokesperson" to the financial world and as a "spokesperson" for those interests.

Generalists are often appointed to head up some of the domestic depart-ments such as Commerce, Transportation, and HUD, while politicians espe-cially close to clientele groups are often appointed head of Agriculture and Interior. President George H.W. Bush appointed members of Congress to head Agriculture, Interior, and Veteran's Affairs departments. President Clinton appointed former governors to head up Interior and Education, and former mayors to head HUD and DOT. George W. Bush appointed former governors to head Health and Human Services, EPA, and the Homeland Security department. Appointing generalists who are unlikely to carry mes-sages and advocate the agenda from interest groups and from partisan con-stituencies advantages the White House over the bureaucracy in the short run, but in the longer run the bureaucrats acting *independently* of their own cabinet secretaries often seek to form their own alliances with clientele groups and congressional committees.

Key aides like Karl Rove, the chief strategist for President George W. Bush, have increased their influence on the executive at the expense of some cabinet members. (*Source:* Copyright © Reuters NewMedia Inc./CORBIS.)

President Clinton's first labor secretary, Robert B. Reich, pointed out the obvious:

> No other democracy does it this way. No private corporation would think of operating like this. Every time a new president is elected, America assembles a new government of 3,000 or so amateurs who only sometimes know the policies they're about to administer, rarely have experience managing large government bureaucracies, and almost never know the particular piece of it they're going to run. These people are appointed quickly by a president-elect who is thoroughly exhausted from a year and a half of campaigning. And they remain in office, on average, under two years—barely enough time to find the nearest bathroom. It's a miracle we don't screw it up worse than we do.[11]

## THE JOB OF THE CABINET MEMBER

Defining the job of the cabinet member depends on one's vantage point. Members of Congress believe a cabinet officer should communicate often and well with Congress and be responsive to legislators' requests. Reporters want a cabinet officer to be accessible, to make news; they applaud style and flair as well as substance. Interest groups want a cabinet member who can speak out for their interests and carry their messages to the White House. Civil servants in a department are generally looking for a cabinet leader who will boost departmental morale and appropriations. White House aides are as keenly concerned about a cabinet officer's loyalty to the president as they are about ability. A president wants a cabinet member who will conserve his or her freedom of action and enhance his or her administration's reputation without embarrassing or overshadowing him or her.[12]

There is little or no training for new cabinet secretaries. They are thrown into the fire and expected to serve many masters. Robert Reich noted the feelings of isolation of a new secretary when he wrote, "As I walk out of her office it suddenly strikes me: I'm on my own from here on. There's no training manual, no course, no test drive for a cabinet secretary. I'll have to follow my instincts, and rely on whomever I can find to depend on along the way. I'll have to listen carefully and watch out for dangers. But mostly I'll have to stay honest with myself and keep perspective. Avoid grandiosity. This is a glamorous temp job."[13]

What is a good cabinet officer? A Carter White House aide summarized how White House staff viewed the cabinet job:

> First, he should be clearly in charge of the department. . . . Second, he should be very sensitive to the department's interest groups and have access to them and fully understand their views. But, third, he should also at the same time be able to distinguish the president's interests and political needs from the department's clientele interests. He should be able to say that this is what they want but it is or is not compatible with your interests. Fourth, the effective cabinet officer is one who can work on most of his congressional relations problems without running to the president for

help. Finally, he should be able to follow-through on presidential policies, that is, to see that they don't get watered down, or lost in the shuffle.[14]

Presidents and their aides repeatedly say the last thing they want to see is a cabinet member who has become a special pleader at the White House for some of the special-interest groups that are strong in the particular department. "The Cabinet officer must certainly be attentive to his departmental business, and he should seek to ensure that the president has timely notice of the impact of other policies on his department's specific interests," a former White House aide writes. "But a Secretary should never choose his departmental interest as against the wider interest of the Presidency."[15]

The greatest test of cabinet members arises from the fact they become tied almost as closely to Congress as they are to a president. Indeed, cabinet officers are legally obligated to obey Congress and the courts as well as the president—even though they may hold contradictory views. In the perpetual tug-of-war between the branches, the cabinet officer is often like the knot in the rope. Bradley Patterson, a longtime civil servant and a staff aide in the Eisenhower White House, pointed this out: "His or her appointment is subject to Senate confirmation. Every power a Cabinet officer exercises is derived from some Act of Congress; every penny he or she expends must be appropriated by the Congress; every new statutory change the Cabinet officer desires must be submitted to the Congress and defended there. A Cabinet officer's every act is subject to oversight by one or more regular or special congressional committees, much of his or her time is accordingly spent at the Capitol and with few exceptions, most of the documents in his or her whole department are subject to being produced at congressional request."[16]

Presidents undoubtedly believe cabinet members should serve as servants of the president and not make decisions independent of the president. When a president makes a decision the cabinet officer is expected to carry it out. In fact, it is inevitable that after a person has been in the cabinet for a time and has become enmeshed in the activities and interests of a department, he or she develops certain independent policy views. A certain hardening of view may set in as the cabinet secretary gets pushed by subordinates, interest-group leaders, or others in a direction that makes it likely he or she will come into conflict with the president. When this happens, the White House typically complains that the cabinet member has "gone native"—he or she has been captured by the interests native to that department. Often, the cabinet officer wants to extract more money out of the president's budget for the department. A budget director once complained that "cabinet members are vice presidents in charge of spending, and as such they are the natural enemies of the presidents."[17]

## THE WEST WING WANTS LOYALTY ALONG WITH COMPETENCE

In reflecting on his old cabinet, former President Lyndon Johnson once blurted out that "I'll always love Dean Rusk, bless his heart. He stayed with me when nobody else did."[18] Though they might not always admit it, those at the White House judge cabinet officers by a formula that weighs ability as primary but ranks loyalty to the president and to the president's political future as a close second. For some White House aides, loyalty to the boss even outweighs competence. Definitions of loyalty not surprisingly vary depending on where you sit. Outsiders often complain that loyalty in the top reaches of the executive branch can too easily lead to mindless servility and a cabinet of "yes-people." Friends and supporters of a president insist a president needs and is entitled to loyalty from cabinet members and staff.

Some presidencies, John Adams' for one, were undermined by cabinet disruptions. Woodrow Wilson had one secretary of state resign in protest and another who persisted in open dissent from the president's policies and even attempted to undermine Wilson's moderate war aims. Jealousies, political ambitions, rivalries, turf fights, and tactical differences can tear an administration apart and can leave considerable doubt in the public's mind as to who is really in charge. However, people with the president's point of view in mind often say loyalty can just as easily be undervalued as overvalued, adding that true loyalty should include the willingness to argue vigorously and speak one's mind—at least within reasonable bounds.

Firing cabinet members is the last thing presidents like to do. When it is done it is usually only after it is "overdue." And they do it at the risk of considerable political backlash. President Andrew Johnson's removal of Secretary of War Stanton contributed to Johnson's impeachment. President Nixon's removal of special prosecutor Archibald Cox and the related resignations of Attorney General Elliot Richardson and Deputy Attorney General William Ruckelshaus badly damaged what remained of Nixon's credibility. Ronald Reagan fired Secretary of State Alexander Haig, White House Chief of Staff Donald Regan, and Secretary of Health and Human Services Margaret Heckler and encouraged some others, such as Raymond Donovan (labor secretary) to resign. George W. Bush eased out several of his top economic advisers at the end of his second year, including his secretary of the treasury. To fire a cabinet member is to acknowledge you made a poor administrative decision in the first place.

President Gerald Ford did not enjoy a good working relationship with Defense Secretary James Schlesinger. Ford considered removing Schlesinger soon after he became president. Later he regretted that he hadn't and he eventually did fire Schlesinger. Why did he wait? Part of the reason was Ford wanted to have a smooth transition from the trauma of Watergate to his own administration. Ford finally fired Schlesinger in part because of Schlesinger's condescending rather than deferential manner. According to one report, Schlesinger seldom looked directly at Ford during cabinet meetings. Instead he looked at Secretary of State Henry Kissinger, as if to imply that his remarks would be lost on Ford.

Nixon fired Interior Secretary Walter Hickel after a celebrated "personal letter" from Hickel to the president was leaked to the press. Hickel was especially frustrated because he only saw the president once or twice for policy discussions. His letter included those pointed sentences: "Permit me to suggest that you consider meeting, on an individual and conversational basis, with members of your cabinet. Perhaps," continued Hickel, "through such conversations we can gain greater insight into the problems confronting us all, and most important, into solutions of these problems."[19] Hickel soon left the cabinet.

Late in his presidency, President Johnson became particularly upset at several of his domestic cabinet members. Oral interviews at the Johnson presidential library in Austin, Texas, indicate several cabinet members were in his doghouse for crossing him on some program or another, or for failure to support the Vietnam War effort enough. More often than not, his chief domestic aide, Joseph Califano (who later, as secretary of Health, Education, and Welfare (HEW), would be fired by Jimmy Carter for lack of loyalty), was ordered to win compliance and greater cooperation from the particular cabinet member in question. Illustrative of Johnson's disappointment with some of his cabinet is his sharp denunciation of his former attorney general, Ramsey Clark: "You know ol' Harry Truman said his biggest mistake was appointing Tom Clark to the Supreme Court. Well, my biggest mistake was appointing Tom's son, Ramsey, as my Attorney General. He couldn't make up his mind about a fish fry." Johnson continued, "Ramsey wanted to go around preachin' bleeding-heart stuff, but he never did a damn thing. I heard Dick Nixon made a campaign speech against Ramsey Clark one night and I had to sit on my hands so I wouldn't cheer it."[20]

From the perspective of the West Wing, these are the questions asked about cabinet members. Have they managed the department well? Do they recruit talented officials to the department? Are they loyal to the president? Can they "handle" the interest groups associated with that department? Have they brought prestige to the department and to the administration? Does their presence in the administration boost confidence in it? Do they help politically as the next election nears? Have they handled the relationships with Congress and the press effectively? Have they come up with fresh and innovative ideas? Have they been able to implement the administration's programs in their department? Have they become an asset or liability? A cabinet-level official sometimes can be both loyal and competent and still be viewed as a political liability.

## THE ROLE OF THE CABINET IN POLICYMAKING

In practice, the cabinet is used as a forum for information exchange, as an occasion for a president to boost morale and highlight priorities, to review major issues that cut across all departments, to go over how members can help push for congressional approval of the president's program, and to discuss ways to improve implementation of major programs. It is, of course, also used as a feedback device through which presidents can obtain political and professional advice on how policies and programs are (or are not) working.

A romantic view of the mythical American cabinet is in part encouraged by presidents themselves. Nixon, Carter, Reagan, and Clinton all emphasized the importance of the cabinet when they picked their original team. Reagan early in 1981 told his cabinet nominees he intended the cabinet to function much like a board of directors in a corporation, the president deliberating with them often and offering input prior to decisions. Truman said, "the cabinet is not merely a collection of executives administering different governmental functions but a body whose combined judgment the president uses to develop fundamental policies of the administration." But one of his biographers argues that "while President Truman used his cabinet to formulate decisions, in practice, important decisions were made by ad hoc groups consisting of cabinet officers and others. He did not wish to create a secretariat and to formalize the meetings."[21]

A consistent pattern seems to characterize president-cabinet relations over time. Just as a president enjoys a distinctive honeymoon with the press and partisan officeholders, White House–cabinet ties are usually the most conflictual or cooperative during the first year of an administration. A newly staffed executive branch, busily recasting the political agenda, seems to bubble over with new possibilities, proposals, ideas, and imminent breakthroughs. Ironically, White House staff, which soon will outstrip most of the cabinet in power and influence, receives less publicity at this time. In the immediate postinaugural months, the Washington political community, and the executive branch in particular, becomes a merry-go-round of cheerful open doors for the new team of cabinet leaders.

But this ends soon. Little over a year in office, Reagan's White House aides developed a distrust for many of their departmental secretaries, saying they had generally become advocates of their own constituencies. "Cabinet government is a myth," said a Reagan staffer. "I'm not sure it has dawned on the [cabinet] members yet that they have been cut out of the decision-making process."[22]

Domestic crises and critical international developments begin to monopolize the presidential schedule. As a president has less time for personal contacts, cabinet members become disinclined to exhaust their personal political credit with him. A president's program becomes fixed as priorities are set, and budget ceilings produce some new rules of the game. Ambitious, expansionist cabinet officers become painfully familiar with various refrains from executive office staff, usually to the effect that there just isn't any more money available for programs of that magnitude; or that budget projections for the next two or three years just can't absorb that type of increment; and, perhaps harshest of all, that a proposal is excellent but will just have to wait until the next term.

A top White House staffer under Nixon captured the complex entanglements of time, presidential priorities, and interactions of people:

> Everything depends on what you do in program formulation during the first six or seven months. I have watched three presidencies and I am increasingly convinced of that. Time goes by so fast. During the first six months or

so, the White House staff is not hated by the cabinet, there is a period of friendship and cooperation and excitement. There is some animal energy going for you in those first six to eight months, especially if people perceive things in the same light. If that exists and so long as that exists you can get a lot done. You only have a year at the most for new initiatives, a time when you can establish some programs as your own, in contrast to what has gone on before. After that, after priorities are set, and after a president finds he doesn't have time to talk with cabinet members, that's when the problems set in, and the White House aides close off access to cabinet members and others.[23]

After the first year or so, presidents become increasingly concerned with leaks from their administration. They worry about saying things or having key decisions made in large groups. They also, in President Carter's words, believe their time is "too precious to waste on many bull sessions among those who have little to contribute. . . ."[24] So what do they do? They begin to hold fewer cabinet meetings and hold smaller sessions with the inner cabinet.

President Kennedy regarded the idea of the cabinet as a collective consultative body largely as an anachronism and told close friends this in blunt terms. He once asked: "Just what the hell good does the cabinet do, anyway?" The nature of a problem, he thought, should determine the group with which he met. Why should the postmaster general sit there and listen to discussions about Indochina, wondered Kennedy. He thought the historical custom of the cabinet should carry with it no special claim on his time. He believed there were few subjects that warranted bringing together, for example, the secretary of labor, the secretary of agriculture, and the secretary of defense. As Kennedy aide Theodore Sorensen recalled:

[Kennedy] had appointed his cabinet members because he regarded them as individuals capable of holding down very difficult positions of responsibility. He did not want to have them sit through lengthy cabinet sessions, listening to subjects which were not of interest to them, not of importance to them, at least not of an interest to their primary duties and their primary skills. So he called cabinet meetings as infrequently as possible. . . .[25]

Richard Nixon had sat through countless formal cabinet meetings during the Eisenhower years. In his memoirs he recalls, "most of them were unnecessary and boring. On the few issues that cut across all departments . . . group discussions would sometimes be informative. But the day had long since passed when it was useful to take an hour and a half to have the Secretary of Defense and Secretary of State discuss the Secretary of Transportation's new highway proposal."[26]

If Nixon found cabinet meetings boring in the Eisenhower period, Elliot Richardson found them the same way in the Nixon years. He wrote that cabinet meetings in both the Nixon and Ford administrations "ordinarily focused on bland common denominators like the economic outlook, displays of budgetary breakdowns, or reviews of the status of administrative proposals."[27]

In short, recent presidents have found it neither comfortable nor efficient to meet frequently with their cabinets as a whole. When they have, it seems to have been as much for purposes of publicity, symbolic reassurance, or appearance of activity as for substantive debate or learning.

On the most important matters, cabinet members as a whole are seldom called on for advice. The president, usually with a handful of senior advisers, makes up his own mind. What one FDR cabinet member said is still generally the case. "We never discuss exhaustively any policy of government. . . . Our cabinet meetings are pleasant affairs, but we only shine the surface of things on routine matters."[28]

Cabinet members come to be judged by the White House on their capacity to generate favorable publicity and to proclaim the virtues of the recent White House achievements. Strong-willed people of independence can hardly be expected to be enthusiastic about performing public relations tasks assigned to them by White House political counselors.

As time passes, cabinet members grow bitter about being left out of White House decisions, though they seldom make their opinions public. Some exceptions exist, of course, and many cabinet officers will talk about the problem privately. The case of Nixon's first secretary of the interior, Walter Hickel, who had only two or three private meetings with his president in the two years before his public protest and subsequent firing, is perhaps extreme. Most cabinet officers have more frequent contact with their president, but few of the domestic cabinet members have been wholly pleased by the quantity or quality of these meetings. A former secretary of commerce in the 1970s once joked of his infrequent ties to the White House by saying that his president "should have warned him that he was being appointed to a secret mission." Secretary of State Alexander Haig said he was "mortally handicapped by his lack of access to the president." And several others such as Cyrus Vance and George Shultz threatened to resign on occasion because they felt bypassed or undercut by White House West Wing aides.

Nixon's increasing centralization of power in the White House was an apparent vote of no confidence in most of his cabinet members, although in naming his original cabinet Nixon claimed to have appointed men who had the potential for great leadership, men with "an extra dimension which is the difference between good leadership and superior or even great leadership." Five years later he had a totally new cabinet. Nixon ran through cabinet members faster than any president in recent history.

Nixon paid a price for keeping his cabinet officers at such a distance. Some of them were so often undercut that they sometimes purposely acted on their own just to show themselves, their departments, and the press that they were capable of independent action. Occasionally this made for a divided administration. At other times, as Nixon later admitted, it threatened to undercut the administration's credibility with foreign countries. More important, Nixon's disuse and downgrading of the cabinet increased his isolation from responsible sources of political and professional advice. An already insecure man—a man who needed friendship and peers—removed himself from a potential source of support. One result was the Watergate scandals.

Why are more spirited and substantive discussions absent from the modern-day cabinet? First, the number attending cabinet sessions is too large. President Ford sometimes had nearly thirty people in attendance. Most cabinet members are unlikely to talk about their troubles or highly sensitive topics in a group that large. The presence of twenty or more cabinet officers and senior aides such as the budget director and chief-of-staff and CIA director sitting around the cabinet table and along the walls permits fewer than three minutes of wisdom per elder per hour. Thus both presidents and cabinet members become disillusioned with government by cabinet meeting. But the alternatives cause problems too. "Of course, if you don't have cabinet government, you have government by a White House staff that has not been confirmed by the Senate," says former Attorney General Griffin Bell. "So you lose one of the checks and balances in our system. Because there is constant friction between the White House staff and the cabinet secretaries, it is extremely difficult to find quality people to serve as cabinet heads."[29]

One of the president's dilemmas is that a fundamental separation of policy formulation and its implementation often develops. Whereas most major policy decisions are made by the president and a smaller number of personal aides, responsibility for enacting these programs rests, for the most part, with the cabinet officers and their departments. The gap between these two functions of the executive has been widening, a result of the transference of power from the more public institution of the cabinet to the relatively hidden offices of the White House staff. The result has been a divorce of the exercise of power from accountability for that exercise.

The very character of the cabinet—a body with no constitutional standing, members with no independent political base of their own and no requirement that the president seek or follow their advice—helps contribute to its lack of influence as a collective body. Ultimately, the influence of the cabinet rests essentially on the role a president desires for it. Most presidents, particularly those since Eisenhower, have made that role an increasingly limited one.

To some extent, this downgrading of the cabinet was imminent from the late 1930s when Roosevelt first began to place top-level advisers in the White House itself. Roosevelt also relied on brain trusters scattered throughout the government in positions other than cabinet posts. Easy and frequent access to the president is an important determinant of an adviser's influence. Equally important, presidents tend to view many of their cabinet officers as parochial and narrow in their outlook, playing only an advocacy role for their own departments.

Ironically, the presidential view of cabinet members as advocates for their departments often proves a self-fulfilling prophecy. Not only have presidents, as a result, tended to use their cabinets to appease interest groups with a supportive ambassador at the head of their relevant department, the limitations presidents place on the time they spend with members forces them to use that precious time to push for their department's needs first. Paradoxically some presidents render the departments less effective in implementing their policies by denying them a say in program development. There is less incentive for cabinet officers or their departments to implement a program efficiently if they believe they have no real stake or say in it.

Experience suggests three basic ways presidents can use the cabinet as a group.

1. For discussing issues and problems in an informal and unfocused manner, primarily to exchange information
2. For focused, regular consideration of specific issues, set forth in papers authored by cabinet members and circulated ahead of time, aided by agendas, concise records of action, and a small secretariat
3. For summit discussions of strategic policy initiatives, which have been through a searching interdepartmental review, with dissents identified and alternative language proposed.[30]

By general consensus the first format was used by Truman, Kennedy, Johnson, Nixon, Ford, Reagan, and Clinton, at least when they were willing to hold cabinet meetings. Eisenhower, however, followed the second alternative. Carter began with aspirations to the second format but, as noted, his patience wore thin. Probably no president has ever used his full cabinet according to format three, although Truman and Eisenhower sometimes did employ their National Security Council in approximately this manner.

## THE REAGAN CABINET COUNCIL EXPERIMENT

More than other recent presidents, Ronald Reagan came to office with a comprehensive ideological program to implement. Although he too espoused the ideals of a strong cabinet, at the heart of his approach to governing was the centralization of policy decision-making in the White House and the Office of Management and Budget.[31] Reagan's advisers deliberately emphasized ideology and loyalty to the president in their appointments throughout the executive branch. Reagan's White House made explicit use of civil service reforms enacted in the Carter years to remove career officials from key posts, and filled them with Reagan supporters. They also used "reductions in force as a legal means of eliminating whole bureaucratic units staffed by careerists. This was done systematically, in the interests of presidential control and successful pursuit of the Reagan agenda."[32]

As governor of California Reagan had been a delegator to his staff and cabinet. He came to the White House prepared to continue this leadership style. He recognized, as had the presidents before him, that a president did not need to convene the entire cabinet to go over plans for defense or urban policy. Thus, Reagan developed a highly compartmentalized structure of cabinet councils, grouped around specific subject areas: economic affairs, human resources, natural resources, food and agriculture, commerce and trade. They retained the statutory National Security Council and set up two additional cabinet councils that addressed items of general management cutting across the executive branch: legal policy, management and administration.

The intention behind these cabinet councils, or so the White House led people to believe, was to integrate both the cabinet officers and Executive Office staff into working bodies that could save the president from convening the whole cabinet and yet would still keep cabinet members involved.

In practice, what happened was that most cabinet members became members of subcabinet policy groups, chaired by a fellow cabinet member but usually directed or orchestrated by a senior White House official. Senior aides loomed large. Meanwhile the president himself did not have to attend many meetings. Cabinet members, however, were forever going to the council meetings!

Participants complained too that the issues often overlapped into the jurisdiction of two or more cabinet councils, creating coordination problems. Cabinet members, many of whom served on at least three cabinet councils, soon complained about the number of meetings, and as their own schedules of congressional testimony and various out-of-town trips inevitably diverted them, they began to send their deputies or even lesser departmental aides to represent them.

After a while, the cabinet council system began to create more problems than it solved. When cabinet members stopped coming, White House aides tended to take control of these councils.

Reagan had centralized and politicized the upper echelons of government more than any president in memory. He had done so deliberately. The conservative agenda of the Reagan presidency had been forged before he took office. A close reading of the books written by Reagan staffers and cabinet officers suggests too that Reagan's top aides, Edwin Meese, in particular, never really intended to allow most of the cabinet a major say in Reagan's policy decisions. To be sure, they had to be involved, but more to ensure they would be loyal cheerleaders and faithful implementers of the Reagan priorities. What he needed most was a means to enact, enforce, and implement his agenda. The cabinet members, through the cabinet councils, would play a role, but not nearly as influential a role as Reagan's White House staff, his Office of Management and Budget and also his Office of Policy Development.

The Reagan cabinet council experiment was judged as a mixed success. For a time it gave cabinet members a sense of involvement. More important, however, it permitted Reagan's top staffers to control the cabinet departments and to protect the president. Policy debates did take place, but coordination of the president's program was at the heart of this process. It is doubtful future presidents will adopt the Reagan system. It suffered from being too diffused and too complicated. It occasioned too many meetings.

Cabinet members soon recognized the councils as another obstacle in the way of talking directly with the president. Reagan, never an avid consumer of advice and information, liked the system while it lasted, yet it also may have been the source of his greatest problems—failure to know what was going on in his own administration and failure to educate his senior people of the legal and constitutional as well as policy responsibilities that came with their jobs at the head of the executive branch.

## A CABINET OF UNEQUALS

Cabinet roles and influence with the White House differ markedly according to personalities, the department, and the times. Each cabinet usually has one or two members who become the dominant personalities. Herbert Hoover's performance as secretary of commerce under Harding was of this type. George Marshall's performance in both State and Defense under Truman was similar. George Humphrey of the Treasury and John Foster Dulles of State clearly towered over others in the Eisenhower cabinet. Robert McNamara enjoyed especially close ties with both Kennedy and Johnson. And James Baker, George Shultz, and Edwin Meese all carried special weight with Ronald Reagan. Robert Rubin, Warren Christopher, and Madeleine Albright became major figures in the Clinton cabinet. Donald Rumsfeld and Colin Powell, along with Dick Cheney, became the major players in the George W. Bush administration.

Certain departments and their cabinet officers have gained prominence in recent decades because every president has been deeply involved with their priorities and missions—Defense and State in the Cold War as well as in the war on terrorism, for example. The Acheson-Dulles-Rusk-Kissinger-Baker tradition of close and cordial ties with their presidents were founded in an era of continuous international tension during which diplomatic and alliance strategy loomed large. Other departments may become important temporarily in the president's eyes, sometimes because of a prominent cabinet secretary who is working in an area in which the president wants to effect breakthroughs: for example, John Kennedy's Justice Department headed by his brother Robert. HEW sometimes was thought to be developing into a presidential department during the mid-1960s when under John W. Gardner it grew rapidly in order to manage Johnson's major educational and health programs. The Department of Energy enjoyed special considerations in the early Carter years for similar reasons. Soon, however, HEW was divided into two departments and Energy was downgraded significantly by Reagan and later presidents.

Much White House–cabinet estrangement undoubtedly arises because presidents simply lack the time to spend with all cabinet officers, let alone the leaders of independent agencies or major bureau chiefs. Most of a president's schedule is consumed with national security and foreign policy matters.

Vast differences exist in the scope and importance of cabinet-level departments. The huge Defense Department and the smaller departments of Labor, Housing and Urban Development, and Education are not at all similar. Certain agencies not of cabinet rank—the Central Intelligence Agency, for example—may be more important, at least for certain periods of time, than certain cabinet-level departments. Conventional rankings of the departments are based on their longevity, annual expenditures, and number of personnel. Rankings according to these indicators can be seen in the first three columns of Table 9.1. Even a casual comparison of these columns reveals unexpected characteristics. Thus, although the State Department is over two hundred years older than some of the newer departments, its expenditures are among the lowest. On the other hand, the Department of Human Services, formerly the Department of Health, Education, and Welfare, officially only about forty years old, ranks very high in expenditures.

The contemporary cabinet can be differentiated also into "inner" and "outer" cabinets, as shown in Table 9.1. This classification, derived from interviews, indicates how White House aides and cabinet officers view the departments and their access to the president. The occupants of the inner cabinet generally have maintained a role as counselor to the president; the

**TABLE 9.1**
**Ways of Looking at the Executive Departments**

| Seniority | Expenditures | Personnel | Inner & outer Cabinet |
|---|---|---|---|
| 1. State | 1. HHS | 1. Defense | *Inner:* |
| 2. Treasury | 2. Treasury | 2. Veterans' Affairs | 1. State |
| 3. War/Defense | 3. Defense | 3. Homeland Security | 2. Defense |
| 4. Interior | 4. Agriculture | 4. Treasury | 3. Treasury |
| 5. Justice | 5. Veterans' Affairs | 5. Agriculture | 4. Justice* |
| 6. Agriculture | 6. Education | 6. Justice | *Outer:* |
| 7. Commerce | 7. Labor | 7. Interior | 5. Agriculture |
| 8. Labor | 8. Transportation | 8. Transportation | 6. Interior |
| 9. HHS† | 9. HUD | 9. HHS | 7. Transportation |
| 10. HUD$‡ | 10. Homeland Security | 10. Commerce | 8. HHS |
| 11. Transportation | 11. Justice | 11. State | 9. HUD |
| 12. Energy | 12. Energy | 12. Energy | 10. Labor |
| 13. Education | 13. Interior | 13. Labor | 11. Commerce |
| 14. Veterans' Affairs | 14. State | 14. HUD | 12. Energy |
| 15. Homeland Security | 15. Commerce | 15. Education | 13. Education |
| | | | 14. Veterans' Affairs |
| | | | 15. Homeland Security |

*Sometimes inner, sometimes outer. "Inner" and "Outer" cabinet is our classification done according to the counseling-advocacy departments.

†HHS, Health and Human Services.

‡HUD, Housing and Urban Development.

*Source:* Expenditures Statistical Abstract of the U.S. 1996, p. 334. Personnel figures from ibid., p. 345. 2004 FY Budget Proposals, *CQ Weekly* (February 8, 2003), p. 332.

departments all include broad-ranging, multiple interests. The explicitly domestic policy departments, with the exception of Justice, comprise the outer cabinet. By custom, if not by designation, these cabinet officers assume a relatively straightforward advocacy orientation that overshadows their counseling role.

## THE INNER CABINET

A pattern in the past several administrations suggests strongly that the inner, or counseling, cabinet positions are vested with high-priority responsibilities that bring their occupants into close and collaborative relationships with presidents and their top staff. Certain White House staff counselors also have been included in the inner cabinet with increasing frequency. The secretary of defense was one of the most prominent cabinet officers during all recent administrations, for each president recognized the centrality of national security issues. Then, too, the defense budget and the DOD personnel, the latter sometimes approaching three million (including the military), makes it impossible for a president to ignore a secretary of defense for very long. Despite the inclination of recent presidents to serve as "their own secretary of state," the top people at the Department of State have nevertheless had a direct and continuous relationship with contemporary presidents. Recent treasury secretaries—George Humphrey, Robert Anderson, Douglas Dillon, John Connally, George Shultz, James Baker, Robert Rubin—also have played impressive roles in presidential deliberations on financial, business, and economic policy. The position of attorney general often, though not always, has been influential in the cabinet.

The inner cabinet, as discussed here, corresponds to George Washington's original foursome and to most memoirs of the Eisenhower through Clinton period. The status accorded these cabinet roles is, of course, subject to ebb and flow, for the status is rooted in a cabinet officer's performance as well as in the crises and the fashions of the day.[33]

### A National Security Cabinet

The seemingly endless series of international crises—Indochina, Central America, South Africa, the Middle East, Bosnia, Afghanistan, and Iraq, and the tensions with the former Soviet Union and North Korea—have made it mandatory for recent presidents to maintain close relations with the two national security cabinet heads. Just as George Washington met almost every day with his four cabinet members during the French crisis of 1793, so also all of our recent presidents have been likely to meet at least weekly and be in daily telephone communication with their inner cabinet of national security advisers. One Johnson aide said it was his belief that President Johnson personally trusted only two members of his cabinet, Secretary of State Rusk and Secretary of Defense McNamara. Kennedy aides say their president viewed his regional assistant secretaries of state as more important officers of the government than most of the cabinet. Harold Brown (Defense) and Cyrus Vance (State) were President Carter's best appointments as well as two of his closest counselors. George H.W. Bush was closest to Secretary of State James Baker and DOD Secretary Dick Cheney. The others were all more remote.

Throughout recent administrations, presidents and their staffs have complained about the operational lethargy of the State Department. Although the secretary of state is customarily considered by the White House to be a member of the president's inner cabinet, the department itself is often regarded as one of the most difficult to deal with. White House staffers invariably cite the State Department to illustrate White House–department conflicts. They scorn the narrowness and timidity of the encrusted foreign service and complain of the custodial conservatism reflected in State Department working papers. In State, more than in the other departments, the method and style of personnel, the special selection and promotion processes, and the protocol consciousness all seem farther removed from the political thinking at the White House. State's personnel invariably become stereotyped by White House aides as preoccupied, cautious, and traditional.

### Attorneys General

The Justice Department is often identified as a counseling department, and its chiefs usually are associated with the inner circle of presidential advisers. That Kennedy appointed his brother, Nixon appointed his trusted campaign manager and law partner, Carter appointed a personal friend, and Reagan appointed his personal attorney and later one of his campaign managers to be attorneys general indicates the importance of this position, although extensive politicization of the department has a long history. The Justice Department traditionally serves as the president's attorney and law office, a special obligation that brings about continuous and close relations between White House domestic policy lawyers and Justice Department lawyers. The White House depends heavily and constantly on the department's lawyers for counsel on civil-rights developments, presidential veto procedures, tax prosecutions, antitrust controversies, routine presidential pardons, the overseeing of regulatory agencies, and for a continuous overview of the congressional judiciary committees and separation-of-power questions. Nowadays, too, fighting terrorism looms large. That these exchanges involve lawyers working with lawyers may explain in some measure why White House aides generally are more satisfied with transactions with Justice than those with other departments.

### Treasury Secretary

The secretary of the treasury continues to be a critical presidential adviser on both domestic and international fiscal and monetary policy, but this person also plays somewhat of an advocate's role as an interpreter of the nation's leading financial interests. Treasury has become a department with major institutional authority and responsibility for income and corporate tax administration, currency control, public borrowing, and counseling of the president on such questions as the price of gold and the balance of payments, the federal debt, and international trade, development, and monetary matters. In addition, Treasury's special clientele of major and central bankers has unusual influence. Also, the treasury secretary is almost always a pivotal figure in crucial negotiations with Congress on tax and trade matters.

The importance of the treasury secretary as a presidential counselor derives in part from the intelligence and personality of the incumbent. Dillon and Connally, for example, were influential in great part because of their self-assuredness and personal magnetism. President Eisenhower found himself responding in a similar manner to George M. Humphrey: "In Cabinet meetings, I always wait for George Humphrey to speak. I sit back and listen to the others talk while he doesn't say anything. But I know that when he speaks, he will say just what I was thinking."[34] Leonard Silk has suggested, however: "Formally, the Treasury Secretary had a mystique and power potential fully comparable to those of the chancellor of the Exchequer in Britain or the Minister of Finance in France. The mystique may not be all that mysterious to explain, it derives from money. Power over money, in the hands of the right man, can enable a Secretary of the Treasury to move into every definite action of government—in military and foreign affairs as well as in domestic economic and social affairs."[35]

Reagan's second-term treasury secretary, James Baker, was regarded as one of the most important individuals in government for several reasons. He had the confidence of the president, he enjoyed a reputation for competence, and he was nearly always a central player in policy decisions concerning the dollar, trade and tariff legislation, tax reform, and our economic relations with key allies. Clinton's Robert Rubin was given considerable credit for the successful economic strategies that helped win Clinton his 1996 reelection. Rubin was regarded as the most influential, member of Clinton's cabinet. George W. Bush had a poor relationship with his first secretary of the treasury and unceremoniously dumped him after one too many embarrassments and disagreements. Bush did not have the rapport with his treasury secretaries that Clinton had with his.

## INNER CIRCLES

Inner-circle cabinet members have been more interchangeable than those of the outer cabinet. Henry Stimson, for example, alternated from being Taft's secretary of war to Hoover's secretary of state and then back once more to war under FDR. Dean Acheson was undersecretary of the treasury for FDR and later secretary of state for Truman. Dillon reversed this pattern by being an Eisenhower undersecretary of state and later a Kennedy secretary of the treasury. When Kennedy was trying to lure McNamara to his new cabinet, he offered him his choice between Defense and Treasury. Attorney General Nicholas Katzenbach left the Justice Department to become an undersecretary of state; Eisenhower's attorney general William Rogers became Nixon's first secretary of state; and John Connally, once a secretary of the navy under Kennedy, became Nixon's secretary of the treasury. Within a mere four and a half years, Elliot Richardson, sometimes called "our only professional cabinet member," moved from undersecretary of state to HEW secretary to defense secretary to attorney general. He became, his unexpectedly short tenure notwithstanding, the fourteenth head of the Justice Department to have served also in another inner-cabinet position. Cyrus Vance, who had served as deputy secretary of defense for LBJ, became Carter's secretary of state. George Shultz, treasury secretary and the Office of Management and Budget (OMB) director under Nixon, served for seven years in the Reagan cabinet as secretary of state. Treasury Secretary Donald Regan moved from treasury secretary to White House chief-of-staff under Reagan, and top White House aide Ed Meese served Reagan later as attorney general. Jim Baker went from White House chief-of-staff to treasury and then under G.H.W. Bush to state and finally back to chief-of-staff. Donald Rumsfeld served as chief-of-staff and later as Secretary of Defense under President Ford and returned to serve as defense secretary for George W. Bush. Occasionally shifts have occurred from inner to outer cabinet, but these have been exceptions to the general pattern.

This interchangeability, or musical chair rotations, may result from the broad-ranging interests of the inner-cabinet positions, from the counseling style and relationships that develop in the course of an inner-cabinet secretary's tenure, or from the already close personal friendship that has often existed with the president. It may be easier for inner-cabinet than for outer-cabinet secretaries to maintain more of a presidential perspective; presidents certainly try to choose people they know and respect for these intimate positions.

In recent years members of the White House staff have performed cabinet-level counselor roles or even assumed cabinet-level roles and prerogatives. Eisenhower, for example, explicitly designated Sherman Adams to be a member of his cabinet ex officio. Kennedy looked upon Theodore Sorensen, McGeorge Bundy, and some of his economic advisers as perhaps even more vital to his decision-making than most of his cabinet members. Johnson and Nixon also assigned many of their staff to cabinet-type counseling responsibilities. Carter adviser Robert Strauss performed several cabinet-level responsibilities in the later 1970s, ranging from anti-inflation matters to diplomatic negotiations. Carter also relied heavily on National Security Adviser Zbigniew Brzezinski. Reagan plainly relied on James Baker and Edwin Meese to supervise or even control cabinet officials. George W. Bush relied heavily on national security assistant Condi Rice and chief political advisor Karl Rove, both of whom enjoyed more access if not status than most cabinet members.[36] He also relied on Dick Cheney.

The people to whom presidents turn for overview presentations to members of Congress and cabinet gatherings are another indicator of inner-counselor status. When Kennedy wanted to brief his cabinet on his major priorities, typically he would ask Secretary Rusk to review foreign affairs, chairman of the Council of Economic Advisers Walter Heller to review questions about the economy, and Ted Sorensen to give a status report on the domestic legislative program. When Lyndon Johnson held special seminars for gatherings of members of the Congress, he would invariably call upon the secretaries of state and defense to explain national security matters and then ask his budget director and his chairman of the Council of Economic Advisers to comment on economic, budgetary, and domestic program matters. Nixon and Ford usually called on Henry Kissinger, the director of the Office of Management and Budget, and one of their chief White House domestic policy counselors. Similarly, Carter and Reagan increasingly turned inward for coordination and crucial political strategy. Clinton relied heavily on OMB Director, then Chief-of-Staff Leon Panetta, as well as White House economic adviser Robert Rubin, who later became secretary of the treasury.

## THE OUTER CABINET

The outer-cabinet positions deal with strongly organized and more particularistic clientele, an involvement that helps to produce an advocate relationship with the White House. These departments—Health and Human Services, HUD, Labor, Commerce, Interior, Agriculture, Transportation, Energy, Education, and Veterans' Affairs—are considered the outer-cabinet departments. The newer Department of Homeland Security is harder to locate because of its many diverse responsibilities. Because most of the president's controllable expenditures, with the exception of defense, lie in their jurisdictions, they take part in the most intensive and competitive exchanges with the White House and the Office of Management and Budget. These departments experience heavy and often conflicting pressures from clientele groups, from congressional interests, and from state and local governments. These pressures often run counter to presidential priorities. Whereas three of the four inner-cabinet departments preside over policies that usually, though often wrongly, are perceived to be largely nonpartisan or bipartisan—national security, foreign policy, and the economy—the domestic departments almost always are subject to intense crossfire between partisan and domestic interest groups.

White House aides and inner-cabinet members may be selected primarily on the basis of personal loyalty to the president; outer-cabinet members often are selected, as mentioned, to achieve a better political, geographical, ethnic, or racial balance. In addition to owing loyalty to their president, these people must develop loyalties to congressional committees that approved them or to those that finance their programs, to laws and programs they administer, and to clientele and career civil servants who serve as their most immediate jury.

President Reagan and majorities in Congress successfully pressed for the creation of a cabinet-level Department of Veterans' Affairs. The Veterans'

Administration and its supporters wanted more recognition and status for their $30 billion program and nearly 250,000 employees. Critics viewed this move as just one more effort to create a "special interest" advocacy cabinet slot.

## THE RISE OF THE ADMINISTRATIVE PRESIDENCY

As presidents fail to get Congress to respond favorably to their legislative proposals, ways are sometimes found to "go around" Congress. Frustrated by congressional nay-saying, presidents look for ways to achieve their policy goals without going through the difficult and cumbersome legislative arena. One strategic approach popular with recent presidents is to devise an administrative agenda for governing.[37] Presidents try to employ managerial or administrative means to policy ends. As Durant and Warber describe:

> ... the administrative presidency is premised on three assumptions. First, congressional opposition to presidential legislative initiatives is the rule rather than the exception. Second, federal agencies make policy as they exercise bureaucratic discretion when implementing statutes. Consequently, presidents have another opportunity to "legislate" that does not require them to mobilize legislative majorities in Congress. Third, and premised on conventional notions of hierarchical control, presidents indirectly can influence policy by naming political appointees to agencies who either substantively or ideologically share their policy agendas. These appointees, in turn, can change agency rules, budgets, structures, and personnel requirements to suit presidential policy goals. In contrast to this more "indirect" (or "contextual") approach of acting through agents, presidents can take a more direct (or "unilateral") approach. They do so when issuing executive orders, proclamations, presidential signing statements, national security directives, and presidential memoranda.[38]

Increasingly, presidents use these administrative devices to make policy. Richard Nixon is credited with "inventing" this strategy, but it did not fully blossom until the Reagan presidency. Reagan aggressively employed a strategy that politicized the managerial side of the presidency in an effort to circumvent Congress and govern on his own terms. President Clinton, learning the lesson well, continued using an administrative strategy to govern, especially after the 1995 Republican takeover of Congress.[39]

Using executive orders, memoranda, signing statements, and a variety of other administrative devices, presidents have been able to make policy without legislative approval and sometimes even against the will of Congress. The Supreme Court has held that executive orders have, under most circumstances, the full force of law (see *Jenkins v. Collard,* IAS U.S. 557, 560–561 [1891]).

An "executive order" is a directive issued by the president of the United States. Its purpose is to assist the president in his or her capacity as chief executive of the nation. Originally, the executive order was intended for rather minor administrative and rule-making functions, to help the nation's chief administrative officer administer the laws more efficiently and effectively. Over time, however, the executive order has become an important and sometimes controversial tool for a president to make policy without obtaining the consent of Congress as required by the Constitution.[40]

As the nation's chief executive, the president bears significant administrative and managerial responsibilities. In order to do his or her job, a president needs the power and authority to issue administrative orders and instructions. The executive order is an "implied" power, not specifically mentioned in the Constitution, but deemed essential for the functioning of government.

George Washington issued the first executive order on June 8, 1789. It instructed heads of departments (cabinet officers) to make a "clear account" of their departments. Under the National Administrative Procedure Act of 1946, all executive orders must be published in the *Federal Register.* Congress, if it wishes, can overturn an executive order. Executive orders can also be challenged in court on the grounds that they may violate the Constitution.

Over time, presidents have gone beyond the use of executive orders for merely administrative matters and have begun to use orders to "make law" on more substantive and controversial matters. Such efforts bypass Congress and sometimes overstep the bounds of what is an appropriate use of the administrative tools of the office. Presidents have been accused, with some justification, of "going around" Congress and "legislating" independent of Congress.

Presidents have used executive orders to implement some very controversial policies. In 1942, during World War II, Franklin Roosevelt interned Japanese-Americans in detention centers. In 1948, Harry S Truman integrated the military. In 1952, Truman attempted to seize control of steel mills. In 1992, Bill Clinton directed the Coast Guard to return Haitian refugees found at sea to Haiti. In 2001, President George W. Bush issued a series of orders aimed at undermining terrorist organizations in the United States and abroad. All these acts were done through executive orders.

Some of the presidential efforts have been challenged in court. In general, the courts have recognized the legitimacy and legality of executive orders, but not all orders pass the test of constitutionality. In 1952, for example, during the Korean War, President Truman seized control of the nation's steel mills to prevent a work stoppage that might have negatively impacted the war effort. The Supreme Court, in *Youngstown Sheet and Tube Co. v. Sawyer,* decided that the president's actions were unconstitutional. Truman was forced to back down, but such limitations are the exception. Overall, presidents have been able to take control of a variety of significant policy areas through the use of administrative tools such as the executive order. Executive orders have become an important weapon in the president's arsenal, and are likely to remain so.

## THE PRESIDENT'S SPOUSE

Presidential spouses have a long history of behind the scenes influence. They certainly enjoy great proximity.[41]

The notable paradox about First Ladies is that the greater their perceived political and policy influence, the more they are criticized because of their unelected and unconfirmed (by Congress) status. Edith Wilson, Eleanor Roosevelt, Betty Ford, Nancy Reagan, and Hillary Clinton became feared or resented, and sometimes both, because they were thought to wield power and influence that had no basis in constitutional provisions.

While the Constitution may be vague concerning the precise powers of the presidency, it is silent on the role of the president's spouse. The First Lady or First Spouse's public position has evolved from a ceremonial hostess role to that of close and sometimes influential policy adviser.[42]

Initially there was confusion over how to address the president's wife. A nation accustomed to royalty and unschooled in the language of democratic politics understandably had a difficult time coming to grips with this new position. Martha Washington was often referred to as Lady Washington, and some even called the president's wife "Presidentress" or "Mrs. President." Over time the lack of (and some would say the desire for) royalty led to a reemergence of regal address, and it wasn't long before the president's wife was regularly referred to as "first lady."

Anthropologist Margaret Mead once said that, "Kings and queens have always focused on people's feelings and since we're not very far from a monarchy, the President's wife, whoever she is, has little choice but to serve as our queen."[43] But almost every president's wife has hated the title First Lady. Jackie Kennedy so loathed it that for a time she forbade her staff to use the term. "The one thing I do not want to be called is first lady," she said. "It sounds like a saddle horse."[44]

At first the role of First Lady was publicly downplayed. This reflected early confusion over the proper place of the president's wife in the public world, and the restricted role of women generally in early American society. Women were relegated to the home, certainly not to the public arena of politics. If First Ladies could not publicly display their political skills, they often exerted significant influence behind the scenes.

The gradual evolution of the First Lady's role from ceremonial/hostess to symbol surrogate, issue highlighter, campaign worker, and political adviser reflects the impact of certain activist First Ladies, the changing role of women in American society, increased power in the executive branch, and the increased public and press attention focused on the presidency's politics and personalities.

The first prominent First Lady was Dolley Madison, who remained a visible social figure for decades. But Dolley Madison was one of the early exceptions—the truly public First Lady. It was not until the time of the Civil War that Mary Lincoln and shortly thereafter Julia Grant basked in the public spotlight.

The first influential First Lady may have been Edith Wilson. When in 1919 her husband had a stroke, Mrs. Wilson became de facto president, prompting Massachusetts Senator Lodge to comment, "a regency was not contemplated in the Constitution."[45]

The outspoken Eleanor Roosevelt would stretch the limits of her role as First Lady. The active and independent Mrs. Roosevelt often served as the eyes and ears of FDR. She vigorously championed civil rights, social justice, and peace initiatives such as the creation of the United Nations and the human rights commission. Her four sons were in the military services even before the Japanese attack on Pearl Harbor and in many ways Eleanor Roosevelt performed as "First Mother" during World War II. For twelve and a half years she traveled the country and the world, volunteered on countless committees and boards, wrote a newspaper column, and played the role of lobbyist, counselor, and sounding board to FDR. Her actions and engagement had a focus. In the words of a sympathetic biographer, Eleanor Roosevelt always "believed that human welfare and social justice should be encouraged and protected under the auspices of an enlightened, caring government."[46]

Edith Mayo, creator of the exhibit at the Smithsonian Institute entitled, "First Ladies: Political Role and Public Image," has written "[i]t is sad and telling that the press and public alike are unaware that Presidential wives since Abigail Adams have been wielding political influence. Further, it is disheartening to find that virtually every First Lady who has used her influence has been either ridiculed or vilified as deviating from women's proper role or has been feared as emasculating."[47]

In fact, the "office" of First Lady has been institutionalized, and is served by a sizable staff and a significant budget. Often the president's spouse is a key player in the internal affairs of the White House.

Since the 1960s, First Ladies have played an even greater public and political role than their predecessors. Jackie Kennedy was a valuable partner with her husband along the campaign trail. Her style and beauty contributed to the Camelot mystique that surrounded the Kennedys. Betty Ford, a strong supporter of abortion and women's rights, outspoken and direct, said she often used "pillow talk" to influence her husband.[48] Rosalyn Carter attended some cabinet meetings, used her position as a platform from which to advance women's issues, and was active in the field of mental health education.

Nancy Reagan was also influential. When her husband went through cancer surgery, Mrs. Reagan somewhat downplayed the vice president's role and announced herself as "the President's stand-in."[49] Mrs. Reagan also held veto power over her husband's schedule, sometimes consulted an astrologer as a guide to her husband's actions, influenced the hiring and firing of key personnel, and along with Michael Deaver, worried a lot about her husband's image and place in history. It is believed that, in the aftermath of the Iran-Contra scandal, Mrs. Reagan encouraged her husband to negotiate an effective arms deal with the Soviet Union in order to advance his reputation.

First Ladies have become increasingly influential and outspoken in recent times. Betty Ford was a strong advocate of many women's rights, sometimes charting a course at odds with the policy views of President Ford. (*Source:* Copyright © Bettmann/CORBIS.)

Hillary Rodham Clinton became one of the most controversial First Ladies. Mrs. Clinton was a successful attorney before her husband decided to seek the presidency, and was active in the legal rights for children movement. Independent and outspoken, Mrs. Clinton rubbed many conservatives the wrong way. Radio talk shows hosts blasted her as a radical liberal and criticized her influence.

Mrs. Clinton was the administration's unofficial leader on health care reform in 1993 and 1994, regularly attended policy strategy meetings, was an influential adviser to her husband, and was a prominent spokesperson for the administration. Her political influence was not, by historical standards, unusual, but her openness about it was. In recognition of the political role of First Ladies, a 1993 U.S. Court of Appeals decision, *Association of American Physicians and Surgeons v. Hillary Rodham Clinton,* concluded that the First Lady was "a full-time employee of the government." Hillary Clinton emerged to political consciousness in an age when the women's movement opened doors for women. She proved to be an invaluable political resource for Bill Clinton both in his 1996 reelection campaign and during the turbulent Monica Lewinsky investigations and impeachment.[50] Hillary Clinton's public approval ratings seemed to rise as she stood by her beleaguered husband.[51] And Hillary Clinton emerged from her eight years in the White House as a celebrity and politician (U.S. Senator, N.Y.) in her own right.

A president's spouse is often in a no-win situation. Expected to pursue a serious issue agenda, she is also held up to ridicule and suspicion if she has too much influence; asked to serve as first hostess and presidential partner, she cannot make the president appear weak or "unmasculine"; expected to support traditional values, she is also accomplished and increasingly has a career outside the home and independent of her spouse. Tensions are inevitable.

Barbara Bush and Laura Bush were seen as more traditional First Ladies. Laura Bush, a former school librarian, made an effort to celebrate books and writers. Yet she and her staff had to cancel an event celebrating poets when some poets planned to use the event as a protest against proposed U.S. military action in Iraq.

In sum, presidential spouses have performed a wide variety of roles and no one doubts that a number of them have been influential and important to presidential policy. Some, like Eleanor Roosevelt and Hillary Clinton, became independent political figures. Some were more inclined to perform family and social responsibilities. No formal job description can exist—the role of presidential spouse will be shaped by the individuals who come as presidential partners.

## THE WHITE HOUSE STAFF

The post–World War II era has witnessed a rise in the size, importance, and power of the president's White House and Executive Office staff and a corresponding decline in the importance and power of the cabinet. As already discussed, many of the functions once performed by the cabinet are now the responsibility of the staff.

Part of the reason for this can be traced to the failure of the cabinet and bureaucracy to supply presidents with the help they believe they need. As noted earlier, presidents come to question the loyalty of some cabinet officials, and the bureaucracy is often a creature of habit where the president may want creatures of politics. The staff has emerged to fill this vacuum.

The way a president organizes his staff depends on *personality, experience,* and *circumstances.* Bill Clinton liked to engage with his staff. This led to an open, unstructured staff arrangement. In Clinton's case it was too unstructured, however, and in 1993 the president replaced Chief-of-Staff Mack McClarty with former Congressman and former OMB Director Leon Panetta. A large part of Panetta's job was to organize and discipline President Clinton, a vain assignment indeed. In stark contrast, the George W. Bush White House was far more structured, heirarchical, and disciplined.[52]

Experience also plays a big role in the choice of staffing structure. Eisenhower, accustomed to a hierarchical and formal command structure from his career in the military, chose a formal staffing system for his presidency. There is not one perfect staffing structure for all seasons. In a crisis, for example, presidents often abandon the more formal or customary staff system and rely on a select few close advisers, as Kennedy did during the Cuban missile crisis, and as Bush did during the Gulf War.

One of the first questions a president must decide when putting together his administration is how strong a chief-of-staff he will have. James P. Pfiffner, a leading student of presidential management, says there are "two firm lessons of White House organization that can be ignored by Presidents only at their own peril: No. 1, A chief of staff is essential in the modern White House; No. 2, a domineering chief-of-staff will almost certainly lead to trouble" (e.g., Sherman Adams under Eisenhower, H. R. Haldeman for Nixon, Donald Regan for Reagan, and John Sununu for Bush). Sununu, instead of catching lightning for President Bush, created it, and was eventually forced out. Pfiffner concludes that "the preferred role for a chief of staff is that of a facilitator, coordinator, and a neutral broker."[53]

Apart from the chief-of-staff decision, presidents must also decide how to organize their staff. There are a variety of different possible models: FDR's competitive approach, which set some staff members against other staff members in a dynamic tension; JFK's collegial style, which sought a cooperative, bonding approach; Nixon's hierarchical model, with a closed, rigid pyramid of access and line of authority; and Reagan's delegating style, which transferred power and authority to key senior West Wing aides.[54]

Each style of staff organization has costs and benefits. The key is for presidents to know themselves, their strengths and weaknesses, and to model the staff in such a way as to take advantage of their strengths while ensuring that their weaknesses do not lead to serious mistakes.

## PROPOSALS FOR IMPROVED WHITE HOUSE DEPARTMENT RELATIONS

White House aides cite several sources of conflict between the White House and the executive departments; they also suggest a number of different remedies. The appropriateness of any suggested reform depends not only on the type of problem but also on which staff functions at the White House and which departments are involved. Rather than calling uniformly for a strengthened presidency, as might be expected, White House staff members often support a middle way, that is, an enhanced cabinet role as well as a strong, assertive White House role.

White House staff aides say that even a strong presidency cannot succeed without an executive branch characterized by strong cabinet and departmental leadership. Many say the president and senior staff had underestimated the importance of these factors in making the government work. In interviews, one aide insisted that allowing the domestic cabinet departments to become so divorced from the White House was a major mistake: "One way to improve things is to have the president and the cabinet members, particularly in domestic areas, meet at least six or seven times a year and talk in great detail and in highly substantive terms about the major priorities of the administration. You have to have better communication. Basically you have to make the cabinet less insecure."[55] Other aides criticized certain of their colleagues for having usurped operational responsibilities of the regular agencies, adding that if they accomplished anything, these aides enlarged their own importance more often than they expedited programs.

The American system is not a parliamentary one, and the cabinet does not and cannot exist as a collegial body in any formal sense. We elect a president, not the cabinet. We do not want a system in which the president is merely the first among equals. The essential question of the role of the cabinet in presidential government is an attitudinal, not a structural, one. A strong and "healthy" cabinet can exist if a president wants it. Multiple-advocacy systems that would enhance the constructive advice he might get cannot be imposed on a president. A president must find it compatible with his style. Ultimately, operating with a strong cabinet requires a president who is at ease with different and new opinions, who has high confidence in both his own personal and political position and the people he appointed. Still, the lesson is clear: presidents will always have strained relationships with several members of their cabinets.

## ADVOCACY CONFLICTS

The White House will generally view outer-cabinet executives as special pleaders for vested clientele interests over the priorities of the president. One of Franklin Roosevelt's commerce secretaries frankly acknowledged his representational and advocacy obligations when he explained: "If the Department of Commerce means anything, it means as I understand it the representation of business in the councils of the administration, at the Cabinet table, and so forth."[56]

Because presidents have less and less time to spend with the outer-cabinet members, the advocate role becomes less flexible and more narrowly defined. Outer-cabinet members find they have little chance to discuss new policy ideas or administrative problems with the president. They must make the most of their limited meetings.

The interpretation of the advocate role by both the outer-cabinet member and a president may vary. It is much easier to listen to an advocate whose point of view fits with the White House philosophy than to one who continually transmits substantively different arguments or who encroaches on other policy arenas. As departments have grown and their administration has become more demanding, fewer of the department heads have had time to be well versed on problems beyond their domain.

Effective presidents have to have the organizational and leadership ability to hear and balance the policy views of both their cabinet members and their White House and political advisors. Political scientist Fred Greenstein writes that a "president's capacity as an organizer includes his ability to forge a team and get the most out of it, minimizing the tendency of subordinates to tell their boss what they sense he wants to hear."[57]

Political scientist Alexander L. George has encouraged presidents to develop a multiple advocacy advising process that allows contrary and minority viewpoints to be weighed alongside conventional advice. His suggestions do not attempt to diminish partisanship, parochial viewpoints, and bargaining in the presidential advisory process. Instead, this system would seek to strengthen the analytical and rational components of standard advisory networks.[58]

## OUTER-CABINET ISOLATION

As tensions build around whether, or to what extent, domestic policy leadership rests with the departments, with the Office of Management and Budget, or with the White House, and as staff and line distinctions become blurred, the estrangement between the domestic department heads and the White House staff deepens. White House aides believe they possess the more objective understanding of what the president wants to accomplish. At the same time the cabinet heads, day in and day out, must live with the responsibilities for managing their programs, with the carrying out of laws delegated to them by Congress, and with the multiple claims of interest groups.

Joseph Califano, HEW cabinet head under Carter, says White House aides were generally both incompetent and hostile. They were constantly leaking negative comments about him and other cabinet members. White House operatives pressured cabinet members to do political chores and make campaign stops, and sometimes they opposed vigorous enforcement of the laws. In Califano's case this meant they would have liked him to ease up on his antismoking campaign and university desegregation efforts. Califano contends he had good, relations with President Carter. But White House staffers under Carter, with one or two exceptions, rarely answered his phone calls, seldom took an interest in his work, and hardly ever made his demanding job any easier. Mutual resentment was the result.

Carter criticized his own White House staffers for failing to establish good relations with cabinet officers. Yet time and again he told his cabinet: "I need your absolute loyalty."[59] He told Califano, one of those he fired, "the problem is the friction with the White House staff. The same qualities and drive and managerial ability that make you such a superb Secretary create problems with the White House staff. No one on the staff questions your performance. . . . But you and some members of the staff . . . have not gotten along."[60]

John Ehrlichman, one of Nixon's senior West Wing aides, wrote that Nixon viewed many of his domestic cabinet officers as "crybabies" and would often threaten to fire them or transfer them to some more remote position. He disliked meeting with them, disliked their demands on his time, and disliked their constant efforts to increase their budgets. Ehrlichman's depiction of the problems in Nixon's cabinet is as revealing about Nixon and Nixon's staff as it is about his cabinet members: "What went wrong with the

Nixon cabinet? Surely something did. Most of the cabinet members were discontented most of the time, and many of them failed to manage their departments well."

At root were the President's own shifting and variable concepts of the cabinet—of what it should be and do—and what the president expected from it. At first, during its selection, he wanted the cabinet to symbolize that all elements of the body politic were to be represented in the Nixon administration. There would be liberals and conservatives, ethnics and even Democrats. At the same time there was some rather vague intention that the cabinet would perform a collegial advisory function.

But soon Nixon changed his view: he looked on the cabinet principally as managers of their respective bureaucracies. A good secretary keeps things under control. Cabinet members were to be spokespersons, too. They should be out in the country making the case for the president and his policies.[61]

Every administration appears to reenact a similar script. Domestic advisers—or the outer cabinet—are led to believe they will be close intimates of the president, key policy advisers, and consulted on a range of matters. For awhile this happens. Typically, however, the president's time becomes scarce. Inevitably, the president's budget director wants to cut the cabinet member's departmental budget and the president usually sides with the budget director. Invariably, too, a president's political advisers grow impatient at a cabinet member's failure to "be more political" or failure to protect a president from politically damaging controversies.

The size of the bureaucracy, distrust, and a penchant for the convenience of secrecy lead presidents to rely heavily on White House staffers. The White House and executive office aides increasingly become involved not only in gathering legislative ideas but also in getting those ideas translated into laws or executive orders and then into programs. Program coordination and supervision, although often ill managed, also become primary White House interests. To an extent, these additional responsibilities transform the West Wing into an administrative rather than a staff agency. Outer-cabinet departments, understandably, begin to lose the capacity to sharpen up their programs, and the department heads feel uneasy about the lack of close working relations with the president.

One of the problems with this tendency to pull things into the White House and to exclude departmental officials is that excellent ideas or proposals that may exist lower down in the bureaus of the permanent government may not get the attention they deserve because, according to people in the departments, nobody asks them or, at least, no one pays them serious attention.

Rather than try to strengthen departmental capacities to come up with broader, more innovative proposals, West Wing aides, impatient for action, instead have developed a wide array of advisory committees, commissions, and task forces or White House operational groups.

## DEALING WITH THE BUREAUCRACY

As the nation's chief executive officer, presidents are supposed to sit at the top of the bureaucracy and control its actions. But their control is incomplete at best. A president operates under a four-year time restraint; the bureaucracy has no such time constraint. The old saying, "Presidents come and go but bureaucrats stay and stay," speaks volumes. The president is the temporary occupant of the White House; the bureaucracy is, at least in relative terms, the permanent government.

The federal bureaucracy, greatly swollen by the New Deal and the Cold War agencies, as well as by Great Society and more recent homeland security programs, is one of the most visible checks on a president. Indeed presidents are quick to fault the bureaucracy for the many problems that beset the implementation and evaluation of presidential programs.

The problem of how to control the bureaucracy has become a major preoccupation for presidents. Even persons who championed the New Deal now recognize that the executive bureaucracy can be a presidential curse. Arthur Schlesinger, Jr., wrote that, "as any sensible person should have known, the permanent government has turned out to be, at least against innovating presidents, a conservatizing rather than liberalizing force."[62] Concern about taming the bureaucracy comes from the right, from the revisionist left, and from moderates. Participants in the Nixon administration constantly

Harry Truman constantly chafed against Washington bureaucracy. His attitude was summed up by the sign on his desk—The Buck Stops Here.
(*Source:* Courtesy of the Harry S. Truman Library.)

embraced the same theme, even to the extent of claiming that their programs were being sabotaged from all directions. One of the key factors in former President Nixon's continuing attempts to centralize more authority either in the White House or in the hands of a few trusted and strong cabinet officials was this suspicion about the loyalties and parochialism of federal civil servants.

Gaining control over existing bureaucracies and making them work with and for the White House is an enormous challenge for the president. They constantly delegate, they must be most precise about what they delegate, and they must know whether and for what reasons the agencies to which they are delegating share their general outlook. They must be sensitive to bureaucratic politics, to the incentives that motivate bureaucrats, and to the intricacies of their standard operating procedures. They must have some assurance (and hence an adequate intelligence system) that what they are delegating will be carried out properly.

Recent presidents have often misunderstood the workings of bureaucracy. They have little appreciation for bureaucrats' considerable concern about organizational essence, organizational morale, and organizational integrity. Presidents and many of their aides mistakenly yet frequently look upon the executive branch as a monolith, and they are especially offended when senior bureaucrats differ with them or otherwise refuse to cooperate.

Presidents too often become defensive and critical of the bureaucracy. They fear, sometimes with reason, that their pet programs will get buried in inert custodial hands. Thus they have often sought shortcuts by setting up new agencies for each of their pet projects and relying increasingly on separate advisory and staff units within the executive office. However, the creation of a new agency does not guarantee presidential control. Indeed, some of the most independent, even maverick, federal agencies were originally set up to bypass the so-called old-line departments. Among such agencies are the Atomic Energy Commission, the Peace Corps, the Office of Economic Opportunity, and the Department of Energy.

Bureau chiefs and career civil servants sometimes do avoid taking risks and responsibility, opting instead for routine and security. The bureaucracy most assuredly has its own way of doing things, perhaps more conservative or more liberal than what the president wants. But that bureaucratic interests and presidential interests often differ does not mean that the permanent employees of the federal executive branch constitute an active enemy force. Bureaucratic organizations act, rather, in rational ways to enhance their influence, budget, and autonomy. And they generally believe that in doing so they act in the nation's interest.

The bureaucracy often defines the national interest differently from the way it is defined in the White House. But a close examination of the two definitions may reveal that both are valid and representative views of what is desirable. The presidential challenge, then, is to understand the strategies and tactics of federal bureaus and appreciate the underlying motivations. Properly understood, the bureaucratic instinct for competition, survival, and autonomy can be creatively harnessed by the White House both to educate itself and to develop cooperative alliances.

## BUREAUCRATIC VETOES

One major cause of the distance and frequent distrust between the presidency and the rest of the executive branch lies in the nature of the bureaucracy and of bureaucrats.

> Consider the official who directs the day-to-day operations of even a broadly defined program; let us call him the bureau chief. He directs the work of large numbers of people, he disposes of large sums of money, he deals every day with weighty, intricate, and delicate problems. He has probably spent most of his adult years in the highly specialized activity over which he now presides. He lives at the center of a special world inhabited by persons and groups in the private sector who stand to gain or lose by what he does, certain members of Congress who have a special interest in his actions, and a specialized press to which he is a figure of central importance. The approbation which is most meaningful to him is likely to be the approbation of the other inhabitants of this special world. The rest of the federal government may seem vague and remote, and the President will loom as a distant and shadowy figure who will, in any event, be succeeded by someone else in a few years. It would be unreasonable to expect this official to see his program in the Presidential perspective.[63]

How entrenched these relations may become can be inferred from the fact that, whereas tenure on the White House staff averages less than three years and even less than that among cabinet appointees, the bureau chiefs, senior members of Congress, senior staff in Congress, and veteran Washington lobbyists often endure in their posts for ten or fifteen years or more. Former Secretary of Health, Education, and Welfare John W. Gardner told the Senate Government Operations Committee:

> As everyone in this room knows but few people outside of Washington understand, questions of public policy nominally lodged with the Secretary are often decided far beyond the Secretary's reach by a trinity consisting of (1) representatives of an outside body, (2) middle level bureaucrats, and (3) selected members of congress, particularly those concerned with appropriations. In a given field these people may have collaborated for years. They have a durable alliance that cranks out legislation and appropriations in behalf of their special interest. Participants in such durable alliances do not want the Department Secretaries strengthened. The outside special interests are particularly resistant to such change. It took them years to dig their particular tunnel into the public vault, and they don't want the vault moved.[64]

Practically any new presidential initiative, therefore, faces a strategically placed potential veto group with major allies within the executive branch itself: a social services bureaucracy to resist a negative income tax, an Office of Education to resist measures that would undermine traditional school-of-education training programs, a defense establishment to resist disarmament agreements, and so forth.

The professionalization of many sections of the federal government has created another potentially powerful constraint on presidential action. Professionals in government—for example, senior engineers and physicists in the National Aeronautics and Space Administration or the Defense Department, physicians and biologists at the National Institutes of Health, and economists throughout the government—are at least equally committed to the values of their profession than to the political fortunes of presidents.

If presidents rarely control the bureaucracy, they still need the bureaucracy to implement their policies. But they are not helpless. Different presidents use different methods to move the bureaucracy. Some presidents do it by placing loyal followers in key positions, others assign a top aide to ride herd, some try to circumvent an unresponsive agency, others create new agencies staffed by their hand-picked administrators. Still other presidents devote their own time and effort to either persuade, bully, or negotiate with an unresponsive bureaucrat.

Bureaucrats can frustrate a president's wishes in a variety of ways. Orders are never self-executing, and it may not be clear exactly what a president wants. Also, some members of the permanent government may disagree with the president's directives and may intentionally sabotage the order by ignoring it, altering it in its execution, or failing to pass it on to the operational level. Delay is another common form of bureaucratic resistance.

## CONCLUSION

Regardless of how organization charts are drawn, future presidential use of the cabinet and White House staff probably will give greater weight to the realities of the differentiated roles and activities of the federal departments. The experience of numerous cabinet councils was an experiment that largely failed in Reagan's first term. But having working groups of cabinet members along the national security, economics, and domestic policy lines makes sense so long as the groups do not preclude occasional full meetings of the cabinet. A president and the White House top advisers need the advice of some individuals who are not directly concerned with a problem.

A redesigned and strengthened outer cabinet might enable the White House staff to abstain more often from the temptation to gather administrative responsibilities to itself. But reorganizational developments will not lessen the need for skillful and decisive executive branch mediators who, with the full confidence of the president, can preside over thorny and complex claims and counterclaims by competing domestic departments, and who also can know when important elements of a debate are being seriously neglected or misrepresented within cabinet-level negotiations. White House aides need to be chosen with these abilities in mind.

No president will be wholly satisfied with the loyalty of department heads. Cabinet members invariably aspire to a president's intimacy, and many in the inner cabinet will indeed become effective counselors and sometimes even friends, yet even some of these will break with a president, often without realizing how serious their differing perspectives have been. A president, however, must welcome advocacy from cabinet officers. And although open and frank discussions in cabinet meetings will sometimes limit a president's discretion, a president will generally profit from using the cabinet and smaller policy clusters of cabinet heads as regular consultative bodies.

The historical record of presidential-executive departmental relations is one of frustration, yet a more realistic view of the cabinet holds out promise for making a presidency more effective and responsible. Structural changes that must take place are minimal relative to the philosophical changes that must take place on the part of a president, White House staff, and cabinet members. In the end, it is a president who determines whether this promise will remain unrealized because of ineffectual disuse or be translated into a means for strengthening presidential leadership.

# *The American Vice Presidency*

What the Vice President will do or is permitted to do
. . . is determined by what the President assigns to him
or permits him to do. . . . The President can bestow
assignments and authority and can remove that authority at will.

> Hubert Humphrey, *Current History,* 67 (1974), p. 58

The job [of vice president] doesn't lend itself to high
profile and decision making. It lends itself to loyally
supporting the president . . . , giving him your best
judgment, and then when the president reaches a decision, supporting it.

> George H. W. Bush, quoted in Michael Duffy and Dan
> Goodgame, *Marching in Place* (Simon & Schuster, 1992)
> p. 40

Cheney is the most powerful deputy ever, and he is also
very much Bush's subordinate; this is not a contradiction so much as a cause and effect. Bush trusts Cheney
because he is loyal, discrete and very clear who is in
charge; that trust in turn is Cheney's trophy, up on the
mantel for all to see.

> Nancy Gibbs, "Double Edged Sword," *Time* (December 30,
> 2002–January 6, 2003), p. 93

During our first 150 years, vice presidents served primarily as ceremonial
ribbon-cutters. They also served as president and presiding officer in the

U.S. Senate. The post was often seen as a semiretirement job for party stalwarts, as a resting place for mediocrities or a "runner-up." Its occupants typically found themselves in a frustrating spectator role. In most administrations a vice president was at best a kind of fifth wheel and at worst a political rival who sometimes connived against the president. Daniel Webster reportedly turned down an invitation to be vice president in 1848, saying, "I do not propose to be buried until I am dead." Thomas Marshall, Woodrow Wilson's vice president, quipped that "once there were two brothers. One ran away to sea, the other became vice president of the United States, and nothing was heard of either of them again." Even Walter Mondale, Jimmy Carter's mostly successful vice president, complained that the job was often "fire hydrant of the nation." The office, said Mondale, is "handmade for ridicule and for dismissal. In the nature of it, you always look like a supplicant, a beggar, a person on a string."[1]

Indeed, until recent decades, Americans were more inclined to joke about the office than think about it. For a variety of sensible reasons, however, presidents now usually take the vice presidency more seriously, and its responsibilities, while still mainly ad hoc, have expanded. As Paul C. Light has noted, "After two hundred years as errand-boys, political hitmen, professional mourners, and incidental White House commissioners, Vice Presidents can now lay claim to regular access to the President and the opportunity to give advice on major decisions."[2]

Still, the vice presidency remains an ambiguous and paradoxical office. To the founding fathers it was pretty much an afterthought. To some scholars it is one of our most conspicuous constitutional mistakes. To some modern-day presidents it still appears to be more of a headache or a threat than an asset. To vice presidents it is often a confusing and unhappy experience. "A damned peculiar situation to be in," said Nixon's vice president Spiro T. Agnew, "to have . . . a title and responsibility with no real power to do anything." Lyndon B. Johnson said that much of the unhappiness in the office stems from knowing you are on "a perpetual death watch." Vice President Hubert Humphrey once said it was "like being naked in the middle of a blizzard, with no one to even offer you a match to keep you warm. . . . You are trapped, vulnerable and alone. . . ."

Paradoxes abound. A vice president's chief importance still consists of the fact that he may cease to be vice president. We yearn for someone to fill the post who has the competence to be president, yet it is a kind of an "off-the-job" training and waiting post. Perhaps the prime paradox is how we select vice presidents. We select our presidential nominees by a process of intensive democratic exposure and deliberation that is long and grueling. But we continue to leave the designation of the vice presidential running mate almost entirely to the personal judgment of the presidential nominee— a judgment that is sometimes made hastily, possibly by an over-extended nominee.

The main purpose of having such a position is to have a stand-by competent leader available if accident befalls the president. Frequently, however, the main criterion used in selecting the vice presidential nominee is balancing the ticket to help win crucial electoral college votes. These two needs, *competence* and *electoral utility,* need not be incompatible, but they often are. The question also arises: How can we get vice presidents of presidential quality if once in office they may have little to do and may be maligned before we really need them, if we need them? Some presidents only share "dirty work," such as press bashing, attacking the opposition party, and funeral duty responsibilities, with their vice presidents. Some do not share much at all for fear of being upstaged and outshone. Others have understandably refused to delegate responsibilities because of sharp policy differences. One student of the office concludes there really can be no deputy or alternate president, because of the "indivisibility of presidential leadership and the lack of place for tandem governance for two."[3]

Because vice presidents are always "a heartbeat away" from becoming president, there is often a strain in relations between vice presidents and their boss. Henry Kissinger wrote that the "relationship between the president and any vice president is never easy; it is, after all, disconcerting to have at one's side a man whose life's ambition will be achieved by one's death."[4] And Lyndon Johnson wrote of his vice presidential days, "Every time I came into John Kennedy's presence, I felt like a goddam raven hovering over his shoulder."[5]

Another paradox is that technically a vice president is neither a part of the executive branch nor subject to the direction of the president. In practice, however, recent vice presidents have shunned their Senate duties and taken up office in the White House, and have served primarily as presidential advisers.

A further paradox is that what it takes to be an effective vice president is vastly different from what it takes to be president. Foremost among the attributes of an effective president are independence and strength of character and skills as a national agenda setter and national unifier. A vice president, on the other hand, even while acting as an "understudy" for the president, must always be loyal and self-effacing while trying to avoid being obsequious. A vice president is constantly aware of the fact that the office and its importance are at least 90 percent dependent on the preferences, and even the whims, of the incumbent president. Political scientist Jeffrey Cohen notes that vice presidents who yearn to become president have to hope the public associates them with the success of the president the serve. This leads vice presidents to become loyal stalwarts in the administration. Yet "a vice president in search of the presidency must also appear to the public as his own person and not merely a pawn or relic of the outgoing administration." Al Gore certainly struggled to do this. Cohen adds, "the vice president must establish his own credentials . . . He must distance himself from the outgoing administration without dissociating from the administration."[6]

Originally the person who received the second highest vote in the presidential election became vice president. This was changed, after a bitter dispute over the election in 1800, when Aaron Burr and Thomas Jefferson both received equal votes. With the Twelfth Amendment to the Constitution (1804), the president and vice president are elected on separate ballots. In recent times, however, more and more presidents essentially dictate the choice of their running mates and successors. Thus Roosevelt, Kennedy, Nixon, and Reagan have picked their own successors, a notion the framers assuredly did not intend. Some people believe the practice of leaving this vital choice of future national leadership to the discretion of a single individual, the presidential candidate or the president, is unacceptable in a nation that professes to be democratic.

Support exists for devising better ways to pick vice presidential nominees. The search is made more urgent by the fact that eight presidents have died in office, four by assassination, four by natural death, and one (Nixon) has resigned. One-third of our presidents were once vice presidents, including six of our last fourteen presidents.

The vice presidency has been significantly affected by two post–World War II constitutional amendments. The Twenty-second, ratified in 1951, imposes a two-term limit for the presidency, which means vice presidents have a somewhat better chance of moving up to the presidency. The Twenty-fifth, ratified in 1967, confirms prior practice that, on the death or resignation of a president, the vice president becomes not acting president but president.[7] Of perhaps greater significance, this amendment provides a procedure, albeit somewhat ambiguous, to determine whether an incumbent president is unable to discharge the powers and duties of the office. Thus the amendment allows an incapacitated president to lay aside temporarily the powers and duties of the office without forfeiting them permanently, as Reagan did for a few hours in 1985 during a cancer operation. The constitutionality of this procedure had previously been in doubt. Further, the amendment creates a mechanism through which a vice president together with a majority of the cabinet may declare the president incapacitated and thus serve as acting president until the president recovers. This procedure answers several problems but also, as shall be discussed, raises new questions.

In addition, the Twenty-fifth Amendment established procedures to fill a vacancy in the vice presidency (a procedure used when Nixon selected Ford and when Ford selected Rockefeller). In the event of such a vacancy, the president nominates a vice president, who takes office upon confirmation by a majority vote of both houses of Congress. This procedure should ensure the appointment of a vice president in whom the president has confidence. If the vice president, under these circumstances, has to take over the presidency, he or she can usually be expected to reflect most of the policies of the person the people had originally elected.

The positive Mondale, Bush, Gore, and Chency (thus far) experiences have prompted reappraisals of the vice presidency. The way in which these men were selected and subsequently used has enhanced the importance of the position. Their experience has increased its prestige as a position of influence. Still, each of them at times either lapsed into or were forced into at times the traditional "cheerleader-in-chief" role. Inextricably, even the best of vice presidents find themselves having to defend administrative policies in which they have had little or no say in shaping.

The Dan Quayle experience—both the way he was selected and his inability to earn the respect of the American public—was a temporary setback to the office.

This chapter looks first at the traditional problems of the office. Then it considers recent vice presidencies. Finally, it treats questions of vice presidential selection and succession.

## TRADITIONAL PROBLEMS

The office, as noted earlier, is often condemned as a superfluous non-job. In fact at the Constitutional Convention of 1787, Benjamin Franklin ridiculed the position by proposing the occupant be called "Your Superfluous Highness." The position, along with any serious duties or prerogatives attached to it, comes only at the pleasure of the president. "I am not in a leadership position," said Vice President Nelson Rockefeller. "The President has the responsibility and the power. . . . The Vice President has no responsibility and no power."[8]

Few offices have been so disdained and lampooned. Our first vice president, John Adams, wrote to his wife in 1793 that: "My country has in its wisdom contrived for me the most insignificant office that ever the invention of man contrived or his imagination conceived." The great Henry Clay is said to have spurned the job twice. John Nance Garner, FDR's first vice president, said the job, "isn't worth a pitcher of warm spit." Gerald Ford could not get himself to accept Ronald Reagan's 1980 offer of running mate because he knew from experience that the job did not amount to much.

American voters send 537 elected officials to Washington. Of these, 536 have a reasonably clear idea of their role and functions. Vice presidents, on the other hand, are never exactly sure whether their functions will change from week to week. Over time, however, the jobs of the vice president have grown. On paper they look somewhat impressive:

1. President of the U.S. Senate
2. Member of the National Security Council
3. Chair of several national advisory councils
4. Diplomatic representative of the president and United States abroad
5. Senior presidential adviser
6. Liaison with Congress
7. Crisis coordinator
8. Overseer of temporary coordinating councils
9. Presider over cabinet meetings in absence of the president

10. Deputy leader of the party and key party fund-raiser
11. Apprentice available to take over job of the president, either on acting or full-time basis
12. President-in-waiting and possible future presidential candidate

Vice presidents have done all of these things. Several vice presidents have served their president and their nation well. Often, however, considerable political, psychological, and structural obstacles stand in the way of the constructive use of vice presidents. As we shall discuss later, Mondale, Bush, Gore, and Cheney have generally been able to overcome some of these.

## PRESIDENT OF THE SENATE

Until about 1940 most presidents and most Americans viewed the vice presidency almost exclusively as a legislative job. Even as late as 1954, the recently retired vice president, Alben W. Barkley, would write that, "The Vice President's principal duty is to preside over the Senate."[9] Vice presidents were to serve as president of the Senate, preside there, and cast an occasional tie-breaking vote.

Originally the Senate comprised a small number of elder statesmen; twenty-six men plus the vice president. Tie votes were frequent: John Adams cast twenty-nine tie-breaking votes. Nowadays, however, mainly because the Senate has grown to one hundred members, tie votes occur less than once a year. Dan Quayle didn't get to cast a single tie-breaking vote in four years. Gore and Cheney cast few.

The Senate was designed in many ways as an ideal place for a vice president to learn the business of government and to serve along with the nation's leading thinkers. The Senate was intended to pass laws, shape national policy, confirm major presidential appointees, oversee the approval of treaties, and, more generally, advise and counsel presidents, particularly in foreign affairs. Over time, the Senate delegated more and more of its powers to the president, cabinet, and even to Executive Office advisers, so much so that the Senate is now almost indistinguishable from the House of Representatives—neither a council of state nor the prime presidential counseling body.

Technically vice presidents could become frequent presiders in the Senate. In practice they have not. The job of presiding over the Senate has become largely thankless and powerless, and today offers little training for the position of chief executive. One observer concluded that

the single job conferred on a Vice President by the Constitution—presiding over the meetings of the United States Senate—can be performed by any six-year old. The presiding officer need do no more than sit there like an elegant dunce, and repeat aloud whatever the parliamentarian stage whispers to him. It is about as challenging as having your hair cut. . . ."[10]

Members of Congress now look on a vice president as a member of the executive branch. Lyndon Johnson, upon election as vice president, for example, sought to retain a certain measure of the control over Democrats that he enjoyed as majority leader. He tried to talk Senator Mike Mansfield into inviting him to preside over Democratic caucus meetings, even though he was about to become vice president. But he was rebuffed.

Vice presidents are rarely used effectively in congressional relations work. This is often because they are not properly prepared by their president. Harry Truman, in his brief tenure as vice president, wanted to become an effective link between Congress and the White House. But this depended on close contact with FDR, and contact was virtually nonexistent. Lyndon Johnson was similarly underused. Johnson was simultaneously rebuffed by both Congress and the White House. Caught both coming and going, he retreated into a nearly three-year sulk.

Franklin Roosevelt's troubles with John Nance Garner were legendary. Garner was an important figure in the Congress and he skillfully assisted the passage of a number of New Deal measures in FDR's first term. But he grew upset with the pace and sweeping scope of later New Deal measures and became outspoken in his opposition to several of them. He opposed Roosevelt's scheme for packing the Supreme Court. He opposed FDR's bid for a third term. Toward the end of his second term, President Roosevelt consciously avoided meeting with Vice President Garner and considered him an impossible person.

The limits of vice presidential influence in the Senate are illustrated by one of Spiro Agnew's transgressions of political convention. Early in his tenure, Agnew tried to interest himself in mastering Senate rules as well as learning the Senate's informal folkways: "But he violated protocol by lobbying on the Senate floor in behalf of the tax surcharge extension supported by the administration. 'Do we have your vote?,' he asked Senator Len Jordan of Idaho, a Republican. The senator replied, 'You did have until now.'" Thus was established Jordan's rule: "When the Vice President lobbies on the Senate floor for a bill, vote the other way."[11] Thereafter, Agnew seemed to lose interest in trying to become presidential emissary on Capitol Hill.

Vice President Hubert Humphrey had served in the Senate for sixteen years before becoming vice president. He was aware that as presiding officer he was to be seen but not heard, except for procedural matters. This was a difficult adjustment for the loquacious Humphrey.

Until recently, a vice president was a full member of neither executive nor legislative branch. The office, because of the duties as presiding officer of the Senate, is clearly a constitutional hybrid, limiting somewhat the use a president can make of a vice president. Thus, President Eisenhower asserted repeatedly in his memoirs that whatever executive assignments the vice president performed were voluntary and by his request.[12]

Some say a vice president should be relieved of traditional Senate functions and freed to participate more directly in executive branch responsibilities. James F. Byrnes of South Carolina, a former senator, associate justice of the Supreme Court, as well as secretary of state, offered this perspective:

> If a motion (in the Senate) does not receive a majority vote, it should be considered lost. It is not wise that the Vice President, a representative of the executive branch of government, should affect the will of the legislators by casting a decisive vote. In short, participation by the Vice President in Senate voting, either in support of his own views or the President's, constitutes a violation of the spirit of the fundamental provision of the Constitution that the three branches of our government shall forever be separated.[13]

Byrnes urged we adopt a constitutional amendment to effect this change.

Constitutional scholar Joseph Kallenbach also favored such a change, contending the vice president could then become a sort of "minister without portfolio," subject to executive assignments as a president may direct. "This would not only insure he would function in a subordinate administrative capacity to the President and not be tempted to become a rival," it would also provide assignments over a period of time that would enable him to acquire a wider knowledge of the operations of government as a whole. "In this way," adds Kallenbach, "he could be given a better opportunity than at present to prepare himself for the responsibility of serving as chief executive in case fate should thrust the role upon him."[14]

This suggestion has been largely ignored, just as most recent vice presidents have dismissed their Senate "job" as largely irrelevant. Vice presidents do show up on certain ceremonial occasions, such as an opening day and when the president addresses a joint session of Congress, but the job of presiding over the Senate is low on the vice president's priority list.

## VICE PRESIDENTS AS "ASSISTANT PRESIDENTS"

George Washington conferred on occasion with Vice President John Adams, but Adams acted in his official executive capacity only once, when he attended a cabinet meeting in 1791. Washington was away and wanted his department heads to get together in his absence, and he requested Adams to join them. Thomas Jefferson, when he served as vice president, declined President John Adam's invitation to attend cabinet meetings. Other vice presidents for the next 120 years stayed away from the cabinet sessions—either by personal or by presidential desire, usually both. Then in 1918 Thomas R. Marshall substituted for Woodrow Wilson when Wilson was in Europe. President Warren Harding invited his vice president, Calvin Coolidge, to regularly attend cabinet meetings.

FDR's second vice president, Henry Wallace, an experienced administrator who had already served two terms as secretary of agriculture, was the first vice president to be assigned major administrative duties. Roosevelt made Wallace chairman, successively, of the Economic Defense Board, the Supply Priorities and Allocations Board, the War Productions Board, and the Board of Economic Warfare. In the latter post Wallace became an aggressive administrator and an outspoken advocate.

Since 1943 vice presidents have, however, been invited to cabinet meetings and related policy councils with some regularity. By a 1949 amendment to the National Security Act of 1947, the vice president now sits as a regular member of the National Security Council. Since the Eisenhower presidency, the vice president has been made the cabinet's acting chairman in the president's absence. Nixon chaired several cabinet sessions during Eisenhower's several illnesses. LBJ and Humphrey chaired several presidential-level councils and commissions, and, like Wallace and Nixon before them, they traveled widely as goodwill ambassadors as well as on some sensitive policy missions. FDR actually began the tradition of sending vice presidents abroad. John N. Garner was FDR's representative at the installation of a Philippine president in 1935, and Henry Wallace as vice president traveled to Latin America as well as to China and Siberia. Nixon traveled to fifty-four countries, LBJ to more than thirty. Humphrey and Agnew were often sent to visit Asia. Mondale conducted a wide range of diplomatic missions to twenty-six nations during his four years as vice president. George H. W. Bush continued this tradition and traveled to even more nations; he logged nearly a million miles during his eight years in the Veep post.

Nearly every vice president in recent times has found it difficult to interfere with the work of cabinet members. The departmental secretaries preside over congressionally authorized departments; hence a vice president is very much an intruder unless a problem arises that is definitely interdepartmental. Even then, what is an interdepartmental matter to some may not be to others. Thus Secretary of State Alexander Haig was reportedly irate in 1981 when President Reagan officially designated George H. W. Bush to be the administration's chief "crisis manager."

Reformers sometime urge that vice presidents be assigned specific cabinet responsibilities, such as secretary of defense or attorney general. This might answer the criticism that the vice presidency is a training ground for nothing at all. Critics of this suggestion say that the existing presidentially approved cabinet members are already hard enough to "keep in line." As an elected department official, a vice president who served as a cabinet secretary/department head would be even tougher to "control" or to "fire." A vice president as department head would also surely be compromised by the narrow clientele constituencies of a single agency. Such a precedent, if established, might also affect the kinds of people a president would pick for vice president. Picking someone who might be a good department head might unwisely subordinate breadth, political talent, or general leadership ability to managerial experience.

Finally, it is not wholly evident that a departmental secretary position provides presidential training. Under some circumstances it might, under others it clearly would not. How many recent department heads come readily to mind as especially promising presidential candidates? To be sure, Jefferson and Madison served as cabinet members prior to their presidencies, but so too did James Buchanan and Herbert Hoover.

Both Presidents Hoover and Eisenhower recommended the creation of an additional appointed vice presidential post. Hoover advocated an administrative vice president; Eisenhower a "first secretary of government" for foreign affairs. Neither proposal received much attention. President Eisenhower's brother and confidant, Milton Eisenhower, urged the creation of two executive vice presidents, to be appointed by the president—one to deal with domestic policy, the other with international affairs, but both to work "in close collaboration with the President."

Eisenhower's suggestion was never taken seriously. Instead presidents rely on key cabinet members or those who serve on their staff.

More radical is a proposal that what we really need to do is to separate the presidency into two functions: the head of state and the chief executive. "What we can do, perhaps, is establish a head of state to greet foreign dignitaries and to visit them abroad, to officiate on occasions when a personification of the nation is required, to become the central figure even at the inauguration of the chief executives, and to live at the White House. The chief executive who would be elected every four years as at present, would live as cabinet members live."[15] Beguiling as this proposal might be, it has generally been considered naive. It smacks too much of importing the royalty feature from Great Britain. Because of this alone it will never gain popularity here. Most experts contend too that the chief executive office would be significantly weakened if the chief of state functions were taken away. Presidents such as the Roosevelts and Reagan clearly mixed the two and strengthened themselves by doing so.

## PSYCHOLOGICAL PROBLEMS OR THE "THROTTLEBOTTOM COMPLEX"

Tensions between a president and a vice president are natural; after all, the vice president is the only officer who works closely with a president who cannot be fired by him.

Alexander Throttlebottom was a character in the entertaining 1930 Broadway play "Of Thee I Sing" by George S. Kaufman and Morris Ryskind. Throttlebottom was a stumbling, mumbling caricature of a decidedly underemployed vice president. Neglected by his president, John P. Wintergreen, Throttlebottom is artfully drawn as an unknown, unwanted, and improbable national leader. Not only did he not want to be vice president or know what was expected of him, but he was even refused the right to resign. The unhappy "Throttlebottom" sat around in the parks and fed the pigeons, took walks, and went to the movies. The character of Throttlebottom provided for splendid satire and comic relief, but the mocking portrait lives on and the name has become a familiar term for the at least occasional reality of contemporary vice presidents.

The estrangement of vice presidents from presidents began with Adams and Washington. Relations between the first president and first vice president were civil but scarcely friendly. Then during his tenure as vice president under President Adams, Thomas Jefferson refused certain diplomatic assignments. Jefferson said of Aaron Burr, his first vice president, that he was a "crooked gun whose aim or shot you could never be sure of." Time and again relations between presidents and vice presidents have been strained, abrasive, and cold to the point of open hostility. A few other examples underscore the mutual frustration.

Roosevelt and John Nance Garner:

> The once cordial relations between the two men had long since turned sour. They had little contact except at cabinet meetings, where Garner, red and glowering, occasionally took issue with the President in a truculent manner. Roosevelt hinted he would desert the Democratic cause before he would vote for the Texan for President (in 1940). By early 1940 even official relations between the two men had almost ceased; Roosevelt was hoping that the Vice President would not show up for cabinet meetings. The President was gleeful about Garner's tribulations as a presidential candidate. . . .[16]

John F. Kennedy and Lyndon B. Johnson:

> They [the White House] made his stay in the vice presidency the most miserable three years of his life. He wasn't the number two man in that administration; he was the lowest man on the totem pole. Though he has never said this to anyone (perhaps because his pride would never let him admit it), I know him well enough to know he felt humiliated time and time again, that he was openly snubbed by second-echelon White House staffers who snickered at him behind his back and called him "Uncle Cornpone."[17]

Richard M. Nixon and Spiro Agnew:

> Nixon barely knew Agnew when he selected him in Miami Beach in 1968. Nixon, himself, had been humiliated in the vice presidential job, a job he called a hollow shell, the most ill conceived and poorly defined position in the American political system. He proceeded nonetheless to visit an even greater humiliation on Agnew. By most accounts Agnew was scorned by the White House staff and given little of importance to do.[18]

Richard Nixon had at best a cool relationship with President Eisenhower. Al Gore enjoyed a much closer relationship with President Clinton, yet it deteriorated in their final year. Dick Cheney's relationship with George W. Bush was more complicated. Bush respected the older, more experienced Cheney and regularly included him in policymaking meetings. Yet they apparently rarely socialized together, and Cheney was in many ways a reserved, often quiet, cheer-leading assistant. For a few months after the 9-11 terrorist attacks, Cheney was kept out of sight in a so-called undisclosed location, presumably for security reasons. This led to an insiders' joke that Cheney's friends apparently told for a while: "Dick Cheney is always at an undisclosed location," they said, "even when he's sitting right in front of you." For the tac-

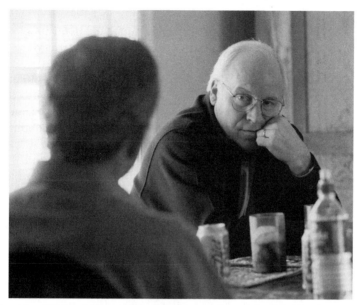

Vice President Richard Cheney is said to be an influential adviser in the George W. Bush White House. (*Source:* Copyright © Brooks Kraft/CORBIS.)

iturn Cheney, discretion has been the key to power and influence. He has made calculated silence his calling card. Whether in meetings with lawmakers on Capitol Hill or in sessions of President Bush's war council, Cheney, as a colleague puts it, "just sits there and listens with that crooked grin on his face. He almost never speaks."[19] Most accounts agree, however, that when Cheney did speak, his views carried weight.[20]

Why does the "Throttlebottom complex" persist? Is there something congenitally or structurally deficient in the relationship between the presidency and the vice presidency? Does the relationship always have to be hollow, hostile, and counterproductive? "Mistrust is inherent in the relationship," wrote Arthur Schlesinger, Jr., because vice presidents are inevitable "reminders of their president's own mortality."[21] This mistrust is also not without historical foundation. Some previous vice presidents have turned against their presidents, mobilizing opposition in the Congress, proposing alternative legislative programs, and preparing to run for the presidency against the president they were then serving. Vice President John Calhoun became so disenchanted that he simply resigned from the office.

There are many reasons for these psychological tensions, but at least one factor is that both the president and the vice president are, or should be, astute politicians, and as Harry Truman once suggested, this often means neither will take the other completely into his confidence.

Although some progress has been made, a psychological barrier, an intangible distance, still seems to prevent a significant delegation of power to a vice president. Presidents fear being upstaged. Their staffs fear it even more.

Some vice presidents refuse to accept demeaning jobs. Nelson Rockefeller did for a while until he lost interest. Lyndon Johnson just went into a retreat. Others willingly become partisan "hit men," straight-arming the press, slashing back at presidential opponents, and stumping endlessly for the reelection of friendly members of Congress. Thus, Spiro Agnew, Nixon's vice president, was used as a mouthpiece and as a surrogate presidential speaker at partisan events, just as the Eisenhower White House had used Nixon. Some of George H. W. Bush's supporters worried that he was hurt by being too loyal a Reagan cheerleader in the 1984 election campaign. Quayle's handlers felt the same way in 1992. Such experiences fit Arthur M. Schlesinger, Jr.'s, generalization that the vice presidency may be less a *making* than a *maiming* experience for its occupants.

Often, it is as if a vice president is entirely unacceptable and unwanted unless he is willing to merge his identity completely with that of the president. Vice presidents, it turns out, often do lose their own identity. They become cheerleaders for their boss. They become expert at laying wreaths at remote ceremonial functions. They become, in a way, part of the furniture in another person's house.

The following passages from a televised "Conversation with Vice President Hubert H. Humphrey" illustrate how one vice president seemingly subordinated his own personal ambitions and vowed nearly feudal homage to his president:

> I did not become vice president with President Johnson to cause him trouble. I feel a deep sense of loyalty and fidelity. I believe that if you can't have that you have no right to accept the office. Because today it is so important that a president and his vice president be on the same wave length. . . . I'd hate to have the president be worried about me, that I may do something that would cause him embarrassment or that would injure his administration. . . . There are no Humphrey people, there are no Humphrey policies, there are no Humphrey programs. Whatever we have we should try to contribute, if it's wanted, to the president and his administration. You can't have two leaders of the executive branch at one time. . . . [22]

In spite of this subservient "leaning over backward," Humphrey was never really trusted by LBJ. Humphrey frequently sought more substantive assignments, only to be disregarded. Johnson would simply exclude Humphrey from his team of insiders whenever the vice president sought independence or tried to develop his own line of thinking. This was especially true in the case of occasional policy differences he had with Johnson over the Vietnam War.

When is loyalty to a president carried too far? Vice Presidents Humphrey, Agnew, Ford, G. H. W. Bush, and Gore sometimes became such apologists for their administrations that they could not help but diminish their credibility, perhaps undermining their own future capacity to provide serious leadership. This raises the question of whether being an apologist isn't inherent in the role of a vice president, at least the role of a trusted vice president. Some promising presidential hopefuls have had their political futures destroyed or at best greatly diminished as a result of their allegiance and their images of being "yes men" to less-than-perfect administrations.

Experience suggests, however, that not only will most presidents not trust their vice presidents but the relationship in terms of real assignments will often be a limited one. Can a vice president, even an outstanding one, become a significant force in the presidential establishment? Or was John Nance Garner correct when he reasoned that a great person may be vice president but can't be a great vice president because the office in itself is unimportant. It is near impossible to assess a vice president's contribution to an administration's policy achievements. For instance, observers who say Mondale, G. H. W. Bush, Gore, and now Cheney, in contrast to Agnew and Quayle, were ideal vice presidents are hard pressed to describe in any rigorous way their precise impact on the Carter-Mondale, Reagan-Bush, Clinton-Gore, or Bush-Cheney records. This is in part due to the "low profile" nature of their duties. What were their own achievements? Can Mondale be relieved of Carter's failures? Can G. H. W. Bush point to his own contributions? On what issues did Gore lead the way? Did Cheney really pull George W. Bush to the right?

Gerald Ford saw tensions and jealousies develop between his own five-hundred-person White House staff and Nelson Rockefeller's vice presidential staff of seventy aides and assistants. Ford allows that he and Rockefeller got along famously. "Nelson was absolutely loyal to me, and he would do anything I asked him to do," writes Ford in his memoir.[23] But Ford, despite the fact he believed Rockefeller was eminently qualified to "step into my shoes" if tragedy struck, went along with his own political advisers' campaign to dump Rockefeller. Ford was motivated almost exclusively in this instance by the political considerations. Later, he acknowledged, "I was angry with myself for showing cowardice in not saying to the ultra-conservatives, 'It's going to be Ford and Rockefeller, whatever the consequences.'"[24]

Despite all these traditional problems, the office has endured, if not prospered. Some of the problems have been diminished somewhat by reducing the physical distance between president and vice president and by providing more staff and perquisites.

Until 1961 vice presidents had to work out of their office in the Capitol. Lyndon Johnson was the first vice president to be given a suite of offices in the old Executive Office Building, across an alley from the west wing of the White House. Spiro Agnew was the first to be given an office in the White House, although he only stayed in it for a few months. In 1975, Nelson Rockefeller was the first modern vice president to be given an official residence. In 1977, Mondale was given his choice of White House offices (excepting only the oval office), and he stayed on the main floor of the west wing for his entire four years, as have all succeeding vice presidents.

## THE MONDALE MODEL

Was Vice President Walter Mondale's influence the result of amplified importance of the vice presidency, or merely the result of Carter's willingness to be persuaded on a number of issues? Or, perhaps, was Mondale's alleged prominence in the Carter White House due mainly to Carter's own lack of Washington experience and thus serious need of advice from a veteran (twelve-year) former member of the U.S. Senate?

The vice presidency "has its frustrations . . . ," said Mondale. "But I went into it with my eyes wide open. I know there is only one president; there is not an assistant president. I'm his adviser."[25] Most students of the vice presidency agree that Mondale enjoyed a closer relationship with his boss, President Jimmy Carter, than any previous vice president. Much of the credit has to go to Carter. Carter not only said he would give his vice president a lot to do; but he tried in earnest to make the vice president as close as one can get to a full working partner. Mondale enjoyed a standing invitation to attend and participate in any of the president's meetings. He had access to all reports and cables. Mondale also had a regularly scheduled weekly luncheon date with Carter.

Mondale came to the job with several helpful assets. He was well known and well liked on Capitol Hill. He knew how Congress and Washington operated. In many respects, he had more of a national base or national following than did Carter. A protégé of Hubert Humphrey's, he nonetheless had an identity of his own.

Perhaps his greatest strength was his ability to get along well with people—all kinds of people. He was a natural team player and not a show-boating, flamboyant credit-seeker. General Eisenhower had once said "There's no limit to how much influence you can have if you are only willing to let others get the credit for it." Mondale was a shrewd politician who understood this proverb.

Mondale also understood the vulnerable "tender nature" of the vice presidency. He knew that nearly everything contributing to his effectiveness as vice president depended on a basic personal relationship of confidence and trust with the president. He knew also that presidential powers are not divisible. He knew he could not long be effective as chief lobbyist or as chief-of-staff at the White House—two jobs that Carter and his staff sometimes tried to give him. Mondale rejected the chief-of-staff post because he knew if he had taken that assignment "it would have consumed vast amounts of my time with staff work and distracted me from important work."

Mondale and Carter overcame some of the traditional problems of the vice presidency by treating Mondale's staff as part of the White House staff. Some senior members of the Mondale staff were assigned high-level White House responsibilities, often with supervisory authority over some White House aides. Mondale's staff won high marks for professionalism, competence, and ability to work with and for Carter as well as with and for their boss. In doing this, Mondale and his staff were able to set a helpful precedent—one that has helped to remove some of the tension and barriers to success so frequently witnessed in the past.

Vice President Mondale is credited with being perhaps the first in that job who regularly exercised substantive policy influence rather than merely an occasional input of ideas. Aides say he moderated certain extreme policies that might otherwise have been announced by the White House. Although he doubtless succeeded in blocking some bad initiatives, he also failed on a number of occasions. The Mondale experience suggests too that even though his views were regularly heard, his role as a policy initiator was usually a limited one. Initiatives typically came from the cabinet departments, from staff agencies, and from Congress. With all the other responsibilities a vice president has, it is difficult for the vice president to take the initiative.

When Carter was asked about his conception of their relationship he put an especially positive gloss on it:

> I probably meet with the Vice President on a daily basis more than all the other staff members that I have combined. . . . there is no aspect of my own daily responsibilities as President that are not shared by the Vice President. . . . I would say without derogating the other members of my staff that there is no one who would approach him in his importance to me, his closeness to me, and also his ability to carry out a singular assignment with my complete trust.[26]

Carter wrote in his memoir that even when Mondale disagreed with him, he always gave him full support. "As we served together, our relationship constantly improved—a pleasant surprise to the two of us as well as to other observers of the White House."[27]

Mondale became someone with whom Carter could sit down and discuss political and policy problems. "What the President needs is not more information, although that is helpful," recalls Mondale, "he needs a few people who can honestly appraise and evaluate his performance. . . . He needs to hear voices that speak from a national perspective. He has no limit to the number of people who want to talk to him, but that does not assure him of the confidentiality he needs to speak freely."[28]

Is the vice presidency a useful understudy position, a place where one can serve a sensible apprenticeship for the presidency? Mondale said it was:

> I think it may be the best training of all (for the presidency). I don't know of any other office, outside of the presidency, that informs an officer more fully about the realities of presidential government, about the realities of federal government and the duties of the presidency that remotely compares to that of the Vice President as it is now being used.
>
> I'm privy to all the same secret information as the President. I have unlimited access to the President. I'm usually with him when all the central decisions are being made. I've been through several of these crises now that a President inevitably confronts, and I see how they work. I've been through the budget process, I've been through diplomatic ventures, I've been through a host of congressional fights as seen from the presidential perspective.

I spent 12 years in the Senate. I learned a lot there, but I learned more here about the realities of presidential responsibilities. I learned more about our country and the world in the last three years than I could any other way.[29]

When his term drew to a close in early 1981 Mondale told his successor, George Bush, that there were some institutional lessons he wanted to pass along. Mondale's chief recommendations were these:

1. Advise the president confidentially. The only reasons to state publicly what you have told the president is to take credit for his success and try to escape blame for failure. Either way there is no quicker way to undermine your relationship with the president and lose your effectiveness.

2. Don't wear a president down. . . . Give your advice once and give it well. You have a right to be heard, not obeyed. A president must decide when the debates must end. . . .

3. As a spokesman for the Administration, stay on the facts. A president does not want and the public does not respect a vice president who does nothing but deliver fulsome praise of a president. . . .

4. Avoid line authority assignments. If such an assignment is important, it will then cut across the responsibilities of one or two cabinet officers or others and embroil you in a bureaucratic fight that would be disastrous. If it is meaningless or trivial, it will undermine your reputation and squander your time.

5. The vice president should remember the importance of personal compatibility. He should try to complement the president's skills and, finally in a real sense the most important of all roles, be ready to assume the presidency. . . . [30]

Did the Mondale-Carter relationship establish a precedent for succeeding administrations? Mondale believed so.

Mondale may have succeeded because he was willing to hew the Carter line and he remained exceedingly loyal—even when close friends of his such as HEW Secretary Joseph Califano were being fired and even when some of his cherished social programs were being cut. One Carter White House aide said virtually no one around the White House challenged Carter seriously, and that Mondale concurred with Carter's preference for "harmony above all other virtues." Others say Mondale's influence stemmed from Carter's dependence on him to explain how Congress worked and to maintain close ties with the labor movement. Carter needed Mondale more than most presidents need their vice presidents. Mondale's patient personality and relative youth meant he (1) could wait for his own chance to become president; and (2) could avoid being a threat to Carter. Even Mondale would admit, that it helps to be seen as a trusted lieutenant yet not be heard as an exponent of too many original views.

## THE GEORGE H. W. BUSH EXPERIENCE

Most observers believe George H. W. Bush enjoyed almost as much influence and probably as good a relationship with Ronald Reagan as Walter Mondale enjoyed with Jimmy Carter. Bush started out in a more compromised position. He had campaigned vigorously against Reagan in the Republican primaries of 1980. His criticisms of Reagan and his proposals had hurt Reagan personally and it is known that for this and perhaps other reasons Bush was not Reagan's first choice for vice president. But Bush was selected and the Reagan-Bush ticket was victorious not only in 1980 but again in 1984. Reagan never wavered in his support for Bush.

Bush benefited from the model established by Carter-Mondale. He inherited the "Mondale office" in the White House both physically and spiritually. He was given access to the president's daily briefing papers and other important paper flow in the White House itself. Bush's stock rose when he acted prudently and professionally during the time of Reagan's assassination attempt and subsequent hospitalization early in the first term. It rose even more as he became an ardent supporter and campaigner for Reagan's economic programs. Bush also performed countless partisan chores with effectiveness.

Gradually the personal friendship and trust between Reagan and Bush developed and indeed often seemed to flourish. At the time of the second inaugural, Reagan enthusiastically toasted his vice president as "the best Vice President this Republic has ever had." Bush, for his part, became about as supportive and cheerful about his president as any vice president had ever become. "I can't think of anything that the president has left undone that he might have done to make me feel more comfortable in my job," he said. "And I guess the best example of that is that I am free to walk three doors down the hall to the Oval Office and walk in there. And I don't have any inhibitions doing that."[31]

Reagan called Bush the most loyal team member that anybody could ever want. Bush even changed some of his views during his first four years of serving Reagan. He had opposed Reagan's supply side economics during the campaign of 1980, calling it "voodoo economics." He also supported the right of women to have an abortion and he endorsed the Equal Rights Amendment to the U.S. Constitution. By 1984, however, he had adopted the Reagan position on each of these issues and supported Reagan on just about everything else. He made it a policy not to discuss his private advice for the president. He rarely spoke at cabinet meetings or at similar forums when the president was present. "I don't ever discuss what I talk to the president about, because if I did, I would undermine the one thing that matters—the confidentiality and the trust that I think exist between us." He prized access and proximity over the ego needs and rewards for public credit. Further, as he put it, "I don't want to end up like Nelson Rockefeller, miserable in the job because the staff cut him off at the knees."[32]

Like those before him, however, George Bush was unable to escape some of the criticism and even ridicule that still seem to come with the job. Thus, during the campaign of 1984 Bush was sometimes portrayed as a man without any ideas of his own. He had become such a "cheerleader-in-chief" that he seemed to have sold out or compromised some of his own views. The cartoon strip "Doonesbury" portrayed him as having "put his political manhood in a blind trust." *Time* magazine wrote that "Bush's emphasis on loyalty and his failure to put his mark on policy cast him in the image of a solid junior executive. His conduct suggests that he has expedient political positions, not deeply held convictions."[33]

Despite Bush's valiant efforts at loyalty, President Reagan refused to endorse him as his successor. Instead, Reagan ducked the press on this issue:

> Well now, you have me between a rock and a hard place, because I have to tell you, I have said that he's been the finest Vice President I ever had any recollection of. He's been an integral part of everything that we're doing. I've always had the feeling . . . But, at the same time in this job, you are titular head of the party and as such you've kind of got a responsibility to let the party function and make its decisions. Now it's not an easy thing for me to think about, but I have to keep that in mind.[34]

Bush, as a member of the National Security Council, also felt the sting of guilt-by-association when the Iran-Contra hearings and the Tower Commission report on the national security policymaking process portrayed a White House that was poorly run and engaged in frequent lying to Congress, the secretary of state, and the American people. Where Bush had gained from Reagan's successes and popular approval through 1985, his effectiveness and leadership abilities were called into question in the more troubled years of the Reagan presidency.

A public opinion survey on Bush and his performance as vice president, seven years into his vice presidency, underscored the liabilities of service as vice president. Roughly half of those polled in a *New York Times*/CBS Survey said "they did not regard the vice presidency as a job that prepared someone to be president" (see Table 10.1). Bush's vice presidency, paradoxically, was both his greatest advantage and his greatest liability. Those surveyed obviously knew him because of his visibility and generally (59 percent) viewed him as honest. Yet only 35 percent of those registered voters held a favorable opinion of him. Why such a low approval rating? Only 42 percent said they had confidence in Bush's ability "to deal with a crisis" or at least would "feel uneasy about him." At least a third of those polled thought Bush lied when he said he did not know that money from the Iranian arms sales was going to help the Contras in Nicaragua. Finally, very few people thought Bush said what he really believed when in fact he did have differences with President Reagan.[35]

**TABLE 10.1**
**The Vice Presidency: Good Training Post for President?**

Q. Which comes closer to your opinion? The Vice President's job gives someone especially good experience that should train him to be President, *or* the Vice President's job is mostly for show and doesn't really prepare someone to lead the country.

| | |
|---|---|
| Doesn't prepare someone for leading the country | 47% |
| Good experience and training/preparation | 44 |
| Don't know/no answer | 10 |

*Source: New York Times*/CBS News Poll, July 21–22, 1987, N-745. Copyright © 1987 by the New York Times Co. Reprinted by permission.

## THE GORE EXPERIENCE

President Clinton continued the trend in relying more heavily on his vice president. Gore was influential in such domestic policy areas as the environment, emerging technology, and the "reinventing government" campaign. In foreign affairs Gore was involved on issues such as U.S. policy toward Russia, South Africa, the Middle East, and nuclear nonproliferation. Al Gore debated Ross Perot on national television over the North American Free Trade Agreement—with great success. And he debated rival vice presidential candidate Jack Kemp in October of 1996—again with success.

Gore was seen by White House staffers, the cabinet, and Washington journalists as a force within the administration, a view President Clinton did not attempt to change. To Gore, the vice presidency became a job of substance, a preparation should the need arise for him to assume the office of president.

As Clinton's labor secretary Robert Reich wrote: "Al [Gore] is the perfect complement to B [Bill Clinton]: methodical where B is haphazard, linear where B is creative, cautious where B is impetuous, ponderous where B is playful, private where B shares his feelings with everyone. The two men need one another, and sense it. Above all, Gore is *patient,* where B wants it all now."[36]

President Clinton seemed less threatened by Gore than many other president–vice president pairings such as Johnson and Humphrey. Clinton was generally able to see Gore as a resource, not a threat, and employ Gore's skills more fully than most vice presidents in history. Yet Gore's reputation was obviously tarnished in Clinton's second term because of the Monica Lewinsky scandal, Clinton's impeachment, and various policy setbacks.

Gore and Clinton had a falling out as Gore was running for the presidency in 1999 and 2000. Gore understandably tried to become more independent and put more than a little distance between himself and the politically weakened Clinton. Clinton, for his part, occasionally disparaged Gore's campaigning abilities and this further eroded their once close friendship. By the summer of 2000 the two were hardly speaking with one another.[37] Nonetheless, for 80 to 90 percent of their two terms in the White House, the Clinton-Gore partnership was both close and effective—so much so that a few observers called Gore the "most influential vice president" in American history.[38]

## THE QUAYLE EXPERIENCE

In sum, the office of the vice presidency took on an improved image in the Carter, Reagan, and Clinton years. The greater visibility and alleged "importance" attached to the office was probably due to the quality of the vice presidents and the fact they worked for the presidents who were outsiders, who hadn't served in the Congress or the cabinet. In light of the different experience with Dan Quayle, it is a safe bet that the office will have its ups and downs, and its definition and effectiveness will continue to depend primarily on the interpretation the incumbent president chooses to give it and who are in the two positions. Much too, of course, will depend on why and how we select vice presidents.

George H.W. Bush's vice president, J. Danforth Quayle, presented something of a problem.[39] A relatively inexperienced Senator from Indiana, Quayle was a surprise pick for vice president. Chosen for his youth and his devoted following among the conservatives in the Republican party (just as Reagan chose the more moderate Bush, when his turn came Bush chose the more conservative Quayle—an ideological balancing act in both cases). Quayle was widely seen by pundits and the general population as not up to the job—and he kept supplying evidence to prove the point.

While Quayle was generally "out of the loop," President Bush did use him to boost the president's standing with the self-proclaimed religious right and other conservative groups. In policy terms, the main area where Quayle had impact was in deregulation of business. Quayle headed the Council on Competitiveness, a pro-business, antiregulatory group that aided business in its efforts to cut government regulations. And Quayle was also marginally involved in policy deliberations on the Gulf War.[40]

While Quayle was more qualified than his media image suggested, there was a widespread feeling among political heavyweights in both major parties that he was not the preferred choice to assume the responsibilities of the presidency should the need arise. Sandwiched among such well regarded and influential vice presidents as Mondale, Bush, Gore, and Cheney, Dan Quayle suffered in comparison.

## THE DICK CHENEY VICE PRESIDENCY

George W. Bush's selection of Dick Cheney in 2000 was a surprise. Cheney had been a secretary of defense, senior White House aide, and a five-term member of the U.S. House of Representatives, but he had also had heart attacks and came from a small, conservative state that just about any Republican presidential candidate could expect to win. Moreover, though a well-regarded insider in Washington, D.C., Cheney was charisma-challenged and hardly a natural campaign-trail politician. However, Bush's selection of Cheney was reassuring to many people who questioned Bush's experience and judgment. Cheney was a seasoned Washington veteran, a plausible voice of stability.

Cheney proved to be a mediocre campaigner, yet he effectively debated Joe Lieberman and this, along with Gore's ineffective debates with Bush, won added support for the Bush-Cheney ticket.

Cheney was unusually visible and played a variety of important policy and personnel roles in the first several months of the Bush presidency—perhaps too visible a role. Both the press and friendly Bush supporters worried that Cheney was virtually running the show. Bush's political advisors grew concerned and made sure Bush and not Cheney was portrayed as the leading man in the administration.

When the September 11, 2001, terrorist attacks occurred, Cheney was relegated to a subordinate and often quite invisible status. The public rationale for this was plausibly enough that, in case anything should happen to the president, the president's advisors wanted to be sure the vice president was protected and could step in to provide emergency national leadership. But Cheney became almost as absent as he had been prominent just months earlier.

Cheney reemerged later and was an uncommonly loyal vice president. He appeared to enjoy the president's confidence and an impressive degree of access to the president. This was especially true of national security matters where Cheney's reputation as a hard-liner appeared to pull Bush to the right as Secretary of State Colin Powell campaigned for more moderate strategies. Cheney and his staff were "not necessarily seen as the forces of evil," according to a White House aide. But their's was "a hardheaded approach focused on how to defend America or how to defend American interests."[41]

Cheney's apparent lack of presidential ambition allowed George W. Bush to use him extensively. Thus Cheney helped recruit dozens of cabinet and Executive Office officials, some of whom, like Secretary of the Treasury Paul O'Neill, didn't work out. He also chaired various policy review committees, including an energy policy task force that became a highly charged political hot-potato when Cheney refused to release copies of their meetings and records.

Cheney, on occasion, gave major talks on national security matters, including a notable one on August 26, 2002, that outlined the justification and the necessity, in his view, for a U.S. attack on Saddam Hussein's Iraq. This particular address attracted international attention because it went beyond the president's stated views and apparently caused the president to ask Cheney to tone down his remarks, especially comments suggesting the futility of U.N. weapons inspectors in Iraq.[42]

In selecting and involving Cheney, George W. Bush was at least in part demonstrating that he had learned a lesson from his father's presidency. This lesson was to err on the side of having an older, experienced vice president rather than someone who, rightly or wrongly, was perceived as a lightweight, lacking "gravitas." The second Bush also had the extra bonus of not having a vice president who would become easily frustrated if he didn't get political credit or political visibility.

Cheney's influence waned a bit after the 9-11 attack, as the President demonstrated greater confidence and assertiveness, and as Bush began to rely more closely on his team of foreign and defense policy advisers. Cheney served as point man on building the case for war with Iraq, pressuring the intelligence agencies, especially the CIA, to issue reports that supported the case for war. This ended up causing the administration embarrassment when in the afterglow of a military victory, serious questions were raised about the legitimacy of the information being distributed.

The presidential aspirations of Rockefeller, Mondale, Quayle, and Gore all came to naught.[43] Dick Cheney's somewhat enhanced and enlarged role in George W. Bush's policymaking process may have been because Cheney had disavowed a desire to be president. In the words of one White House aide, "For the first time since Truman, you have a Veep who does not dream, does not wonder, does not think every day about being president."[44]

Questions remain—perhaps they can be called the paradoxes of the modern vice presidency. Vice presidents have to give their advice in private. They may give candid advice to presidents but they have to keep that advice to themselves. And then, whatever the president decides, the vice president has to support. Must they become apologists and cheerleaders even when they disagree with presidents? Also, can vice presidents earn election in their own right when they have had to be that loyal and when their major contributions (if they have made any) have to remain mostly or even entirely off the record? Few vice presidents are likely to solve these puzzles.

## SELECTION

As noted, apart from the problem of what to do with vice presidents, there is the enduring problem of how best to recruit people to the office and to fill it when vacancies occur. For years the vice presidential nomination process has tempted the fates. It's a pig-in-a-poke system, critics say, that not only is often abused but also denigrates the office.[45]

The process invariably begins with a search for someone who will strengthen the presidential ticket but often ends with a search for someone who will not weaken the ticket. The search for someone who will "balance the ticket" causes countless problems. Sometimes it means choosing party workhorses whose chief virtue is that they have antagonized nobody. Sometimes it means choosing persons mainly because they come from a politically crucial region of the nation. Sometimes this practice means nominating someone from a rival political wing of the party. Sometimes it involves a "unite the party by picking the person who came in second" approach. And then there is always the gamble or "bold stroke" approach of selecting someone who will be a big surprise and put everyone off balance, such as Nixon's choice of Spiro Agnew in 1968, Mondale's choice of Geraldine Ferraro as a 1984 running mate, and, to some extent, George W. Bush's selection of the older, more experienced Dick Cheney in 2000.

In recent years the identity of the presidential nominee has been determined well in advance of the party convention. Not so the vice president. Some are last-minute choices (McGovern and Shriver), some surprises (George H.W. Bush and Quayle, or Dole and Kemp), some bizarre (Reagan offering former President Ford a "co-presidency" role if he accepted the vice presidential spot in 1980).

In general, the president is free to choose whomever he wishes as his vice presidential running mate. In practice however, presidential nominees choose someone they believe will help them get elected.

Pressure builds up to subordinate considerations of proven leadership ability to those of vote-getting power. (Ticket balancing has allowed the Andrew Johnsons, Arthurs, Henricks, Tompkins, Nixons, and Agnews to rise from relative political obscurity to become vice president.) A problem with nearly all the approaches mentioned above is that after all the excitement fades, the presidential candidate must live with the choice and the country sometimes gets the person as the next president.[46]

Is it right to entrust the selection of the vice president to the presidential nominee? How many vice presidents have been merely an afterthought at the national convention? The 1972 selection of Senator Thomas Eagleton of Missouri by George McGovern and the 1968 Governor Spiro Agnew of Maryland selection by Richard Nixon prompted various reappraisals, as did the Dan Quayle selection and election.

In 1973 the Democratic Party created a Commission on Vice Presidential Selection, chaired by former Vice President Hubert Humphrey. The Commission made several suggestions, including these:

1. Extending the convention for a day, permitting a forty-eight-hour interval between the nomination of the president and the nomination of vice president.

2. To ensure even more deliberation, the selection of the vice president could be put off for three weeks or more and the nominee could then be ratified by the party's national committee in a mini-convention (a procedure used in 1972 when McGovern's choice, Thomas Eagleton, withdrew and Sargent Shriver was approved as the vice presidential nominee).[47]

Other reformers suggested that every aspirant for the presidential nomination might pick his vice presidential nominee about sixty days before his party's national convention. At the convention, the two would run as a ticket.

This method might, its sponsors say, allow the vice presidential choice to emerge with more stature.

Another proposal suggests that to democratize the convention selection, the presidential nominee could be required to submit several names for vice president to the delegates. Others have suggested convening the party committee perhaps a month or so after the national convention to act on a recommendation by the presidential nominee. Still another variation would have the national convention delegates vote on the recommendation of their standard bearer by mail-in secret ballot a month or so after the convention.[48]

Still another proposal urged that national conventions nominate only the presidential nominee. Then the November election winner would announce a choice of a vice president in December, and the new Congress meeting in January would consider the choice before inauguration day. If the first name was not approved, the new president would submit another. This proposal might not require a constitutional amendment, since the president would in essence be following procedures provided in the Twenty-fifth Amendment.

The most radical proposal of all would require a constitutional amendment: abolishing the vice presidency altogether. The idea of abolishing the office has been occasionally proposed since the beginning of the Republic. This measure was embraced by a dozen writers in the mid-1970s in the wake of Watergate and two periods of vacancy in the vice presidency. Frustrated by the abuse and misuse of the office, critics said: let's get rid of the office before it sinks us. If a president dies or becomes disabled or resigns, let a designated cabinet member (secretary of state or defense or treasury) take over for one hundred days and meanwhile let's conduct a special election for a new democratically elected president. Arthur M. Schlesinger, Jr., a proponent of this plan, concluded that the multiple problems that now depreciate the vice presidency could simply be eliminated by eliminating the office itself:

> There is no escape . . . from the conclusion that the Vice Presidency is not only a pointless but even a dangerous office. A politician is nominated for Vice President for reasons unconnected with his presidential qualities and elected to the Vice Presidency as part of a tie-in sale. Once carried to the Vice Presidency not on his own but as second rider on the presidential horse, where is he: If he is a first-rate man, his nerve and confidence will be shaken, his talents wasted and soured, even as his publicity urges him on toward the ultimate office for which, the longer he serves in the second place, the less ready he may be. If he is not a first-rate man he should not be in a position to inherit or claim the presidency. Why not therefore abolish this mischievous office and work out a more sensible mode of succession?[49]

The Throttlebottom complex would be solved. We would stop elevating to the presidency individuals who have not really won election. Presidents could appoint one or more vice presidents. "If the principle be accepted—the principle that if a president vanishes, it is better for the people to elect a new president than endure a vice president who was never voted for that office, who became vice president for reasons other than his presidential qualifications and who may very well have been badly damaged by his vice presidential experience—the problem is one of working out the mechanics of the intermediate election. This is not easy but far from impossible."[50]

At the heart of the matter is whether we want to be a government of and by the people. It is widely acknowledged that we sometimes choose vice presidents for the wrong reasons. It is equally clear, however, that today the vice presidency has become a stepping stone either to the presidency directly or at least to presidential nomination. Nearly 25 percent of our presidents did not serve out the terms they were serving. And nearly a third of the presidents were vice presidents first (Table 10.2).

The issues at stake, especially in this proposal, are issues of democratic procedure and political legitimacy. Many say that the nation could not afford a special election after a presidential death, as in 1945 or in 1963, but many other Western nations do so regularly. Others say intermediate elections violate the tradition of quadrennial elections. But what is so compelling or virtuous about waiting until that fourth year if what is at question is the quality and character of the nation's leadership? Moreover, the special election would merely be to fill out the remainder of the departed president's term. Would this new arrangement be a departure from the intent and spirit of the founding fathers? Although strictly speaking they opposed direct popular election, it would reaffirm their general view. They opposed selection of the president by the Congress. As much as possible they wanted the people to have the main say. What could be more sensible for a self-governing democracy than that the president must, except for the briefest periods, be a person elected to that office by the people?

There are, however, several disadvantages to the idea of abolishing the vice presidency and conducting a special election to fill a presidential vacancy. First, it would invite instability and turmoil during the succession

**TABLE 10.2**
**Vice Presidents Who Became President**

| Year | Vice president | President served | Reason for obtaining office |
|------|----------------|------------------|-----------------------------|
| 1797 | John Adams | George Washington | Elected to office |
| 1801 | Thomas Jefferson | John Adams | Elected to office |
| 1837 | Martin Van Buren | Andrew Jackson | Elected to office |
| 1841 | John Tyler | William Henry Harrison | Harrison died |
| 1850 | Millard Fillmore | Zachary Taylor | Taylor died |
| 1865 | Andrew Jackson | Abraham Lincoln | Lincoln killed |
| 1881 | Chester A. Arthur | James A. Garfield | Garfield killed |
| 1901 | Theodore Roosevelt | William McKinley | McKinley killed |
| 1923 | Calvin Coolidge | William G. Harding | Harding died |
| 1945 | Harry S Truman | Franklin D. Roosevelt | Roosevelt died |
| 1963 | Lyndon B. Johnson | John F. Kennedy | Kennedy killed |
| 1968 | Richard M. Nixon | Dwight D. Eisenhower | Elected to office |
| 1974 | Gerald R. Ford | Richard M. Nixon | Nixon resigned |
| 1989 | George H. W. Bush | Ronald Reagan | Elected to office |

period. Second, it is doubtful that a sixty- or ninety-day campaign in a nation this large would allow for the clarification of competing issues. It is one thing for Canada or France to conduct a short campaign, but the United States is substantially larger and has weaker political parties, and it usually takes longer here for issues to get sharpened. Finally, most people, rightly or wrongly, are not displeased by the existing system. Neither are they displeased by those who have become vice presidents through the current arrangements.

In sum, the vice presidential nomination process has had a mixed history. We now have had nine examples of what happens when a vice president is forced by necessity to become president. Several became respected presidents. Yet at least half were major disappointments. More disturbing, however, is that an assessment of those who have mercifully not become president, from Aaron Burr to Spiro Agnew to Dan Quayle, is not in the least reassuring.

None of the reform proposals suggested in the recent past are without liabilities. Even the most casual of political science students can discern most of the trade-offs and the deficiencies. Nor has any of them captured a following. Most people are resigned to living with the existing system.

However, even if we stick with the present system for selecting vice presidential nominees, several sensible modest improvements can be made. None of these requires a constitutional amendment and most are merely the product of learning from past mistakes. In a condensed form, these are the recommendations most frequently made:

- Presidential candidates should have their staffs recommend and consider several vice presidential candidates, well in advance of the convention. Whenever possible the presidential nominee should interview these candidates, also well in advance.

- Presidential candidates should give highest priority to the need for ideological compatibility, treating "electoral balancing" as a secondary factor. Note, however, that the "two are neither mutually exclusive nor naturally contradictory."[51]

- National parties should provide for a flexible convention schedule, permitting an extra day if necessary for presidential nominees to deliberate over the vice presidential nominee choices. Provisions should be made, in special cases, for a delay of a few weeks and the approval of the running mate at a miniconvention. Such special cases might be on such occasions as when a classic "dark horse" or last-minute compromise candidate wins the presidential nomination and he or she had not expected to win and hence was unprepared for the vice presidential selection responsibility.

- The candidates should make a list of serious preferences for the vice presidency before the convention, to facilitate media and public examination; and they are encouraged to initiate direct contact and staff liaison with potential running mates.[52]

Common-sense suggestions such as these will not guarantee an error-proof selection process, but they should reduce the risks.

Walter Mondale outlined a helpful list of job qualities he thought were important to keep in mind as presidential candidates select a vice presidential running mate. He provided this at the time he was engaged in selecting his own running mate in June of 1984. "My choice" he said "will be guided by the need to select someone totally qualified to assume the office of the President should that be necessary." Then he went on to say there were many ways a vice president can help a president govern. For example:

1. The vice president, the only other official elected nationwide, can advise a president from a national perspective.

2. Without specific ties or allegiances, the vice president can help break through the bureaucracy and solve complex problems.

3. A vice president can speak for the president on Capitol Hill and help advance the president's legislative program.

4. The vice president can be the president's most effective spokesperson with the public.

5. The vice president can extend the president's reach in foreign policy by conducting negotiations at the highest levels and serving as the president's eyes and ears abroad.[53]

This list will vary from presidential candidate to presidential candidate yet is a good beginning, and journalists and party leaders should press candidates to acknowledge these qualities and possible roles whenever the selection process is taking place. Still, presidential nominees will choose their running mates with their probable impact on the electoral outcomes in mind. Nor is this concern for political considerations unreasonable. "A party facing an election of such great consequence as the race for the White House would be irrational not to weigh heavily the probable political impact of prospective running mates," wrote Joel Goldstein. He added, "A two-party system provides many advantages to a democracy. It simplifies voter choice, promotes consensus, adds stability to a society, and allows majorities to form. But every virtue has its costs. Compromise is part of the price. The use of the vice presidential nomination to placate disgruntled factions is part of the mortar that holds the political system together."[54]

## SUCCESSION

Despite all of the other problems associated with the vice presidency, the office has done one thing reasonably well—solving our succession problem. Many nations have faltered or even been torn apart by civil upheavals because they failed to provide for a prompt, orderly means of transition. Our citizens, like most people, long for system stability and for a heightened sense of continuity with an understood heritage.

Americans used to joke about vice presidents who because of some emergency became "His Accidency" or president-by-chance. However, most Americans are grateful when the leadership vacuum is replaced and the new leader, endowed with legitimacy, acts with confidence and dispatch. Our vice presidential succession process may be imperfect, but one of its virtues is the stability it brings to our governance arrangements. Trauma, chaos, and instability are avoided, as people know well in advance that there is a plan, a legitimate plan that will be put into effect. Whatever one may think of the succession plan, the reassurance rendered is somewhat remarkable.

The framers provided that the vice president should be first in the order of succession, but they left it up to Congress to establish the rest of the order of succession. Three statutes and one constitutional amendment speak to this matter. In the first presidential succession act, passed in 1792, the president pro tempore of the U.S. Senate (by custom the senior member of the majority party in the Senate) was named first in line behind the vice president, followed by the speaker of the House of Representatives. If a double vacancy occurred (that is, if something happened to both the president and vice president), this same 1792 act provided that the president pro tempore of the Senate would become acting president "until a president be elected." Hence an immediate special election of some kind would have been called to elect a new president, unless the vacancy occurred in the last months of the presidential term.

This first statute was superseded in 1886 when the heads of the cabinet departments, beginning with the secretary of state, were named as the line of succession. This may have been done to avoid violating the principle of separation of powers. Many people, however, believe an elected official should stand first in line to fill the presidency. Harry Truman, while serving out FDR's fourth term, urged a return to succession by elected congressional officials. In 1947, Congress approved this change, placing the speaker of the House first behind the vice president, followed by the Senate's president pro tempore, followed by the cabinet officers in terms of the departmental seniority—secretary of state and so on.

Some people understandably question the wisdom of having the Senate's president pro tempore, usually the senior and often the oldest member of the Senate's majority party, in this line of succession. Not too long ago this put Senators Strom Thurmond of South Carolina and Robert Byrd of West Virginia as third in line to serve as president. They were both well past their prime. One political scientist urged, in the aftermath of terrorist attacks on the United States, that Congress should consider ex-presidents and governors from the most populous states in the line of succession. "Why not allow former presidents, who do not normally live in Washington and already have Secret Service protection into the order of succession?"[55]

Before the Twenty-fifth Amendment to the Constitution, the vice presidency had been vacant eighteen times for a total of about forty years. Fortunately, during these periods there had been no need to go down the line of presidential succession. Section 2 of the Twenty-fifth Amendment, ratified in

1967, now provides that "whenever there is a vacancy in the office of the vice president, the president shall nominate a vice president who shall take office upon confirmation by a majority vote of both Houses of Congress."

Some critics of this provision say it gives too much power to the president. Defenders of the provision counter the criticisms as follows:

> In giving the President a dominant role in filling a vacancy in the vice presidency, the proposed amendment is consistent with present practice whereby the presidential candidate selects his own running mate who must be approved by the people through their representatives. It is practical because it recognizes the fact that a vice president's effectiveness in our government depends on his rapport with the president. If he is of the same party and of compatible temperament and views, all of which would be likely under the proposed amendment, his chances of becoming fully informed and adequately prepared to assume presidential power, if called upon, are excellent.[56]

Some say this provision is overly vague on certain points. Thus some would amend it to add deadlines against stalling by either the White House or Congress. Others wondered what would happen if a president resigned or died while his nomination of a vice president was still pending. Would the nominee still stand? Or would the speaker of the House, who had just become president, have the right to nominate his choice? "Would Congress have the right to choose between the two nominees? The fact that there are any open questions about presidential succession is, of course, dangerous, for there is nothing more threatening to a constitutional democracy than doubts about who has the legitimate right to govern."[57]

When Nixon was Eisenhower's vice president they had come to an informal agreement about when the vice president would take over in cases of emergencies; obviously it would sometimes be up to the determination of the president, or Nixon along with the president's doctors. By the same token, Eisenhower said, "I will be the one to determine if and when it is proper for me to resume presidential responsibilities."[58]

Section 3 of the Twenty-fifth Amendment provides for presidents to delegate presidential powers and duties to the vice president for a specified period. Debates had long raged over questions of presidential inability or disability. Many presidents have been temporarily unable to fulfill their responsibilities, and two presidents had serious disabilities—Garfield for two and a half months before he died, and Wilson for about a year. In each case their vice presidents did not assume presidential duties, in part because they wished to avoid usurping the powers of that office. Now a president can temporarily step aside. Section 3 reads:

> Whenever the President transmits to the President pro tempore of the Senate and the Speaker of the House of Representatives his written declaration that he is unable to discharge the powers and duties of his office, and until he transmits to them a written declaration to the contrary, such powers and duties shall be discharged by the Vice President as Acting President.

But will a president invoke this section, save in extraordinary occasions? Reagan's aides chose not to do so during his operations for bullet wounds after the March 1981 attempt on his life. Reagan's aides did not believe the president would be totally incapacitated for more than a few hours—which was the case, although the first couple of days were rough. But there are political implications as well. Invoking this section of the Twenty-fifth Amendment might alarm the public, might dramatize the president's vulnerability, might weaken the image of strength of the incumbent.

In July of 1985, President Reagan signed a letter which read in part: "I have determined and it is my intention and direction that Vice President George Bush shall discharge [presidential] powers and duties in my stead, commencing with the administration of anesthesia to me." With these words, Reagan—without formally invoking Section 3 of the Twenty-fifth Amendment—made Vice President George H.W. Bush acting president. Reagan would be operated on for colon cancer, and from the time he was anesthetized until seven hours and fifty-four minutes later, power was transferred to his vice president.

While this was a controversial step, the president wanted to avoid repetition of the chaos that resulted after he was shot in 1981, when Secretary of State Alexander Haig marched before television cameras to announce "I am in control here." During his hours as acting president, George Bush wisely played a low-key role, and that evening when President Reagan signed another letter stating that he was prepared to once again discharge his duties as president, all power was returned to the president.

President Reagan, wisely if reluctantly, followed the sensible procedures provided in the Twenty-fifth Amendment to permit the vice president to serve as acting president when he underwent surgery. Yet Reagan acted in a way that raises questions about Section 3. Reagan's letter to the president pro tempore of the Senate and the speaker of the House of Representatives included the following curious sentence: "I do not believe that the drafters of this amendment intended its application to situations such as the instant one." Reagan was probably wrong. No doubt he and his aides feared that Reagan might have further illnesses and operations and that frequent invoking of this section might diminish Reagan's leadership image. Anyone who has ever worked in the White House appreciates how much a president's influence rests on how the Congress and the public perceive the president's strength, energy, and ability to persuade.

George H.W. Bush, by the way, exercised no presidential responsibilities during the nearly eight hours of that historic July thirteenth in which he was, in effect, president. Curiously, Reagan shied away from referring to Bush as the "acting president," yet that is the term specified in the amendment. Bush apparently was not informed of the exact time he was assuming (or was supposed to assume) his responsibilities. For practical purposes, the then White House chief-of-staff, Donald Regan, was the man in charge during this interval, and, perhaps, for most of the time Reagan was undergoing surgery. Bush remained at the vice presidential residence ready to act if needed, yet dependent on the chief-of-staff who, along with Reagan's wife, remained at the president's side.

There is confusion too about when a vice president is formally put in the position of discharging the powers and duties of the presidency. Is it when the White House staff telephones him? Is it when a president signs the required letters to the leaders of Congress? Is it when those leaders receive the letters?

Less than eight hours after his surgery, Reagan signed a second letter to the congressional leaders reclaiming his responsibilities. Bush was presumably also notified at the same time. Should these notifications be by letter, telephone, fax, or e-mail? White House aides inevitably will play the intermediary role in most of these circumstances, but this first test suggests there are additional questions and procedures to be ironed out.

Confusion only increased when in May of 1991, President George H. W. Bush announced that,in the event his irregular heartbeat required electric shock therapy, power would be turned over to Vice President Quayle. While such a transfer of power was never required, the process again raised troubling questions.

What if there is contention about whether the president is disabled or fit? Section 4 of the Twenty-fifth Amendment speaks to this, though here again, the provisions invite ambiguous interpretation. The beginning of this section reads:

> Whenever the Vice President and a majority of either the principal officers of the executive departments or of such other body as Congress may by law provide, transmit to the President pro tempore of the Senate and the Speaker of the House of Representatives their written declaration that the President is unable to discharge the powers and duties of his office, the Vice President shall immediately assume the powers and duties of the office as Acting President.

The "principal officers of the executive departments" refers implicitly, if not explicitly, to the members of the cabinet. However, nowhere in the Constitution or anywhere else is there a formal definition of who is in the cabinet. It varies not only from president to president but from season to season, depending on whom the president wishes to include.

Another problem in this section that may raise uncertainty in the future involves the provision,of how a president may regain his powers. A president, so the amendment provides, can inform the leaders of Congress that no inability exists and ask to resume the powers, but the vice president, together with a majority of the cabinet, can contest the president's assertion. What then? Well, says the provision, Congress has to decide quickly whether the president is able or unable. Complications can plainly arise in the vague wording of this section. A president could conceivably keep stating he was able to continue. Meanwhile, while Congress would be debating the issue, two persons could both be attempting to exercise the powers and duties of the presidency.

These problems can be cleared up without resorting to any changes in the Twenty-fifth Amendment. Informal agreements and unambiguous precedents will help diminish the confusion. The amendment is plainly a compromise of many different proposals, none of which is entirely satisfactory. Constitution writing is always hard, and to try to accommodate every possibility is impracticable. Not every contingency can be controlled by law or constitutionally specified protocol. The amendment is an improvement, although not definitive for every situation. Judgment on its overall effectiveness must await the inevitable future tests of its various provisions.[59]

## CONCLUSION

What of the vice presidency? Ambiguous and fragile though it may be, this office is here to stay, paradoxes, uncertainties, tensions, and all. The office solves our nation's succession problems and can be made into a useful learning and advisory position. The job will remain attractive to aspiring politicians precisely because it is one of the major paths to the presidency. The Mondale, George H. W. Bush, and Gore experiences, on balance, have added to its prestige.

Vice presidents will continue to have, and perhaps should have, a more or less undefined set of troubleshooting and advisory functions. Different incumbents will bring different skills and strengths to the office. Some will be better at diplomatic functions. Some will be gifted political negotiators and coalition builders. Some will be excellent liaisons with mayors and governors. A certain flexibility is needed.

Given all its problems and all the ambiguities of the position, a case can be made to abolish it. Yet this is highly unlikely. Our tradition, Constitution, and political tendencies all point toward retaining the office. Moreover, amending the Constitution to make more explicit that vice presidents should now be executive and not legislative branch officials would not be worth the effort. However, if there is ever a constitutional convention or a comprehensive constitutional amendment concerning the presidency it would be prudent to relieve vice presidents of their senate responsibilities—including the presiding *and* the casting of tie-breaking votes. Those responsibilities, as noted earlier, are no longer relevant.

Efforts in the past several presidencies to make the office function more effectively should continue. The most obvious way of upgrading the vice presidency is to enhance the quality of the vice presidential selection process.

In the end, although the office may remain puzzling, the person holding the office is usually important and the presidential–vice presidential partnership is almost always a critical one in the overall success of a presidency. Still, a central paradox remains: nearly all the credit for a successful presidency goes to the president. Vice presidents almost always lose their independence and sometimes even their identity. The most damning and illustrative example of this was when President Dwight Eisenhower was asked toward the end of his presidency to cite an example of a major idea that Vice President Nixon had contributed to the Eisenhower presidency. Eisenhower responded with the embarrassing comment: "If you give me a week, I might think of one. I don't remember." Eisenhower's remark haunted Nixon later in Nixon's 1960 presidential campaign as well as in subsequent campaigns.[60] Thus the vice presidency often remains both a training and a maiming experience for many of its occupants.

# Presidential Leadership and Constitutional Democracy

If men were angels, no government would be necessary. If angels were to govern man, neither external nor
internal controls in government would be necessary. In
framing a government which is to be administered by
men over men the great difficulty lies in this, you must
first enable the government to control the government
and in the next place oblige it to control itself. A
dependence on the people is no doubt the primary
control on the government. But experience has taught
mankind the necessity for auxiliary precautions.

James Madison, *Federalist Papers* No. 51 (1788)

A strong president is a bad President, a curse upon the
land, unless his means are constitutional and his ends
democratic, unless he acts in ways that are fair, dignified, and familiar, and pursues policies to which a 'persistent and undoubted' majority of the people has given
support. We honor the great Presidents of the past, not
for their strength, but for the fact that they used it
wisely to build a better America.

Clinton Rossiter, *The American Presidency* (Harcourt,
Brace and World, 1956), p. 257

How did we reach our present comfort level with illegality and executive abuse of power? For decades, professors of history, law, and political science have
indulged in idolatry and hagiography in their writings
about the presidency. Readers are treated to a long list
of imaginary virtues and strengths, with the highest
accolade placed on action. . . . Unless we restore

> respect for checks and balances, we can expect . . .
> constitutional violations by presidents and White
> House officials.
>
> Louis Fisher, "Epilogue," in David Gray Adler and Michael
> Genovese, eds., *The Presidency and the Law* (Lawrence:
> University Press of Kansas, 2002), p. 207

Novelist W. Somerset Maugham once said "There are three rules for writing a novel. Unfortunately, no one knows what they are." Similarly, we are tempted to conclude there are three rules to being an effective president, yet no one knows exactly what they are.

As discussed, the presidency changes from season to season, occupant to occupant, issue to issue. We may never unravel many of the paradoxes of the American presidency. Yet there are things the American people and presidents can do to encourage effective presidential performance.

As noted, we want to be led, yet we cherish our independence and freedom. We want a "take charge" leader in the White House, yet we demand accountable and responsive leadership. Many Americans are now less content to hold presidents to account only every four years when they go to the polls, they yearn for more regular accountability. Our system is built on distrust of powerful leaders and the need for their accountability.

Popular conceptions of the presidency have changed dramatically over time. During the Depression and World War II we demanded a powerful, heroic presidency. During the Cold War we wanted a powerful foreign affairs presidency to thwart the rising threat of communism's spread. Yet abuses of power, the war in Vietnam, and Watergate led to accusations of an imperial presidency, and we sought to clip the wings of the president.

For a time we were content with a constrained presidency, but as problems grew and the president and Congress deadlocked, we grew impatient for direction and leadership. It was not until the tragic terrorism of 2001 that the conditions were right for the reemergence of a strong presidency.

It seems we want the presidency to be there always, ready when we call, to rise when the demand grows and diminish in less pressing times. We want a presidency with the potential to be heroic when we need it, but constrained and limited at other times.

This chapter will examine the need for and challenge of holding presidents accountable, and will discuss some existing and proposed checks on the president.

## HOLDING PRESIDENTS TO ACCOUNT

As our theme in these chapters suggests, any discussion of presidential leadership and accountability must take into account the ever-present paradoxes of the presidency. Some part of us wants a larger-than-life, two-gun, charismatic Mount Rushmore leader. Harrison Ford in the film *Air Force One* (1997) vivified this yearning. Still, there is the remarkably enduring antigovernment, antileadership, chronic-complainer syndrome. We want strong, gutsy leadership to operate on alternate days with a "national city manager." We want presidents to have a wealth of power to solve our problems, yet not so much they can do lasting damage.

Accountability implies not only responsiveness to majority desires and answerability for actions but also taking the people and their views into account. It also implies a performance guided by integrity and character. Accountability implies as well that important decisions could be explained to the people to allow them to appraise how well a president is handling the responsibilities of the office.

To whom is accountability owed? No president, it would seem, can be more than partially accountable to the people, for each president will listen to some people and some points of view more than to others. If we have learned anything in recent years, however, it is that the doctrine of presidential infallibility has been rejected. Arbitrary rule by powerful executives has always been rejected here. But what should be done when there are sharp differences between experts or when expert opinion differs sharply from the preponderance of public opinion? How much accountability, and what kind, is desirable? Is it not possible that the quest for ultimate accountability will result in a presidency without the prerogatives and independent discretion necessary for creative leadership?

As Michael Lind reminds us, "Presidential democracy is not democracy."[1] A too-strong presidency jeopardizes freedom. A too-weak presidency jeopardizes stability. An imperial presidency is not democracy, yet an imperiled presidency is equally troubling. The dilemma for any democracy is both to empower and to control those who govern.

The modern presidency, in fact, may be unaccountable because it is too strong and independent in certain areas and too weak and dependent in others. One of the perplexing circumstances characterizing the modern presidency is that considerable restraints sometimes exist where restraints are least desirable and inadequate restraints are available where they are needed. Also, presidential strength is no guarantee that a president will be responsive or answerable. Indeed, significant independent strength may encourage low answerability when it suits a president's short-term personal power goals.

## THE PRESIDENCY AND DEMOCRATIC THEORY

How do you grant yet control power? Can leaders be empowered yet also democratized?

These are classic questions our framers faced and these have been central to debates in democratic political theory. Leadership implies power, accountability implies limits. Contradictions aside, accountability is a fundamental piece of the democratic puzzle. In essence it denotes that public officials are answerable for their actions. But to whom? Within what limits? Through what means?

There are essentially three types of accountability: *ultimate accountability* (which the United States has via the impeachment process), *periodic accountability* (provided for by general elections and occasional landmark Supreme Court decisions), and *daily accountability* (somewhat contained in the separation of power).[2] James Madison believed elections provided the "primary check on government" and that the separation of powers ("ambition will be made to counteract ambition") plus "auxiliary precautions" should take care of the rest.[3]

There *are* times when presidents abuse power or behave corruptly. But even in the two notable bouts with presidential abuses, Watergate and the Iran-Contra scandal, the president was stopped by the countervailing forces of a free press, an independent Congress, an independent judiciary, and eventually an aroused public.

We may hold presidents accountable, but can they be held responsible? That is, can they muster enough power to govern? One means to improve accountability and also empower leadership is to strengthen the party system in America. Our parties are, at least by European standards, relatively weak, undisciplined, and nonideological. A stronger party system could organize and mobilize citizens and government, diminish the fragmentation of the separation of powers, and mitigate against the atomization of our citizenry. If the parties were more disciplined and programmatic, the government's ability to push through its programs would doubtless be enhanced.

A more responsible party system would also ground presidents in a more consensus-oriented style of leadership, and thereby diminish the independent, unconnected brand of leadership so often attempted by recent presidents. A more robust party system can help join president and Congress together in a more cooperative relationship.[4]

All presidents work to be successful, yet what does it mean to be a success? Great popularity? A good historical reputation? Achieving your policy goals? A high congressional box score for getting your legislative priorities adopted into law? Getting your way?

If success is measured merely by getting one's way, then many bullies would be judged successful. But success means more than getting what one wants. In determining success, we must always ask "power for what *ends?*," because power divorced from purpose is potentially dangerous and democratically undesirable.

Presidential politics should always be concerned with central issues and values. Candidates who run for the White House and thereby seek the power to influence the lives of millions of Americans ought to do so because they have a vision of building a better and more just America. If this is not the case, those candidates who are merely seeking power for its own sake should be smoked out in the election process.

If we look on government as the enemy and politics as a dirty word, our anger turns to apathy, and power (but not responsibility) slips through our hands. We often look at politics not as a means to achieve public good, but as an evil; we see elections as the choice between the lesser of two evils; we presume that our democratic responsibilities are satisfied merely by the act of voting every so often, or we drop out of politics. Consequently many people abandon politics altogether.

This is why politics and elections matter so much. People who give up on politics in effect abdicate the possibility of implementing their most cherished policy ideas. People who give up on politics and parties are essentially giving others power over their lives.

In a democracy, a successful president pursues and uses power, not for selfish ends, not to aggrandize his or her own status, but to help solve problems and help citizens enjoy the blessings of freedom and opportunity.

The best of democratic leaders are teachers who both understand and educate all of us about the promise and mission of America. They move the government in pursuit of the consensus generated from the values of the nation. They appeal to the best in citizens and attempt to lead the nation towards its better self.[5]

Franklin Roosevelt suggested that the presidency "is preeminently a place of moral leadership."[6] Thus, presidents may use their office as a "bully pulpit" to appeal to our better instincts, and lead democratically. It was through politics and government that the nation's progressive social movements helped move us toward greater racial and gender equality, devised policies to expand education and opportunities to a wider segment of the population, attempted to protect and expand the rights of citizens. These battles are far from over. As a nation we have a long way to go before we can truly grant the blessings of liberty and prosperity to all citizens, yet it is through politics—and only through politics—that we can achieve these goals. And if we want our politics and our government to succeed, we must find ways for citizens to guide and encourage responsible presidential leadership.

Presidents may and have also used the powers of the presidency to promote economic stability and economic growth in America. The Roosevelts, Wilson, Kennedy, Reagan, and Clinton all strived to stimulate the economy and promote favorable trade programs that in turn created jobs and economic security. Presidents generally know what is expected of them as promoters of economic development, yet, here again, they are likely to respond to the yearnings and lobbying of those who become actively engaged in the political process and party politics.

The ends power serves are important, but in presidential terms, virtue is not enough. A successful president must have *character* and *competence*. Character without competence (resources, skill, power) gives us noble but ineffective leaders; competence without character may lead to government by demagogues or rogues.

Presidents who lead in the democratic spirit can encourage leaders, foster citizen responsibility, and inspire others to assume leadership responsibilities in their communities. Democratic leaders establish a purposeful vision, pursue progressive goals, and question, challenge, engage, and educate citizens.

The United States needs a strong presidency and a democratically controlled presidency, and this in turn necessitates a strong civic culture.[7] Political theorist Benjamin R. Barber notes the challenge inherent in such a quest:

> At the heart of democratic theory lies a profound dilemma that has afflicted democratic practice at least since the eighteenth century. Democracy requires both effective leadership and vigorous citizenship: yet the conditions and consequences of leadership often seem to undermine civic vigor. Although it cries for both, democracy must customarily make do either with strong leadership or with strong citizens. For the most part, depending on devices of representation in large-scale societies, democracy in the West has settled for strong leaders and correspondingly weak citizens.[8]

The American presidency operates within a system of shared power, one in which the claims of many groups constantly compete. Presidential struggles with other governmental and extragovernmental centers of power stem from the larger societal conflicts over values and the allocation of wealth and opportunity. As a result, the presidency becomes a place in which few radical decisions are made; most of its domestic policies are exploratory, remedial, or experimental modifications of past practices.

Limitations on a president's freedom of action are, to be sure, often desirable. Many of the checks and balances that are still at work today were deliberately designed by the framers of the Constitution. In some measure, presidents should be the agents of their campaign commitments, their parties, and their announced programs. They should be responsive most of the time to the views of the majority of the American people. Presidential behavior should be informed by the Constitution, existing laws, and the generally understood values that define democratic procedure. The notion that party programs, spelled out in campaigns, allow the public some control over policy through the election process is a valuable brake, one that needs, if anything, to be revitalized. Other brakes that limit presidential discretion may be viewed as positive or negative, depending on an individual's political and economic views. The constraining of a president by the bureaucracy and by special interests is implicitly, if not explicitly, a kind of accountability, even if it is not exactly the kind we want as our prime constitutional safeguard against the abuse of power.

A president's leeway for achievement can be determined by the degree to which consensus or conflict exists among elite interest groups within a particular arena of public policy. If the policy elite of a given profession or industry share wide agreement on a particular issue, it is difficult for a president to effect an opposing point of view. Occasional exceptions such as Medicare, automobile safety devices, and homeland security legislation are not persuasive, because the profession or industry in question seldom lost much and the costs for such programs were in most cases passed on in some way to the consumer or taxpayer. If, however, cleavage or confusion occurs over substantive or procedural matters, a president has some independent influence; although even then, the scope and type of his influence will be shaped by the character of the conflict among these elite. Thus, Johnson's efforts to create model cities as demonstrations of how social and physical planning could produce decent and livable cities soon was heavily influenced by pressures from home builders, developers, real-estate associations, big-city mayors, and other strategically positioned interests.

Likewise, despite widespread public support for rapid progress on the environmental front, Carter's environmental protection recommendations soon became influenced by the views of the automobile manufacturers as well as by the unions potentially affected by stringent standards and too rapid implementation. Clinton's efforts at health care reform met with fierce opposition from insurance companies and medical care providers who felt threatened by the proposed reforms. Sometimes a consensus among policy elites may be the product of presidential commitment, but the reverse is more likely to be the case.

In the end, all three branches of government and the bureaucracy listen more attentively and usually yield to the ideas from those segments of society able to represent themselves, able to shape the character of those branches, and able to supply precisely that information and argumentation needed to make the system move. Thus the many well-heeled interests continue to enjoy a special advantage in any contest with a president who is a progressive or a reformer.

The founders would have been pleased to see how the system of checks and balances has thwarted executive tyranny. But they would, we believe, be less pleased with the gridlock that so often characterizes relations between the president and Congress.

Is the separation-of-powers model *the* problem? Does it create deadlock and paralysis? To presidents, there must be times when it seems so. Woodrow Wilson, writing in 1884 long before he became president, saw the separation as creating a massive political escape clause for blame and responsibility. Wrote Wilson:

> Power and strict accountability for its use are the essential constituents of good government. . . . It is, therefore, manifestly a radical defect in our federal system that it parcels out power and confuses responsibility as it does. The main purpose of the Convention of 1787 seems to have been to accomplish this grievous mistake. . . . Were it possible to call together again the members of that wonderful Convention . . . they would be the first to admit that the only fruit of dividing power had been to make it irresponsible.[9]

Upon reflection we are reminded of the positive benefit of separating, sharing, and overlapping power. If one values, as we do, deliberation, discussion, and debate; if we accept a model of democratic governing based on consensus and cooperation, then the reform agenda will be short. But some see the separation as the likely suspect in the crime of stalemate and gridlock.

Americans are great fixers. Americans have proposed hundreds of amendments to our Constitution in the hopes of improving our republic. The presidency is the subject of many such proposed reforms. We will now discuss some of them. Most of these proposals, we believe, are undesirable and would only make things worse.

## THE SIX-YEAR NONRENEWABLE TERM

One of the more curious remedies persistently suggested in discussions of reforming the presidency is the idea of a single six-year presidential term. This is certainly not a new idea, having been originally proposed in Congress as early as 1826. It has been reintroduced more than 150 times since then and has won backing from at least ten presidents, including Johnson, Nixon, and Carter. This reform could only be achieved by amending our Constitution.

In April 1979 President Carter allowed that the press would ascribe purer motives to his policies if he did not have the option of seeking reelection. And so he endorsed the six-year term as a sensible reform.

Proponents contend the single six-year term would remove a president from the negative kind of partisan politics. The assumption is that once elected to such a term, with no possibility of reelection, presidents would cast aside partisan calculations and provide leadership for all of the people. Presidents would do what is right even if this meant that their party would lose votes, their friends would suffer financial losses, or their own political future would be damaged.

In short, the case in favor of the single six-year term is based on several expectations, namely, that it would:

- reduce the role of politics in the White House
- liberate a president from the worries and indignities of a reelection effort
- allow more time to concentrate on policy planning and program implementation
- liberate a president from the pressures of special-interest groups and party-line politics, allowing him to exercise greater independence of judgment and nonpartisan leadership
- eliminate the advantages of incumbency from presidential elections
- allow a president to make decisions free from the temptation of political expediency
- enforce the common-sense idea that a period of six years is enough even for the most robust individual

Despite a few attractive features, the six-year term would cause more problems than it would solve. The required reelection after four years is one of the most democratic aspects of the presidency. It affords an opportunity

Arguments for and against a single, six-year term have raged for decades. Woodrow Wilson argued against it when the Senate passed a resolution in favor of the reform in 1913. (*Source:* Reproduced from the collections of the Library of Congress.)

for assessment. It enhances the likelihood that a president will carefully weigh the effects of whatever he or she does on his reelection chances. At the core of our system is the belief that our president should have to worry about reelection and be subject to all the same vicissitudes of politics as other elected officials. Moreover, a political party should retain the threat of dumping a president as a check on the incumbent and the office, especially on a president who refuses to honor his or her party's pledges.

When the U.S. Senate in 1913 passed a resolution in favor of the single six-year term, Woodrow Wilson argued against it and his reasoning still seems valid: "The argument is not that it is clearly known now just how long each President should remain in office. Four years is too long a term for a President who is not the true spokesman of the people, who is imposed upon and does not lead. It is too short a term for a President who is doing, or attempting, a great work of reform, and who has not had time to finish it." Wilson also contended that "to change the term to six years would be to increase the likelihood of its being too long without any assurance that it would, in happy cases, be long enough. A fixed constitutional limitation to a single term of office is highly arbitrary and unsatisfactory from any point of view."[10]

The proposed divorce between the presidency and politics presupposes a significantly different kind of political system from that of the United States, which is glued together largely by ambiguity, compromise, and the extensive sharing of powers. In light of the requisites of democracy, the presidency must be a highly political office and the president an expert practitioner of the art of politics. Quite simply, there is no other way for presidents to negotiate favorable coalitions within the country, Congress, and the executive branch and to gather the authority needed to translate ideas into accomplishments. A president who remains aloof from politics, campaigns, and partisan alliances does so at the risk of becoming the prisoner of events, special interests, or his own whims.

The very means for bringing a president in touch with reality is the process of political debate and political bargaining, with all of the necessary uncertainty, changes of course, arguments, and listening to other points of view. What makes domestic politics so distasteful to presidents, that it is full of groups to persuade and committees to inform, is precisely its virtue; indeed, it is the major hope for maintaining an open presidency, one neither bound by its own sources of information nor aloof to the point that it will no longer listen.

One way to prevent future abuses of presidential power, as others have noted, is to make the White House more open; and one way to do that, as has not been suggested so often, is to begin regarding a president as a politician once again. *Politics,* in the best sense of that term, is the art of making decisions in the context of debate, dialogue, and open two-way conversations, the art of making the difficult and desirable possible. This kind of politics at the White House should not be diminished. Indeed, as pointed out above, it is highly desirable that presidents be great practitioners of the craft of politics. They, as well as Congress and our parties, would profit from more politics, not less.

Most of the effective presidents have been highly political. They knew how to stretch the limited resources of the office, and they loved politics and enjoyed the responsibilities of party leadership. The nation has been well served by sensitive politicians disciplined by the general thrust of partisan and public thinking. Many of the least political presidents were the least successful and seemingly the least suited temperamentally to the rigors of the office. The best have been those who listened to people, who responded to majority as well as to intense minority sentiment, who saw that political parties are often the most important vehicle for communicating voter preferences to those in public office, and who were attentive to the diversity and intensity of public attitudes even as they attempted to educate and to influence the direction of opinion.

If national leaders do become isolated or insulated from the mood of the public, then electing presidents for longer terms would only encourage this tendency.[11] Frequent elections necessarily remain a major means of motivating responsive and responsible behavior. An apolitical president, disinterested in reelection, motivated by personal principle or moralistic abstractions, and aloof from the concerns of our political parties, could become a highly irresponsible president. Elections customarily force an assessment of presidential performance. They are welcomed when promises have been kept and feared when performance has been unsatisfactory. Was it, for example, a mere coincidence, or was President Nixon's Vietnam troop-withdrawal rate calculated with the election of 1972 in mind? Was the Johnson-Humphrey bombing halt of 1968 aimed toward that year's election? Nixon's economic game-plan reversal in 1971, Johnson's vain efforts at peace negotiations in 1967 and 1968, and Bill Clinton's 1996 embrace of several of the House Republicans' key issues were unmistakenly related to the positive, constructive, and dynamic character of American elections.

There is yet another practical consideration about the six-year term: If we elect an exceptional president under this reform we have him or her in the White House for two years less than under the present practice that would have provided eight years. If we elect a really bad president we are stuck for two years more than under the present system that provides for getting rid of such types at the end of four years.

The single-term proposal has a comforting ring of good, old-time government and nonpartisanship to it. Yet it represents the last gasp of those who cling to the hope that we can separate national leadership from the crucible of politics and of those who contend our presidency is too beholden to the workings of a patronage or spoils system. Neither is the case: the former remains an impossibility—it is impossible to take the politics out of public leadership in a democracy—whereas the latter is a problem whose time largely has passed. Equally undesirable is the notion that intense conflict over policy choices, that is, intense political activity, somehow can be removed from the presidency. The conflicts that surround the presidency and require a president to act as a public mediator, mirror those existing and potential conflicts over values that exist within the American society at large. If presidents were not required to resolve political conflicts by making political choices, they would not be fulfilling those responsibilities we rightly associate with democratic leadership.

## A PLURAL EXECUTIVE IS ALSO NOT NEEDED

The job of the president, some think, has now become too complex and its reach too extended to be entrusted to one individual's fallible judgment. What can be done to lessen our excessive dependence on the accident of presidential personalities? One solution is to have several presidents.[12] The idea of a plural executive received consideration and some support at the 1787 Constitutional Convention.

The vast responsibilities of an executive who is also chief-of-state and top party leader are expected nowhere else. Political scientist Herman Finer was sufficiently alarmed by the growth of presidential power that he came out strongly in favor of introducing some kind of plural or collegial element to our national leadership: "The burdens . . . are necessarily so multifarious that to avoid a fatal collapse of efficiency and responsibility the President would have to be a titan and a genius. A collective Presidency might have these qualities, but not a solitary man. A solitary President is a gamble this nation cannot afford."[13] Hence, Finer suggested having one president and eleven vice presidents.

The defects of most plural executive schemes are fairly self-evident: competition and conflict within the executive, a further swelling of the size of the presidency, and a diffusion and confusion of responsibilities. In times of crisis the members of a truly collective presidency would be expected to show unanimity. But what if they did not come to an agreement? Would the public have confidence in a major policy arrived at by a three or two to one decision? Surely the bureaucracy might heed such decisions less assiduously. Might not a collectivized presidency court paralysis or indecision, or both, in a terrorist attack or in an international monetary crisis, when swiftness and decisiveness would be most needed?

Perhaps the most frequent complaint about the plural executive idea is that it would create great difficulties in assigning accountability. Alexander Hamilton argued that the restraints of public opinion on the presidency would lose their efficacy if there were several executives rather than one. Whom should the people blame when things went wrong? Which one or set of executives should be impeached? Far better that there should be a single person for the people to oversee. Hamilton's 1788 brief in behalf of a single executive remains compelling:

> ... the plurality of the Executive tends to deprive the people of the two greatest securities they can have for the faithful exercise of any delegated power, first, the restraints of public opinion, which lose their efficacy as well on account of the division of the censure attendant on bad measures among a number, as on account of the uncertainty on whom it ought to fall; and, second, the opportunity of discovering with facility and clearness the misconduct of the persons they trust, in order either to their removal from office, or to their actual punishment in cases which admit of it.[14]

In general, suggestions for institutionalizing more help for presidents by fixing into law or grafting onto the Constitution any plan for a plural executive should be rejected. The presidency, as opposed to the president, is already a collective entity, and individual presidents usually have ample discretion to organize their own office as they please.

## NO TO "VOTES OF NO CONFIDENCE"

One of the boldest responses to Watergate and the abuse of power by Richard Nixon was a proposed constitutional amendment providing for a vote by Congress of no confidence in a president. The effect would be similar to the recall, now provided for in about sixteen states. Introduced in Congress by Representative Henry Reuss on August 15, 1974, H. J. Resolution 1111 gained little attention and little support.[15] But it merits some attention in our discussion of presidential accountability, if only because it poses a rather strong alternative to current practices. Indeed, the vote of confidence, if enacted here, would have far-reaching consequences, so much so that it might substantially transform the system of government in the United States as we now know it.

How would the no-confidence amendment work? A three-fifths vote of the members of each House present and voting would be necessary. Such a resolution would take priority over any other pending issue before Congress. If adopted, Congress would fix a date, between 90 and 110 days, for a special election for the president and vice president as well as for members of Congress. If it occurs near the regular congressional election date, that date would be used. Note that the incumbent president is eligible to stand for reelection even though he was the target of the no-confidence vote.

A reason put forward in defense of the no-confidence proposal is that the presidency in modern times has grown too powerful, especially in crisis contexts and in foreign affairs. Presidential power, it is argued, has risen above the level where the system of checks and balances can be effective in countering presidential actions. More bluntly, however, advocates of the no-confidence or similar national recall proposals believe that the four-year fixed term is a liability if and when we have incompetent presidents who lose the confidence of the nation. Incompetence, they point out, is not an impeachable offense. A "no-confidence" vote might also be a way to reconstitute a hopelessly deadlocked or failed government.

A goal of the proposed vote of confidence is to make future presidents more accountable to Congress, as well as more accountable to the American people. A president, it is assumed, would realize that he or she is accountable for his actions, proposed programs, negotiations, policies, and decisions and would have to face up to criticisms by Congress. The commission of high crimes and misdemeanors would no longer be needed to justify a president's dismissal. Maintaining the confidence of Congress and the general public would be an ongoing necessity. Matters such as Vietnam policy, for example, would have to be discussed in greater detail with congressional leaders to ensure that a president had the support of Congress. The vote of no confidence would be a means of retaliation against a president who too often worked behind the scenes or otherwise manipulated the spirit of checks and balances. Advocates reason that major decisions would have to be made by consultation, instead of by one person. To some extent, then, this constitutional amendment would introduce a certain amount of plural or shared decision making in our national government. The fundamental dangers of decisions by a Lone Ranger president would be thereby reduced.

A primary advantage of the Reuss amendment, of course, was that it did not require proof of illegal conduct. With the impeachment process, high crimes and misdemeanors must be proved. But as James Sundquist wrote, "In today's meanings of those words, a president who has simply lost his capacity to lead and govern because of bungling, betrayal by ill-chosen subordinates, or any of the other weaknesses that can lead to misuse of presidential power, cannot for that reason be relieved of power."[16] The Reuss proposal, however, could be used as a clear statement of dissatisfaction with a president's leadership abilities or his policies or lack thereof.

In a nutshell, the chief arguments in favor of the vote of no confidence are these:

- Impeachment is an inefficient check. At best it protects against gross criminal violations of the public trust but not against presidential incompetence.

- The president would be more disposed to working with Congress, explaining his policies and educating Congress and the general public about his plans and conduct in office.

- This proposal would force more presidential consultation with Congress and the leaders of the major parties and should lessen the secrecy surrounding presidential policymaking.

- The proposal does not take power away from the president; it only makes him more responsible for how he uses his power. It might prevent a president from trying to be "above politics" and from isolating himself from criticism.

- It would allow Congress to act in the face of negligence, gross incompetence, and disastrous policies, not just explicitly criminal abuses.

Critics viewed the Reuss amendment as an example of "good intentions, bad policy." Congress, they pointed out, has plenty of resources with which to check a president if only they would use them. Further, even though presidents have become paramount in the conduct of foreign affairs, Congress has numerous means at its disposal to oversee this exercise of power.

In certain situations it would seem a vote of no confidence would give Congress the power to frustrate continually a president with whom it disagreed. The alternatives are a government of continuous presidential elections and overall paralysis or a government in which president and Congress are so close as to defeat the basic concept of the separation of powers so fundamental to our system. Perhaps this latter condition of power centralized in an overly united president and Congress would, under certain circumstances, be more dangerous to the basic freedom and spirit of the United States than any single "imperial" president.

There is also the argument that a vote of no confidence could actually be used to strengthen the hand of an already strong leader, much as Hitler and de Gaulle used plebiscites to weaken their opposition. If timed properly, a president who wins a vote of no confidence with a strong show of votes can use it as a false rally of support. One imagines, for example, that Lyndon Johnson could have won a vote of no confidence on his Vietnam policy in 1966. Or Richard Nixon might have won a vote of no confidence during the early stages, say the spring or summer of 1973, of his Watergate crisis. In both cases, these "victories" might have strengthened the hand of those men in defiance of a more responsive, accountable posture.

A vote of no confidence arrangement might lead presidents to avoid making significant changes in policy that would antagonize Congress. Innovative leadership would be thwarted, as presidents might gear most of their actions to public opinion polls or to the wishes of the majority at the expense of minority rights. The proposal could lead a president to concentrate on short-term or immediately popular initiatives to "create" favorable public approval at the expense of long-term planning.

In short, the cure would doubtless be worse than the occasional ailment.[17] The vote of no confidence procedure would not necessarily improve the quality of presidential leadership, nor would it enhance accountability in any significant way. Presidents do not intentionally make poor decisions. What could result might be far worse than the rare arrogant president we have had to endure. This measure might make presidents too dependent on Congress, or conform too closely with popular opinion. This measure might give us an endless line of unsuccessful short-term presidents and as a result a paralyzed nation. We risk the unwise weakening of the presidency by such an amendment. Abuses of presidential power do need to be curbed, but this proposal is not the way to do it. We need better and wiser leadership, not a weakened presidency.

## THE ILLUSION OF THE THIRD PARTY PANACEA

One of the more appealing (on the surface) political reforms is the idea that perhaps a major third party could, if it were able to organize and win a respectable following, produce better presidential candidates and straighten out the existing two parties.

Congressman John Anderson preached this reform in 1980 when he challenged Reagan and Carter in the presidential general election. Businessman Ross Perot, who won nearly 19 percent of the popular vote in 1992 and 8 percent in 1996, tried in vain to build a third party he called the Reform Party. Ralph Nader, especially in 2000, tried to build a new third party comprised of environmental and antiglobalization activists. Anderson, Perot, and Nader raised important issues and forced the Democrats and Republicans to explain their policies. Third parties in America are at their best when they call attention to controversial issues and criticize the establishment parties for neglecting to do what they have promised to do.

Our seemingly entrenched two major parties have made it difficult for an existing or future third party to become a major party. The last time this happened was in the late 1850s! And, of course, no third party has won the presidency since 1860. Third parties have never shaped national policy from inside the government. And, although their points of view often get absorbed into one of the major parties, third parties and their candidates have rarely had much influence on national policy.

The political realities are that third parties do not have bright prospects in the next several years, and past experience is clear in demonstrating that serious third parties are readily put out of business when they do not have compelling policy ideas. Simply put, one of the major two parties will steal, modify, and adapt such ideas into their own platforms and promises.[18] That's what Nixon did with some of George Wallace's ideas in 1968 and 1972. That's what Democrats and Republicans did with some of Ross Perot's better ideas.

Doubtless our two-party system needs to be challenged and shaken up. Doubtless, too, a serious multiparty system in America would stir more people to participate in politics and elections, and this would be healthy. Yet the two-party system has also served this country well. It needs challenge and revitalization, but this can be done as well—and perhaps better—from within the parties as outside of them.

Strengthening, reforming, and improving the two-party system offers more hope and is more realistic than the search for the magical third party. It is highly unlikely that a third party will provide the answers to most of the pressing economic, social, and international problems facing the United States in the twenty-first century.

In contrast to the six-year term idea, the idea of a plural presidency, notions of votes of no confidence, and the illusions of the third party panacea, there are existing checks that work reasonably well. These need better appreciation. There are also additional ways to make our system of governance and the presidency act in a more accountable and responsible manner.

## THE ULTIMATE CHECK: IMPEACHMENT AND REMOVAL

Impeachment is obviously one of the most potent checks against the abuse of executive power, yet over the nation's history it has been the least used check. For practical purposes, it is a political action, phrased in legal terminology, against an official of the federal government. The Constitution deals with the subject of impeachment and conviction in six places, but the scope of the power is outlined in Article II, Section 4.

> The President, Vice President and all civil officers of the United States, shall be removed from Office on Impeachment for, and Conviction of, Treason, Bribery, or other high Crimes and Misdemeanors.

In the impeachment process, the House of Representatives acts as the prosecutor and the Senate serves as judge and jury. Any member of the House may initiate impeachment proceedings by introducing a resolution to that effect in the House. The House Judiciary Committee may conduct hearings and investigations. The committee then decides either in favor of or against an impeachment verdict and sends its conclusions on to the full house. A 50-percent vote in the House is needed to impeach. Select members of the House, if an impeachment is enacted, would then try the case before the U.S. Senate. In the Senate a two-thirds vote of those members present is needed for conviction and removal.

Only fourteen national officials have been impeached by the House since 1789. Of these, only four were convicted, although one resigned before the Senate took action. Nine of these cases involved federal judges, one involved a senator, one a secretary of war, and two presidents, Andrew Johnson and Bill Clinton. Both were impeached but not convicted.

The impeachment and removal of a president has been a much misunderstood and an obviously cumbersome means of accountability. Its use is fraught with emotion and hazardous side effects, and it necessarily remains a device to be used only as a last resort.

Impeachment is plainly a time consuming and highly traumatic instrument to deploy. Yet there is no reason to suppose in most instances that impeachment would be any more traumatic than having a person such as Richard Nixon continue in office for another two years when he has long since lost the ability to govern effectively. The impeachment and removal powers may well be an elaborate and difficult-to-use means to hold presidents to account, but as the Andrew Johnson and Richard Nixon cases attest, each in its own way, it can be used. Even though it can be abused, as in the Clinton case,[19] its availability is a reminder to presidents that their power must be exercised in an accountable manner.

## THE NEED FOR OCCASIONAL INDEPENDENT COUNSELS

Only a handful of the more than one hundred Watergate-related reform bills ever made it through Congress. One of the more controversial ones that did was a provision that would establish, under certain circumstances, a temporary special prosecutor to investigate and prosecute executive branch conflict-of-interest allegations. Later legislators would rightly substitute the name *independent counsels* for the more biased term *special prosecutors*.

Watergate demonstrated that the executive branch could not investigate itself lest there be the appearance—if not the reality—of a conflict of interest. After considerable debate Congress passed the Special Prosecutor Act in 1978. This law allowed the attorney general to appoint a special investigator under certain circumstances.

Under this legislation it is up to the attorney general to determine whether a case of conflict of interest is valid enough to warrant further investigation and prosecution. This would apply in the cases of about one hundred top executive office and Justice Department posts and top officers of a presidential election campaign. The statute mandates the appointment by a designated panel of three federal judges of an independent counsel whenever charges of a violation of federal criminal law arise in connection with these top officials.

Did the Congress overreact in creating the special prosecutor law? No. Presidents, like all executives, set the moral tone for their administrations, give clues as to acceptable and unacceptable behavior, establish norms and limits. Presidents demonstrate by words and deeds the kind of behavior that will be tolerated and the standards applicable to the entire administration. Independent counsels, while perhaps overused in recent years, can serve a useful purpose when employed in appropriate circumstances.

If politics is, or appears to be, scandal ridden, if self-interest and not pursuit of the public interest appears to be the chief motivating force in politics, then it should not surprise us that the general public sees "politics" as a dirty word. But this may undermine democracy and the respect for the rule of law, as well as drive people out of the political process. Thus, it is vital to the health of constitutional democracy that corruption be exposed and the wrongdoers punished.

Critics have argued that some independent counsels have politicized their investigations and that in some cases, such as the Iran-Contra affair and in the more recent Whitewater and campaign financing investigations, investigations have gone on for too long.

Some critics think too that the independent counsels are too independent. But this independence may be necessary if the process is to have integrity. Legal scholar Peter Shane suggests:

> The relative independence of the independent counsel is secured not only by his or her judicial appointment but also by statutory protection against discharge. Independent counsels ordinarily have job tenure until they determine that all matters within their jurisdiction are adequately resolved. They may be removed only by personal action of the Attorney General, and then only for "good cause, physical disability, mental incompetency, or . . . other condition that substantially impairs" the independent counsel's job performance. As a consequence, the Attorney General—and, thus, the President—is without power to threaten an independent counsel with removal because of disagreements about the conduct of an investigation or prosecution. Decisions regarding the sufficiency of evidence for an indictment, the appropriateness of alternative investigative techniques, witness selection and so on, are entirely within the independent counsel's discretion.[20]

Former Watergate special prosecutor Archibald Cox was probably correct in writing that "In the rare national crises that arise when there is serious evidence of criminal misconduct by a president or other high executive official, only an independent counsel, chosen by a judicial panel, can provide the best assurance of thorough and impartial investigation followed by fair-minded prosecution or public dismissal of the charges."[21]

Cox believes the potential for abuse of this process can be reduced by a number of changes. He suggests the independent counsel provisions should be limited just to the president and cabinet-level officials. It should also, he believes, be limited to crimes committed in national office. "The benefits of allowing investigation of earlier wrongdoing are outweighed," Cox writes, "by the risk of encouraging opposing politicians to dig for stories of past misdeeds."[22] The process should probably also have a time limit of up to a year. Most important, Cox adds, "independent counsels must see their function not as pursuit of a target to be wounded or destroyed, but as an impartial inquiry with as much concern for public exoneration of the innocent as for indictment of the guilty."[23]

The independent counsel law was challenged in *Morrison v. Olson,*[24] but in 1988 the Supreme Court upheld its constitutionality. Yet its abuses and overuse led Congress to let the law authorizing its use expire. Actions by presidents in the future will probably cause the American people to encourage Congress to reinstitute some type of independent counsel procedure. The lessons of the 1980s and 1990s will prove useful, and a new process, with proper cautions and limits, is possible and may be desirable.[25]

## THE CLINTON INVESTIGATION AND IMPEACHMENT

William Jefferson Clinton is the only elected president in history to be impeached. The Clinton impeachment reveals both the strengths and weaknesses of the impeachment process. Yes, a president can be held to account for his actions. But is impeachment the most effective means of doing so?

Clinton sometimes seemed to attract scandals like a magnet. Even before he became president he faced questions about past sexual relations, and almost immediately upon assuming office, Republicans began investigating his past business dealings. In his first year in office, Clinton faced inquiries into an Arkansas land deal (Whitewater), the firing of Travel Office employees, accusations that he was responsible for the death of White House aide Vince Foster (who had committed suicide), as well as court proceedings relating to accusations of sexual improprieties leveled by Paula Jones. Clinton also faced investigations into his fund-raising efforts ("renting" out the Lincoln bedroom to fat-cat donors) and, finally, independent counsel Ken Starr's investigation of "Monicagate," in which the president had an improper sexual relationship with a White House intern (Monica Lewinsky), lied about it to the public, and lied about it under oath. In 1998, this sparked a move to impeach the president.

Despite Clinton's 60-percent job approval rating, the House of Representatives pressed for impeachment. The Judiciary Committee passed four articles of impeachment on a straight party-line vote. The grounds for impeachment included perjury, obstruction of justice, and abuse of power. For only the second time in history, the full House was asked to impeach a president.

When the House convened on December 19, 1998, to deal with the impeachment of William Jefferson Clinton, speaker-designate Robert Livingstone shocked the nation by announcing his resignation. Livingstone's own extramarital affair was about to be made public. Then Henry Hyde, who headed the Judiciary Committee, admitted that the stories about his own affair were true. Instead of resigning, Hyde led the charge against the president.

Eventually the House approved two articles of impeachment against the president: perjury and obstruction of justice. Impeachment cases are tried in the Senate with a two-thirds vote required for conviction. On January 7, 1999, the trial began. Members of the House Judiciary Committee made the case for impeachment, but in spite of the fact that the Republicans held control of the Senate, both articles of impeachment failed to get even a simple majority. Article One (perjury) failed 45–55, with ten Republicans voting against the charge. Article Two (obstruction of justice) ended in a 50–50 tie, with five Republicans voting against it.

The Republicans failed to oust the president, but the office of the independent counsel continued to pursue Clinton, eventually spending more than $60 million. Shortly before Clinton left office, he made a deal with the counsel to end the inquiry. Clinton admitted that some of the answers he gave "were false," and agreed to a five-year suspension of his Arkansas law license as well as a $25,000 fine.

The Clinton experience reminds all of us that impeachment is a complex, tumultuous, and unpredictable process. It also affirms that the framers were wise in placing the final decision in the U.S. Senate and not in the U.S. House of Representatives. In Clinton's case, there was no doubt he was guilty of serious wrongdoing and stupidity, but as political scientists David Gray Adler and Nancy Kassop conclude:

> the lying and cover-up of his reckless affair with a White House intern . . . did not involve the abuse of power to political ends or the subversion of the Constitution, nor did it constitute the sort of "great and dangerous offenses" by "great offenders" or the crushing threat to the Republic that the Framers of the Constitution contemplated when the fashioned the impeachment power as an instrument for placing a "bridle on the executive."[26]

Clinton deserved some form of punishment, "but in the form of sanctions imposed by the criminal and civil justice systems rather than by a court of impeachment."[27]

## THE NEED FOR GREATER CAMPAIGN FINANCE INTEGRITY

As stated in Chapter 2, running for president is a very costly enterprise. Candidates must raise vast sums of money, and the sheer magnitude of this fund raising poses serious questions for democratic accountability and integrity. The dependence of candidates on the largess of big donors raises the appearance, if not the reality, of corruption.

In the 1960s, presidential campaigns were funded by less public means than today. Joseph Kennedy, father of John Kennedy, once scolded his son for spending too much on the 1960 race, complaining that he was interested in financing a victory, not a landslide. During the 1960s the costs of presidential campaigning began to skyrocket. The main cause of this was television. The costs of television caused candidates to spend more and more time raising money to pay for costly TV advertising.

The scandals of the 1972 Nixon reelection campaign caused a backlash, prompting the Congress to attempt to reform the method of financing presidential elections. A series of laws and amendments to the laws sought to limit the impact of money on the selection process, but the laws had loopholes that were soon exploited by various campaigns. One of the biggest loopholes was the "soft money" contribution, where money was given to the political party and not directly to the candidate, thus allowing candidates to bypass the legal limits imposed on their campaigns.[28]

In 1992, Democrats spent $85 million in "hard" money to the Republicans' $164 million. In soft money the Republicans outspent the Democrats $46 million to $31 million. By 1996, costs soared. Republicans spent $278 million in hard money to the Democrats' $146 million. In soft money they spent $121 million to the Democrats' $106 million.[29] In 2000, the Republicans spent over $249 million in soft money. The Democrats spent over $245 million.

President Clinton suffered a number of embarrassments when disclosures of his 1996 fund-raising efforts revealed questionable judgment relating to money taken from a number of foreign sources and reports that for $25,000 a donor could attend an "event" at the vice presidential mansion, for $50,000 could meet with the president at the White House, and for $100,000 or more, could dine with the president at the Hay Adams Hotel or be an overnight guest at the White House.[30]

Clearly the reform efforts of the 1970s had not worked as intended. Is there a solution to this continuing problem? Some call for tightening the loopholes in current law; others suggest stricter limits on donations; and others want stiffer penalties for violations of current law. Still others suggest that television stations be required to give free prime-time spots to candidates in hopes that this will diminish the need for such large sums of money.[31]

As the 1970s campaign finance reform efforts indicate, creative and determined candidates are usually able to find a loophole to frustrate reformist intent. Limits on soft money contributions and free television time for major candidates is now needed to guarantee the integrity of our political process. Congress has now acted on the former but not on the latter proposal. It is probably not wise to rely on legal prohibitions alone to control the campaign finance mess. Here, as in many cases, the most hopeful corrective is an aroused, educated, and demanding public. Yes, full disclosure of sources of funding and spending; and yes, closing loopholes offers some help. But in the end, it must be the voters who demand better of their candidates. Laws alone will not do the job; laws backed by an informed public may.

## THE NECESSITY FOR POLITICS AND HEALTHY POLITICAL PARTIES

A basic question throughout this book is not whether government by the people is possible or even desirable in the modern world but rather how the political system and the relationship between leadership and citizens can be transformed so they will approach more closely the ideals of democracy. This argument explicitly rejects the view that things must remain as they are because that is the way underlying forces make them. These pages have often emphasized the need for a strong yet also a lean and accountable presidency, a presidency that could achieve peace, economic prosperity, and the reforms and innovative changes that would broaden the economic and political opportunities of everyone.

The simplistic notion that returning to the drawing boards and coming up with a new charter or a new constitution will provide the needed solutions is rejected. A new constitutional convention is not needed. Solving major policy problems and keeping presidents honest and responsible are more likely to be accomplished by political than any additional *constitutional* means. No single institutional innovation we have ever heard of could guarantee a commitment to truth, compassion, and justice. Formal constitutional provisions to guard against presidential isolation, such as the institutionalization of government-sponsored votes of confidence or a lengthened presidential term, are not sensible ways to increase accountability.

That the American political system and leaders are asked to undertake much of what the rest of society refuses to do is a continual problem in this nation. The promise of the presidency symbolizes the hopes of the people, and certainly there is nothing wrong in calling on our president to summon up exalted national commitments. But the attempt to reconstitute any single institution in a large, complex society may be rather futile if the fundamental purpose of that institution is to represent and respond to the dominant values of the society. There is little doubt that this society's values are rooted in a strong faith in political and social gradualism, in a deep fear of revolutionary change, and in a steadfast devotion to most of what constitutes the existing order.

Political controls, however, do need to be sharpened and strengthened to ensure a continual public and congressional scrutiny of presidential activity. Openness and candor often have been lacking. Presidents and their aides sometimes supply disappointingly little information to the press, to Congress, or to the public on matters of executive agreements, vetoes, executive orders, complex arms sales, and how they raise campaign contributions. In the seemingly endless attempt to accentuate the positive, White House spin controllers too often have distorted news and thereby aggravated difficulties in credibility by claiming too much credit for fortuitous events or for policy initiatives that may or may not achieve sustained or desirable ends and by projecting the appearance of boldness, usually at the expense of candid discussions of the complexity of problems, the modesty of proposed solutions, and the realities of who must pay and how much.

A free society must mean a society based explicitly on free competition, most particularly competition in ideas and opinions, and by frank discussions of alternative national purposes and goals. Elected leaders and a vigorous press must ceaselessly attack ignorance, apathy, and mindless nationalism—the classic enemies of democracy. The citizen must resist sentimental patriotism that espouses everything as a matter for top priority but in practice eschews the tough political programs that must be implemented. Needed is a far more thoughtful way of looking at the presidency, leadership, and citizen responsibilities.

Also, Congress, the press, and the public must use existing political controls as a means to inspire as well as to check presidents. Citizens must insist presidents lend their voice and energies to those who are not represented by well-heeled lobbyists. Strengthening the have-not sectors of society and promoting opportunities for the nation's disadvantaged minorities will always remain major presidential responsibilities and an essential part of the legitimacy of the modern presidency.

We may want to change the presidency, yet *we* also must change. We must make the presidency work, but we must also strengthen Congress, modify public expectations and demands, and strengthen the party system. The interconnectedness of the American system—not the reform of one branch, but the reform of the American governmental system—should be the goal. And while ours is primarily a presidentially driven system, it is also a system driven by cooperation and engagement between the separate institutions that share power.

A precondition of making the separation of powers work better is the need to develop a *consensus* around particular governing ideas. This does not mean that all Americans must march in lockstep behind the will of the majority, nor does it mean that we must, or even can, come together on such issues as abortion, welfare, or prayer in school, but it does point to the need for a people joined together in common pursuit of the common good; a nation, not merely an aggregation of individuals. The routine division between Congress and president reflects not merely the institutional battles between two branches of government but also reflects deeper conflicts and divisions that divide the nation and its people.

Ideal conditions for presidential accountability are difficult to spell out, but the public should know what a president's priorities are, how they will be financed, who will gain and who will lose, and what the alternatives are. The public and its representatives in normal circumstances should be given a chance to evaluate presidential priorities and give their views. Where strong majorities exist, Congress should be able to compete with a president in shaping the nation's policy agenda. Substantial controversy exists, however, over the extent to which public opinion should shape or dictate presidential choices. Government by public opinion, however it is devised, can never guarantee justice or wisdom.

No one seriously proposes that a president's decisions should merely reflect majority opinion. The structure of the office in part reflects the desire of its designers to prevent presidents from being threatened or rushed into action by the shifting gusts of public passion. The definition of acceptable limits for presidential accountability will vary over time. If the standards for presidential accountability tilt too far in the direction either of public opinion or of independence and isolation, a president is less able to provide those subtle accommodating and mediating elements of leadership that are essential for effective democratic government. No task defines the essence of presidential leadership in a pluralistic society better than that of devising a workable and purposeful adjustment of the conflicting views of experts, elite groups, and the people as a whole.

With the proliferation of public opinion polls, presidents are barraged with nearly minute-by-minute CNN, Fox, and MSNBC reports on everything from "How is the president doing?" to the most trivial of minutiae. The time frame for presidential decision-making and problem-solving has been shortened. Issues cannot percolate up or ripen; problems cannot be debated, discussed, analyzed. Our instant-gratification culture wants immediate answers.

Although certain presidents have tried on occasion to govern without the benefit of public and partisan support, they seldom succeed. Presidents are in fact usually heavily influenced by their anticipation not only of the next election but also of tomorrow's headlines and editorials, next week's Gallup poll, next month's congressional hearings, and possible reprisals against their programs by Congress, the Supreme Court, the opposition party, and other institutions. In what other nation can a chief executive be overruled in the courts? A judicial check on a chief executive seldom exists in parliamentary systems if the leader retains his party's backing. In what other countries do the legions of newspapers, pamphleteers, tabloids, talk radio, and bulletin-board chat groups flourish with such tolerance and even encouragement?

One of the more confusing aspects of presidential accountability is the way the American people find it convenient to blame presidents for a whole range of problems, regardless of whether the problems have been subject to presidential control. We generally withhold our applause when a president's work is good, but we seldom fail to hiss presidential blunders. As noted earlier, no matter what presidents do, their popularity is likely to decline. When news is good, a president's popularity goes down or stays about the same; when news is bad, it merely goes down faster. Decline in approval of a president is in large part a function of the inability and unlikelihood of a president to live up to the buildup received during the presidential honeymoon.

Ultimately, being paradoxical does not make the presidency incomprehensible. Can we rid the presidency of all paradoxes? We couldn't, even if we wanted to do so. Nothing is wrong with some ambiguity. It is in embracing the paradoxical nature of the American presidency that we may be able to arrive at understanding. And with understanding may come enlightened or constructive criticism. This is the basis for citizen democracy.

The American presidency is a dynamic, not a static institution. While there are standard role expectations and responsibilities faced by all occupants of the office, such uniformity must be seen as the other side of the coin of the rich variety each president brings to the office. Each president brings a unique set of skills, experiences, goals, and styles to the presidency, yet the office and the requirements of the times place certain demands on every president. Each new president has to both emulate the master performances of Washington, Lincoln, and FDR, yet each must invent his or her own approach that will help build a better America. It is this mix of the unique and the expected that makes the presidency such a fascinating institution. Since all presidents are expected to "lead," how individual differences impact the institution often give us a clue of how well or poorly a president will perform.

In the end, presidents will be kept in line only if the people, according to their own personal views, exercise their rights and their political responsibilities. If the people insist both at and between elections that there be more respect for the doctrine of self-restraint, which all branches, including presidents, violate on occasion, it may happen.

James Madison was right. A constitutional democracy must insist on the effectiveness of our "auxiliary precautions"—Congress, parties, the courts, the press, the Bill of Rights, concerned citizen groups—if we are to have acceptable presidential leadership and preserve our constitutional democracy.

# *Notes*

CHAPTER 1

1. Barbara Tuchman, *The Distant Mirror* (New York: Knopf, 1978), p. xvii.

2. F. Scott Fitzgerald, *The Crack-Up* (New Directions, 1956), p. 69.

3. Erwin C. Hargrove, *The President as Leader: Appealing to the Better Angels of Our Nature* (University Press of Kansas, 1998), p. 49.

4. Alexis de Tocqueville, *Democracy in America,* Vol. II (Wordsworth Classics, 1998), Chapter 5, p. 359.

5. See Harvey C. Mansfield, Jr., "The Ambivalence of Executive Power," in Joseph Bessette and Jeffrey Tulis, eds., *The Presidency in the Constitutional Order* (Baton Rouge: Louisiana State University Press, 1981), pp. 314–33; and Walter Berns, "The American Presidency: Statesmanship and Constitutionalism in Balance," *Imprimis* (January 1983).

6. Lance Morrow, "Keeping up the Presidential Style," *Time* Magazine, June 15, 1981, p. 52.

7. William Davison Johnston, *TR, Champion of the Strenuous Life* (Theodore Roosevelt Association, 1958), p. 95.

8. Eugene Kennedy, "Political Power and American Ambivalence," *The New York Times Magazine,* March 19, 1978.

9. Richard M. Nixon, *Leaders* (New York: Warner Books, 1983), p. 341.

10. Saul Alinsky, *Rules for Radicals* (New York: Random House, 1971).

11. Michael Maccoby, *The Gamesman: The New Corporate Leaders* (New York: Simon & Schuster, 1976).

12. Alan Ehrenholt, "The Paradox of Corrupt Yet Effective Leadership," *The New York Times,* September 30, 2002, p. A23.

13. Robert J. Morgan, *A Whig Embattled: The Presidency under John Tyler* (University of Nebraska Press, 1954), p. 183.

14. James MacGregor Burns, *Roosevelt: The Lion and the Fox* (San Diego: A Harvest/HBJ Book, 1984).

15. Quoted in *U.S. News & World Report,* January 28, 1985, p. 40.

16. Editorial, "Presidents and Politics," *The Washington Star,* January 10, 1981.

17. Ibid.

**18.** Harold J. Laski, *The American Presidency* (New York: Harper & Brothers, 1940), pp. 34–35.

**19.** James MacGregor Burns, *Leadership* (New York: Harper & Row, 1978).

**20.** Bruce Miroff, *Pragmatic Illusions: The Presidential Politics of John F. Kennedy* (New York: David McKay, 1976), p. 31. See also Thomas E. Cronin, "John F. Kennedy: President and Politician" in Paul Harper and Joann P. Krieg, eds., *John F. Kennedy: The Promise Revisited* (Greenwood, 1988), pp. 1–21. For a somewhat similar treatment of several earlier presidents, see Richard Hofstadter, *The American Political Tradition* (New York: Vintage, 1948).

**21.** Arthur M. Schlesinger, Sr., *Paths to the Present* (Boston: Houghton Mifflin, 1964), p. 93.

**22.** See David H. Donald, *Lincoln* (New York: Simon & Schuster, 1995).

**23.** Laski, note 18, p. 93.

**24.** For interesting accounts of the Gulf War and the military efforts in Afghanistan by the two Bushes see Bob Woodward, *The Commanders* (Simon & Schuster, 1991) and Bob Woodward, *Bush at War* (Simon & Schuster, 2002).

**25.** John Keegan, *The Mask of Command* (New York: Penguin Books, 1987).

**26.** *Boston Globe,* January 7, 1976, p. 19.

**27.** Bob Woodward, *The Agenda: Inside the Clinton White House* (New York: Simon & Schuster, 1994), p. 165.

**28.** This is how one of our students put it in a class discussion a few years ago.

**29.** Former President Jimmy Carter, in a seminar at the U.S. Air Force Academy, August 26, 1985.

**30.** Stephen Skowronek, *The Politics Presidents Make: Leadership from John Adams to George Bush* (Cambridge: Belknap, 1993).

**31.** See J. David Greenstone, *The Lincoln Persuasion: Remaking American Liberalism* (Princeton: Princeton University Press, 1993).

**32.** Nelson Mandela, *Long Walk to Freedom* (Back Bay Books, 1993), p. 625.

## CHAPTER 2

**1.** Gerald M. Pomper, "The Presidential Election," in Gerald M. Pomper, ed., *The Election of 2000* (New York: Chatham House, 2003), chap. 6, p. 125.

**2.** See Pomper, ibid.; Jack N. Rakove, ed., *The Unfinished Election of 2000* (New York: Basic Books, 2001); and James Ceaser and Andrew Busch, *The Perfect Tie: The True Story of the 2000 Presidential Election* (Lanham, Md.: Roman and Littlefield, 2001).

**3.** Karlyn Bowman, "Do You Want to Be President?" *The Public Perspective* (February–March 1997), pp. 39–41.

**4.** Henry E. Brady, "Trust the People: Political Party Coalitions and the 2000 Election," in Jack N. Rakove, ed., *The Unfinished Election of 2000* (New York: Basic Books, 2001), pp. 67–68.

5. William R. Keech, "Selecting and Electing Presidents," in Thomas E. Cronin and Rexford G. Tugwell, eds., *The Presidency Reappraised* (New York: Praeger, 1977), p. 98.

6. Erwin Hargrove, "What Manner of Man?," in James David Barber, ed., *Choosing the President* (New York: Prentice-Hall, 1974), p. 19.

7. James David Barber, *The Presidential Character,* rev. ed. (New York: Prentice-Hall, 1992).

8. See an essay by Michael Nelson on "Presidential Character" in Leonard W. Levy and Louis Fisher, eds., *Encyclopedia of the American Presidency,* Volume 4 (New York: Simon & Schuster, 1994), pp. 1200–1202. See also the analysis of Barber's approach in Fred I. Greenstein, *The Presidential Difference: Leadership Style from FDR to Clinton* (New York: Free Press, 2000), pp. 253–56.

9. Martin Walker, book review of Robert Wilson's *Character Above All, The Washington Monthly* (April 1996), p. 54. See also Robert A. Wilson, ed., *Character Above All* (New York: Simon & Schuster, 1995).

10. On this point see Rexford G. Tugwell, *The Brains Trust* (New York: Viking, 1968), pp. 410, 423–24.

11. Emmett H. Buell, Jr., "The Invisible Primary," in William G. Mayer, ed., *In Pursuit of the Presidency* (Chatham N.J.: Chatham House, 1995).

12. See David B. Magleby, ed., *Financing the 2000 Election* (Washington, D.C.: The Brookings Institution, 2002); and Charles Lewis and the Center for Public Integrity, *The Buying of the President* (New York: Avon Books, 1996).

13. Quoted in *The Los Angeles Times,* February 2, 1995, p. E4.

14. Quoted in *The New York Times,* October 19, 1974, p. E18.

15. Jill Abramson and Thomas Petzinger, Jr., "Deja Vu: Big Political Donors Find Ways around Watergate Reforms," *Wall Street Journal,* June 11, 1992.

16. Michael Duffy, "The Money Chase," *Time* Magazine, March 13, 1995, p. 93.

17. Quoted in Jasper B. Shannon, *Money and Politics* (New York: Random House, 1959), p. 35.

18. Jane Mayer, "Inside the Money Machine," *The New Yorker,* February 3, 1997, pp. 32–37; and Anthony Corrado, "Financing the 1996 Elections," in Gerald Pomper, ed., *The Election of 1996* (Chatham, N.J.: Chatham House, 1997).

19. Scott Martelle, "'Soft Money' Became a Runaway Train This Election," *The Los Angeles Times,* December 11, 2000, p. A24. See also Magleby.

20. Arthur T. Hadley, *The Invisible Primary* (New York: Prentice-Hall, 1976), pp. 14–15. See also Richard Ben Cramer, *What It Takes* (New York: Random House, 1992); and Lou Dubose, Jan Reid, and Carl M. Cannon, *Boy Genius: Karl Rove, the Brains Behind the Remarkable Political Triumph of George W. Bush* (New York: Public Affairs Press, 2003).

21. A useful and balanced analysis can be found in William R. Keech and Donald R. Matthews, *The Party's Choice* (Washington, D.C.: Brookings, 1976). See also William J. Crotty, *Political Reform and the American Experiment* (Crowell, 1977), chap. 7.

22. See the provocative analysis in Robert D. Loevy, *The Flawed Path to the Presidency* (Albany, N.Y.: SUNY Press, 1995).

23. Quoted in Michael Kelly, "Glasshouse Conventions," *The New Yorker,* September 9, 1996, p. 39.

24. Robert T. Nakamura and Denis G. Sullivan, "Party Democracy and Democratic Control," in Walter Dean Burnham and Martha W. Weinberg, eds., *American Politics and Public Policy* (MIT Press, 1978), p. 33.

25. Ibid., p. 38. See also Denis G. Sullivan's review of the Kirkpatrick volume, *American Political Science Review* (September 1978), pp. 1068–69.

26. Edward R. Tufte, *Political Control of the Economy* (Princeton, N.J.: Princeton University Press, 1978), pp. 2–3.

27. Gerald Pomper, ed. *The Election of 2000* (New York: Chatham House, 2001), p. 141.

28. See Thomas E. Patterson, *The Vanishing Voter: Public Involvement in Our Age of Uncertainty* (New York: Alfred A. Knopf, 2002).

29. Robert A. Dahl, "Myth of the Presidential Mandate," *Political Science Quarterly* 105 (Fall 1990), pp. 355–72. But see also Patricia H. Conley, *Presidential Mandates: How Elections Shape the Natural Agenda* (Chicago: University of Chicago Press, 2001).

30. Jimmy Carter, comments at a meeting in Atlanta, March 26, 2001, quoted in Jack N. Rakove, "The E-College in the E-Age," in Jack N. Rakove, ed., *The Unfinished Election of 2000* (New York: Basic Books, 2001), p. 201.

31. See Jack N. Rakove, ibid., and Shlomo Slonim, "Designing the Electoral College," in Thomas E. Cronin, ed., *Inventing the American Presidency* (Lawrence: University Press of Kansas, 1989). See also Thomas E. Cronin, "Foreword: The Electoral College Controversy," in Judith A. Bast, ed., *The Choice of the People? Debating the Electoral College* (Lanham, Md.: Rowman and Littlefield, 1996), pp. vii–xxv.

32. Arthur Schlessinger, Jr., "The Electoral College Conundrum," *Wall Street Journal,* April 4, 1977. See also his "It's a Mess, But We're Been Through It Before," *Time* Magazine, November 20, 2000, p. 64.

33. Nelson W. Polsby and Aaron Wildavsky, *Presidential Elections,* 9th ed. (Chatham, N.J.: Chatham House, 1995), p. 3.

34. Stephen J. Wayne, "Let the People Vote Directly for President," in Stephen J. Wayne and Clyde Wilcox, eds., *The Quest for the White House* (New York: St. Martin's Press, 1992), pp. 313–14.

35. *Electing the President: A Report of the Commission on the Electoral College Reform* (Washington, D.C.: American Bar Association, January 1967), p. 3.

36. A strong case is made for the direct vote system in Lawrence D. Longley and Neal R. Peirce, *The Electoral College Primer 2000* (New Haven: Yale University Press, 1999). See also the helpful analyses in Paul D. Schumaker and Burdett A.

Loomis, eds., *Choosing a President: The Electoral College and Beyond* (New York: Chatham House, 2002).

37. See, for example, Douglas Amy, *Real Choices/New Voices: The Case for Proportional Representation in the United States* (New York: Columbia University Press, 1993); and Stephen J. Brown, *The Presidential Election Game* (New Haven: Yale University Press, 1978).

38. See William Keech, *Winner Take All: Report of the Twentieth Century Fund Task Force on Reform of the Presidential Election Process* (New York: Holmes and Meier, 1978). See also Thomas E. Cronin, "Choosing a President," *The Center Magazine,* September–October, 1978, pp. 5–15; and Thomas E. Cronin, "The Direct Vote and the Electoral College: The Case for Meshing Things Up!," *Presidential Studies Quarterly,* (Spring 1979), pp. 144–63.

39. Such a system was supported by a group called the Center for Voting and Democracy, as well as by the Ralph Nader inspired Public Interest Research Group. See www.votersdecide.com. Australia uses a similar system for its parliamentary elections, and Ireland uses it to elect their president, the ceremonial head of state.

## CHAPTER 3

1. Arthur M. Schlesinger, Jr., "The Ultimate Approval Rating," *The New York Times Magazine,* December 15, 1996, pp. 46–51. See also Steve Neal, "Putting Presidents in Their Place," *Chicago Sun-Times,* November 19, 1995, pp. 30–31. See also the special issue on presidential rankings in *White House Studies,* Vol. 3 No. 1, (Spring 2003).

2. See, for example, Marjorie Connelly, "Americans Are Still Voting for JFK," *The New York Times,* Sunday, August 18, 1996; and New York Times/CBS News Poll, July 11–13, 1996, "Presidential Favorites," from *The New York Times* poll watcher service.

3. See, for example, Forrest McDonald, *The American Presidency* (Lawrence: University Press of Kansas, 1994); and Sidney Milkis and Michael Nelson, *The American Presidency: Origins and Development,* 2d ed. (Washington, D.C.: Congressional Quarterly Press, 1994).

4. Roberta S. Sigel and David J. Butler, "The Public and the No Third Term Tradition: Inquiry into Attitudes toward Power," *Midwest Journal of Political Science* 8 (1964), p. 54.

5. Walter Berns, "The American Presidency: Statesmanship and Constitutionalism in Balance," *Imprimis* (January 1983), p. 3.

6. See David H. Donald, *Lincoln* (New York: Simon & Schuster, 1995), pp. 128–29.

7. See Max J. Skidmore, "Ranking and Evaluating Presidents: The Case of Theodore Roosevelt," *White House Studies,* Vol. 1, No. 4 (2001), pp. 495–504. Nathan Miller, *Theodore Roosevelt: A Life* (New York: Quill, 1992).

8. See Woodrow Wilson, *Constitutional Government in the United States* (New York: Columbia University Press, 1908). See also James Ceasar et al., "The Rise

of the Rhetorical Presidency," in Thomas E. Cronin, ed., *Rethinking the Presidency* (Boston: Little, Brown, 1982).

9. James L. Sundquist, *The Decline and Resurgence of Congress* (Washington, D.C.: Brookings, 1981), p. 33.

10. Jack Citrin and Donald Philip Green, "Presidential Leadership and the Resurgence of Trust in Government," *British Journal of Political Science* (October 1986), p. 450.

11. Stephen Skowronek, "Presidential Leadership in Political Time," in Michael Nelson, ed., *The Presidency and the Political System* (Washington, D.C.: C.Q. Press, 2003), p. 114. See also Stephen Skowronek, *The Politics Presidents Make: Leadership from John Adams to Bill Clinton* (Cambridge: Harvard University Press, 1997); and Erwin C. Hargrove and Michael Nelson, *Presidents, Politics, and Policy* (New York: Knopf, 1984).

12. Brian Newman, "Bill Clinton's Approval Ratings: The More Things Change, the More They Stay the Same," *Political Science Quarterly* (December, 2002), p. 797. See, in general, Joe Klein, *The Natural: The Misunderstood Presidency of Bill Clinton* (New York: Doubleday, 2002).

13. Haynes Johnson, *The Best of Times: America in the Clinton Years* (New York: Harcourt, 2001); and William C. Berman, *From the Center to the Edge: The Politics and Policies of the Clinton Presidency* (Lanham, Md.: Rowman and Littlefield, 2001).

14. John Steinbeck, *America and Americans* (Bonanza Books, 1966), p. 46.

15. Roberta S. Sigel, "Image of the American Presidency: Part II of an Exploration into Popular Views of Presidential Power," *Midwest Journal of Political Science* (February 1966), pp. 123–37.

16. William W. Welch, "Tax Cut Supporters Walking a Tightrope," *USA Today,* April 3, 1995, p. 10A.

17. Samuel Kernell, *Going Public: New Strategies of Presidential Leadership* (Washington, D.C.: Congressional Quarterly Press, 1986), p. 174.

18. Anthony Downs, "Up and Down with Ecology—the Issue Attention Cycles," *Public Interest* (September 1972), p. 38.

19. Paul Brace and Barbara Hinckley, *Follow the Leader: Opinion Polls and the Modern Presidents* (New York: Basic Books, 1992).

20. Richard E. Neustadt, *Presidential Power and the Modern Presidents* (New York: Free Press, 1990).

21. George C. Edwards, *Presidential Influence in Congress* (San Francisco: W.H. Freeman, 1980), pp. 86–100.

22. Quoted in George C. Edwards and Stephen Wayne, *Presidential Leadership,* 3rd ed. (New York: St. Martin's Press, 1994), p. 90.

23. Arthur M. Schlesinger, Jr., "The Ultimate Approval Rating," *The New York Times Magazine,* December 15, 1996, p. 51.

24. Jeffrey E. Cohen, *Presidential Responsiveness and Public Policy* (Ann Arbor: University of Michigan Press, 1997), p. 247.

**25.** In addition to Cohen, see Lawrence R. Jacobs and Robert Y. Shapiro, *Politicians Don't Pander: Political Manipulation and the Loss of Democratic Responsiveness* (Chicago: University of Chicago Press, 2000).

**26.** David W. Brady and Craig Volden, *Revolving Gridlock* (Boulder: Westview Press, 1998).

**27.** George Edwards, *The Public Presidency* (New York: St. Martin's Press, 1983), p. 233.

**28.** Ibid.

**29.** Kristen R. Monroe, *Presidential Popularity and the Economy* (New York: Praeger, 1984), pp. 145–46. But see also Samuel Kernell, "Explaining Presidential Popularity," *American Political Science Review* 72 (June 1978), pp. 506–22; and James A. Stimson, "Public Support for American Presidents," *Public Opinion Quarterly* 40 (1976), pp. 1–21.

**30.** Summaries of the literature on the impact of the economy can be found in Kernell, note 17, chap. 7; and Edwards, note 27, chap. 6.

**31.** Thomas E. Yantek, "Public Support for Presidential Performance: A Study of Macroeconomic Effects," *Polity* (Winter 1982), p. 278. For somewhat differing but parallel studies see Samuel Kernell, "The Presidency and the People" in Michael Nelson, ed., *The Presidency and the Political System* (Washington, D.C.: Congressional Quarterly Press, 1984), pp. 233–63. See Richard Brody, "Public Evaluations and Expectations and the Future of the Presidency," in James Young, ed., *Problems and Prospects of Presidential Leadership in the Nineteen Eighties,* vol. 1 (University Press of America, 1982), pp. 37–55; and Charles W. Ostrom, Jr., and Dennis M. Simon, "Promise and Performance: A Dynamic Model of Presidential Popularity," *American Political Science Review* (June 1985), pp. 334–58.

**32.** See William C. Berman, *From the Center to the Edge: The Politics and Policies of the Clinton Presidency* (Lanham, Md.: Rowman and Littlefield, 2001); and Joe Klein, *The Natural: The Much Misunderstood Presidency of Bill Clinton* (New York: Doubleday, 2002); and Brian Newman, note 12.

**33.** James W. Ceaser, "The Reagan Presidency and American Public Opinion," in Charles O. Jones, ed., *The Reagan Legacy: Promise and Performance* (Chatham, N.J.: Chatham House, 1988), p. 220.

**34.** But see the valuable analysis provided in Stanley A. Renshon, *The Psychological Assessment of Presidential Candidates* (Albany: New York University Press, 1996).

**35.** See Gary M. Maranell and Richard D. Dodder, "Political Orientation and the Evaluation of Presidential Prestige: A Study of American Historians," *Social Science Quarterly* (September 1970), p. 418. These authors found that conservatives rated Lincoln, Washington, and Jefferson slightly higher in prestige than did liberals, while the liberal "experts" not surprisingly rated FDR, Truman, Wilson, Jackson, and Kennedy somewhat more favorably than did the conservative experts. Authors who suggest the problem of the liberal bias in these polls are Thomas A. Bailey, *Presidential Greatness* (Appleton-Century, 1966), pp. 25–28; and Daniel Bratton, "The Rating of Presidents," *Presidential Studies Quarterly* (Summer 1983), pp. 400–4. See also the special issue of *White House Studies,* Vol. 3, No. 1. (Spring 2003).

**36.** James Lindgren, *Rating the Presidents of the United States, 1789–2000: A Survey of Scholars in History, Political Science, and Law* (Washington, D.C.: The Federalist Society, 2000), mimeographed report. See also James Lindgren and Steven Calabresi, "Ranking the Presidents," *The Wall Street Journal,* November 16, 2000, p. A26.

**37.** See Skowronek, note 11; and Richard Ellis and Aaron Wildavsky, *Dilemmas of Presidential Leadership* (New Brunswick, N.J.: Transaction Publishers, 1989).

**38.** Henry Steele Commager, *Parade Magazine,* May 8, 1977, p. 17. For an innovative effort by a political psychologist to examine this, see Dean Keith Simonton, *Why Presidents Succeed* (New Haven: Yale University Press, 1987).

**39.** Bailey, note 35, p. 292.

**40.** See James P. Pfiffner, "George Washington's Character and Slavery," *White House Studies,* Vol. 1, No. 4. (Winter 2001), pp. 451–61.

**41.** Bruce Miroff, *Icons of Democracy: Heroes, Aristocrats, Dissenters, and Democrats* (New York: Basic Books, 1993).

**42.** Schlesinger, note 23, p. 46.

**43.** See Steve Neal, "Putting Presidents in Their Places," *Chicago Sun-Times,* November 19, 1995, pp. 30–31.

**44.** Bailey, note 35, p. 259. Also see Simonton, note 38, chap. 6.

**45.** George F. Will "The Presidency in the American Political System," *Presidential Studies Quarterly* (Summer 1984), pp. 328–29. See also Garry Wills, "What Is Political Leadership?" *Atlantic Monthly* (April 1994), pp. 63–80.

**46.** Fred Greenstein, "What the President Means to Americans," in James D. Barber, ed., *Choosing the President* (New York: American Assembly, 1974), pp. 130–31.

**47.** Theodore J. Lowi, *The Personal President: Power Invested, Promise Unfulfilled* (Ithaca, N.Y.: Cornell University, 1985).

**48.** Brace and Hinckley, note 19, p. 1.

**49.** Michael B. Grossman and Martha Joynt Kumar, *Portraying the President* (Baltimore, Md.: Johns Hopkins University Press, 1981), pp. 255–63.

**50.** Michael J. Robinson et al., "With Friends Like These . . . ," *Public Opinion* (June/July 1983), pp. 2–3. See also James Fallows, *Breaking News: How the Media Undermine American Democracy* (New York: Vintage, 1997).

**51.** Larry Sabato, *Feeding Frenzy* (New York: Free Press, 1993), p. 1.

**52.** Joe Klein, *The Natural: The Misunderstood Presidency of Bill Clinton* (New York: Doubleday, 2002), p. 208.

**53.** See Martha Joynt Kumar, "Does This Constitute a Press Conference? Defining and Tabulating Modern Presidential Press Conferences," *Presidential Studies Quarterly* (March 2003), pp. 221–37.

**54.** John Maltese, *Spin Control: The White House Office of Communications and the Management of Presidential News* (Chapel Hill: University of North Carolina

Press, 1992). See also, for an inside view, Michael K. Deaver, *Behind the Scenes* (New York: William Morrow, 1987).

55. Kernell, note 17.

56. Mark Hertsgaard, *On Bended Knee: The Press and the Reagan Presidency* (New York: Schocken Brooks, 1988).

57. See series by David Shaw, *Los Angeles Times,* September 15, 16, and 17, 1993, for an examination of the media's treatment of the Clinton presidency.

58. Arthur M. Schlesinger, Jr., "Rating the Presidents: Washington to Clinton," *Political Science Quarterly* (Summer 1997), p. 186.

59. James MacGregor Burns, commentary at a Hofstra University conference on presidential rankings, published in *White House Studies,* Vol. 3, No. 1 (Spring 2003).

60. See Richard M. Pious, "Reflections of a Presidency Rater," *White House Studies,* Vol. 3, No. 1 (Spring, 2003).

## CHAPTER 4

1. Bruce Miroff, *Icons of Democracy: American Leaders as Heroes, Aristocrats, Dissenters, and Democrats* (New York: Basic Books, 1993).

2. Charles O. Jones, *The Presidency in a Separated System* (Washington, D.C.: Brookings, 1994).

3. Michael A. Genovese, *The Presidential Dilemma: Leadership in the American System,* 2d ed. (New York: Longman, 2003), chap. 2.

4. Samuel P. Huntington, *American Politics: The Promise of Disharmony* (Cambridge, Mass.: Harvard University Press, 1981), pp. 4, 33.

5. Clinton Rossiter, *Conservatism in America* (New York: Vintage, 1962), p. 72.

6. Max Lerner, *America as a Civilization* (New York: Knopf, 1957), p. 718.

7. Alexis de Tocqueville, *Democracy in America* (New York: Knopf, 1969), p. 430.

8. See Robert Bellah, Richard Masden, William Sullivan, Ann Swidel, and Steven Tipton, *Habits of the Heart* (New York: Harper & Row, 1985). Also see Arthur M. Schlesinger, Jr., *The Disuniting of America* (New York: Norton, 1991).

9. Warren Bennis, *Why Leaders Can't Lead: The Unconscious Conspiracy Continues* (San Francisco: Jossey-Bass Publishers, 1989), p. 46.

10. See Stephen Skowronek, *The Politics Presidents Make* (Cambridge, Mass.: Belknap Press, 1993).

11. Bert Rockman: *The Leadership Question: The Presidency and the American System* (New York: Praeger, 1984), p. 84.

12. Stephen Skowronek, "Presidential Leadership in Political Time," in Michael J. Nelson, ed., *The President and the Political System,* 3rd ed. (Washington: *Congressional Quarterly Press,* 1990), pp. 117–62.

13. Valerie Bunce, *Do New Leaders Make a Difference?* (Princeton, N.J.: Princeton University Press, 1981).

14. Paul C. Light, *The President's Agenda* (Baltimore, Md.: Johns Hopkins University Press, 1982).

15. Arthur M. Schlesinger, Jr., *The Cycles of American History* (Boston: Houghton Mifflin, 1986), pp. 22–27.

16. Ibid., p. 34.

17. See William W. Lammers and Michael A. Genovese, *The Presidency and Domestic Policy: Comparing Leadership Styles from FDR to Clinton* (Washington, D.C.: CQ Press, 2000), chap. 1. See also David Nathan, "President Eager to Test Agenda-Setting Power," *CQ Weekly* (January 25, 2003), pp. 180–89.

18. Many constitutional scholars contend that the framers were explicit in limiting and constraining governmental powers. See the useful collection of essays in David G. Adler and Larry George, eds., *The Constitution and the Conduct of Foreign Policy* (Lawrence: University Press of Kansas, 1996).

19. Edward S. Corwin, *The President: Office and Powers,* rev. ed. (New York: New York University Press, 1957).

20. de Tocqueville, note 7, p. 126.

21. Lyndon Johnson to Richard Nixon, quoted in Bobby Baker with Larry Nixon, *Wheeling and Dealing* (Norton, 1978), p. 265.

22. This work has gone through several revisions: Richard Neustadt, *Presidential Power. The Politics of Leadership with Reflections on Johnson and Nixon* (New York: Wiley & Sons, 1976). The latest edition (New York: Free Press, 1990) includes commentary up to and including the Reagan presidency. All quotes are drawn from the 1976 edition. See also Charles O. Jones, ed. *Preparing to be President: The Memos of Richard E. Neustadt* (Washington, D.C.: AEI Press, 2000); and Robert Y. Shapiro, et.al, eds., *Presidential Power: Forging the Presidency for the Twenty-First Century* (New York: Columbia University Press, 2000).

23. Ibid., p. 229.

24. Ibid., 230.

25. Ibid., p. 239.

26. Ibid., p. 33.

27. John Hart, "Presidential Power Revisited," *Political Studies* (March 1977), p. 56.

28. Charles E. Lindblom, "The Market as Prison," *The Journal of Politics* 44 (1982), pp. 324–36; and William F. Grover, *The President as Prisoner* (Albany, N.Y.: SUNY Press, 1989).

29. Bruce Miroff, *Pragmatic Illusions* (New York: David McKay, 1976).

30. Others make the case for strong presidents and a strong presidency because they see the possibilities of principled conservative leadership. One example is Terry Eastland's *Energy in the Executive: The Case for the Strong Presidency* (New York: Free Press, 1992).

31. Quoted in Henry Etzkowitz and Peter Schwab, eds., *Is America Necessary?* (West Publishing, 1976), p. 579.

32. Eastland, note 30; and L. Gordon Corvitz and Jeremy A. Rabkin, eds., *The Fettered Presidency: Legal Constraints on the Executive Branch* (Washington, D.C.: America Enterprise Institute, 1989). And Republican contenders for the (1996 and 2000 Republican nomination also saw the White House and the presidency as important tools to advance a conservative political agenda. But see also the helpful revisionist commentary on Neustadt's analysis by Fred Greenstein, *The Presidential Difference* (New York: Free Press, 2000), pp. 251–53.

33. Hedrick Smith, *The Power Game: How Washington Works* (New York: Ballantine, 1988).

34. Robert Shogan, *The Riddle of Power* (New York: Dutton, 1991), p. 5.

35. Robert A. Dahl, *Pluralist Democracy in the United States* (New York: Rand McNally, 1967), p. 90.

36. James P. Pfiffner, *The Strategic Presidency: Hitting the Ground Running,* 2d ed. (Lawrence: University Press of Kansas, 1996).

37. James MacGregor Burns, *Roosevelt: The Lion and the Fox* (San Diego: Harcourt Brace Jovanovich, 1956), p. 197. See also Ronald Heifetz, *Leadership without Easy Answers* (Cambridge, Mass.: Belknap Press, 1994).

38. Corwin, note 19.

39. John F. Kennedy, "Foreword" to Theodore C. Sorensen, *Decision-Making in the White House* (New York: Columbia University Press, 1963), p. xi. Kennedy's noted speechwriter maintained that vigorous presidential leadership with a strong Democratic party is the best prescription for solving our nation's problems. See Theodore C. Sorensen, *Why I Am a Democrat* (New York: Henry Holt, 1996).

40. Warren Bennis and Burt Nanus, *Leaders* (New York: Harper & Row, 1985), pp. 39 and 42. See also Warren Bennis and Patricia Ward Biederman, *Organizing Genius* (Reading, Mass.: Addison Wesley, 1997).

41. Lance Blakesley, *Presidential Leadership: From Eisenhower to Clinton* (Chicago: Nelson-Hall, 1995).

42. Quoted in Sidney Blumenthal, "The Education of a President," *The New Yorker,* January 24, 1994, p. 33.

43. Erwin C. Hargrove, "Presidential Personality and Leadership Style," in George C. Edwards, John H. Kessel, and Bert A. Rockman, eds., *Researching the Presidency: Vital Questions, New Approaches* (Pittsburgh: University of Pittsburgh Press, 1993), p. 70. See also Erwin C. Hargrove, *The President as Leader* (Lawrence: University Press of Kansas, 1998).

44. Ibid., p. 82.

45. For a view that suggests we should spend less time studying skill and more studying institutional pressures, see Terry M. Moe, "Presidents, Institutions, and Theory," in Edwards, Kessel, and Rockman, note 43, pp. 337–85.

46. Burns, note 37, p. 264.

**47.** See James David Barber's oft criticized but influential work, *The Presidential Character: Predicting Performance in the White House,* 4th ed. (Englewood Cliffs, N.J.: Prentice-Hall, 1992).

**48.** James P. Pfiffner, *The Managerial Presidency* (Pacific Grove, Calif.: Brooks/Cole, 1991).

**49.** Pfiffner, note 36, p. 4.

**50.** See James Perry, "For President Bush, the First 100 Days Offer Little to Provide Strength for Tough Times Ahead, Political Experts Contend," *Wall Street Journal,* April 28, 1989. But see retired President George H.W. Bush's retrospective and, not surprisingly, more positive view, "An Interview with Former President George Bush," *Parade Magazine,* December 1, 1996, pp. 4–6.

**51.** David Gray Adler and Michael A. Genovese, eds. *The Presidency and the Law: The Clinton Legacy* (Lawrence: University Press of Kansas, 2002).

**52.** James Bryce, *The American Commonwealth,* vol. 2 (New York: MacMillan & Co., 1888), p. 460.

**53.** Benjamin R. Barber, "Neither Leaders nor Followers: Citizenship under Strong Democracy," in Michael R. Beschloss and Thomas E. Cronin, eds., *Essays in Honor of James MacGregor Burns* (Englewood Cliffs, N.J.: Prentice-Hall, 1989), pp. 117–32.

**54.** Miroff, note 1, p. 1.

**55.** Arthur M. Schlesinger, Jr., *The Cycles of American History* (Boston: Houghton Mifflin, 1986), p. 430. See also how several authors wrestle with this enduring tension in David G. Adler and Larry George, eds., *The Constitution and the Conduct of Foreign Policy* (Lawrence: University Press of Kansas, 1996).

**56.** Willard Sterne Randall, *Thomas Jefferson: A Life* (New York: Henry Holt, 1993). See also Merrill D. Peterson, ed., *The Portable Thomas Jefferson* (New York: Viking Press, 1975).

**57.** Jimmy Carter, "Prayer and Civic Religion," *The New York Times,* December 29, 1996, p. A13.

## CHAPTER 5

**1.** For an examination of these conflicting views, see Charles Beard, *An Economic Interpretation of the Constitution* (New York: Macmillan, 1913); and Robert E. Brown, *Charles Beard and the Constitution* (Princeton, N.J.: Princeton University Press, 1956). See also Leonard W. Levy, *Original Intent and the Frames' Constitution* (New York: Macmillan, 1988).

**2.** Alexander Hamilton, James Madison, and John Jay, *The Federalist Papers, No. 51* (New York: New American Library, 1961), p. 322.

**3.** Madison, *The Federalist Papers, No. 45,* Hamilton, *The Federalist Papers, No. 70,* respectively.

**4.** Edward S. Corwin, *The President: Office and Powers, 1978–1984,* 5th ed. (New York: New York University Press, 1984; originally published in 1940). See also

Joseph M. Bessette and Jeffrey Tulis, *The Presidency in the Constitutional Order* (Baton Rouge: Louisiana State University Press, 1981); and Louis Fisher, *The Constitution between Friends* (New York: St. Martin's Press, 1978).

**5.** James P. Pfiffner, *The Modern Presidency* (New York: St. Martin's Press, 1993), p. 13.

**6.** For a history of the presidency, see Michael A. Genovese, *The Power of the American Presidency: 1789–2000* (New York: Oxford University Press, 2001).

**7.** Glenn A. Phelps, *George Washington and American Constitutionalism* (Lawrence: University Press of Kansas, 1993). See also Garry Wills, *Cincinnatus: George Washington and the Enlightenment* (Garden City, N.Y.: Doubleday, 1984).

**8.** Leonard White, *The Federalists: A Study in Administrative History* (New York: Macmillan, 1967), p. 99.

**9.** Stephen Showronek, *The Politics Presidents Make: Leadership from John Adams to George Bush* (Cambridge, Mass.: Belknap Press of Harvard University Press, 1993).

**10.** Willard Sterne Randall, *Thomas Jefferson: A Life* (New York: Henry Holt, 1993).

**11.** Robert V. Remini, *Andrew Jackson* (New York: Harper & Row, 1966).

**12.** Herman Belz, *Lincoln and the Constitution: The Dictatorship Question Reconsidered* (Fort Wayne, Ind.: Louis A. Warren Lincoln Library and Museum, 1984); James G. Randall, *Constitutional Problems under Lincoln,* rev. ed. (Urbana: University of Illinois Press, 1951); and David Donald, *Lincoln* (New York: Simon & Schuster, 1995).

**13.** Jeffrey K. Tulis, *The Rhetorical Presidency* (Princeton, N.J.: Princeton University Press, 1987).

**14.** Theodore Roosevelt, *The Autobiography of Theodore Roosevelt* (New York: Charles Scribner's Sons, 1941), pp. 197–98.

**15.** Arthur S. Link, *Wilson and the New Freedom* (Princeton N.J.: Princeton University Press, 1956); and Hendrick A. Clements, *The Presidency of Woodrow Wilson* (Lawrence: University Press of Kansas, 1992).

**16.** William E. Leuchtenburg, *In the Shadow of FDR: From Harry Truman to Ronald Reagan* (Ithaca, N.Y.: Cornell University Press, 1983). See also the revisionist discussions in Raymond Tatalovich and Thomas S. Engeman, "The Emerging Scholarly Consensus on Presidential Leadership: A New Realism, and Old Idealism" *White House Studies,* Vol. 2., No. 2 (2002), pp. 123–37.

**17.** Fred I. Greenstein, *The Hidden-Hand Presidency: Eisenhower as Leader* (New York: Basic Books, 1982).

**18.** Clinton Rossiter, *The American Presidency* (New York: Harcourt, Brace & World, 1956).

**19.** Ibid., p. 251.

**20.** Alfred DeGrazia, *Congress and the Presidency* (Washington, D.C.: American Enterprise Institute, 1967) and *Republic in Crisis: Congress against the Executive Force* (New York: Federal Legal Publications, 1965).

**21.** George Will, "The Veep and the Blatherskite," *Newsweek,* June 29, 1992, p. 72.

**22.** Sir Michael Howard, "Smoke on the Horizon," *Financial Times* (London) September 6, 2002, p. 16.

**23.** Editorial, *The New York Times,* September 22, 2002, p. 12.

**24.** See Spencer Ackerman and John B. Judis, "The First Casualty: The Selling of the Iraq War," *The New Republic* 228 (June 2003), pp. 14–25.

**25.** John F. Kennedy, quoted in Richard Nixon, *RN: Memoirs of Richard Nixon* (Grosset & Dunlap, 1978), p. 235.

**26.** See the discussion in Michael R. Beschloss and Strobe Talbott, *At the Highest Levels: The Inside Story of the End of the Cold War* (Boston: Little, Brown, 1993), pp. 463–74.

**27.** Richard Nixon, quoted in Theodore White, *The Making of the President 1968* (Atheneum, 1969), p. 147.

**28.** Leonard Garment, quoted in White, note 27, p. 52.

**29.** Aaron Wildavsky, "The Two Presidencies," *Trans-Action* (December 1996), in Widavsky, ed., *Perspectives on the Presidency* (Boston: Little, Brown, 1975), p. 7. See also Barbara Kellerman and Ryan J. Barilleaux, *The President as World Leader* (New York: St. Martin's Press, 1991); and Cecil V. Crabb and Kevin V. Mulcahy, *American National Security* (Pacific Grove, Calif.: Brooks/Cole, 1991).

**30.** See Ryan C. Hendrickson, *The Clinton Wars: The Constitution, Congress, and War Powers* (Nashville: Vanderbilt University Press, 2002); and David G. Adler and Larry George, eds., *The Constitution and the Conduct of Foreign Policy* (Lawrence: University Press of Kansas, 1996).

**31.** But see Louis Fisher, *Presidential War Power* (Lawrence: Universty Press of Kansas, 1995).

**32.** Jon R. Bond and Richard Fleisher, *The President in the Legislative Arena* (Chicago: University of Chicago Press, 1990), p. 171. See also David P. Forsythe and Ryan C. Henderson, "U.S. Use of Force Abroad: What Law for the President?" *Presidential Studies Quarterly* (Fall 1996), pp. 950–61.

**33.** Marcia Lynn Whicker, James P. Pfiffner, and Raymond A. Moore, eds., *The Presidency and the Persian Gulf War* (Westport, Conn.: Praeger, 1993).

**34.** See Bob Woodward, *Bush at War* (New York: Simon and Schuster, 2002).

**35.** For a full examination of the presidency and crisis management, see Graham T. Allison, *Essence of Decision: Explaining the Cuban Missile Crisis* (Boston: Little Brown, 1971); Alexander L. George, *Presidential Decision-making in Foreign Policy: The Effective Use of Information and Advice* (Boulder, Colo.: Westview, 1980); and Alexander L. George, *Avoiding War: Problems of Crisis Management* (Boulder, Colo.: Westview, 1991).

**36.** Thomas S. Langston, *With Reverence and Contempt: How Americans Think about Their President* (Baltimore: Johns Hopkins University Press, 1995).

**37.** Richard Brookhiser, *Founding Father: Rediscovering Washington* (New York: Free Press, 1996). See also Garry Wills, note 7.

**38.** Barry Schwartz, *George Washington: The Making of an American Symbol* (New York: Free Press, 1987).

**39.** Clinton Rossiter, *The American Presidency* (New York: Mentor Books, 1960), pp. 102–3.

**40.** Bruce Miroff, "Abraham Lincoln: Democratic Leadership and the Tribe of the Eagle," in Miroff, *Icons of Democracy: American Leaders as Heroes, Aristocrats, Dissenters, and Democrats* (New York: Basic Books, 1993). See also David Donald's account in *Lincoln* (New York: Simon & Schuster, 1995).

**41.** On the impact and significance of Lincoln's celebrated Gettysburg address, see Garry Wills, *Lincoln at Gettysburg: The Words That Remade America* (New York: Simon & Schuster, 1992).

**42.** Quoted in Arthur M. Schlesinger, Jr., *A Thousand Days* (Boston: Houghton Mifflin, 1965), p. 127.

**43.** See Irving I. Janis, *Victims of Groupthink* (Boston: Houghton Mifflin, 1972).

**44.** G. Calvin Mackenzie, "The Politics of the Appointment Process," mimeo, 1977, pp. 66–67. See also F. V. Malek, *Washington's Hidden Tragedy* (New York: Free Press, 1978), chap. 4.

**45.** Benjamin Ginsberg and Martin Shefter, *Politics by Other Means* (New York: Basic Books, 1990), pp. 164–65.

**46.** See, for example, Charles O. Jones, *The Presidency in a Separated System* (Washington, D.C.: Brookings, 1994).

**47.** Two classic studies of implementation are Jeffrey Pressman and Aaron Wildavsky, *Implementation* (University of California Press, 1973); and Eugene Bavdach, *The Implementation Game* (Cambridge: MIT Press, 1977).

**48.** Marver Bernstein, "The Presidency and Management Improvement," *Law and Contemporary Problems* (Summer 1970), p. 516. See also Otis I. Graham, Jr., *Toward a Planned Society: From Roosevelt to Nixon* (Oxford University Press, 1976).

**49.** Hugh Heclo, *A Government of Strangers* (Washington, D.C.: Brookings, 1977).

## CHAPTER 6

**1.** James S. Young, *The Washington Community, 1800–1828* (New York: Columbia University Press, 1966), pp. 75–76.

**2.** James A. Thurber, ed., *Rivals for Power: Presidential-Congressional Relations* (Washington, D.C.: Congressional Quarterly Press, 1996).

**3.** Emmet John Hughes, *The Living Presidency* (New York: Coward, McCann & Geoghegan, 1973), p. 208.

**4.** Jon R. Bond and Richard Fleisher, *The President in the Legislative Arena* (Chicago: University of Chicago Press, 1990).

**5.** Robert J. Spitzer, *President and Congress: Executive Hegemony at the Crossroads of American Government* (New York: McGraw-Hill, 1993), p. xx.

6. Lance T. LeLoup and Steven A. Shull, *Congress and the President: The Policy Connection* (Belmont, Calif.: Wadsworth, 1993).

7. Clinton Rossiter, *The American Presidency* (New York: Harcourt, Brace & World, 1980), p. 26.

8. Roger H. Davidson, "The Presidency and Congress," in Michael Nelson, ed., *The Presidency and the Political System* (Washington, D.C.: Congressional Quarterly Press, 1984), pp. 363–91.

9. George C. Edwards III, *At the Margins: Presidential Leadership of Congress* (New Haven, Conn.: Yale University Press, 1989).

10. *Youngstown Sheet and Tube Co. v. Sawyer,* 343 U.S. 579, 635 (1952).

11. Jean Edward Smith, *George Bush's War* (New York: Henry Holt, 1992). See also Bob Woodward, *The Commanders* (New York: Simon & Schuster, 1991).

12. Anthony Lewis, "'On His Word Alone,'" *The New York Times,* January 12, 1992, p. E19. See also several of the essays in David G. Adler and Larry George, *The Constitution and the Conduct of Foreign Policy* (Lawrence: University Press of Kansas, 1996).

13. Jane Mayer and Jill Abramson, *Strange Justice: The Selling of Clarence Thomas* (New York: Plume, 1995); and John Danforth, *Resurrection: The Confirmation of Clarence Thomas* (New York: Free Press, 1994).

14. David Rogers and Jackie Calmes, "Thomas Is Confirmed by Senate," *The Wall Street Journal,* October 16, 1991, p. A18.

15. David Nathan, "President Eager to Test Agenda-Setting Power," *CQ Weakly,* (January 25, 2003), pp. 180–189.

16. Lester G. Seligman and Cary R. Covington, *The Coalitional Presidency* (Chicago: Dorsey Press, 1989).

17. Roger H. Davidson and Walter J. Oleszik, *Congress and Its Members,* 5th ed. (Washington, D.C.: Congressional Quarterly Press, 1996), p. 289. See also Mark A. Peterson, *Legislating Together* (Cambridge, Mass.: Harvard University Press, 1990); and David Mayhew, *Divided We Govern* (New Haven, Conn.: Yale University Press, 1991).

18. Edwards, note 9; Bond and Fleisher, note 4.

19. Paul Brace and Barbara Hinckley, *Follow the Leader* (New York: Basic Books, 1992); see Douglas Rivers and Nancy Rose, "Passing the President's Program: Public Opinion and Presidential Influence in Congress," *American Journal of Political Science* 29 (May 1985), 183–96; and Richard Brody, *Assessing the President: The Media, Elite Opinion, and Public Support* (Stanford, Calif.: Stanford University Press, 1991), p. 21.

20. Bond and Fleisher, note 4, p. 218; Edwards, note 9; and Aage R. Clausen, *How Congressmen Decide: A Policy Focus* (New York: St. Martin's Press, 1973).

21. Terry Sullivan, "Headcounts, Expectations, and Presidential Coalitions in Congress," *American Journal of Political Science* 32:(3) (August 1988), pp. 567–89.

22. Edwards, note 9, p. 216.

**23.** Rowland Evans and Robert Novak, *Lyndon B. Johnson: The Exercise of Power* (New York: New American Library, 1966), p. 104. See also, for a study of Johnson as a senate leader, Robert A. Caro, *Master of the Senate* (New York: Knopf, 2002).

**24.** Douglas Jehl, "Clinton Assails G.O.P. Delays in Bitter Tones," *The New York Times,* July 27, 1993, p. 1.

**25.** See Mark A. Peterson, *Legislating Together* (Cambridge, Mass.: Harvard University Press, 1990).

**26.** On the veto power, see Robert Spitzer, *The Presidential Veto* (Albany, N.Y.: SUNY Press, 1988).

**27.** Barbara Hinkson Craig, *The Legislative Veto* (Boulder, Colo.: Westview Press, 1983).

**28.** 77 I. Ed 2d 317 (1983).

**29.** Daniel P. Franklin, "Why the Legislative Veto Isn't Dead," *Presidential Studies Quarterly* (Summer 1986), p. 499.

**30.** Louis Fisher, quoted in Martin Tolchin, "The Legislative Veto, an Accommodation That Goes On and On," *The New York Times,* March 31, 1989, p. A8. See also Louis Fisher, *Constitutional Dialogues: Interpretation as Political Process* (Princeton, N.J.: Princeton University Press, 1988).

**31.** Leonard W. Levy, *Original Intent and the Framers' Constitution* (New York: Macmillan, 1988), p. 30.

**32.** Stephen A. Ambrose, "The Presidency and Foreign Affairs," *Foreign Affairs* (Winter 1991–92), p. 137.

**33.** Ibid., p. 136.

**34.** Arthur M. Schlesinger, Jr., *The Imperial Presidency* (Boston: Houghton Mifflin, 1973).

**35.** On the importance of executive orders and similar direct presidential actions, see Phillip J. Cooper, *By Order of the President* (Lawrence: University Press of Kansas, 2002); and Kenneth R. Mayer, *With The Stroke of a Pear* (Princeton, N.J.: Princeton University Press, 2001).

**36.** Leonard C. Meeker, "The Legality of U.S. Participation in the Defense of Vietnam," *Department of State Bulletin,* March 28, 1966, pp. 484–85.

**37.** See James Sundquist, *The Decline and Resurgence of Congress* (Washington, D.C.: Brookings Institution, 1981).

**38.** John Hart Ely, *War and Responsibility* (Princeton, N.J.: Princeton University Press, 1993); and Louis Fisher, *Presidential War Power* (Lawrence: University Press of Kansas, 1995).

**39.** Ronald Reagan, quoted in Christopher Madison, "Despite His Complaints Reagan Going Along with Spirit of War Powers Law," *National Journal,* May 19, 1984, p. 990.

**40.** President George H.W. Bush to Congress, January 11, 1991, reprinted in *Congressional Quarterly,* January 12, 1991, p. 70.

**41.** Michael Ross, "House Defeats GOP Effort to Kill War Powers Act," *Los Angeles Times,* June 8, 1995, p. A4.

**42.** Senator Leverett Saltonstall (R-Mass.), quoted in Henry Howe Ransom, *The Intelligence Establishment* (Cambridge, Mass.: Harvard University Press, 1970), p. 169.

**43.** Stansfield Turner, *Secrecy and Democracy: The CIA in Transition* (Boston: Houghton Mifflin, 1985).

**44.** See, for example, Bob Woodward, *Veil: The Secret Wars of the CIA* (New York: Simon & Schuster, 1987).

**45.** Bill Bradley, "Congress at Its Worst," *The Washington Post National Weekly Edition,* October 28, 1985, p. 29. See Warren Rudman's vivid personal account of it in Rudman, *Combat: Twelve Years in the U.S. Senate* (New York: Random House, 1996), chap. 2.

**46.** James A. Thurber, "The Impact of Budget Reform on Governance," in Thurber, ed., *Divided Democracy* (Washington, D.C.: Congressional Quarterly Press, 1991), p. 167. See also John B. Gilmour, *Reconcilable Differences: Congress, the Budget Process and the Deficit* (Berkeley: University of California Press, 1990).

**47.** Christopher J. Deering, "Damned if You Do and Damned if You Don't: The Senate's Role in the Appointment Process," in G. Calvin MacKenzie, ed., *The In-and-Outers: Presidential Appointees and the Problems of Transient Government in Washington* (Baltimore, Md.: Johns Hopkins Press, 1987), chap. 5.

**48.** Stephen L. Carter, *The Confirmation Mess* (New York: Basic Books, 1994).

**49.** John Massaro, *Supremely Political: The Role of Ideology and Presidential Management in Unsuccessful Supreme Court Nominations* (Albany, N.Y.: SUNY, 1990).

**50.** Stephen L. Elkin, "Contempt of Congress: The Iran-Contra Affair, and the American Constitution," *Congress and the Presidency* 18 (1) (Spring 1991), p. 3.

**51.** Lloyd Cutler, "Party Government under the Constitution," in Donald L. Robinson, ed., *Reforming American Government: The Bicentennial Papers of the Committee on the Constitutional System* (Boulder, Colo.: Westview Press, 1985); and Donald L. Robinson, *To the Best of My Ability: The Presidency and the Constitution* (New York: Norton, 1987).

**52.** James L. Sundquist, *Constitutional Reform and Effective Government* (Washington, D.C.: Brookings, 1986), p. 15.

**53.** Ibid., p. 135.

**54.** Ibid., p. 203–4.

**55.** Ibid., p. 205.

**56.** James M. Burns, *The Power to Lead: The Crisis of the American Presidency* (New York: Simon & Schuster, 1984), p. 117. See also James MacGregor Burns and Georgia J. Sorenson, *Dead Center: Clinton-Gore Leadership and the Perils of Moderation* (New York: Scribners 1999)

**57.** See the analysis and critique of Burns's proposal in Thomas E. Cronin, "James MacGregor Burns and the Idea of a Vigorous, Programmatic, Partisan, Yet

Accountable Presidency," in Michael R. Beschloss and Thomas E. Cronin, eds., *Essays in Honor of James MacGregor Burns* (Englewood Cliffs, N.J.: Prentice-Hall, 1989), pp. 38–65.

## CHAPTER 7

1. James W. Davis, *The President as Party Leader* (New York: Praeger, 1993), pp. ix–x.

2. Robert V. Remini, "The Emergence of Political Parties and Their Effect on the Presidency" in Philip C. Dolce and George H. Skau, eds., *Power and the Presidency* (New York: Scribners, 1976), p. 32.

3. Ibid., p. 33. See also Robert Remini, *Martin Van Buren and the Democratic Party* (New York: Columbia University Press, 1959).

4. Quoted in Arthur B. Tourtellot, *The Presidents on the Presidency* (New York: Doubleday, 1964), p. 387.

5. Ibid., p. 5.

6. Michael Duffy and Dan Goodgame, *Marching in Place: The Status Quo Presidency of George Bush* (New York: Simon & Schuster, 1992).

7. See Lou Dubose, Jan Reid, and Carl M. Cannon, *Boy Genius: Karl Rove, the Brains Behind the Remarkable Political Triumph of George W. Bush* (New York: Public Affairs, 2003).

8. See Thomas E. Patterson, *The Vanishing Voter* (New York: Knopf, 2002). See also Ray A. Teixeira, *The Disappearing American Voter* (Washington D.C.-Brookings Institution, 1992).

9. Roger G. Brown and David M. Welborn, "Presidents and their Parties: Performance and Prospects," *Presidential Studies Quarterly* 12 (3) (Summer 1982).

10. Robert Harmel, "President-Party Relations in the Modern Era: Past, Problems, and Prognosis," in Harmel, ed., *Presidents and Their Parties: Leadership or Neglect* (New York: Praeger, 1984), p. 250.

11. Arthur Schlesinger, Jr., "Crisis of the Party System, I," *Wall Street Journal,* May 10, 1979, editorial page.

12. See David Frum, "It's His Party," *The New York Times,* January 5, 2003, p. 11

13. Sidney M. Milkis, *The President and the Parties* (New York: Oxford University Press, 1993).

14. See also Kay Lawson, "Party Renewal and American Democracy," in Michael R. Beschloss and Thomas E. Cronin, eds., *Essays in Honor of James MacGregor Burns* (Englewood Cliffs, N.J.: Prentice-Hall, 1989); and James MacGregor Burns, *The Power to Lead: The Crisis of the American Presidency* (New York: Simon & Schuster, 1984).

15. See David Magelby, ed., *Financing the 2000 Election* (Washington, D.C.: Brookings Institution, 2002).

16. Austin Ranney, *The Federalization of Presidential Primaries* (Washington, D.C.: American Enterprise Institute, 1978), p. 39.

**17.** See Martin Wattenberg, *The Decline of American Parties, 1952–1980* (Cambridge, Mass.: Harvard University Press, 1984).

**18.** Quoted in Donald Robinson, "Cleaning Up Campaigns: How to Reform Election Finances Without Hurting Political Parties," *Chronicle of Higher Education,* December 20, 1996, p. 134.

## CHAPTER 8

**1.** David Gray Adler and Michael A. Genovese, eds., *The Presidency and the Law: The Clinton Legacy* (Lawrence: University Press of Kansas, 2002).

**2.** See, for example, Albert R. Hunt, "Symmetry in Judicial Nominations," *Wall Street Journal,* February 20, 2003, p. A13.

**3.** Terry Eastland, *Energy in the Executive: The Case for the Strong Presidency* (New York: Free Press, 1992), p. 235.

**4.** Selections from the *Correspondence of Theodore Roosevelt and Henry Cabot Lodge, 1884–1918* (New York: Charles Scribner's Sons, 1925), vol. 2, p. 519. For a good study of President Harding's appointment of a Supreme Court justice, see David J. Danelski, *A Supreme Court Justice Is Appointed* (New York: Random House, 1964).

**5.** Henry J. Abraham, *Justices and Presidents: A Political History of Appointments to the Supreme Court,* 2d ed. (New York: Oxford University Press, 1985), p. 65. See also Robert J. Steamer, *Chief Justice: Leadership and the Supreme Court* (Columbia: University of South Carolina Press, 1986). For a useful study of Lyndon B. Johnson's criteria and political decision making in the appointment of judges, see Neil D. McFeeley, *Appointment of Judges: The Johnson Years* (Austin: University of Texas, 1987), esp. chaps. 5 and 6.

**6.** Stephen L. Carter, *The Confirmation Mess* (New York: Basic Books, 1994).

**7.** Jane Mayer and Jill Abramson, *Strange Justice: The Selling of Clarence Thomas* (New York: Houghton Mifflin, 1994); and John C. Danforth, *Resurrection: The Confirmation of Clarence Thomas* (New York: Viking, 1994). For a reaction to both the Bork and Thomas nominations, see Carter, note 5.

**8.** Quoted in David G. Savage, "Bush's Judicial Nominations Go 28 for 80 in the Senate," *The Los Angeles Times,* December 31, 2002, p. A12.

**9.** James Gerstenzang, "Bush Urges Judicial Process Changes," *The Los Angeles Times,* October 31, 2002, p. A10.

**10.** *Brown v. Board of Education,* 347 U.S. 483 (1954).

**11.** Stephen E. Ambrose, *Eisenhower: The President* (New York: Simon & Schuster, 1984), p. 90. See also the oral history of top Eisenhower aide Sherman Adams, conducted for Columbia University, April 11, 1967, vol. 2 of 4, p. 121. Eisenhower Library, Abilene, Kansas.

**12.** Robert Scigliano, *The Supreme Court and the Presidency* (New York: Free Press, 1971), pp. 146–47. Another study concludes that most presidents by and large do rather well in appointing individuals who will be supportive of the administration that supports them, at least during their first few years on the Court. "After that initial period, there is an apparent falling off." See Roger Handberg and Harold F. Hill, Jr., "Predicting the Judicial Performance of Presidential Appointments to the United States Supreme Court," *Presidential Studies Quarterly* (Fall 1984), pp. 538–47.

13. *Marbury v. Madison,* 5 U.S. (1 Crouch) 137 (1803); *Ex-parte Milligan,* 4 Wall. 2 (1966); *Youngstown Sheet and Tube Co. v. Sawyer,* 343 U.S. 579 (1952); and *U.S. v. Nixon,* 418 U.S. 683 (1974).

14. Robert H. Jackson, *The Struggle for Judicial Supremacy* (New York: Vintage, 1941), p. 314.

15. Scigliano, note 12, p. 159. This view is echoed in David M. O'Brien, *Storm Center: The Supreme Court in American Politics* (New York: Norton, 1986), chap. 2.

16. Quoted in *Time* magazine, May 23, 1969, p. 24.

17. *Dred Scott v. Sandford,* 60 U.S. (19 How.) 393 (1856).

18. *Ex-parte Merryman,* 17 Fed. Case No. 9487 (1861). See also on this clash, David M. Silver, *Lincoln's Supreme Court* (Urbana: University of Illinois Press, 1957).

19. Clinton Rossiter, *The Supreme Court and the Commander in Chief* (Ithaca, N.Y.: Cornell University Press, 1951), p. 25. See also the interesting political theory interpretation offered in Brian F. Danhoff, "Lincoln, Machiavalli and American Political Thought," *Presidential Studies Quarterly* (June 2000), pp. 290–311.

20. Richard N. Current, "The Lincoln Presidents," *Presidential Studies Quarterly* (Winter 1979), p. 32. See also Arthur M. Schlesinger, Jr., *The Imperial Presidency* (Boston: Houghton Mifflin, 1973), pp. 64–67; and J. G. Randall, *Constitutional Problems under Lincoln,* rev. ed. (Urbana: University of Illinois Press 1951), pp. 513–22. For a broader context, see David Donald, *Lincoln* (New York: Simon & Schuster, 1995).

21. Robert H. Jackson, *The Struggle for Judicial Supremacy* (New York: Vintage, 1941).

22. Philip Abbott, *The Exemplary Presidency: Franklin D. Roosevelt and the American Political Tradition,* chap. 7, "They Have Retired into the Judiciary" (Amherst: University of Massachusetts Press, 1990).

23. David Gray Adler, "Court, Constitution, and Foreign Affairs," in Adler and Larry George, eds., *The Constitution and the Conduct of American Foreign Policy* (Lawrence: University Press of Kansas, 1996), p. 25.

24. David J. Danelski, "The Saboteurs' Case," *Journal of Supreme Court History* 1 (1996), p. 80. (Complete essay pp. 61–82.)

25. *Korematsu v. United States,* 323 U.S. 214 (1944).

26. See the discussion of Truman's plight in this case in Robert J. Donovan, *Tumultuous Years: The Presidency of Harry S. Truman, 1949–1953* (New York: Norton, 1982), pp. 382–91. Also see Maeva Marcus, *Truman and the Steel Seizure Case: The Limits of Presidential Power* (New York: Columbia University Press, 1977);

and Alan Westin, *The Anatomy of a Constitutional Law Case* (New York: Macmillan, 1958).

27. Bill Clinton acted in this manner on many occasions. See Ryan C. Hendrickson, *The Clinton Wars: The Constitution, Congress, and War Power* (Nashville: Vanderbilt University Press, 2002); and Louis Fisher, "The Law: Legal Disputes in the Clinton Years," *Presidential Studies Quarterly* (September 1999), pp. 697–707.

28. Stanley K. Kutler, *The Wars of Watergate* (New York: Knopf, 1990); and Fred Emery, *Watergate* (New York: Touchstone, 1995).

29. Theodore Draper, *A Very Thin Line: The Iran-Contra Affair* (New York: Touchstone Books, 1991); Jane Mayer and Doyle McManus, *Landslide: The Unmaking of the President, 1984–1988* (Boston: Houghton Mifflin, 1988); and Lawrence E. Walsh, *Firewall: The Iran-Contra Conspiracy and Cover-up* (New York: Norton, 1997).

30. Nancy V. Baker, *Conflicting Loyalties: Law and Politics in the Attorney General's Office, 1789–1990* (Lawrence: University Press of Kansas, 1992); Katy J. Harriger, *Independent Justice: The Federal Special Prosecutor in American Politics* (Lawrence: University Press of Kansas, 1992); and Rebecca Mae Salokar, *The Solicitor General: The Politics of Law* (Philadelphia: Temple University Press, 1992).

31. See Harold Hongju Koh, *The National Security Constitution: Sharing Power after the Iran-Contra Affair* (New Haven, Conn.: Yale University Press, 1990).

32. Daniel P. Franklin, *Extraordinary Measures: The Exercise of Prerogative Powers in the United States* (Pittsburgh: University of Pittsburgh Press, 1991).

33. John Locke, *Treatise of Civil Government and a Letter Concerning Toleration* (New York: Appleton-Century-Crofts, 1937), chap. 14, p. 109.

34. Ibid., p. 113.

35. Jean Jacques Rousseau, *The Social Contract and Discourses* (New York: E. P. Dutton, 1950), Book IV, chap. 6, p. 123.

36. J. Malcolm Smith and Cornelius P. Cotter, *Powers of the President during Crises* (Washington, D.C.: Public Affairs Press, 1960), p. 7.

37. Clinton Rossiter, *Constitutional Dictatorship: Crisis Government in the Modern Democracy* (Princeton, N.J.: Princeton University Press, 1948).

38. Abe Fortas, "The Constitution and the Presidency," *Washington Law Review* 49 (August 1974), p. 100.

39. Edward S. Corwin, *Total War and the Constitution* (Westminister, Md.: Knopf, 1947), p. 80.

40. Rossiter, note 37, p. 12.

41. *The New York Times,* September 8, 1942, p. 1.

42. See Harold Hongju Koh, "Why the President Almost Always Wins in Foreign Affairs," in Adler and George, note 23, pp. 158–80.

43. Richard Longaker, Introduction to Rossiter, *The Supreme Court and the Commander in Chief,* exp. ed. (Ithaca, N.Y.: Cornell University Press, 1976), p. xii.

**44.** See Hendrickson, and Fisher, note 27, and David Gray Adler and Michael A. Genovese, eds., *The Presidency and the Law: the Clinton Legacy* (Lawrence: University Press of Kansas, 2002).

**45.** See Nancy V. Baker, "The Law: The Impact of Antiterrorism Policies on Separation of Powers: Assessing John Ashcroft's Role," *Presidential Studies Quarterly* (December 2002), pp. 765–78.

**46.** Glendon Schubert, *The Presidency in the Courts* (Minneapolis: University of Minnesota Press, 1957), pp. 4, 354.

**47.** See, for example, David G. Adler, "Foreign Policy and the Separation of Powers under the Constitution: The Influence of the Judiciary," paper delivered at the 1987 Annual Meeting of the Western Political Science Association, Anaheim, California, March 26–28, 1987; and his more specialized book *The Constitution and the Termination of Treaties* (New York: Garland Publishing, 1986). See also Francis D. Wormuth and Edwin B. Firmage, *To Chain the Dog of War* (Dallas: Southern Methodist University Press, 1986). For a more modified verdict see Louis Fisher, *The Politics of Shared Power,* 2d ed. (Washington, D.C.: Congressional Quarterly Press, 1987), pp. 105–7. For a much more modified view, see Robert Scigliano, "The Presidency and the Judiciary," in Michael Nelson, ed., *The Presidency and the Political System* (Washington, D.C.: Congressional Quarterly Press, 1984), p. 414. See also a helpful quantitative study by Craig R. Ducat and Robert L. Dudley, "Presidential Power in the Federal Courts during the Post War Era," paper delivered at the 1985 Annual Meeting of the American Political Science Association, New Orleans, August, 1985.

**48.** *The Prize Cases,* 67 U.S. (2 Black) 635 (1863).

**49.** *In re Neagle,* 135 U.S. 1 (1890).

**50.** *In re Debs,* 158 U.S. 564 (1895).

**51.** *Myers v. United States,* 272 U.S. 52 (1926).

**52.** *United States v. Curtiss-Wright Export Corporation,* 299 U.S. 304 (1936).

**53.** *United States v. Belmont,* 301 U.S. 324 (1937).

**54.** Hugo Black, *Korematsu v. United States,* 323 U.S. 214 (1944).

**55.** Eugene V. Rostow, book review, *The Washington Post National Weekly Edition,* January 2, 1984, p. 34. See also Peter Irons, *Justice at War. The Story of the Japanese American Internment Cases* (New York: Oxford University Press, 1983).

**56.** David G. Adler, *The Constitution and the Termination of Treaties* (New York: Garland Publishing, 1986), p. 306. For other views see Louis W. Koenig et al., eds., *Congress, the Presidency and the Taiwan Relations Act* (New York: Praeger, 1985).

**57.** *Dames and Moore v. Reagan,* 453 U.S. 654 (1981).

**58.** William H. Rehnquist, *All the Laws but One: Civil Liberties in Wartime* (New York: Knopf, 2001).

**59.** Michael A. Genovese, *The Supreme Court, the Constitution, and Presidential Power* (Lanham, Md.: University Press of America, 1980), p. 121.

**60.** *Marbury v. Madison,* 1 Cranch 137, 2 L. Ed. 60 (1803).

**61.** *Little v. Bareme,* 2 Cranch 170 (1804).

**62.** *Humphrey's Executor v. United States,* 295 U.S. 602, 628 (1935).

**63.** See Louis Fisher, "Congress and the Removal Power," *Congress and the Presidency* (Spring 1983), pp. 64–65.

**64.** Robert J. Donovan, *Tumultuous Years* (New York: Norton, 1982), p. 387.

**65.** Ibid., p. 391.

**66.** *New York Times Co. v. United States,* 403 U.S. 713 (1971).

**67.** Ibid., 712.

**68.** *United States v. U.S. District Court,* 407 U.S. 297 (1972).

**69.** See David Gray Adler and Michael A. Genovese, eds., *The Presidency and the Law: The Clinton Legacy* (Lawrence: University Press of Kansas, 2002).

**70.** *Clinton v. Jones,* 520, U.S. 681, 1977.

**71.** This is nicely shown in Ducat and Dudley, note 47.

## CHAPTER 9

**1.** Peri E. Arnold, *Making the Managerial Presidency* (Princeton, N.J.: Princeton University Press, 1986), p. 361.

**2.** See Alexander L. George, *Presidential Decisionmaking in Foreign Policy: The Effective Use of Advice and Information* (Boulder, Colo.: Westview Press, 1979); Irving L. Janis, *Groupthink: A Psychological Study of Foreign Policy Decisions and Fiascoes* (Boston: Houghton-Mifflin, 1982); Lawrence E. Walsh, *Firewall: The Iran-Contra Conspiracy and Cover-Up* (New York: Norton, 1997); and Jeffrey H. Birnbaum, *Madhouse: The Private Turmoil of Working for the President* (New York: Times Books, 1996).

**3.** See MaryAnne Borelli, *The President's Cabinet: Gender, Power, and Representation* (Boulder, Colo.: Lynne Rienner, 2002); Shirley Anne Warsaw, *Powersharing: White House-Cabinet Relations in the Modern Presidency* (Albany: State University of New York, 1996); and Anthony J. Bennet, *The American President's Cabinet* (New York: St. Martin's, 1996). Finally, see Robert B. Reich's curious memoir from the Clinton years, *Locked in the Cabinet* (New York: Knopf, 1997); and George Stephanopoulos, *All too Human: A Political Education* (Boston: Little, Brown, 1999).

**4.** Jimmy Carter, *Keeping Faith: Memoirs of a President* (New York: Bantam, 1982), p. 60.

**5.** Henry Barret Learned, *The President's Cabinet: Studies in the Origin, Formation and Structure of an American Institution* (Burt Franklin, 1912, reissued in 1972), p. 119. This is a useful study of the origins of the cabinet. The best study of the cabinet in the mid-twentieth century was that of Richard Fenno, *The President's Cabinet* (New York: Vintage, 1959).

**6.** Lyndon B. Johnson, quoted in Charles Maguire, oral history, August 19, 1969, Lyndon B. Johnson Presidential Library, Austin, Texas, p. 28.

**7.** See the useful study of gender and cabinet selections in MaryAnne Borelli, *The President's Cabinet: Gender, Power, and Representation.*

**8.** Richard Nixon, *RN: The Memoirs of Richard Nixon* (Grosset & Dunlap, 1978), p. 338.

**9.** Keith Nicholls, "Presidential Cabinets: The Politics of Selection from Washington to Reagan," *Congress and the Presidency* (Autumn 1989).

**10.** See Paul C. Light, "Our Tottering Confirmation Process," *Public Interest* (Spring 2002), pp. 57–83. See also Calvin G. MacKenzie, ed., *Innocent Until Nominated: The Breakdown of the Presidential Appointments Process* (Washington, D.C.: The Brookings Institution, 2001); and Stephen L. Carter, *The Confirmation Mess* (New York: Basic Books, 1994).

**11.** Robert B. Reich, *Locked in the Cabinet* (New York: Knopf, 1997), pp. 51–52.

**12.** Shirley Anne Warshaw, *Powersharing: White House–Cabinet Relations in the Modern Presidency* (Albany, N.Y.: SUNY Press, 1996).

**13.** Reich, note 11, pp. 43–44.

**14.** Carter White House aide, interview with Thomas E. Cronin.

**15.** McGeorge Bundy, *The Strength of Government* (Harvard University Press, 1968), p. 39.

**16.** Bradley H. Patterson, Jr., *The President's Cabinet: Issues and Questions* (American Society for Public Administration, 1976), pp. 17–18. See also his *The White House Staff: Inside the West Wing and Beyond* (Washington, D.C.: The Brookings Institution, 2000).

**17.** Quoted in Kermit Gordon, "Reflections on Spending," in J. D. Montgomery and Arthur Smithies, eds., *Public Policy* (Cambridge, Mass.: Harvard University Press, 1966), p. 15.

**18.** Lyndon B. Johnson, quoted in Bobby Baker, with Larry King, *Wheeling and Dealing* (Norton, 1978), p. 265.

**19.** Walter J. Hickel, *The New York Times,* May 7, 1970, p. C18.

**20.** Lyndon B. Johnson, note 18, pp. 265–66. It should be noted that this statement was made some four years after LBJ had left the White House.

**21.** Harold Gosnell, *Harry S Truman* (New York: Greenwood Press, 1980).

**22.** Quoted in *U.S. News & World Report,* March 29, 1982, p. 28.

**23.** Interview at the White House with Thomas E. Cronin.

**24.** Jimmy Carter, *Keeping Faith: Memoirs of a President* (New York: Bantam, 1982), p. 59.

**25.** Theodore C. Sorensen, transcript of a panel discussion at the Annual Meetings of the American Society for Public Administration, New York City, March 22, 1972, p. 22. Reprinted as "Advising the President: A Panel," *Bureaucrat* (April 1974), p. 33.

**26.** Nixon, note 8.

**27.** Elliot Richardson, *The Creative Balance* (Holt Rinehart and Winston, 1976), p. 74.

**28.** Harold L. Ickes, *The Secret Diaries of Harold L. Ickes,* vol. 1 (New York: Simon & Schuster, 1953), p. 308.

**29.** Griffin B. Bell and Ronald J. Ostrow, *Taking Care of the Law* (New York: Morrow, 1982), p. 47.

**30.** Patterson, note 16, p. 113.

**31.** See, for example, David A. Stockman, *The Triumph of Politics: Why the Reagan Revolution Failed* (New York: Harper & Row, 1986), chap. 4.

**32.** Terry M. Moe, "The Politicized Presidency," in John E. Chubb and Paul E. Peterson, eds., *The New Direction in American Politics* (Washington, D.C.: Brookings, 1985), pp. 260–61.

**33.** Keith Nicholls, "The Dynamics of National Executive Service: Ambition Theory and the Careers of Presidential Cabinet Members," *Western Political Quarterly* (March 1991).

**34.** Quoted in Richard H. Rovere, "Eisenhower: A Trial Balance," *The Reporter,* April 21, 1955, pp. 19–20.

**35.** Leonard Silk, *Nixonomics* (New York: Praeger, 1972), p. 81.

**36.** See Jeanne Cummings, "Bush Relies on Cheney-Rove Dynamic Duo," *Wall Street Journal,* January 3, 2003, p. A4; Lou Dubose, Jan Reid, and Carl M. Cannon, *Boy Genius: Karl Rove, the Brains Behind the Remarkable Political Triumph of George W. Bush* (New York: Public Affairs, 2003); and Evan Thomas, "The Quiet Power of Condi Rice," *Newsweek,* December 16, 2002, pp. 26–34.

**37.** Charles E. Walcott and Karen M. Hult, *Governing the White House* (Lawrence: University Press of Kansas, 1995). See also Richard W. Waterman, *Presidential Influence and the Administrative State* (Knoxville: University of Tennessee Press, 1989).

**38.** Robert F. Durant and Adam L. Warber, "Networking in the Shadow of Heirarchy: Public Policy, the Administrative Presidency, and the Neoadministrative State," *Presidential Studies Quarterly,* Vol. 31, No. 2 (June 2001), pp. 221–244.

**39.** Richard Nathan, *The Administrative Presidency* (New York: Wiley, 1983); Robert F. Durant, *The Administrative Presidency Revisited* (New York: State University of New York Press, 1992); and Peri E. Arnold, *Making the Managerial Presidency* (Lawrence: University Press of Kansas, 1998). See also Phillip J. Cooper, *By Order of the President: The Use and Abuse of Executive Direct Action* (Lawrence: University Press of Kansas, 2002).

**40.** See Cooper, note 39, and Kenneth R. Mayer, *With the Stroke of a Pen: Executive Orders and Presidential Power* (Princeton, N.J.: Princeton University Press, 2001).

**41.** Myra Gutin, *The President's Partner* (New York: Greenwood Press, 1989); and Edith Mayo, "The Influence and Power of First Ladies," *The Chronicle of Higher Education,* September 15, 1993, sec. A; Alice E. Anderson and Hadley V. Baxendale, *Behind Every Successful President: The Hidden Power and Influence of America's First Ladies* (Shapolsky Publishers, 1992); Carl S. Anthony, *First Ladies: The Saga of the President's Wives and Their Power* (William Morrow, 1990); Lewis L. Gould, "Modern First Ladies and the Presidency," *Presidential Studies Quarterly*

20 (1990), pp. 677–83; Lewis L. Gould, "First Ladies," *The American Scholar* 55 (1986), pp. 528–35; and Karen O'Connor, Bernadette Nye, and Laura van Assendalft, "Wives in the White House: The Political Influence of the First Ladies," *Presidential Studies Quarterly* 26 (1996), pp. 835–53.

**42.** Betty Boyd Caroli, *First Ladies* (New York: Oxford University Press, 1987).

**43.** Margaret Mead, quoted in *The New York Times,* December 12, 1974, sec. VI, p. 36.

**44.** See, in general, Mary Van Rensselaer Thayer, *Jacqueline Kennedy, The White House Years* (Boston: Little, Brown and Co., 1967).

**45.** Donald Young, *American Roulette: The History and Dilemma of the Vice Presidency* (New York: Viking, 1974), p. 134.

**46.** Lois Scharf, *Eleanor Roosevelt: First Lady of Liberalism* (Boston: Twayne Publishers, 1987), p. 110.

**47.** Mayo, note 41, p. 2; and Edith Mayo and Denise Meringolo, *First Ladies: Political Role and Public Image* (Washington, D.C.: Smithsonian Institute, 1994).

**48.** MaryAnne Borelli, "Competing Conceptions of the First Ladyship: Public Responses to Betty Ford's *60 Minutes* Interview," *Presidential Studies Quarterly* (September 2001) pp. 397–414.

**49.** *The New York Times,* July 16, 1985, p. 1.

**50.** On Hillary Clinton's role in public policy matters in Bill Clinton's first years in the White House, see Jacob Hacker, *The Road to Nowhere: The Genesis of President Clinton's Plan for Health Security* (Princeton, N.J.: Princeton University Press, 1998).

**51.** On the difficulty of explaining public attitudes toward First Ladies using Hillary Clinton as an example, see Jeffrey E. Cohen, "The Polls: Public Attitudes Toward the First Lady," *Presidential Studies Quarterly* (June 2000), pp. 374–81. See Hillary Clinton's own story in her autobiography, *Living History* (New York: Simon & Schuster, 2003).

**52.** See the personal recollections of these staff differences in Colin Powell, *My American Journey* (New York: Random House, 1995). See also Charles E. Walcott, Shirley Anne Warshaw, and Stephen J. Wayne, "The Chief of Staff," in *Presidential Studies Quarterly* (September 2001), pp. 464–89.

**53.** James P. Pfiffner, "The President's Chief of Staff: Lessons Learned," Working Paper 92, Institute of Public Policy, George Mason University, October 1992, p. 19.

**54.** See Warshaw, note 12; see also Richard T. Johnson, *Managing the White House* (New York: Harper & Row, 1974).

**55.** Personal interview conducted by Thomas E. Cronin.

**56.** Jesse Jones, quoted in Richard Fenno, "President-Cabinet Relations and Pattern and a Case Study," *American Political Science Review* (March 1958), p. 394.

**57.** Fred I. Greenstein, *The Presidential Difference* (New York: Free Press, 2000), p. 195.

**58.** See Alexander L. George and Eric K. Stern, "Harnessing Conflict in Foreign Policy Making: From Devil's to Multiple Advocacy," *Presidential Studies Quarterly* (September 2002), pp. 484–508. See also David Gergen, *Eyewitness to Power: The Essence of Leadership from Nixon to Clinton* (New York: Simon & Schuster, 2000).

**59.** Joseph A. Califano, Jr., *Governing America: An Insider's Report from the White House and the Cabinet* (New York: Simon & Schuster, 1981), p. 407.

**60.** Ibid., p. 434–35.

**61.** John Ehrlichman, *Witness to Power: The Nixon Years* (New York: Simon & Schuster, 1982), pp. 110–11.

**62.** Arthur M. Schlesinger, Jr., *The Crisis of Confidence* (New York: Houghton Mifflin, 1969), p. 291.

**63.** Kermit Gordon, "Reflections on Spending," in J. D. Montgomery and A. Smithies, eds., *Public Policy* (Cambridge, Mass.: Harvard University Press, 1966), pp. 13–15.

**64.** John W. Gardner, testimony before the Senate Government Operations Committee, *Congressional Record,* 92nd Congress, 1st session, June 3, 1971, S.8140.

## CHAPTER 10

**1.** Walter Mondale, as quoted in David S. Broder and Bob Woodward, "Waiting in the Wings to Play the Lead Role," *The Washington Post National Weekly Edition,* January 27–February 2, 1992, p. 10. And see also Jules Whitcover, *Crapshoot: Rolling the Dice on the Vice Presidency* (New York: Crown, 1992); and Vance R. Kincade, Jr., *Heirs Apparent: Solving the Vice Presidential Dilemma* (Westport, Conn.: Praeger, 2001).

**2.** Paul C. Light, *Vice Presidential Power: Advice and Influence in the White House* (Baltimore, Md.: Johns Hopkins University Press, 1984), p. 1.

**3.** Allan P. Sindler, *Unchosen Presidents* (Berkeley: University of California Press, 1976), p. 41.

**4.** Henry Kissinger, *White House Years* (Boston: Little, Brown, 1979), p. 713.

**5.** Doris Kearns, *Lyndon Johnson and the American Dream* (New York: Harper & Row, 1976), p. 164.

**6.** Jeffrey E. Cohen, "Popular Views of the Vice President: Vice Presidential Approval," *Presidential Studies Quarterly* (March 2001), p. 143.

**7.** The most comprehensive account of the Twenty-fifth Amendment is by John D. Feerick, *The Twenty-fifth Amendment* (New York: Fordham University Press, 1976).

**8.** *Time,* January 20, 1975, p. 23.

**9.** Alben W. Barkley, *That Reminds Me: The Autobiography of the Veep* (Garden City, N.Y.: Doubleday, 1954), p. 209.

**10.** James M. Naughton, "Above the Battle," *The New York Times Magazine,* June 24, 1973, p. 49.

11. Donald Young, *American Roulette: The History and Dilemma of the Vice Presidency* (New York: Holt, Rinehart & Winston, 1972), pp. 353–54.

12. Paul T. David, "The Vice Presidency: Its Institutional Evolution and Contemporary Status," *Journal of Politics* (November 1967), p. 733. President Eisenhower's dealings with his own vice president, Richard Nixon, were also affected by his ambivalence toward Nixon. According to his leading biographer, Ike often doubted Nixon's maturity and thought him overly ambitious. "The more Eisenhower tried to praise him [Nixon], it somehow seemed, the more tongue-tied he got; the more he tried to endorse Nixon's leadership qualities, the more doubtful he sounded." Stephen E. Ambrose, *Eisenhower: The President* (New York: Simon & Schuster, 1984), p. 297.

13. James F. Byrnes, *All in One Lifetime* (New York: Harper & Brothers, 1958), p. 233.

14. Joseph E. Kallenbach, *The American Chief Executive* (New York: Harper & Row, 1966), pp. 234–35.

15. Michael Novak, *Choosing Our King* (New York: Macmillan, 1974), pp. 263–64.

16. James MacGregor Burns, *The Lion and the Fox* (New York: Harcourt, Brace, 1956), p. 414.

17. Sam Houston Johnson, *My Brother Lyndon* (New York: Cowles, 1970), p. 109.

18. And, of course, Agnew would be forced to resign as a result of allegations of tax evasion and political bribery. See Richard M. Cohen and Jules Witcover, *A Heartbeat Away: The Investigation and Resignation of Vice President Spiro T. Agnew* (New York: Viking Press, 1974). These authors say Agnew "was a slick snake-oil salesman" (p. 360). For Agnew's own more complicated assessment of his final year in office, see Spiro T. Agnew, *Go Quietly . . . or Else* (New York: William Morrow and Co., 1980).

19. James Carney, "Seven Clues to Understanding Dick Cheney," *Time,* December 30, 2002–January 6, 2003, p. 104.

20. See, for example, David M. Shribman, "He Is the Very Model of a Modern 2nd Fiddle," *The Boston Globe,* July 2, 2002, p. A. 3, and Glenn Kessler and Peter Slevin, "The Department of Dick Cheney," *The Washington Post National Weekly Edition,* October 21–27, 2002, p. 8. See also Elisabeth Bumiller and Eric Schmitt, "Cheney, Little Seen by Public, Wielding Influences on Security," *The New York Times,* January, 31, 2003, pp. 1, A14.

21. Arthur M. Schlesinger, Jr., "Is the Vice Presidency Necessary?" *Atlantic* (May 1974), p. 37.

22. Hubert H. Humphrey, "A Conversation with Vice President Hubert H. Humphrey," National Educational Television, April 1965. See also Hubert H. Humphrey, *The Education of a Public Man: My Life in Politics* (Minneapolis: University of Minnesota Press, 1991).

23. Gerald R. Ford, *A Time to Heal* (New York: Harper & Row/Reader's Digest, 1979), p. 327.

24. Ibid., p. 328. For the Rockefeller side of this story see Joseph E. Persico, *The Imperial Rockefeller: A Biography of Nelson A. Rockefeller* (New York: Simon & Schuster, 1982); and Michael Turner, *The Vice President as Policy Maker: Rockefeller in the Ford White House* (Westport, Conn.: Greenwood Press, 1982).

**25.** Walter F. Mondale, quoted in *National Journal,* December 1, 1979, p. 2016.

**26.** President Jimmy Carter news conference, *The New York Times,* September 30, 1977, p. A18.

**27.** Jimmy Carter, *Keeping Faith: Memoirs of a President* (New York: Bantam, 1982), p. 40. See also *The New York Times,* November 13, 1980, p. 14. See also Joel K. Goldstein *The Modern American Vice Presidency* (Princeton, N.J.: Princeton University Press, 1982); and Paul C. Light, *Vice-Presidential Power* (Baltimore: Johns Hopkins Press, 1984).

**28.** Walter F. Mondale, lecture on "The American Vice Presidency" at the University of Minnesota, Minneapolis, February 18, 1981, mimeo, p. 3.

**29.** Walter F. Mondale, interview, *National Journal,* December 1, 1979, p. 2016.

**30.** Adapted and condensed from Mondale, note 28, p. 7.

**31.** *The Houston Post,* May 1, 1983, p. 1.

**32.** *Time,* February 22, 1982, p. 22.

**33.** Ibid. A later criticism along these lines is found in Dale Russakoff, "Bush: The Loyal Subordinate. . . . ," *The Washington Post,* January 21, 1985, pp. G4–5.

**34.** Ronald Reagan, interviewed by reporters from *The New York Times,* February 12, 1985, p. 6.

**35.** E. J. Dionne, Jr., "Bush's Presidential Bid Is Shaky . . . , Poll Finds" *The New York Times,* July 26, 1987, pp. 1, 14.

**36.** Robert B. Reich, *Locked in the Cabinet* (New York: Knopf, 1997), p. 241.

**37.** See Joe Klein, *The Natural: The Misunderstood Presidency of Bill Clinton* (New York: Doubleday, 2000), pp. 200–201.

**38.** See, for example, Elizabeth Drew, *On the Edge: The Clinton Presidency* (New York: Simon & Schuster, 1994), p. 227.

**39.** David S. Broder and Bob Woodward, *The Man Who Would Be President: Dan Quayle* (New York: Simon & Schuster, 1992).

**40.** Jean Edward Smith, *George Bush's War* (New York: Henry Holt, 1992); and Burt Solomon, "War Bolsters Quayle's Visibility, but Hasn't Increased His Stature," *National Journal,* March 2, 1991. See Quayle's own accounts in Dan Quayle, *Standing Firm* (New York: Harper Paperbooks, 1995).

**41.** As quoted in Glenn Kessler and Peter Slavin, "The Department of Dick Cheney," note 20. See also Bob Woodward, *Bush at War* (New York: Simon & Schuster, 2002).

**42.** For Cheney's speech, see Elizabeth Bumiller and James Dao, "Cheney Says Peril of a Nuclear Iraq Justifies Attack," *The New York Times,* August 27, 2002, pp. 1, 8. See also, John Burry et al., "The Quiet Power of Condi Rice," *Newsweek,* December 16, 2002, p. 26.

**43.** See David W. Romero, "Requiem for a Lightweight: Vice Presidential Candidate Evaluations and the Presidential Vote," *Presidential Studies Quarterly* (September 2001), p. 454.

**44.** Quoted in Nancy Gibbs, "Double-Edged Sword," *Time,* December 30, 2002–January 6, 2003, p. 93.

**45.** Thomas M. Durbin, *Nomination and Election of the President and the Vice President of the United States* (Washington, D.C.: U.S. Government Printing Office, 1988).

**46.** Jules Witcover, *Crapshoot: Rolling the Dice on the Vice Presidency* (New York: Crown, 1992).

**47.** See *Official Report of the Vice Presidential Selection Commission of the Democratic Party,* December 19, 1974, mimeo. See also "Hearings of the Vice Presidential Selection Commission of the Democratic National Committee," *Congressional Record,* October 16, 1973, S19245 ff; and Allan P. Sindler, *Unchosen Presidents* (Berkeley: University of California Press, 1976).

**48.** Some of these proposals are discussed and assessed in Joel K. Goldstein, *The Modern American Vice Presidency* (Princeton, N.J.: Princeton University Press, 1982), p. 282ff.

**49.** Arthur M. Schlesinger, Jr., *The Imperial Presidency* (New York: Popular Library, 1974), p. 481. For an earlier version, see Lucins Wilmerding, Jr., "The Vice Presidency," *Political Science Quarterly* (March 1953), pp. 17–41.

**50.** Ibid., p. 493.

**51.** Report of the Study Group on Vice Presidential Selection, Institute of Politics, Kennedy School of Government, Harvard University, June 14, 1976, monograph, p. 7. This report contains several of the proposals summarized here.

**52.** Ibid.

**53.** Bernard Weinraub, "Mondale Outlines Job Qualities of Running Mate," *The New York Times,* June 13, 1984, p. B11.

**54.** Goldstein, note 48, p. 89.

**55.** Paul Sracic, "A Change is in Order," *The Washington Post National Weekly Edition,* December 9–15, 2002, p. 23.

**56.** John D. Feerick, "The Proposed Twenty-fifth Amendment to the Constitution," *Fordham Law Review* (December 1965), p. 197. See also Feerick's *The Twenty-fifth Amendment* (Bronx, N.Y.: Fordham University Press, 1976); and Herbert L. Abrams, "Shielding the President from the Constitution: Disability and the 25th Amendment," *Presidential Studies Quarterly* (Summer 1993), pp. 533–53.

**57.** J. W. Peltason, *Understanding the Constitution,* 8th ed. (New York: Holt, Rinehart and Winston, 1979), pp. 232–33.

**58.** Stephen E. Ambrose, *Eisenhower: The President* (New York: Simon & Schuster, 1984), p. 440.

**59.** For a negative assessment of the Twenty-fifth Amendment and some alternative remedies, see Herbert L. Abrams, *The President Has Been Shot* (New York: W. W. Norton, 1992).

**60.** See John M. Murphy and Mary E. Stuckey, "Never Cared to Say Goodbye: Presidential Legacies and Vice Presidential Campaigns," *Presidential Studies Quarterly* (March 2002), pp. 46–66.

## CHAPTER 11

1. Michael Lind, "The Out-of-Control Presidency," *The New Republic,* August 14, 1998, p. 21.

2. Theodore C. Sorensen, *Watchmen in the Night* (Cambridge, Mass.: MIT Press, 1975).

3. James Madison, *The Federalist Papers,* No. 51. (Modern Library, 1937).

4. Sidney M. Milkis, *The President and the Parties* (New York: Oxford University Press, 1993).

5. See, especially, Erwin C. Hargrove, *The President as Leader: Appealing to the Better Angels of Our Nature* (Lawrence: University Press of Kansas, 1998); and Bruce Miroff, *Icons of Democracy* (New York: Basic Books, 1993), chap. 1.

6. James M. Burns, *Roosevelt: The Lion and the Fox* (San Diego: A Harvest/HJB Book, 1956, renewed 1984), p. 151.

7. Benjamin Barber, *Strong Democracy: Participatory Politics for a New Age* (Berkeley: University of California Press, 1984).

8. Benjamin R. Barber, "Neither Leaders nor Followers: Citizenship under Strong Democracy," in Michael R. Beschloss and Thomas E. Cronin, eds., *Essays in Honor of James MacGregor Burns* (Englewood Cliffs, N.J.: Prentice-Hall, 1989), p. 117.

9. Quoted in Larry Berman, *The New American Presidency* (Boston: Little, Brown, 1987), p. 344.

10. Woodrow Wilson, letter placed in the *Congressional Record,* 64th Congress, 2d Session, August 15, 1916, 53. pt. 13:12620.

11. The possibility also exists that a six-year term, or "a term-and-a-half" as some call it, with reelection precluded, would intensify the presidential selection process. Certainly in such a winner-take-more situation, there is the likelihood that ideological competition would be more aggressive and perhaps more bitter than at present. Conflict would assuredly be heightened. How harmful this would be is difficult to assess, but judging from how corrupt the 1972 reelection campaign became, this factor must be considered.

12. Thomas A. Baylis, *Governing by Committee: Collegial Leadership in Advanced Societies* (Albany, N.Y.: SUNY Press, 1989).

13. Herman Finer, *The Presidency: Crisis and Regeneration* (University of Chicago Press, 1960), p. viii. See also a more recent plea for a more collective presidency: Milton Eisenhower, *The President Is Calling* (Doubleday, 1974).

14. Alexander Hamilton, *The Federalist Papers,* No. 70 (Modern Library, 1937), pp. 460–67.

15. The constitutional amendment proposed by Representative Henry S. Reuss can be found in Congressional Record, II 7158, July 21, 1975. The one place where it received attention and scrutiny was in the *George Washington Law Review,* which contained a symposium on the no-confidence proposal (January 1975), pp. 328–500.

**16.** James Sundquist, "Needed: A Workable Check on the Presidency," *Brookings Bulletin* 10 (4) (1973), p. 7. See also, Sundquist, *Constitutional Reform* (1986).

**17.** Samuel H. Beer puts it well from a comparative perspective: "The lesson of British experience, and indeed of comparative government generally, is that the vote of confidence device might unduly weaken the executive, or unduly strengthen the executive, or, possibly, bring about the nice adjustment that Representative Reuss desires. In short, the consequences of the proposed reform are incalculable. In view of the further fact that the impeachment process did work in the case of President Nixon, these prospects indicate to this author that Congress should leave things as they are." *George Washington Law Review* (January 1975), p. 371.

**18.** The best history and political analysis of third parties is Steven Rosenstone, Roy Behr, and Edward Lazarus, *Third Parties in America: Citizen Response to Major Party Failure* (Princeton, N.J.: Princeton University Press, 1984).

**19.** See Richard A. Posner, *An Affair of State: The Investigation, Impeachment and Trial of President Clinton* (Cambridge: Harvard University Press, 1999). See also Peter Baker, *The Breach: Inside the Impeachment and Trial of William Jefferson Clinton* (New York: Scribner, 2000) and Jeffrey Toobin, *A Vast Conspiracy: The Real Story of the Sex Scandal That Nearly Brought Down a President* (New York: Touchstone, 1999).

**20.** Peter M. Shane, "Independent Counsel," in Leonard Levy and Louis Fisher, eds., *Encyclopedia of the American Presidency* (New York: Simon & Schuster, 1994), p. 816.

**21.** Archibald Cox, "Curbing Special Counsels," *The New York Times,* December 12, 1996, p. A21.

**22.** Ibid.

**23.** Ibid. See also "Keep the Independent Counsel," *The New York Times,* December 21, 1996, p. 18, editorial.

**24.** *Morrison v. Olson 487* U.S. 654 (1988).

**25.** See Robert J. Spitzer, "The Independent Counsel and the Post-Clinton Presidency," in David Gray Adler and Michael A. Genovese, eds., *The Presidency and the Law: The Clinton Legacy* (Lawrence: University Press of Kansas, 2002), pp. 89–107.

**26.** David Gray Adler and Nancy Kassop, "The Impeachment of Bill Clinton," in Adler and Genovese, eds., *The Presidency and the Law,* p. 155.

**27.** Ibid.

**28.** Fred Wertheimer, "Stop Soft Money. Now," *The New York Times Magazine,* December 22, 1996, pp. 38–39.

**29.** Michael Duffy and Nancy Gibbs, "Money and Politics," *Time* magazine, November 11, 1996, p. 33.

**30.** Ibid.

**31.** Anthony Corrado, *Paying for Presidents: Public Financing in Presidential Elections* (New York: Twentieth Century Fund Press, 1993).

# Selected Bibliography

## MAJOR REFERENCE WORKS ON THE PRESIDENCY

Genovese, Michael A. *The Encyclopedia of the American Presidency*. New York: Facts-on-File, 2004.

Goldsmith, William M. *The Growth of Presidential Power: A Documented History*. 3 vols. New York: Chelsea House, 1974.

Graff, Henry F., ed. *The Presidents: A Reference History*. New York: Scribner's, 1984.

Greenstein, Fred I., Larry Berman, and Alvin S. Felzenberg with Doris Lidtke. *Evolution of the Modern Presidency: A Bibliographical Survey*. Washington, D.C.: American Enterprise Institute, 1977.

Levy, Leonard W., and Louis Fisher, eds. *Encyclopedia of the American Presidency*. 4 vols. New York: Simon & Schuster, 1994.

Nelson, Michael, ed. *Guide to the Presidency*. Washington, D.C.: Congressional Quarterly Press, 1989.

———. *The Presidency, A to Z*. Washington, D.C.: Congressional Quarterly Press, 1992.

Shane, Peter M., and Harold H. Bruff, eds. *The Law of Presidential Power*. Durham, N.C.: Carolina Academic Press, 1988.

Whitney, David C., and Robin Vaughn Whitney, eds. *The American Presidents*. 8th ed. Pleasantville, N.Y.: Reader's Digest, 1996.

## OTHER IMPORTANT WORKS

Abraham, Henry J. *Justices and Presidents*. 2d ed. New York: Oxford University Press, 1985.

Abrams, Herbert L. *"The President Has Been Shot": Confusion, Disability and the 25th Amendment*. Stanford: Stanford University Press, 1994.

Adler, David Gray, and Larry N. George, eds. *The Constitution and the Conduct of Foreign Policy*. Lawrence: University Press of Kansas, 1996.

———, and Michael A. Genovese, eds. *The Presidency and the Law: The Clinton Legacy*. Lawrence: University Press of Kansas, 2002.

Arnold, Peri E. *Making the Managerial Presidency*. Princeton, N.J.: Princeton University Press, 1986.

Asher, Herbert. *Presidential Elections and American Politics*. 5th ed. New York: Harcourt Brace, 1992.

Baker, Nancy V. *Conflicting Loyalties: Law and Politics in the Attorney General's Office. 1789–1990*. Lawrence: University Press of Kansas, 1992.

Barber, Benjamin R. *The Truth of Power: Intellectual Affairs in the Clinton White House*. New York: W. W. Norton, 2001.

Barber, James David. *The Presidential Character: Predicting Performance in the White House.* 4th ed. Englewood Cliffs, N.J.: Prentice-Hall, 1992.

Bennett, Anthony. *The American President's Cabinet: From Kennedy to Bush.* New York: St. Martin's, 1996.

Bennis, Warren, and Bert Nanus. *Leaders: Strategies for Taking Charge.* New York: HarperCollins, 1986.

Berman, Larry. *The New American Presidency.* Boston: Little, Brown, 1987.

Bessette, Joseph M., and Jeffrey Tulis, eds. *The Presidency in the Constitutional Order.* Baton Rouge: Louisiana State University Press, 1984.

Best, Judith A., et al. *The Choice of the People? Debating the Electoral College.* Lanham, Md.: Rowland & Littlefield, 1996.

Birnbaum, Jeffrey H. *Madhouse: The Private Turmoil of Working for the President.* New York: Times Books/Random House, 1996.

Blakesley, Lance. *Presidential Leadership: From Eisenhower to Clinton.* Chicago: Nelson-Hall, 1995.

Blessing, Time H., and Robert K. Murray. *Greatness in the White House: Rating the Presidents, Washington through Carter.* University Park: Pennsylvania State University Press, 1988.

Bond, Jon R., and Richard Fleisher. *The President in the Legislative Arena.* Chicago: University of Chicago Press, 1990.

———, eds. *Polarized Politics: Congress and the President in a Partisan Era.* Washington, D.C.: C.Q. Press, 2000.

Borrelli, MaryAnne. *The President's Cabinet: Gender, Power, and Representation.* Boulder, Colo.: Lynne Rienner, 2002.

Brace, Paul, and Barbara Hinckley. *Follow the Leader: Opinion Polls and the Modern Presidents.* New York: Basic Books, 1992.

Brody, Richard A. *Assessing the President: The Media, Elite Opinion, and Public Support.* Stanford, Calif.: Stanford University Press, 1991.

Buchanan, Bruce. *The Presidential Experience: What the Office Does to the Man.* Englewood Cliffs, N.J.: Prentice-Hall, 1978.

Bunce, Valerie. *Do New Leaders Make a Difference?: Executive Successions and Public Policy Capitalism and Socialism.* Princeton, N.J.: Princeton University Press, 1981.

Burke, John P. *The Institutional Presidency.* Baltimore: Johns Hopkins University Press, 1992.

Burns, James MacGregor. *Leadership.* New York: HarperCollins, 1978.

———. *Deadlock of Democracy.* Englewood Cliffs, N.J.: Prentice-Hall, 1963.

———. *The Power to Lead: The Crisis of the American Presidency.* New York: Simon & Schuster, 1984.

———. *Presidential Government: The Crucible of Leadership.* Boston: Houghton Mifflin, 1965.

———. *Roosevelt: The Lion and the Fox.* San Diego: Harvest/HBJ, 1984.

———. *Roosevelt: Soldier of Freedom.* New York: Harcourt Brace, Jovanovich, 1970.

———, and Georgia J. Sorenson. *Dead Center: Clinton-Gore Leadership and the Perils of Moderation.* New York: Scribners, 1999.

Campbell, Colin. *Managing the Presidency: Carter, Reagan and the Search for Executive Harmony.* Pittsburgh: University of Pittsburgh Press, 1986.

Cannon, Lou. *President Reagan: The Role of a Lifetime.* New York: Touchstone, 1991.

Carter, Jimmy. *Keeping Faith: Memoirs of a President.* New York: Bantam Books, 1982.

Carter, Stephen L. *The Confirmation Mess: Cleaning Up the Federal Appointments Process.* New York: Basic Books, 1994.

Caroli, Betty Boyd. *First Ladies.* New York: Oxford University Press, 1987.

Ceasar, James W. *Presidential Selection.* Princeton, N.J.: Princeton University Press, 1979.

———, and Andrew Busch. *The Perfect Tie: The True Story of the 2000 Presidential Election.* Lanham, Md.: Rowman and Littlefield, 2001.

Clinton, Hillary. *Living History* New York: Simon & Schuster, 2003.

Conley, Patricia H. *Presidential Mandates: How Elections Shape the National Agenda.* Chicago: University of Chicago Press, 2001.

Corvitz, L. Gordon, and Jeremy A. Rabkin, eds. *The Tethered Presidency.* Washington, D.C.: American Enterprise Institute, 1989.

Corwin, Edward S. *The President: Office and Powers, 1978–1984.* 5th ed. New York: New York University Press, 1984.

———. *Total War and the Constitution.* Westminister, Md.: Knopf, 1947.

Covington, Cary R., and Lester G. Seligman. *The Coalition Presidency.* Chicago: Dorsey Press, 1989.

Cox, Gary W., and Samuel Kernell, eds. *The Politics of Divided Government.* Boulder, Colo.: Westview, 1991.

Crabb, Cecil V., and Pat Holt. *Invitation to Struggle: Congress, the President, and Foreign Policy.* 3rd ed. Washington, D.C.: Congressional Quarterly Press, 1989.

———, and Kevin V. Mulcahy. *American National Security: A Presidential Perspective.* New York: Harcourt Brace, 1990.

———. *Presidents and Foreign Policymaking.* Baton Rouge: Louisiana State University Press, 1986.

Cramer, Richard Ben. *What It Takes: The Way to the White House.* New York: Random House, 1992.

Cronin, Thomas E., ed. *Inventing the American Presidency.* Lawrence: University Press of Kansas, 1989.

———, ed. *Rethinking the Presidency.* Boston: Little, Brown, 1982.

———. *The State of the Presidency.* 2d ed. Boston: Little, Brown, 1980.

———, and Sanford Greenberg, eds. *The Presidential Advisory System.* New York: Harper & Row, 1969.

———, and Rexford Tugwell, eds. *The Presidency Reappraised.* New York: Praeger, 1977.

Dallek, Robert. *Hail to the Chief: The Making and Unmaking of American Presidents.* New York: Hyperion Books, 1996.

———. *An Unfinished Life: John F. Kennedy, 1917–1963.* Boston, Mass: Little, Brown and Co., 2003.

Darman, Richard. *Who's in Control? Polar Politics and the Sensible Center.* New York: Simon & Schuster, 1996.

Davis, James W. *The American Presidency.* 2d ed. Westport, Conn.: Praeger, 1995.

———. *The President as Party Leader.* New York: Praeger, 1992.

DeGrazia, Alfred. *Congress and the Presidency.* Washington, D.C.: American Enterprise Institute, 1967.

Donald, David H. *Lincoln.* New York: Simon & Schuster, 1995.

Draper, Theodore. *A Very Thin Line: The Iran-Contra Affair.* New York: Touchstone Books, 1991.

Dubose, Lou, Jan Reid, and Carl M. Cannon. *Boy Genius: Karl Rove, the Brains Behind the Remarkable Political Triumph of George W. Bush.* New York: Public Affairs, 2003.

Eastland, Terry. *Energy in the Executive: The Case for the Strong Presidency.* New York: Free Press, 1992.

Edwards, George C. *At the Margins: Presidential Leadership in Congress.* New Haven, Conn.: Yale University Press, 1989.

———. *Presidential Influence in Congress.* San Francisco: W.H. Freeman, 1980.

———. *The Public Presidency.* New York: St. Martin's Press, 1983.

———, John H. Kessel, and Bert A. Rockman, eds. *Researching the Presidency: Vital Questions, New Approaches.* Pittsburgh: University of Pittsburgh Press, 1993.

———, and Stephen Wayne. *Presidential Leadership: Politics and Policy Making.* 3rd ed. New York: St. Martin's Press, 1994.

Ellis, Richard, and Aaron Wildavsky. *Dilemmas of Presidential Leadership.* New Brunswick, N.J.: Transaction Publishers, 1989.

Fishel, Jeff. *Presidents and Promises.* Washington, D.C.: Congressional Quarterly Press, 1985.

Fisher, Louis. *The Constitution between Friends.* New York: St. Martin's Press, 1978.

———. *The Politics of Shared Power: Congress and the Executive.* 4th ed. College Station: Texas A & M University Press, 1998.

———. *Presidential War Power.* Lawrence: University Press of Kansas, 1995.

Franklin, Daniel P. *Extraordinary Measures.* Pittsburgh: University of Pittsburgh Press, 1991.

Frum, David. *The Right Man: The Surprise Presidency of George W. Bush.* New York: Random House, 2003.

Gardner, John W. *On Leadership.* New York: Free Press, 1990.

Genovese, Michael A. *The Power of the American Presidency, 1787–2000.* New York: Oxford University Press, 2001. The Presidential Dilemma: Leadership in the American System. 2d ed. New York: Longman, 2002.

———. *The Nixon Presidency: Power and Politics in Turbulent Times.* Westport, Conn.: Greenwood Press, 1990.

———. *The Presidency in an Age of Limits.* Westport, Conn.: Greenwood Press, 1993.

———. *The Supreme Court, the Constitution, and Presidential Power.* Landham, Md.: University Press of America, 1980.

Gergen, David. *Eyewitness to Power.* New York: Simon & Schuster, 2000.

Goldstein, Joel K. *The Modern American Vice Presidency: The Transformation of a Political Institution.* Princeton, N.J.: Princeton University Press, 1982.

Gould, Lewis L. *The Modern American Presidency.* Lawrence: University Press of Kansas, 2003.

Greenstein, Fred. *The Hidden-Hand Presidency: Eisenhower as Leader.* New York: Basic Books, 1982.

———. *The Presidential Difference: Leadership Style from FDR to Clinton.* New York: Free Press, 2000.

Gregg, Gary L. *The Presidential Republic: Executive Representation and Deliberative Democracy.* Lanham, Md.: Rowland & Littlefield, 1997.

Grover, William F. *The President as Prisoner.* New York: State University of New York Press, 1989.

Hamilton, Alexander, James Madison, and John Jay. *Federalist Papers.* New York: New American Library, 1961.

Han, Lori Cox. *Governing from Center Stage: White House Communication Strategies During the Television Age of Politics.* Cresskill: New Jersey: Hampton Press, 2001.

Hargrove, Erwin C. *The Power of the Modern Presidency.* New York: Knopf, 1974.

———. *The President as Leader: Appealing to the Better Angels of Our Nature.* Lawrence: University Press of Kansas, 1998.

———, and Michael Nelson. *Presidents, Politics and Policy.* Baltimore: Johns Hopkins University Press, 1984.

Harriger, Katy J. *Independent Justice: The Federal Special Prosecutor in American Politics.* Lawrence: University Press of Kansas, 1992.

Hart, Roderick. *The Sound of Leadership.* Chicago: University of Chicago Press, 1987.

———. *The Presidential Branch.* Chatham, N.J.: Chatham House, 1995.

Henderson, Ryan C. *The Clinton Wars: The Constitution, Congress and War Powers.* Nashville: Vanderbilt University Press, 2002.

Hess, Stephen. *Organizing the Presidency.* Washington, D.C.: Brookings, 1976.

Hughes, Emmet John. *The Living Presidency.* New York: Coward, McCann and Geoghegan, 1973.

Hyman, Sidney. *The American President.* New York: Harper & Brothers, 1954.

Jamieson, Kathleen Hall. *Packaging the Presidency.* New York: Oxford University Press, 1996.

Johnson, Haynes, and David Broder. *The System.* Boston: Little, Brown, 1996.

Johnson, Loch K. *Bombs, Bugs, Drugs and Thugs: Intelligence and America's Search for Security.* New York: New York University Press, 2002.

———. *Fateful Decisions: Inside the National Security Council.* New York: Oxford University Press, 2003.

———. *Secret Agencies: U.S. Intelligence Agencies in a Hostile World.* New Haven, Conn.: Yale University Press, 1996.

Johnson, Richard T. *Managing the White House.* New York: HarperCollins, 1974.

Jones, Charles O. *The Presidency in a Separated System.* Washington, D.C.: Brookings, 1994.

Kallenbach, Joseph E. *The American Chief Executive.* New York: Harper & Row, 1966.

Kernell, Samuel M. *Going Public: New Strategies of Presidential Leadership.* Washington, D.C.: Congressional Quarterly Press, 1993.

———, and Samuel Popkin, eds. *Chief of Staff.* Berkeley: University of California Press, 1986.

Kessel, John H. *Presidential Campaign Politics.* Chicago: Dorsey Press, 1988.

King, Gary, and Lyn Ragsdale. *The Elusive Executive: Discovering Statistical Patterns in the Presidency.* Washington, D.C.: Congressional Quarterly Press, 1988.

Klein, Joe. *The Natural: The Misunderstood Presidency of Bill Clinton.* New York: Doubleday, 2002.

Koenig, Louis W. *The Chief Executive.* 5th ed. San Diego: Harcourt Brace Jovanovich, 1986.

Koh, Harold Kongju. *The National Security Constitution: Sharing Power After the Iran-Contra Affair.* New Haven, Conn.: Yale University Press, 1990.

Kutler, Stanley K. *The Wars of Watergate.* New York: Knopf, 1990.

Lammers, William W. *Presidential Politics: Patterns and Prospects.* New York: Harper-Collins, 1976.

———, and Michael A. Genovese. *The Presidency and Domestic Policy.* Washington, D.C.: C.Q. Press, 2000.

Langley, Lawrence D., and Neal R. Peirce. *The Electoral College Primer 2000.* New Haven, Conn.: Yale University Press, 1999.

Laracey, Mel. *Presidents and the People: The Partisan Story of Going Public.* College Station: Texas A & M University Press, 2002.

Laski, Harold. *The American Presidency.* New York: Harper & Brothers, 1940.

LeLoup, Lance T., and Steven A. Shull. *Congress and the President: The Policy Connection.* Belmont, Calif.: Wadsworth, 1993.

Leuchtenburg, William E. *In the Shadow of FDR: From Harry Truman to Ronald Reagan.* Ithaca, N.Y.: Cornell University Press, 1983.

Levine, Myron A. *Presidential Campaigns and Elections.* Itasca, Ill.: F.E. Peacock, 1995.

Light, Paul C. *The President's Agenda.* 3rd ed. Baltimore: Johns Hopkins University Press, 1998.

———. *Vice Presidential Power: Advice and Influence in the White House.* Baltimore: Johns Hopkins University Press, 1984.

Loevy, Robert D. *The Flawed Path to the Presidency.* Albany: State University of New York Press, 1995.

Lowi, Theodore J. *The Personal President: Power Invested Promise Unfulfilled.* Ithaca, N.Y.: Cornell University Press, 1985.

MacKensie, G. Calvin, ed. *Innocent Until Nominated: The Breakdown of the Presidential Appointments Process.* Washington, D.C.: The Brookings Institution, 2001.

Maltese, John. *Spin Control: The White House Office of Communications and the Management of Presidential News.* Chapel Hill: University of North Carolina Press, 1992.

Mansfield, Harvey C., Jr. *Taming the Prince: The Ambivalence of Presidential Power.* New York: Free Press, 1989.

Maraniss, David. *First in His Class: The Biography of Bill Clinton.* New York: Touchstone, 1995.

Mayer, Jane, and Doyle McManus. *Landslide: The Unmaking of the President, 1984–1988.* Boston: Houghton Mifflin, 1988.

Mayer, Kenneth R. *With the Stroke of a Pen: Executive Orders and Presidential Power.* Princeton, N.J.: Princeton University Press, 2001.

Mayer, William G., ed. *In Pursuit of the Presidency: How We Choose Our Presidential Nominees.* Chatham, N.J.: Chatham House, 1995.

Mayhew, David. *Divided We Govern.* New Haven, Conn.: Yale University Press, 1991.

Milkis, Sidney M. *The President and the Parties.* New York: Oxford University Press, 1993.

———, and Michael Nelson. *The American Presidency: Origins and Development.* 3rd ed. Washington, D.C.: Congressional Quarterly Press, 2003.

Miroff, Bruce. *Icons of Democracy.* New York: Basic Books, 1993.

———. *Pragmatic Illusions: The Presidential Politics of John F. Kennedy.* New York: David McKay, 1976.

Morris, Richard S. *Behind the Oval Office: Winning the Presidency in the 1990s.* New York: Random House, 1997.

Mosley, Zelma, Joseph Pika, and Richard A. Watson. *The Presidential Contest.* Washington, D.C.: Congressional Quarterly Press, 1992.

Mullen, William F. *Presidential Power and Politics.* New York: St. Martin's Press, 1976.

Murray, Robert K., and Tim H. Blessing. *Greatness in the White House: Rating the Presidents, Washington through Carter.* University Park: Pennsylvania State University Press, 1988.

Nathan, Richard. *The Administrative Presidency.* New York: John Wiley and Sons, 1983.

Neustadt, Richard E. *Presidential Power.* New York: Wiley, 1960.

———. *Presidential Power and the Modern Presidents.* New York: Free Press, 1990.

O'Toole, James. *Leading Change: The Argument for Values-based Leadership.* New York: Ballentine Books, 1996.

Patterson, Bradley H., Jr., *The White House Staff: Inside the West Wing and Beyond.* Washington D.C.: The Brookings Institution, 2000.

Patterson, Thomas E. *Out of Order.* New York: Vintage Books, 1994.

———. *The Vanishing Voter: Public Involvement in an Age of Uncertainty.* New York: Alfred A. Knopf, 2002.

Peterson, Mark A. *Legislating Together.* Cambridge, Mass.: Harvard University Press, 1990.

Pfiffner, James P., ed. *The Managerial Presidency.* 2d ed., College Station: Texas A&M University Press, 1999.

———. *The Strategic Presidency: Hitting the Ground Running.* 2d ed. Lawrence: University Press of Kansas, 1996.

Phelps, Glenn A. *George Washington and American Constitutionalism.* Lawrence: University Press of Kansas, 1994.

Podhoretz, John. *Hell-of-a-Ride; Backstage at the White House Follies, 1989–1993.* New York: Simon & Schuster, 1993.

Polsby, Nelson W. *Political Innovation in America.* New Haven, Conn.: Yale University Press, 1985.

———, and Aaron Wildavsky. *Presidential Elections.* 10th ed. New York: Chatham House, 2000.

Posner, Richard A. *An Affair of State: The Investigation, Impeachment and Trial of President Clinton.* Cambridge, Mass.: Harvard University Press, 1999.

Quayle, Dan. *Standing Firm.* New York: Harper Paperbacks, 1995.

Ragsdale, Lyn. *Presidential Politics.* Boston: Houghton Mifflin, 1993.

Reich, Robert. *Locked in the Cabinet.* New York: Knopf, 1997.

Reagan, Ronald. *An American Life: The Autobiography.* New York: Simon & Schuster, 1990.

Reeves, Richard. *President Nixon: Alone in the White House.* New York: Touchstone, 2001.

Rimmerman, Craig A. *Presidency by Plebiscite.* Boulder, Colo.: Westview, 1993.

Robinson, Donald L. *"To the Best of My Ability": The Presidency and the Constitution.* New York: Norton, 1987.

Rockman, Bert. *The Leadership Question: The Presidency and the American System.* New York: Praeger, 1984.

Rose, Richard. *The Postmodern President: The White House Meets the World.* Chatham, N.J.: Chatham House, 1991.

Rosenstiel, Tom. *Strange Bedfellows: How Television and the Presidential Candidates Changed American Politics, 1992.* New York: Hyperion Books, 1993.

Rossiter, Clinton. *The American Presidency.* New York: Harcourt, Brace and World, 1956.

———. *Constitutional Dictatorship: Crisis Government in the Modern Democracy.* Princeton, N.J.: Princeton University Press, 1948.

Rozell, Mark J. *Executive Privilege: Presidential Power, Secrecy, and Accountability.* 2d ed., rev. Lawrence: University Press of Kansas, 2002.

Rudalevige, Andrew. *Managing the President's Program: Presidential Leadership and Legislative Policy Formulation.* Princeton, N.J.: Princeton University Press, 2002.

Sabato, Larry. *Feeding Frenzy.* New York: Free Press, 1991.

Schlesinger, Arthur M., Jr., *The Cycles of American History.* Boston: Houghton Mifflin, 1986.

———. *The Imperial Presidency.* Boston: Houghton Mifflin, 1973.

Schraf, Lois. *Eleanor Roosevelt: First Lady of Liberalism.* Boston: Twayne Publishers, 1987.

Schumaker, Paul D., and Burdett A. Loomis, eds. *Choosing a President: The Electoral College and Beyond.* New York: Chatham House, 2002.

Shogan, Robert. *The Riddle of Power.* New York: Dutton, 1991.

Shull, Steven A., ed. *The Two Presidencies: A Quarter Century Assessment.* Chicago: Nelson-Hall, 1991.

Shultz, George P. *Turmoil and Triumph: My Years as Secretary of State.* New York: Scribners, 1993.

Simonton, Dean Keith. *Why Presidents Succeed.* New Haven, Conn.: Yale University Press, 1987.

Sindler, Allan P. *Unchosen Presidents.* Berkeley: University of California Press, 1976.

Skowronek, Stephen. *The Politics Presidents Make.* Cambridge, Mass.: Belknap, 1993.

Smith, Hedrick. *The Power Game: How Washington Works.* New York: Ballantine, 1988.

Sorensen, Theodore C. *Watchman in the Night.* Cambridge, Mass.: MIT Press, 1975.

———. *Why I Am a Democrat.* New York: Henry Holt, 1996.

Spitzer, Robert J. *President and Congress: Executive Hegemony at the Crossroads of American Government.* New York: McGraw-Hill, 1993.

———. *The Presidential Veto: Touchstone of the American Presidency.* Albany: State University of New York Press, 1988.

Stewart, James B. *Blood Sport: The President and His Adversaries.* New York: Simon & Schuster, 1996.

Stockman, David A. *The Triumph of Politics: The Inside Story of the Reagan Revolution.* New York: Avon, 1987.

Stuckey, Mary E. *The President as Interpreter-in-Chief.* Chatham, N.J.: Chatham House, 1991.

———. *Strategic Failures in the Modern Presidency.* Cresshill, N.J.: Hampton Press, 1997.

Sundquist, James L. *Constitutional Reform and Effective Government.* Washington, D.C.: Brookings, 1986.

Thurber, James A., ed. *Divided Democracy.* Washington, D.C.: Congressional Quarterly Press, 1991.

———, ed. *Rivals for Power: Presidential-Congressional Relations.* Washington, D.C.: Congressional Quarterly Press, 1996.

Tulis, Jeffrey K. *The Rhetorical Presidency.* Princeton, N.J.: Princeton University Press, 1987.

Troy, Gil. *Affairs of State: The Rise and Rejection of the Presidential Couple since World War II.* New York: McGraw Hill, 1997.

———. *See How They Ran: The Changing Role of the Presidential Candidate.* New York: Free Press, 1991.

Troy, Tevi. *Intellectuals and the American Presidency: Philosophers, Jesters or Technicians.* Lanham, Md.: Rowman and Littlefield, 2002.

Walsh, Kenneth T. *Feeding the Beast, the White House vs. Press.* New York: Random House, 1996.

Walsh, Lawrence E. *Firewall.* New York: Norton, 1997.

Warshaw, Shirley Anne. *Powersharing: White House–Cabinet Relations in the Modern Presidency.* Albany: State University of New York Press, 1996.

———. *The Domestic Presidency.* Boston: Allyn and Bacon, 1997.

Watson, Richard A. *Presidential Vetoes and Public Policy.* Lawrence: University Press of Kansas, 1993.

Wayne, Stephen J. *The Road to the White House, 2000.* New York: St. Martin's Press, 1999.

Weko, Thomas J. *The Politicizing Presidency: The White House Personnel Office, 1948–1994.* Lawrence: University Press of Kansas, 1995.

Whitcover, Jules. *Crapshoot: Rolling the Dice on the Vice Presidency.* New York: Crown, 1992.

Wills, Garry. *Certain Trumpets: The Call of Leaders.* New York: Simon & Schuster, 1994.

Wilson, Robert A., ed. *Character Above All: Ten Presidents from FDR to George Bush.* New York: Simon & Schuster, 1995.

Woodward, Bob. *The Agenda: Inside the Clinton White House.* New York: Simon & Schuster, 1994.

———. *Bush at War.* New York: Simon & Schuster, 2002.

# Timeline of Presidential
# Elections and Tenure

| 1789 | 1796 | 1800 | | 1808 | 1816 |
|---|---|---|---|---|---|
| George Washington (no party) | John Adams (Federalist) | Thomas Jefferson (Dem-Rep) | | James Madison (Dem-Rep) | James Monroe (Dem-Rep) |

| 1848 | 1852 | 1856 | 1860 | 1868 |
|---|---|---|---|---|
| Zachary Taylor (Whig) | Franklin Pierce (Democrat) | James Buchanan (Democrat) | Abraham Lincoln (Republican) | Ulysses S. Grant (Republican) |
| died 1850 | | | died 1865 | |
| Millard Fillmore (Whig) | | | Andrew Johnson (Republican) | |

| 1904 | 1908 | 1912 | 1920 | 1924 | 1928 |
|---|---|---|---|---|---|
| Theodore Roosevelt (Republican) | William H. Taft (Republican) | Woodrow Wilson (Democrat) | Warren G. Harding (Republican) | Calvin Coolidge (Republican) | Herbert C. Hoover (Republican) |
| | | | died 1923 | | |
| | | | Calvin Coolidge (Republican) | | |

| 1960 | 1964 | 1968 | 1976 | 1980 |
|---|---|---|---|---|
| John F. Kennedy (Democrat) | Lyndon B. Johnson (Democrat) | Richard M. Nixon (Republican) | Jimmy Carter (Democrat) | Ronald Reagan (Republican) |
| died 1963 | | resigned 1974 | | |
| Lyndon B. Johnson (Democrat) | | Gerald R. Ford (Republican) | | |

1824
John Q.
Adams
(Dem-Rep)

1828
Andrew Jackson
(Democrat)

1836
Martin
Van Buren
(Democrat)

1840
William H.
Harrison
(Whig)

died 1841

John Tyler
(Whig)

1844
James K.
Polk
(Democrat)

1876
Rutherford B.
Hayes
(Republican)

1880
James A.
Garfield
(Republican)

died 1881

Chester A.
Arthur
(Republican)

1884
Grover
Cleveland
(Democrat)

1888
Benjamin
Harrison
(Republican)

1892
Grover
Cleveland
(Democrat)

1896
William McKinley
(Republican

died 1901

Theodore Roosevelt
(Republican))

1932
Franklin D. Roosevelt
(Democrat)

died 1945

Harry S. Truman
(Democrat)

1948
Harry S.
Truman
(Democrat)

1952
Dwight D. Eisenhower
(Republican)

1988
George H.W.
Bush
(Republican)

1992
Bill Clinton
(Democrat)

2000
George W. Bush
(Republican)

# Presidential Election Results, 1789–2000

| Year | Presidents/ Vice-Presidents/ Other Candidates | Party | Popular Vote | Electoral Vote |
|------|---------------------------------------------|-------|--------------|----------------|
| 1789 | George Washington John Adams | | | 69 |
| | John Adams | | | 34 |
| | Others | | | 35 |
| 1793 | George Washington John Adams | | | 132 |
| | John Adams | | | 77 |
| | George Clinton | | | 50 |
| | Others | | | 5 |
| 1796 | John Adams Thomas Jefferson | Federalist | | 71 |
| | Thomas Jefferson | Democratic-Republican | | 68 |
| | Thomas Pinckney | Federalist | | 59 |
| | Aaron Burr | Democratic-Republican | | 30 |
| | Others | | | 48 |
| 1800 | Thomas Jefferson Aaron Burr | Democratic-Republican | | 73 |
| | Aaron Burr | Democratic-Republican | | 73 |
| | John Adams | Federalist | | 65 |
| | Charles C. Pinckney | Federalist | | 64 |
| 1804 | Thomas Jefferson George Clinton | Democratic-Republican | | 162 |
| | Charles C. Pinckney | Federalist | | 14 |
| 1808 | James Madison George Clinton | Democratic-Republican | | 122 |
| | Charles C. Pinckney | Federalist | | 47 |
| | George Clinton | Independent-Republican | | 6 |
| 1812 | James Madison Elbridge Gerry | Democratic-Republican | | 128 |
| | DeWitt Clinton | Federalist | | 89 |
| 1816 | James Monroe Daniel D. Tompkins | Democratic-Republican | | 183 |
| | Rufus King | Federalist | | 34 |
| 1820 | James Monroe Daniel D. Tompkins | Democratic-Republican | | 231 |
| | John Quincy Adams | Independent-Republican | | 1 |
| 1824 | John Quincy Adams John C. Calhoun | Democratic-Republican | 108,740(30.5%) | 84 |
| | Andrew Jackson | Democratic-Republican | 153,544(43.1%) | 99 |
| | Henry Clay | Democratic-Republican | 47,136(13.2%) | 37 |
| | William H. Crawford | Democratic-Republican | 46,618(13.1%) | 41 |
| 1828 | Andrew Jackson John C. Calhoun | Democratic | 647,231(56.0%) | 178 |
| | John Quincy Adams | National Republican | 509,097(44.0%) | 83 |
| 1832 | Andrew Jackson Martin Van Buren | Democratic | 687,502(55.0%) | 219 |
| | Henry Clay | National Republican | 530,189(42.4%) | 49 |
| | William Wirt | Anti-Masonic | | 7 |
| | John Floyd | National Republican | 33,108(2.6%) | 11 |
| 1836 | Martin Van Buren Richard M. Johnson | Democratic | 761,549(50.9%) | 170 |
| | William H. Harrison | Whig | 549,567(36.7%) | 73 |
| | Hugh L. White | Whig | 145,396(9.7%) | 26 |
| | Daniel Webster | Whig | 41,287(2.7%) | 14 |

| Year | Presidents/ Vice-Presidents/ Other Candidates | Party | Popular Vote | Electoral Vote |
|------|-----------------------------------------------|-------|--------------|----------------|
| 1840 | William H. Harrison John Tyler | Whig | 1,275,017 (53.1%) | 234 |
|      | Martin Van Buren | Democratic | 1,128,702 (46.9%) | 60 |
| 1844 | James K. Polk George M. Dallas | Democratic | 1,337,243 (49.6%) | 170 |
|      | Henry Clay | Whig | 1,299,068 (48.1%) | 105 |
|      | James G. Birney | Liberty | 63,300 (2.3%) | |
| 1848 | Zachary Taylor Millard Fillmore | Whig | 1,360,101 (47.4%) | 163 |
|      | Lewis Cass | Democratic | 1,220,544 (42.5%) | 127 |
|      | Martin Van Buren | Free Soil | 291,163 (10.1%) | |
| 1852 | Franklin Pierce William R. King | Democratic | 1,601,474 (50.9%) | 254 |
|      | Winfield Scott | Whig | 1,386,578 (44.1%) | 42 |
| 1856 | James Buchanan John C. Breckinridge | Democratic | 1,838,169 (45.4%) | 174 |
|      | John C. Fremont | Republican | 1,335,264 (33.0% | 114 |
|      | Millard Fillmore | American | 874,534 (21.6%) | 8 |
| 1860 | Abraham Lincoln Hannibal Hamlin | Republican | 1,865,593 (39.8%) | 180 |
|      | Stephen A. Douglas | Democratic | 1,381,713 (29.5%) | 12 |
|      | John C. Breckinridge | Democratic | 848,356 (18.1%) | 72 |
|      | John Bell | Constitutional Union | 592,906 (12.6%) | 79 |
| 1864 | Abraham Lincoln Andrew Johnson | Republican | 2,206,938 (55.0%) | 212 |
|      | George B. McClellan | Democratic | 1,803,787 (45.0%) | 21 |
| 1868 | Ulysses S. Grant Schuyler Colfax | Republican | 3,013,421 (52.7%) | 214 |
|      | Horatio Seymour | Democratic | 2,706,829 (47.3%) | 80 |
| 1872 | Ulysses S. Grant Henry Wilson | Republican | 3,596,745 (55.6%) | 286 |
|      | Horace Greeley | Democratic | 2,843,446 (43.9%) | 66 |
| 1876 | Rutherford B. Hayes William A. Wheeler | Republican | 4,036,571 (48.0%) | 185 |
|      | Samuel J. Tilden | Democratic | 4,284,020 (51.0%) | 184 |
| 1880 | James A. Garfield Chester A. Arthur | Republican | 4,449,053 (48.3%) | 214 |
|      | Winfield S. Hancock | Democratic | 4,442,035 (48.2%) | 155 |
|      | James B. Weaver | Greenback-Labor | 308,578 (3.4%) | |
| 1884 | Grover Cleveland T. A. Hendricks | Democratic | 4,874,986 (48.5%) | 219 |
|      | James G. Blaine | Republican | 4,851,931 (48.2%) | 182 |
|      | Benjamin F. Butler | Greenback-Labor | 175,370 (1.8%) | |
| 1888 | Benjamin Harrison Levi P. Morton | Republican | 5,444,337 (47.8%) | 233 |
|      | Grover Cleveland | Democratic | 5,540,050 (48.6%) | 168 |
| 1892 | Grover Cleveland Adlai E. Stevenson | Democratic | 5,554,414 (46.0%) | 277 |
|      | Benjamin Harrison | Republican | 5,190,802 (43.0%) | 145 |
|      | James B. Weaver | Peoples | 1,027,329 (8.5%) | 22 |
| 1896 | Wiliam McKinley Garret A. Hobart | Republican | 7,035,638 (50.8%) | 271 |
|      | William J. Bryan | Democratic; Populist | 6,467,946 (46.7%) | 176 |
| 1900 | William McKinley Theodore Roosevelt | Republican | 7,219,530 (51.7%) | 292 |
|      | William J. Bryan | Democratic; Populist | 6,356,734 (45.5%) | 155 |

| Year | Presidents/ Vice-Presidents/ Other Candidates | Party | Popular Vote | Electoral Vote |
|------|-----------------------------------------------|-------|--------------|----------------|
| 1904 | Theodore Roosevelt Charles Fairbanks | Republican | 7,628,834(56.4%) | 336 |
|      | Alton B. Parker | Democratic | 5,084,401(37.6%) | 140 |
|      | Eugene V. Debs | Socialist | 402,460(3.0%) | 0 |
| 1908 | William H. Taft James S. Sherman | Republican | 7,679,006(51.6%) | 321 |
|      | William J. Bryan | Democratic | 6,409,106(43.1%) | 162 |
|      | Eugene V. Debs | Socialist | 420,820(2.8%) | 0 |
| 1912 | Woodrow Wilson Thomas R. Marshall | Democratic | 6,286,820(41.8%) | 435 |
|      | Theodore Roosevelt | Progressive | 4,126,020(27.4%) | 88 |
|      | William H. Taft | Republican | 3,483,922(23.2%) | 8 |
|      | Eugene V. Debs | Socialist | 897,011(6.0%) | 0 |
| 1916 | Woodrow Wilson Thomas R. Marshall | Democratic | 9,129,606(49.3%) | 277 |
|      | Charles E. Hughes | Republican | 8,538,211(46.1%) | 254 |
| 1920 | Warren G. Harding Calvin Coolidge | Republican | 16,152,200(61.0%) | 404 |
|      | James M. Cox | Democratic | 9,147,353(34.6%) | 127 |
|      | Eugene V. Debs | Socialist | 919,799(3.5%) | 0 |
| 1924 | Calvin Coolidge Charles G. Dawes | Republican | 15,725,016(54.1%) | 382 |
|      | John W. Davis | Democratic | 8,385,586(28.8%) | 136 |
|      | Robert M. La Follette | Progressive | 4,822,856(16.6%) | 13 |
| 1928 | Herbert C. Hoover Charles Curtis | Republican | 21,392,190(58.2%) | 444 |
|      | Alfred E. Smith | Democratic | 15,016,443(40.8%) | 87 |
| 1932 | Franklin D. Roosevelt John Nance Garner | Democratic | 22,809,638(57.3%) | 472 |
|      | Herbert C. Hoover | Republican | 15,758,901(39.6%) | 59 |
|      | Norman Thomas | Socialist | 881,951(2.2%) | 0 |
| 1936 | Franklin D. Roosevelt John Nance Garner | Democratic | 27,751,612(60.7%) | 523 |
|      | Alfred M. Landon | Republican | 16,681,913(36.4%) | 8 |
|      | William Lemke | Union | 891,858(1.9%) | 0 |
| 1940 | Franklin D. Roosevelt Henry A. Wallace | Democratic | 27,243,466(54.7%) | 449 |
|      | Wendell L. Wilkie | Republican | 22,304,755(44.8%) | 82 |
| 1944 | Franklin D. Roosevelt Harry S. Truman | Democratic | 25,602,505(52.8%) | 432 |
|      | Thomas E. Dewey | Republican | 22,006,278(44.5%) | 99 |
| 1948 | Harry S. Truman Alben W. Barkley | Democratic | 24,105,812(49.5%) | 303 |
|      | Thomas E. Dewey | Republican | 21,970,065(45.1%) | 189 |
|      | J. Strom Thurmond | States' Rights | 1,169,063(2.4%) | 39 |
|      | Henry A. Wallace | Progressive | 1,157,172(2.4%) | 0 |
| 1952 | Dwight D. Eisenhower Richard M. Nixon | Republican | 33,936,234(55.2%) | 442 |
|      | Adlai E. Stevenson | Democratic | 27,314,992(44.5%) | 89 |
| 1956 | Dwight D. Eisenhower Richard M. Nixon | Republican | 35,590,472(57.4%) | 457 |
|      | Adlai E. Stevenson | Democratic | 26,022,752(42.0%) | 73 |
| 1960 | John F. Kennedy Lyndon B. Johnson | Democratic | 34,227,096(49.9%) | 303 |
|      | Richard M. Nixon | Republican | 34,108,546(49.6%) | 219 |

| Year | Presidents/Vice-Presidents/Other Candidates | Party | Popular Vote | Electoral Vote |
|------|---------------------------------------------|-------|--------------|----------------|
| 1964 | Lyndon B. Johnson<br>Hubert H. Humphrey | Democratic | 43,126,233 (61.1%) | 486 |
|      | Barry Goldwater | Republican | 27,174,989 (38.5%) | 52 |
| 1968 | Richard M. Nixon<br>Spiro T. Agnew | Republican | 31,783,783 (43.4%) | 301 |
|      | Hubert H. Humphrey | Democratic | 31,271,839 (42.7%) | 191 |
|      | George C. Wallace | American Independent | 9,899,557 (13.5%) | 46 |
| 1972 | Richard M. Nixon<br>Spiro T. Agnew | Republican | 46,632,189 (61.3%) | 520 |
|      | George McGovern | Democratic | 28,422,015 (37.3%) | 17 |
| 1976 | Jimmy Carter<br>Walter F. Mondale | Democratic | 40,828,587 (50.1%) | 297 |
|      | Gerald R. Ford | Republican | 39,147,613 (48.0%) | 240 |
| 1980 | Ronald Reagan<br>George H. W. Bush | Republican | 42,941,145 (51.0%) | 489 |
|      | Jimmy Carter | Democratic | 34,663,037 (41.0%) | 49 |
|      | John B. Anderson | Independent | 5,551,551 (6.6%) | 0 |
| 1984 | Ronald Reagan<br>George H. W. Bush | Republican | 53,428,357 (59%) | 525 |
|      | Walter F. Mondale | Democratic | 36,930,923 (41%) | 13 |
| 1988 | George Bush<br>James D. Quayle III | Republican | 48,881,011 (53%) | 426 |
|      | Michael Dukakis | Democratic | 41,828,350 (46%) | 111 |
| 1992 | Bill Clinton<br>Albert Gore | Democratic | 38,394,210 (43%) | 370 |
|      | George Bush | Republican | 33,974,386 (38%) | 168 |
|      | H. Ross Perot | Independent | 16,573,465 (19%) | 0 |
| 1996 | Bill Clinton<br>Albert Gore | Democratic | 45,628,667 (49%) | 379 |
|      | Bob Dole | Republican | 37,869,435 (41%) | 159 |
|      | H. Ross Perot | Reform | 7,874,283 (8%) | 0 |
| 2000 | George W. Bush<br>Richard Cheney | Republican | 50,456,169 (48%) | 271 |
|      | Al Gore | Democrat | 50,996,116 (48%) | 266 |
|      | Ralph Nader | Green | 2,767,176 (3%) | 0 |

# Index

# Other Titles by the Authors

*Also by Thomas E. Cronin*

*The Presidential Advisory System*. New York: Harper & Row, 1969

*The Presidency Reappraised*. New York: Praeger, 1974, 1977

*The State of the Presidency*. Boston: Little, Brown & Co., 1975, 1980

*U.S. v. Crime in the Streets*. Bloomington: Indiana University Press, 1981

*Direct Democracy: The Politics of Initiative Referendum and Recall*. Cambridge: Harvard University Press, 1989

*Essays in Honor of James MacGregor Burns*. Englewood Cliffs, NJ: Prentice Hall, 1989

*Inventing the American Presidency*. Lawrence: University of Kansas Press, 1989

*The Write Stuff: Writing as a Performing and Political Art*. Englewood Cliffs, NJ: Prentice Hall, 1990, 1993

*Colorado Politics and Government*. Lincoln: University of Nebraska Press, 1993

*Government by the People*. Upper Saddle River, NJ: Prentice Hall, 1975, 2004

*State and Local Politics*. Upper Saddle River, NJ: Prentice Hall, 1976, 2004


*Also by Michael A. Genovese*

*The Supreme Court, the Constitution, and Presidential Power*. Lanham, MD: University Press of America, 1980

*Politics and the Cinema*. Lexington, MA: Ginn Press, 1986

*The Nixon Presidency: Power and Politics in Turbulent Times*. Westport, CT: Greenwood Press, 1990

*Women as National Leaders*. Newbury, CA: Sage Publishing, 1993

*The Presidency in an Age of Limits*. Westport, CT: Greenwood Press, 1993

*The Political Film*. New York: Simon & Schuster, 1998

*The Watergate Crisis*. Westport, CT: Greenwood Press, 1999

*The Presidency and Domestic Policy: Comparing Leadership Styles, FDR to Clinton*. Washington DC: CQ Press, 2000

*The Power of the American Presidency, 1789–2000*. New York: Oxford University Press, 2000

*The Presidency and the Law: The Clinton Legacy*. Lawrence: University Press of Kansas, 2002

*The Presidential Dilemma*. 2d ed. New York: Longman, 2003

*Polls and Politics*. Albany: SUNY Press, 2004

*The Encylcopedia of the American Presidency*. New York: Facts-On-File, 2004